Foreign Policy
in
World Politics

THIRD EDITION

PRENTICE-HALL, INC., *Englewood Cliffs, New Jersey*

Foreign Policy in

ROY C. MACRIDIS, Editor

World Politics

CONTRIBUTING AUTHORS

VERNON V. ASPATURIAN

George I. Blanksten

KARL W. DEUTSCH

LEWIS J. EDINGER

LEON D. EPSTEIN

ROY C. MACRIDIS

HANS J. MORGENTHAU

Richard L. Park

ROBERT A. SCALAPINO

KENNETH W. THOMPSON

Allen S. Whiting

Foreign Policy

in

World Politics

3rd Edition

Roy C. Macridis, Editor

Current printing (last digit):
10 9 8 7 6 5 4 3 2 1

Prentice-Hall International, Inc., *London*
Prentice-Hall of Australia, Pty. Ltd., *Sydney*
Prentice-Hall of Canada, Ltd., *Toronto*
Prentice-Hall of India Private Ltd., *New Delhi*
Prentice-Hall of Japan, Inc., *Tokyo*

Library of Congress Catalog Card No.: 67-12251

Printed in the United States of America

Preface

When the first edition of this volume appeared in the spring of 1958, we had no way of knowing that it would be received as well as it was. We knew that we were involved in subject matter that was new, and all that we could hope for was to give to the student and the teacher supplementary material for courses in comparative government and international relations. This third, revised, edition is now being presented with the assurance that at the level of college instruction there is a deep concern with the comparative study of foreign policy.

The third edition maintains essentially the format of the previous ones. We have updated most of our material and rather extensively rewritten the chapters on France, India, Japan, and Soviet foreign policy, adding a new chapter dealing, in part, with the Sino-Soviet split. We have also added an entirely new section on foreign policy issues and processes in Latin America.

It is our hope that the volume will continue as an introduction to the recently developed courses in comparative foreign policy and that it will continue to serve as a supplement to the study of comparative government and international relations. My deepest thanks for help and cooperation again go to all the contributors and to James J. Murray, III, and his staff, at Prentice-Hall.

R. C. M.

Waltham, Massachusetts

Contents

3

FRENCH FOREIGN POLICY   *62*
ROY C. MACRIDIS

4

FOREIGN POLICY OF THE GERMAN FEDERAL REPUBLIC   *102*
KARL W. DEUTSCH and LEWIS J. EDINGER

5

SOVIET FOREIGN POLICY   *156*

VERNON V. ASPATURIAN

8

9

10

11

Foreign Policy
in
World Politics

1

The Comparative

KENNETH W. THOMPSON and ROY C. MACRIDIS Study

# of Foreign Policy

TWO BASIC APPROACHES TO FOREIGN POLICY

Two approaches to foreign policy have vied with one another in Western thought at least since the days of the French Revolution. One is the *ideological* approach, according to which the policies of states vis-à-vis the rest of the world are merely expressions of prevailing political, social, and religious beliefs. In this approach, foreign policies are classified as democratic or totalitarian, libertarian or socialist, and peace-loving or aggressive. The second approach to foreign policy is *analytical*. At the heart of this viewpoint is the proposition that policy rests on multiple determinants, including the state's historic tradition, geographical location, national interest, and purposes and security needs. To understand foreign policy, the observer must take into account and analyze a host of factors.

The ideological approach

In the twentieth century, it has been commonplace for critics to proclaim that the United States, or Britain, or France has no foreign policy or has been unfaithful to liberal or socialist or conservative principles, as the case

may be. This is one way to think about foreign policy; to the present day it is perhaps the prevailing approach. Periodically, the domestic political arena rings with angry charges that a set of political leaders, a political party, or an administration is opportunistic in foreign affairs and faithless to its political creed or ideology. Governments are condemned for not supporting democracy, or free enterprise, or a particular social class everywhere around the world. This dominant approach views foreign relations primarily in psychological terms; it looks to the motives or ideologies of leaders or governments as the essential, if not the sole, determinant of policy. It maintains that a democratic regime pursues one type of foreign policy, an autocratic government another, a communist government a third, and a democratic-socialist administration still another. There is a fairyland-like simplicity about this that makes it widely acceptable and easily understood. Foreign policy is considered a function of a political system in action or of the preferences or convictions of political leaders who carry out its programs.

The analytical approach

There is a second approach to foreign policy, however, which has at

1

least as respectable a heritage. It was a ruling point of view throughout much of the eighteenth and nineteenth centuries, whether in doctrines of *raison d'état* or in broader historical interpretations, and it is being revived in our day by a handful of analysts and scholars.

Its renaissance is partly an outcome of the apparent shortcomings of the psychological or ideological approach, especially in accounting for present-day international developments. That approach has been shaken and discredited by inner contradictions, and it has faltered and failed in describing the continuities of objective and purpose in the policies of states. Regardless of the party in power or the leaders and their private or public philosophies, British, American, French, and Russian foreign policies display unities that transcend individual beliefs or ideologies. In the early postwar period, the Labor government in England, despite long-standing protests against Tory imperialism and power politics, turned inevitably to the protection—in Western Europe, in the countries of the British Commonwealth, in the Iberian Peninsula, and in the Near and Middle East—of substantially the selfsame interests that Tories and Whigs had considered vital for several centuries. In the United States, the Dulles-Eisenhower and the Kennedy-Johnson-Rusk foreign policies have looked to the central goals with which the administrations of Roosevelt and Truman were concerned. The means, methods, or techniques may have changed, but the interests and objectives have been relatively constant.

Therefore, in a period of a little more than a decade there has been a reaction against the ideological approach to the study of international relations. It should perhaps have been obvious that a conception in which foreign policy is nothing more than a by-product of domestic politics could hardly do justice to the elements of continuity in national policy. At some point, it became necessary to recognize that objective requirements of the national interest place certain irremovable limits upon any statesman seeking to formulate foreign policy. Regardless of the intentions, social philosophy, or religious outlook of individuals, there are broad strategic interests intimately bound up with a nation's geographic position and international role that must be safeguarded if its independence is to be preserved. Not only are these interests permanent for Bolsheviks as well as Tsars, but continuity also appears in the approach of a nation's statesmen, who stand guard over their country's security and whose conception of that security has been formed and molded by the same institutions and traditions. However intangible, the "national mind," which interprets the national interest, is itself a factor in the permanence of foreign policy. Out of the interplay of a durable international position with permanent traditions and institutions, the larger nation-states have fashioned foreign policies which, in broadest outline, have been consistently maintained over long periods, even in the face of drastic changes on the domestic political scene.

According to this second approach, foreign policy demands, of policy makers, choices and discriminations of a basic order. Not only are the interests of a nation permanent in character, but they range themselves in a hierarchy of greater and lesser interests. In a classic statement intended as a guide in the formulation of Belgium's foreign policy but with relevance for all foreign policy, Monsieur Paul-Henri Spaak observed:

There must be a hierarchy in international obligations. The nations of a continent cannot reasonably be asked to consider with the same realism and sincerity of judgment affairs which directly concern them and events which are taking place thousands of kilometers away in regions where they have neither interests nor influence.

Certain interests must be defended at all costs; others should be safeguarded under particular circumstances; and certain others, although desirable, can almost never be defended. It is the task of foreign policy, in the first instance, to determine its own hierarchy of interests and, next, to examine the scale of interests revealed in the principles or practice of other nations' foreign policies. Even when national leaders forswear the formulation of hierarchies of interests, the hard tests of practice often evoke underlying conceptions of vital interests. The United States' decision, in World War II, to bring the fighting to a successful conclusion in Europe and the North Atlantic before turning to destroy the enemy in the Pacific, or Britain's waiting, at the turn of the nineteenth century, until Poland was attacked and other nations were invaded before forming coalitions against Napoleon—these are examples of action in terms of a basic perception of interests.

The interests of states, and their power to pursue their claims, are of course immutable for any given historical period only in the sense that they set broad limits within which choices in foreign policy are made. They set the framework within which the domestic political contest over external policies must be waged. In the same way that no German political party today can afford to ignore the sometimes latent but ever-present demands for German reunification, no

American government can take steps that would compromise the security of the Western Hemisphere. It is obvious that both power and interests can be made responsive to the forces of change. For example, a so-called peace-loving nation, faced by threats to its security, can translate its resources into military power, its influence into foreign bases and real estate, and its industrial and military potential into forces in being. This has, in effect, been the trend of postwar American foreign policy. Or a state may suffer a loss of power, as Britain did in World War II, with the consequent need for revising its estimates of national interest. Technology can require continuing reappraisals of national security and of the means of preserving it, and may lead to changes in the ranking of the great powers. Britain may have fallen in the hierarchy of powers as other nations belatedly experienced the industrial revolution, but it may recapture at least some of its vaunted supremacy in an era of atomic energy and hydrogen bombs. The existence of continuities in the foreign policies of states is admittedly more subject to debate in an era when one of the few certainties is the continual unrelenting pace of technological change.

Yet most students of international politics are persuaded that those recurrent patterns of the foreign policies of nations which most diplomats appear to take for granted are amenable to study and analysis by the modern scholar. These patterns have been approached along several distinct if parallel lines. Scholars have engaged in more general studies of the geographical, industrial, and physical position of nations, of the peculiar historical circumstances in which these conditions have operated, of the actual adjustment of nations on the basis of their objective position to successive historical circumstances, and of the claims and declarations made by statesmen engaged in pursuing a certain historic foreign policy. Obviously, the intent of the studies in this volume is not to do basic research in any or all of these areas, but significantly, and almost without exception, each separate inquiry starts with an examination of some aspect of the objective patterns and conditions of foreign policy in the respective countries. At the same time, in successive chapters, the writers go on to consider the role of ideology, of those changing institutions and domestic political factors which give to the policies of states that endless subtlety and richness that throws into question every simple generalization about the conduct of states. In effect, the theme of the book is one of continuity and change, of unities and coherences alongside the unique and particular in foreign relations. The authors, although wary of what Burckhardt described as "grand simplifications," are nevertheless compelled by their interests as political scientists to examine what can be said in general about foreign policy. This provides a unifying theme or central core of intellectual interests, not everywhere made explicit but unquestionably at hand for those who seek understanding in this complex and fascinating realm.

THE ELEMENTS OF FOREIGN POLICY

The study of foreign policy, despite the two major approaches described above, provides no ready-made categories that can be applied to every nation. Perhaps even in the physical sciences, the effort to uncover total systems, at least in these terms, is less fruitful than is sometimes imagined. In any event, there is marked diversity in the categories of analysis by which foreign policy has been studied in the present volume. To a considerable ex-

tent, this results from differences in national context. For example, social stratification has implications for the making of foreign policy in Britain that it seems not to have in the Soviet Union, and the policy-making process in Britain has greater continuity and tradition even than the American system. *A fortiori*, the newer states cannot point to the same political experience and diplomatic tradition in which the older nations can take pardonable pride. Despite these individual variations in the species, the nation-states whose policies are described have much in common. Their foreign policies are susceptible of analysis in terms of a check list of elements that exist, that can be identified, and that merge and compromise the bases of foreign policy.

The elements of foreign policy may be thought of in terms of concentric circles. At the center are certain elements that are more or less material in character. Some of these are relatively permanent, such as geography and natural resources. Others, like the economic, industrial, and military establishments, are more responsive to change and human manipulation. Then there are human factors, largely quantitative in the case of population, and qualitative as regards national character, social structure, national morale, political institutions and experience, and an effective tradition of diplomacy. From these elements and the instrumentalities of the policy-making process, the substance of foreign policy derives, and major historic policies and the vital interests of countries emerge.

It may be worth at least passing mention that students of international politics have for the most part concentrated their attention on the elements of foreign policy. By contrast, writers on comparative politics have dealt more particularly with the policy-making process, including the influence of political parties, interest groups, effective political ideologies, and the peculiar executive-legislative relations in a country. The attempt has been made in the present volume to marry these two approaches, and to combine the study of objective factors in foreign policy with the study of processes by which decisions are reached and policies implemented.

SIGNIFICANT FACTORS IN THE STUDY OF FOREIGN POLICY

The Elements of Foreign Policy
A. The relatively permanent material elements
 1. Geography
 2. Natural resources
  a. Minerals
  b. Food production
  c. Energy and power
B. Less permanent material elements
 1. Industrial establishment
 2. Military establishment
 3. Changes in industrial and military capacity
C. The human elements: quantitative and qualitative
 1. Quantitative: population
 2. Qualitative
  a. Policy makers and leaders
  b. The role of ideology
  c. The role of information

The Foreign Policy-Making Process
A. The governmental agencies
 1. Executive (e.g., prime minister, relevant ministries, and interministerial or interdepartmental organizations)
 2. Legislature (including relevant committees)
B. The nongovernmental agencies
 1. Political parties
 2. Interest groups
 3. Media of communication
 4. Characteristics of public opinion

Trends and Issues
A. National purposes
 1. Peace as national purpose
 2. Security as national purpose
 3. Power as national purpose
 4. Prosperity and economic development as national purpose

B. Diplomacy
 1. Diplomatic practices
 2. The transformation of diplomatic practices
 3. The rediscovery of diplomacy
C. Democratic and totalitarian systems
D. The impact of the Cold War

The relatively permanent material elements

Geography. The more or less permanent elements of foreign policy obviously include geography, perhaps the most stable factor undergirding a nation's policies. It is not without significance that "except for Japan . . . Britain has been the only major power of modern times to be based on an island rather than a large continental area."[1] Its separation from the European continent by a narrow but strategic body of water, the English Channel, proved as decisive in frustrating the designs of Hitler and Napoleon as it had those of Julius Caesar or Philip II. No less an authority than Sir Eyre Crowe observed: "The general character of England's foreign policy is determined by the immutable conditions of her geographical situation on the ocean flank of Europe as an island State with vast oversea colonies and dependencies, whose existence and survival as an independent community are inseparably bound up with the possession of preponderant sea power."[2] This passage gives a clue to an important source of one of the most successful foreign policies in history. Going back to the fifteenth and sixteenth centuries, England, with but two exceptions, has neither been invaded nor defeated; and the exceptions

[1] See Chap. 2.
[2] Eyre Crowe, "Memorandum on the Present State of British Relations with France and Germany, January 1, 1907," in *British Documents on the Origins of the War: 1898–1914*, ed. G. P. Gooch and H. Temperley (London: Her Majesty's Stationery Office, 1938), III, 402–3.

—the American Revolution and the Afghan Wars—are hardly impressive evidence to challenge the importance of its geographic position. Even today, England remains an island with what Winston S. Churchill described as threefold commitments to Europe, the British Commonwealth, and the "New World." Historically and down to the present, it has striven to retain for itself sufficient freedom of action to harmonize its commitments in each of these orbits, and only at points where they overlapped have new undertakings been possible. It is true that technology, through inventions like the airplane and submarine, has transformed the character of Britain's location, and there are signs that its interests today are drawing it ever closer to Europe. In part, political factors have prompted this trend, including the British failure to pursue a successful independent foreign policy when its interests were in conflict with those of the super-powers, as in the Suez crisis in the autumn of 1956. But in Arnold Toynbee's apt words ". . . in this postwar age, the English Channel is no broader—in the subjective human terms of measurement which have to be applied in this context— than a Dutch dyke in the age of Alva and William the Silent; and the Atlantic itself is no broader than the Channel at the time when Napoleon's army of invasion was encamped at Boulogne."[3] Nonetheless, there are reasons for treating with some reserve claims about the annihilation of distance, for this statement dates back to 1934—only a few short years before the backbone of Nazi strategy was broken by an island state whose geography continued to make a difference.

No one would doubt that communi-

cations and modern warfare have shifted the emphasis that can properly be laid on geographic location, but its influence continues in various ways, not least in the case of the great powers. The territorial expanse of the Soviet Union, whose land mass extends over one-seventh of the land area of the earth, or the vast reaches of the Chinese empire—both make military conquest and control problematical even with absolute weapons. The policies that the United Nations was able to pursue in Korea were circumscribed by the magnitude of the military effort of fighting a successful war on the seemingly endless terrain of the mainland of China. At the same time, the difficulties of maintaining communication networks within these vast areas can be a source of weakness in defense. For Russia, the lack of natural frontiers in the west or of natural obstacles to invasion across the plains of Poland and Eastern Germany has been a source of conflict and weakness from the fourteenth century up to the present day. This condition must be considered at least partly responsible for Soviet policies toward the satellites and for the insistence of the late Premier Stalin that "Poland is a matter of life and death."

Consequently, experienced diplomats like Ambassadors Charles E. Bohlen and Llewelyn Thompson warn that the most probable *casus belli* for the Russians could be a sudden change in the status of Eastern Europe. Short of a general settlement, they would fight to preserve their position in this area.

Natural resources. The crisis in the Middle East provides a reminder that natural resources continue to be a vital element in foreign policy. The decisive importance of the countries in the Arabian peninsula rests largely in

[3] Arnold J. Toynbee, *A Study of History* (London: Oxford University Press, 1934), III, 353.

the control they exert over oil. In practice, modern technology has made Middle Eastern oil production an increasingly vital necessity, especially for regions like Western Europe. Instruments of production, transportation, and war require oil as a source of energy—Clemenceau once observed that "one drop of oil is worth one drop of blood of our soldiers"—and its importance has led to a shift in the relative power of major regions of the world (as in the rise to importance of the Middle East) and of some of the major nations. Self-sufficiency in this natural resource has enhanced the power of Russia and the United States while Britain and other European nations have been made weaker by their want of oil. The Middle East furnishes about 80 per cent of Western Europe's oil supplies and, barring major conflicts, this figure was expected to increase. Other estimates suggest that with the expansion of industrial production and national income and the flagging output of Europe's coal industry, Western European oil consumption may be trebled in twenty years. Hence control of oil becomes a crucial stake in world politics, and "oil diplomacy" has emerged as a term of art among policy makers.

Other natural resources influence foreign policy; the most basic has tended to be food production. Germany's military and political strategy in two World Wars was influenced by the need to gain a comparatively early victory before its limited food reserves were exhausted. For much the same reason, Britain, which before World War II produced only 30 per cent of its food, ran the risk of destruction when its external lines of communication were threatened by submarines and air power. Britain, by economic enterprise, had extended its influence until, by the 1930's, there was no part of the world not economically linked in some way with London, but its security became more precarious in proportion to its dependence on tenuous and extended lines of communication. Liberals, prompted by their zeal for international trade, frequently decry a nation's quest for autonomy and self-sufficiency, yet in wartime self-sufficiency becomes a decisive source of strength. Food and energy are the lifeblood of a nation; its leaders must find ways, whether domestically or internationally, to satisfy these needs.

Less permanent material elements

Industrial establishment. The twin forces of the industrial revolution and the contemporary political revolution, symbolized by the fact that approximately 60 new nations have gained recognition since World War II, underscore the vital importance of another element of foreign policy. In the nineteenth and twentieth centuries, the industrial establishment of a country has been the most basic index of world power. So long as Britain had no equal as an industrial power, its weight in the balance of power was bound to be decisive. With the increase in industrial strength of Germany and the Soviet Union or of Italy and Japan, to say nothing of the United States, Britain's capacity to influence the course of world politics was substantially reduced. Britain, having lost its industrial supremacy, also lost its capacity to serve as a balancer. France's industrial decline in relation to Germany meant that it was no longer able to resist German expansionism. Industrial capacity in both World Wars, even more than peacetime military preparedness, proved to be the *ultima ratio*. It was the latent power of the United States, reflected in its industrial resources, that tipped the scales and gave the victory to the allied powers:

In any comparison of the potential resources of the Great Powers the United States, even before Hitler's war, far outstripped every other nation in the world in material strength, in scale of industrialization, in weight of resources, in standards of living, by every index of output and consumption. And the war, which all but doubled the American national income while it either ruined or severely weakened every other Great Power, has enormously increased the scale upon which the United States now towers above its fellows.[4]

The realities of industrial capacity can therefore be ascertained and measured, at least in approximate terms. India, for example, seems to have been lacking in the industrial resources essential to a great power. Although it has substantial deposits of coal and iron and ranks high in manganese production, it has in the past lagged far behind the first-rate powers in the level of its industrial establishment. Only a tiny percentage of its total population has been engaged in industry, and its industrial plants have been severely limited. India is but one of a number of new nations whose rising political expectations are echoed in their demands for expanded industrial capacity. Its Five Year Plans are in part the expression of the drive for economic development and industrialization. Most of the nations that have only recently attained independence seek economic growth as the indispensable prerequisite of status in the international society. For some, the quest for rapid industrialization cannot be other than abortive. The observer can suggest that they might play a more significant role if they held to a more modest view of their destiny and cast

4 *The Economist* (London), May 24, 1947, p. 785.

their lot with neighboring states in a regional development program. In so doing, however, they would accept a permanently inferior position in which their freedom of action would be hedged about, and this they are unwilling to do.

Military establishment. The military establishments of nations comprise another, and possibly the most explicit, element of foreign policy. Diplomacy and military strength go hand in hand. In an earlier day, the great powers sent gunboats up the rivers of states they were seeking to influence; today a show of strength involves air forces, fleets, and satellites. The postwar distribution of power was an outcome of the position of the Red Army at strategic points in the heart of Europe. Germany's demoniacally successful diplomacy in the period between World Wars I and II was clearly the direct outgrowth of superior military preparedness. The explosion and testing of atomic weapons by the Soviet Union has been joined with strategic moves in the Cold War. The frontiers separating the spheres of influence of warring states often demarcate the limits of their effective military forces, as, for example, in Korea. As long as force remains the final arbiter of rivalries among nations, the comparative strengths of military establishments will set boundaries to actions in foreign affairs.

Military strength quite obviously lacks the permanence of the elements of geography or natural resources. Throughout history it has been subject to the compulsions of technological changes that have brought far-reaching shifts in power. The phalanx was the key to Sparta's victory over Athens in the Peloponnesian War of 431–404 B.C. Its effectiveness lay in the use of heavy infantry in close-order formation and in reliance upon shock techniques. The Athenians recovered from their defeat and, thirty-three years later, employed swarms of light infantry to conquer the Spartans. Somewhat later, the Thebans improved the phalanx by distributing its power in depth, thus introducing an element of surprise which had been missing. The Macedonians revamped the Spartan phalanx, made use of Greek mercenaries, and put their stress on a war of movement. But Macedonia was succeeded by the military genius and mobile legions of Rome. Hardened in civil and border wars, the Roman army proved versatile enough to fight as skirmishers or heavy armed infantrymen in open country and in villages and towns. However, the battle of Adrianople against heavily armed cavalrymen from the east brought the challenge Roman military leaders had foreseen but for which they were unprepared. In modern times, technology has given dramatic opportunities to those military leaders who proved capable of adaptation and innovation. By contrast, failure to respond to change has usually meant failure even for those whose traditional military resources appeared to be adequate. The Germans were defeated in World War I because they used the strategy of 1870 against their opponents' order of battle of trench warfare and economic blockade. The French, expecting another costly and brutal war of attrition, built the Maginot Line in the 1930's to fight the kind of struggle that military technology had already rendered obsolete. Short of warfare itself, the failure of military establishments to keep pace with fast-moving technological changes can also reduce nations' influence in the chancelleries of the world. This was the tragedy of France before World War II.

The difficulties inherent in maintaining military establishments that will not suffer defeat are more complex than mere responses to technological change. A nation may recognize the need for military organs capable of supporting the foreign policies it pursues but be limited in the margin of its economic resources that can be turned to military use. Some countries exhaust their resources in attaining a viable economy; others, like the United States, have a surplus with which to meet foreign military and political commitments. Belgium cannot afford to devote the same part of its gross national product to military ends as can the Soviet Union or the United States. Thus, both in absolute and relative terms, the military establishment of smaller powers must lag behind.

Three errors are commonly made in appraising the military component of foreign policy. First, military power is often confused with national power, and a nation's capacity to impose its will is equated with its military establishment. Military power is like the fist whose force depends on the health and vitality of the body politic and the whole society. Troops are an important determinant of a successful foreign policy, but without other foundations they will not suffice. Second, the military element is often viewed in more static terms than is appropriate. The democracies, although the last to arm in two World Wars, rallied their forces to gain the victory in the end. Third, it is difficult to analyze and foresee, in advance of a particular war, the most effective distribution of the components of military force. For example, what comprises a strong military force today? Is it large ground forces, hydrogen bombs, or intensive research? Is a small, highly specialized army more desirable than a large number of ground forces, or are both essential for a nation that seeks to be strong? The answers to these questions will probably be decisive in determining a state's future influence in the world, yet it is sobering that estimates must be made on the basis of contingencies that cannot now be foreseen. We know in a general way that an effective foreign policy must be supported by a military program that can safeguard national security. But this leaves those who make decisions with the painful task of distributing resources among alternative means of defense without any certainty of the kind of war they may have to fight.

Changes in industrial and military capacity. Beyond this, the weapons of today may not be used in future wars because technology has rendered them obsolete. It is said that conventional weapons are fast being supplanted by new and more deadly weapons and, that therefore, traditional armaments fail to provide an adequate basis for foreign policy. On the other hand, there are military experts who question whether atomic and hydrogen weapons will ever be used, given the prospect of mutual annihilation. Is it not fair then to ask whether the stockpiling of an unlimited supply of weapons that no nation would dare to use furnishes a state with the requisite military support? A military establishment grounded in conventional weapons may fall short of providing a defensible military posture, but so may a military program aimed at superior atomic capacities. These are the horns of the dilemma on which defense strategists could be impaled.

The human elements: quantitative and qualitative

Quantitative: population. Students of foreign policy have stressed another set of elements that make up a third concentric circle of factors of policy. They constitute the human forces—both quantitative and qualitative. Population is a quantitative factor that obviously must be considered in every calculation of the capacity of states. The Middle East provides an example of the weight that policy makers give to the fact that Arabs are more numerous than Jews. The importance of China and India rests partly in the size of their populations, which exceed 400 million people; both the Soviet Union and the United States, numbering less than half the populations of these countries, have shown respect for their potential. Conversely, nations with falling birth rates have lost influence among the society of nations, as France did after World War I. In the past, the wide diversity in technological skills, for instance between an Englishman and a Chinese, meant that population was not a factor. In recent years, this situation has been changing. The 50 million people now living in the United Kingdom enjoy a high degree of scientific skill, but there is no longer any certainty that the peoples of underdeveloped areas may not eventually approach them, or even that the combined skills of so large a population may not compensate for a persistent technological lag.

The use of population statistics and forecasts suggests that the science of estimating and predicting the relative populations of states is simple and precise. Yet demography is subject to many of the vicissitudes to which other research in the social sciences is exposed. For example, World War I virtually wiped out a whole generation of Frenchmen. France's casualties from 1914 to 1918, numbered 1,400,000 young men. By 1938, the French birth rate no longer compensated for the death rate, and in World War II, France lost 625,000 men—almost three times America's losses in a country one-fourth America's size. Yet, since World War II, the French birth rate has reversed itself, and, since 1946, the surplus of births over deaths has been about 300,000 a year—a surplus greater than that of Italy or West Germany. France, which had been static and immobile between the Wars, has witnessed a renewal of its rate of growth. In more general terms, then, population is an element of foreign policy which is not absolutely predictable and which depends on other related elements. It may enable or prevent a state from achieving its national purposes but, in either role, it is also subject to change and fluctuation.

Qualitative: policy makers and leaders. Another crucial element of policy is the role of policy makers within a political system. The study of the methods, style and quality of the process by which policies are implemented is the concern of students of both international and comparative politics. Moreover, the capacity for rational and responsible foreign policy varies greatly from state to state.

From a formal point of view, a policy maker is the official empowered with making the relevant decisions in foreign policy. In some political systems, the officials are the effective decision makers, as is the case in stable democratic systems and well-established authoritarian systems. In other cases, the officials are not the effective decision makers. The matter is one for empirical observation, knowledge of existing domestic systems, and study of historical patterns of foreign policy action. In most cases, observation will disclose the effective wielders of power and the real centers of decision making, but there will always be some doubt, especially when competing groups and elites have different views or when there is conflict on goals or on the

means of achieving them. In societies where the officials are not the true wielders of power, the search for the centers of power may lead us to the political party, the military, the trade unions, the tribal chiefs, or the intellectuals. No prediction about foreign policy trends can be made, for many countries, without a careful assessment of the relative strength of the students, the trade unions, the military, the church, and the business groups.

Formal or informal decision makers reflect the existing balance of forces in any given political society, from the most consensual to the most divided and fragmented. There are some long-range trends, however, that are very relevant to the study of foreign policy. These include the growing managerial control of advanced industrialized societies, the growing influence of the natural scientists, both as policy makers and as an important group, and the relative independence of the military. Industrialization and technological improvement, together with rising material expectations and their satisfaction, create similar societies in which ideologies progressively give place to pragmatic and technical considerations. Ideological conflicts become secondary. Such a trend inevitably leads to emphasis upon peace, since material satisfaction and the utilization of technology for this purpose are possible only if there is peace. Although there are qualifications to be made, one might well hypothesize that present industrial and technical developments put primacy upon fulfillment of material goals and satisfaction of material expectations, rather than upon international conflict. However, the growing importance of the military in all contemporary societies is *prima facie* evidence of the reverse trend.

Political leadership, in most societies, acts in order to maintain the security of the national state. An indispensable ingredient of security is power. The "realists" in international relations claim that power is a primary consideration in the behavior of the ruling groups of any nation-state, and that ideology and all other considerations are subordinate. This is undoubtedly true, and the quest for power often comes into conflict with national welfare or even internal status; thus, groups in power, in order to increase the power of the nation-state, may sometimes undermine their own position. The extent to which considerations of power will come into conflict with considerations of internal status, wealth, and leadership is a matter for empirical and historical study. In order to study comparative foreign policy, we ought to know how well entrenched are the effective wielders of power, and how likely is it that their decisions will be obeyed. International conflict will strengthen or weaken leadership, depending on the existing constellation of the various groups in a society. It is important to discover the circumstances under which an external threat leads to the consolidation of the power of an existing leadership group and when it leads to an undermining of that leadership.

It is also important to define the relations between the various decision makers or wielders of power. The question applies with equal relevance to the "Soviet world" and the "free world."

The role of ideology. What is the role of ideology within the international system? The term "ideology" applies not only to the manner in which objectives are shaped, but also to how the given objectives will be pursued. There is a range of means, extending from outright violence to attachment to the established procedures. As long as international rules for the adjustment and

accommodation of conflict have a very low degree of legitimacy, conflict will always involve a threat of violence. At what point is conflict likely to lead to war? It is difficult to make an accurate prediction, but certain obvious alternatives can be envisaged.

Some nation-states and their political leadership are likely to resort to violence more readily than others.

The available instruments of violence are an important consideration in assessing the likelihood of war. The more destructive the weapons available, the less likely their use; hence, the effort will be to accommodate conflict. "Total" destructive power in the hands of only two powers may lead to a number of alternatives: progressive disarmament of all other political systems; progressive polarization, in the form of alliances under the leadership of the two states, or an effort to redress the balance by the manufacturing of weapons by a third power or bloc, as by de Gaulle's France. Polarization may be stable if it brings about either complete disarmament of the rest of the world, with the express or tacit agreement of the two states involved or the physical division of the world into two clearly demarcated and integrated spheres. All other situations are bound to be highly unstable.

This appears to be the case some twenty years after the end of World War II. The two superpowers unable to reach an agreement have permitted a slow drift towards multicentrism. France and China have developed their atomic weapons while the Atlantic alliance and the Russian-controlled bloc are going through a process of disintegration. Thus we have again entered a period of instability mitigated only by the continuing predominance of the United States and the Soviet Union. The Sino-Soviet conflict, the growing United States involvement in

Southeast Asia, DeGaulle's withdrawal from NATO, the nationalist stirrings in West Germany, and finally the Franco-Soviet rapprochement are all indications of the fluidity of the present situation in which the only discernible pattern is the reassertion of nationalist aspirations by independent sovereign states.

Possibilities of surprise attack and retaliation obey essentially simple rules if there are only two nuclear powers. The moment ultimate weapons are available and held by many states—a threat implicit in the so-called n^{th} country problem—there can be no stabilizing force such as the one implicit in the balance-of-power theory. The situation is one in which there is no possible balancer; each nation-state, once it possesses a given number of ultimate weapons, is relatively as powerful as the other. At this point, instability is so great that it is safe to predict that conflict inevitably will lead to violence on an unprecedented scale. Our world will approximate Hobbes' model of the state of nature.

The role of information. What importance does information have in shaping policy? The problem of available information, which forms the basis of the policy makers' decision, is very complex. The theory of games postulates its free flow, much as the liberal economics assumed perfect mobility and price competition. The "liberal model" is useful because, on its basis, we can make inferences about events and developments even when empirical reality does not fit the model. The theory of games does not have this advantage, because it assumes a game without telling us what the game is about—i.e., whether it is war, peace, accommodation, maintenance of the *status quo*, surprise attack, or annihilation. Despite the theory's emphasis

upon the "rules," we cannot understand what they are unless we assume that the participants have similar objectives, norms, and leadership characteristics, a situation that obviously never obtains. If the participants all play different games with different rules, we have no game amenable to rational observation. Therefore, where and how reality differs from the model cannot be shown in any terms. The theory of games, useful in military analysis when we consider the use of weapons and force, is not relevant to the study of foreign policy.

To undertake a discussion of the relationship between information and policy making or formulation of objectives, we would have to consider: (*a*) information available to decision-making and governing elites; (*b*) information as a source of conflict among elites; (*c*) possession of information as a source of power and influence among certain of the political elites or decision makers; (*d*) the manner in which information is perceived; and (*e*) the serious problem of the disparity between the information available to the public and that available to various public policy-making and leadership groups. A subsidiary problem is that of the manufacturing of "information" in different degrees in all political systems.

It is hard to relate the above meaningfully and arrive at certain hypothetical generalizations. The Wilsonian theory, that the free flow of information would keep opinion alert and pave the way to the resolutions of all conflicts without resort to war, was based on the notion that decision makers and governing elites are more prone to conflict and war than are the people. It was further based on the assumptions that the public, when given all the facts, would make rational judgments, and that rational judgment excludes war. There are reasonable doubts, however, that public opinion is the more rational or that it is more easily modified in the light of information received. There is also less evidence than had been assumed that the withholding of information by the decision makers, or the limiting of access to it to only a small group of persons with leadership positions is more likely to lead to war.

Diplomacy: national purposes

Another element of foreign policy is the quality of a nation's diplomacy. At one level, this involves a clear conception of national purposes; at another, it involves prudence and skill in the use of the tools of statecraft. For purposes of analysis, both can be examined in the context of American foreign policy.

It is well to remind ourselves that issues confronting the makers of American foreign policy compete for attention, crowding out and succeeding one another in headlines of the daily press. Korea, Indochina, Formosa, Israel, Laos, Berlin, and Cuba, to say nothing of the overriding attention to Vietnam, flash kaleidoscopically across each of our horizons as we seek to understand international affairs. Sensing this process, it is tempting to second-guess the future. When one is asked what will be the most compelling and troublesome problems of the next six months or a year, he can prophesy the threat of war in the Middle East, orderly transition to independence or self-government in former colonial areas, or agreement on atomic controls. But behind these issues and affecting their resolution are deep-seated, underlying questions relating to this country's basic goals and national purposes. What do Americans seek in the world? Is it peace? Power? Prosperity? Each of these goals is often set forth as a national fundamental

aim. Sometimes peace, especially in this atomic age, is made an absolute purpose; prosperity sometimes seems to emerge as the one end Americans seek above all others in the conduct of their affairs in the world. We shall look in turn at each of these goals, seeking to ascertain its relevance to the real issues in America's foreign affairs.

Peace as national purpose. It is sometimes considered a mark of bad judgment to recite a succession of "great generalities" at the outset of any discussion. However, the present crisis imposes upon us responsibilities of perceiving more clearly the ebb and flow of certitude and truth with respect to the root principles of world affairs. Recent events have shaped and molded the dimensions of the international problem in a manner that few anticipated. Take, as an example, the issue of peace. For the first time in centuries, rational men have been claiming—apparently with some accord—that war has become obsolete as an instrument of national policy. President Eisenhower reiterated this view, and he maintained again at the First Geneva Conference that victor and vanquished alike would be casualties in any nuclear or hydrogen war. His successor, President Kennedy, continued negotiations until the Limited Nuclear Test Ban Treaty was signed and ratified by the Senate in 1963. But does this mean that peace is inevitable and atomic warfare impossible? Apparently not, if we consider recent policy statements, the informed opinions of experienced leaders, or events in the Middle East and above all, in Southeast Asia, without mentioning, of course, the Sino-Soviet conflict.

Power as national purpose. The most celebrated and controversial policy statements in the mid-Fifties were those attributed by *Life* writer James

Shepley to Secretary of State John Foster Dulles. In discussing the policy of "massive retaliation," Mr. Dulles observed: "The ability to get to the verge without getting into the war is the necessary art. If you cannot master it, you inevitably get into war. If you try to run away from it, if you are scared to go to the brink, you are lost." Earlier, he had said that a potential aggressor must know that his acts would be met by such retaliation and that he would lose more than he could gain. Specific targets for retaliation had to be selected and agreed upon in advance. "The way to deter aggression is for the free community to be willing and able to respond vigorously at places and with means of its own choosing." Its response should be massive and overwhelming.

If we separate the chaff from the wheat, the political from the inescapable truth in this contested statement, it seems clear that the possibility of resort to military measures has not been cast out from the armory of American foreign policy. Since the Eisenhower administration stressed, wherever possible, the replacement of manpower with decisive weapons, the risk of warfare with ultimate weapons can hardly be said to have passed. Nor is this possibility made any less ominous by the boasts of Soviet leaders that they too have developed a strategy of retaliation. The Soviet resistance to a neutral administrator of a disarmament agreement and their refusal to accept other suggested procedures are further evidence. In this situation an accident, a miscalculation, or an act of desperation could easily set off the conflict that Geneva was said to have made impossible.

Prosperity and development of national purpose. Turning to the issue of prosperity, we enter the presence of the most appealing of the current trends of informed thinking on our foreign affairs. This trend of thought maintains, with varying reservations, that most of the tensions between the West and the uncommitted countries of the world are the result of mutual suspicions, and that these can be composed through economic cooperation and aid. Put in the proper perspective, a policy of contributing modestly and consistently to prosperity and the raising of standards of living in the world is a viable, if not an utterly essential goal, of American foreign policy. Its emphasis is all the more crucial because of the neglect of this facet of American thinking in the past. However, prosperity, like peace, is at best a proximate guide to action. It offers no panacea to all the ills that engulf the world. Tensions may be eased when the fruits of economic development and growth are more widely shared at home and abroad, yet American experiences of intense strife and national division during the past decade should caution us against excessive optimism.

On a world scale, the limits of a form of inverted Marxism that looks to economic development as a miraculous device for purging tensions and strife are even more graphic. India and the United States have not been deterred from misunderstandings by India's phenomenal economic growth. The fact that India has literally raised herself by her own bootstraps, that she increased real income 15 per cent in the period from 1949 to 1954, and attained, in 1953–'54, the highest rate of economic growth in the world has, if anything, prompted her to press claims more vigorously, even when they conflicted with those of the West.

Furthermore, those who would lay the disparities in standards of living throughout the world on the conscience of the West sometimes seek to exact a heavier tribute than any nation or civilization can fulfill. These developments in other countries are intimately bound up with cultural traditions, with political order and stability, with resources, attitudes, population pressures, and a thousand local conditions that Western powers can only slightly shape or affect. If Western efforts can assist others to inch their way to a happier and more promising state of economic well-being and political justice, this will be enough, and it may even stem the advance of hostile forces. However, it can lead at best to public disillusionment and perhaps a deep and festering embitterment with the West's role in the world if public justification of these programs claims more than is warranted.

That the West should be left to find its way gropingly, painfully, and with uncertainty can come as a shock only to those who forever seek simple absolutes and an easy pathway. Peace, more than ever before in America's history, is a paramount goal of American foreign policy. However, it is a goal that knows its limits. Power throws a spotlight on those dark corners of American action which were but dimly lighted throughout the era of intellectual pacifism and political neutralism. Prosperity—especially in Asia, Africa, and the Middle East—must be as much America's aim as military security, particularly since the foe becomes ever more cunning and resourceful in his pursuit of this enterprise. Yet prosperity is a means and not an end. The interests of progressive, no less than oppressed, states clash and must be accommodated. Diplomats and not the experts in technical assistance must be called to this task.

We will be on surer ground if we recognize that peace, power, and prosperity are rough guide lines to action. They show us the perimeters within which to work, but in no way remove the demands placed on leaders for political judgment and practical wisdom.

Diplomacy and democracy

Democratic theory rests on the supposition that the very broad goals of foreign policy must be decided by the people, but the concrete decisions and implementation within these goals is the function of the political leadership, primarily the executive branch of the government. Bryce argued, in the heyday of the Wilsonian "populism" in matters of foreign policy, that the broad ends of foreign policy should be decided by the people, and he produced evidence to show why democracies had displayed more "wisdom" than despotisms in the formulation of such broad objectives. Most democratic theorists tempered their remarks with a realization that popular awareness and popular infallibility were more restricted in matters of foreign policy than in domestic matters. Bryce himself put this in the following terms: ". . . one of the strongest arguments for democratic government is that the masses of the people, whatever else they may not know, do know where the shoe pinches, and are best entitled to specify the reforms they need. In foreign policy this does not apply . . ."[5]

These basic presuppositions about the role of public opinion and the relationship between leadership and public opinion require comparative analysis and study. To begin with, the rationalist assumptions about public opinion have been subjected to careful criticism and reconsideration ever since the publication of Walter Lippmann's *Public Opinion* and the *Phantom Public*. Secondly, the apathy of

[5]James Bryce, *Modern Democracies* (New York: The Macmillan Company 1921), II, 370.

public opinion in matters of foreign policy in contemporary systems calls for the reconsideration of those presuppositions. When the European Defense Community sharply divided the French Parliament and stalemated any legislative action in the second legislature of the Fourth Republic, ". . . four-fifths of the public [in France] had heard about the project but [were] uncertain as to whether the plan had been voted or not . . ."[6] The surveys carried on by the Institute of Public Opinion in France reveal the colossal ignorance of foreign policy matters of an electorate that has been traditionally considered alert and sophisticated. In the United States, 75 per cent of the electorate have been considered as unaware of, or uninformed on, foreign policy questions.[7] Strangely enough, if public opinion polls have any relevance, the postwar German public opinion has been consistently more alert and informed than that of the traditionally democratic and enlightened nations. Third, Professor Almond's careful study of opinion, curiously enough, has not brought forth parallel studies for other countries, although his analysis of the structure and organization of public opinion could probably be widely applied. A recent study indicates the same general division between an informed active minority and a large mass of uninformed and passive public. It may be warranted, therefore, to raise this

[6]Pierre Gerbet, "L'influence de l'opinion publique et des partis sur la politique étrangère en France," in La politique étrangère et ses fondements, ed. Jean-Baptiste Duroselle, (Paris: Librairie Armand Colin, 1954).

[7]Lester Markel, ed., Public Opinion and Foreign Policy, Martin Kriesberg, Dark Areas of Ignorance. When Secretary of State Dean Acheson was under severe attack for the Truman-Acheson foreign policies, only 23 per cent of those polled could identify the Secretary of State.

fundamental question as an invitation to comparative study of foreign policy. Are the democratic presuppositions valid? If not, why? If so, under what conditions do they obtain?

Diplomatic practices and diplomacy. In diplomacy, the choice of methods and techniques is no less vital than clarity about objectives. Democracies sometimes assume that the demands of coherence and consistency in diplomacy fall less heavily upon them than upon other states. In part, this stems from the prevailing outlook about democracy and foreign policy.

The first two decades of the twentieth century witnessed the flowering of a philosophy of international politics that was unambiguously simple, straightforward, and capable of engendering widespread popular appeal. Those who held this view looked, in a spirit of buoyant optimism, to democracy and national self-determination as the twin sources of international peace and order. The creation of popular regimes on the Anglo-American model everywhere throughout the world was heralded as a sure corrective to the harsh conflicts that for centuries had wracked international life. New nations, brought into existence at the will of a self-conscious community of peoples, would dissolve the rivalries and frictions that had always led to conflict among contiguous social groups. The faith of modern Western *Homo sapiens* in man's potentialities for unending progress found its expression on the international scene in the assurance that a brave new world merely awaited the fulfillment of these goals.

It is ironic that this illusion, based on an excess of faith in what is essentially the divine right of the *vox populi* has, in the recent past, been rudely shaken on numerous fronts.

The phenomenon of totalitarian democracy, unknown in the nineteenth century, has not only left political rivalries and conflict intact but has heightened and made virtually irreconcilable the disputes among the new collectivities. Inflamed public passions, playing on statesmen, have made moderation and compromise more difficult of attainment. National leaders, by pandering to popular passions, have often reduced the alternatives open to responsible makers of foreign policy. Nationalism has not led to more peaceful relations among peoples who rested content with their political status, but instead has bred the most embittered antagonisms between new nations and their former colonial masters or between non-Western states and their erstwhile exemplars in the West. National self-determination and democracy can hardly be said to have ushered in a new era; our more serious observers find deep anguish in the steep and sudden decline of influence and self-confidence of the Western democracies. The West succeeds in engendering resentment and suspicion more often than it earns respect. Yet many students and statesmen insist on talking in bated breath about the causes and conditions of our decline. The bulk of those who assume leadership in intellectual and political life are singularly inhibited when it comes to diagnosing the source of our ills. It is commonplace to respond to a critical evaluation of the conduct of foreign policy in a democracy by pointing the finger of scorn at nondemocratic societies that are still more obviously the authors of our most recent historic catastrophes. The key to this difficult problem is surely not loss of faith in democracy. It is rather a deeper awareness of the methods of diplomacy.

Democratic diplomacy, like all diplomacy, must adhere to certain sound principles and rules. It must prove its consistency with the diplomatic tradition and the imperatives of effective negotiation. Majority votes in multilateral conference, dialectics, invective, or propaganda may hold a certain fascination for the spectators of world affairs. But more often than not, their effect is to sow international distrust and to increase, rather than alleviate, world conflicts. The first principle worth noting is that, historically, diplomacy and foreign policy have not been considered identical. Foreign policy has been viewed as the legislative aspect, and diplomacy as the executive aspect, of managing foreign relations. Diplomacy has called for experts with freedom of action; policy is a matter for the most responsible branches of government, including at some point the legislature. Diplomacy is not the framing of policy, but rather its execution. It is no more a point of focus for public attention than is the execution of the national budget, as distinct from its authorization.

The Oxford English Dictionary states: "Diplomacy is the management of international relations by negotiation; the method by which these relations are adjusted and managed by ambassadors and envoys; the business or art of the diplomatist." This definition suggests a second principle. The test of diplomacy is not the vindication of some abstract moral principle or the rewarding or punishment of virtuous or evil forces. It is rather the most effective accommodation of state relations that are sometimes in harmony, but other times in conflict.

Third, diplomacy calls for an intimate knowledge of the mechanics of negotiation, for endless patience in the use of numberless expedients in working out agreements, and for consummate skill in adjusting national proposals and making them acceptable at home and abroad without sacrificing vital objectives.

In recent years, many serious writers have questioned whether or not diplomacy has measured up to the standards inherent in these principles. Hugh Gibson, who has few peers among twentieth-century American diplomatists, wrote:

What we have come to call diplomacy in the course of the past twenty years has failed to achieve results and has led into all sorts of disasters. But it wasn't really diplomacy. It was the usurpation of diplomatic functions by politicians and inept amateurs; it was the new method of having the negotiation of infinitely complicated world problems handled by politicians, amateurs, and adventurers; the forcing on the world in critical times of new and untried methods; publicity stunts and hurried personal discussions between the political leaders, who should stay at home and be the heavy artillery in reserve rather than trying to direct operations on hurried visits to the front-line trenches.[8]

These words have even greater relevance today than they had a little more than a decade and a half ago.

The transformation of diplomatic practices. For nearly four centuries, the statecraft of Europe had certain salient features. It sought, in theory at least, to mitigate and reduce conflicts by means of persuasion, compromise, and adjustment. It was rooted in the community of interests of a small group of leaders who spoke the same language, catered to one another as often as to their own people, and played to one another's strengths and weaknesses. When warfare broke out, they drew a ring around the combatants and sought to neutralize the struggle. The old dip-

[8]Hugh Gibson, *The Road to Foreign Policy* (Garden City, N.Y.: Doubleday & Company, Inc., 1944), p. 63.

lomats carried on their tasks in a world made up of states that were small, separated, limited in power, and blessed, ironically enough, by half-hearted political loyalties. Patience was a watchword; negotiations were often as protracted during war as in peace. It was taken for granted that talks would be initiated, broken off, resumed, discontinued temporarily, and reopened again by professionals in whose lexicon there was no substitute for "diplomacy."

Today not one of these conditions any longer prevails, and the search for new formulas in diplomacy has gone on apace. The first and most novel pattern to crystallize after World War II found expression in the United Nations and in what is called "popular diplomacy." International forums and majority votes in the General Assembly were to substitute for the tortuous paths of traditional diplomacy. It must be said that this choice was expressed more rigorously in practice than in the United Nations Charter, which emphasized talks among the parties to a dispute before placing an issue on the agenda. Popular diplomacy reflects the faith in parliamentary procedures, in the rule of the people, and in straightforward, rational, and open discussion. It is the joint product of an age of rationalism and an age of popular government. It translates into global terms supreme political attainments of free people within the democratic state. Popular diplomacy, despite the role of the Great Powers in the Security Council, marks a swing of the pendulum to diplomacy by all the peoples of most of the nations. It is the antithesis of secret diplomacy by a concert of leaders of the pre-eminent countries.

Because popular diplomacy has been the basis of much of our postwar diplomacy, we are able to make a modest estimate of its success. To use Lester

Pearson's phrase, we find that the problems of "diplomacy in a gold fish bowl" are more intractable than we had supposed. Publicity has been both a virtue and a vice. It has kept the spotlight of public opinion on world affairs, but it has encouraged the actor in world politics to take inflexible positions from which it is difficult to retreat. Majority votes on Korea have demonstrated who controlled greater support; they have left conflicts of interest unaffected or have actually contributed to their increase. When this new pattern of diplomacy has worked, it has been flavored with more ancient techniques, as with the private diplomacy of Mr. Ralph Bunche in Palestine and of Mr. Jessup on Berlin, and the "quiet diplomacy" of the late Secretary-General of the United Nations on Suez and the Belgian Congo.

These successes, however noteworthy, failed to arrest the sharp swing of the pendulum to another type of international diplomacy. The Eisenhower administration espoused personal diplomacy as a means of correcting the excesses of public negotiations. The first Geneva Conference, the United States-Canadian-Mexican Conference at White Sulphur Springs, and the meeting with India's Prime Minister Nehru and with Prime Minister Macmillan of England illustrated a new and emerging pattern. It was a pattern based upon the President's partiality "for talking things out rather than negotiating things out" in an atmosphere of genial informality. It reflected the view that some of the roots of conflict would dissolve when leaders from other nations, sitting across a table from Mr. Eisenhower, became persuaded of his good intentions. The personal touch of a famous personality has been placed on the scales of world diplomacy. It is perhaps too early to assess the style

and the successes or failures, of the late President Kennedy and of President Johnson. The first combined successfully personal diplomacy and negotiations with what we have called "popular diplomacy." The Cuba crisis and the manner in which he handled the Soviet thrust there was an excellent display of a combination of diplomacy and power. His successor has shown a greater penchant for popular diplomacy. With President Johnson there has also appeared a shift away from a realistic approach in favor of ideological commitments—so common in American foreign policy.

The rediscovery of diplomacy. The two novel approaches—personal and parliamentary diplomacy—are at opposite poles of the spectrum. One emphasizes public speeches, mass assemblies, and resolutions emerging from open forums; the other stresses informality and man-to-man conferences free of protocol, agendas, and advance preparation. (At White Sulphur Springs, on the eve of the so-called Little Summit Conference, the Canadians didn't know the topics to be discussed.) Yet these new patterns, so divergent in conception and design, share one thing in common. They constitute a revolt against traditional diplomacy.

For diplomats, the first rule has always been that negotiations are essential when national interests are in conflict. Since such conflicts arise from causes more basic than personal hostility, personal amiability can hardly resolve them. Sir Harold Nicolson has argued:

Diplomacy is the art of negotiating documents in a ratifiable and dependable form. It is by no means the art of conversation. The affability inseparable from any conversation . . . produces illusiveness, compromises, and high intentions.

Diplomacy if it is ever to be effective, should be a disagreeable business, and one recorded in hard print.

The trouble with approaches that set aside the lessons of the past is that history has a way of returning to haunt us. Both popular and personal diplomacy have their place, especially if we safeguard them against their excesses. The best way of doing this is to remember that foreign policy has a memorable tradition, not all of which is folly.

REFLECTIONS ON THE STUDY OF FOREIGN POLICY IN THE CONTEXT OF THE COLD WAR

Theories of social science run the risk of departing too sharply from social reality. By contrast, advances in the medical sciences are often accounted for by the phrase, "the scientist is never too far from the patient in the sickbed." The scientist is close to nature so long as he poses relevant and researchable questions. The focus of his interest must be "operationally relevant." Economics, particularly since Walras and more notably since Keynes, has become at once more scientific and more useful. Practitioners of foreign policy are often critical of the unfortunate irrelevance of much theorizing in approaches such as the theory of decision making and behaviorism. They charge that theories remain on the drawing board without being tested or applied against reality.

At the same time, policy makers are the first to signal the need for principles of wider application or for a manageable body of doctrine on foreign policy. Public leaders need help, not merely from efficiency experts, but also from political and constitutional theorists, on problems involved in the organization of the government for the conduct of foreign policy. How should foreign policy be carried on in a democracy? Who takes responsibility and who should be the coordinator of policies and programs? What aspects of foreign policy are the appropriate concern of appointed or elected officials? What part is the responsibility of the whole of the body politic? What are the objectives of foreign policy, how should they be ranged, and in what hierarchical order? For example, how should statesmen order and relate the goals of most Western countries, which include national security, avoidance of thermonuclear war, the preservation of Western values, and support for the rising expectations of newly independent peoples?

These issues are clearly amenable to study, to the ordering of facts and data, to trial and error in testing alternative hypotheses, and to building a body of more generalized theory with relevance for practice. Propositions put forward by one observer will invariably be challenged by others. This is the story of evolving knowledge. If scholars and writers with commitments to rigorous and systematic analysis leave this rich field to others, understanding will suffer. Yet it is disheartening to note how many serious scholars prefer the simpler if tidier tasks of abstracting from reality those problems on which great masses of data are at hand, regardless of their significance.

The elements of foreign policy and the forces of international politics may seem abstract, remote, and distant when conceived of in principle or viewed in the light of an historical past. However, the present conflict between the Soviet Union and the United States is approached more meaningfully if seen in terms of the scheme of the basic factors that lie at the roots of foreign policy. The Cold War is more than two decades old by now, and is plainly visible as a conflict with at least two aspects. At one level, the struggle is for men's minds; the vitality and universality of communism and democracy are at stake. At the other level, the struggle engages two great configurations of power who, by necessity or design, reach out to influence others. A treatise on foreign policy is perhaps not the most appropriate place to analyze the comparative strengths and weaknesses of democracy and communism, for in one sense this is chiefly an issue in political theory, albeit theory in action. Soviet-American rivalry, however, is more clearly a problem in foreign relations.

Both the Soviet Union and the United States have been blessed with the most favorable of geographic situations. The United States is surrounded in the north and south by friendly and weaker states, and bounded and safeguarded in the east and west by two great ocean moats. The geographic area of the Soviet Union, constituting about one-seventh of the earth's surface, has historically swallowed up any would-be invader, although its western boundaries are exposed by the open terrain of the European plains. The natural resources of both powers are immense, and their technology is far advanced. In conventional military weapons, Russian strength probably exceeds American, but in the production of new weapons—first of an offensive type but more recently of a defensive kind—the Russians despite their progress with satellites, have lagged behind. Russia's population is slightly greater than America's, although their per capita technical skill is probably less. American political institutions should in the long run prove superior, but the Russians may temporarily enjoy the advantages that flow from a system in

which instantaneous decision making and personal initiative are possible. National morale, particularly in the hydrogen age, is difficult to measure before a crisis. The quality of diplomacy on both sides is subject to the broader tendencies and problems that have been described.

Americans live by the faith that other peoples will come to embrace a political creed involving a decent respect for the dignity of mankind, and that an international order may be founded on respect for the rights and interests of other sovereign states. However, there are three obstacles that confound American policy makers and that must at least be mitigated if the struggle is to be won.

Policy and public opinion. The first obstacle is inherent in the problem of marshalling domestic support for American policies while at the same time putting America's best foot forward in the eyes of the rest of the world. To mobilize support for policies, Americans say things to themselves that, from the standpoint of other peoples, might better be left unsaid. (In this, the United States is, of course, not unique.) America is a vast sprawling continent of great diversity of political and religious beliefs; in its constitutional system, power and responsibility are broadly diffused, although less so in foreign affairs than in the conduct of domestic affairs. Thus Americans speak in many voices, some raucous and strident, as they seek to persuade one another of the right course to follow. The language of domestic politics is not the language of political theory. It aims to unite as many as will join to support policies or programs. It looks to a common denominator that can more often be found in broad principles and moral generalities than in specific directives of strategy which, like military policies, must be cast in practical alternatives to meet circumstances. It prefers militant slogans to qualified truths, a crusade to public conversations about a problem.

Above all, it is a permanent part of the landscape of international relations that American foreign policy must draw its support from a union of the experts, the public, and friends and allies abroad. History demonstrates that no American statesman can ignore any point on the triangle without courting disaster. Before World War II, the public ostensibly lagged behind the thinking on foreign affairs of experts and allies. Following World War II and up to 1950, American policy—especially for Europe—was acceptable alike to the authoritative views of the experts, to the public, and to the members of the postwar Grand Alliance. This day has passed, and the demands of the three groups have tended increasingly to go their separate ways. America's allies have more and more viewed their national interests as not necessarily identical with the United States'; ironically, at a time when American policies are vulnerable to criticism by experts at home and abroad, they enjoy broad endorsement at all levels of American life to the point of becoming virtually untouchable. By stressing one side of the triangle and striving above all for harmonious domestic political relations, the Eisenhower administration, and more recently the Johnson administration, created difficulties for itself at the other points on the triangle. In this way, it illustrated a perennial problem in the conduct of foreign relations.

Colonialism. Another obstacle stems from the colonial dilemma, which reaches beyond America's national life and touches conflicting interests at work throughout the rest of the world. We know that the colonial problem stands at the top of every agenda for discussion of American foreign policy. Responsible officials are encouraged to issue proclamations and to throw America's weight behind independence movements. In this setting, it is tempting to take general and sweeping positions and to express an American doctrine on the rights of peoples everywhere to independence and self-government. This is particularly true because Americans' own experience is so rich in its lessons and apparently pregnant with meaning. The fruits of attempts thus far made to propound a dogma should serve, however, to give us pause, for the record of America's efforts to align itself squarely with either colonial or anticolonial powers is sprinkled with as many failures as successes.

Nevertheless, Americans face new situations today and demands crowd in upon them for new and more vigorous policies. Nationalism is on the march in Asia, the Middle East, and Africa, and Americans implore one another to identify their country with these movements rather than appearing to stand in their pathway. Unhappily, the colonial problem is less tractable than those exhortations suggest. For at the same time as the fight is waged to end old imperialisms, a new and more demoniac expansionism threatens. To meet it, some feel that America must cleave to its trusted friends and allies with whom it has interests and military bases in common, striving to preserve a more stable world balance of power. Yet, in itself, this is not likely to be enough. The present equilibrium of power will be upset unless America can join with new forces in the so-called underdeveloped areas. We may say, therefore, that the

United States faces the triple challenge of stemming the tide of Russian imperialism and Chinese communism, uniting the other Western states, and drawing closer to non-Western peoples only recently emerging as independent states. In a manner of speaking, policy makers must keep three balls in the air. This is the unenviable task of American statesmanship.

The pathos of our present position may be illustrated briefly from events in the last decade. First there was the statement on Goa, recognizing Portugal's authority in the tiny enclave in India, prompted doubtless by the zeal of European officers in the State Department to display a sense of community with Portugal. This provoked deep resentment in India and, perhaps, throughout much of Asia. Next came the expression of "sympathy" for Greek feelings in the Cyprus dispute, by the United States Ambassador to Greece, Cavendish W. Cannon, which loosed a torrent of British protest. Then the Dutch voiced dismay at Mr. Dulles' warm and friendly comments during a visit to the Indonesian Republic. More recently, the United States aroused its European friends by appearing to take sides with Egypt and Middle Eastern friends by reassuring Turkey against Syria and Russia. More recently the changing objectives of Soviet foreign policy, the emergence of a new and independent but powerful communist China in Asia, the specter of communism of the Castro variety in the neighboring countries of Latin America have underscored the predicament of American foreign policy. The Soviet image is rapidly changing among our Western allies and the need of accommodation with the Soviet Union is beginning to be shared by many American experts. Yet we remain somehow still committed to an "anticommunist posture" that paralyzes our

reflexes and makes more difficult negotiations on common interest between the two countries. Similarly there is a tendency to view the war in Vietnam in global and absolute terms—as the extension of communist aspirations for domination and expansion instead of considering it as a manifestation of a limited and negotiable area of conflict. Events in Latin America have shown an increasing nervousness with popular revolutions, whose champion we often were in the past, and a tendency to equate them with anti-American subversive moves directed and inspired by "world communism." Such attitudes have accounted for the progressive decline of our influence and position in Western Europe.

Perceiving these problems, can we say anything about this perplexing picture that will offer some guidance to the juggler or policy maker of whom we have spoken? Perhaps there are guidelines or principles we can enunciate to spotlight a few of the darker corners of this colonial problem. First, we must start with the presumption that the colonial problem is fraught with dilemmas with which America must learn to live. Dogmas for or against colonialism will not waft them away. Solutions must be worked out case by case; and as, for example, Tunisia is not identical with Algeria, policies must be shaped to meet individual needs. Second, timing is of the essence. The statement supporting Indonesia stirred up a hornets' nest because Dutch-Indonesian tensions at that time were great, over the trial of a former Chief of Dutch Military Intelligence charged with plotting to overthrow the Indonesian government, over the conflict for Netherlands New Guinea, and over the unilateral abridgment by Indonesia of certain financial and economic treaties. Third, if any general solution can be found, it rests in the coordinating of mutual interests, not in the wholesale sacrifice of one set of interests to another. In North Africa, the French, American, and African interests appeared to coincide, in that all wanted "liberal solutions." Likewise, in other regions, the goal should be the harmonizing of interests. This calls for a judicious balancing of claims. Fourth, it is one of the ironies of history that force may be necessary to preserve colonial arrangements, not in order to perpetuate them, but that their orderly liquidation may be achieved. Fifth, it will not do to call every conflict of view between America and its European allies a colonial issue. On October 2, 1956, in what one commentator called a "Freudian slip that betrayed the main lines of American thinking," Mr. Dulles noted that Britain and America were at odds over Suez on the question of the "shift from colonialism to independence." He treated Suez as an issue between the "colonial powers" and "the powers which are primarily and uniquely concerned with the problem of getting their independence as rapidly as possible." Walter Lippmann was prompt to point out that Egypt could hardly be considered a colony, especially as it sought to expand its national power. A British journal observed:

The American desire to keep the goodwill of the Arab states is good sense . . . but it will defeat itself in the end if, in pursuing it, the Americans think in anti-colonial conventions which are current. . . . In that way they will merely seek to please everybody, committing their strength to the support of local weak men, and overlooking that the conflicts which trouble the region, being real conflicts, require solutions of substance which are bound to give offense to some.[9]

Finally, conflicts of interest—as past

[9] *The Economist* (London), December 8, 1956, p. 853.

conflicts between Britain and India or between the Dutch and the Indonesians —may be swept along by powerful historical movements until one side emerges supreme. It may be necessary for American policy makers to choose sides, and so inevitably give offense. These facts need not preclude prudence and restraint, but the end of the colonial era has changed the form, if not the substance, of choices Western leaders must make.

The moral problem. A final obstacle has roots in the moral problem. The question of right and wrong is continuously raised in international relations, as in all the other social orders. Nations as individuals either seek to do, or claim to have done, what is right. The nature of Western values, as embodied in American culture, assures that America persistently aspires to justice and to the goal of international order. We are pained when some aspect of national conduct cannot be justified in broader international terms, yet we can take comfort from the fact that, historically, this has been among the most baffling philosophical problems. The question is whether an action shall be called "good" if it serves the group of primary loyalty, or whether it must serve a more inclusive purpose. Political morality, as distinct from pure law or justice, dictates the answer in terms that give it a unique flavor. We must look for the point of concurrence between the particular and the general value or interest, rather than calling for the sacrifice of the part to the whole. Politically, there always remains a residual egotism or self-interest which represents the creative potential of individuals and groups. The nascent international community must guard against extreme forms of parochial loyalty, which end in nations claiming too much and reserving to themselves the right to suppress and overwhelm weaker neighbors. Short of this, however, the larger community is able to harness, beguile, and deflect the more limited national purposes even though it cannot easily transcend them. In Reinhold Niebuhr's words: "The individual or the group may feel called upon to sacrifice an immediate value for the sake of the more ultimate or general interest. But the community cannot demand this sacrifice as its right." Nor, one might add, can another sovereign state.

America's policy makers look for shortcuts to the moral problem. They talk a great deal more about promoting the impact of morality than about determining its content. They seize on the most available expressions congenial to their tastes and interests, like "majority rule" and "the will of the United Nations." The workings of political machinery are invested with all the trappings of a religious exercise, and political pronouncements are equated with the glorification of God. Repelled by all the talk of "missions" and "crusades," one of our most sensitive critics has said: "I would rather *be* moral than claim to be it; and to the extent we succeed in lending moral destruction to the conduct of our affairs, I would rather let others discover it for themselves." The deep pathos of the moral problem calls more for Christian humility than for a moralistic self-righteousness, which can win few friends abroad and serves only to lower the currency of moral principles.

CONCLUSION

When it comes to studying foreign policy in its various manifestations, and most particularly international conflict including war, the social scientist is in a difficult position. He is asked to ex-

plain and predict attitudes whose complexity makes a mockery of the few "scientific" tools we have. The layman presses us to predict American or Chinese foreign policy; to unwrap the famous riddle of the Soviet foreign policy; or to explain the nature and conditions of conflict in our contemporary world.

The more stubborn and complex the material, the greater the temptation to move into the realm of abstraction. The canons of science call for simplicity and economy in the formulation of hypotheses that are to be tested. It is only when simple hypotheses are tested that the scientist moves into the more complex, slowly relating and checking his findings with the outside world. We, in contrast, find that we cannot test. As a result, many of us today find it easier *not* to relate our speculations to the outside world at all, and to create propositions, conceptual schemes, and models that have logical coherence, but fail to pass the test of empirical relevance. There is much futility in this.

The way out, in our opinion, is to assume from the start that the range of indeterminacy in our social and political world is great. This is even more applicable to the behavior of states that goes under the name of "foreign policy." To attempt to construct generalizations and models that will give us a rigorous scientific understanding and prediction of foreign policy is a hopeless task.

As we move more into the realm of abstraction in the name of "science," we become more likely to evade—and perhaps evasion is the basic reason for the "scientific" trend toward a high degree of abstraction and conceptualization—our responsibilities in advancing an understanding of politics, notably in international relations and conflict. We would, for instance, suggest a better understanding and study of the existing laboratory, i.e., history. (We cannot understand why simulated war games are more important to devise and study than actual or historical conflict from which all degree of simulation is eliminated by the stark and brutal necessity of real choice and decisions.) Second, we believe that case studies of the individual foreign policymaking process, including conflict of various states in terms of the descriptive categories suggested, would give us considerable food for thought and might lead us to more fruitful hypotheses.

One of our aims should be to find regularities in the behavior of nations and to develop general propositions by setting forth carefully the conditioning factors that account for types of behavior. Thus we may hope to reduce the range and degree of indeterminacy. But ours is also a world where exercise of will and choice calls for more than a scientific knowledge of man and nations.

The analytical approach to foreign policy, as distinct from the ideological approach, is no miracle-working device for understanding the complex problems of international affairs. It gives no clue to the specific decisions that must be reached daily. It is not a cookbook with recipes for action to fit every contingency. It does, however, provide a way of thinking about the foreign policy of any country and ordering the factors that contribute to the conduct of foreign relations. If prediction is still beyond the reach of scholars, analysis in the face of varying contingencies may be attainable. In some form or another, this method is useful in studying the acts of great and small powers. Amid all the variations of individual scholars writing about unique national policies, the present book serves to demonstrate the role and the limits of the systematic analysis of foreign policy.

SELECTED BIBLIOGRAPHY

Almond, Gabriel A., *The American People and Foreign Policy.* New York: Frederick A. Praeger, Inc., 1960.

Aron, Raymond, *A Century of Total War.* Garden City, N. Y.: Doubleday & Company, Inc., 1954.

———, *Peace and War: A Theory of International Relations.* Garden City, N.Y.: Doubleday & Company, Inc., 1966.

Beloff, Max, *Foreign Policy and the Democratic Process.* Baltimore: Johns Hopkins Press, 1955.

Buchanan, William, *How Nations See Each Other: A Study in Public Opinion.* Urbana: University of Illinois Press, 1953.

De Visscher, Charles, *Theory and Reality in Public International Law.* Princeton, N. J.: Princeton University Press, 1956.

Duroselle, Jean-Baptiste, *La politique etrangere et ses fondements.* Paris: Librairie Armand Colin, 1954.

Fehrenbach, T. R., *This Kind of Peace.* New York: David McKay, Inc., 1966.

Gross, Feliks, *Foreign Policy Analysis.* New York: Philosophical Library, 1954.

Haas, Ernest B., and Allen S. Whiting, *Dynamics of International Relations.* New York: McGraw-Hill Book Company, 1956.

Halle, Louis J., *Civilization and Foreign Policy.* New York: Harper & Row, Publishers, Inc., 1955.

Hinsley, F. H., *Power and the Pursuit of Peace.* New York: Cambridge University Press, 1963.

Hoffmann, Stanley (ed.), *Contemporary Theory in International Relations*. Englewood Cliffs, N. J.: Prentice-Hall, Inc., 1960.

Kennan, George F., *Realities of American Foreign Policy*. Princeton, N. J.: Princeton University Press, 1954.

———, *American Diplomacy: 1900–1950*. Chicago: University of Chicago Press, 1951.

Marshall, C. B., *The Limits of Foreign Policy*. New York: Holt, Rinehart & Winston, Inc., 1955.

Morgenthau, Hans J., *Politics Among Nations*. New York: Alfred A. Knopf, Inc., 1954.

———, *The Purpose of America*. New York: Alfred A. Knopf, Inc., 1960.

———, and Kenneth W. Thompson, *Principles and Problems of International Politics*. New York: Alfred A. Knopf, Inc., 1951.

Nicolson, Harold, *Diplomacy*. New York: Harcourt, Brace & World, Inc., 1933.

———, *The Evolution of Diplomatic Methods*. New York: Harper & Row, Publishers, Inc., 1955.

Thayer, Charles W., *Diplomat*. New York: Harper & Row, Publishers, Inc., 1959.

Thompson, Kenneth W., *Christian Ethics and the Dilemmas of Foreign Policy*. Durham, N. C.: Duke University Press, 1959.

———, *Political Realism and the Crisis of World Politics*. Princeton, N. J.: Princeton University Press, 1960.

———, *The Moral Issue in Statecraft*. Baton Rouge, Louisiana: Louisiana University Press, 1966.

———, *American Diplomacy and Emergent Patterns*. New York: New York University Press, 1962.

Wadsworth, James, *The Glass House*. New York: Frederick A. Praeger, Inc., 1966.

2

BRITISH
FOREIGN
POLICY

LEON D. EPSTEIN

British foreign policy making has often been regarded as a model for other countries, particularly for the United States. Much of the world has been willing to admire the method, if not always the substance, of British policy, assuming that Britain's policy-making process was calculated to serve the national interest, and that the wisdom and shrewdness of diplomacy prevailed over political emotions and parochial concerns. Britain's diplomatic prestige was almost inevitable during the centuries when so small an island kingdom existed as a world power. The reputation of the process by which British foreign policy was made and executed was enhanced by its success.

It has been more difficult to sustain this reputation during the last few decades of decline in Britain's status among the great powers. Neither the adjustment to second place in a military alliance nor the accommodation to massive imperial withdrawal, even if graciously accomplished, appears as impressive as the policies that had previously established Britain's leadership and empire. No nation has ever so successfully surrendered so much in so short a time as has Britain since 1945, but the world has not been awed in the way that it was by the original accumulation of territory and power. Nor is the world likely to be impressed by Britain's current attempts to discover a lesser but still influential role.

THE NATIONAL BACKGROUND

Economic geography

Except for Japan, whose days of glory were few, Britain has been the only major power of modern times to be based on an island rather than a large continental area. It is easy to forget how small the British island home is. The whole of the United Kingdom, including the six counties of Northern Ireland plus England, Wales, and Scotland, comes to just over 94,-000 square miles—an area smaller than Oregon and only slightly larger than Minnesota. Over 53 million people now live in the United Kingdom, and about 46 million of this total are in England and Wales, which together have one of the highest population densities of any white community of comparable size. Over ten million persons live in London and its immediate environs, and almost every Englishman is within a day's rail journey of London.[1] This densely populated island is separated from the northwest coast of Europe by only 21 miles of open water, but even this distance has been sufficient for British life to develop its own distinctive pattern. Al-

though isolation from European power struggles (in the nineteenth-century American manner) has never been feasible, the British long avoided identification as a purely European power.

Britain's island location and the absence of a nearby frontier, either in Britain or on the continent, made it natural for Englishmen to seek their fortunes in faraway places. This meant sea trade as well as colonial settlement, and both ventures were highly developed before the industrial revolution. Almost from the start, British factories supplied an established overseas trade in addition to a domestic market. By the mid-nineteenth century, the large-scale exchange of domestic manufactures for overseas raw materials and foodstuffs had become the cardinal feature of the British economy. Abundant coal, only recently expensive to mine, provided an important base for the early British industrial supremacy. Not until 1870 did this supremacy begin to fade in relation to the more rapid industrial growth of Germany and the United States.[2]

Nineteenth-century industrialization made the British almost entirely an urban people, and reduced agriculture to a decidedly secondary status. Now fewer than 5 per cent of the nation's gainfully employed workers are engaged in agriculture—a lower proportion than in any other country in the world.[3] Despite recent successful efforts to increase agricultural production, the British must remain predominantly a manufacturing people and also a people largely dependent on outside sources of food and raw materials. Well over half of the nation's

[1] Demographic and economic data are published by the Central Statistical Office, *Annual Abstract of Statistics* (London: Her Majesty's Stationery Office).

[2] W. Stanford Reid, *Economic History of Great Britain* (New York: The Ronald Press Company, 1954), pp. 337, 377.

[3] P. Sargent Florence, *The Logic of British and American Industry* (London: Routledge & Kegan Paul, Ltd., 1953), p. 5.

food is now imported, and in order to pay for the food Britain must export a very high percentage of its manufactured products. Although British real income, per capita, stands relatively high in the world, it rests heavily and uneasily on the vicissitudes of international economic relations.

Social structure

Class differentiation, on various bases, is treated more openly as a fact of life in Britain than in the United States, and this may lead to an exaggeration of the relative importance of class in British politics. It is true, however, that working-class consciousness has, at least until very recently, been definite and substantial. Despite the occupational rise of many Englishmen in each generation,[4] a rise resembling American patterns of mobility, the working class long retained a distinctive status resting on the assumption that most children of workers would themselves become workers. The sense of status, especially in the past, was linked to a deferential attitude toward a traditional ruling class, but it has also been significantly associated with the solidarity of manual laborers, both in industrial unions and in political movements. Class consciousness of this kind appears stronger in Britain than in the United States because of the residue of a feudal past and because of the sharply unequal distribution of the benefits of early industrialization. An important sense of differentiation remains despite the material advantages afforded the working class by the egalitarian governmental policies of the 1940's and the general prosperity of the 1950's and 1960's. Status may now be more fully identified with occupation than with

income, and also with intangibles such as style of life or manner of speech.

An important part in the preservation of class distinctions is played by the British educational system. This is obviously true of the famous "public schools," which are really private boarding or day schools attracting, at the secondary level, almost all children whose parents can afford the fees. These schools remain the most prestigious, and the best of them provide an education of extremely high quality. Government grammar schools also provide secondary education of quality, but only for the minority who display sufficient academic promise in the examinations given the children when they are about eleven years old. The remaining students of secondary age go to less academic government schools, most of which were created after World War II. Comprehensive schools which, like American high schools, are designed to give courses under one roof for students of different abilities, have until recently developed only in some areas. The older pattern, in publicly supported secondary education, is to separate students sharply on the basis of ability. The best students are given the kind of education that fits them to compete, along with the students of the private schools, for the very limited number of places available in British universities and for the scholarships that subsidize a large percentage of university students. It is clear that this system produces an able intellectual elite, selected largely on the basis of merit.[5] Now that ability counts heavily, along with wealth and family background, the talented and motivated child of the working class can secure both a grammar-school and a university education. In doing so, he

[4] D. V. Glass, ed., *Social Mobility in Britain* (London: Routledge & Kegan Paul, Ltd., 1954), p. 20.

[5] Michael Young, *The Rise of the Meritocracy* (London: Thames and Hudson, 1958).

enters an elite of the middle and upper classes, distinguished in educational experience and attainment from the bulk of the population, so that the tradition of class status is maintained even though the opportunity to rise is modernized. This distinction may be observed in the wide gulf between the newspapers of the elite, notably the *Times* and the *Guardian*, and those of the mass, still mainly characterized by an extremely low quality.

On the other hand, there are many ways in which the British people are markedly homogeneous. The population, despite substantial immigration in the 1950's from the West Indies, India, and Pakistan, is still 98 per cent white, and the immigration controls enacted in the early 1960's are designed to maintain the proportion. The white population is overwhelmingly of a "British stock," formed by successive invasions of long ago. The Scots and the Welsh preserve distinctions, but their national background is assuredly British. Irish immigrants must be noted separately, but they, along with smaller numbers of continental refugees, are decidedly exceptional minorities. The great bulk of Britain's inhabitants, unlike the Americans, have no national background save their present one. The British also have a considerable religious homogeneity. The nation is largely Protestant, with about four million Roman Catholics and a half-million Jews.

Political experience

Not only are the British old as a people, but they are also old as a nation. The unity of England and Wales goes back to the Middle Ages, and the union with Scotland dates from the beginning of the eighteenth century. The island was small enough to be dominated early by a single political authority, mainly representing the numerically superior English population. National political institutions are of such long standing that loyalty to them can be taken for granted in a way that would be difficult in a more recently created nation.

The supremacy of Parliament, in relation to the monarch, has been constitutionally established since 1688. Traditionally, the parliamentary regime was liberal and aristocratic: it was liberal in the sense of standing for the liberty of individuals and of property, and it was aristocratic in that relatively few were eligible to choose parliamentary representatives. Like British society in general, the political system was non-egalitarian until late in the nineteenth century, when the vote was extended to the mass of the population. That the political institutions, managed over centuries by a special ruling class, should thus have been democratized without revolution distinguishes British history from much of the European continent's. That history is also distinguished from America's, in that Britain had a long predemocratic political experience and that it adapted universal suffrage to an old institutional pattern.

The liberalism of the British tradition has been associated particularly with the toleration of dissenting and unpopular opinions. Although there have been exceptions, respect for individual liberty of expression has been characteristic of modern British history. To some degree, this is the heritage of Protestant religious differences which, since the seventeenth century, have been tolerated for the sake of internal peace. Whatever the source, there is no doubt about the vitality of the tradition in political as well as in religious matters. It means toleration of eccentrics and even of those regarded as subversive elsewhere in the democratic world.

Persistent external concerns

Historically, Britain has had two major international concerns. The first has been to maintain oceanic access to the rest of the world, and the second to prevent any potentially hostile power from dominating the continent of Europe. Both concerns have been vital to the national interest. Without overseas connections, Britain would have been cut off, not just from imperial possessions or Commonwealth partners but also from the world trade which sustains British life. Even more directly would Britain have been adversely affected if any single nation controlled Europe and threatened to dominate Britain as well.

In the days when the British Empire was at its zenith and when most of the now equal partners in the Commonwealth were imperial colonies, the simplest way to maintain overseas access was for Britain itself to command the seas. This is just what Britain did on its own until about the time of World War I. As long as "Britannia ruled the waves," the nation's trade routes were secure and so were its military communications with the Empire. The growth of American naval power ended exclusive British control of the seas, but the advantages of that control remained because the United States became an ally and not an enemy. The most direct threat first came from the German navy, and especially from German submarines in both world wars. For the first time in modern history, an enemy was equipped with a force that could just possibly cut the British lifeline to the outside world. And this was not yet all. The airplane and the rocket bomb threatened the island even more dramatically during World War II. Ruling the waves, although still within the power of Britain joined by the United States, was no longer enough to pro-

vide security for the island and its people. It is surely not enough now.

The classic British concern with the European balance of power has sometimes been explained as a corollary of the nation's general position in the world. In his famous Foreign Office memorandum of 1907, Eyre Crowe assumed that Britain's capacity to command the seas, which he regarded as essential, would inspire fear and jealousy among other countries.[6] To avert an anti-British combination based on such fear and jealousy, Crowe thought, Britain needed to make special efforts to develop a policy that harmonized with the interests of other nations. First among these interests, he wrote, was independence, and therefore Britain had rightly championed (and should continue to champion) the independence of nations against any single powerful and ambitious state. In practice, this meant a grouping of forces against first one strong European power and then another, "but ever on the side opposed to the political dictatorship of the strongest single State or group at a given time."[7] So explained, Britain's policy in Europe was a striking instance of high-mindedness coinciding with national self-interest.

Neither of Britain's major concerns has diminished in the nuclear age. Access overseas, even without large imperial possessions, remains vital for economic reasons, and the avoidance of hostile domination of continental Europe is politically as well as economically important. It is the means for dealing with these concerns which have changed. With limited resources

[6]Memorandum by Eyre Crowe, in *British Documents on the Origins of the War: 1898–1914*, ed. G. P. Gooch and Harold Temperley (London: Her Majesty's Stationery Office, 1928) vol. III.

[7]*Ibid.*, p. 403. On the balance of power, see also Harold Nicolson, *Diplomacy* (London: Oxford University Press, 1950), p. 135.

in a new world of super powers, Britain's old command of the seas is impossible, and even a joint Anglo-American oceanic mastery provides much less security in the age of nuclear missiles than was achieved in times past. Similarly, the means of preventing hostile domination of the European continent have drastically altered. Britain itself cannot supply the crucial element in a coalition against the single strongest continental power. This is even clearer when that power is Russia, as it has been since World War II, than when it was Germany. In both instances, the United States, rather than Britain, became the decisive force.

Yet another and newer circumstance has rendered Britain's balance-of-power policy obsolete in Europe. This is the rapidly growing integration of the Western continental nations which threatens Britain economically, although not militarily, unless Britain can actually join the new European community. But joining would represent as sharp a break with traditional British methods as would a complete elimination of British influence in continental affairs.

THE POLICY-MAKING PROCESS

In discussing the conduct of British foreign affairs, observers sometimes hold that there has been a change from control by a nineteenth-century executive elite to control by a twentieth-century legislative democracy.[8] This seems to overstate what has happened. Now as before, the initiative remains in the hands of the executive branch. It may be granted that the contempo-

[8]That such a change has taken place is accepted, admiringly, by many left-wing writers, and it is also accepted as a fact, though an unfortunate one, by a more conservative critic like Walter Lippmann, *The Public Philosophy* (Boston: Little, Brown and Company, 1955), p. 24.

rary executive, in exercising its initiative, responds to a broader public than did nineteenth-century statesmen, whose concern was limited to an upper-and-middle class electorate. But the concern to secure support for a given foreign policy was no less real for a popular and successful nineteenth-century Foreign Secretary like Lord Palmerston, just because his public was smaller than it is in present-day democratic Britain.[9] Moreover, the informed public, regularly concerned with foreign affairs, is by no means overwhelmingly large in our own time.

Governmental agencies

The executive authority. The basic constitutional principle is that the Crown is responsible for British policy. In modern times this means that responsibility is exercised by ministers of the Crown—the government. Although ministers hold office only by having the confidence of a majority in the House of Commons, the conduct of foreign policy is firmly in their hands and rarely subject to concessions necessary to retain that parliamentary confidence. Policy is not conceived as the product of legislative deliberation, but only as matter for debate after it has been submitted by the government. Practically speaking, the government usually consists of a Cabinet of fifteen to twenty ministers, chosen by the Prime Minister from among his party's most important political leaders. The members of the Cabinet are supposed to share executive responsibility in a way that American departmental secretaries do not. Although in principle, the Prime Minister is not so dominant as is a President of the United States in relation to his Cabinet, there is little doubt that the British doctrine of col-

[9]Charles Webster, *The Foreign Policy of Palmerston* (London: G. Bell & Sons, Ltd., 1951), I, 44–51.

legial executive authority is modified in practice by a strong and determined Prime Minister. In foreign affairs, perhaps even more than in domestic affairs, he can make the crucial decisions, assisted by no more than a few inner Cabinet colleagues of his own choosing, and subsequently obtain the support of the remainder of the Cabinet. This much can be said without subscribing to the new, unorthodox theory that British executive authority has become so focused in a single person as to make for "prime-ministerial" government, approximating presidential rather than traditional cabinet government.

The Prime Minister himself assumes a special responsibility in all major foreign policy matters even though ordinarily—and always since 1924— the foreign secretaryship is entrusted to another member of the cabinet. The Foreign Secretary is much more than the Prime Minister's agent, but he is not free to make policy without the approval of his chief and, ultimately at least, of the Cabinet.

Contrary to general impression, the foreign secretaryship has not always, especially in recent years, gone to a man greatly experienced in international affairs. Sir Anthony Eden did have such an orientation even before he first became Foreign Secretary, but Labour's two postwar appointees, Ernest Bevin and Herbert Morrison, had both been concerned almost exclusively with domestic matters before assuming the Foreign Secretary's duties. So had Michael Stewart, chosen in 1965 for Harold Wilson's Labour government. Considerations other than experience in foreign affairs plainly influenced these selections. General ability and political status have sometimes been decisive. It may be important to choose a man well-equipped to lead party members in support of governmental policy, or a man in whom the Prime Minister has great personal confidence with respect to the carrying out of the Prime Minister's policy. Winston Churchill reposed such confidence in Anthony Eden, who served as his Foreign Secretary from 1940 to '45 and from 1951 to '55, Eden in Selwyn Lloyd in 1956, and Harold Macmillan in Lord Home from 1960 to '63. Home, incidentally, was the first Foreign Secretary, since before World War II, to serve while in the House of Lords. The expectation, treated as doctrine by the Labour Party, is that the Foreign Secretary, like the Prime Minister, should be a member of the House of Commons and so directly answerable to that body.

The Prime Minister and the Foreign Secretary are not the only members of the political executive (that is, of the government) who deal with foreign affairs. Since World War II, there have been at least four additional ministers, not of Cabinet rank, in this area. Wilson's Labour government of 1964 had five, of whom four were ministers of state for foreign affairs, and one an under-secretary. Each had a separate responsibility—for example, one minister represented Britain at the United Nations and another was primarily concerned with disarmament negotiations. Three of the five were in the Lords, and two in the Commons. This division, as well as the total number and the assignment of responsibilities, can vary from government to government. Beyond these particular appointments, there are other ministers whose work relates to foreign affairs. The Chancellor of the Exchequer and the Defense Secretary, plus the ministers of the Army, Navy, and Air Force, are always concerned, and so generally is the Secretary for Commonwealth Relations and the Secretary for the

Colonies (which have recently been combined in a single ministry). What must be said of all ministers dealing with foreign affairs, whether or not they are directly assigned to that sphere, is that they are primarily politicians and only secondarily specialists in the subject matter of their ministries. The Foreign Secretary, like any minister, exercises executive authority as a member of his government, and the government is the political leadership of the nation.

The foreign service. Deliberately and carefully differentiated from the political level in the conduct of foreign affairs is the career service. As a distinguished retired career officer explained, "The Foreign Service is an instrument of Government; it does not formulate policy." However, he grants that the foreign service, by presenting all the material facts, "advises the Secretary of State on what his policy should be."[10] Obviously the giving of advice in this manner contains an element of influence. Even though the power to make policy remains in the hands of the political authority, which has been known to act against the advice of career officials, the description of the foreign service's role as limited to carrying out policy must be qualified by the inevitable indefiniteness of any line between formulation and execution.

A sense of profession is highly developed and of long standing in the foreign service. Admission to the Foreign Office itself, as well as to the diplomatic service, has been firmly based on open competitive examinations since the 1870's, when a similar procedure was adopted in the British

civil service generally. Recruitment, then as now, was separate from recruitment of members of the home service, and the development of special standards of competition gave the foreign service a prestige of its own. Until after World War I, there was even a separation between diplomatic personnel and Foreign Office (or headquarters) personnel. This separation has disappeared and indeed, since the large-scale reorganization of 1943, the foreign service now includes the formerly distinct Consular and Commercial-Diplomatic Services, plus auxiliary services. The whole of this enlarged foreign service remains distinct from the bulk of civil service employees.

The traditionally prestigious elements of the foreign service have been the diplomats and the top-level personnel of the Foreign Office. It is they who occupy the positions for which independent means and social status were once requisites and for which the intellectual and personal standards have been so high as to favor those with the very best educational backgrounds. Ordinarily this has meant high-ranking graduates of Oxford and Cambridge, and there is little evidence of any recent change in this respect. Intellectually, the method of selection is as rigorous as ever, but whether this implies a class bias in recruitment is less certain. The large-scale state scholarship program allows poorer students to compete at Oxford and Cambridge, as well as at other universities, and so also to compete in foreign service examinations.[11]

Important career opportunities have been afforded by the foreign service because the very top positions, with rare exceptions, have been reserved

---

[10]Frank T. Ashton-Gwatkin, *The British Foreign Service* (Syracuse, N.Y.: Syracuse University Press, 1950), p. 49.

[11]On recruitment, see Lord Strang, *The Foreign Office* (New York: Oxford University Press, 1955), chaps. 4–5.

for members of the service. British practice has differed notably from the once-prevalent, and still occasionally practiced, American custom of giving the best foreign posts to politicians and businessmen as rewards for their contributions to successful presidential campaigns. It is equally important to appreciate that the British promotional ladder also includes the extremely important positions involving administrative direction of the Foreign Office, particularly the post of Permanent Under-Secretary for Foreign Affairs. "Permanent," in this context, distinguishes the civil service position from those secretaries and undersecretaries who are political appointees of the government of the day. Among career officers, the Permanent Under-Secretary is the main official adviser to the Foreign Secretary, and he is also the administrative head of the foreign service. His advice on policy matters may be ignored or overridden, as it was by the Chamberlain government in the 1930's, but this is hardly regarded as normal or desirable in the British system.

Members of the foreign service have vigorously defended their position as *the* British specialists in international matters. For example, there were strong protests against the Treasury's effort, during the years between World War I and II, to maintain the same control over Foreign Office personnel procedure as was exercised by the Treasury over the domestic civil service. Such control by outsiders, it has been argued, was so serious as to contribute to the ineffectiveness of British foreign policy during the 1930's.[12] Since World War II, the independence of the Foreign Office has been secured, at least in the sense that the authority of the Secretary of the

[12]Ashton-Gwatkin, pp. 26–27.

Treasury, as Head of the Civil Service, does not extend to foreign service personnel. No doubt much can be said for the spirit with which the service guards its own standards, but this very spirit has caused outsiders to suspect that the foreign service might have too much confidence in its own members. In particular, it has been suggested that the service was slow in recognizing serious faults in the records of two subsequently notorious members, Maclean and Burgess, who defected to the communists.[13]

One last point about the foreign service deserves notice. Its members, even the Permanent Under-Secretary, do not assume public responsibility for government policy, although their advice has helped to formulate it. The responsibility is the minister's and the government's. So well established is this principle, in custom and in law, that career officials remain entirely outside the arena of political debate over policy. Any attack on the government's policy is directed to political ministers, not to foreign service officers. Mistakes, if there are any, have to be accepted by politicians.

Parliament. While the British legislative authority does not make foreign policy, it is the most significant focal point for debate and controversy. Parliament thus exerts a great indirect influence, similar to the influence it exerts in domestic affairs. This holds despite the fact that the House of Commons does not exercise its constitutional power to reject government policy. The Commons is expected to contain a majority of the party which regularly supports the government and

[13]Ernest Davies, "The Foreign and Commonwealth Services," *The Civil Service in Britain and France,* ed. William A. Robson (New York: The Macmillan Company, 1956), p. 67.

its policy, and although not all members of the party always like all of their leaders' policies, only rarely does one of them vote against the leadership on a parliamentary question involving confidence in the government.

If individual members of the majority influence their government's policies, it is through intraparty discussion and pressure. Regular occasions are provided for communication between back-benchers and their parliamentary leaders. The M.P.'s in a party meet as a whole from time to time, and also have subject-matter committees. For example, each party has a foreign affairs committee for interested M.P.'s, and the appropriate minister meets with his party's committee on request. But whatever the arguments here between back-bencher and minister, the policy that emerges, whether or not it is influenced by the arguments, will regularly be supported in parliamentary voting by a cohesive and disciplined party.[14] The minority party, or parties, provides the opposition vote in the Commons, but it is always supposed to lose.

Since the Parliament is not an independent center of authority, there is nothing comparable to the loci of power represented by American congressional committees and their chairmen. Individual M.P.'s do not share in policy making in foreign affairs, or ordinarily in any other area, unless they are also members of the government, and particularly of the Cabinet which is *the* significant committee of the House of Commons. Nor can M.P.'s outside the responsible executive authority exert the direct influence on the administration of policy that is

within the capacity of American legislators.[15]

Freed from independent decision making, Parliament exists to debate the policies of the government. It does so vigorously and significantly. The popularly elected Commons is the main forum, but occasionally there are important foreign affairs debates in the House of Lords as well. Always, however, it is in the Commons that the government is expected to make the principal defense of its policies against the opposition and, although each parliamentary party contains a variety of individual views which find expression in debate if not in voting, major attention is ordinarily focused on the give-and-take between party leaders. On an important occasion, the government's policy will usually be presented and defended by the Foreign Secretary, one or two of his political aides, and the Prime Minister; the opposition will then be represented by appropriate members of its "shadow cabinet"— that is, particularly by its prospective Foreign Secretary and its prospective Prime Minister (the opposition leader). Thus a Commons debate is mainly between those responsible for policy and those who would like to be and might well become responsible. It is a discussion between a government and its alternative.[16]

How much does a debate really matter, in the face of the fact that a poor governmental showing does not

[14]This subject is treated at length in Leon D. Epstein, "Cohesion of British Parliamentary Parties," *American Political Science Review*, L, (June, 1956), 360–77.

[15]Max Beloff, *Foreign Policy and the Democratic Process* (Baltimore: Johns Hopkins Press, 1955), pp. 25–26.

[16]The most dramatic example was the prolonged debate between the Labour opposition and the Conservative government over Britian's Suez intervention, reported in 558–560 *House of Commons Debates, passim* (October 30–November 8, 1956). See also Leon D. Epstein, *British Politics in the Suez Crisis* (Urbana, Ill.: University of Illinois Press, 1964), chap. 5.

modify majority approval in the immediate circumstances? It can weaken the position of the Cabinet leaders within their own party, and so possibly lead to changes in personnel or policy. And it can strengthen the opposition party in the country, thus influencing future elections. Similarly, a weak opposition case can damage the leadership of the minority party. There is not much doubt that British politicians place great store by performance in debate, and no minister is likely to survive if his own supporters find him a poor spokesman for the government and the party.

Foreign policy debates in the Commons occur, in one form or another, with considerable frequency. Usually they are scheduled in order to discuss a currently controversial policy or subject, so that the interval between debates varies with the number of international crises. However, there is a foreign affairs debate about every three or four weeks. The politically conscious members of the community may follow the full reports in the nation's best newspapers and read the columns of critical comment in the serious intellectual weeklies. Although little parliamentary news is carried in the large popular dailies, the serious press keeps the sizable educated minority informed of the course of parliamentary discussion.

In addition to full-fledged debates on foreign affairs, the government is subject to attack during the regularly scheduled Commons question period—the first hour of each of the first four meeting days of the week. During this period, questions are addressed to ministers concerning their various policies. Foreign affairs receives its share of questions, both from opposition members and from members of the majority party. Sometimes the questions are directed to the Prime Minister instead of to the Foreign Secretary or his political aides. More often than is possible for other subjects, foreign affairs questions can be turned away on the ground that to answer would violate national security. However, there are many questions, sometimes difficult and embarrassing, that government spokesmen attempt to handle, for it is politically unwise for ministers to dodge too many questions. The question period, as well as the general debate, serves to exemplify the usefulness of Parliament's role with respect to policy making: to question and criticize, but not to defeat the government.

Apart from strictly party criticism designed to embarrass the government for the opposition's benefit, there are some parliamentary remarks that, although not unrelated to party considerations, reflect an individual M.P.'s concern with a particular aspect of world affairs. The most imposing case in point is the parliamentary performance of Winston Churchill in the 1930's. As a nonministerial member of the governing Conservative Party, Churchill used the Commons as the principal forum for his views on the dangers of British military weakness in relation to Hitler's Germany. Much less famously, the left-wing Labour critics of Britain's postwar anti-Soviet alliance with the United States tried to employ parliamentary speeches as a way of gaining attention and support for their protests against the policies, first of their own Labour government and later of the Conservative government. Similarly, a number of imperialist Conservative M.P.'s used their parliamentary opportunities in the late 1950's to protest what they regarded as the scuttling of the Empire—illustrated in their minds especially by British withdrawal from the Suez Canal

Zone. Again, in the 1960's left-wing Labour M.P.'s pressed their argument, especially for unilateral nuclear disarmament, and attempted in the Commons as well as outside to move their party from its commitment to the Atlantic alliance.

Nongovernmental agencies

Political parties. Although there are wide areas of agreement on some critical occasions, as illustrated by wartime coalitions, it is normal and legitimate for the party out of power to attack either the substance or the execution of the foreign policy of the party in office. Outside of Parliament, both major parties (and the recently revived Liberal Party as well) maintain large mass organizations with rather loosely defined relations to the respective parliamentary parties and their leaders. These extraparliamentary organizations are not simply cadres of office-holders and prospective office-holders,[17] nor are they skeletonized structures to be filled out only during election campaigns. Rather they contain large numbers of regular dues-paying members.

On this score, the Conservative structure is simpler than Labour's. Conservative membership is entirely individual and direct. The member joins a Conservative constituency association, which is affiliated to the National Union of Conservative and Unionist Associations. Total membership has been between two and three million. Labour's more complicated structure allows both direct and indirect memberships. In addition to about one million who belong to Labour constituency associations, over five million are counted as members

because they belong to trade unions that are affiliated to the Labour party and that pay dues to the Party.

From the viewpoint of each party's parliamentary leadership the principal purpose of the mass membership is undoubtedly to help win elections. Advice, let alone direction, on policy questions is hardly desired, but this does not prevent the organized membership from offering and even urging such advice. Regular dues-paying members have often become active in the first place in order to have a role affecting policy. There are two levels at which rank-and-file members can try to influence decisions. The first is through the constituency organization, which in each case, Conservative or Labour, selects its parliamentary candidate, and would therefore appear to have the means to influence decisively the position of an M.P. How much and how often this channel of influence is used cannot readily be discovered. Certainly there are very few instances of sitting M.P.'s being locally rejected for subsequent candidacy because of policy disagreements, and in such cases (as those occurring after the Suez crisis of 1956) the M.P.'s have been rejected because they violated national party positions.[18] Indeed the constituency associations seem to reinforce national party leadership by using their candidate-selection power to make it unlikely that any M.P.'s would move toward the parliamentary opposition. This is understandable, since members of a constituency association are recruited on the basis of loyalty to the national party cause. They may tolerate M.P.'s who occasionally deviate toward a position more extreme than that of party leaders—that is, a position farther removed from that of the other party—but they do not want

[17]The fullest account of the relationship of mass to parliamentary parties is by R. T. McKenzie, *British Political Parties* (London: William Heinemann, Limited, 1963).

[18]Epstein, *British Politics in the Suez Crisis*, chap. 6.

M.P.'s whose deviation tends to help the opposition. This means, among other things, that a constituency association is unlikely to press an M.P. to adopt a policy at variance with that of the national party leaders. That an association would have such a policy is itself unlikely in the highly centralized system of British politics.

The second level for rank-and-file influence is the national conference held annually by each major party. The conference seems designed for this purpose, and avowedly so in the Labour case. Delegates to each conference, chosen by the various units of the national party, have the opportunity to present, discuss, and vote on policy resolutions. On foreign affairs as on other matters, the mass membership of each party has had distinctive views which it has sought, via conference resolutions, to persuade or pressure party leaders to adopt. The Conservative conference has done so without claiming the power to fix the parliamentary leadership's policy, but the Labour conference has often acted as though it and the executive committee elected by the conference did have such power. The Labour Party constitution does give the external mass organization the power to decide general policy, but this is at odds with the usual British conception that policy is made by parliamentary representatives who are individually and collectively responsible to the electorate. It is also at odds with much of Labour's own practice, especially in the really significant period of 1945–1951, when the Party formed the government. Then Labour government leaders succeeded in getting the Party conference to support foreign policy positions already adopted by the government. And these parliamentary leaders were able, during most of the subsequent decade after Labour went into opposi-

tion, to keep the initiative and to persuade the conference delegates to accept official policy, occasionally in compromised form. Only in 1960 did the Labour conference adopt foreign policy resolutions advocating unilateral nuclear disarmament, which were flatly opposed by the parliamentary leadership, and then the leadership, under Hugh Gaitskell, refused to accept these resolutions as binding on the parliamentary party. Whether Gaitskell would eventually have been forced either to adopt the conference's policy or to resign was never answered, because he succeeded in a campaign to have the next annual conference, in 1961, reverse its position. The fact, however, that he and the bulk of the Labour M.P.'s persisted in a year's defiance of conference resolutions is pretty strong evidence of the primacy of the elected M.P.'s and their leadership. That primacy, especially of the leadership, was even more striking after Labour returned to power in 1964.

Regardless of their disputed role in determining policy, organized parties do serve, much more regularly than in the United States, as media for the expression of public opinion and, thus, as agencies of popular pressure if not of popular control. This is plainer and more significant in the Labour Party, largely because of the already-noted claims of the annual conference. The left-wing critics within the Labour Party have been numerous and persistent, whether defeated, as on a variety of resolutions in the 1950's, or temporarily successful, as on unilateral nuclear disarmament in 1960. They represent a strong tendency among many Party activists and trade union leaders, and their persistent left-wing advocacy in foreign affairs is rooted in both socialism and pacifism. Opposition to "power politics" and "imperialism" has been traditional Party ideology; so has a commitment to a distinctively "socialist foreign policy." Thus, the left-wing opposed German rearmament, suspected the Anglo-American alliance, and rejected nuclear weapons.[19] It is true that these left-wing views have not become official Labour policy and that their chance of becoming so receded as the party approached and finally reached power in the mid-1960's. Certainly Prime Minister Wilson yielded little to his left-wing supporters during the first years of Labour's return to office.

Clear even earlier was the now diminishing role of the comparable, although ideologically contrary, force which sought in the recent past to move the Conservative party away from the foreign policy supported by moderate opinion. More accurately called "imperial" rather than "right-wing," this was a substantial force at Party conferences and among Conservative M.P.'s until the late 1950's. "Empire" long remained the emotive word for Conservatives, as "socialist" has been for Labour. Without so openly challenging established Party leadership as did the Labour Left, the Conservative imperialists used postwar annual conferences to urge various measures to preserve the "Empire"—a term that Conservatives often preferred to "Commonwealth" even when they meant the latter. Speeches and resolutions were ordinarily general and exhortative, but occasionally the Party was asked to take a specific stand. A case in point was opposition to the General Agreement on Trade and Tariffs (GATT) on the ground that free trade sacrificed the Imperial Pref-

erence system. Also, in one way or another, delegates to Conservative conferences in the 1950's demonstrated their uneasiness about how well the Empire was being protected, as well as their desire that the Conservative leadership adopt a tougher line against Britain's enemies than was typical of postwar government policy, Conservative or Labour.[20] In particular, there was a rank-and-file Conservative element, not always a dominant one, that preferred the use of military force to the surrender of British interests, and so rallied readily to support the kind of action taken by Eden's government in Suez in 1956. But the whole imperialist movement is disappearing along with the Empire itself. Suez may have been a last fling. Even the lingering Conservative identification with British settlers in east and central Africa seems obsolete now that power has generally been yielded to native African majorities. Southern Rhodesia, in the mid-1960's, was exceptional in still serving as a focal point for some Conservatives.

Rank-and-file pressures in constituencies and in party conferences are often closely related to differences of opinion between the party's M.P.'s. It is really the M.P.'s who are the direct objects of whatever influence the external organizations can bring to bear. Despite the advantages, already described, of the party's leadership in maintaining parliamentary cohesion—especially when they hold government office—the fact remains that the few hundred M.P.'s who compose a majority party have a final authority. Their backing for a policy has to be secured by a government. And when a party is out of power, its M.P.'s even have

---

[19]For examples, see the *53rd Annual Report of the Labour Conference* (1954), pp. 69–89; the *54th Annual Report of the Labour Conference* (1955), pp. 137–51; and the *59th Annual Report of the Labour Conference* (1960).

[20]See the *74th Annual Report of the Conservative Conference* (1954), p. 51; and the *75th Annual Report of the Conservative Conference* (1955), pp. 27, 33.

room for some initiative. Labour formally gives control of its opposition policy to its M.P.'s, and the Conservative Party maintains an equivalent, though less clear-cut, means for backbenchers to express their opinions, which may also be the opinions of their constituency followers.

In discussing the role of parties it should be pointed out that, despite extremists within each party, the moderate Conservative and the moderate Labour leaders have occupied a good deal of common ground with respect to Britain's postwar foreign policy. The really important matters of maintaining a substantial defense establishment, preserving the American alliance, and surrendering imperial possessions have not been basically at issue between the two major parties (or between them and the Liberal Party). Insofar as the parties have disagreed on these matters, it has ordinarily been at the margins of policy. For example, the Labour Party officially disputed, from 1960 to '64, the Conservative government's policy that Britain should have an independent nuclear arsenal, but its alternative was to place Britain's nuclear force into a joint Atlantic force with the United States and to rely openly on American military capacity. Much more unusual was the sharp and nearly total Labour opposition to the Conservative government's Suez campaign of 1956. But Suez was the dramatic case, in the whole of the postwar period, of an entirely partisan division over foreign policy. Something like it was developing from Labour's opposition to the Conservative government's proposed entry into the Common Market in the early 1960's, but France's veto of British entry put that issue in abeyance during the 1964 election. The disagreement was revived less sharply in 1966.

There is a danger of overstating the importance of British parties in foreign policy making simply by calling attention to their greater organization and cohesion around policy positions in comparison with American parties. The fact remains that British parties do not regularly present competing foreign policies to the electorate. Even when they seem to present marginally different policies, as on the independent nuclear force in the 1964 general election, the issue may not be especially relevant to the voters. Party appeals have usually focused on domestic issues, and there is convincing evidence from opinion surveys in 1964 that the British electorate regards these issues as much more important than any defense or foreign policy question.[21] The 1964 electorate is probably not exceptional in this respect. Without a notable crisis in world affairs, it now seems that most British voters are unlikely to regard their electoral decisions as primarily about international questions. Perhaps they never did have any such view, but it would have been less unrealistic to have expected it several decades ago, when Britain was a more consequential force in world affairs.

Interest groups. The old view of the unimportance of interest groups in the British political process has been abandoned. The study of such groups has disclosed that they play a large role, at least in domestic matters, and no one now doubts that, on such questions as tariffs, British manufacturers, unions, and farmers have means of effectively conveying their preferences to the government. However, it is evident that British interest groups, though as multifarious as those anywhere else, operate differently from

[21]National Opinion Polls, Ltd., *Political Bulletin* (London), October, 1964, Appendix A.

their American counterparts. The very fact that political parties are national in character and cohesive in parliamentary organization makes it of limited value to pressure legislators, directly or through constituents, for individual votes. To affect the main lines of government policy, certainly in foreign affairs, a British interest group would have to influence a party's leadership, or more remotely the bulk of its M.P.'s. Neither of these avenues seems feasible except for the biggest interest groups, although on lesser matters, particularly those involving administrative decisions, it may be assumed that smaller groups exert influence. Certainly it is established government practice to consult representatives of interest groups likely to be affected by contemplated policies. This practice is highly institutionalized.

Major British interest groups tend to have direct connections with a political party. The outstanding example is that of the trade unions, most of which are affiliated to the Labour Party and thus share directly, often dominantly, in that party's policy making. The unions also have a general organization, the Trades Union Congress, which is not part of the Labour Party and which confers with the governments, regardless of which party is in power, in behalf of union interests. Somewhat similarly, the cooperative movement works both within and outside the Labour Party. The Conservatives have no precise organizational counterparts, but industrial leaders maintain close connections with the Party. This they do personally, as important Conservatives themselves, and through the usual business organizations established in particular trades and in general categories like manufacturing. Trade associations, like individual trade unions, may maintain communication with party leaders on

policy matters of direct concern. A distinctive feature of this political communication, from the American point of view, is that individual M.P.'s often openly serve as agents for interest groups—business, union, farm, and others. M.P.'s are even subsidized for this purpose by the groups they represent.

Generally, the most substantial interest groups concerned with foreign policy decisions are not organized primarily to influence such decisions. This holds for the important domestic economic groups noted above, and also for other types of organizations. Churches are plainly in this category. Through their official representatives, they express opinions bearing on British foreign policy, although the expression of such opinions is only incidental to their main role. Veterans' groups are another case in point, although their efforts to influence general policy are less prominent in Britain than the efforts of comparable groups in the United States. The same can be said, for a different reason, of the activities of ethnic groups. Such groups are simply less significant in Britain because of the absence of large ethnic minorities of the sort that compose so much of the American population. Although there are, and almost always have been, continental refugees in Britain, their numbers have not been sufficient to constitute serious pressure on British foreign policy making. Even the Jewish population of half a million cannot be said to be an electoral factor in determining British policy toward Israel, despite a vigorous Zionist movement—represented particularly in the Labour Party. Neither is the Irish minority, largely centered in a few seaports and manufacturing centers, a major influence, although it does, like the Zionists, have parliamentary spokesmen.

In addition to the groups whose varying influence on foreign affairs is incidental to their other purposes, there are also many British groups organized entirely around foreign policy issues. These may be less substantial, but they are often most active propagandistically. Some organizations are devoted to particular causes, such as justice or freedom for certain people in a certain place, and they wax and wane with the excitement of the issue. Others are broader in scope and more durable. One example is the United Nations Association; another, operating at a scholarly and almost official level to influence opinion makers, is the Royal Institute of International Affairs; a third, also of limited membership, is the newer Institute of Strategic Studies. At an altogether different level of activity is the mass-membership organization, the Campaign for Nuclear Disarmament. Developed in the late 1950's to oppose Britain's retention of nuclear weapons, the C.N.D. undoubtedly mobilized the residual pacifism and neutralism of socialists, students, intellectuals, and miscellaneous middle-class citizens. Their most spectacular demonstration was a well-publicized protest march each spring from a nuclear weapons center to a Trafalgar Square rally. The Nuclear Disarmers became active not only in this way and through a flood of speeches and literature, but also in the Labour Party, where their position was accepted by important trade-union leaders as well as by many constituent party workers. To a large degree, the Labour Party conference's decision in 1960 to support unilateral nuclear disarmament was a victory for the campaign of the previous few years. Afterward, the campaign lost momentum.

Media of mass communication. The most basic point to note about British mass media is their national character. Strictly local and regional newspapers are of minor importance in relation to the media centered in London. The British magazine, radio, and television audience is essentially national. Opinion concerning foreign policy, like that concerning most domestic policy, is formed nationally and not regionally.

British communication has also been given a special character by the continued monopoly of radio broadcasting by the government-owned British Broadcasting Corporation (B.B.C.), and by a similar monopoly of telecasting, which lasted until 1955, when supervised commercial television began to compete with the B.B.C. The government-owned service has avoided the editorialized commentary on the news typical of American radio and television. The news is reported straight and without dramatization, and a similar standard is expected of commercial television. Radio and television facilities are used by government spokesmen, particularly the Prime Minister and the Foreign Secretary, for official expositions of foreign policy, the importance of this means of communication with the nation having been firmly established by the successful wartime speeches of Winston Churchill. Some radio and television time is divided, according to an agreed-upon formula, between political parties for a presentation of their views on international as well as other issues. Occasionally, too, there are programs devoted to discussion of foreign policy. Television, as in the United States, is the important means of reaching a mass audience, but in no case is there any purchase of time for the presentation of opinions.

The neutrality of British radio and television is in contrast to the sharply partisan attachments of the press. A majority of papers lean toward the Conservatives, but the largest London paper, the *Daily Mirror*, is often pro-Labour. Although none of the mass-circulation dailies, like the *Daily Mirror* and its several pro-Conservative counterparts, give much serious attention to international affairs, it is through their headlines, often slanted by partisan considerations, that a large share of the British population forms its perspective on international policies. Nevertheless, the quality press, even with its small circulation, deserves more attention as a molder of opinion,[22] for it reaches most Englishmen who have opinion-making roles. Except in Scotland, where there are equivalent newspapers, almost every person seriously concerned with national or international affairs reads either the quasi-official *Times* of London or the liberal *Guardian*. If "seriously concerned" is defined more broadly, the category should include the readers of the Conservative *Daily Telegraph*, which is unusual in that its news presentation stands between the popular press and the quality press. Moreover one of three Sunday papers, the *Observer*, the *Sunday Times*, and the *Sunday Telegraph*, is read by virtually the whole of the serious English public. In addition, the special importance of the weekly *Economist* should be noted: more than other intellectually oriented weeklies, like the *Spectator* and the left-wing *New Statesman*, the *Economist* reaches the influential. Although these various papers and periodicals often present divergent views, there is an intimacy about the English circle of discussion that is absent in a larger and less centralized political community.

[22]An excellent study emphasizing the role of the quality press in opinion formation is R. Bassett, *Democracy and Foreign Policy, A Case History: The Sino-Japanese Dispute, 1931–1933* (London: Longmans, Green & Company, Ltd., 1952).

Other media of communication also play an important role in Britain. Pamphlets, for instance, are still widely used by party and party-affiliated groups to reach the public. Furthermore, Britain is a book-reading nation, and it is worth mentioning that both scholarly and popular volumes on foreign policy reach the attentive public. Speeches at public meetings, even though they are declining in popularity as a result of television, are still a means of influencing political audiences. A speech by a major public figure remains an important occasion, at least for the membership of a political party.

The role of public opinion

Many of the "non-governmental agencies" just discussed are often conceived as representing public opinion, in contrast to the official agencies of governmental policy making. For analytical purposes it has been useful to adhere to this distinction, but there is a considerable overlapping of persons and functions. The term "Establishment," now widely used in the United States, seems to have been invented in Britain to refer to an inner circle of important ministers, top civil servants, editors of quality newspapers, and a miscellany of academic and other public figures all capable of informal consultation with each other. Based on common social and educational backgrounds, the members of this Establishment, it is thought, both make policy and expound it. The small, homogeneous nature of the British community lends credibility to this notion, especially when we are considering the somewhat detached area of foreign policy.

No doubt there is more divergence among the influential British than the concept of an Establishment conveys. But with or without the term, the British community frankly recognizes the leadership groups that, in Gabriel Almond's phrase, "carry on the specific work of policy formulation and policy advocacy."[23] As Almond has also pointed out (though in reference to the United States), an elite of this sort does not operate independently of "certain policy criteria in the form of widely held values and expectations."[24] The British public, like publics elsewhere, sets such criteria, and the policy makers are limited thereby —as, for instance, by the public's manifest desire for peace. The subtlety of these relations was well described by Kenneth Younger, a former Minister of State for Foreign Affairs. Control of foreign policy, he said, was more oligarchic than control of domestic policy, and on first reflection he thought of no occasion when he or his superiors "had been greatly affected by public opinion in reaching important decisions."[25] But this first impression, he realized, was misleading because public opinion did affect ministers in a general way. "The Government," he wrote, "tends to identify itself almost unconsciously with a vaguely sensed general will, and no clear formulation of the pressure of public opinion upon Government policy ever occurs."[26] Younger believed that a government identified itself especially with its own supporters.

THE SUBSTANCE OF FOREIGN POLICY

Ordinarily it is assumed, whatever respective party positions happen to be, that major elements in British foreign policy are not subject to drastic change.[27] No such change was evident, for example, in the transfer of office from the Conservative to the Labour Party in 1945, from Labour to Conservative in 1951, or from Conservative back to Labour in 1964. The definition of the national interest remains fairly stable, and the world situation allows a government only limited choices, often confined to methods, tone, and timing.

Commonwealth relations

Properly speaking, Britain's Commonwealth policy may not belong in the sphere of foreign affairs, and the details of that policy cannot be specified here. However, in international matters the British themselves have often viewed the Commonwealth (or Empire as it has, at least until recently, been called by its oldest champions) as an overseas extension of the British nation and, thus, as an entity through which Britain could play a larger role in the world than as an island kingdom standing alone. As a British ambassador to the United States declared: "It would be misleading to talk about the British contribution to the free world solely in terms of the efforts and the economy of the fifty million people in the British Isles. Britain lies at the heart of the Commonwealth, and the Commonwealth contains over six hundred million people, more than a third of the population of the free world."[28]

[23]Gabriel Almond, *The American People and Foreign Policy* (New York: Harcourt, Brace & World, Inc., 1950), p. 5.

[24]*Ibid.*, p. 6.

[25]Kenneth Younger, "Public Opinion and Foreign Policy," *British Journal of Sociology*, VI (June, 1955), 169.

[26]*Ibid.*, p. 171.

[27]Basic material on British policy of the recent past may be found in E. L. Woodward and Rohan Butler, eds., *Documents on British Foreign Policy: 1919–1939* (London: Her Majesty's Stationery Office, 1947–1954). For a general historical account, see A. W. Ward and G. P. Gooch, eds., *The Cambridge History of British Foreign Policy: 1783–1919* (London: Cambridge University Press, 1922–1923).

[28]Roger Makins, "The Commonwealth in World Affairs," *Labour and Industry in Britain*, XIV (September, 1956), 116.

The Commonwealth has not fulfilled much of this British aspiration for a mid-twentieth century substitute for the old imperial influence, but it is an imposing residual institution. By 1965, twenty former British dependencies of one sort or another had chosen to be Commonwealth members after achieving self-government, and a few more are likely to join as they, too, become self-governing. The continued association of these nations lessened the shock of Britain's rapid imperial surrenders of the postwar years. The method of association had already been established by the earlier Commonwealth of Canada, Australia, New Zealand, the Union of South Africa, and Britain. To this heavily British group there were added, in the postwar years, the overwhelmingly large Indian nation and the numerous other formerly British dependencies in Asia and Africa which have secured their independence. Their numbers did much more than compensate for the withdrawal of South Africa in the early 1960's; they transformed the Commonwealth from a relatively homogeneous white man's club to a multiracial gathering of obviously diverse interests. The nations of the new Commonwealth, like those of the old, regularly confer with each other, and may reach certain agreements although there is no legal compulsion to do so. Each member nation finds it convenient, economically at least, to maintain the tie. The symbol of free association is the Queen, acknowledged by all as Head of the Commonwealth and by some member nations as their own crowned head. In the latter category are Britain itself and those other Commonwealth members closest to Britain in ethnic origin, language, and customs: Australia, New Zealand, and Canada. Significantly, the first new postwar members, India, Pakistan, and Ceylon, became republics. In their different view of the Queen, as in other more substantial ways, these nations, which contain a large majority of the Commonwealth's population, caused the whole structure to appear less united than the British preferred. However, to hold within the Commonwealth the Asian members, and then the new African states, Britain has been willing to make the structure even more flexible and informal than it was when it was originally developed in the period between World War I and World War II.

Technically within the Commonwealth, but not member nations, are the remaining small and scattered British dependencies. A few may become self-governing and subsequently choose Commonwealth membership, but others are not potentially viable as nations. Some, like Gibraltar, are of primarily strategic importance. Few represent problems of imperial withdrawal like those which Britain successfully met in Malaya, where a communist revolt had to be suppressed before independence was granted, or in Kenya, where British settlers had to accept minority status in an African nation. Nor are any complicated in the manner of Cyprus, where a Greek majority and a Turkish minority had different ideas about self-government. The one substantial imperial difficulty still outstanding in 1966 was Southern Rhodesia. Its white settlers, a numerous minority, had long been self-governing in domestic affairs, and were treated, for some purposes, as though they were a member nation of the Commonwealth. This status was not decisively affected by their inclusion, in the 1950's, in an abortive Central African Federation which was broken up by the insistence of its other two components (both almost entirely native African territories) that they become separately self-governing. Southern Rhodesia remained dominated by its white settlers, and their refusal to provide for rapid enfranchisement of the native African majority kept Britain from acknowledging its independence. In 1965, the white settlers unilaterally asserted Southern Rhodesia's independence, and in 1966 they defied the efforts of British authority, moved by Asian and African pressure, to use economic pressure against the independent government. These British efforts, successful or not, illustrate the choice which Britain finally made in its postwar Commonwealth policy. It has been to champion rapidly achieved majoritarian self-government in each of its old Asian and African territories, even when such self-government meant minority status for an appreciable number of British settlers. One result has been the alienation of the Union of South Africa, which is rigidly governed by its large white minority, and perhaps of Southern Rhodesia also, if it remains dominated by its European settlers. But another result has been the continued voluntary association of Asian and African nations in the Commonwealth.

No doubt this association is worth something in terms of a general international purpose of communication, between developing and advanced nations and across racial as well as economic barriers, but how much it is worth to Britain itself is open to question. Symbolically, Britain benefited during its twenty years of imperial withdrawal, 1945–'65, by having the Commonwealth to substitute for the old Empire. It helped Englishmen to assuage what has been aptly called a "sense of personal loss—almost of amputation,"[29] which they regularly felt when some colony became independent. At the very least, the new

[29]John Strachey, *The End of Empire* (New York: Frederick A. Praeger, Inc., 1964), p. 204.

Commonwealth seemed better than no association at all, and there was really no serious possibility of maintaining the Empire. Withdrawal was not merely a choice based on the desirability of creating a Commonwealth to include Asian and African nations. After World War II, it was probably impractical for any Western nation to resist native nationalist movements, and certainly it was impractical for Britain, with its limited resources, to do so. Despite internal criticism, postwar British governments recognized the necessity, and so Britain, the most successful modern imperial power, conducted the most successful imperial retreat. On the whole, it did so graciously. The major exception was the belated effort to reassert British power at Suez in 1956 and, significantly, this was an area where the former imperial control had been less direct than in India or tropical Africa, and where the control had not been succeeded by Commonwealth membership.

However useful the Commonwealth has been as a transitional symbol, the need for such a symbol is bound to be temporary. Now that the transition from imperial mastery has been virtually accomplished, what advantages can Britain derive from the Commonwealth? The new multiracial Commonwealth is hardly a sufficiently cohesive group to lend itself to many common policies in world affairs, and Britain itself is not large enough or rich enough to dominate its affairs. The new Asian and African states have, it is true, a common heritage of former British rule. They therefore use certain British governmental procedures and have an elite educated in these procedures and in the English language and culture. But this heritage is not deep enough to withstand the rising nationalism of their native masses. And even though anticolonialism is losing its relevance, there is hardly an identity of interest between the newly developing but still impoverished Asian and African nations and Britain, a white and relatively wealthy developed nation. The new Commonwealth nations view the world differently from Britain and from the West generally. The difference has already been observed in Britain's relations with India, the largest member nation and the major contender for leadership of the Asian and African countries, be they Commonwealth members or not. The Commonwealth front was surely broken in the postwar world as Britain joined the American-led effort to contain Russia and India became persistently neutral. This and other differences remain. They do not prevent Britain from helping Asian and African Commonwealth nations, economically and otherwise, but they stand in the way of the kind of leadership that many Englishmen had once expected their nation to be able to exercise within the new Commonwealth. It was, unlike the former imperial role, to have been a leadership freely accepted on the basis of experience and mutual interest, but it was nevertheless to have been the way in which Britain could be a great power in the mid-twentieth century. The substance for such status turns out to be lacking.

In certain respects, however, Britain has continued to act as a responsible great power, especially in relation to the Commonwealth. Britain has sought, even in the 1960's, to help Malaysia defend itself against Indonesian military threats, and to help India prepare to meet Chinese offensives. For such purposes, defense bases are maintained at considerable expense in many parts of the world, often straining British economic resources. One can argue that the imperial legacy which the Commonwealth represents is misleading Britain into maintaining or assuming burdens beyond its capacity, but there is still a residuum of British effort, represented by the self-governing Commonwealth nations, in which Englishmen understandably take sufficient pride to want to help defend. Whatever guilt they may have felt for Britain's earlier accumulation of imperial possessions, on which the community was and is divided, there can be little doubt that Englishmen now feel sadly misunderstood when their country is denounced as an oppressive colonial power. Such denunciations are resented not only because Britain has rapidly liquidated its empire, but also because the attacks often come from powers that have themselves expanded their territories over a continental land mass. Criticism from such sources seems to be based on the salt-water fallacy: overseas expansion is evil in a way that continental expansion is not.

Cultural and ideological ties

Of a different sort, but probably stronger in the long run than the Commonwealth are the uninstitutionalized ties based on culture and ideology. Britain has such ties with both Commonwealth and non-Commonwealth countries. Canada, Australia, and New Zealand would be regarded as kindred nations even without a Commonwealth structure. Their populations are heavily British in origin, their language is English (with a large exception in Canada), and their political institutions are direct adaptations of the British model. Together with Britain and the United States they constitute the nongovernmental entity that Englishmen, and Sir Winston Churchill in particular, have called the "English-speaking peoples."[30] The term is partly

[30]As, for instance, in Winston Churchill's famous Fulton, Missouri, speech. See the *New York Times*, March 6, 1946, p. 4.

a euphemism for "Anglo-Saxon world," and yet it conveys much of the feeling associated with a racial or ethnic bond. Within the English-speaking world, the British recognize the United States as a very special case. Although similarities in many matters, including an English political heritage, are acknowledged and even overstated, relations are complicated by the differences between American and British customs.[31] Sometimes these differences are regarded as unfortunate deviations from a British norm, like the American adoption of the separation of powers in government instead of using the parliament and cabinet system. More significantly, in postwar years, the British have found it difficult to accustom themselves to American military and economic predominance. The United States, a newcomer in international affairs, has sometimes seemed to Englishmen to be a brash usurper of Britain's former leading role, particularly in the Middle East. Irritation with American ways, however, has not prevented the broad central sector of British opinion from considering the postwar alliance with the United States to be natural and right. Ideologically, the American connection has been uncongenial only to left-wing socialists who objected to American capitalism, and to imperialist Conservatives who interpreted American criticism of the British Empire as national rivalry. Even many of these ideological critics objected mainly to the terms of the alliance, admitting, though bitterly, Britain's overriding need for American power. The imperialists are a vanishing breed; their last great anti-American campaign came during the Suez crisis of 1956,

when the United States opposed the Anglo-French intervention. Nor does left-wing socialism appear to be a rising force in British politics.

For the bulk of the British public, notably the attentive political public, it is a customary fact of life to maintain what is conceived as a "special relationship" with the United States. As the *Economist* editorialized in the spring of 1965, at a time when there was widespread British questioning of President Johnson's foreign policies: "Should Britain go *all* the way with LBJ? Can it? On the other hand, can it go anywhere else?"[32] Finding anywhere else to go is not solely a matter of obtaining adequate military and economic support. The United States, as can be observed, is useful to Britain in these respects, but it also is relatively compatible in language, culture, and historical background. Canada, Australia, and New Zealand have the same or greater compatibility, but not the power.

Beyond the United States and the English-speaking members of the Commonwealth, Britain's cultural and ideological ties are less definite. A general attachment to political democracy causes Englishmen to identify more readily with some nations than others, and a minority in the Labour Party sympathizes particularly with professedly socialist countries and with ideological neutralism of India. There is a cultural link with the nations of Western Europe, but its strength is less than that of the English-speaking Atlantic community. This is so despite the heavy volume of British travel to the continent, and despite the communion in an old and threatened culture which British intellectuals share with their continental counterparts. For most Englishmen, the barriers of

[31]The problems of the postwar Anglo-American relationship, as seen by Englishmen, are treated in Leon D. Epstein, *Britain: Uneasy Ally* (Chicago: University of Chicago Press, 1954), chap. 2.

[32]*Economist*, CCXV (May 22, 1965), 883.

language and unstable continental politics have outweighed geographic proximity. Germany has been a particular difficulty. Its aggressive enmity of the recent past has made it hard for popular links to be established. Consequently, any entry into an integrating Western Europe, such as Prime Minister Macmillan tried to negotiate in the early 1960's and as may again be attempted, will have to be achieved without a prior European identification on the part of the bulk of the British public. The identification might then grow in response to economically and politically integrative forces.

With respect to all of Britain's broad ties with other countries, the claim is often made that foreign policy has been developed apart from such considerations, particularly of ideology, and solely on the basis of a calculated national interest.[33] But even if it is true that policy is arrived at independently of ideological and cultural preferences, there can be no doubt that support for a given policy can be more readily obtained when that policy is in line with the attachments of the British community.

Foreign economic policy

Britain's dependence on overseas trade means that economic matters are always in the forefront among foreign policy issues. Since World War II, the most constant national worry has been to maintain a sufficient volume of exports to pay for needed imports of food and raw materials. During much of the first postwar decade, Britain required outside help in the form of loans and Marshall Aid in order to

[33]Note, for example, Winston Churchill's rejection of the ideological case against Franco's Spain, in his *The Second World War* (Boston: Houghton Mifflin Company, 1951), v, p. 627.

bridge the dollar gap. That is, Britain had to be given dollars, over and above those earned, so as to allow the purchase of goods from the United States and Canada. The more recent American military aid has also involved a degree of dependency.

The general postwar economic policy of seeking to increase exports has been complicated by Britain's leading role among the nations associated in the sterling bloc. Within this bloc, free exchange is encouraged, and earnings of gold and dollars are pooled for dealing with countries outside the bloc. The sterling bloc consists of all parts of the Commonwealth except Canada, plus a few other small nations. It is not Britain alone, but this bloc as a whole that seeks a balance of trade with the rest of the world. Britain serves as banker for the bloc, and thus its currency, the pound sterling, is subject to important pressures and fluctuations. In this arrangement, there are advantages for British trade and prestige. Besides helping to maintain London as a major center of international exchange, the sterling bloc facilitates the exchange of British manufactured goods for food and raw materials produced in Commonwealth countries. To assist in the economic development of the bloc's non-Western sections, some of which, like Malaysia, are large dollar earners, Britain has sought to encourage investment of the relatively small amount of capital that the nation now has available for export. Investment on a larger scale within the sterling bloc has been envisioned and even projected in what is known as the Colombo Plan, but Britain itself has found it difficult to produce the surplus needed to reestablish its prewar status as an overseas investor. That status was largely lost as a result of forced wartime sale of British assets. Reestablishing British overseas investments has also been complicated by the home market's increased attractiveness and need for capital during Britain's recently prosperous years.

The marks of an economic policy geared to Britain's tenuous position in world trade were most obvious in the early postwar years, but many remained even in the 1960's. The government has closely controlled foreign exchange, limiting in particular the exchange of pounds for dollars and thus the purchase of American goods. In addition, Englishmen have been restricted from purchasing many of their own products, either by high sales taxes or by the establishment of quotas, so that such products might be exported in order to earn the foreign currency with which to buy necessities from abroad. For a similar reason, the British government has regulated the flow of industrial investment so as to secure the expansion of productive facilities most likely to manufacture goods saleable abroad and especially in the United States. The efforts to sell overseas in order to live met with enough success to permit considerable relaxation of the immediate postwar policies of enforced austerity. Increases in the volume of British goods sold in the United States were impressive, but their continuance has been insecure and, with it, Britain's whole economic situation. From time to time there is a balance of payments crisis—meaning that Britain is buying more abroad than it is selling. The crisis can temporarily be met by reducing home consumption, especially of imports, as it was in 1964 through the imposition of a special tariff surcharge, but in the long run the problem is to increase exports sufficiently to purchase the imports desired and needed by the British population. Increasing exports requires not only aggressive salesmanship, but also more efficient and economical production of British manufactures.

Given the national need for external trade, it might be expected that Britain would have a low tariff policy. This was true in the nineteenth century. Then British manufactures were able to compete with those of almost any other country, and Britain was willing to encourage the importation of food from abroad both because it was cheaper and because the nations that sold food to Britain could buy its manufactured products. There was no high protective tariff for industry or agriculture. In the twentieth century, however, this free-trade formula ceased to be so evidently to Britain's net advantage. British manufacturers encountered difficulties in foreign markets from newer industries of other countries; some of these newer industries were more efficient, some employed cheaper labor, and some were protected in their own markets by tariffs. Additional cause for the British to reexamine their trade policy was the difficulty of importing food in a time of siege, first evident during World War I. The result of all these circumstances, coupled with strongly nationalistic trends elsewhere, was a substantial British retreat from its tradition of free trade during the early decades of the twentieth century. Domestic agriculture was subsidized in various ways, including tariffs on foreign products. Selected manufacturing industries were also protected by fairly high tariffs. Moreover, the necessarily stringent postwar limitations on imports of foreign goods also served to protect British manufactures against competition in the home market, although this was not the purpose of such limitations, which in any event were meant to be temporary during Britain's shortage of foreign exchange. Generally free trade is again a goal despite the retreats of the last several decades.

Closely linked to Britain's modest protective system has been Imperial (now, properly, Commonwealth) Preference. Under this arrangement, like the tariff policy itself a product largely of the years between the two World Wars, Britain and other Commonwealth nations negotiated reciprocal tariff advantages. The object was to encourage intra-Commonwealth trade and, from the British standpoint, to have a protected market for manufactured goods in exchange for preferential importation of food and raw materials from these other Commonwealth nations. Substantial mutual preferences of this nature were established in the 1930's, and their extension in the direction of a general Commonwealth free trade was advocated then, and later, by the heirs of the old turn-of-the-century belief in Joseph Chamberlain's imperial economic union. Commonwealth trade preference became, in fact, the last bastion of imperialist ambition. In the eyes of its champions, Imperial Preference, by establishing material advantages in Commonwealth relations, might be the beginning of a new and potent British-led economic and political unit. It represented an alternative to reliance on American trade and American power. Such hopes for the development of Imperial Preference failed to be realized after World War II, however. Some of the other Commonwealth nations did not find it in their interests to extend preference on a broad front, and Britain's own need for more American trade was not compatible with enlarged discrimination in favor of Commonwealth producers. The alternative presented by the postwar American encouragement of a general free trade policy was simply more attractive. Consequently, the relative importance of Imperial Preference declined in the postwar

years. Not only were new preferences not negotiated, but the existing ones were not as significant, in terms of competitive advantage, as they had been in the 1930's.[34]

Still, Imperial Preference retained enough importance to play a part in molding opposition to British participation in the various European supranational economic arrangements of the 1950's. Britain's special economic relations with Commonwealth nations long provided an argument for standing outside both the Schuman Plan, to establish a common Western European market for coal and steel, and the later European Economic Community, to establish a common market over a broad range of products. In the latter case especially, the British were reluctant to eliminate their economic preferences for food from Commonwealth nations.

The reluctance to abandon Imperial Preference was genuine, both for economic and political reasons which derived from the cherished Commonwealth connection, but it turned out to be no insurmountable obstacle in the way of the Macmillan government's attempt, in the early 1960's, to enter the European Economic Community (the Common Market established by France, Italy, Germany, and the Benelux countries).[35] The failure of the attempt had almost nothing to do with Imperial Preference. Before President de Gaulle imposed a French veto against British entry, the Macmillan government's negotiators had already made the crucial concessions by way of long-run curtailment of the special trading arrangements with

[34] Political and Economic Planning, *Commonwealth Preference in the United Kingdom* (London: George Allen & Unwin, 1960), p. 5.

[35] *The United Kingdom and the European Economic Community*, Cmd. 1565 (London: Her Majesty's Stationery Office, 1961).

the Commonwealth. The government would have liked to maintain these arrangements, while joining the Common Market, but it was willing to give them up in order to obtain what seemed the greater economic opportunities of European integration.[36] Not only had the significance of Imperial Preference declined by the 1960's, but Commonwealth trade in general was not so promising as European trade. It was notable that the Macmillan government was able to obtain the support of its Conservative party, in Parliament and in the extra-parliamentary organization, for the virtual abandonment of a traditional Conservative position. In fact, the internal political difficulty on this score was less than seemed to be involved in obtaining support for the surrender of some political sovereignty, which membership in the Common Market would eventually require. That there would have to be any such surrender was camouflaged during Macmillan's period of negotiations.

The decision to try to join the Common Market represented the triumph of economic thinking over all of the various ideological, political, and cultural objections which had once prevailed. That is, such economic perceptions triumphed in the Macmillan government, the organized Conservative following, the Liberal Party (committed even earlier to the Common Market), and the bulk of Establishment opinion. On the other hand, Hugh Gaitskell, leading the Labour Party in opposition to the terms of entry being negotiated in 1962, did not think the economic advantages of joining Europe were sufficient to outweigh other considerations. The deci-

[36]Miriam Camps, *Britain and the European Community: 1955–1963* (Princeton, N.J.: Princeton University Press, 1964), chaps. 9–10.

sive veto wielded by President de Gaulle was influenced primarily by noneconomic perceptions, that is, that Britain was linked, politically and militarily, to the United States rather than to Europe. But Britain had never seriously considered abandoning its overwhelmingly important "special relationship" to the United States as the price of entry into the European Common Market, nor did the United States, itself pressing for British entry, contemplate that Britain should exchange an Atlantic alliance for a purely European one. Britain's economic needs were not that great, or at any rate they were not yet so in the early 1960's.

Even by the late 1950's, however, the progress of European economic union had become sufficiently impressive to cause Britain to reconsider its postwar aloofness. The continental nations were increasing their production and prosperity faster than Britain. Moreover, the six Common Market countries, by reducing their tariffs on each other's products and by adopting a common tariff for goods from the rest of the world, threatened to discriminate against British sales in Europe. French and German automobiles, for example, would enjoy tariff advantages over British automobiles throughout the Common Market, including the Netherlands, where Britain had long sold cars in the absence of a domestic product. The first British response, once the Common Market started to succeed, was to try to persuade the six continental nations to join with Britain and several other European nations in a looser free-trade area. The unwillingness of the six to place themselves in this larger organization led Britain, one of seven non-Common Market nations, to form the more or less rival European Free Trade Association. By the mid-1960's this association was a going concern, having brought about the reduction of tariffs among its members—Britain, Sweden, Denmark, Norway, Portugal, Austria, and Switzerland. But it differed greatly from the Common Market. It was much less supranational in its political implications, and it did not provide for a common tariff in relation to the rest of the world.

Membership in the European Free Trade Association was entirely compatible with Britain's pre-existing relationships with the Commonwealth, the United States, and the world in general. As a method of increasing trade, it was therefore ideal from the standpoint of British interests. But substantively it was inadequate. The Association members, all of them except Britain having small populations, provided too limited a market, so that the benefits of increased trade among the seven would almost certainly be overshadowed by the disadvantages of exclusion from the larger and booming Common Market. It is no wonder that in the early 1960's the Macmillan government, while seeking to preserve the Association connection, did not view it as a real alternative to the Common Market. Nor is it likely to be so viewed in the future, if Britain should again believe that there is an opportunity to enter the Common Market. Indeed, certain other members of the European Free Trade Association will probably seek entry in the Common Market, with or without Britain.

The really serious problem for Britain is to make future Common Market membership compatible with its relationship with the non-European world, particularly with the United States, and still, to some extent, with the Commonwealth. Britain remains and wants to remain a major factor in world trade, looking outward beyond the oceans for its economic as for its political ties. An exclusionary European policy, such as de Gaulle envisions, would (as de Gaulle rightly said) represent a sharp departure for Britain. But the Common Market may not always have exclusionary implications. It may not even seem so after President de Gaulle ceases to wield power.

Security policy

The reasons for Britain's assumption that it cannot protect itself against aggression without help are obvious. The island's location, vulnerability, and limited resources require that protection come from collective arrangements with other nations. Strictly speaking, modern Britain never relied solely on its own military capacities. Its tradition of trying to maintain a European balance of power necessarily involved joining some nations against others. And before World War I, this policy, combined with command of the seas, allowed Britain considerable freedom of action and certainly a sense of having the national destiny in its own hands. The change in Britain's relative position may not have been fully appreciated until World War II, but in 1940 even the magnificent stand against Hitler could not conceal Britain's inability to protect its far-flung interests without the aid of a stronger power.

After World War II, and partly as its consequence, Britain appeared distinctly less imposing than either of the superpowers, Russia and the United States. Security against Russian domination of the continent required American help. Accordingly, the cornerstone of Britain's postwar European policy was to obtain an American commitment, of a sort denied before World War II, to defend Western Europe and by this means to deter aggression. Thus, American involvement in the

North Atlantic Treaty Organization (NATO) was considered a prime diplomatic success. As a leading British diplomatic historian wrote of the treaty, "It is indeed in one sense the culmination of British policy during the last half century."[37] Britain had at last, through an outside ally, succeeded in righting the European balance of power. From this viewpoint, British participation in the military arrangements of the Western European Union, though a sharp departure in British policy, became decidedly subordinate to membership with America in the North Atlantic Treaty Organization.

Being a junior partner in an alliance has, however, been a new experience for Britain, and there have been British misgivings about the United States and its dominance. Since 1947, the British have tended to be fearful that American policies toward Russia would be too provocative, too zealously anticommunist, and too uncompromising. These fears have risen and fallen with particular circumstances, but they have never disappeared. The British government, supported by its public, has regularly urged conciliatory summit meetings of Western leaders with the Russians. Moreover, Britain has been less completely hostile to Soviet China, whose government the British recognized in accord with traditional diplomatic practice although they have not so far pressed hard to overcome American opposition to Chinese admission to the United Nations. Certainly, Britain has made it clear that it is reluctant to be involved in any full-fledged war with China. For this reason, as well as because Britain preferred American military efforts to be concentrated in Europe, there has been a dislike for any proposed American military action against China. In late 1950, when the Korean War threatened to involve a major American commitment, Winston Churchill was surely expressing general British feelings when he said that the sooner "the Far Eastern diversion" could be stabilized, the better. It is in Europe, he said, that the world cause will be decided. "Perhaps," Churchill noted, "we are biased by the fact that we all live there or thereabouts. But none the less, one cannot conceive that our natural bias has in any way distorted the actual facts."[38] The subsequent American decision to strengthen the North Atlantic Treaty Organization met with a strongly positive British response. Britain's substantial contribution to European defense, paid as part of the price for greater American efforts, left no doubt about the primacy of British concern.

That concern, while it remained dominant, appeared to lose some of its urgency in British minds by the late 1950's. This was partly because the Russian threat was conceived to be less directly military in Europe and because the Eastern European nations exhibited nationalist sentiments of their own. China, it is true, had become powerful and more plainly bellicose than Russia, but it did not directly menace Europe. Where China impinged on British interests, especially in India, Britain responded with military assistance. It also so responded in Malaysia, when the menace was from communist-allied Indonesia. But none of these Asian responses took the place of the established British concern with security in Europe. The successive Berlin crises kept that concern alive, and Britain continued to join the

[37]Charles Webster, in *United Kingdom Policy*, ed. Charles Webster (London: Royal Institute of International Affairs, 1950), p. 26.

[38]481 *House of Commons Debates* 1336 (November 30, 1950).

United States in preserving the island of West Berlin from encroachment by East Germany and its Russian sponsors.

In the 1950's, participation in NATO was still the cornerstone of defense policy, but, instead of building a really large conventional military force, Britain and its allies began to rely increasingly on nuclear weapons as a deterrent to Russian aggression. Britain sharply reduced its total military force, particularly in 1957, and finally put an end to conscription in 1960. What conventional forces remained were either in NATO's limited establishment or spread thinly over the reduced, but still widespread, imperial possessions. Their expense was still considerable, but no large military reserve for conventional warfare was maintained. The potential power thus abandoned, largely because of cost, was supposed to be compensated by British development of nuclear weapons over and above those already in American hands. Britain produced its own H-bomb in the late 1950's, and so became the third nuclear power in the world. But, before the decade ended, the significance of this achievement was reduced by the realization that Britain was going to find it too expensive to develop its own system for delivering missiles.

This experience is a telling one, for it illustrates the frustration of the British attempt to be a great power in the nuclear age. Unquestionably, being a great power requires membership in the "nuclear club." But to be a full-fledged club member involves owning a delivery system as well as the nuclear bomb. Britain's delivery system was its V-bomber fleet, good only as long as manned aircraft remained useful for strategic bombing. To prepare for the predictable time when such aircraft became obsolete,

the British government, in the 1950's, spent a large amount on its own projected rocket, called Blue Streak. When it had to be abandoned as impractical in 1960, the development of another rocket seemed prohibitively expensive. Accordingly, Britain arranged to purchase the supposedly forthcoming American Skybolt, a missile to be released from an aircraft; but this was not produced. Then Britain arranged, in late 1962, to purchase American missiles designed for Polaris submarines, which Britain would manufacture according to American specifications. It was this delivery system, so largely supplied by the United States, that the Conservative government claimed, in 1963–'64, provided Britain with an independent nuclear deterrent. The Labour Party, as already noted, rejected this claim, but when it came to office in 1964, its government retained nuclear bombs for use in the aging V bombers and continued part of the Polaris arrangement. The Labour government, however, did not conceal its preference for an eventual pooling of Britain's nuclear capacity in an Atlantic force, presumably dominated by the United States and so spelling the end of Britain's effort to be an independent nuclear power. Much informed British opinion, regardless of party, supports such a policy as the only one compatible with Britain's resources, and a Conservative government might eventually adopt the same position.

With or without its own nuclear bomb, Britain remains linked to the vital American military capacity. To that capacity the British have already contributed, supplying bases for American bombers, sites for intermediate-range ballistic missiles, and harbors for missile-carrying submarines. Britain thus has been in the front line of American and allied nuclear war strategy. Britain may become less useful to the United States in this respect, if America relies more fully on intercontinental missiles, but the British dependence is not likely to diminish. Neither is Britain's military dependence on the United States in other areas. Almost nowhere, be it Malaysia, East Africa, or the eastern Mediterranean, does Britain seem able to act in protection of its interests, often derived from old imperial ties, without American support of some kind. Much of this dependence, it must be stressed, flows from the continued British preference for the role of a responsible power. Naturally, if Britain chose instead to abdicate responsibility outside of Europe, it would have less need for American help. And if Britain went so far as to become a neutral power even in Europe, it would renounce the American nuclear shield. Such reversals, the second of which is much more unlikely than the first, would probably also mean the end of British support for various American moves.

Putting such radical speculation to one side, it is clear at least in 1966, that Britain is more definitely wedded to American military policy than it has ever been—certainly, more so than most European nations. Neither the Conservative government of the early 1960's nor the Labour government in 1964–'66 showed any tendency to prefer President de Gaulle's proposals for French-led European security. Indeed, Macmillan's Conservative government, in the Nassau agreement of late 1962, so sharply chose to continue its junior partnership with the United States as to lead de Gaulle to exclude Britain from even the Common Market. Wilson's Labour government still more evidently pursued the same policy, and conspicuously supported American policy in Vietnam during 1965 and '66, when France was opposing it and other Western nations were plainly dubious.

Britain's difficulties in going it alone, that is, without the United States, have been illustrated by its postwar experiences in the Middle East. Here, Britain emerged from World War II temporarily reestablished as the dominant power, but without the resources to maintain its traditional interests in the sea routes to India and Australia or its newer interests in Persian Gulf oil. Arab nationalism became increasingly hostile to the indirect British imperial control, especially in the period between the two World Wars, and Britain retreated with less graciousness than anywhere else in the postwar world. British weakness in the whole Mediterranean area became apparent as early as 1947, when the defense of Turkey and Greece from communist aggression was abandoned to the United States, and when Britain failed to solve the postwar Palestine problem to anyone's satisfaction. Yet the British tried to hold what they still regarded as their strategic interest in the Middle East. This centered about the Suez Canal. As a distinguished British soldier wrote during the postwar years, "It has been an axiom of British policy that no hostile Power should be allowed to establish itself within striking distance of Suez, and we have fought immense campaigns in support of this policy."[39] The same interest caused Britain to maintain troops on the Canal until early 1956, and to attempt, along with France, to return troops later the same year, after the Suez Canal Company was seized by the Egyptian government and at the time of Israeli-Egyptian hostilities. It was the failure of this move, in the face of American and United Nations' condemnation, that seemed to be the climactic event in Britain's decline as a Middle Eastern

[39]Ian Jacob, in *United Kingdom Policy*, p. 51.

power. A loss of influence in Iraq followed in 1958, and only remnants of British tutelage subsequently remained in the Arab world. Leadership of the Western effort to court the growingly intransigent Arab nationalism and to counter communist influence in the Middle East now passed to the United States. For Englishmen, particularly Conservative imperialists, this was ironic, since they had previously complained of American unwillingness to back British efforts in the Middle East.

The Suez misadventure of 1956 was a bench mark for British decline in a broader area than the Middle East. The ignominy of the forced withdrawal from Suez brought home the reality of Britain's new position in the world. Large-scale British action anywhere simply could not be carried out without the assurance of an American sympathy sufficient, at least, to provide economic assistance. Certainly no war against a major enemy could be risked without the United States.

A point that remains to be discussed is British membership in the United Nations. As one of the founding Big Five, Britain is a permanent member of the Security Council and a prominent participant in U.N. affairs generally. Except in the Suez altercation, Britain has tended to join in majority decisions of the organization. However, it has never been official British policy to rely primarily on the United Nations as the agency for securing England against aggression. Although many Englishmen, particularly liberals and Labour Party members, display a considerable emotional attachment to U.N. ideals, British policy makers have understandably found alliances like the North Atlantic Treaty Organization sturdier shields than the U.N. Charter. Britain has been anxious primarily to maintain the United Nations as a gathering place for all nations, including communist nations, so that opportunities for discussion, negotiation, and compromise are available.

SUMMARY

The best way to summarize recent British foreign policy is to say that it has sought to meet immense responsibilities with severely limited resources. The diminution of British power, relative to the rest of the world, is a cardinal feature of the international situation in the twentieth century. It may have been less noticeable than the rise of new great powers or of Asian nationalism, but the consequence for the rest of the world, as well as for the British themselves, may be just as serious.

A drastic alternative, which the British have not accepted, is to drop out entirely as a world power and assume the "little England" role that was advocated in the mid-nineteenth century. The model might be the Netherlands, Switzerland, or Sweden. For the present, however, Britain does not intend willingly to abdicate its power and influence. Even the accommodations that Britain has made to nationalist elements in the Commonwealth have been designed to retain British status in a revised form. Furthermore, the British have maintained a considerable share of the responsibility of defending themselves and others from communist aggression. Neutralism has, so far, been well in the background of British consciousness. Most Englishmen have been able to view the United States as a powerful ally brought in to help a common cause, and not as a nation using Britain for its separate purposes.

That Britain will continue to regard itself as an American ally is probable, but not absolutely certain. As the popularity of unilateral nuclear disarmament within the Labour Party in 1960 demonstrated, neutralism can appeal to a substantial minority of the public. It would even have the virtue of bringing Britain in line with most of the Asian and African nations in the Commonwealth. Chiefly, however, it is presented as a means of eliminating the risk believed to flow from participation in American nuclear war strategy. Conceivably, the willingness to assume this particular risk, as well as to assume responsibility in general, might diminish as a new British generation becomes conscious of the nation's loss of status as a great power. The surrender of imperial possessions, while it has removed a source of friction with anticolonialist America, may have the incidental effect of giving Englishmen less cause to participate in the defense of the world against aggression. They now appear to have less of their own to lose, and identification with American power and American interest is incomplete. Yet, in 1966, Britain is not retreating from its active membership in the American-led alliance; indeed, Britain remains virtually America's most dependable ally.

The American connection might not even be drastically affected by Britain's membership in an integrated Western Europe. Joining a European union, likely to become more meaningful politically as well as economically, would allow Britain to play a role different from that of a "little England" or of a pretender to a Commonwealth hegemony. Britain might in time become a leader of a powerful new European community, but any such community in which Britain plays an important part would most probably be an outward-looking ally of the United States rather than an independent, Gaullist-minded Europe.

SELECTED BIBLIOGRAPHY

Bull, Hedley, The Control of the Arms Race: Disarmament and Arms Control in the Missile Age. New York: Frederick G. Praeger, Inc., 1961.

Camps, Miriam, Britain and the European Community: 1955–1963. Princeton, N.J.: Princeton University Press, 1964.

Epstein, Leon D., British Politics in the Suez Crisis. Urbana, Ill.: University of Illinois Press, 1964.

Miller, J. D. B., The Commonwealth in the World. London: Gerald Duckworth & Co., Ltd. 1959.

Mulley, F. W., The Politics of Western Defence. London: Thames and Hudson, 1962.

Nicolson, Harold, Diplomacy. London: Oxford University Press, 1950.

Northedge, F. S., British Foreign Policy. New York: Frederick A. Praeger, Inc., 1962.

Snyder, William P., The Politics of British Defense Policy. Columbus, Ohio: Ohio State University Press, 1964.

Strang, Lord, The Foreign Office. New York: Oxford University Press, 1955.

Thornton, A. P., The Imperial Idea and Its Enemies. London: Macmillan & Co., Ltd., 1959.

Ward, A. W., and G. P. Gooch, eds., The Cambridge History of British Foreign Policy: 1783–1919. London: Cambridge University Press, 1922–'23.

Younger, Kenneth, Changing Perspectives in British Foreign Policy. London: Oxford University Press, 1964.

FRENCH
Foreign Policy

3

Roy C. Macridis

INTRODUCTION

The dilemma confronting French foreign policy may be stated in rather simple terms. France, one of the great powers of the nineteenth century, has found her position in the world progressively declining, while the aspiration and the illusion of greatness and strength have persisted.

France emerged from World War II militarily weak, drained of manpower, with her economy seriously undermined after four years of occupation, facing urgent problems of economic and social reconstruction at home. Her situation was such that she was dependent upon Britain and, primarily, upon the United States. In terms of Walter Lippmann's axiom that commitments in foreign policy must be commensurate with strength, it was very clear that there were few commitments that France could undertake and carry out successfully without Anglo-American support. France's lib-

erty of action, therefore, was limited. Her aspiration to remain a top-rank power seemed to be at variance with her capabilities.

Thus, the dilemma involved either the acceptance of the realities of the post-World War II situation, or a continuation of France's "vocation of greatness" without the physical and economic resources to implement it. This problem needed to be confronted throughout the years after the Liberation. Neither the political system nor the political parties and the press managed to present it to the public in clear-cut terms. There was no "great debate" for the purpose of redefining the French position and status in the world.

To explain the nature of the dilemma will be the purpose of this chapter. We shall discuss the background that has shaped France's foreign policy —her geographic position, economic and social development, and culture, the more persistent interests pursued by France, and both the objectives and the institution of foreign policy making in the Fifth Republic.

BACKGROUND FACTORS

A number of interacting factors constitute the setting in which foreign policy operates. Some of these factors are objective ones; they can be easily measured and compared. Others are subjective, and constitute a community's image of itself in the world. Among the objective factors, the most important are the nation's economic strength, its geographic position, its military potential, its technological skill, its culture, and the diffusion of its culture in other parts of the world. The subjective factors are primarily ideological; they can be studied with reference to the various elites of the system and to the particular conception the elites have of their country's role in the world. Important among those elites is, of course, the political leadership.

Subjective and objective factors constantly interact to give to foreign policy a dynamic and ever-changing pattern; however, such interaction may be impeded for various reasons, so that reality, i.e., the objective factor, may be at variance with ideology, i.e., the subjective factor. As we have pointed out, this might be a tenable hypothesis for the study of French foreign policy in the twentieth century.

The economic foundations

The most significant feature of the French economy has been, until the last decade, its gradual decline. While industrialization went forward rapidly throughout the nineteenth century in England, Germany, Japan, and the United States, and also in the Soviet Union in the twentieth century, France's economy advanced at a snail's pace.

Yet France began with a marked head start over *all* other countries. During the Napoleonic era and until the middle of the nineteenth century, France was one of the most economically developed nations of the world. From then on, despite a wealth of resources and skilled labor, her economy declined in comparison with almost all the countries of Western Europe. Her total national income, between 1870 to 1940, rose by about eighty per cent; that of Germany increased five times; that of Great Britain, three times and a half. In the years between the two World Wars (1918–1940), investment declined to a point below zero—that is, France was living on her capital, using her factories and equipment without replacing them in full. She was going through a period of disinvestment. The destruction wrought by World War II, estimated at approximately fifty billion dollars, was an additional setback. With her industrial equipment destroyed or dilapidated and her transportation network paralyzed, France's economy was in a state of collapse.

There were many long-range factors associated with this stagnation: notably, the very slow growth of population, a backward agriculture, the protectionist policies of the state and, finally, the attitudes of the business groups.

Population. In 1800, France had the largest population of any country in Europe and the Americas, excepting only that of Russia. The Napoleonic armies were recruited from, and supported by 26 million French men and women, when England had only 11 million inhabitants, the United States had 5.5 million, and the German states, including Austria, had about 23 million. France maintained this advantage until about 1860, when she had about 38 million. From then on, her population remained virtually static. In 1940, for instance, it was almost exactly 40 million, while that of the United States was close to 150 million, that of Great Britain was 50 million, and that of Germany (West and East, but without Austria) was 65 million. In the years between 1930 and 1940, the French population actually declined—that is, there was an excess of deaths over births. Two wars had taken a heavy toll, also, of the young and active part of the population. The percentage of the aged (over 65) became disproportionately heavy, thereby contributing to economic stagnation.

Agriculture. France's agricultural problem developed in the period between 1870 and 1940. The proportion of farmers—about 35 to 40 per cent of the active population—was the largest in Western Europe excepting Italy and Spain, but their productivity was one of the lowest in Europe. There were a great number of small, marginal farms, divided and subdivided into parcels to which new techniques and mechanization could not be applied. Until 1940, France used less fertilizer than any other Western European country, and the use of tractors remained insignificant.

Protectionism. That much of the population remained on relatively unproductive farms was due partly to the tariff policies of the state. Agricultural interests formed powerful lobbies which demanded and got a high protectionist tariff, sheltering French business and agriculture from foreign competition. They also received special subsidies and guaranteed price supports. Not only wheat producers and growers of beets (from which large quantities of alcohol are distilled) profited from these measures, but also wine growers, fruit growers, and dairy interests. High tariffs also sheltered manufacturing concerns. The state was perpetuating and supporting a situation that consecrated the weakness of the economic system.

Business attitudes. Industrialists and business groups did not show, in France, the initiative and willingness to take risks that we generally associate with capitalism. Many business enterprises were family affairs. Production remained geared to a limited demand instead of seeking new markets. Profits were often saved, instead of being reinvested.

A particularly vulnerable sector of the economy was in the distribution sector. Large chain stores were the exception, and small merchants and shopkeepers eked out a living through a limited volume of trade. As a result, efficient techniques to reduce costs and bring prices down did not develop. Retail prices kept far ahead of wholesale prices, with the many middlemen who handled the product making small profits. This unduly inflated the price the consumer paid. The middlemen in France, like the agricultural population, formed an oversized and relatively unproductive sector of the economy. They, too, organized in strong pressure groups and demanded subsidies and protection.

The end of World War II brought to light the weaknesses of the country and accentuated a number of them. The greater part of the foreign assets and investments of France had been wiped out, millions had lost their lives or health as a result of the war and the enemy occupation, and the industrial equipment of the country had reached obsolescence. The tasks ahead were to stop inflation and put the currency back on a healthy basis, to rebuild the communication systems as well as the schools, factories, and homes, to improve the productive resources in order to bring production up to the prewar level and surpass it, and to rationalize and reorganize the agriculture.

Geographic position

France's geographic position created contradictory interests and commitments. On the one hand, she has been a continental power with frontiers that include, to the east, Belgium, Germany, Switzerland, and Italy, and, to the southwest, Spain; on the other hand, she has had a colonial empire with possessions throughout Asia and Africa and in the Pacific, Indian, and Atlantic oceans.

The French Empire had been developed and consolidated by the end of the nineteenth century. On the continent, the Spanish frontier, and that facing Belgium and Switzerland, presented no problems. The threat came from Germany—a Germany that after 1870 had been unified and that after 1930, despite its defeat in 1918, confronted France once more with a population of some 65 million and an economic and industrial system more productive than her own. At the same time, the Empire required everlasting vigilance against potential marauders, particularly England, and against nationalist independence movements. This required the maintenance of a strong army at home as well as a strong navy. The position of France, therefore, involved heavy economic sacrifices.

This situation accounted for the existence of two distinct groups within the French political leadership. One tended to favor a rapprochement with Germany. It was anti-British, since the traditional obstacle to French imperial ambitions and naval power had been Great Britain. The other tended to emphasize the continental position of France, to plead for a strong army, and to underplay her imperial commitments. It tended to be pro-British and anti-German. Neither point of view could or did prevail. Germany was naturally in favor of encouraging France's imperial commitments, in exchange for a free hand in Europe—particularly in Eastern Europe and in the Middle East, which ultimately would endanger France's position in Europe. England, on the other hand, was anxious to encourage France in her continental policy, with the full realization that a strong French army would be a deterrent against Germany and hence would allow England to concentrate on its naval strength and the development of its own empire, ultimately at the expense of the interests of France in the world.

From whichever point of view one looks at the situation as it developed in the latter part of the nineteenth century, one cannot help but realize that the French predicament was a serious one. France, more than any other country of the world, had to assume the heavy burdens both of a continental power and of an empire. The end of World War II and the subsequent developments indicate, as we shall see, that France stubbornly attempted to preserve both positions.

Cultural diffusion

It would hardly be an exaggeration to say that France was, in the nineteenth century, the cultural center of the world. In politics, art, literature, and education, French thought radiated everywhere. The French Revolution had given to the cause of freedom a clear-cut formulation which was carried to all parts of Europe by Napoleon's armies. The French Napoleonic code was plagiarized by almost every Latin-American and European nation. The French language was the medium of communication in international conferences and the second language of the educated classes of the world. France's philosophers, intellectuals, and scientists pioneered the cause of human and scientific knowledge.

Innumerable cultural ties linked France with most other countries. Such links constituted, without any doubt, a capital that, like the *Marseillaise*, was just as important as ships and soldiers, just as important as the investment of the British merchants and storekeepers in the British Empire. But it was the kind of capital whose logic calls for continuous reinvestment. It was also the kind of capital that tends to pervert the lender. With the relative decline of the French economy in the twentieth century, other nations began to attract scientists and intellectuals. The use of the French language in diplomacy and in other aspects of international relations began to be challenged. The French political system itself showed signs of strain, as her colonial policy revealed obvious incompatibilities with the universal ethical postulates that the French Revolution promulgated. The colonial elite, who had studied in France and for whom French was a second language, chose to engage her in a dialogue in which the lessons they had learned became increasingly embarrassing for the teacher. But at the very moment the dialogue was engaged—particularly between the colonies and the metropolis—French cultural pre-eminence had become permanent and incontrovertible in the minds of the French. It became a myth, an *idée fixe* which could allow no exception and permit no argument. French cultural supremacy was taken for granted. This produced innumer-

able reflexes which account for some of France's recent actions: her prolonged reluctance to change her policy with regard to the Empire; her extreme sensitivity to criticisms from abroad; a blind pride, considering her own system as superior to that of any other nation in the world; and finally a strong belief in the unique mission of France —to educate, to cultivate, and to humanize.

Persistent patterns

A number of patterns underlie the French conception of foreign policy. In the nineteenth century they reflected France's strength, but they slowly crystallized into dogmas and myths that were ultimately separated from twentieth-century reality. It is, nonetheless, in terms of such myths that France's post-World War II foreign policy has been shaped, rather than in terms of the new factors that developed partly as a result of the war and partly as the result of a number of social, economic, and ideological forces that stirred the world.

The basic objectives of foreign policy remained: (a) the continuation of France's imperial position and (b) continental strength. The first meant, as we have seen, the maintenance of the far-flung Empire with all the financial difficulties and obligations it entailed. Not for a moment was the notion of federalism and self-government for its members seriously entertained. The Empire was conceived as a part of France's mission and as a continuous challenge to French culture and influence. The resurrection of France as a continental power was also an automatic reflex; no political leader doubted it. The end of World War II by the defeat of Germany was, in a sense, their revenge for the German occupation of France. Victory, it was thought, simply reestablished the prewar balance. To implement France's continental position, the same alliances with the West and with the East were contemplated—all of them directed against a Germany that lay prostrate and divided. The fact that the Soviet Union had gained a foothold in the heart of Europe did not alter, for a long time, the traditional French reflexes; Germany was the enemy of France. A weak Germany and a Franco-Russian Alliance remained the condition of French security. When General de Gaulle visited Moscow and signed the Franco-Russian treaty in December, 1944, he was preserving French security according to the best traditions of the nineteenth century. Underlying his actions was the belief that France, with her Empire, and secure from the resurrection of German might and German attack, was once more a great power ready to fill the power vacuum that lay in the heart of Europe; moreover she was poised to throw her weight on one or the other side of the scale of the conflict for power that emerged between the Soviet Union and the United States.

THE SUBSTANCE OF FOREIGN POLICY: TRENDS AND PROBLEMS

France has followed two basic foreign policy objectives ever since the eighteenth century. The first is the policy of *natural frontiers* and the second is the policy of what might be called *European status quo,* or *balance of power* in Europe.

The natural frontiers of France have been considered to be on the Rhine and on the Alps. They include Belgium, Holland, Luxembourg, and the German territories that lie west of the Rhine. This was interpreted to mean that France's strategic and military interests extended to those areas, and that no other power could set foot there without jeopardizing her interests. The continuity of this policy is remarkable. Danton stated in 1793: "The frontiers [of the Republic] are marked *by nature.* . . . They are the Rhine, the Alps and the Pyrennean mountains." Clemenceau affirmed in 1919: "The move towards the Rhine was the tradition of our ancestors. . . . It was the tradition to create a frontier, a *true* frontier marking the French territory." General de Gaulle, in 1944, demanded, in the name of a weak and defeated country: "The Rhine *is* French security and I think the security of the whole world. But France is the principal interested party. . . . She wishes to be solidly established from one end to the other of her *natural frontier.*"[1]

The policy of *status quo,* on the other hand, was based upon three assumptions that became in turn three basic objectives of policy:

1. France was not interested in any European conquest.

2. No single power should gain preponderant strength in Europe. The *status quo*—consisting of a number of competing political units, small if possible—should be maintained so as to give France the role of an arbitrator.

3. France became the protector of small states throughout Europe, since it was owing to the existence of many of them that she could effectively play the role of arbitrator and maintain her position of supremacy in Europe. As Vergennes wrote, in 1777: "France, placed in the center of Europe, has the right to influence all the great developments. Her King, like a supreme judge, can consider his throne as a tribunal established

[1]See the excellent article by J. Raoul Girardet, "L'influence de la tradition sur la politique étrangère de la France" *La Politique étrangère et ses Fondements,* ed. Jean-Baptiste Duroselle, (Paris: Librairie Armand Colin, 1954), pp. 143–63.

by Providence to guarantee the respect for the rights and properties of the sovereigns."[2]

This providential role of France has been restated many times.

In 1919, the two policies converged. The theory of natural frontiers led to the demilitarization of the Rhine area, to the control of the Saar, and to the military hegemony of France over the Low Countries. The policy of the *status quo,* as redefined, led to an effort to divide Germany, to the breakup of the Austro-Hungarian Empire, and to the establishment of a number of new nations all over Eastern and Southeastern Europe, with which France established close political, economic, and military ties. Of course, a number of other factors entered into the picture. The Wilsonian idea of self-determination encouraged the establishment of small states which France was only too pleased to take under her protection, while the creation of a number of small states east of Germany formed a *cordon sanitaire* against the Soviet Union and, at the same time, prevented Germany from moving east.

By 1919, then, the two traditional French foreign policies had found a happy reconciliation. Despite a number of difficulties (the dismemberment of Germany did not take place, for instance), the general settlement gave France both a position of preponderance in Europe and a great degree of security and safety. If only the world had stood still, France might have maintained that position.

The policy of a European balance of power, plus security, also became France's worldwide policy. The Empire had been consolidated by the end of the nineteenth century and World War I. The imperial vocation, and with it the world vocation of France, continued side by side with its continental

[2]Quoted by J. Raoul Girardet, *Ibid.*

vocation in the years after World War II—years that we intend to discuss now. We shall divide our discussion into three parts: France and Europe; France and the Empire; and France and the world.

France and Europe: the insoluble dilemma

The immediate reaction of France after the Liberation was to attempt to reestablish her traditional position of security in Europe and of independence as a world power. From 1944 until mid-1947, a policy was followed that for all practical purposes was identical to that of 1919. France proposed the following:

1. The dismemberment of Germany and prolonged occupation of the country.
2. Heavy reparations and tight control of German industrial output.
3. The reestablishment of French control in the area west of the Rhine by the detachment of these territories from Germany.
4. A prolonged occupation, if not annexation, of the Saar.
5. The independence of the small nations of Europe.
6. An alliance with Russia directed against a threat to French security from Germany.
7. An alliance with Great Britain.

Under the government of General de Gaulle, this policy was pursued with great tenacity. After the Liberation in December, 1944, a Treaty of Mutual Assistance was signed with the Soviet Union. The two countries agreed to take "all the necessary measures in order to eliminate any new menace coming from Germany and to take the initiative to make any new effort of aggression on her part impossible." [Article 3.] Immediately after the signature of the pact, General de Gaulle declared: "Because two of the principal powers of the world—free from any conflict of interest in any part of the world—decide to unite under specific conditions, it does not mean that either the one or the other envisages to organize the world and even its security without the help of other nations."[3]

But one might ask whether the haste with which General de Gaulle went to Moscow to sign the treaty was not motivated by considerations other than the security of France from an attack by Germany, which lay literally prostrate before the Anglo-American and Russian armies. By the treaty with Moscow, France was indeed serving notice to her former British and American allies that she intended to pursue an independent policy.

Throughout 1946, every effort was made by France to gain the support of *either* the Soviet Union *or* the United States and Great Britain in the implementation of her German policy. Neither of her two allies, however, responded favorably, since they both hoped to see, ultimately, an economically and politically unified Germany *on their side,* something that would have meant the end of French aspirations for European security and leadership. When the Soviet Foreign Minister, Molotov, declared himself, in July, 1946, in favor of a politically unified Germany, the author of the *Année Politique* wrote: "There was reason for France, which could count on the support of her ally in the East *against* the Anglo-Americans, to be disappointed."[4]

There were more disappointments to come. The Soviet Union feared that France would ultimately become part of the Anglo-American camp, and refused to support her aspirations to see the Ruhr and the Rhine provinces detached from Germany. The Soviet-American conflict at the time revolved

around the control of the whole of Germany, and the prize seemed far more important than France. By the time it became quite clear that the conflict could not be resolved except by a partition of Germany, France had discovered that her policy had failed; she had failed to gain the support of either the Soviet Union or the United States. She was faced with the dilemma of either accepting the division of Germany into two zones, a division that could confront France with a highly industrialized and powerful West Germany, or of following an independent policy by maintaining her occupation of a small part of West Germany and the Saar.

The Cold War and the development of Western alliances. The Cold War, whose origin can be traced to Yalta and Potsdam, erupted in the middle of 1947. The two conferences, held in Moscow and in London, had failed to produce any kind of agreement on the problem of Germany. The lines were being drawn, and the division of Germany into two zones—Soviet and British-American—became a certainty. The conflict implied the strengthening of both zones, and hence the development of a strong West German Republic supported by the United States and England.

France managed to maintain control over the Saar, but failed in all her other claims. After June, 1947, the whole of Western Europe and Great Britain received massive American aid to develop their economy. In 1948, the Brussels Pact brought together the Benelux countries, France, and Great Britain. It provided for a permanent consultative council, for negotiations to promote economic development of the countries concerned, and included a military clause calling for immediate consultations to take common action against a German attack or aggression

[3] *Année politique: 1944–45*, p. 89.
[4] *Année politique: 1946*, p. 400.

and to cope with a situation that constituted a menace to peace, no matter where it occurred or from where it came. In 1949, the creation of a large military umbrella was logically called for. Not only the Brussels signatories, but also all the Western countries, including ultimately Greece and Turkey, participated. The United States became a permanent part of this alliance that still continues as the North Atlantic Treaty Organization (NATO). Article 5 stipulated that an attack against any one of the signatories, either in Europe or in North America, would be considered to be an attack against all. It further provided (in Article 9) for a permanent deliberative organization and the establishment of a common military command. West Germany was originally excluded from NATO.

These developments determined France's position. She became a member of NATO and of the various Western alliances, under the over-all leadership and military direction of the United States. Such an alliance underwrote her security and, in general terms, the integrity of her Empire. The exclusion of Germany continued to give her a strategic position in Western Europe, as well as the semblance, if not the reality, of national power and independence. But the question of Germany's future had been only postponed. A military Western alliance without Germany hardly represented a solution of the problems of military defense. Furthermore, as the struggle between the East and the West not only continued but was intensified with the Korean War, the prize of Germany became more important for the two major opponents. For the United States, the rearmament of West Germany seemed, rightly or wrongly, the logical step for the construction of a strong defensive wall in the West against a potential Soviet attack.

For France, however, such a rearmament was a threat. German economic development and the revival of German strength across the Rhine evoked the traditional reflexes. Yet by 1950 or '51, as we pointed out, there could be no imminent danger to France's security. The military alliance with Great Britain, the Brussels Pact, NATO, and the presence of American and British forces on the continent constituted adequate guarantees. Only France's notions of independence and European supremacy were really at stake. A Western Alliance in which an armed West Germany participated might, to the French mind, come under the domination of the strongest country—West Germany.

The European Defense Community and its alternatives. The defensive arrangements of the Western world and the Atlantic powers did not include West Germany. Yet West German resources were considered indispensable by the United States. The problem, therefore, was to integrate West Germany's power within the frame of a Western alliance, without alienating France and the signatories of the Brussels Pact.

It was, strangely enough, the French who came forth with the answer: the creation of a West European army —the European Defense Community (EDC)—involving a genuine integration of national forces, a unified and, if possible, a supranational command. The United States became convinced that such a policy was preferable to the rearming of West Germany within NATO. There were many tangible indications of a widespread movement in favor of European cooperation. The Council of Europe, representing the Western European nations, and with a European Assembly, had been established in 1949; the Organization of European Economic Cooperation was a European body studying the resources and needs of Western Europe and attempting to liberalize trade relations. The Western European Payments Union was functioning in order to control and regulate the deficits in the balance of payments of various European countries. Above all, the Coal and Steel Community, initiated by France, had become a reality that involved a supranational authority with power to make decisions on matters of investment, production, and transportation of coal and steel among the six signatory powers—West Germany, France, the Benelux countries, and Italy. The establishment of a European army, ambitious though it appeared to be, was welcome in the context of these moves toward European cooperation and integration.

No sooner had the European Defence Community been announced and formulated, however, than it provoked a storm of protest in France. The political parties were actively for or against it. Extreme right-wing and extreme left-wing parties joined hands against the treaty, which was defended by a sharply divided center. To French public opinion, the most controversial part of the treaty was the envisaged German rearmament. A majority of the members of the National Assembly considered German rearmament, even within the EDC, to be a direct challenge to French sovereignty, clearly spelling the end of France's aspirations to remain a leading European nation. The memory of Nazi Germany was too fresh in the minds of many; the possibility that West Germany, once rearmed, might attempt to provoke a war with Russia in order to achieve its unification, and thus drag the whole of Europe into a war, was pointed out; the assumption by Germany of a predominant role in Europe, at a time

when France was heavily engaged in protecting her Empire, was also mentioned. Each party and each parliamentary group saw specific reasons for refusing to accept the treaty, while its proponents defended it also for different reasons. Since there was no genuine majority[5] for or against the treaty, it was on a procedural motion that, in August, 1954, the EDC was rejected by the French National Assembly. In the meantime, all its prospective members had honored the signature of their governments. Only the French Assembly used its constitutional prerogatives and refused to ratify the treaty. The rejection climaxed four whole years of equivocation. It was only in December, 1954, that the National Assembly, six months after defeating the EDC for fear of German rearmament, allowed Germany to become a member of NATO and to rearm herself within the context of the NATO alliance.

A third force? While the EDC was being debated and criticisms against it multiplied, the movement in favor of neutralism assumed great importance. It is hard to define or describe it briefly without doing injustice to its manifold aspects and characteristics. Essentially, it was a movement that answered the profound hopes of the French people that, in case of war, France would be allowed to remain out of it. Some 70 per cent of the French people answering a poll conducted by the French Institute of Public Opinion expressed this hope in 1951, when the Cold War was at its highest. At the same time,

[5]The division of the political system in the French Parliament and in the various coalition Cabinets reflected very closely the division of public opinion. In July, 1954, 36 per cent of those asked were "for" or "rather for" the EDC, 31 per cent were "against" or "rather against," and 33 per cent did not answer.

neutralism was a movement that tended to reassert the traditional French claims to independence and a balance of power. Since the world was divided between two camps, France alone, or France at the head of Western Europe, could afford to say "A plague on both your houses!" and, if need be, to arbitrate between them.

The neutralist position was advanced by the Communist Party and by some left-wing intellectuals for other motives. Essentially, they wanted to weaken American predominance over Western Europe. Many of the left-wing intellectuals were motivated by subtler considerations: the independence of the French nation to continue to develop her own way of life; the rejection of the realities of a polarized world; an emphasis upon France's cultural and intellectual vocation. For some, it was mere anti-Americanism and a declaration of France's independence from American tutelage; for others, it was the belief that France had more to gain than to lose from a pro-Soviet orientation; for many others, it was a constructive step towards the building of a solid Western alliance with Great Britain as a partner, which would develop enough strength to play the role of Third Force that France could not play alone. Neutralism and nationalism were often linked.

But the German problem was again an obstacle. A Third Force in Europe, without West Germany and without wholehearted British commitment, could not be strong enough. A Third Force with Germany, however, was one in which Germany, rather than France, might assume a preponderant role. The real tragedy was that France, weak alone, found that any form of European integration and alliance underscored her weakness and subordination—to the United States, to the

Soviet Union, or possibly to England or West Germany. By 1954, therefore, France found herself, after interminable zigzags, equivocations, and soul-searching, in the Atlantic camp to which a fifteenth member had been added—West Germany.

France and the Empire

France emerged from World War I as one of the three big powers. Russia lay in the throes of Revolution; the United States still was unwilling to assume international responsibilities that involved continuous commitments abroad; elsewhere in the world, the stirrings of nationalist awakening were making themselves heard, but not sufficiently to cause concern to the colonial powers, of whom England and France were the most important.

The French Empire extended over every continent of the world. Its administration was a vestige of the Napoleonic conceptions of a highly centralized bureaucratic system—an administration in which Paris, through the colonial officials, made the ultimate decisions and legislated for the whole Empire. Its cementing ideology was that of "assimilation"—the notion that ultimately every inhabitant would become a French citizen and be represented in the French Parliament—a notion at marked variance with the Anglo-Saxon conception, according to which political and cultural evolution of the colonial peoples would ultimately bring about political autonomy and self-government.

In 1944, the basic charter of colonial policy had been drafted at the Brazzaville conference. There it was decided that "the purpose of the civilizing work accomplished by France in the colonies excludes any idea of autonomy, any possibility of an evolution outside of the French Empire. The establishment, even in the remote future, of 'self-government' in the colonies must not be considered."[6] In 1945, when a Trusteeship Committee was appointed within the United Nations, the French made it quite clear that they would not accept its jurisdiction. The Empire was French, and hence a matter of domestic policy.

In almost every case, the French insisted upon assimilation and maintenance of French sovereignty. In 1945, France refused to withdraw her army from Syria and Lebanon. Within a year she had to give in. In 1947, she refused to enter into negotiations with Ho-Chi-Minh, and engaged in a war that lasted until 1954. The war in Indochina cost France more than a billion dollars a year, drained her of resources, retarded her internal investment policy, and paralyzed her alternate plans for an economic and social reconstruction of the North African territories. It was primarily responsible for France's inability to keep pace with German economic reconstruction in Western Europe.

But the Indochinese war brought other problems to a head. In Algeria, Tunis, and Morocco, the independence movements were gaining strength. These movements, however, envisaged continued cooperation with France. In every case, the French political leaders and representatives and the various military leaders in command of the French troops reiterated the philosophy of the French vocation. Time after time, the legitimate interests of France were evoked. Time after time, the representatives of the French government and army intervened. By 1956, both Morocco and Tunisia became independent. The refusal to grant self-government left only one alternative: secession.

This situation was most evident in Algeria, where there was a very strong

movement in favor of self-government after the Liberation. It gained strength after the independence of Morocco and Tunisia. Yet there were many opportunities to cope with the Algerian situation, and progress was made in 1947, when special legislation granting considerable political autonomy to Algeria was passed, although never implemented. Claims of French sovereignty in Algeria and assertions that France "intends to stay there," made in the last years of the Fourth Republic, sounded very similar to the assertions made about Syria, Lebanon, Indochina, Tunis, and Morocco.

France and the world: the vocation of greatness

The explanation of the predicament of the French Empire lies in the postwar vocation of France to maintain her top-rank power status in the world. The French Empire, as a French commentator wrote in an excellent but highly optimistic analysis of the prospects of the French Union, "corresponds without any doubt to the profound interest of France. . . . France cannot aspire to play an important international role except in terms of her ability to represent a powerful association of peoples."[7]

The fate of France was invariably presented in terms of the destiny of the nation in the world. The answer was given in terms of traditional historical reflexes—France's military power, her cultural superiority, her civilizing mission, and her Empire. Over and above these misconceptions, the assessment of national strength was also couched in terms of nineteenth-century imperial perspectives. The equation, however, was no longer valid in view of the develop-

[6] Année politique: 1944–45.

[7] "L'union Française: Bilan politique de l'année 1947," in Année politique: 1947, p. 275.

ment of colonial nationalism. The British saw in it something the French refused to realize: that to maintain an Empire by force is far more expensive and far more debilitating to a nation's strength than to abandon it.

THE LEGACY OF THE FOURTH REPUBLIC (1946–1958)

ELEMENTS OF STABILITY

Speaking on October 28, 1966, in his 14th Press Conference, General de Gaulle stated with remarkable succinctness the objectives of French foreign policy in terms that apply to the Fourth Republic as well. "In the world as it is," he said, "people sometimes feign surprise over the so-called changes and detours of France's action. And there are even those who have spoken of contradictions or Machiavellism. Well, I believe that while the circumstances are changing around us, in truth there is nothing more constant than France's policy. For this policy, throughout the extremely varied vicissitudes of our times and our world—this policy's essential goal is that France be and remain an independent nation."

Despite the divisions of the political system under the Fourth Republic and the fact that they often spilled over into the area of foreign policy, there was continuity in the pursuit of basic objectives of foreign policy. The political elite, the political parties (with the exception of the communists), and the public remained steadfast in their attachment to the traditional interests of France, in spite of rapidly changing world conditions. Discontinuities were occasionally introduced, but only in the form of decisive choices. This was the case in 1954–'55, with the termination of the Indochinese war, the granting of autonomy and later independence to Morocco and Tunisia, and the Paris agreements that consecrated West German sovereignty and allowed for German participation in NATO. The political system remained, by and large, committed to the following objectives: (a) the maintenance of an Atlantic and world position that implied a weak Germany and a militarily independent France; (b) a European rapprochement in terms of which France could gain strength at the head of Western Europe; and (c) the maintenance of a top-rank world position.

What has been called *la politique du grandeur* ("the policy of greatness"), according to which France's vocation is that of a world power and therefore a partner in the development of world strategy or—under propitious conditions—an independent force, was ever present. General de Gaulle's policy, since his return to power on June 1, 1958, has been a faithful expression of the broad objectives pursued by the political leadership of the Fourth Republic.

The Empire: the foundation of a new policy. It was only in the last two years of the Republic, between 1956 and '58, that France's leadership decided to move ahead of the irresistible trend of colonial emancipation rather than attempt to oppose it. In 1956, the French Parliament began consideration of new legislation to put an end to the theory and practice of assimilation. A *loi-cadre* ("framework law") empowered the government to enact executive orders in order to give considerable autonomy to the African republics and Madagascar. They became semi-independent republics, with their own parliaments and responsible executives. France retained jurisdiction over important areas of policy making such as defense, foreign policy, trade and education. But the first path toward gradual political emancipation had been made, and it proved to be irreversible.

Economic and military policy. The Fourth Republic also laid the groundwork of France's economic and military recovery. The Atomic Energy Commissariat, founded in 1945, continued in operation throughout the years when the Cabinet was unstable, and it was endowed with adequate credits. The possession of an atom bomb in a world in which three powers had developed nuclear weapons became associated, in the eyes of the French political leaders and public alike, with France's national independence and security. Throughout the latter years of the Republic, all French governments favored the suspension of the fabrication of the bomb *and* the gradual destruction of nuclear weapons. Only if the latter condition were accepted would France have been willing to abandon her manufacture and testing of the bomb.

Although favoring the Atlantic alliance, the political leaders of the Fourth Republic never agreed to play a secondary role and acquiesce to American or British and American supremacy. They did not accept any genuine integration of military command within NATO and, alleging their colonial obligations, insisted on maintaining autonomy over their military forces. They remained reluctant to permit the United States to establish stockpiles of nuclear weapons on French soil or to construct launching sites. The same fear of integration of the military forces applied to a purely European army, as we have seen.

Thus, while accepting participation in an Atlantic and European military alliance, the French governments made sure that these alliances never took a form that undermined France's independence and freedom to use her own military forces at her own discretion. By the same token, they were unwilling to participate in any defense system with the British and the Americans unless France were given full and equal power on all global decisions and strategy.

Public opinion[8]

Studies of opinion throughout the Fourth Republic indicate that there was a striking coincidence of the action of the political leaders and public opinion. French attitudes toward the Cold War, the Soviet Union or the United States, the problem of French military independence and West Germany, and European cooperation show stability and continuity.

The Cold War. Generally, the attitude of the French with regard to the Cold War can be summed up as one of neutrality and considerable hostility to both protagonists. One out of every ten Frenchmen polled believed that the United States was to be blamed, two out of ten put the blame on the Soviet Union and four out of every ten on both. At the same time, the French public thought that neither the United States nor the Soviet Union were doing all they could to avert the Cold War. Fifty-two and 57 per cent of those interrogated in 1957 believed that the United States and the Soviet Union respectively, were not doing as much as possible. From 1952 until 1957, the public expressed itself as

[8]I am indebted to the summary of public opinion trends, *"La politique étrangère de la France et l'opinion publique: 1954–1957,"* *Sondages: Revue Française de l'opinion publique*; Nos. 1 and 2 (1958).

follows: *To which camp should France belong?*

		The West	The East	Neither
Sept.,	1952	42%	4%	43%
Nov.,	1954	36%	2%	39%
June,	1955	18%	3%	57%
Aug.,	1955	23%	4%	51%
Dec.,	1955	35%	5%	45%
May,	1957	28%	4%	39%
Dec.,	1957	21%	3%	51%

If there were a war between the United States and the Soviet Union, to which camp should France belong?

		U.S.	U.S.S.R.	Not take part
Sept.,	1952	36%	4%	45%
Nov.,	1954	22%	2%	45%
June,	1955	19%	3%	58%
Aug.,	1955	25%	5%	51%
Sept.,	1957	15%	3%	62%

Europe. While the French continued to fear West Germany and to be reluctant to see her rearm, there was a general resignation to Germany's participation in European cooperation schemes. From 1947 until December, 1957, French public opinion favored a European union. Fifty-five to 70 per cent were in favor, and those opposed never exceeded 21 per cent. In only two polls, taken in 1955, did less than 50 per cent favor a European union. Support for the European Common Market for the Schuman Plan, and for the European atomic cooperation program was equally strong. The rearmament of West Germany, however, was considered, until 1954, to be a danger, and the consensus of opinion favored a demilitarized Germany. In 1955, 53 per cent were against the participation of West Germany in the defense of Western Europe.

Atomic weapons, NATO, and the United States. Although they still chose neutrality and condemned the manufacture and potential use of atomic weapons, the French, in December, 1957, favored "giving more attention to atomic weapons" for the defense of their country. Forty per cent were in favor; 20 per cent opposed, and 40 per cent declined to answer.

In December, 1957, the French were also asked, "Under the present circumstances, how can France best assure her security?" Sixteen per cent favored the maintenance of the existing alliances in Western Europe, within NATO and with the U.S.A.; 5 per cent favored a military alliance limited to Western Europe only; 21 per cent favored a general security system including the United States, Western Europe and the Soviet Union; and 34 per cent favored withdrawal *from all alliances* and the assumption of an independent and neutral posture.

In the same context, the general reaction of the French public with regard to NATO was one of indifference. Not more than 50 or 60 per cent were prepared to answer on the basis of any knowledge of the organization. Of those answering, only a small percentage favored the organization and considered it important for the security of France. Such a reaction was not caused by the intervention of the United States in the Suez expedition or the delivery of arms to Tunisia—generally considered to be acts inimical to France. It stemmed primarily from the realization that the United States was exerting too much influence on French foreign policy. Forty to 42 per cent of the French interrogated between 1952 and December, 1956, found that the United States had too much influence. In the same manner, more than 60 per cent believed, in 1956 and 1957, that France was not treated by the United States as an equal in matters concerning the two countries. Some 27 to 40 per cent believed that Americans and French had common interests, while some 25 per cent believed that the interests of the two countries were different. More than 33 per cent of those asked in December, 1956, believed that a European union would diminish American influence, and 35 per cent of them believed that such a diminution of American influence would be "a good thing."

Thus throughout the period of the Fourth Republic, the public, even if badly informed, reacted with a remarkable degree of unity in favor of neutrality and European cooperation, feared Germany, suspected NATO, and in general agreed that independence and security could be based only on national strength and freedom of action. Despite an underlying realization of France's reduced world status, the public continued to cling to the image of a strong and independent France. They deplored the reduction of French strength and accepted European unity as an instrument for the realization of national security vis-à-vis both the United States and the Soviet Union.

Foreign Service

An important factor in the continuity of the French foreign policy was the existence of a small but competent body of civil servants attached to the Ministry of Foreign Affairs. A hard core of some four thousand foreign service officers constitute the administrative network of the foreign service; about a thousand are in Paris, and roughly three thousand are scattered over the various embassies, legations, consulates, and other foreign services. They are admitted into the foreign service on the basis of competitive examinations and, since 1945, all candidates complete two or three years of study in the National School

of Administration. Thus a greater percentage of candidates of modest fortune may enter the foreign service. Less than 5 per cent of the applicants pass the examination, which requires a high level of intellectual competence.

The structure and the personnel of the Ministry of Foreign Affairs has not undergone serious modification in the last century. The consular and the diplomatic corps have been combined, and a number of foreign service personnel were purged after the Liberation. The organization of the Ministry continues to be based on functional rather than geographic divisions: it includes the General Office of Political and Economic Affairs, the General Office of Personnel and General Administration, the General Office of Cultural and Technical Affairs, the Office of Administrative and Social Affairs, the Office of Protocol, the Archives, and the Legal Service section. However, there are certain broad geographic subdivisions: (a) Europe and European organizations; (b) Asia and Oceania; (c) Africa and the Middle East; and (d) America.

The hard core of the foreign service has been a stable and efficient body, but it has shared and, in a way, contributed to the perpetuation of many of the myths on which French diplomacy has been based, such as the supremacy of French culture and the top rank of France. What is more, it has long remained, because of the education of many of its officers, tradition-bound and legalistic. Problems have not been considered in terms of the dynamics of the ever-changing relations of power in our world.[9]

[9]As Prof. J.-B. Duroselle points out ". . . the service remains a caste ever prone to believe in its omniscience."—Kertesz and Fitzsimons, eds., *Diplomacy in a Changing World* (Notre Dame, Ind.: University of Notre Dame Press, 1959), p. 227.

A new economic policy. There was a clear perception among most of the political leaders of the Fourth Republic that France could not recover its prewar position without drastic economic effort. A rapid modernization of the French economy and a gradual movement toward increasing European cooperation were required. A strong France in a well-integrated western European economy could be far stronger than if she acted alone. Therefore, the Fourth Republic, after many equivocations, moved after 1956 in the direction of the European Economic Market, providing for liberalization of trade, lowering and ultimately elimination of all tariffs, and free movement of capital and labor among West Germany, Italy, France, and the Benelux countries. The European Market Treaty was signed in Rome in 1957, and put into effect on January 1, 1959.

The beginning of economic modernization. The task facing the country immediately after World War II was twofold: reconstruction and productive investment, to renew the industrial equipment of the nation and to expand its weak sectors. This was the objective of the first Monnet Plan (1947–1950).

Production and modernization programs for *six basic industries*—coal mining, electric power, steel, cement, farm machinery, and internal transportation—were adopted for 1947, 1948, 1949, and 1950. A second and third plan were developed. These began to build upon healthier foundations. Whatever the weaknesses of the Fourth Republic, whatever the vacillations of the various governments, massive public investment was followed scrupulously and expansion and growth became the commonly accepted policy. By 1956–'57, the impact of the economic plans was clearly discernible.

France was modernizing fast, at a tempo that began to compare favorably with that of Germany in 1952–'56. By 1958, the gross national product had almost doubled. The population also began to grow, registering a rise for the first time since 1870. It grew by about 15 per cent since the end of the war, and should reach about 50 million by 1968.

ELEMENTS OF INSTABILITY

The governmental institutions of the Fourth Republic adversely affected the implementation of the long-range objectives, but only to a degree. Despite the instability of the Cabinet—there were twenty Cabinets under the Fourth Republic—foreign policy was directed by only a very small number of Foreign Ministers. Under the Fourth Republic there were, in all, five Ministers of Foreign Affairs: Robert Schuman and Georges Bidault (from the MRP), Edgar Faure and Pierre Mendès-France (from the Radical Socialists), and Christian Pineau (of the Socialist Party). Divisions, however, in domestic and colonial issues and growing parliamentary interference provided serious internal difficulties and a marked immobility in policy making. This was the cause, for instance, of the equivocation on the European Defense Community. The instability of the Cabinet undermined consistency in execution of policies.

The formulation of foreign policy, like the formulation of any other policy at the governmental level, involved the cooperation of the Prime Minister and his Cabinet with the Parliament. As a result, its formulation suffered because of certain inherent weaknesses of the governmental process in France. These weaknesses were: (*a*) the coalition character of the Cabinet, and (*b*) the instability of the Cabinet.

Coalition Cabinet. In France the Cabinet was, and to a great extent continues to be, composed of the leaders of a number of political parties. Ever since the establishment of the Third Republic, hardly a party or a combination of two parties managed to provide a majority in the legislature. The Cabinet was a coalition of the leaders of many parties and groups. As a result, the desired homogeneity of views on policy in general and on foreign policy in particular was lacking. Very often, the members of one and the same Cabinet held opposing views on matters of foreign policy. That happened, for instance, between 1952 and 1954, when members of the same Cabinet were in favor and against the European Defense Community.

Instability of the Cabinet. In France, the average life of a coalition Cabinet has been short. In the last two decades of the Third Republic, the average life of a Cabinet hardly exceeded eight months. From the establishment of the Fourth Republic to the middle of 1958 there were twenty Cabinets. The succession of Cabinets at this rate was responsible for the following consequences:

1. Lack of continuity in the implementation of foreign policy.
2. Lack of planning for goals.

Both these evils were to some degree alleviated, as we have noted, by the relative independence of the Minister of Foreign Affairs and by his continuity in office. However, this continuity in office of the Minister of Foreign Affairs could not compensate for the instability of the Cabinet, since issues of foreign policy could not be dissociated from other issues of policy. They were part of a whole that engages the Cabinet and, as a result, called for common policy and planning in the Cabinet.

The only two semipermanent coordinating Cabinet committees were (*a*) the general secretariat attached to the Organization of European Economic Cooperation (OEEC), composed primarily of civil servants of the various economic ministries; and (*b*) the permanent secretariat of the National Defense, operating under the Ministry of the National Defense—a staff organization with rather limited functions and a turbulent history of continuous reorganizations. All the other existing coordinating organizations operated either at the administrative level and were composed of civil servants or were *ad hoc* organizations formed to deal with a particular problem. As Professor Duroselle pointed out, "there were no coordinating agencies between the different bureaus of the *Quai d'Orsay* (the Ministry of Foreign Affairs) and the other Ministries."[10] There were some ministerial committees but, because of the instability of the Cabinet, they were just as short-lived as the Cabinet itself. Furthermore, there was no permanent planning agency. To quote again Professor Duroselle, "the most striking fact is the complete absence of planning organisms. French policy was organized exactly as if decisions were to be taken on a day-to-day basis."[11]

The only planning agencies that existed, it may be argued, were the Ministry of Foreign Affairs and the Cabinet as a whole. But the first, as we have pointed out, was unable to cope with the volume and the complexity of the work involved, while the instability of the latter made planning in foreign

[10]Jean-Baptiste Duroselle, "L'élaboration de la politique étrangère française," *Revue Française de la science politique*, VI, No. 3 (July-September 1956), 418.
[11]*Ibid.*, p. 516.

policy impossible. It was generally admitted that, since the Liberation, and despite the continuity of her objectives, France had no foreign policy on many grave matters that concerned her. There were many Algerian policies, a number of European policies, a great number of North African policies, succeeding each other, but never forming a whole and never followed in terms of a coherent plan.

Such a situation could not but invite growing parliamentary interference, which aggravated the situation. Disagreements on foreign policy inevitably reached the Parliament and became, in turn, matters over which political parties and parliamentary groups took sides, thus intensifying party warfare in the National Assembly, causing frequent dislocations of the existing majorities, and accentuating the instability of the Cabinet.

Conclusion

Tenacity and continuity in the perception of common goals; inability to implement these goals because of great disparity between aspiration and means, a disparity brought about by the influence of stronger powers, notably the United States, and a deadlock created by the sharp internal divisions that produced discontinuities and vacillations in the over-all carrying out of foreign policy—this is perhaps the best way to summarize the foreign policy of France in the twelve-odd years of the Fourth Republic.

It was only at the very end that, after numerous setbacks, a new note of realism was injected into the relations between France and her western neighbors. The domestic economic efforts were beginning to pay off, and the French business elite became increasingly reconciled to the notions of de-

colonization and of European unity. The Schuman plan had functioned moderately well, and the prospect of an enlarged European market began to appeal to many French manufacturers, undermining the traditional protectionist mentality of business groups. By 1957, most political parties were willing to go along with the establishment of the European Common Market. For many, however, close economic and political European cooperation implied something else—the creation of a strong European bloc, possibly under the leadership of France, that would give her an opportunity to play a genuinely independent role in world affairs.

Colonial disengagement, economic modernization, the abandonment of a protectionist economic policy, the rapid development of resources including the discovery of rich deposits of oil and gas both on the soil of France and in Sahara, were beginning to provide a sense of strength and recovery where in the past there had been only a feeling of weakness and frustration. The dismal way in which the Fourth Republic came to an end, and the difficulty of finding a solution to the Algerian problem, did not hide from the vast majority of French men and women the promise that lay ahead.

THE FIFTH REPUBLIC AND GENERAL DE GAULLE

The failure of the Fourth Republic to rapidly and effectively translate into action the commonly shared foreign policy objectives was one of the major reasons for its ultimate downfall. France's diminished status in the world, the successive defeats or withdrawals in the many and elusive colonial wars, the failure of France and Great Britain in Suez, the growing strength of West Germany in NATO and in Western Europe under a stable political leadership were all factors in the growth of a spirit of nationalism in the country, contrasting sharply with governmental instability. Parliament and coalition Cabinets continued to mirror the perennial and multiple divisions of the body politic at the very time when the public demanded unity and the realization of national objectives.

Whatever the factors and the immediate causes associated with the uprising of May 13, 1958, in Algeria, it was to General de Gaulle that most of the political groups and leaders turned. Army officers, veterans, the political parties from the Socialists to the Independents, and a great number of intellectuals—some with considerable misgivings—turned to de Gaulle as the symbol and the person around whom this new spirit of French nationalism could find expression.

The basic assumptions

De Gaulle's basic assumptions, what we may call his over-all philosophy, begin and end with the notion that there is one social force—the "reality of the nation" (*le fait national*)—that overshadows all others. No other force or forces, ideological, social, or economic, have succeeded in undermining the nation-state as the focal point of the ultimate loyalty of man.

From the postulate of national reality a number of inferences flow. They do not always have the logical consistency that an academician would desire; but consistency is not a necessary ingredient of statecraft. Situations change so fast in our world that the only consistency lies in the ability to adjust.[12] Consistency means, in the last analysis, realism. Yet the inferences that follow from the postulate on national reality constitute guides to action and must be spelled out.

The reality of the nation and the means of achieving independence. The reality of the nation requires power in order fully to manifest itself. Surveying the world situation before the Allied victory in Europe, de Gaulle could not restrain his bitterness. "How dull is the sword of France at the time when the Allies are about to launch the assault of Europe."[13] Though not the only one, the basic ingredient of power is the military. In the ruins of France after the Liberation, de Gaulle set himself to recreate the French Army. He was haunted with the certainty that the Allies were blocking his efforts because they were unwilling to allow France to develop the military strength that would enable her to become an equal. When the matter of Germany's occupation seemed in doubt, he ordered his divisions onto German soil, suspecting, perhaps rightly, that the Allies might prevent France from participating in settling the future of Germany and remembering, also, that in war possession is nine-tenths of the law. His vision remained the same throughout the months following the Liberation—to recreate the French armed forces. When there was not enough gas to heat French stoves, he established a Commission for Atomic Energy.

[12]Almost always, for instance, de Gaulle, speaking on international issues, will insert the phrase "given the present conditions in the world," or "in the actual state of developments," or "things being as they are."

[13]Charles de Gaulle, *War Memoirs*, II: *Unity* (New York: Simon & Schuster, Inc., 1959), p. 245.

But there are other important factors in the equation of power. De Gaulle recognizes many and has used them all: alliances; diplomacy and skill in negotiations; cultural relations; spiritual influence; economic resources; and population.

A strong ingredient of power, indeed the only valid expression of a nation, is the state and its political organization. Gaullist revisionism, both before and throughout the Fourth Republic, was predicated upon de Gaulle's ideas about world relations and the role of the French nation. To play the proper role, France needed a strong state. In this state, one man, the President of the Republic, should make foreign policy on behalf of the nation—the "real France"—incarnating the national interests over and above the welter of particular interests and ideological factions.

A third ingredient of power that de Gaulle has evoked very frequently since he returned to office has led him to follow policies to which he seemed firmly opposed only a decade ago. This is what he calls the imperative of the *grands ensembles* (the "great wholes"). Nations must establish cooperative "wholes" that provide the structural bases and the resources for the economic development and defense of each one and all. This is not contrary to his emphasis upon national uniqueness, nor does it lead him to the espousal of projects of military integration. The building of large wholes creates more than an alliance and less than a federation. It is a close association and cooperation between nation-states which, by pooling some of their resources, find the strength to sustain a common purpose. Whether it stems from a profound realization on de Gaulle's part of contemporary economic trends or is simply a tactical answer to the "two great empires"

(the Soviet Union and the United States), whether it applies to Western Europe or to the French community, he has been one of its most forceful advocates, reminding the African republics time after time that independence nowadays is a fiction, unless sustained by strength, and that strength can never be attained by geographically small political fragments that go under the name of "sovereign states."

The idea of balance. De Gaulle's emphasis upon the reality of the national phenomenon and its concomitant accessories—power, both military and political—leads him to a theory of international relations that is often referred to as "realist." International relations comprise an arena of conflict in which every participant nation-state attempts to increase its strength at the expense of the other. Every political leadership, no matter what ideology inspires it, acts in terms of national consideration. *If so, it is only power that can check power—and the only possible international world is one in which an equilibrium of powers is reached.* This leads de Gaulle to follow conclusions that directly shape his actions.

The present balance is unnatural, precarious, and unwise. Unnatural, because it involves a growing polarization of the world and the creation of political satellites, which are inconsistent with the secular realities and interests of nations; precarious, because both the big and small nations are continuously on the brink of war; unwise, because it gives to the two of the less qualified nation-states—the United States and the Soviet Union— full liberty to act, the independence to decide their fate and with it the fate of the world.

Both the American and the Russian efforts are expressions of national power, in one form or another, and de Gaulle has no illusions about either. If they are allowed free sway, they might enter upon armed conflict. If they find a temporary accommodation, it will be in order to establish a joint hegemony over the world. *Either eventuality will be to the detriment of the other nation-states* and of course, of France and Europe. This can be avoided only by creating a balance of power consistent with the growing realities of the world, in which the economic and political development of Europe is bound to play a growing role.

General de Gaulle's conception of a balance has been a permanent trait of his thinking and action ever since he became a public figure. It has taken a number of forms.

In the third volume of his *Memoirs*, de Gaulle pointed out that the only way to keep Russia out of the heart of Europe was to dismember Germany. Thus the threat of a new Germany would be eliminated, and the fears of the Soviet Union and the Eastern European nations alleviated. Moreover, a treaty with the Soviet Union, directed against the revival of German power, would free France to pursue her other world obligations. It was the failure of Yalta to revive the pre-World War II arrangement in Europe that also accounted for the bitter denunciations against the settlement. Though France received a number of compensations, perhaps far beyond what the French leadership had a right to expect in terms of her real power at the time, Yalta became slowly identified with a betrayal of Europe and France by the Anglo-Saxons.

De Gaulle made an open offer to Churchill in November, 1944, to combine forces so that the two countries with their far-flung empires would be able to act independently of the Rus-

sians or the Americans. It is worth quoting his remarks to Churchill:

You can see, France is beginning to recover. But whatever my faith in her is, I know that she will not recover soon her former strength. You, English, will finish this war on the other hand with glory. But nonetheless your relative position may well be weakened in view of your losses and sacrifices, the centrifugal forces that undermine the Commonwealth and above all the ascendancy of America and Russia, and later on of China. Well then, our two ancient countries are both weakened at the time when they are to confront a new world. . . . But if England and France agree and act together in the future negotiations, they will have enough weight to prevent any decision that will not be acceptable to them. . . . It is this common will that must be the basis of the alliance that you are proposing to us. . . . The equilibrium of Europe . . . the guarantee of peace on the Rhine, the independence of the states on the Vistula, the Danube and the Balkans, the keeping on our side of the peoples to whom we opened up civilization in all parts of the world, the organization of the nations in a manner that will provide something else than a battlefield for the quarrels of the Russians and the Americans, finally the primacy in our policy of a certain conception of man, despite the progressive mechanization of the societies, . . . is it not true that these are the great interests of the Universe? These interests, let us put them together and safeguard them together.[14]

A third scheme involved an alliance with the Soviet Union, directed against German recovery and guaranteeing the *status quo* of Europe. Speculating before his trip to the Soviet Union in December, 1944, only a few weeks after he had made his offer to Churchill, de Gaulle wrote wistfully, "Per-

[14]*War Memoirs*, III: *Salvation* (New York: Simon & Schuster, Inc., 1960), p. 52. Author's translation.

haps it might be possible to renew in some manner the Franco-Russian solidarity, which even if misunderstood and betrayed in the past, was nonetheless compatible with the nature of things *both with regard to the German danger and the Anglo-Saxon efforts to assert their hegemony.*"[15]

A fourth and perhaps more persistent effort to recreate a balance is the revival of Europe as a Third Force. What "Europe" means to de Gaulle, exactly, is a difficult matter. In his *Memoirs* he spoke of an organization of the peoples of Europe from "Iceland to Istanbul and from Gibraltar to the Urals." Sometimes Russia is part and sometimes it is not, though emphasis is often put on the European destiny of Russia. Sometimes it is Western Europe and sometimes the whole of Europe. Sometimes "Europe" implies a dismembered Germany, sometimes a divided Germany, and sometimes a Franco-German rapprochement without qualifications. Two things are certain: "Europe," whatever it is, is distinct from the "Anglo-Saxon powers." It is also separate from Soviet Russia, without, however, always denying the European position of Russia and hence its participation.

With the economic recovery of West Germany and the continuing division of this country into two blocs, de Gaulle's conception of Europe became clearer. A strong France in Western Europe can assume the leadership of the Western bloc and speak for it. But to be strong in Western Europe, France must maintain good relations with a West Germany that is, all the same, never to be allowed to match France's leadership. So, underlying the new conception of balance in which Western Europe is perhaps to become

for the first time a genuine Third Force, there is always an emphasis on France's interest, which means France's strength. A leader of Western Europe, France, can put all her weight, in the name of the new force, into world strategy and world leadership.

In the name of balance, de Gaulle has in the course of less than twenty years envisaged the following alliances: (*a*) with the British, in order to create an independent bloc vis-à-vis the Russians and the Americans; (*b*) with the Soviet Union, in order to maintain French supremacy in Europe vis-à-vis Germany; (*c*) with all against the revival of a unified, militarized, and strong Germany; and (*d*) with West Germany and the West European states, in order to create an independent bloc—a Third Force in Europe that might lead to drastic changes in the balance of power.

A new style

Harold Nicolson, in his *The Evolution of Diplomacy*, distinguishes between the "old" diplomacy and the "new." The distinction has both procedural and substantive traits. Substantively, the old diplomacy assumed the primacy of Europe, the objective gradation of nations in terms of power, and the responsibility of the big powers for the course of international events and, more particularly, for matters of peace and war. Procedurally, the old diplomacy used diplomacy and negotiations and shied away from appeals to world opinion, large conferences, and ideologic confrontations. The "new" diplomacy is the work of secular forces that changed the balance of forces. Europe was progressively overshadowed. It was also the work of Woodrow Wilson, who introduced diplomacy by conference, utilized ideological slogans, and stressed the equality of all nations.

---

[15] *Ibid.*, p. 54. Author's translation. [Italics supplied.]

All of de Gaulle's sympathies remain with the old diplomacy. While conceding basic alterations in the balance of forces that ought to be considered, he has no patience with the new procedures. The old Concert of Europe, he is willing to concede, ought to become the new Concert of the World in which the United States has a permanent place—perhaps, also, China and even India. But Europe is still, in his mind, a dominant—perhaps, under the proper conditions, *the* dominant—force. The powers that have global interests and global responsibilities are few; they must continue to play a leading role in all matters of international relations, and particularly in matters of war and peace.

Negotiations and carefully prepared treaties must be once more the rule. Such negotiations must be conducted by experts, as in the past, in secret, and communicated at the appropriate time to parliaments and publics. Neither the United Nations, as organized today, nor the various summit meetings, past, present, or future, have appealed to de Gaulle. In his press conference of November 10, 1959, he specifically criticized assemblies whose only purpose seemed to be the airing of grievances and the agitation of public opinion. Again, when France decided no longer to provide funds for the United Nations operations in the Congo, de Gaulle explained in his press conference of April 11, 1961, why support had been withdrawn. The Security Council, where decisions were to be made by five big powers, had lost virtually all power, he said. Power had shifted to the General Assembly. "It [the General Assembly]," he pointed out acidly, "has assumed all powers. It can deliberate on everything." This Assembly, furthermore would soon consist of some 120 states,

"many of which are improvised states and believe it their duty to stress grievances or demands with regard to the older nations." The meetings of the United Nations "are no more than riotous sessions." "As the United Nations," he concluded, "becomes a scene of disturbance, confusion, and division, it acquires the ambition to intervene in all kinds of matters." France, he hinted, would maintain its aloofness toward "these United, or Disunited, Nations."[16] At the end of July, 1961, France refused to acknowledge the competence of the United Nations in dealing with the French-Tunisian conflict in Bizerte.

The execution of treaties must be constantly in the hands of the Great Powers; their good faith must be taken for granted, and sanctions must follow any breach. Action, however, must be based in all events upon the free exchange of information by those concerned and must be taken in terms of the global interests of all concerned. As in the years between the two World Wars, the French position remains that matters of war and peace are both global and indivisible. Regional alliances, like NATO, must be put into this context.

De Gaulle's actions ever since he assumed the Presidency—indeed, ever since he returned to power on June 1, 1958—exhibit all the traits associated with the "old" diplomacy: his firm commitment to European revival under the leadership of France; his emphasis upon the global responsibilities and global strategy of the Great Powers; his underplaying of the United Nations and NATO (to the extent to which it consecrates the hegemony of the Anglo-Saxons and allows only them,

[16]News conference, April 11, 1961, in *Speeches and Press Conferences*, trans. Press and Information Service, French Embassy (New York), No. 162, pp. 7–8.

86

especially the United States, freedom of action); and, above all, the exclusive jurisdiction he has assumed as President of the Republic for foreign affairs.

The new style is reflected in the constitutional arrangement and institutional development of the Fifth Republic.

The new Constitution. The Constitution of the Fifth Republic provides that the Cabinet "shall determine and direct the policy of the nation" and "it will be responsible to Parliament." "The Prime Minister is responsible for national defense" (Articles 20 and 21). The President of the Republic, on the other hand, "shall be the guarantor of the national independence, of the integrity of the territory, and of the respect . . . of treaties" (Article 5). He "shall negotiate and ratify treaties" and "he shall be informed of all negotiations leading to the conclusion of an international agreement" (Article 52). All major treaties, however, must be "ratified by law" (Article 53).

The contrasts with the constitutional arrangement of the Fourth Republic lie primarily in the conception of the role of the President. He was given both implicitly and explicitly broader powers. The President is the guarantor of the national integrity, the commander-in-chief, presiding over the meetings of the various defense councils, and the possessor of large emergency powers. He is the "moderator" (*arbitre*), making presumably final decisions whenever there appears to be division and conflict in the country or his Cabinet. He has the power to dissolve the legislature and to ask the public, in a referendum, to endorse or reject his policy.

Under de Gaulle, the Presidency has become the coordinating office for the major decisions: military policy; foreign policy; and colonial policy, including the Algerian problem. Cabinet meetings are simply for the execution and implementation of the decisions made by the President and his immediate advisers. De Gaulle is not simply informed of foreign policy negotiations. He negotiates directly with foreign representatives, prime ministers, and heads of state; he outlines the goals of the government—at times taking even the Cabinet and the Prime Minister by surprise. Matters pertaining to NATO, to the ties among the members of the Common Market, to negotiations concerning suspension of atomic tests, to the advisability of a summit meeting—all are decided by General de Gaulle.

In order to implement the personal character of his foreign policy, de Gaulle has sought to strengthen the Ministry of Foreign Affairs and, at the same time, remove foreign policy issues from legislative interference. The new Minister of Foreign Affairs is a career diplomat (for the first time in many decades), a former Ambassador to Washington, London, and Bonn. Foreign policy matters are coordinated and handled through the Ministry of Foreign Affairs and the foreign service, under the over-all supervision of de Gaulle.

The role of Parliament is greatly diminished. Negotiations and formulations of policy are kept secret in the best tradition of the old diplomacy. Only general developments and over-all policy have been discussed in Parliament. Since the establishment of the Fifth Republic, there have been at least five major foreign policy debates, lasting two or three days each. Debate, however, is limited to the exposition of the Prime Minister's or Minister's views and to foreign policy pronouncements by various party leaders.

The parliamentary committee on Foreign Affairs of the National Assembly has heard the Minister of Foreign Affairs frequently, and many questions on foreign policy have been addressed to the Prime Minister and the Minister. Both the replies and the controversy have been perfunctory, however. Since the possibility of engaging the responsibility of the President of the Republic and the Cabinet is lacking, in the first place, and highly restricted in the second, debate is little more than academic.

Occasions for the expression of dissatisfaction have not been lacking, however. For instance, when the debate on the government's program on atomic weapons and the development of a retaliatory atomic force for France took place (in connection with the voting of military credits), the Senate twice defeated the measure that had been passed in the National Assembly. The opposition in the National Assembly had the opportunity to introduce a motion of censure which was endorsed on the last two occasions by 215 and 217 votes—some 60 votes short of the majority required to bring the Cabinet down. Again in the spring of 1966 de Gaulle's decision to withdraw from NATO led to a full-dress debate triggered by a censure motion against the government. Not more than 140 deputies out of 482 voted for the motion.

Realism and the vocation of greatness

Without abandoning the basic objective of French independence and national power, de Gaulle has been able, since his return to power, to inject into France an element of realism that was lacking in the past. This is only too clear with regard to the colonial and economic policy he has pursued.

The end of empire. In 1958, General de Gaulle pledged to all overseas territories a new political arrangement— the French Community—and, if they wished it, their independence. All of the territories, with the exception of Guinea, entered the French Community. They became republics federated with France. They were governed by the President of the French Republic, who was also President of the Community, with the assistance of an Executive Council which consisted of the President of the Republic, a number of French ministers charged with Community affairs, and the prime ministers, or their delegates, of the African republics and Madagascar. A Community Senate, with primarily consultative powers, was also established, as well as a Community arbitration court, to hear and pass on controversies among the member states.

In the course of 1959–1960, the Community was abandoned. It still exists in name, but its institutions have been set aside. Speaking in Dakar, Senegal, in December, 1959, de Gaulle promised to grant "international sovereignty"—that is, complete independence to all the African territories. Special accords between France and the member states were passed and ratified by the French Parliament, providing for diverse modes of cooperation between France and the individual republics in economic, social, cultural, and military affairs. All provisions can be renegotiated and possibly cancelled by new accords in the future. All the African republics have become independent, and all of them have become members of the United Nations as independent, individual states with the freedom to vote as they please at the United Nations Assembly and to participate in its organs and specialized commissions.

Thus France, under de Gaulle, put an end to colonialism. In doing so, she improved her position in Africa, where she is assured of a reservoir of goodwill. Large subsidies to the African republics and to Madagascar guarantee a good rate of modernization and industralization there, which is bound to favor French trade and investments in Africa and improve the living standards of the Africans themselves. Thus, politically and economically, the road was paved for better relations.

Algeria. It was not until July 3, 1962, after a series of zigzags and equivocations into which we need not enter here, that Algeria was finally granted her full independence. The leaders of the rebellion were released from jail, and the French settlers began their return to France. Between 1962 and 1965, almost one million European French citizens and a sizeable number of Algerians who had fought in the French army or in territorial units were resettled in the metropolis with substantial financial aid from the state. Thus the war in Algeria (1954–1962) that, like the war in Vietnam, had sapped the energy of the country, that had provoked sharp and, at times, irreconcilable conflicts, that had seriously qualified France's freedom of action, that had gravely undermined her prestige among her former colonies, particularly in Africa, came to an end. France retained a temporary foothold, the naval base of Mers-el-Kebir and her atomic and space testing grounds in Sahara. As for her rapidly growing oil installations in Algeria, the French companies were allowed to continue their exploitation subject to negotiated agreements with an independent Algerian government. The last military adventure had come to an end, and in 1962, for the first time since World War II, French soldiers were no longer fighting anybody, anywhere. Relations with Algeria itself rapidly improved, and France continued to extend considerable economic and cultural aid to the newly created state.

The national economy. Since de Gaulle's return to power, the economic development of the country has continued to improve. The improvement was partly due to the measures originally suggested by a "special" committee of experts appointed by General de Gaulle in 1958, a program of austerity designed to eliminate inflationary tendencies and restore monetary stability. As stated by General de Gaulle himself, this plan aimed "to restore to France its international status" in the economic field and "to establish the nation on a foundation of truth and severity, which alone can enable it to build its prosperity."

In order to achieve a sounder monetary position and a better competitive position for French goods in foreign markets, the franc was devalued by 17.5 per cent in December, 1958. France restored the convertibility of the franc, thus giving foreign companies the guarantees necessary to enable them freely to invest and remit profits. Foreign capital began to flow into the country, contributing appreciably to the improvement in the balance of payments. The new price of the franc made it again possible to liberalize trade, and enabled France to fulfill its commitments towards its Common Market partners. On January 1, 1959, France implemented, in full, the European Common Market Treaty provisions for the reduction of customs duties and the liberalization of trade. Moreover, because devaluation had lowered the prices of French goods, the country's foreign trade improved rapidly. In May, 1959, for the first time in a very long period, France's foreign trade balance showed a surplus. Her gold and foreign exchange reserves steadily mounted, to over five billion dollars by 1966. Exports rose at a rapid rate. Industrial production, after a slight decline in 1963–'64, resumed its upward trend and was followed by a steady rate of increase that has since averaged 4.5 per cent.

The memorandum of September 23, 1958. Immediately after his return to power, de Gaulle asserted that it was not the purpose of France to limit her foreign policy "within the confines of NATO." On September 23, 1958, he addressed a memorandum, still technically secret, to Henri Spaak, Prime Minister Macmillan, and President Eisenhower. It is, however, common knowledge that the memorandum was a diagnosis of the problems facing NATO, and a statement of French policy. De Gaulle indicated the common responsibilities imposed upon the Alliance in case of war, but pointed to the inequality in armaments and, what is more, to the disparity in the freedom of the member states to make decisions. Events in Egypt and Algeria contrasted sharply with those in the Near East, Formosa and, later, Vietnam. He proposed, therefore, the establishment within NATO of a "directorate" of three—England, France, and the United States—with responsibility for elaborating a common military and political strategy for the whole of the planet, for the creation of Allied commands for all theaters of operation, for joint deliberations about strategy, and for joint decision on the use of atomic weapons. "The European states of the continent," he stated on April 11, 1961, ". . . must know

exactly with which weapons and under what conditions their overseas allies would join them in battle."[17] He reminded President Kennedy, who was to visit him within a matter of weeks, that "the threats of war are no longer limited to Europe" and that NATO should accordingly revise its organization to meet joint non-European problems. There was also a threat in the memorandum: France would reconsider its NATO policy in the light of the response of England and the United States.

Though ostensibly addressing problems related to NATO, de Gaulle was actually attempting to place France on a level to which no other European power in NATO could aspire. NATO was to remain a broad organization, but with three of its members —France, England and the United States—jointly in charge of global strategy. The three great powers were, in the best tradition of the old diplomacy, to be in charge, at the NATO level, of the Atlantic problems, and jointly in charge of planetary strategy. De Gaulle has remained adamant. When his suggestions were rejected, France withdrew the Mediterranean Fleet from NATO command; she refused to integrate her air defense with NATO; she prevented the building of launching sites and the stockpiling of atomic warheads over which she could have no control. But this stand against military integration was to bring France in conflict with West Germany. This became painfully evident during Adenauer's visit in December, 1959, and throughout 1960, when de Gaulle and his advisers talked freely about an "independent" Western European strategy and apparently foresaw even the pos-

[17]News Conference, April 11, 1961 in *Speeches and Press Conferences*, No. 162, pp. 7–8.

sibility of the withdrawal of American forces.

The atom bomb. Since the Allies seemed unwilling to subordinate overall strategy and the use of atomic weapons to a "directorate," France proceeded with the explosion of her own atom bomb. A number of additional reasons were given: the uncertainty about the use of the bomb by the United States, except in self-defense; the need of a French deterrent to war; the injection of a new pride and a higher morale in an army that had experienced one frustration after another; and, finally, the worldwide commitments of France. As long as other powers have nuclear weapons, the only policy consistent with French interests, according to de Gaulle, is to develop nuclear weapons. At the Geneva disarmament conference, the French continue to favor the liquidation of stockpiles of weapons and delivery missiles before the suspension of manufacturing and testing of nuclear weapons.

The European Common Market. De Gaulle's acceptance of the Common Market was motivated, in part, by economic reasons and, in part, by considerations favoring the development of a European "whole." The crucial reason, however, was political. It gave him a bargaining position with the British in respect to the demands of his memorandum of September 23 and on a number of other issues, notably Berlin, atomic weapons, and the agenda of the ill-fated summit conference of June, 1960. In repayment for Adenauer's participation in the Common Market, and as a compromise of their disagreements about the extent and nature of military integration in NATO, de Gaulle became a staunch

supporter of the Berlin *status quo*. However, he also accepted Germany's existing frontier arrangements with Poland. Many still think, on the basis of his *Memoirs*, that he continues to consider the future of Germany to be the crucial problem of our times, and they believe that under no circumstances is he prepared to make any concession to Germany other than on Berlin, which has only a symbolic value and does not alter the balance of forces.

Thus de Gaulle emerged in control of an array of strong bargaining weapons in order to accomplish what he sought in the year after Liberation —the realization of a top rank for France.

Tactics and objectives

A shrewd use of all the trumps that France held characterizes the Gaullist diplomacy. France has appeared to be both European and Atlantic. De Gaulle has blocked England's entry to the Common Market, but has never for a moment claimed that this was a final decision. He has attempted to build the foundations of European power on the basis of a Franco-German alliance but, at the same time, has held out the prospect of a new Franco-Soviet agreement, first with the visit of his Foreign Minister to Moscow in the winter of 1965 and later, in the summer of 1966, visiting Moscow himself. While urging the drastic reform of NATO, he has never come out openly in favor of the abandonment of his close contacts or, indeed, the alliance with the United States. While ridiculing and deriding the United Nations, he has not refrained from using it to advance the cause of the admission of China. Disclaiming all colonial ambitions, he has reasserted, much to the embarrassment of the United States, France's interests in the peace and security of Vietnam, and in the neutralization of that area in which France fought a long and unsuccessful war. Finally, neither his rapprochement with the Soviet Union nor his profession of strong Atlantic ties stopped him from recognizing China and establishing trade relations with it. The goal is one and only one —the assertion and the realization of French independence. To achieve this, he will pick and choose allies, promote French interests as the situation shifts and changes, and exploit any opportunity in order that France climb once more to the level of both a continental and world power.

As André Fontaine wrote, with justice, in the influential *Le Monde*:

Everything is aimed to accomplish an objective, however remote. A Europe to its full geographic limits, with African, Near Eastern and—who knows—South American extensions . . . A Europe that will no longer be divided between American and Soviet zones of influence, a Europe which might even receive Russia the day it becomes "Russian" as it is predestined by history, a Europe that will once more become the nerve center of the world and which might if it were necessary arbitrate between the great empires.[18]

De Gaulle's objectives then appear to be the following: the liquidation of the European *status quo* as created by Yalta, and its substitution by something that resembles more closely the situation that existed in Europe before 1939—but without the resurrection of German strength; a free hand for France to exert political, cultural, and economic influence in all parts of the world; and, ultimately, the freedom to reconsider all alliances and commitments to the West or, as the case may be, to the East.

[18]*Le Monde* (Paris), March 10, 1960.

The atom bomb and French strategic thinking

On February 13, 1960, France exploded her first atomic device in the Sahara. Since then, there have been seven additional atomic tests in the atmosphere and a number of underground ones. Nuclear devices are scheduled to be exploded soon in the Polynesian possessions of France in the Pacific. By 1967, France had a minimum of a hundred atomic bombs, averaging in strength, at least three times that of the first bomb which fell on Hiroshima. With nuclear capabilities to be added soon General de Gaulle estimated France's force to exceed 100,000 kilotons by 1970. The army has been trimmed down and increasing emphasis has been placed on atomic weapons and the production of delivery vehicles, some of which will be operational before 1970.

The reality of French nuclear capability, even if limited, was bound to cause a reconsideration of strategic thinking. General de Gaulle himself has been particularly anxious not to allow France to confront a crisis with antiquated ideas and weapons. Atomic weapons are considered today to be the best deterrent against war, by giving to the nation possessing them the possibility of retaliating against the centers of an aggressive enemy's power. However, given the nuclear capabilities of the United States and the Soviet Union, the confrontation of American and Soviet forces in the heart of Europe and, finally, the particular interests of France in Europe, the French hope to perform a number of interrelated and often contradictory strategic tasks. France wishes to maintain a special and privileged position in Western Europe, including West Germany, without, however, allowing herself to be overshadowed by Germany; to keep the substance of the Atlantic alliance, without conceding to the United States a free hand in Western Europe; and to promote a *détente* with Eastern Europe. To do so, she must reconcile these goals with Germany's interest in reunification and with American strategic and military interests.

The French atomic weapons are of course not calculated to provide a solution to the above problems. The atomic weapon itself is only a means to *one* goal—independent French action—rather than part of a comprehensive strategy. The acquisition of military independence, or at least of a semblance of independence, can and will provide freedom for France to move in one or another direction as the world situation changes. This is the heart of Gaullist doctrine, and it is, of course, at odds with American efforts to reduce to a minimum anything and everything that might upset our own control and initiative.

A French *force de frappe*, wielded by France under the control of the French government, provides for a certain degree of independence. It gives France a degree of freedom, especially within a decade or so, to do away with American protection, which virtually all now consider necessary; it maintains France's superior position in Western Europe vis-à-vis Germany; it has given the French impressive reasons for reconsidering NATO. These points, taken one by one, appear to be only mildly persuasive, but if we were to accept the central argument of French government circles and of de Gaulle—i.e., if we were to accept the uniqueness of the nation-state and the exclusively national character of defense and military preparedness—then the *force de frappe* indeed gives the French nation-state a weight and a

position that it did not and could not have before. This is especially so in the light of the contingent and fluid nature of international politics and the narrow margin of resources and power that often spells the difference between national survival and national disaster.

Thus, the French *force de frappe*, when viewed in the abstract, can, or at least *may*, play a number of roles. Which role it will play, in political or military terms, cannot be assessed *à priori*, however. The important thing, for France, is to have the bomb and be ready to play *any* given role that the situation demands. It strengthens France's position in NATO, if NATO is still desired, or it can give France the freedom to move completely out of NATO; it gives France the possibility of assuming the military leadership of Western Europe, but at the same time the possibility of breaking away from the confines of a European context and coming to terms with the Soviet Union on matters concerning at least Western and Eastern Europe. It may be the strongest argument against MLF, controlled exclusively by the United States, but it is also one of the strongest trumps in France's hands if it suits her interests to reshape MLF; it is both an argument with which to silence Germany's desires to get nuclear weapons and to undermine American efforts to provide Germany with such weapons and it also gives Germany a strong incentive (how strong depends upon a number of factors) to enter a European military arrangement and share in the control of a European strategy. Thus, the French bomb can destroy European unity or become the basis for European common military arrangements. It can cause proliferation, or it can help put an end to it, if the powers that have the bomb now—including France and China—were to be given the proper voice in the deliberations against proliferation. The bomb might conceivably hasten American withdrawal from Europe, but it can well have the opposite effect. It may incite the Russians to greater belligerence in Europe, but it may also provide the basis for a Franco-Soviet understanding with regard to a new settlement of European problems, particularly the German problem.

In sum, it is highly unrealistic to condemn the French effort because of the contradictions it involves. These contradictions do not impede choice; on the contrary, they allow, depending on the circumstances, for choice. This, in itself, enhances freedom of choice. And this is the basic postulate of a sound strategy! The bomb is only a condition for the development of strategy. It would, therefore, be a mistake and perhaps irrelevant to speculate at length on the exact character of French strategy. There is little of it, and what does exist is rather primitive. It is only in the last few years that French military, political, and intellectual leaders, as well as the various "clubs" have entered into the debate about atomic weapons; in this connection the interested reader is referred to *Le grand débat*, Raymond Aron's succinct exposition and criticism of the French position.[19]

[19]Publications on French nuclear strategy are rapidly increasing in number. The most important are the following: General Gallois, *Stratégie de l'âge nucléaire* (Paris: Calman-Levy, 1960), General Beaufre, *Introduction à la stratégie* (Paris: Librairie Armand Colin, 1963); and Alexander Sanguinetti, *La France et l'armée atomique* (Paris: Julliard, 1964). Jules Moch: *Non à la force de frappe* (Paris: Robert Lafont, 1963); Club Jean Moulin, *La force de frappe et le citoyen* (Paris Editions du Seuil, 1963); Club de Grenelle, *Siècle de Damocles: Du nouveau sur la force de frappe* (Paris: Les éditions Pierre Coudere, 1964); Raymond Aron, *Le grand débat:*

The Common Market and England

Since 1960, the political and military reasons that accounted for de Gaulle's acceptance of the economic provisions of the Common Market have become increasingly apparent. The Common Market suggested the possibility that a larger European whole could be placed under the leadership of France, armed with atomic weapons that were denied to Germany by virtue of the Paris Accords. Britain's participation was highly desirable, provided Britain was willing to abandon the intimate Atlantic connections that underwrote the dominance of the United States, and also provided that Britain brought into a European pool —under some form of Franco-British control—her atomic and hydrogen weapons and knowhow. Britain's nuclear power was to be its dowry in the contemplated marriage with the Common Market. When it became clear that England was unwilling to cut her intimate ties with the United States, de Gaulle decided to refuse entry to England. His decision became a foregone conclusion when, after meeting with President Kennedy, Macmillan virtually placed British nuclear weapons under the control of the United States. In his now famous press conference of January 14, 1963, de Gaulle, alleging economic and cultural reasons, rejected England's entry. The heart of the matter, however, was political and strategic; England, de Gaulle feared, would remain under the domination of the United States, and her

Initiation à la stratégie atomique, 1964.

The reader will find a review of some of the most important recent publications in "*Le grand débat nucléaire*," *Bulletin sedeis*, No. 910, Supplement, (February 10, 1965). Significant articles have also appeared in "*La politique étrangère*," Nos. 1 and 2 of *Sondages* (1958).

entry into the Common Market would reinforce America's influence.

With England at least temporarily out of the picture, de Gaulle turned to Germany. A Franco-German alliance providing for frequent consultations, and possibly for the elaboration of common policy on military, foreign, cultural and economic questions, would provide the hard core that would consolidate Western Europe and, given France's military superiority, safeguard French leadership at the same time. In January, 1963, a Franco-German Treaty, embodying the principle of consultations on matters of defense, foreign policy, and cultural affairs, was signed. However, the very logic of the Treaty raised serious questions. It was again based on the assumption that West Germany would accept French, rather than American, leadership and protection. But in the light of its military and economic ties w,th the United States, and especially in the light of the overwhelming superiority of the United States, it was unlikely that any German political leader would acquiesce to this. Gradually, the Treaty was bypassed and the policies of the two countries on military and foreign policy questions began to diverge, with Germany supporting the United States. Thus, what accounted for de Gaulle's rebuff of Britain seemed to be also called into play by Germany. It was only de Gaulle, and only France, that seemed to believe that Western Europe could do without the United States, and it was only France that pressed for a European solution of the European problems at the very time when the heart of the European defense establishment continued to lie across the Atlantic.

But the Common Market remained a successful economic arrangement. It had, by 1965, reached the stage when increasing commitments to su-

pranationality were to be made, and when some decision could be made by a qualified majority of the participants. In other words, the Market had moved to the critical stage when it was about to assume, even to a limited degree, genuine supranationality. However, such a supranationality is, as we have seen, contrary to de Gaulle's basic assumptions about the nature of international relations. Alleging the unwillingness of the other five members to accept common agricultural policies (policies, incidentally, quite advantageous to French agriculture), de Gaulle instructed his ministers, in the middle of 1965, to withdraw from the Council of Ministers of the Common Market. He also attacked the supranational character of the Rome Treaty and claimed that the assumption of power by a body of "stateless" functionaries was prejudicial to the independence of the sovereign member states. The Treaty of Rome, he concluded, had to be revised in order to do away with all supranational clauses. In effect, he urged that the Market remain a purely economic arrangement, held together by the will of sovereign and independent states, and subject to the veto power of each and all. How hard he was to press this claim, how serious he was about it, and what compromise solutions he was willing to accept remained to be seen.

The reform of NATO

After the memorandum of September 23, 1958, de Gaulle continued to simultaneously emphasize France's Atlantic commitment and her European and world vocation. His emphasis on France's European vocation inevitably raised the question of the status of NATO. As a treaty signed at the time of the peak of the Soviet peril in 1949, when Western Europe was still suffering from the economic, social and, to some extent, political aftereffects of World War II, NATO consecrated American hegemony and placed Western Europe under American military tutelage. The United States could deploy its strength and assert its interests in other parts of the world, but the European nations, especially France, found themselves tied to a regional alliance that deprived them of freedom of action in Europe and elsewhere. According to General de Gaulle, the situation was unacceptable on both counts. As the European nations developed in strength, as France began to withdraw from the heavy imperial commitments she had assumed in Asia and in North Africa, as her economy began first to recover and then to move rapidly ahead, and as, finally, she began to develop atomic weapons, the contradiction between the conditions of 1949 and those of the 1960's became increasingly apparent.

With the end of the Algerian War, there was no doubt at all as to where de Gaulle stood and what he wanted. First, European problems had better be left to the European nations. This involved even the problem of German reunification. Second, European nations, notably France, had worldwide commitments that transcended the regional limits of NATO, just as did the United States. Hence the future of the national armed forces and their deployment and posture was a national matter belonging to France. Third, without ever stating it, de Gaulle seemed to infer that the presence of American troops in Europe was becoming, at least politically, a liability. Fourth, NATO and its integrative aspects were to be thrust aside and replaced, at most and on the basis of expedience and contingency, by a classic alliance among individual and separate states—an alliance that was to be negotiated and renegotiated as the circumstances demanded. De Gaulle has never rejected the desirability of such a classic alliance, but while insisting on its form—a pact between individual sovereign states—he has never specified its content. It has seemed clear, however, that such an alliance was to be construed narrowly. The partners would be free to differ on everything that did not involve their defense against a specified foreign attack under the stipulated conditions. France would be free to move in her own way in China, in Southeast Asia, and in Latin America, as well as reconsider her relations with the Eastern European countries or the Soviet Union. De Gaulle's revisionist policy with regard to NATO was, in other words, an explicit reformulation of France's full-fledged independence to act as a world power. If and when the interests of the United States and France converged, so much the better; if they diverged, each would be free to act independently of the other. This, in effect, would put an end to NATO. To quote a pronouncement at some length:

Nothing can make a law enforceable, without amendment, when it no longer agrees with the ways of the times. Nothing can make a treaty wholly valid when its object has changed. Nothing can make an alliance remain as such when the conditions in which it was concluded have changed. It is therefore necessary to adapt the law, the treaty and the alliance to the new factors, failing which the texts, emptied of their substance, will, if circumstances so require, be nothing more than useless papers in the archives, unless there is a harsh break between these obsolete forms and the living realities.

Well! If France considers, today still, that it is useful to her security and to that of the West that she be allied with a certain number of States, particularly with America, for their defense and for hers in the event of agression against one of them; if the declaration made in common on this subject, in the form of the Atlantic Alliance treaty signed in Washington on April 4, 1949, still remains valid in her eyes, at the same time she recognizes that the measures for implementation taken subsequently no longer correspond to what she deems satisfactory, with respect to herself, in the new conditions.

I say, the new conditions. For it is quite clear that, owing to the internal and external evolution of the countries of the East, the Western world is no longer threatened today as it was at the time when the American protectorate was set up in Europe under the cover of NATO. But, at the same time as the alarms were dying down, there was also a reduction in the guarantee of security —one might say absolute—that the possession of the nuclear weapon by America alone gave to the Old Continent, and in the certainty that America would employ it, without reservation, in the event of aggression. For Soviet Russia has since that time equipped itself with a nuclear power capable of striking the United States directly, which has made the decisions of the Americans as to the eventual use of their bombs at least indeterminate, and which has, by the same token, stripped of justification—I speak for France—not the Alliance, of course, but indeed integration.

On the other hand, while the prospects of a world war breaking out on account of Europe are dissipating, conflicts in which America engages in other parts of the world—as the day before yesterday in Korea, yesterday in Cuba, today in Vietnam—risk, by virtue of that famous escalation, being extended so that the result could be a general conflagration. In that case Europe—whose strategy is, within NATO, that of America—would be automatically involved in the struggle, even when it would not have so desired. It would be so for France, if the intermeshing of her territory, of her communications, of certain of her forces, of several of her air bases, of some of her ports with the military system under American command were to continue much longer. Moreover, our country, having become for its part and by its own means an atomic power, is led to assume itself the very extensive strategic and political responsibilities that this capacity involves and that, by their nature and by their dimensions, are obviously inalienable. Lastly, France's determination to dispose of herself, a determination without which she would soon cease to believe in her own role and be able to be useful to others, is incompatible with a defense organization in which she finds herself subordinate.

Consequently, without going back on her adherence to the Atlantic Alliance, France is going, between now and the final date set for her obligations, which is April 4, 1969, to continue to modify successively the measures currently practiced, insofar as they concern her. What she did yesterday in this respect in several domains, she will do tomorrow in others, while taking, of course, the necessary measures so that these changes take place gradually and so that her allies cannot be suddenly, and because of her, inconvenienced. In addition, she will hold herself ready to arrange with one or another of them, and in the same manner in which she has already proceeded on certain points, the practical relations for cooperation that will appear useful on both sides, either in the immediate present or in the eventuality of a conflict. This naturally holds for allied cooperation in Germany. In sum, it means re-establishing a normal situation of sovereignty, in which that which is French as regards soil, sky, sea and forces, and any foreign element that would be in France, will in the future be under French command alone. This is to say that it in no way means a rupture, but a necessary adaptation.[20]

Subsequently, in three separate memoranda—on March 11, March 29, and April 22, 1966—the French government communicated its decision

[20]News conference, February 21, 1966, in *Speeches and Press Conferences.*

to withdraw its forces from NATO on July 1, 1966, and demanded the withdrawal, by April 1, 1967, of all United States forces and personnel and of all NATO instrumentalities from the French soil. The only remaining possibility was that American forces could be stationed in France, and French forces in Germany, on the basis of bilateral arrangements, a possibility that, if accepted, would in effect lead to NATO's destruction as an integrative military alliance. The alternative left the United States was to persist in the continuation of NATO without France, but with the support of England and West Germany. This appears to be the official position of the three governments concerned. Such an attitude raises serious tactical and logistic problems for the United States, but even more serious are the political problems. What will be the status of the French forces in Germany? Any request that they either withdraw or remain integrated will, since integration is unacceptable to the French, provoke sharp dissension between Germany and France; this in turn, may force the United States to enhance its special relationship with Germany. But this would arouse the traditional French fears of the resurgence of German strength, make unification impossible, give additional support to de Gaulle's plans to bring about a rapprochement with the Soviet Union and, as long as the latter commits no acts of aggression gradually alienate many of the United States' European allies and erode its position in Western Europe.

The "opening to the East"

As we have seen, de Gaulle never accepted the arrangements made at Yalta. Yet it was quite obvious that, as long as the Soviet threat continued and Soviet power was countered by American power, the division of Europe along the lines laid down at Yalta was inevitable. With the emergence of the Sino-Soviet split, with the relative weakening of the Soviet Union's expansionist trends, with the growing preoccupation of the Russians with many internal problems, and last, with the emerging aspirations of many Eastern European nations for independence, the time appeared propitious to reopen the Yalta settlement. This necessitated, first, a reconsideration of the problem of German reunification and, second, the assumption by Western Europe of a relative degree of independence vis-à-vis the United States. For as long as NATO remained what it was, and as long as there was direct Soviet-American confrontation in the heart of Europe, there would be no relaxation of Soviet controls in Eastern Europe.

De Gaulle's emphasis upon a "European Europe," his often-repeated statements about a Europe stretching from the Urals to the shores of the Atlantic, were designed to suggest such a relaxation. Its implementation proved to be a much harder problem. One way was to achieve a genuine Franco-German entente within the context of the Common Market, and then to begin a dialogue with the Soviet Union on matters of German reunification. This proved difficult because of the unwillingness of the Germans to substitute French protection for American, and because of the legitimate doubts of American policy makers about the advisability of such a course of action. De Gaulle then made repeated overtures in the direction of the Eastern satellites. Cultural and economic ties were stressed; visits were exchanged, a number of leaders of Eastern European countries visiting Paris; and France refused to consider any arrangement that would give the Germans a say about nuclear arms. Thus, under de Gaulle, France is returning increasingly to the pre-World War II arrangements—in which an understanding with the Soviet Union is indispensable to the maintenance of peace in Europe, and in which Germany must reenter the concert of European powers, but without the ultimate weapons. This might well have been the objective of General de Gaulle's visit to Russia in the summer of 1966 and of Premier Kosygin's return visit to France six months later.

De Gaulle as a national spokesman

Since 1958, de Gaulle's foreign policy has, according to all public opinion polls, received widespread approval. There was never an occasion when less than 65 per cent approved of his foreign policy. In the first direct presidential election, on December 5 and 19, 1965, he failed, it is true, to receive an absolute majority on the first ballot and received only 55 per cent on the second. It is doubtful, however, except for Lecanuet, who firmly advocated a European community endowed with supranationality and who received 16 per cent of the votes on the first ballot, that the foreign policy issues were sharply drawn.

Polls of the opinion both of the elite and the public indicate a fairly wide approbation of the Gaullist position, at least with regard to NATO, France's independence vis-à-vis the United States, her worldwide commitments, and the prospect of cooperation with Germany and the Soviet Union. De Gaulle is regarded by the public as a European, but the opinion of the elite is far more reserved on this. In the summer of 1964, 49 per cent of the elite groups approved of General de Gaulle's foreign policy, 35 per cent disapproved, and 12 per cent

were indifferent or didn't know.[21] Only 41 per cent, however, felt that a national nuclear arsenal was a prerequisite of a country's independence, and 52 per cent thought it was not. Forty-three per cent thought it was worth the cost, and 44 per cent felt it was not. Thirty-one per cent thought that the French nuclear capacity was credible to France's enemies, and 51 per cent thought it was not. Even more significantly, only 22 per cent thought that the *force de frappe* would be kept and strengthened after de Gaulle, while 48 per cent thought it would be "supranationalized." "Supranationalization," however, must be understood in the context of Europe, or of the Europe of the Six and England, but not of NATO. Both the public and the elite have been hostile or indifferent to a NATO force or to MLF. Though a sizeable fraction of the elite followed de Gaulle's original position in favor of a drastically reformed and overhauled NATO, their preference was overwhelmingly for a European or a Franco-British nuclear arsenal. It is perhaps in this respect, and perhaps in this respect only, that de Gaulle is supported by the public at large but fails to secure the same approbation from the elite. A majority are in favor of a political supranational arrangement in Europe, and though they are not hopeful that this is likely to occur in the near future, they blame de Gaulle for his intransigence. They feel that military problems and matters of defense and security can no longer be solved within the framework of the national state; they also are strong believers in increasing economic integra-

---

[21]For a detailed account of the opinion of the elite groups, see Deutsch, Edinger, Macridis, and Merritt, *France, Germany, and the Western Alliance* (New York: Charles Scribner's Sons, 1967).

tion, and they actively support growing political arrangements in the direction of supranationality. They feel, as they do about the *force de frappe*, that de Gaulle's departure will signify a new effort to provide for political integration, and they are hopeful that Great Britain will then be allowed to join the Six.

Retrospectively, France under de Gaulle has assumed the stance that France had assumed with or without de Gaulle between 1944 and 1947. This was a period when the stark realities of a weakened nation produced an effort toward independence that took a number of forms—the occupation of parts of Germany, the Franco-Soviet pact, the demand for the internationalization of the Ruhr, the occupation and control of the Saar, the war in Indochina and, above all, the notion of the Third Force. By the end of 1947, the French effort had virtually collapsed except for her long-drawn colonial battles, and France became dependent on the United States. The Fourth Republic lived with this situation until 1954, when it revolted against the United States and torpedoed the European Defense Community. The famous "No" to its five partners and to John Foster Dulles, accompanied later by a renewed effort to independently produce fissionable material and a *force de frappe*, culminating in the abortive Suez adventure, were in a real sense the prelude to the Gaullist policy. De Gaulle managed to revive the notion of independence and to implement policies that were expressly designed to symbolize the independence of France vis-à-vis the United States and to redefine her new role as an independent state. He accepted only temporarily the reforms made by his predecessors, like the Common Market, as well as those

elements of American foreign policy that were essential to the economic well-being and security of France. He rejected or seriously qualified most of the others. He returned to the idea of a Third Force and, thanks to European unity, decolonization, and the burdens of American commitments elsewhere, he was able to implement it better. Weakening and abandoning NATO without doing away with the American guarantee, recognizing China, making overtures to the Soviet Union and Eastern Europe, making efforts to reassert France's lost influence in Southeast Asia, and visiting Latin America and Cambodia were not acts undertaken for the sake of prestige alone: they were positive efforts to implement the idea of a Third Force in Europe, led by France and supported by a powerful economic and industrial complex.

It is not necessary to assume that, with de Gaulle's death, a docile France will return again to the Atlantic fold. Nor is it necessary to assume that, with his death, the Fifth Republic will collapse without leaving any trace on domestic institutions and foreign policy. France is more powerful, has a better sense of its role in the world, has tasted the fruits of independence and the poison of the atomic era, and has regained the posture she had temporarily lost after the shattering defeat of 1940. But it will be also difficult to believe that, in the years to come, France will be in a position to maintain her present intransigent attitude of independence. There will be no return to a position of tutelage and dependence upon the United States, as happened after 1947, but it is unlikely that there will be a full-fledged separation and independence from the Atlantic commitment. It is also unlikely that the development of closer European ties can be thwarted. To begin with, the demands for national independence will have to be qualified by a return to what France refused to accept in 1954—a common European military arrangement. Second, European political and military unity will require that one member of the "Anglo-Saxons"—England—be invited to participate. Finally, Europe will inevitably assume greater independence in the world, still, however, requiring the American guarantee and perhaps even the presence of American soldiers. NATO will therefore have to be reconsidered, not as underwriting French dependence, but rather as an indispensable instrument of protection and common strategy, unless and until de Gaulle's great vision of integrating the Soviet Union into Europe is realized.

SELECTED BIBLIOGRAPHY

Année politique. Annual volumes published since 1944. It constitutes one of the best sources of material on French foreign policy.

Aron, Raymond, and Daniel Lerner, France Defeats the EDC? New York: Frederick A. Praeger, Inc., 1957.

———, France, Steadfast and Changing: The Fourth to the Fifth Republic. Cambridge, Mass.: Harvard University Press, 1960.

Beloff, Nora, The General Says "No." Baltimore: Penguin Books, Inc., 1964.

Brogan, D. W., France Under the Republic: 1870–1939. New York: Harper & Row, Publishers, Inc., 1940.

De Gaulle, Charles, War Memoirs. Vol. I, The Call to Honour, New York: The Viking Press, Inc., 1955; Vol. II, Unity, New York: Simon & Schuster, Inc., 1959; Vol. III, Salvation, New York: Simon & Schuster, Inc., 1960.

Deutsch, Karl W., et al., Elite Attitudes and Western Europe. New York: Charles Scribner's Sons, 1966.

Duroselle, J. B., La politique étrangère et ses fondements. Paris: Librairie Armand Colin, 1954.

Furniss, Edgar, Jr., France: Troubled Ally. New York: Harper & Row, Publishers, Inc., 1960.

Grosser, Alfred, La politique extérieure de la 4iéme République. Paris: Librairie Armand Colin, 1963.

———, La politique extérieure de la 5iéme République. Paris: Edition Sevil, 1963.

Hoffmann, Stanley, "De Gaulle's Memoirs: The Hero in History," World Politics, No. 1, (October, 1960), pp. 140–56.

———, et al., In Search of France. Cambridge, Mass.: Harvard University Press, 1964.

Howard, J. E., Parliament and Foreign Policy in France. London: Cresset Press, 1948.

Kissinger, Henry, The Troubled Alliance. New York: McGraw-Hill Book Company, 1965.

Luethy, Herbert, France Against Herself. New York: Frederick A. Praeger, Inc., 1955.

Kertesz, Stephen D., and M. A. Fitzsimons, Diplomacy in a Changing World. South Bend, Ind.: University of Notre Dame, 1959. See the section by Prof. J.-B. Duroselle, "French Diplomacy in Post-World War," pp. 204–50.

McKay, Donald D., United States and France. Cambridge, Mass.: Harvard University Press, 1951.

Macridis, Roy C., De Gaulle—Implacable Ally. New York: Harper & Row, Publishers, Inc., 1966.

———, "De Gaulle's Foreign Policy and the Fifth Republic," *Yale Review*, Winter, 1961.

———, and Bernard E. Brown, *The De Gaulle Republic: Quest for Unity.* The Dorsey Press, 1960.

Steel, Ronald, *The End of Alliance: America and the Future of Europe.* New York: The Viking Press, Inc., 1964.

Sondages: *Revue Française de l'opinion publique, "La politique étrangère de la France et l'opinion publique: 1954–1957,"* Nos. 1 and 2, 1958.

Williams, Philip, *Politics in Post-war France.* New York: Longmans, Green & Co., Inc., 1954.

De Gaulle's major pronouncements are indispensable. They are translated by the Press and Information Service of the French Embassy, 972 Fifth Avenue, New York 21, New York. The most important are the press conferences of October 23, 1958; March 25, 1959; November 10, 1959; September 5, 1960, April 11, 1961; February 14, 1963; September 9, 1965; February 21, 1966, and October 28, 1966. The major addresses are those of September 16, 1959; December 13, 1959 (delivered at Dakar); January 29, 1960.

Foreign Policy of the German Federal Republic

KARL DEUTSCH AND LEWIS J. EDINGER

4

THE HISTORICAL SETTING
AND BASIC ATTITUDES

In all countries, the making of foreign policy is influenced by the legacy of the past. Among the small groups of influential persons, as well as among the broad masses of the voters, memories of the past help to shape the images of what foreign policy is and what it could be. Such memories guide men's imagination as to what tasks any present or future foreign policy could accomplish, what persons and institutions should accomplish them, and by what methods. People turn to memories for answers to their basic questions: "Who are we?" "What do others expect of us?" and "What should we expect of ourselves?" In all countries, memories thus fashion expectations; everywhere they influence the interplay between foreign policy and the ongoing process of national self-perception and self-definition. In Germany, however, these historical memories are, in some respects, more self-contradictory than in any other large country.

The heritage of memories

From the tenth to the thirteenth century, the medieval German Empire was the leading power of Europe, claiming the symbolic and, at times, the actual leadership of Western Christendom. For another three centuries, from the thirteenth to the sixteenth century, German princes and cities, German knights and German merchants were predominant in Central and Eastern Europe without finding serious rivals. Generations of German school children have had impressed upon them those three centuries of universal greatness, and those six centuries of unchallenged German predominance in Central Europe; but they have been given a far less clear picture of the processes that were at work in the centuries of decline and catastrophe that followed.

By the sixteenth century, although Germany had had no effective central government for almost three hundred years, it had not suffered any serious risk of foreign military invasions. With the rise of more effectively organized states in Western Europe, this situation changed. France, at times allied with Sweden, fought the Spanish and Austrian empires on German soil for almost two centuries, leaving the country divided into innumerable independent states. The political fragmentation of Germany was made far deeper by the religious cleavages of the Reformation of the early sixteenth century, which left the German people approximately two-thirds Protestant and one-third Catholic. In the same period, the routes of world trade shifted away from Central Europe to the Atlantic coast, and to the ocean lanes to countries overseas. These economic processes were subtle and anonymous, but their results were disastrous and conspicuous, like the decline of a patient who is weakened by a serious disease of which he remains ignorant. In any case, it seemed as if the world were turning cold and hostile toward Germany. Many of the prosperous German cities declined, while French and English trade centers increased in size and influence. These unfavorable economic developments left the German middle class economically and culturally backward, as well as politically weak and lacking in self-reliance, during the period when the middle classes became more prosperous and more self-reliant in the West.

Throughout the sixteenth and seven-teenth centuries, German states, German cities, and German politics remained, on the whole, petty; no effective economic or political centers for the entire area developed. Both in spite and because of this situation a new concept—Germany (*Deutschland*)—came into use, and a vague notion spread that the Germans were a single people with some sort of common identity, some common destiny, and some common need for safety and prestige.

Early in the seventeenth century, when economic decline and political frustration had become well established on the German scene, the full force of political catastrophe struck. From 1618 to 1648, about one-third of the German people perished in a Thirty Years War, waged essentially by foreign countries for reasons of European power politics, with no significant result for the German people other than sufferings and devastation. During the rest of the seventeenth and eighteenth centuries, Germany remained a battlefield of foreign powers; in the course of these two centuries, Germans acquired an image of Germany as the "land of the middle," helplessly exposed to attacks, surrounded by hostile powers, and condemned to be the perpetual victim of foreign aggressors because of her own lack of unity, organization, and concentrated military power.

By the end of the eighteenth century, two major patterns of response to this situation had become widespread. One consisted in accepting the political and religious division of the country, and the almost total absence of significant military power on the part of most of the petty states into which the country was divided. Resigned to viewing politics as hostile and evil—as Martin Luther had already pictured it—some Germans felt free to concentrate their energies on diligent productive work in trades and crafts, in economic activity, and, perhaps most important of all, in the arts and sciences.

A contrasting but related pattern of response developed in the state of Brandenburg-Prussia: if politics was evil, force and cunning were its only realistic methods. This view stressed the strengthening of the state as the only organization that could safeguard the individual in a world of enemies. To make this state ever larger, stronger, more efficient, and more disciplined was believed the only way of ensuring a minimum of security and dignity for its population. The subjects of the King of Prussia might at least live in a state of law, with an orderly administration and some security against the arbitrary whim of foreign powers. Political passivity and military assertiveness—symbolized by Potsdam, the town of the Prussian soldier-kings, and Weimar, the town of the German poets—became the two equal and opposite responses of the Germans to their predicament.

In the course of the nineteenth century, these two German traditions were partly fused under the impact of the German industrial revolution and of the German political unification movement, which culminated, in 1871, in the establishment of a united German Empire under Prussian leadership. The new political and social system linked much of the German intellectual and literary heritage to the Prussian tradition of widespread public education and instruction. The German intellectuals of the generation that reached maturity after 1809, and that experienced the closing phases of the Napoleonic Wars, were receptive to nationalism and impressed with the need for national political power. It was not only the memories of the humiliating French occupation in the days of Napoleon that made national military

power seem ever more important; the growth of German industry and commerce created a whole series of conflicts with the neighbors of Germany. There were disputes with the Netherlands about the shipping tolls on the lower Rhine, and with Denmark about the duchies of Schleswig and Holstein and, hence, about the territory of the future German Kiel Canal between the Baltic and the North seas, for example. Only military power seemed likely to prevent endless frustrations in these conflicts and to resolve them in accordance with what were considered German needs.

In the course of the nineteenth century, and particularly after 1848, the German middle class and the German liberal parties turned increasingly to an alliance with their own princes, with the aristocracy and the military castes of Germany and, in particular, to an alliance with the Prussian state. Bismarck's policy of "blood and iron," which accomplished the reunification of Germany in three wars, between 1864 and 1871, found in the end the overwhelming support of the German intellectuals and the German middle class, as well as of most of the German people. The coming of the railroads and the triumph of industrialization and urbanization took place in the same decades as these triumphs of power politics, and Bismarck's Empire was credited with all.

To this day, Bismarck's popularity has remained remarkable. In July, 1962, 23 per cent of a cross section of West German adults said that, among great men, Bismarck had done most for Germany; ten years earlier, in 1952, 36 per cent of a similar cross section of voters had given the same answer.[1] No other German historical figure even ap-

[1] Elisabeth Noelle and Erich Peter Neumann, *Jahrbuch der oeffentlichen Meinung: 1958–1964* (Allensbach am Bodensee: Verlag fuer Demoskopie, 1965), p. 297. All

proaches this popularity, but in the late 1950's, a living statesman, Chancellor Konrad Adenauer, began to surpass Bismarck. In May, 1963, 28 per cent of a representative cross section of the West German population thought that Adenauer, who at that time was still in office, had done most for Germany, while 21 per cent of the respondents decided for Bismarck. In popular memory, the Empire that Bismarck founded, which endured from 1871 to 1918, lived on as a golden age. By October, 1951, 45 per cent of the West Germans polled identified the time of this Empire as the period in which they felt Germany had been best off. Twelve years later, however, by December, 1963, this nostalgic group had dwindled to 16 per cent.

But the memories from the period of Bismarck's empire are by no means all idyllic. They include memories of international rivalries in the age of imperialism, and images of the envy and resentment of foreign countries at German commercial and political successes. They include the beginning of the themes of a German bid for "living space," for a "place in the sun," and the double image of the empire-building and colony-owning Western powers, such as France and England. These countries were seen as models and reference groups whom the Germans should imitate and from whom they had to learn how to get on in the world; at the same time, they were viewed as envious enemies ready to encircle and destroy Germany.

By 1914, a very large number of Germans saw themselves engaged, at one and the same time, in a bitterly

competitive struggle for world power and a desperate defensive effort for national survival. They welcomed the seemingly clear-cut state of open war as a long-awaited release from the tensions and frustrations of the pre-war years. The outbreak of World War I was thus accepted with enthusiasm; about three million poems celebrated the event within the first nine months of its outbreak in August, 1914. At the beginning, volunteers for combat duty were numerous, and the fighting morale of front-line troops remained high until close to the end. Even after 1918, many Germans refused to accept the fact of defeat; about one-quarter of the German voters continued to support parties that insisted that with better home-front morale the war would have been won.

Some of these memories of an inevitable power struggle against foreign envy and hostility were revived and reinforced by the impact of the great economic depression that hit Germany in 1929, and which, by early 1933, had produced six million unemployed, almost one-third of the industrial labor force. The image of a hostile international environment, the image of a German empire, similar to the British Empire, as a solution to Germany's difficulties, the image of a desperate bid for living space and a place among the leading imperial nations of the world— all played their part among the appeals by which Hitler rose to power. At the beginning of the Nazi terror, in the elections of March, 1933, as many as 43 per cent of the German voters supported Hitler's National-Socialist party; another 8 per cent supported Hitler's close allies in matters of foreign policy at that time, the German Nationalist party. Fifteen years later, in October, 1948, 41 per cent of a cross section of West German voters recalled that they themselves had approved of the Nazi

---

data in this yearbook are for samples of the adult population, i.e., above 16 years, unless otherwise indicated. Unless otherwise specified, all data cited in this chapter concerning opinions and attitudes come from this source.

seizure of power in 1933. In the same month, 57 per cent agreed that National Socialism was a good idea that had been badly carried out. How views on these matters had developed by the mid-1960's will be reported in later sections.

The German defeat at the end of World War II, so much more shattering than that at the end of World War I, is vividly remembered. Four West Germans out of every five in a cross section of the adult population interviewed in October, 1948, remembered aerial bombardments or fire at the front; almost one in four still dreamed of these experiences; about one out of every six reported these dreams as exciting, terrifying, frequent, or intense. In June, 1954, almost two West Germans out of every five expressed the belief that, in the future, Germany would be once again one of the most powerful states of the world. Another two-fifths of the same sample did not believe that this would ever again happen; the rest were undecided. By June, 1962, those who rejected the vision of restored German national power had become a majority of 53 per cent, while the number of those still believing in it had dwindled to about 20 per cent.

Compared to the glories and terrors of two World Wars, the civilian interlude of the Weimar Republic, between 1918 and 1932, is remembered as relatively colorless. Less than one-tenth of the West Germans interviewed in October, 1951, remembered it as the best period for Germany in the twentieth century; one month later a somewhat smaller percentage named it as the worst. The same colorless image was reported in similar surveys in 1959 and 1963.

The legacy of German history is thus a profoundly ambiguous background for future German foreign policy decisions. It includes memories that counsel fear of remaining weak in a world of ruthless foreign interests, but it is also rich in memories of the suffering and defeat which followed on reckless bids for world power. It is rich in memories of success in fields requiring economic, technical, or scientific performance, but it lacks, for much of a thousand-year period, any impressive memories of sustained political successes following on unaggressive foreign policies and peaceful development of democratic and constitutional practice. Dictatorship and war are remembered by perhaps three-fifths of the West German people as terrible failures; but democracy and peaceful international relations are not at all widely remembered as successes. This store of memories is likely to limit the number of West German voters who will support a consistent and firm commitment to democracy and to wholehearted cooperation with the Western powers. But historical memories also influence German attitudes on foreign policy in other ways.

Images of foreign policy objectives

Perhaps more than most other large peoples, West Germans view their foreign policy in terms of their own collective status and prestige in the world at large. Foreign policy is expected not only to procure material advantages, or to maintain peace, it is also expected to contribute to the respect of the world for the Germans and thus, indirectly, to bolster German self-respect. More than two out of every three West Germans interviewed in a survey in May, 1959, believed that the Germans were unpopular in the world because of their particular qualities. Only one-fifth of the respondents blamed this on their good qualities, particularly their diligence and ability, while as many as one-half believed that their bad qualities—their loudness, lack of adaptability, their intolerance, and their political legacy—made the Germans unpopular abroad.

During the first years of political consolidation of the newly established Federal Republic, the largest world power and one of the smallest—the United States and Switzerland—emerged as the countries most admired in West Germany; 8 per cent of the persons asked, in a survey in July, 1954, said they would like most of all to live in the United States, another 7 per cent picked Switzerland, and another 8 per cent scattered their preferences over the rest of Europe. In November, 1953, a cross section of young people between fifteen and twenty-four years old was asked whether the Germans could learn anything from other peoples, and if so, from what people. Almost two-thirds of the youngsters answered that Germany could indeed learn from others; 23 per cent then named, as a model, the United States; 10 per cent named England; 7 per cent, Switzerland; 5 per cent, France; 3 per cent, Sweden; the rest were scattered.[2]

Attitudes toward the United States. Germany today is a country in search of friends, just as she is a country in search of herself. Clearly, the political friendship that is most popular is that with the United States. Large majorities in opinion surveys have consistently favored close association between the Federal Republic and the United States. In February, 1963, 76 per cent of the West Germans polled expressed "good" feelings for the United States; only 1 per cent reported either "bad" or "very bad" feelings for their American ally. During the last decade, when asked to choose between "East" and "West" under peacetime conditions, a majority

of West Germans have consistently expressed overwhelming preference for the West; only 1 to 3 per cent have declared themselves in favor of cooperation with the East.[3]

The appeal of neutralism. Organized and overt expressions of neutralism have diminished drastically in recent years. However, polls indicate that a sizeable minority, between one-fourth and one-third of the West Germans who were willing to express a view on this problem between 1952 and 1961, continue to wish that the Federal Republic remain neutral in a conflict between East and West. Confronted with the more specific problem of the withdrawal of Western troops from the Federal Republic in return for a withdrawal of Russian troops from Eastern Europe and East Germany, 56 per cent of the West Germans favored such a development in a poll in March, 1958, and only 16 per cent opposed it. On this matter, the West German leaders differed somewhat from their people; when the same question was put to a cross section of the West German Parliament, 54 per cent opposed reciprocal troop withdrawal and 45 per cent favored it.

More recent surveys suggest that the gap between public opinion and that of the elite on the question of a reciprocal withdrawal of troops is likely to have widened. In a 1964 survey, 72 per cent of the articulate elite were opposed to regional arms reduction in Central Europe. Mass opinion was more inclined toward neutralism, particularly in the event of war. In the event of a Russian attack on the United States, 52 per cent of a cross section of West

[2]Karl-Georg von Stackelberg, ed., *Jugend zwischen 15 und 24: Eine Untersuchung zur Situation der Deutschen Jugend im Bundesgebiet* (Bielefeld: Emmid-Institut, 1954), p. 87.

[3]Data are drawn from Noelle and Neumann, *Jahrbuch, III: 1958–1964*, p. 533; and from Donald J. Puchala, "Western European Attitudes on International Problems: 1952–1961," (Yale University, 1965) pp. 6–7. Mimeographed.

German voters polled in December, 1958, wanted their country to remain neutral, 13 per cent favored giving the United States merely nonmilitary support in such a conflict, and only 17 per cent were willing to live up to the Federal Republic's obligation under NATO to give military aid to its American ally.[4] Similarly, in October, 1958, although 63 per cent of the West German respondents generally favored the siding of their country with the West against the East, only 38 per cent wanted West Germany to side with the United States against Russia in case of war. In February, 1961, endorsement of the American military alliance had shrunk to 40 per cent, and 42 per cent preferred neutrality.[5] By contrast, when a Russian attack on West Germany was hypothesized, 61 per cent of the West Germans polled in the same year expected United States' military support in such a conflict and, by 1963, 79 per cent favored the stationing of American troops on German territory for this very reason.[6] In general, while West Germans overwhelmingly reject communism, favor the Western way of life, and choose cooperation with the United States in the event of a military encounter between the two major powers, neutrality still seems a prudent policy to quite a few of them, and only a minority seems willing for West Germany to actually fight on the side of the West in a major war.

[4]DIVO Institut, *Umfragen: Ereignisse und Probleme der Zeit im Urteil der Bevoelkerung* (Frankfurt am Main: Europaeische Verlagsanstalt, 1959), II, 21–23, 36.
[5]From data in Karl W. Deutsch, *Arms Control and the Atlantic Alliance* (New York: John Wiley & Sons, Inc., 1966); and *Jahrbuch,* III, See also Karl W. Deutsch *et al., France, Germany and the Western Alliance* (New York: Charles Scribner's Sons, 1966).
[6]DIVO Institut, *Pressedienst,* (Frankfurt am Main: Europaeische Verlagsanstalt 1964), I, 7; *Jahrbuch,* III, 556.

Popular notions of the relative strength of the United States and the Soviet Union no doubt play a part in these considerations. In December, 1952, 66 per cent of the West Germans surveyed thought that the West would in the long run become preeminent over the East. Seven years later, December, 1959, this proportion had dropped to 36 per cent, and the proportion of those believing that both camps would emerge equally strong had risen from 7 to 18 per cent.[7] By February, 1960, only 29 per cent of the West Germans polled expected the United States to be the stronger after twenty to twenty-five years, just as large a proportion expected the Soviet Union to emerge on top, 19 per cent believed that the two superpowers would be equal in strength, and 23 per cent expressed no opinion.[8] German faith in the military superiority of the United States had also diminished drastically. In June, 1955, 39 per cent of the West Germans polled still thought the West stronger in atomic weapons than the Soviet Union, but by May, 1960, only 16 per cent believed this to be the case, more than 20 per cent thought the West was weaker than the U.S.S.R., and 34 per cent thought both camps were equally strong in atomic weapons. However, likely as a result of the strong position taken by the United States during the 1958–1962 crisis in Berlin and the 1962 crisis over missiles in Cuba, West German faith in the military superiority of the United States revived somewhat. By October, 1963, only 11 per cent of the West Germans polled believed that the Soviet Union would emerge victorious from an assumed third world war, almost 33 per cent ex-

[7]DIVO, *op. cit.,* 3/4, p. 9.
[8]See poll results from a confidential USIA survey, reported in "The United States in Foreign Eyes: 1960," *New York Times,* November 2, 1960.

pected the United States to win such an encounter, and another 33 per cent thought that neither of the powers would win.[9]

West German policy makers thus can count on popular approval of their efforts to maintain a general climate of friendly relations with the United States, but they must be careful not to arouse fears of dangerous commitments, which could unite a majority of voters against them. At the same time, West German politicians who prefer a closer approach to neutrality in international affairs must be careful not to arouse fears of a loss of American friendship. As long as the West German voters view the Western alliance as primarily defensive and peaceful, these two attitudes can be reconciled. A considerable amount of agreement on basic foreign policy has, in fact, developed among the major parties and among the great majority of the electorate. If, however, new and major tangible commitments should be demanded from Germany by her allies, or if the international situation should approach the brink of war, much of this consensus might disintegrate.

National reunification and the eastern territories. Other foreign policy aims on which there is a great deal of popular agreement stem directly from Germany's defeat and partition in World War II.

Germany, after her defeat in 1945, was an exhausted, partly destroyed, and half-starved country, occupied by four foreign powers. Since no central government was set up in Western Germany until 1949, the tasks of procuring a minimum of food and shelter fell to the occupying powers and to the new local and provincial governments that were set up under their supervision. When a federal government for Western Ger-

many was established, its first and basic task appeared to be the gradual regaining of national independence. The public agreed: more than two-thirds of all the West German respondents, and more than three-quarters of all the men, said in August, 1949, that they were "ready to commit all their strength to make Germany self-supporting and independent, politically and economically." This goal seemed to have precedence even over the maintainance of friendship with the United States and the regaining of a respected position among the Western powers. The fact that the Adenauer government was able to pursue all these goals simultaneously, between 1949 and 1957, contributed much to its strength.

Other goals also arose directly from the German postwar situation. First of these, in the minds of most West German voters, appears to be the reunification of East and West Germany, substantially on the basis of those political and social institutions that prevail in the German Federal Republic. Polls have consistently indicated an overwhelming desire for such reunification; in January, 1965, almost half of all West Germans polled believed that the reunification of Germany was "the most important question for people in West Germany today."[10] The belief that reunification could be achieved by peaceful means has, however, declined over the years. Late in 1961, shortly after the building of the Berlin Wall, half the West Germans polled did not regard peaceful means as a possible avenue of reunification, although half still did.[11]

There was also the question of the

[9]DIVO, *op. cit.*, 3/4, p. 8; *Jahrbuch*, III, 556.

[10]Institut fuer Demoskopie Allensbach, *Informationsdienst* (Allensbach am Bodensee), May, 1965. Adding the 4 per cent who gave top priority to the Berlin problem brings the total level of this essentially national concern to 51 per cent. *Ibid.*
[11]*Jahrbuch*, III, 481.

German expellees from Eastern Europe and the former German territories east of the Oder and Neisse rivers. Over ten million persons of German language and sympathies were expelled from such Eastern European countries as Poland, the Baltic countries, Czechoslovakia, Hungary, Rumania, Yugoslavia, and from those parts of prewar Germany east of the Oder and Neisse rivers which came under Polish or Russian administration after 1945. Many of these expellees wanted to regain their former lands, properties, and social positions; their aspiration had the approval, mild or strong, of many German voters. The regaining of territory, particularly the former German Oder-Neisse territories which include coal-rich Silesia, thus became a long-range goal of German foreign policy.

Public sentiment for regaining these lost territories seem to have decreased over the years, however. Although 35 per cent of all West Germans polled in 1959 believed that these territories would again belong to Germany, only 29 per cent still thought so in 1962. In 1959, only about one-third of the respondents believed that these territories were lost to Germany, and by 1962, this fraction increased to almost half. Furthermore, the desire to regain the territories must be considered as relatively weak. In April, 1959, only 6 per cent of all West German adults, and 8 per cent of all expellees, regarded war as a possible strategy for regaining these territories, and more than 80 per cent of both groups rejected the possibility of war. On the other hand, almost 40 per cent of the expellees said they would return to their former homelands if Germany ever recovered them.[12]

The fear of war. The fact seems to be, judging from many polls, that a majority of Germans believe in the foreign poli-

cy objectives we have discussed above, but that they would be unwilling to fight for most of them. Asked in June, 1956, whether Germans should fight "to defend Europe" against an armed Soviet attack, only 26 per cent said "Yes"; 36 per cent said that war should be avoided, above all; and 38 per cent were undecided.[13] Today, however, this attitude seems to be subject to one qualification: over the last decade, West Germans have increasingly come to accept their country's obligation to maintain a national army which has, as its official mission, the defense of the country's chosen way of life and values. Between 1956 and 1961, the proportion of West Germans who favored the maintenance of the Federal Army (*Bundeswehr*) increased from 38 to 60 per cent, and the proportion of those who approved of West Germany's integration into the North Atlantic Treaty Organization (NATO) rose from 52 per cent, in November, 1955, to 67 per cent, in September, 1963.[14]

West German public opinion, thus, seems largely united in disliking and distrusting communism and communist governments; in fearing and rejecting war, except to ensure its own security; in seeking at least political equality with other Western powers, such as France and the United Kingdom; and in desiring to remain friends with the United States. Large majorities also wish for eventual national reunification and, less urgently, for the recovery of former German territories in the East. Smaller, but still appreciable, majorities also desire West German participa-

[13]*Jahrbuch*, II, 361. It seems interesting that only 26 per cent of West German respondents at that time seemed willing to fight for Europe, while a larger minority, 38 per cent, said, in October, 1958, that they would be willing to have their country side with the United States in case of war.

[12]*Jahrbuch*, III, 504–5.

[14]*Jahrbuch*, III, 470, 539.

tion in some form of European cooperation and integration.

Opinion about a Western European union. In September, 1955, more than two-thirds of the West Germans polled said that they would vote in favor of forming a United States of Europe. Almost three-fifths considered the formation of a United States of Europe a practical possibility, only 17 per cent finding it an impossible idea. In general, this favorable attitude seems to have persisted and even grown: by 1961, the proportion in favor of a European union had increased to 81 per cent. However, on the more qualified question of choosing between two "solutions for the future—the rebuilding of West Germany as a completely independent national state with its own customs frontiers, or West Germany as an equal member of a European union," —a bare majority of 51 per cent chose membership in a European union, in September, 1956, while 43 per cent preferred an independent national state.[15] By May, 1960, in answer to a somewhat differently worded question, the proportions had changed drastically: only 42 per cent chose a supranational solution, while 50 per cent preferred independent national governments in Europe.[16]

Thus, the favorable West German attitude toward European integration seems subject to two qualifications: though not necessarily impractical, European union seems remote; furthermore, it must not take away from West Germany the sovereign right of ultimate decision. Only 29 per cent of the West Germans questioned in 1965 believed that they would live to see the

Western European countries unite to form the United States of Europe;[17] and in April and May, 1960, only 42 per cent were willing to concede to a European parliament the right of ultimate decision in questions touching West German national interests, as against 50 per cent who insisted that ultimate decisions must remain with the national parliament or government of the individual country. There the matter seems to have remained.

Most of the more specific institutions of European cooperation did not become popular foreign policy goals. The proportion of those endorsing the European Coal and Steel Community (ECSC) declined from 39 per cent in June, 1950, to 21 per cent in January, 1952, and it kept declining for a while. A year later (March, 1953), only 19 per cent said it had "not been a mistake" for Germany to join in this arrangement, while 75 per cent were either undecided (15 per cent) or uninformed (60 per cent). By April, 1956, however, the popularity of ECSC had again reached the 1950 level: the fraction of undecided and uninformed respondents had dwindled to 43 per cent, and West Germany's membership in the ECSC was endorsed by 38 per cent of all the West Germans polled.[18] In later years, questions about the European Coal and Steel Community were dropped out of West German opinion surveys.

The project of a European Defense Community (EDC), which was to include German troops under a common European command, was endorsed by 33 per cent in March, 1950, and, in September, 1954, 37 per cent expressed regret for the failure of the project. Throughout the period, however, polls always recorded more opponents than

---

[15]Typescript summary of poll results on German ideologies and politics, Spring, 1957, from EMNID Institute, Bielefeld, p. 9; henceforth cited as "Ideologies."
[16]DIVO, *op. cit.*, 3/4, p. 18.

[17]Institut fuer Demoskopie Allensbach, *Informationsdienst* (Allensbach a.B.), January, 1966, p. 3.
[18]*Jahrbuch*, II, 349.

supporters of any West German troop contribution to a Western European defense force, but the levels of both support and opposition usually remained below those for or against an independent West German army. There are ample indications that, in 1954, unlike the voters, a majority of West German leaders supported the EDC project. Ten years later, however, in mid-1964, 44 per cent of a sample of leaders of the rearmed Federal Republic opposed EDC, and only 35 per cent still supported it.[19]

West German membership in NATO has apparently become more popular in recent years. When Chancellor Adenauer succeeded in securing parliamentary ratification of the treaty, popular support was quite small. In April, 1954, only 24 per cent of the West Germans asked in a survey could approximately identify NATO. By June, 1960, 83 per cent had heard of NATO, and, in a survey taken in September, 1963, more than half of all the West Germans polled were able to provide correct information about the goals and structure of the organization. On the other hand, only 33 per cent of those polled, in 1960, had great confidence in the organization's ability to provide security against a Russian attack. Fifty-four per cent had only "some," "a little," or "no confidence" in NATO's ability to defend Western Europe. However, it remained popular: in 1963, only 9 per cent of all respondents believed that the disadvantages resulting from West Germany's membership exceeded the advantages of participation.[20]

The notion of a common market in Europe became a foreign policy image before the actual creation of the Euro-

pean Economic Community (EEC) by the Rome agreement in March, 1957, and almost half the West Germans polled in January, 1957, had already heard of the project. In a survey taken in June, 1960, more than three West Germans out of every four knew of their country's membership, and almost three in every five favored Germany's participation.[21]

Franco-German reconciliation. Judging from a considerable number of French and German public opinion polls between 1952 and 1962,[22] mutual friendliness between the two peoples increased considerably during that decade—but mutual trust appears to have increased much less! General "good" feeling for France, as reported by West German polls, rose spectacularly, from 12 per cent, in 1954, to 46 per cent, in early 1963, and French "good" feeling about Germany rose similarly, from 9 per cent, in 1954, to 53 per cent, in early 1964. Thus French goodwill toward the Germans surpassed, for the first time, French sympathies for the United States, although the West German good feeling toward France, reported by a minority of 46 per cent, fell far below the 76 per cent majority which clearly favored the United States.

Poll data for the period 1954–1961, however, reveal that mutual trust is of a different order. Answers to the specific question, "Which country would you trust as an ally in a case of war?" show that the percentage of West Germans expressing "a great deal" of trust in France as a military ally rose, but only from 7 per cent, in 1952, to 20 per cent, in 1961; similarly, the fraction of

[19]Deutsch, *Arms Control and the Atlantic Alliance*; Deutsch *et al., France, Germany, and the Western Alliance.*

[20]DIVO, *op. cit.*, 3/4, pp. 36–38; *Jahrbuch*, III, 538–39.

[21]*Jahrbuch*, III, 542–44.

[22]Data reported in Karl W. Deutsch, *"Arms Control and European Integration: A Survey of Findings,"* (Yale University, 1965), pp. 105–10, with references. Mimeographed.

French respondents who would trust Germany as an ally increased only slightly, from 9 per cent to 21 per cent during these nine years. Thirteen per cent of the West Germans, and 23 per cent of the French, as polled in 1961, declared that they did not trust the other country at all, and a majority of both Frenchmen and West Germans avoided a decision by saying "Up to a point," or "Don't know."

Questioned about the particular issue of the Franco-West German Friendship Treaty of 1963, 51 per cent of all West Germans polled in July, 1963, favored the agreement, 17 per cent thought it "rather bad" for Germany, and 32 per cent were uninformed or undecided.[23]

It seems likely, in the light of this evidence, that most West German and French voters have become attracted by the prospect of Franco-German reconciliation, as well as to a long-range possibility which would be spurred by such a reconciliation, of European union—but that most of them have not yet overcome their mutual distrust or, at least, the reservations which are the legacy of past Franco-German conflict.

The unpopularity of nuclear armament proposals. Among major foreign policy goals, one is conspicuous by the limited and reluctant popular support it finds: West Germany's national rearmament and the country's quest for nuclear weapons. In thirteen polls, from November, 1950, to February, 1955, opposition to an independent West German army declined from 48 to 43 per cent, but support only rose from 33 to 39 per cent. By November, 1956, after the Hungarian uprising, 46 per cent endorsed the setting up of a German federal army, but an equal number opposed it. In recent years, popular

support has further increased: by August, 1961, three West Germans out of five favored the retention of the Federal Army, as against one in every four who opposed it.

Any proposal for nuclear armament, however, is still met with overwhelming rejection. In a survey of mass opinion conducted in May, 1960, 62 per cent of all the West Germans questioned objected to nuclear equipment for the Federal Army, and only 18 per cent favored such a move.[24] Among West German leaders commenting, in a mid-1964 survey of opinion on this issue, a West German national deterrent to nuclear war was rejected by 96 per cent as "not worth its cost."[25] What the German government does in the way of rearmament is thus less a response to any pressure of domestic opinion, but a result of international considerations and, conceivably, of the attitudes of small minorities within the West German political and military elite.

Regardless of popular feelings on any matter of foreign policy, however, West German foreign policy makers have a great deal of leeway so far as domestic opinion is concerned. There is a long-standing German tradition of leaving such complicated matters to experts and persons of authority; and the West German government may count on popular acquiescence even to relatively unpopular foreign policy moves. Thus, in the past, governmental decisions—and without encountering serious domestic opposition—have been far more accommodating toward France on the issues of the Saar territory and farm-price agreements within the EEC, and to Israel on the issue of German

[23]*Jahrbuch*, III, 566.

[24]*Jahrbuch*, III, 470; DIVO, *op. cit.*, 3/4 p. 15.

[25]For sources, see Deutsch, *Arms Control and the Atlantic Alliance*; and Deutsch et al., *France, Germany and the Western Alliance.*

reparations, than the public opinion would have liked.

Ideologies and classes

The Germans of the Federal Republic are largely an urban and industrial people. By 1961, one-third of the West Germans older than sixteen lived in large cities of more than 100,000, and another 16 per cent lived in middle-sized cities, of between 20,000 and 100,000 inhabitants. This left 28 per cent for small towns (2,000-20,000 population), and 22 per cent in smaller, mostly rural, communities. The rural sector of West German society lost 4 per cent of the population between 1950 and 1961, and might well lose another 4 per cent during the 1960's. Partly because of war casualties, 54 per cent of the population were women and only 46 per cent were men. They were an old people, compared to other countries. Nearly 23 per cent of the total were 60 years or older, 27 per cent were under 30, and the rest was almost evenly divided between those above and below 45 years of age. In 1961, the ranks of men in their forties had been depleted in World War II.

As to occupation, almost half the labor force were industrial workers, and another 1.6 per cent were rural laborers. For the first time in many decades, manual workers formed only a minority of the West German population. This shift was mainly due to the decline in the proportion of rural laborers after 1950, and to the widespread importation of foreign laborers from Southern Europe. Twenty-three per cent were privately employed white-collar workers, and 7 per cent (2 per cent more than a decade earlier) were public officials, bringing the total proportion of wage or salary earners to more than 80 per cent, or four-fifths, of the total. The remaining fifth were

self-employed persons; of these, 9 per cent were peasants or farmers (a drop of one-fourth since 1950), a little less than 11 per cent were businessmen and artisans, and 1.5 per cent were professionals such as doctors, architects, or lawyers. Altogether, the people of the Federal Republic had become, during the 1950's, more middle-class, more urban, and far less agricultural than they had been before.

They had not yet become much better educated, however, and educational levels are still not very high. In 1962, only 5 per cent of West Germans over sixteen had the equivalent of a junior college (*Abitur*) education, 1 per cent more than in 1950. Another 16 per cent had the equivalent of ten grades in school, 3 per cent more than in 1950. The remaining 79 per cent had no more than the equivalent of eight school years (*Volksschule*).

No political group can win a majority in West Germany without the support of at least part of these urban and industrial groups. But there are enough peasants, white-collar workers, and others of middle-class status or aspirations to permit a variety of political combinations, and to reward political appeals designed to unite at least some wage and salary earners with some self-employed groups. This situation limits the effectiveness of class appeals and favors politicians who can present their views as serving the interests of the nation.

Other conditions also reduce the effectiveness of sectional or denominational politics and encourage the appeal of national interests. Almost one-quarter of the West Germans over sixteen are expellees or refugees who cannot be expected to support policies based on the interest of a single region or section. Many of these expellees are of middle-class background and, whatever their present occupation may be, their memories and their attitudes are still at least partly middle-class.

To the 50 per cent of West Germans who are now in middle-class or white-collar occupations, there must be added an appreciable group of wage earners with middle-class aspirations—all of whom could lend their support to policies expressed in national terms. A similar consideration applies to the religious groups. With the population over sixteen almost unchangingly and evenly divided—51 per cent are Protestants and 44 per cent are Roman Catholics (but these are somewhat better organized)—religion would prove too divisive a basis for decision. Finally, the ideological cleavages inherited from the days of the Empire, the First (Weimar) Republic, the Nazi dictatorship, and two World Wars all cut largely across regional, religious, and class boundaries.

The most important underlying cleavage in West Germany is that between friends and enemies of the Republic, between supporters of democracy and adherents of dictatorship. In practical terms, this still means the latent, but persistent, difference between Nazi and anti-Nazi—between those who would like to see some equivalent of the Hitler dictatorship restored and those who wish to maintain democratic institutions.

Communism is a negligible domestic issue in West Germany. Only 8 per cent of the West Germans polled indicated a favorable view of it in April, 1950, and by March, 1955, this had slipped to 2 per cent. The Communist Party of Germany (KPD) has been outlawed in West Germany since 1956. A survey made in April, 1957, showed that almost three West Germans out of every ten were opposed to this action by the Federal Constitutional Court and viewed it as "not necessary," while an equal proportion of voters regarded

the decision as "necessary." In 1960, more than half of a cross section of West German adults believed that the Communist Party was working underground and influencing the political process in West Germany, but, by 1962, only 5 per cent of those polled regarded the possible readmission of the communists as a crucial issue for the incoming Erhard government.[26] In respect to world politics, however, 38 per cent of a cross section of German youth between sixteen and twenty-four years of age, polled in 1956, expected the influence of communism to increase, while only 20 per cent expected its decline. Their expectations, however, differed from their preferences. Confronted with the question of whether "communist ideas" or "Western ideas" had greater attraction for them, 38 per cent of the youths in this survey indicated that Western ideas had "much greater attraction," and 23 per cent thought that they had "somewhat greater attraction." Only 5 per cent found communist ideas far more attractive, and 8 per cent found them somewhat more attractive.[27] The large majority of West Germans of all ages appear to be against communism as they are against sin. Nazi sympathizers are alternately vehement in denouncing communism, or are ready to play with the thought of making alliances with communists against the West, in line with the old Stalin-Hitler pact of 1939, and with some more recent "national-bolshevist" propaganda themes. But it is in their appeal to the traditions of nationalism and authoritarianism that the potential strength of the Nazis must be sought; it is here that the supporters of democratic institutions will have to resist them.

[26]*Jahrbuch*, III, 309, 455–56.
[27]DIVO, *Basic Orientation and Political Thinking of West German Youth and Their Leaders, 1956: Report on a Nation-wide Survey* (Frankfurt am Main: 1956), p. 81.

On most questions, about one-third of the West German electorate are consistent defenders of democracy. On some issues, their number rises to half or even more. Thus, in 1961, 43 per cent of all West German respondents denied that Hitler would have been a great statesman even if there had been no war, and 53 per cent of the respondents, in May, 1964, regarded the Third Reich as a criminal regime and a state of injustice. In the same survey, 52 per cent of all West Germans above sixteen years of age endorsed the intentions of the members of the anti-Hitler resistance; and 30 per cent, contrasted with only 20 per cent in 1956, approved of naming a school after one of the heroes of the German resistance against Hitler during World War II. One West German out of two, in 1959, placed the main guilt for World War II on Germany, a substantial increase over the 32 per cent who had done so in 1951. A slightly higher percentage of respondents (52 per cent), in July, 1960, indicated a clear awareness of the connection between dictatorship and acts of violence.

Constitutionalism is finding popular support. Three West German voters out of five approved of the Constitution, the so-called Basic Law of the Federal Republic, in 1956. In November, 1961, more than half the respondents—53 per cent, and nearly twice as many as in 1954—favored the black, red, and gold colors of the German Federal Republic over the black, white, and red of the Hohenzollern Empire and the Nazis. In 1952, as many as 71 per cent demanded that a "good" political party should be "democratic," and, in 1959, the multiparty system was endorsed by 77 per cent—a significant increase over the 61 per cent who did so in 1951.[28]

On the other side, there is still a hard core of unreconstructed Nazis and a penumbra of sympathizers. In West Germany, between 1950 and 1958, about one West German in eight could be counted, for most political purposes, a Nazi. That is, in polls taken during this period, between 7 and 15 per cent said that they liked Hitler and Goebbels, professed Nazi race doctrines about Jews, and announced that they would welcome the return of a new National Socialist party to power. Of the young people between fifteen and twenty-five years of age, the polls of November, 1953, 1954, and 1955 showed, about 10 per cent professed favorable opinions of Hitler and of National Socialism.[29] In a 1956 survey, 25 per cent of West German adults, and 41 per cent of the youths between sixteen and twenty-four, wanted "again" to have a "single strong national party which merely represents the interests of all classes of all people." Sixteen per cent of the adults believed that "we should again have, as before, a national leader who rules Germany with a strong hand for the welfare of all," and 21 per cent of the young people also supported this sentiment.

Sentiment in favor of a single political party appears to have declined sharply in the later 1950's. In August, 1958, in a poll question not phrased with specific reference to the Nazi regime and its leaders, less than one out of ten West Germans favored a one-party system. On the whole, women, younger people, the less educated, and those living in small communities appeared to favor a single strong national party and a powerful national leader more frequently than others in West Germany.

[28]*Jahrbuch*, II, 172–73, 278; *Jahrbuch*, III, 233–34, 256; Institut fuer Demoskopie, *Informationsdienst*, July, 1964.

[29]Rolf Froehner, *Wie stark sind die Halbstarken? Dritte Emnid Untersuchung zur Situation der deutschen Jugend* (Bielefeld: Stackelberg Verlag, 1956), pp. 119–21, 305–10.

Despite the efforts of government authorities to acquaint German youths with the activities of the Nazi regime, 62 per cent of the West German youth were unable, in the 1956 survey, to name any of the "chief aims" of Nazism.[30] Similarly, in a poll taken in January, 1960, only two West Germans out of five identified antidemocratic attitudes and the "Fuehrer-principle" as dominant characteristics of Nazism, and a somewhat smaller fraction named anti-Semitism.[31]

About one West German in four was, during the 1950's, an emotional supporter of the Nazis in general, professing a predominantly favorable opinion of Hitler, his deputy Hess, and the Nazi Youth leader, von Schirach. In November, 1961, about the same proportion of West Germans expressed an unfriendly attitude toward democracy and favored the colors of the Hohenzollern Empire and the Nazis over those of the Federal Republic. Ten years earlier, in 1951, an equal proportion had felt that the main responsibility for the outbreak of World War II lay with the Western powers, and that Germany had lost the war mainly because of domestic sabotage and treason. By 1959, these fractions had dwindled, to 11 and 15 per cent, respectively. But five years later, in 1964, 16 per cent of all West Germans polled still viewed war-time resistance against Hitler as treason, while, as we noted earlier, 52 per cent approved of it and 32 per cent were undecided.[32]

On many specific issues, a much larger number of West Germans held nationalistic views that made them potential allies or supporters of a revival of Nazi tradition or politics on these particular questions. As many as 54 per cent of a cross section of West German voters polled in 1961 said that they could not consider, or could not have considered, marrying a person of Jewish descent. (As many as 70 per cent had said so in 1949; the prejudice had declined 16 percentage points in 12 years.) On the other hand, overt anti-Semitism is on the decline, and it has ceased to be respectable for the great majority of Germans. In 1952, about 40 per cent of the West Germans polled opposed a legal penalty for anti-Semitic propaganda and agreed that it was better for Germany not to have any Jews; but by January, 1960, only 7 per cent expressed opposition to a legal penalty for anti-Semitic propaganda, and 78 per cent favored such action. By May, 1963, less than 20 per cent of the West Germans polled agreed that it was better for Germany not to have any Jews. But almost half the West Germans polled in 1960 had reservations about a Jew becoming Chancellor of the Federal Republic (a question few persons would have thought of asking in the 1950's) and only 57 per cent had similar reservations about former leading Nazis holding high positions in the federal government.[33]

About one-third of all West Germans over sixteen years of age opposed the admission of former anti-Hitler refugees to high positions in the Federal Republic, in 1954. In the same year, roughly the same proportion expected Germany to become once again one of the most powerful states in the world, but by June, 1962, this fraction had dropped to one-fifth. Slightly more than half of the West Germans polled in 1951 favored lifting the ban on the wearing of Nazi World War II decorations with the swastika symbol (almost every second German man had at least one such decoration), and they op-

---

[30] DIVO, *Basic Orientation, 1956*, pp. 36–39, 45.

[31] *Jahrbuch*, III, 222.

[32] Institut fuer Demoskopie, *Informationsdienst*, July 1964, p. 4.

[33] *Jahrbuch*, III, 215–16, 223.

posed the idea of reissuing these decorations with the swastika omitted. A majority rejected the notion of German war crimes. More than half (55 per cent) felt, in 1953, that the German soldiers of World War II had nothing to reproach themselves for in their behavior in the countries occupied. As many as one-quarter of the respondents, in a survey in July, 1960, lacked any clear awareness of the link between dictatorship and acts of violence. Thus, in a poll published in 1961, as many as 36 per cent said that even "if after 1933 a person was firmly convinced that wrongs and crimes had been committed under Hitler," he should not have offered any resistance; and three years later, in 1964, more than one-third refused the notion of "state of injustice" (*Unrechtsstaat*) and "regime of criminals" (*Verbrecherregime*) to describe the Nazi period.[34]

The limited but significant improvements in popular sympathies for democracy thus far have not changed the political balance in the German Federal Republic, nor the relative immobility of many policies that reflect it. Most of the large majorities on particular foreign policy issues seem to arise in those cases where many or all of the democrats (about 25 to 30 per cent of the population), and many or all of the antidemocratic Nazi sympathizers (about 20-25 per cent) can agree. When they agree, a considerable part of the usually undecided or ambivalent persons may be likely to join in. We have surveyed the main issues that tend to produce this kind of agreement between pro- and anti-Nazis, adherents of nationalistic dictatorship and of democracy, friendly and hostile critics of the United States, France, and the United Kingdom. They are the familiar

issues: opposition to communism; a preference for Western economic and political connections and living standards; and a desire for restoring and increasing national prosperity, German international prestige, and West German bargaining power.

The nature of this consensus implies its limits. Most voters will not follow nationalist goals to the brink of war; most democrats would not increase West German international bargaining power to the point where extreme nationalists and militarists would actually regain major power in domestic politics; and most of the right-wing extremists do not wish to deepen their alliance with the West to the point where they would have to drop their anti-Semitism, their admiration for much of the Nazi system, and their contempt for democracy. Wherever those limits of consent are reached, democrats and Nazi sympathizers separate again, and a considerable part of their countrymen withdraw into silence or indifference. Policy decisions, though sometimes delayed or compromised, are carried on by the government in line with the democratic sectors of opinion and in line with what is judged to be the relevant international opinion.

Wanted: a foreign policy of caution

Altogether, the structure of West German public opinion, in the mid-1950's, favored a foreign policy of firm symbolic attachment to the West, coupled with caution and a preference for limiting the extent of actual commitment. There was a clearly accepted general goal—the prosperity and prestige of the West German people, on a level with that of the leading Western nations—and there were at least four specific goals which were agreed upon. Three of these had been, in fact, attained and merely had to be preserved: (*a*) the preservation of peace and of

[34]*Jahrbuch*, III, 234; Institut fuer Demoskopie, *Informationsdienst*, July, 1964, p. 3.

a Western style of life in the Federal Republic; (b) the retention of United States friendship and support for West German aspirations; and (c) the exclusion of any major communist influence from West Germany. The fourth was felt as missing: the reunification of East and West Germany, substantially on West German terms. The first three of these goals were so much taken for granted that most poll respondents did not mention them as salient or problematic. The fourth—national reunification—was put at the top of the unresolved problems. Two further unattained goals were endorsed by majorities, but they were perceived as less urgent for the time being, and perhaps also as less important in the long run. These less salient goals were the political integration of Western Europe and the recovery of the former German territories east of the Oder and Neisse rivers.

Above all, West German opinion wanted to avoid unpalatable choices. It rejected anti-communism at the price of war, as well as peace at the price of communist rule. It rejected national reunification at the price of either communist penetration or the loss of Western friendship. It favored neutrality, provided it could be coupled with continuing close and friendly association with the West, but it would not favor any overt displays of neutralism that might alienate West Germany's Western allies.

These preferences correspond fairly well to the very limited range of opportunities available to West German foreign policy makers in the present international situation. Although qualitatively and structurally in a period of transition, the two great power blocs, led by the United States and the U.S.S.R., respectively, appear to have reached a near stalemate. Neither side can count on a clear and certain shift of power in its favor in the immediate years ahead. More than one-third of the West Germans polled in October, 1963, viewed the outcome of an assumed world war between the two blocs as undecided. At the same time, all the major countries in Europe are committed to one of the two blocs. There is no effective bloc of neutral countries; only Sweden, Finland, Austria, and Switzerland are neutral in military terms, and Yugoslavia is not firmly committed to either side. These countries could not form any effective combination that would offer any positive attractions or opportunities to West Germany.

Under these conditions, some of the determinants of West German foreign policy were likely to be negative: to avoid or delay any decisions that might make matters worse. As long as really attractive positive opportunities were lacking or, like Western European integration, seemed very slow in coming, West German public opinion was most likely to favor a policy of cautious advance, designed to limit West German risks and to increase, quietly and steadily, the extent of West German bargaining power. But what any major political or economic shift, such as a major political crisis or a severe economic depression, would do to this alignment of opinion, no one could foretell.

This, then, was the popular image of the tasks of West German foreign policy. What was the popular image of the leadership, of the makers of that policy? They should be experts, competent to make all necessary changes within the broad limits of the goals outlined. They should be cautious, but determined on essentials; they should be persevering, persistent, and resourceful; they should try every promising approach, but not make any major concessions or compromises at the expense of long-run goals. They did not have to be open or explicit; they should not bother the voters with the burden of decisions; above all, they should be united. If they could also be "crafty" or "foxy," so much the better. "Prudence," "diplomacy," "smartness," and "foxiness" were all considered major traits of former Chancellor Adenauer, during the late 1950's when his popularity was high.[35]

There is less public concern about the constitutional, legal, and administrative details of the way in which foreign policy was supposed to be made. Nevertheless, these arrangements are important, and it is to them that we must now direct our attention.

THE ROLE OF GOVERNMENTAL AND NONGOVERNMENTAL INSTITUTIONS IN THE MAKING OF FOREIGN POLICY

Under the Constitution of the German Federal Republic, foreign policy is the responsibility of the federal government. The ten constituent states of the Republic, and their governments, are bound by federal actions in the realm of foreign policy; if required, they are expected to pass enabling legislation to incorporate into state law commitments undertaken by the federal government toward foreign governments. To a limited extent, the states participate in the formation of foreign policy through the upper house of the federal legislature (*Bundesrat*); this house is composed of representatives of the ten state governments, and each state has from three to five votes, according to the size of its population. This chamber has an absolute veto over all constitutional changes, but only a suspensive veto over ordinary legislation. Prior to the conclusion of treaties affecting the particular interest of one or more states, the state governments have the

[35]*Jahrbuch*, III, 273.

right to make their views known, but these opinions are not binding on the federal government and may formally be ignored by it, though political considerations may induce the federal government to take them into account in deciding a course of action. As under the constitution of the Soviet Union (and unlike our own system) the states have the right to conclude treaties of their own with foreign nations—subject to the approval of the federal Chancellor—when these deal with matters not specifically reserved for federal jurisdiction or with subjects of concurrent jurisdiction not yet pre-empted by the federal government. These, however, are minor matters; in the main, foreign policy is federal in theory and practice.

The key role of the Chancellor

Within the federal government, the federal Chancellor (*Bundeskanzler*) is constitutionally the principal decision maker in the realm of foreign policy. His Cabinet, the federal President, the two chambers of the federal legislature, and the federal constitutional court may, under certain circumstances, share in the decision-making process but, constitutionally, the final source of authority is the Chancellor, who alone has the power and responsibility for determining public policy.

The framers of the Basic Law of 1948—the Constitution of the Federal Republic—deliberately endowed the Chancellor with considerable power in the hope of avoiding the sort of governmental instability that is common in many countries where an all-powerful legislature is divided into many bitterly antagonistic factions. At the same time, they wanted to prevent a recurrence of the sort of irresponsible executive absolutism that had prevailed in Germany before 1918 and in the early 1930's. Designed for the traditional German multiparty system, the Basic Law strives for executive responsibility by providing for a chief of government elected by and responsible to a majority of the popularly elected lower house of the federal legislature. It strives for governmental stability by providing that a Chancellor remain in office until: (*a*) a majority, or at least a plurality, of the lower house agrees on a replacement; or (*b*) a new lower house is elected; or (*c*) the incumbent Chancellor dies, resigns, or is convicted of certain criminal acts. The Chancellor cannot be impeached. Thus, it was hoped by the fathers of the Constitution, neither the disintegration of a coalition nor the opposition of a parliamentary majority unable to agree on a replacement should force the fall of a government. Chancellor government (*Kanzlerregierung*) is intended to make the head of the government less dependent upon the legislature than under a pure parliamentary system, yet more so than under our own presidential form of executive leadership.

In accordance with these principles, the Chancellor alone—and not the entire government—is supposed to determine government policy, see to its execution, and account for it to the legislature. There is no collective responsibility of the entire government. Accordingly, the Chancellor, in effect, appoints and dismisses the members of his Cabinet; his recommendations are binding on the federal President, who has the formal power of appointment and dismissal. In turn, the ministers of the Chancellor's government are solely responsible to him as his advisors and subordinate administrators, and their tenure ends automatically with his.

Constitutionally, neither the President nor the legislature can compel the Chancellor to include anyone in his government or to dismiss any minis-

ter. Chancellor Adenauer successfully maintained this point in 1955, when one of the parties in his coalition broke with him and sought to withdraw its representatives from the government. The ministers, Adenauer insisted, were his agents once they joined the government, and not those of their party. Subsequently, he dropped some Cabinet members on his own because their presence in the government apparently no longer seemed politically advisable to him. Adenauer's actions underlined the fact that a strong Chancellor, who commands a majority in the lower house of the legislature, can afford to defy suggestions concerning the composition and size of his government. On the other hand, a weak Chancellor —that is, one who did not command such a majority, or even a plurality— presumably would have to be far more considerate toward the leaders of parties whose support he sought in connection with the makeup of his Cabinet. In order to gain such support he might be forced to accommodate them, to give ministerial portfolios to representatives of parties whose support he wanted, and perhaps to create new portfolios or appoint ministers without portfolios. He might have to offer important ministries to powerful political leaders who were not necessarily qualified for these posts, but who would bring him the parliamentary support he needed.

Other offices and officials

Individually, the members of the Chancellor's government are supposed to administer the affairs of their ministries in accordance with the general policy determined by their chief. As in the case of the Chancellor himself, the personality, experience, and qualifications of the incumbent play an important part in determining the actual role he plays in the decision-making process, and in the extent to which he relies on subordinate officials.

Chief among the ministries concerned with foreign policy is, of course, the Foreign Office (*Auswärtiges Amt*). It is officially charged with "attending to foreign affairs," and unless the Chancellor makes special exceptions (as in the case of the Minister for Economic Cooperation, in the second Adenauer Government), other ministries may deal with foreign governments and international organizations only with its approval. Jurisdictional conflicts are resolved either by the entire Cabinet or by the Chancellor alone. Other ministries directly or indirectly concerned with foreign policy decisions are those of Defense (*Bundesministerium für Verteidigung*); Finance (*Finanzen*); Economics (*Wirtschaft*); the Ministry for Expellees, Refugees, and Victims of War (*Vetriebene, Flüchtlinge und Kriegsbeschädigte*), especially created to attend to the interests of some twelve million citizens who fled or were expelled from German and East European territories now dominated by the Soviet Union; and the Ministry for All-German Affairs (*Gesamtdeutsche Fragen*), which has special responsibility for matters pertaining to the reunification of divided Germany. Since 1961, the Ministry for Economic Cooperation (*Bundesministerium fuer Wirtschaftliche Zusammenarbeit*), previously responsible for questions pertaining to European economic cooperation, deals exclusively with economic aspects of West German foreign policy toward the developing countries. (European matters are now dealt with by the competent ministries in cooperation with the European agencies at Brussels.)

Collectively, the ministers form the Chancellor's Cabinet and, as such, are supposed to advise him on matters of general policy and to decide on government proposals to be submitted to the legislature. The actual role of the Cabinet and its individual members in decision making would also appear to depend very largely upon the personalities and relative political power of the Chancellor and his ministers. A strong Chancellor, such as Adenauer, could largely dictate policy; a less determined incumbent, like Erhard, depends more upon the approval and support of at least the most powerful of his ministers, and of the parties or factions which they represent.

A relatively recent creation is the Federal Defense Council (*Bundesverteidigungsrat*), a sort of inner cabinet, somewhat similar to the American National Security Council, whose members are selected and appointed by the Chancellor. The membership varies; normally, only select members of the Cabinet are included, but other ministers and important officials may be invited to attend meetings, at the Chancellor's discretion.

Two other agencies of the executive branch of the federal government have, in recent years, played a considerable role in the making of West German foreign policy, largely owing to the intimate relationships existing between their respective chiefs and the incumbent Chancellor. The first of these, the Chancellor's Office (*Bundeskanzleramt*), is formally charged with assisting the Chancellor in his relations with other branches of the government and important nongovernmental agencies, with keeping him informed on political developments at home and abroad, and with preparing for the decisions that the Chancellor may decide to take on the basis of this information. The second, the Press and Information Office of the Federal Government (*Presse und Informationsamt der Bundesregierung*), is supposed to assure close relations between the executive branch and the media of mass communication—both foreign and domestic—to gather and evaluate data on public opinion, and, generally, to interpret the policies, decisions, and actions of the government to the public at home and abroad. In terms of actual as well as potential influence over the foreign policy-making process, leading officials in both these offices are important members of the decision-making elite within the executive branch, the extent of their influence varying with the prevailing relationship between their incumbents and the Chancellor.

The powers of the President

The role of the federal President in the foreign policy-making process is normally insignificant. Although he has the right to nominate a candidate for the Chancellorship to the lower house of the legislature, he must appoint the choice of the majority of the deputies, whether he approves or not. The incumbent Chancellor is supposed to keep the President informed, and consult with him on the policies of his government, but the President, for his part, is constitutionally bound to co-operate loyally with a man who has the support of a majority of the deputies. He must sign such treaties, bills, and decrees as are submitted to him by the Chancellor or his ministers, appoint or dismiss officials on the Chancellor's advice and, in general, exercise his formal powers at the discretion of the chief of government, who bears ultimate responsibility for the actions of the executive branch. Some constitutional commentators would concede the President's limited influence over diplomatic negotiations, but, even here, a strong Chancellor would appear to have the final word, as principal decision maker.

A few constitutional commentators have claimed that the powers of the President, particularly in foreign policy making, might be used more decisively in the hands of a powerful incumbent. Such an interpretation may have led Chancellor Konrad Adenauer to consider exchanging the Chancellorship for the Presidency in 1959. His decision not to become a candidate for the Presidency, and his subsequent efforts to maneuver the popular Minister of Economics, Ludwig Erhard, into running for the office so he could not succeed Adenauer as Chancellor, seemed to indicate that the President has little or no influence on policy making under present circumstances.

The President's role might become more important if the Parliament should be so deeply divided that its members would neither support the incumbent Chancellor nor agree upon a successor. Given the present division of Parliament into two major parties, more or less tightly organized and united, such a development is not likely. Should a multiparty system re-emerge at some future date, as seems unlikely today, and should a deadlock then develop between the incumbent Chancellor and a majority of the deputies, the role of the President might temporarily become more significant.

The powers of Parliament: the Bundestag

Of the two chambers of the federal legislature, the lower house (*Bundestag*) has by far the greater power in most matters, including foreign policy. Treaties that regulate the political relations of the federation, or that relate to matters of federal legislation, can become the law of the land only with its consent. Similarly, the transfer of sovereign rights of the state to international institutions, such as the EEC, require legislative action. Finally, all treaties and other legislation that conflict with the Basic Law require constitutional amendments, which must be approved by two-thirds of the membership of the lower house.

Apart from its legislative functions, the lower house is granted certain other powers which are designed to give the members a voice in the foreign policy-making process. A majority elects a Chancellor and can dismiss him by choosing a successor. The deputies of the lower house provide half the votes in the Federal Assembly (*Bundesversammlung*) which, every five years, chooses a federal President, and which can initiate impeachment proceedings against him before the federal constitutional court.

In the lower house, the deputies have the right to investigate and criticize the actions of the executive in plenary sessions or in committees. They may summon and question members of the government when they choose; the latter, for their part, have the right to demand to be heard by the deputies at any time, providing themselves with potential opportunities to influence important deliberations of the house at decisive moments.

Most of the important contacts between the executive branch and the deputies occur in the sessions of the standing and select committees of the lower house, rather than in plenary sessions. It is here that experts from the various parties examine the actions and requests of the government and question its members thoroughly. The vote in the committee is usually decisive, and committee recommendations are usually approved in subsequent plenary sessions. With respect to foreign policy issues, the key committees are Foreign Affairs (*Auswärtige Angelegenheiten*), Defense (*Verteidigung*), Budget (*Haushalt*), Expellees (*Heimatsvertriebene*), All-Ger-

man Affairs (*Gesamtdeutsche Fragen*), and Border Questions (*Grenzlandfragen*).

The role that the deputies of the lower house may play in West German foreign policy appears to depend primarily on the authority that the Chancellor exercises in the chamber. If he commands a stable majority— or better, two-thirds of the votes—his powers are fairly absolute and his position firm. However, if he lacks such strength, his freedom of action would seem to be more limited; he may be forced to rely on the cooperation of uncertain and demanding allies in order to see his program through the legislature and to prevent the election of a successor.

In the event of constitutional disputes arising out of foreign policy issues, the federal constitutional court may enter the picture. It may be called upon to adjudicate jurisdictional disputes between the federal government and the states or between the executive and the legislative branches of the national government. The court may also be asked to render advisory opinions on the constitutionality of certain pending actions, either upon the joint request of the executive and the legislature, or upon that of the federal President alone. The President has the right to refuse to place his signature on treaties, acts of the legislature, or government decrees pending an advisory opinion from the court. Thus, in 1952, President Theodore Heuss tried to withhold his signature from the treaty providing for the arming of the Federal Republic until the constitutional court had advised him that it did not conflict with the Basic Law, but he finally signed the treaty on Chancellor Adenauer's advice.

To summarize what has been said about the formal role of various governmental institutions in making of foreign policy: foreign affairs are a federal matter; and, within the federal government, the principal decision maker is the Chancellor, while lesser roles are assigned to the ministers, President, legislature, and constitutional court of the Republic. How this formal arrangement actually functions depends primarily on the prevailing relationship between a Chancellor and the lower house of the legislature. A strong Chancellor, who commands a comfortable majority in the lower house, will have a great deal of freedom in the conduct of foreign affairs; a Chancellor who lacks such support is likely to be far more dependent on the cooperation of the legislature and the President.

Experience during the first sixteen years of the Republic's existence indicates that the Chancellor's position vis-à-vis both Parliament and legislature rests largely on his relationship to his party and on that party's strength and cohesion. A future Chancellor might not necessarily be a party man at all—not even a member of the legislature—nonetheless, his power to make decisions would still depend primarily on his ability to gain the support of the majority party or coalition in the legislature. The formal organization of the foreign policy-making process thus becomes a functioning party system, though it does provide the Chancellor with some limited means of governing temporarily without parliamentary support, should the parties fail to produce a stable majority behind him.

The role of the political parties

The Basic Law of the Federal Republic is unique in its specific recognition of the decisive role of political parties in the formulation of national policy. Through their representatives in the executive and legislative branches of the national government, the parties are supposed to act as the responsible agents of the electorate in the conduct of government. The existing electoral law compels all aspirants for seats in the popularly elected lower house to belong to a party and, thus to identify themselves with, and bear responsibility for, its policies and actions. Referenda, plebiscites, and other devices for "direct democracy" which bypasses parties and legislature, have been deliberately omitted from the Constitution; its framers were all too aware of the antidemocratic uses to which such devices had been put in the past by demagogues who appealed to the "popular will" against the "selfish" interests of parties.

Anyone may organize a political party in the Republic, as long as its objectives and organization accord with the democratic principles of the Constitution and do not aim at the overthrow of the present state. In fact, however, the electoral laws have made it almost impossible for any party receiving less than 5 per cent of the electoral votes to gain representation in the national legislature.

Contrary to the apparent expectations of the framers of the Constitution, the traditional German multiparty system has been gradually eliminated, and the two major parties have become the principal representatives of the electorate. These are the Christian Democratic Union (CDU) and the Social Democratic Party (SPD). Between them, these parties received 60 per cent of the votes and 67 per cent of the seats, in the 1949 election; 74 per cent of the votes and 83 per cent of the seats, in 1953; 82 per cent of the votes and 88 per cent of the seats, in 1957; 82 per cent of the votes, and 87 per cent of the seats, in 1961; and 87 per cent of the votes and 90 per cent of the seats, in 1965.

The Christian Democratic Union (*Christlich Demokratische Union*), operating in Bavaria as the Christian Social Union (*Christlich Soziale Union*), CSU, is a departure from the traditional German parties. Instead of following the traditional pattern of parties in Germany and becoming closely identified with some particular ideology, religious group, or economic interest, this Party has managed to attract the support of rather heterogeneous elements among the voters in the name of its "Christian principles." It is moderately conservative in its domestic economic and social program, and has faithfully followed the lead of its first and long-time chairman, Konrad Adenauer, in the realm of foreign policy. Its professed aims have been the reunification of Germany "in peace and freedom"; the peaceful recovery of the German lands presently "administered" by Poland and the Soviet Union; permanent and intimate collaboration with the Western powers; and the economic, military and—ultimately—political integration of the states of Western Europe.

The Social Democratic Party (*Sozialdemokratische Partei Deutschlands*), is more strongly rooted in the past than the CDU, or CSU—both in terms of its objectives and its supporters. The SPD is primarily a workers' party, as it was before the advent of Hitler and its prohibition in 1933, and many of its supporters have been adherents for many decades. Heretofore far more homogeneous in both membership and electorate than the CDU, or CSU, the SPD has lately made strenuous efforts to broaden its support among the voters. Most West Germans appear unwilling to cast their ballots for a "workers' party," however, and even many manual workers no longer want to be considered proletarians. Seeking to become a progressive "peoples'

party" similar to the Scandinavian labor parties, the SPD has thrown overboard most of its traditional Marxist principles. In its domestic program, the party has gone far toward accepting the social and economic tenets of the Christian Democrats, while in foreign affairs it has abandoned its former neutralist inclinations and embraced rearmament and NATO membership. These efforts have had only limited effect in changing the image of the SPD among the general electorate. In the September, 1965, elections, the SPD still remained limited to about 40 per cent of the national vote.

None of the minor parties represented in the national legislature has played a very significant role in matters of foreign policy. The largest, the Free Democratic Party (*Freie Demokratische Partei*), aspires to hold the balance of power between the two major parties. With almost 13 per cent of the national vote in 1961 and 9.5 per cent in 1965, it has oscillated between opposing and supporting the CDU, but its range of policy choices remains limited by its dependence on many of the same sources of social, business, and financial support.

Until 1967 extremist parties have been conspicuous by their absence; the insignificant Communist Party had no representation in the national legislature even before it was outlawed in 1956; a small neo-Nazi party was also banned by the constitutional court; other extremist parties—such as the neo-Nazi National Democratic Party, which polled only 2 per cent of the national vote in 1965—have been singularly unsuccessful in gaining support among the electorate.

The formulation of West German foreign policy has, thus, been primarily in the hands of the two major parties. As the governing party since the establishment of the Federal Republic in

1949, the CDU has borne the prime responsibility for initiating and executing foreign policy decisions. The SPD has been compelled to play the role of a permanent opposition, endeavoring, with mixed success, to influence foreign policy through criticism of the government, through attempts to amend government bills in the national legislature, and through efforts to mobilize public opinion to compel the government to modify its position. During much of the 1950's, both parties sought, between elections, to establish a clear distinction in the public mind between their respective policies, in order to present the electorate with a decisive choice at election time. In the early 1960's, however, these distinctions became increasingly blurred. In any case, in foreign affairs, the exigencies of the situation in which the Federal Republic has found itself have made it difficult for the Social Democratic opposition to formulate convincing alternative proposals for the conduct of West German foreign policy.

The role of the interest groups

The Constitution grants all West Germans the right to form organizations to represent their particular political, economic, or religious interests, as long as such groups are not directed against "the principle of international understanding." As in the United States, there exist in the Federal Republic numerous associations that, in one way or another, seek to influence the conduct of foreign affairs in accordance with their perceived interests. However, West German interest groups are more inclusive, more tightly organized, and occupy a more privileged position in public life than do their counterparts in this country. On the other hand, the West German public tends to be more critical and suspicious of the influence of such interest groups than the Americans.

Economic and political interests are organized into large national organizations (*Spitzenverbände*), all of which are ostensibly nonpartisan, but by no means nonpolitical. Religious interests are primarily represented by the two major churches, the Roman Catholic and the Protestant, and their affiliated lay organizations.

In general, the influence of interest groups on the conduct of foreign affairs has increased in direct proportion to the gradual restoration of West German sovereignty and the recovery of independence of action by the government of the Federal Republic. Most of them have endeavored to exercise their influence over national policy through the political parties and, particularly, through party leaders in the executive and legislative branches of the federal government.

Economic interest groups in the Federal Republic fall roughly into two major categories: (*a*) employers' organizations; and (*b*) organizations representing employees, independent farmers, independent craftsmen, and the professions. The employers' groups have the greater financial resources, but the others have a greater voting strength to offer to political leaders and parties. Reliable figures on financial support are lacking, but some of the potential voting power of different economic interests may be apparent from the 1955 percentage figures of gainfully occupied persons and their dependents, given earlier in this chapter, under the heading "Ideologies and classes."

German employers are organized both regionally and by economic sectors. Every employer must belong to one of the eighty-one regional Chambers of Industry and Commerce, which are represented nationally by the Association of German Chambers of Industry and Commerce (*Deutscher Industrie-und Handelstag*), perhaps the most powerful of the employer groups. Next in importance is the Association of German Industry (*Bundesverband der deutschen Industrie*), which represents the interests of the thirty-eight branches of German industry. The Coordinating Committee of German Trade and Industry (*Gemeinschaftsausschuss der deutschen gewerblichen Wirtschaft*) includes all major employer groups and acts as a coordinating agency among the component interest groups. Other important employer interest groups concerned with foreign affairs are the Federal Association of Private Banking (*Bundesverband des privaten Bankgewerbes*), the Association of German Wholesalers and Exporters (*Gesamtverband des deutschen Gross- und Aussenhandels*), the Central Organization of German Retailers (*Hauptgemeinschaft des deutschen Einzelhandels*), the German Shipowners Association (*Verband der deutschen Reeder*), the German Section of the International Chamber of Commerce (*Deutsche Gruppe der internationalen Handelskammer*), and the Committee for Foreign Trade of German Business (*Arbeitsgemeinschaft Aussenhandel der deutschen Wirtschaft*). In addition to these permanent national organizations, various business groups frequently form temporary alliances for special ends, such as export drives or tariff reform.

Among employee groups, by far the largest and most important is the German Confederation of Trade Unions (*Deutscher Gewerkschaftsbund*). With 6.5 million members as of 1964, it not only includes all wage earners' unions, but it is also the largest organization of salaried employees and civil servants. About 41 per cent of all wage earners, 13 per cent of all salaried employees,

and 46 per cent of all civil servants in the Federal Republic belong to the Confederation. Seventy-nine per cent of the members of the Confederation are wage earners (an additional 12 per cent are salaried employees, and 9 per cent more are civil servants), and the large industrial enterprises are the most thoroughly organized and represented within the Confederation. IG Metall, the largest industrial union, contributes almost one-third of the total membership of the Confederation. Two more specialized white-collar organizations also have prospered. The German Employees Union (*Deutsche Angestelltengewerkschaft*), with some 475,000 members (as of 1964), includes about 8 per cent of all salaried employees; and the German Federation of Civil Servants (*Deutscher Beamtenbund*) with some 692,000 members (in 1964), represents about 53 per cent of all civil servants. Among them, the three groups include about 41 per cent of the wage earners, 21 per cent of the salaried employees, and a staggering 99 per cent of the civil servants in the Republic. Individually or collectively, these organizations endeavor to influence the foreign policy-making process whenever they consider their special interests to be involved.[36]

The chief farm organization is the League of German Farmers (*Deutscher Bauernverband*), which represents more than three-quarters of the country's 1.8 million independent farmers. Despite the shrinking of the agricultural sector since 1950, West German farm organizations still have considerable political influence. This influence has been effectively directed toward specific demands, such as agricultural subsidies, prices of pro-

[36] Figures from the *Statistisches Jahrbuch fuer die Bundesrepublik Deutschland*, 1965, p. 153; and *Jahrbuch*, III, 4.

duce and, especially, the accommodation of West German agricultural prices within the framework of the European Economic Community. As a result, German farming remained remarkably well protected through the mid-1960's. Under a 1966 European agricultural agreement, French, Italian, and Dutch agricultural products are to be admitted more freely to the West German market from 1967 onward, but West German agriculture is likely to continue to be effectively compensated for its high costs through governmental subsidies.

The League of German Artisans (*Zentralverband des deutschen Handwerks*), which has 864,000 members, includes practically all the independent craftsmen in the nation. Its interest in foreign affairs appears to be limited primarily to the protection of its members against cheaper imports and the promotion of the export of their products.

Organizations concerned with such matters as migration, trade, investment, tourism, and banking are obviously interested in asserting influence in the foreign policy-making process. Other groups, too, may take a strong interest when their particular economic sector is thought to be affected, as in the case of tariffs, international marketing arrangements, and wage-price agreements. Special issues may lead to temporary alliances between groups that may disagree on other subjects. Farm and industry groups may jointly seek tariff protection; employer and employee organizations within particular industries may temporarily unite, to fight for or against proposed international agreements that affect them; or export industries may ally themselves to gain government support for trade expansion.

Only a few of the special interest groups play any significant role in the Federal Republic. The most important of these are the organizations of expellees—German citizens and ethnic Germans who fled or were expelled from German lands east of the Oder-Neisse line which are presently administered, under the Potsdam Agreement of 1945, by Poland and the Soviet Union, and from other parts of Eastern and Southeastern Europe. About 9.3 million of these expellees live in the Federal Republic today, constituting about 16 per cent of the total population, and approximately half of them are former residents of Silesia and the Sudetenland. Only a fraction of the expellees are organized into the various groups that claim to defend their common interests. The most important of these are the League of Expelled Germans(*Zentralverband Vertriebener Deutscher*) and the League of Regional Groups (*Verband der Landsmannschaften*), with its major affiliates of Silesians (*Landsmannschaft Schlesian*) and Sudeten Germans (*Sudetendeutsche Landsmannschaft*). There are also more than 4 milion refugees from the Russian zone of Germany in the Federal Republic (about 7.5 per cent of the population) but, although there are numerous organizations that would like to represent their interests, few of the refugees belong to them. Together, expellees and refugees number more than 13 million persons, almost one-quarter of the population, but most of them appear to have found adequate representation of their interests within the major political parties.

Mention should also be made of close to 1,200 veterans' organizations, though few, if any, of them appear at this time to exercise any major influence in German politics. The largest, and potentially the most influential, is the League of German Soldiers (*Verband deutscher Soldaten*), primarily an organization of present and former professional soldiers. Among its stated objectives are "loyalty to an undivided fatherland," the rehabilitation of all "defamed" former soldiers, and the liberation of still-imprisoned soldiers convicted of war crimes. The pre-Hitler, right-wing veterans' organization, Steel Helmet (*Stahlhelm*), is a much smaller association with apparently little influence. The same is true of the Air Force Circle (*Luftwaffenring*), which is composed of former members of the German air force.

According to the 1961 census, 51.1 per cent of the population of the Federal Republic professed the Protestant religion and 44.1 per cent, the Roman Catholic religion, as compared with 60.6 and 33.3 per cent, respectively, in prewar Germany. In terms of relative strength, thus, the potential influence of the Roman Catholic Church in national affairs has increased considerably. However, no more than 11 million West Germans—about half of those professing the Roman Catholic faith—are thought to be active members of their church; in the case of the Protestants, the proportion is about one-eighth. Of the two major churches, the Roman Catholic is probably the more politically active and influential.

The supreme organ of the Roman Catholic Church, the annual meeting of the hierarchy at the town of Fulda (*Fuldaer Bischofskonferenz*), also claims jurisdiction in the Russian-controlled German Democratic Republic. Nonetheless, the influence of the Church is largely restricted to the Federal Republic, for less than 20 per cent of the Germans living in East Germany are Roman Catholics, and their government has greatly restricted contacts between the West German hierarchy and the East German Roman Catholics. In the Federal Republic, the Church maintains a liaison office at the capital to represent its interests. With the encouragement of the hierarchy, the members of numerous lay groups affiliated with the Church endeavor to translate Catholic interests into Catholic action by playing an active role in public life. Thus, a 1958 survey found that almost two-thirds of the Roman Catholics, but only about half the Protestants, expressed approval of one of the two major parties. In addition, the Catholics appeared to be more concentrated than Protestants: 47 per cent of the Catholics expressed a preference for the CDU, and only 15 per cent approved of the SPD, while almost equal proportions of Protestants (26 and 28 per cent, respectively) endorsed both parties.[37]

The German Evangelical Church (*Evangelische Kirche in Deutschland*), EKD, is a union of German Protestant Churches in both the Federal Republic and the Democratic Republic. Since over 80 per cent of the Germans living under communist rule are Protestants and their church still exercises considerable influence over them, the EKD and its member churches have considerably stronger ties to, and interest in, the population of the Democratic Republic than has the Roman Catholic Church. The Synod, Council, and Conference of the Evangelical Church used to be recognized representatives of the Protestants in both parts of the divided country, but in recent years the Protestants have found it increasingly difficult to maintain the religious unity of Germany. The Evangelical clergy in East Germany has been hard-pressed by the communist government. Through its Office for Foreign Affairs (*Kirchliches Aussenamt*), the church maintains relations with other churches in both communist and non-communist countries.

The orthodox Lutherans among the

[37]DIVO, *op. cit.*, II, 56.

German Protestants have traditionally shunned political action on behalf of their church. Today, too, they exert only indirect influence in political affairs through their tacit support of the dominant liberal leadership of the Evangelical Church. The leaders of this liberal wing, although numerically in the minority, occupy most of the positions in the EKD and, in this capacity, endeavor to exercise some influence in both the Federal Republic and the Democratic Republic. In the Democratic Republic, this has involved the church in many bitter clashes with the communist rulers; in the Federal Republic, its participation in public life is neither as extensive nor as intensive as that of the Roman Catholic Church. Although individual church leaders occasionally speak out on public issues, organized Protestant groups have played a comparatively small role in the political process. In late 1965, however, in the face of the government's inaction on the questions of Germany's eastern frontiers and of her present and future relationship toward her Eastern European neighbors, the German Evangelical Church took a public stand in a widely discussed memorandum, and thus brought that question back into the political arena of the Federal Republic.

THE SYSTEM IN OPERATION: THE SUBSTANCE OF FOREIGN POLICY

The actual operation of West German foreign policy making is heavily influenced by three factors: the aims of West German policy makers; the pressure of various interest groups; and, to a lesser extent, the involvement of the West German economy with the United States, first through various forms of United States aid, during the late 1940's and early 1950's, and, later, through private business relations. The

intra-German factors will be discussed below, but the West German stake in its political and economic relations with the United States is so substantial that we must say something about its magnitude at the outset.

The economic influence of the United States

To indicate even the order of magnitude of the American dollar flow into the Federal Republic and West Berlin during the immediate postwar decade is not an easy task. The aid has been given in a large variety of ways, under a bewildering succession of alphabetical agencies: GARIOA; ECA; MSA; FOA; and others. Although these accounted publicly for their operations, data for other channels of dollars into the West German economy have not been so readily available. In West Germany, as in some other countries, many of these extraordinary dollar receipts, as a report of the U.N. Economic Commission for Europe points out, ". . . belong to the twilight zone of quasi-strategic information: at best, only general orders of magnitude are known."[38]

What is this general order of magnitude? The German Federal Ministry for Economic Cooperation acknowledged, in 1956, that West Germany had received almost $10 billion up to June 30, 1956, presumably for a period since early 1948.[39] Of the exact total, $9,935 million, $6,355 million was listed as aid to the Federal Republic in general, and $3,580 million

[38]United Nations, Department of Economic Affairs, Economic Commission for Europe, *Economic Survey of Europe in 1953* (Geneva, 1954), pp. 19–20.

[39]Bundesministerium für wirtschaftliche Zusammenarbeit, *Der europäische Wirtschaftsrat—OEEC: Handbuch, 1956* (Godesberg: Verlag für Publizistik), p. 70.

as aid to West Berlin.[40] Even if one assumes that this total includes all dollar aid since 1946, one would arrive at an average of $1 billion per year, approximately $20 per year for every German man, woman, and child.

The value of these dollars to the West German economy was greatly increased by the manner in which they were employed and by the efficient response of West German management and labor. Through counterpart funds and other devices, a considerable part was used to increase capital investment, and thus the technological equipment of West German industry, without any of the sacrifices that consumers would have otherwise had to make for an investment program of this magnitude. The result was an increase in both capital equipment and consumer goods. An official West German publication sums it up thus:

To use a medical term, it was "dollar therapy" and the tonic effect of an American blood transfusion. . . . Every Marshall Plan dollar spent in Germany has resulted in $10 to $20 worth of goods produced and services rendered.[41]

The Federal Republic's economy remains fundamentally dependent on the United States. Although the increasing consolidation and growth of the German economy has translated this dependence from one-sided aid to a mutual interplay, West Germany's need for warm relations with the United States has remained greater than the United States' need for even minimal good relations with West Germany. West German exports, as well as domestic goods, continued to depend in good part on American defense installations, and American tax and tariff

policies, as well as on the continuing confidence of American investors. A decline of the American stock market, such as that of Blue Monday, May 28, 1962, has an immediate effect on the economy of the Federal Republic. American taxes on the investments of its nationals abroad, or fears among American and European investors of military or political instability in West Germany could alter the country's prosperity and balance of payments very rapidly, indeed.[42]

The economic influence of the United States is heavily reinforced by psychological, social, and military considerations that make American friendship appear to be the most important basis of what security the makers of West German foreign policy can hope for in this uncertain world. The results of this relationship have been conspicuous. In almost every major West German foreign policy decision, the government of the United States has been an invisible—and sometimes not so invisible—partner.

Nevertheless, there has been a growing autonomous component in West German foreign policy. The interplay of West German aims and United States influence with the various West German domestic interests can be seen best by glancing briefly at a few actual cases. The questions of West German membership in the European Coal and Steel Community, of West German rearmament, of West Germany's role in the European Economic Community, and of negotiations with the Soviet Union about German reunification— are the cases in which we shall try to watch the making of West German foreign policy.

[40]*Ibid.* The latter sum may have included orders placed in West Berlin for work done elsewhere in the Federal Republic.

[41]*Germany Reports*, 1953, pp. 239–43.

[42]Cf. also Karl W. Deutsch, "The German Federal Republic," in *Modern Political Systems: Europe*, ed. Roy Macridis and Robert E. Ward. (Englewood Cliffs N.J.: Prentice-Hall, Inc., 1963), pp. 301–2.

Toward the recovery of German influence

A primary objective of West Germany's foreign policy, since the creation of the Federal Republic in 1949, has been the recovery of West German influence in international affairs. There have been differences among the elite and among the public at large over the means to be employed, but there is solid unanimity about the general objective. The man primarily responsible for the conduct of West German foreign policy from 1949 to 1963, Chancellor Konrad Adenauer, was singularly successful in his efforts to regain independence of action in the conduct of foreign policy without losing the political, military, and economic support of the West, particularly the United States. Adenauer's policy was to establish West Germany as the leading power and the senior partner of the United States on the European continent, by means of adroit and subtle moves which gained for the Federal Republic full sovereignty and a leading position within the Western alliance in the course of a few years. In the face of frequently bitter opposition at home, particularly from the Social Democratic leadership, and often without the specific support of public opinion, he gained his ends through close collaboration with the Western powers, particularly the United States. Adenauer gambled, successfully, that temporary concessions would eventually lead to major gains for West German foreign policy, and that the voters would sustain him at election time. He owed his success to a combination of factors: his unrivalled position as the leader of the governing political group; his remarkable prestige, both inside and outside West Germany; his ability to enlist the support of crucial West German leaders for specific foreign policy moves, in the face of public opposition or indifference; his influence among leading policy makers in Western countries; and last, but not least, the exigencies of the international situation. In general, Adenauer exploited, to the fullest, his great formal and informal powers as Chancellor and as leader of the largest West German party—if necessary, in the face of widespread public opposition at home and abroad—in order to gain his ends in foreign affairs.

The European Coal and Steel Community Treaty. The first step toward the recovery of West German sovereignty and liberation from allied controls, after the creation of the Federal Republic, was taken with the creation of the European Coal and Steel Community (ECSC), popularly known as the Schuman Plan. Under the Occupation Statute of 1949, the new West German state gained only limited independence from control over its affairs by the three Western occupation powers—the United States, Great Britain, and France. A tripartite Allied High Commission was established, endowed with broad powers designed to assure that the Federal Republic would conform to Western plans for a democratic and demilitarized Germany and that it would honor the political and economic obligations it had undertaken in return for allied agreement to the establishment of the new state. The Allied High Commission controlled the organization and operation of German business, endeavoring to prevent its reconcentration in cartels and trusts, and diverting a considerable share of the production of the Ruhr's coal to foreign countries who had been victims of German aggression. The Commission regulated political and economic relations between the new state and foreign countries, and, for all practical purposes, represented the interests of the Federal Republic and its citizens abroad.

The new West German government, a coalition led by Adenauer, immediately sought ways and means of gaining freedom from allied supervision. These efforts were helped immeasurably by the rapid economic recovery of the new German state and by the intensification of the conflict between the Western allies and the Soviet Union. The failure to achieve agreement with the Soviet Union on the reunification of Germany, and the belief that Russia might attack Western Europe through the territory of the Federal Republic, led the Western occupation powers to yield to Adenauer's demands for complete sovereignty. Even before the outbreak of the Korean conflict in July, 1950, Western policy toward West Germany had begun to change. Instead of continuing to treat the Federal Republic as a defeated enemy, the West began to seek its inclusion in the Western alliance as a major bulwark against Russian aggression. These developments played directly into the hands of the leaders of the Federal Republic, who offered intimate collaboration to the Western powers in return for independence and West German equality in the councils of the Western alliance. Their first opportunity to move toward their objective came almost as soon as the new state had come into being, in May, 1950, when French Minister Robert Schuman called for the pooling of French and German coal and steel production in an economic union which he invited other interested European states to join.

The French Foreign Minister made his proposal for a variety of political, economic, and military reasons, including the desire to prevent the restoration of an independent West German power on the continent, one that might once more become a threat to French security. Conscious of the rapid recovery of German power, Schuman sought to make a virtue of apparent necessity by proposing a close organic bond between the Federal Republic, France, and other states of Western and Eastern Europe which, he hoped, would permit resurgent West German power to benefit, rather than threaten, the anti-communist nations of Europe. Schuman advertised his proposal as the first step toward the economic and political unification of Europe, which, he claimed, would put an end to past Franco-German conflicts and prove advantageous to all participating states.

Chancellor Adenauer immediately hailed Schuman's proposal as "epoch-making" and called for its speedy implementation in the form of a treaty. However, the spokesmen of the Federal Republic let it be known that their country would join the proposed community only if all existing restrictions on the Republic's sovereignty, imposed by the Occupation Powers, were removed. The Occupation Statute of 1949, thus, was gradually revised in the course of the negotiations leading to the signing of the ECSC treaty in April, 1951. The Federal Republic was given partial control over its foreign relations, and some of the most severe allied controls over its domestic affairs were gradually dropped. In January, 1952, the Bundestag approved the ECSC treaty by a vote of 232 to 143.

Bundestag approval of the ECSC treaty was not due to overwhelming public support. The "attentive public" in favor of the proposed coal and steel community declined steadily during negotiations, and the opposition to it increased. The largest number of West Germans appear to have become increasingly indifferent toward the issue, however, leaving the final decision to the makers of foreign policy.

West German armament as an instrument of foreign policy. On the morning of May 9, 1955, the black, red, and gold flag of the German Federal Republic rose at the Supreme Headquarters, Allied Powers Europe (SHAPE), while the band played the old German national anthem, *Deutschland, Deutschland über alles, über alles in der Welt.* It signified the admission of a free and sovereign West German state to NATO—almost ten years to the day since its new allies had dictated armistice terms to a vanquished state. After almost six years of determined efforts to throw off Western allied controls over German affairs, Chancellor Adenauer and his associates appeared at last to have obtained their goal. In exchange for the promise of a German military contribution to the defense of Western Europe, they had gained for the Federal Republic "the full authority of a sovereign state over its internal and external affairs," a national military establishment, a major voice in the councils of the Western powers, assurances of Western military and political support against the Soviet Union, and, finally, Western recognition of the Bonn government as "the only German Government . . . entitled to speak . . . as the representative of the [entire] German people in international affairs."[43]

As in the case of ECSC, the negotiations leading to the abolition of Western controls and the recognition

of the Federal Republic as a sovereign and equal member of NATO demonstrated the far-reaching and generally uncontested independence of West German foreign policy decision makers from the influence of domestic public opinion. The price that the Adenauer government agreed to pay for sovereignty and NATO membership was the setting up of a national military establishment, a decision repeatedly opposed, during the period of negotiations, by more Germans than supported it.

Adenauer and his closest associates sought to achieve their objective—as in the case of the ECSC—in the name of European integration. In December, 1949, Adenauer launched a trial balloon by suggesting that the West Germans should contribute to the defense of Europe in a European army. Apparently anticipating that the West would soon demand a West German contribution to European defense, and basing this prediction on formal and informal suggestions from Western political and military leaders, he maintained his position in the following months despite violent opposition both in the Federal Republic and abroad. Adenauer sought to impress Western leaders with the value of the Federal Republic as an ally and to prove to them that it might play a crucial role in a future conflict between the Soviet Union and the NATO powers. He claimed that the industrial and demographic resources of the Federal Republic might prove decisive in a future war; and he stressed the danger of large-scale Russian troop concentrations in central Germany and of the growing power of the People's Police of the communist-dominated German Democratic Republic, suggesting that, short of a military contribution from the Federal Republic, the Western powers lacked the forces to repel an attack

[43]See United States Senate, *Protocol on the Termination of the Occupation Regime in the Federal Republic of Germany and Protocol to the North Atlantic Treaty on the Accession of the Federal Republic of Germany,* 83d Congress, 2d Session, Executives L and M (Washington, D.C.: Government Printing Office, 1954).

from the East. For political as well as military reasons, Adenauer maintained, the Western powers needed the loyal support of the people of the German Federal Republic; he offered it in exchange for an end to allied controls and the termination of existing limitations on the sovereignty of the Federal Republic.

To gain his objective, Adenauer was willing to risk Russian threats against the Federal Republic and the possibility that the reunification of Germany might be deferred indefinitely; as in the case of ECSC, he was prepared to sacrifice *potential* sovereign rights in return for the surrender of *actual* sovereign powers by other nations participating in the creation of a European defense community. The same ideological motives that influenced the CDU, under Adenauer's leadership, to support the Schuman Plan of May, 1950, also led it to support concurrent proposals for the creation of a European army, even though every one of ten opinion polls, between 1950 and 1954, showed more opponents than supporters for the plan.

However, political considerations were every bit as important. Membership in a European integration scheme held out, for a West German state both wealthier and more populous than any other continental state, the prospect not only of equality but of potential leadership of the democratic nations of continental Europe. Instead of remaining merely a rump German state, facing the prospect of indefinite occupation and control by foreign powers, the Federal Republic might become "first among equals," playing a leading role in international affairs as the leader of the continental nations, particularly in relation to the United States and the Soviet Union, the two superpowers of the world. Finally, such a role for Germany in a

European military union promised to make it less dependent on foreign powers and to give its leaders a greater voice in matters affecting the defense of the Federal Republic against attack from the East. To gain these ends, Adenauer was prepared to defy popular opposition to German rearmament. Sovereignty and equality for the Federal Republic, through European integration, were to him worth the price of a West German military contribution, as Adenauer's official biographer was to note.[44]

Adenauer's arguments for a German military contribution to the defense of Western Europe against communist attack seemed substantiated by the North Korean attack on South Korea in July, 1950. Particularly in the United States, government, military and political leaders—some of whom had favored a German military contribution, at least since 1949—reportedly interpreted the unexpected invasion as a clear warning that either the Soviet Union herself, or her East German satellite, might invade the Federal Republic, too. Western allied forces in Germany, never very strong, and further weakened by the diversion of military resources to Korea, appeared inadequate to meet the threat. Simultaneously, the French government informed the United States that it was not interested in an allied strategy that depended primarily on American atomic weapons, but wanted Western Europe to be defended by ground forces, as far east as possible.

While the United States sought desperately to stem the North Korean sweep down the peninsula, Chancellor

[44]See Paul Weymar, *Konrad Adenauer: Die autorisierte Biographie* (München: Kindler, 1955), pp. 500, 557. See also Fritz René Allemann, *Bonn ist nicht Weimar* (Köln-Berlin: Kiepenheuer and Witsch, 1956), pp. 187–212.

Adenauer pointed with increasing emphasis to the exposed situation of his country, and of Western Europe in general. In August, 1950, he suggested to the Western allies the formation of a "special force of German volunteers" of the same size and strength as the People's Police in the Russian Zone of Germany—estimated at 50,000 to 80,000 trained soldiers. He coupled this appeal with the renewed suggestion that the Federal Republic might make a sizeable contribution to a European army in return for an end to allied controls and complete equality within a defense arrangement. Simultaneously, Adenauer appointed a former general to head a new office in the federal government that was to lay plans for such a West German military contribution.

The United States government, responding to the urgings of its own military leaders, replied to Adenauer's proposals by openly calling for the use of West German productive resources and military manpower for the defense of Western Europe. Secretary of State Dean Acheson asked the British and French to agree to the inclusion of about ten German divisions in the NATO forces in Europe. But, in the face of French opposition to the creation of an independent German army, the three Western governments agreed that the West German military contribution demanded "by democratic leaders in Germany" should become part of an integrated European army.

Urged on by the United States, the governments of the Federal Republic of Germany, France, Italy, Belgium, the Netherlands, and Luxembourg hammered out a scheme for a European Defense Community (EDC) that would more or less parallel the pattern agreed upon for the Coal and Steel Community. French negotiators, led by Adenauer's friend, Foreign Minister Robert Schuman, sought to limit West German influence in the proposed military arrangement, but the representatives of the Federal Republic demanded complete equality and the termination of allied controls over West German affairs. The West Germans were aided, not only by strong United States support but, paradoxically, by popular opposition to rearmament in West Germany itself. Pointing to gains for the opposition Social Democrats—strongly opposed to the scheme—in various local elections, Adenauer extracted major allied political concessions for the more "cooperative" West German leaders.

When the EDC treaty was finally signed, in May, 1952, it provided for the creation of twelve German divisions, an air force, and a small navy, which were to become major components of a European military establishment. True, the German Federal Republic was not yet admitted to NATO, but Chancellor Adenauer had no doubts that membership would follow as soon as the German defense contribution had begun to take concrete form. Simultaneously with the signing of the EDC treaty, the Federal Republic concluded a Contractual Agreement with the three Western occupation powers which was to replace the Occupation Statute of 1949. In effect, this agreement terminated the occupation and put an end to practically all allied controls. However, Western forces, remaining in Germany as "allies," retained the right to intervene in case the democratic order in the Federal Republic should be threatened either from within or without.

In May, 1953, the Bundestag approved the two agreements by a majority of 59 votes, a considerably smaller margin of victory than Adenauer's policies had achieved for the

ECSC, only a few months earlier. The treaties became the major issues in the parliamentary election which followed ratification. The Christian Democratic Union, supported only diffidently by leaders of the smaller parties in the Adenauer coalition, claimed a major political victory for Germany. The opposition came largely from a peculiar alignment of militarists, pacifists, nationalists, and neutralists who feared that military alignment with the West would prevent any Russian agreement to the reunification of Germany. The Social Democratic and trade union leaders, this time united, claimed that rearmament would restore the antidemocratic and bellicose German military leadership of the past and perpetuate the division of Germany. The Protestants were divided. Important members—like the Social Democratic leaders who were particularly sensitive to the needs of their silent constituents living under Soviet control in central and East Germany— claimed that membership in EDC would constitute a "betrayal" of their "oppressed brethren." The old military elite was also divided into proponents and opponents of EDC. Some supported Adenauer's claim that the political and military gains for Germany outweighed whatever disadvantages the agreements might include. Others maintained that the limitations imposed on a new West German military establishment were unacceptable, and asked that rearmament be deferred until political conditions and popular opinion had become more favorable.[45] Strenuous communist efforts, directed from East Germany, to draw the various opposition groups into a united "patriotic" front proved unsuccessful.

[45]See, for example, excerpts from a memorandum by former Fleet Admiral Heinrich Gerlach, reprinted in *Der Spiegel*, April 3, 1957, p. 16.

Despite widespread popular opposition to rearmament, the promised restoration of German sovereignty and the gains in Germany's international position impressed many voters. Adenauer won a resounding personal victory in the election of 1953. His prestige and reputation as an effective representative of German interests gave the Christian Democrats an absolute majority in the Bundestag, for the first time; the ruling coalition now commanded the two-thirds majority required for the constitutional changes which rearmament might require. Adenauer's policy of German political recovery in international affairs through European integration was dealt a setback in August, 1954, however, when the French Chamber of Deputies rejected the EDC treaty and thus defeated the scheme. Following this defeat, interestingly enough, only 37 per cent of the respondents in a West German poll expressed regret for the failure of the project.

The German Chancellor immediately demanded complete sovereignty for the Federal Republic, maintaining that it had fulfilled its part of the bargain and was not to blame for the failure of the armament scheme. However, the British and American governments insisted that a West German military contribution, agreed to by the French, remained the *sine qua non* of political sovereignty. On British initiative, representatives of the United States, Britain, Canada, and the six continental countries that had signed the EDC treaty, formulated a hasty substitute. It provided for the creation of a national West German military establishment, and the admission of the Federal Republic to NATO as a sovereign and equal partner, subject only to certain limitations of its future military power and the retention of a few formal rights by the former Occupation Powers, pertaining to West Berlin and German reunification. By May, 1955, all the governments concerned had ratified these Paris Agreements. A major goal of Adenauer's foreign policy since 1949 had been achieved, though not exactly in the manner the Chancellor had intended. The immediate political gains for the Federal Republic were even greater than under the proposed EDC arrangement; however, many of the West German proponents of European integration paid the price only reluctantly. The immediate gains of sovereignty, NATO membership, and a national military establishment did not appear to them to be worth the sacrifice of the European army scheme and its apparent promise of German leadership of a European political union.

Originally NATO was promised 500,000 troops by 1957, but the projected pace was subsequently slowed, so that only about 400,000 West German troops were under arms by early 1966. The percentage of West German national income spent for defense purposes, however, climbed from about 4 per cent, during most of the 1950's to about 7 per cent, in the early 1960's, close to that of France and Britain but less than the roughly 11 to 12 per cent spent by the United States in 1965–'66 and the perhaps still higher level of the Soviet Union.

Efforts toward further integration: the European Economic Community

The movement for the progressive integration of the six countries which were partners in the Coal and Steel Community did not come to an end with the defeat of the European Defense Community. Its protagonists—particularly, Belgium's Foreign Minister, Paul Henri Spaak, and Chancellor Adenauer—were too deeply convinced of the need for unity, and too resolute-

ly determined to achieve it, to consider the EDC's failure as more than a temporary setback. For West Germany, it marked the end of one approach to European unity, but also—subject only to certain limitations on its rearmament and the few formal rights reserved by the former Occupation Powers—it marked the country's return into the community of politically equal nations of the Western alliance. It also meant an increasing concentration on Bonn's most effective strategy, the pursuit of European integration through the use of Germany's economic strength.

In late 1954, the Common Assembly of the ECSC called for a special committee to study ways of enlarging the common market created by the Coal and Steel treaty. The Conference of Foreign Ministers, at Messina, in June, 1955, then set up an Intergovernmental Conference at Brussels to prepare the creation of a customs union between the six countries, as well as to establish a joint organization for the utilization of atomic energy. When the Brussels conference met, in 1955–'56, following the unsuccessful EDC venture of 1954, supranationalism was clearly in disrepute. Accordingly, Dr. Adenauer did not again advocate his proposals for fuller integration, but stressed the provisional character of the projects under consideration, which he viewed as stages in the working out of full European integration. Real power, he suggested, should remain with the individual governments, and the powers of "supranational technocrats" should be clearly delimited.[46]

The treaty establishing the European Economic Community (EEC) and the European Atomic Energy Commission (Euratom) was signed in Rome, on

[46]Wilhelm Grewe, *Deutsche Aussenpolitik der Nachkriegszeit* (Stuttgart: Deutsche Verlagsanstalt, 1960), p. 104.

March 25, 1957. It provided for the progressive abolition of customs duties, quantitative restrictions, and similar barriers to trade, and for the establishment of a common external tariff. This was to take place in three stages, over twelve to fifteen years, and to be completed in 1969–1972. By then, the six countries were to have achieved a customs union, with free movement of goods, capital, and labor within the union and with a single common tariff on the goods of all other countries. In regard to institutions, the treaty followed the example of the ECSC and provided for executive, parliamentary, judicial, and intergovernmental organs. The powers of the executive bodies were more limited, however, than those of the High Authority of the ECSC, and lacked the supranational character of the latter.

Although almost two years had elapsed since the original decision to establish the EEC was taken at the Messina conference, the negotiations were spurred by the determination of its promoters to have the treaty signed and ratified before the elections for the German Bundestag in September, 1957, and, if possible, while the Mollet government was still in office in France. The West German negotiators were bound by a general directive from Chancellor Adenauer to consider the political importance of the treaty and, particularly, the adherence of France, as of overriding concern. They appeared, therefore, much less determined on specific economic matters than might have been assumed from remarks made by other West German leaders, especially by Herr Ludwig Erhard, their Minister of Economics. Adenauer's policy led to a number of concessions to France in regard to agriculture, some relatively high tariffs, the arrangements made for the French colonies, and the concentration of the

powers of decision in the hands of the Council of Ministers. Adenauer successfully pressed these concessions, overriding considerable criticism from his own government, as well as from other members of the prospective community. His goal was progress toward a further integration of Western Europe and, in particular, toward a further reconciliation with France; and he used his country's economic capability for these political goals. On July 19, 1957, the Bundestag endorsed the Chancellor's strategy and, with the support of the Social Democrats (representatives of certain economic, mainly agricultural, interests were opposed) ratified the EEC and Euratom Treaty by a large majority, 400 to 97.

From the outset, the project of a Common Market seems to have caught the attention of a considerable segment of West German public opinion. By January, 1957, three months before the signing of the Rome treaty, almost half the West Germans questioned said that they had heard about the Community, and almost one-third could provide "correct" or "almost correct" information about the ideas and goals behind the project. The government's decision to join the EEC soon had overwhelming public support. By June, 1960, almost three West Germans out of five believed that the advantages of Germany's participation in the Community exceeded the possible disadvantages, and only one in twenty voiced any objection to the treaty and to West Germany's membership in the Community. Two-thirds of these objections were for economic reasons, most often negative influences on the German farm industry.[47]

In 1962, the chief question remaining before the six members of the EEC was the admission of Great Brit-

[47]*Jahrbuch*, III, 542–44.

ain, under conditions lenient enough to permit her to retain some of her special trade relations with the Commonwealth (particularly, the importation of cheap foodstuffs from the Commonwealth countries) during a long period of transition. Since the French government, under President de Gaulle, seemed rather unwilling to make any substantial concession to British interests, much hinged on the attitude of the West German government. Both industrial rivalry and Chancellor Adenauer's policy of close cooperation with France tended to range West Germany against Britain on this issue, while the French policy permitted West Germany to remain inconspicuously in the background of the conflict. On January 28, 1963, after months of tight negotiations at Brussels, France vetoed Britain's entry into the Common Market. In a survey taken in February, 1963, more than two-thirds of the West Germans polled expressed dissatisfaction about the outcome of the Brussels negotiations, and about the same proportion blamed the result on France or President de Gaulle. However, while 66 per cent of the West Germans indicated that the federal government had done "enough" to support Britain's attempt for membership, 19 per cent believed that France's decision was the result of Germany's disinterest and inactivity in furthering the cause of Great Britain.[48]

Within the next two years, the appearance of Franco-German unity vis-à-vis Britain and the non-European powers disappeared. According to the Rome Treaty, the EEC was to shift from unanimous agreement to majority rule in 1966, but 1965 was to bring the final technical arrangements for putting into effect the financial concessions to French agriculture, to

[48]DIVO, *Pressedienst*, May, 1963, pp. 1–5.

which Germany and the other EEC partners had already agreed in principle. Neither of these matters progressed smoothly. The French had misgivings about any situation in which France could be outvoted, on matters of major national interest, by a majority of foreign governments. The West German government was in no hurry to implement what seemed, to many West Germans, unduly generous financial concessions to the French, particularly at a time when French relations with Germany's closest ally, the United States, were becoming somewhat strained by differences about NATO.

In this situation, the Bonn government supported a new Dutch demand that France should accept somewhat greater supranational political powers for the organs of EEC and its Brussels secretariat, headed by Germany's Walter Hallstein, before the financial concessions promised to France were effectuated. De Gaulle's government treated this as a breach of promise and withdrew its representatives from the major policy-making EEC committees, bringing their work to a standstill. Only the carrying through of the promised financial arrangements in favor of French agriculture (which, in fact, were to be financed primarily by West Germany) and the reduction of the powers of the EEC bureaucracy, and particularly of Dr. Walter Hallstein, it was suggested in Paris, would bring France back to the conference table.

By the late spring of 1966, the crisis was mitigated by mutual concessions. An EEC agreement gave France the substance of her economic demands, largely at West Germany's expense, as envisaged in the original understanding; but for the time being Dr. Hallstein remained in office at Brussels and the EEC administrative structure was preserved unchanged. The delicate matter of future voting was deferred; the details of the future merger of the three chief European organizations— ECSC, EEC, and EPC—were left to be negotiated later; and the way to new negotiations with Britain about her entry into the Common Market, under somewhat less stringent conditions, seemed once again open. The entire affair illustrated the precarious condition of European supranationalism and the persistence of national interests, but it also illustrated the resilience of German and French diplomacy and of European institutions.[49]

An unresolved foreign policy issue: German reunification and relations with the Soviet Union

The preceding analysis has suggested repeatedly that the makers of foreign policy in the Federal Republic have tended to show a great deal of independence from the pressure of public opinion. To this, there has been one conspicuous exception. On the issue of German reunification, no important leader has dared suggest that the Federal Republic is more than a provisional arrangement pending the "liberation" of the Soviet zone. During the years that German policy makers concentrated on gaining sovereignty and freedom of action for the "rump" German state, reunification took second place, leading many non-German observers to underestimate its importance. Since 1955, however, it has become increasingly apparent that peaceful reunification, through some sort of arrangement with the Soviet Union, is one of the most crucial foreign policy

issues confronting decision makers in the Federal Republic, one that is likely to affect significantly the future relationship between the Republic and its Western allies.

Professions, by official government spokesmen, of support for European integration have tended to obscure the existence of considerable sentiment for German reunification, particularly among the refugees from the Soviet zone. Some indication of the intensity of this sentiment may be gotten from comparing the attitudes of the young West Germans (between fifteen and twenty-four) on the subjects of European integration and German reunification. In 1956, 50 per cent of a cross section of West German youth expressed themselves as "very strongly" in favor of reunification at the present time, and 30 per cent were "strongly" in favor of it, as compared, respectively, to 34 per cent and 31 per cent of adults polled on the same issue. On the other hand, only 66 per cent of the young West Germans were in favor of efforts to unite Western Europe, while 79 per cent of the adults favored such efforts.[50] Thus, in 1956, sentiment for reunification appeared to be a good deal stronger, among West German youth, than sentiment for European unification, particularly as compared to the adult population. By January, 1965, the preference had become even more explicit. While 50 per cent of the young West Germans surveyed (aged sixteen to twenty-nine) regarded German reunification as the "most important question for people in West Germany today to be concerned with," only 5 per cent accorded this degree of urgency to European unification. By that time, also, most of their elders agreed with them.

Deep-rooted loyalties to the idea of

[49]Cf. Carl A. Erhardt, "Die haerteste Belastungsprobe der EWG," *Aussenpolitik,* XVI, no. 9 (September, 1965), 620–33; and "Dokumente zur Entwicklung der Krise in der EWG," *Europa-Archiv,* XX, no. 24 (December, 1965), D605–26.

[50]DIVO, *Basic Orientation, 1956,* pp. 123–39.

a united German nation appear, then, to be far stronger than support for the supranational ideal of European unification. Moreover, intimate personal bonds link a large number of citizens of the Federal Republic to German lands and people presently under communist domination. Over 27 per cent of the makers of foreign policy,[51] and about 24 per cent of the population, are natives of central and eastern Germany. In December, 1960, 34 per cent of the respondents in a poll of public opinion claimed to have either relatives or friends living in the German Democratic Republic. When one adds to these the number of West Germans with personal acquaintances, the share of West Germans with such personal contacts should be well over half the population of the Federal Republic. Many of these human contacts have remained active; in July, 1959, almost one West German out of every five said he "often" wrote letters to the "East zone," and almost two out of five did so "sometimes."[52] Before the border was sealed off completely by the Berlin Wall in August, 1961, several thousand refugees from East Germany used to enter the Federal Republic monthly, serving as a constant reminder that seventeen million Germans remained outside the present "rump" German state.

In addition to national and personal sentiments, visions of potential political and economic gains motivate the demand for reunification. With a population of seventy-five million and the largest area, by far, of all European states, a united Germany would once more rank among the leading powers

of the world—second only to the United States and the Soviet Union. Trade between the Federal Republic and the communist countries is negligible—even trade with the Soviet zone amounted to only about 2 per cent of its total foreign trade—but reunification might open up vast new markets.

The magnitude and intensity of popular pressure for German reunification is evidenced by the attitudes of West Germany's leaders. Leaders of opinion have sought to outdo each other in denouncing the division of Germany as intolerable, and in labeling reunification the most important national duty confronting the government. General agreement exists that reunification must be achieved peacefully, and by free elections of a national assembly throughout Germany, not through negotiations with the "puppet" regime of the Russian zone. Views diverge, however, on the strategy that should be employed by the government of the Federal Republic in achieving reunification.

Most German leaders acknowledge—however reluctantly—that the government is not a free agent in the matter of reunification. German unity, they admit, depends, in the last analysis, on agreement between the United States and the Soviet Union. Both Chancellor Adenauer and his successor, Erhard, have taken the position that the best means of obtaining such an agreement consists in inducing the West—the United States, in particular—to adopt this German national objective as their own, and to treat it as more important than any other American interest that might conceivably be served by any Russo-American settlement of other issues. Any general settlement of outstanding East-West differences, it is argued, would then have to include the unification of Germany on terms satisfactory to the govern-

51This proportion held in samples studied in 1955 and 1964. For sources, see Karl W. Deutsch *et al., French and German Elite Responses, 1964: Code Book and Data* (New Haven: Yale University Political Science Research Library, 1966), p. 211.

52*Jahrbuch,* III, 5.

ment of the Federal Republic. To gain such support, however, the Republic and its leaders must convince Western leaders of their devotion and loyalty to the Western Alliance; above all, they must convince them that a reunified Germany would be no threat to the peace of the world. According to the government of the Federal Republic, the most effective way to earn such confidence and support is for the Federal Republic to take the leadership in the movement for European union. Chancellor Adenauer, during his terms in office, repeatedly claimed that without the unification of Europe there could be no unification of Germany.

In recent years, West Germans appear to have become increasingly pessimistic regarding the chances for reunification of their country in the near future. While professing the desire for reunification with undiminished strength, West German opinion polls have reflected such pessimism. In March, 1958, 33 per cent of the West Germans surveyed thought that the chances for reunification were "bad," and 7 per cent thought they were "very bad"; by January, 1964, 37 per cent thought the chances were "bad," and 17 per cent thought they were "very bad."[53] The Social Democratic Party, heretofore identified with efforts to seek reunification through neutralization, dropped all references to reunification and neutralization from its Godesberg program, implying the acceptance of the status quo. Leaders of the Protestant Church, who in the past were often critical of Adenauer's pro-Western policies, have, in the face of Russian intransigence, adopted a "more realistic" point of view. They, too, are no longer to be found in the forefront of the neutralist, pacifist, and nationalist elements who, in the past,

[53]DIVO, Pressedienst, I, 11.

believed that the cause of German unity would be better served by loosening the ties that the Chancellor had forged between the Federal Republic and the West. Without enthusiasm, many West Germans have come to accept the present split of Germany. There appears to be a reluctant acceptance of a fact unacceptable to most West Germans in the past, that the status quo is likely to be perpetuated indefinitely by a tacit understanding between the great powers to shelve the issue of German unification indefinitely, for the sake of compromise on other issues, such as Berlin, disarmament, and the preservation of peaceful relations at the European boundaries of the communist world.

In 1966, Germany seemed further away from reunification than in 1949. At best, the foreign policy of the Bonn government appeared to be preserving the status quo; at worst, it seemed to be aggravating the division of the nation. However, the government's failure to register any concrete gains for reunification seemed not to be counted against it by the voters, as evidenced by the opposition's ceasing to charge that the government had merely paid lip service to the cause of reunification. Earlier claims that the predominantly Roman Catholic, western and southern German conservative elite, which had supported Adenauer, had influenced his foreign policy through their fear of the political and economic effects of unification, are no longer being heard, perhaps also because Erhard is a Protestant and has appointed a larger proportion of Protestants to high Cabinet office.

Both elite and mass opinion appear to be that reunification lies beyond the control of the West German policy makers. Indeed, this was vividly demonstrated in 1963–'64, when Foreign Minister Gerhard Schroeder proposed the creation of a standing four-power body, composed of the signatories of the Potsdam agreement and France, which would keep the German question under review. This proposal merely provided for the creation of machinery which would allow the Western powers to probe Russian ideas about a lasting European security system and discuss the possible conditions of German reunification. The proposal, however, was rejected by the United States, on the grounds that it was risky to undertake such negotiations on German reunification and a future peace treaty, so long as the Western powers, including the Federal Republic, were not in agreement on the substance of a political bargain with the Soviet Union.[54]

Thus, German foreign policy makers are faced with a double deadlock on the formula for German unity: the stalemate between the Soviet Union and the United States on the one hand, and the lack of clear agreement among Western leaders—not only between Germany and France, but perhaps even between West Germany and the United States—on the other. In respect to the Russo-American deadlock, both sides conceive the potential status of a united Germany as a matter so vital to their respective interests that they have found it impossible to make the concessions that a compromise solution would require. Western leaders see the terms for reunification proposed by the Russian leaders as designed to give control over this strategic area to the U.S.S.R., while the latter insist that a Germany united according to Western plans would constitute a menace to the Soviet Union and its allies in Eastern Europe. The resulting

deadlock has aroused widespread suspicions in the Federal Republic that neither the West nor the Soviet Union is genuinely interested in resolving the issue—protestations by both sides to the contrary—while the West German government seems unable to do anything about it. "The German people . . . [are merely] the subjects of negotiations between foreign powers which pursue only their own interests," observed the leading foreign affairs journal in the Federal Republic after ten years of inconclusive four-power negotiations on German unification. This sense of exasperation and frustration has repeatedly led to demands that the leaders of the Federal Republic take matters into their own hands and negotiate directly with the Soviet Union. However, attempts in this direction have been singularly unsuccessful. This was illustrated by Adenauer's visit to Moscow in September, 1955.

The termination of the occupation regime in May, 1955, was, to many influential leaders of the Federal Republic, the signal for the start of direct negotiations with the Soviet Union on reunification. Such sentiments were strengthened by the failure of the Geneva four-power talks on German unification the following July. Therefore, when Russian leaders invited Adenauer to come to Moscow in September, 1955, he accepted, evidently sharing the widespread West German view that his bargaining position was strong enough to extract favorable terms from the Russian government. It turned out, however, that he had overestimated his own position and underestimated that of the Russian leaders. The latter refused to discuss reunification, but suggested that he negotiate directly with the leaders of the German Democratic Republic—the satellite regime in the Russian Zone of Germany—

[54]Richard Lowenthal, "The Germans Feel Like Germans Again," *New York Times Magazine*, March 6, 1966, pp. 36–50.

which no political leader in the Federal Republic was then, or is now, willing to do. Adenauer refused, but he agreed to the establishment of diplomatic relations between the Federal Republic and the Soviet Union in return for the release of several thousand German prisoners of war still in captivity. To many leading West Germans, it seemed that Adenauer had walked into a Soviet trap. By agreeing to the establishment of diplomatic relations, he seemed to have accepted the Russian claim that there were two German states, both represented in Moscow, and that unification could only come about by negotiations between their respective governments. However, Adenauer quickly sought to dispel the impression that he had abandoned the claim of the Federal Government to be the only German government and that he was moving toward recognition of East Germany. In fact, he had obtained the release of some prisoners, which his Western allies had failed to procure. The presence of a Russian ambassador in Bonn, and of a West German ambassador in Moscow, represented a relative increase in German independence and bargaining power vis-à-vis the West; and Adenauer had gained these points without injuring in any way his reputation for rock-solid reliability as an ally of the Western powers. However, it was evident that the Federal Republic could ill afford to go much further in the way of independent negotiations with the Soviet Union, and that it still depended upon the Western powers—particularly the United States—to achieve the professed major foreign policy objective of its leaders: German unity.

Between 1949 and 1956, West German makers of foreign policy were highly successful in obtaining their objectives in negotiations with the Western occupation powers, primarily be-

cause the West was willing and able to pay the price demanded. To obtain the political, military, and economic participation of the Federal Republic in the Western alliance against the Soviet Union, they agreed to Adenauer's demands for sovereignty and equality. Reunification is another matter. As long as international tensions remain acute, a united Germany may seem too dangerous to either side in the East-West contest. Small or unarmed countries can be neutral in the sense that neither side is forced to count them as enemies or allies, but a large, armed country would be not so much neutral as merely uncommitted; it might keep everyone in fear of what it might decide to do with its concentrated power. In the case of Germany, now still divided, neither Eastern nor Western leaders seem overly eager to hasten the day when such fears might become real. Although German reunification often has been described—particularly by German leaders—as a major means of lessening tensions between East and West, it seems possible that a reduction of international tensions, through compromises on some other issues, might make German reunification more acceptable to the other powers.

Thus, the great threat to West German desires for a reunited nation is the possibility of a tacit agreement between the great power leaders to leave the issue indefinitely in abeyance—as they did in divided Korea and Indochina. This possibility has become particularly acute in the light of recent attempts to halt the armament race between the Soviet Union and the United States.

To the West German mind, however, this threat seems remote. In a survey taken in September, 1962, 44 per cent of the West Germans rejected the possibility that the United

States might recognize the partition of Germany as the price of an agreement between the United States and the Soviet Union, although 23 per cent regarded it as a likely development.[55] Prodded by Chancellor Adenauer, Western leaders had formerly insisted that agreement on German reunification must precede agreement on disarmament, but indications have been abundant that their position need not remain rigid: German unification, unlike disarmament, has little appeal outside Germany.

West German leaders could render the achievement of such East-West compromises on other issues more difficult. If they chose, they could exercise their influence to hamper, or even block, agreement on disarmament; they probably could intensify and dramatize the daily East-West frictions in divided Germany. But it is difficult to see how any such action would bring reunification closer. At most, they could use their insistence on the priority of reunification as a bargaining technique, in order to exact concessions, from both East and West, on other and more manageable matters.

PROSPECTS FOR GERMAN FOREIGN POLICY

The study of the background of foreign policy making in the German Federal Republic, among the various policy-making institutions, interest groups, and sectors of public opinion, reveals a limited area of agreement, surrounded by substantial cleavages of attitudes and interests and by the possibility of deadlocks.

Government, interest groups, and the general public all desire, by and large, a peaceful return of Germany to leadership and power in Europe—

[55] *Jahrbuch*, III, 558.

and through Europe, perhaps in a larger area of the world. A substantial majority want peace, freedom from communist control, and economic and political links with the United States— and they do not want to have to choose between these aims. Second to these primary goals comes German reunification, a long-range aim.

"The First Servant of Europe"

European integration takes only third place; it is often seen as a road to West German leadership or to the attainment of other West German goals, rather than as an end in itself. Among the West German elite, as well as among the electorate, there are many who are likely to show little enthusiasm for remaining in any close European community that would prove unresponsive to West German leadership or major influence. Other groups —though perhaps less strong—might be willing to accept a more modest role for West Germany in a united Europe. The cleavage between those who want West Germany to lead a Western European community and those who want her merely to join it has been adroitly bridged, for the time being, by the formulation of a prominent CDU leader and former diplomat, Kurt Sieveking:

England and France . . . will always . . . be preoccupied by extra-European tasks. . . . Italy is . . . not yet developed to its full strength. From this it is evident that Germany will become ever more the natural nucleus of crystallization for Europe. . . . Above all it must be made absolutely clear that this German foreign policy is far from any thought of any hegemony over Europe and that Germany, as one put it in a well-known saying, is "the first servant of Europe."[56]

[56] Kurt Sieveking, "Die europäische Aufgabe der deutschen Aussenpolitik," *Aussenpolitik*, VI, No. 3 (March, 1957), 150–51.

The "well-known saying" so aptly recalled by Herr Sieveking is indeed well known to almost every educated German: it is the classic eighteenth-century phrase in which the absolute ruler of Prussia, King Frederick the Great, called himself "the first servant" of the State, and thus pictured his enlightened despotism as a matter, not only of right, but of duty. Nationalists may take heart from what they may well read as a broad hint of future aspirations, whereas more liberal-minded "Europeans" may take comfort from the explicit rejection of any thought of German hegemony which prefaces it in the same sentence. Like many a present-day political leader, Herr Sieveking is raising here two sets of overtones and expectations in the same statement, and thus appealing at one and the same time to different sections of his variegated audience.

In the meantime, the Fifth French Republic, under President de Gaulle, has reduced her overseas commitments, particularly in Asia and Africa, and has increased her efforts at influencing the political future of the European continent. In England, a considerably larger sector of the population is once again becoming aware of Britain's interest in continental European affairs. West German governments may find it increasingly difficult, therefore, to lead in European politics without taking increasing account of French and British interests. Rather, Bonn's leaders may have to count with an increased French and British presence in European affairs, and they may have to pursue German interests in this changed context.

How much stress on military power?

In practice, Bonn's policy of cautious advance toward greater power within the Western alliance may mean that German reunification will remain largely in the realm of rhetoric. The Soviet Union has no motive, for the time being, to concede German reunification on Western terms, and the Western powers have no way of changing Russian policy. Even granting that the Russian attitude toward Germany has more to do with military fear than with ideological expansionism, Western policy toward German reunification was likely to be sterile. The limits of this policy have been put illuminatingly in a recent analysis of the problems involved:

The Western approach made sense only on the assumption that either the Soviet weakness would eventually drive the Communists to accept the uneven bargain, or that . . . West Germany could be amalgamated into Western military and economic arrangements while mere lip-service continued to be paid to reunification.[57]

It is the second alternative which has come true. Faced with a deadlocked international situation in regard to the question of German reunification, West Germany, for the time being, will have to accommodate her demands to the limits allowed by her chosen allies. To reconcile public opinion to this state of affairs, however, the Federal Republic will have to achieve a bargaining position of her own.

This necessarily involves a consideration of Bonn's future military policy. Will Germany accept, as her share in the common defense effort of the West, the provision of the moderately strong conventional forces provided for in her treaties of the mid-1950's? Or will she press for nuclear weapons

[57]Frederick H. Hartmann, *Germany Between East and West: The Reunification Problem* (Englewood Cliffs, N.J.: Prentice-Hall, Inc., 1965).

and a more competitive role toward other Western powers?

One of the most prominent spokesmen for the nuclear armament of West Germany, former Defense Minister and present CSU Chairman Franz-Josef Strauss, made it clear that this policy did not necessarily imply any inclination toward military adventures, despite repeated charges to that effect by the East. All it implies, Strauss has insisted, is a desire to make West Germany so strong, as a military and nuclear power, that she will become an "indispensable" partner or party in all future confrontations or negotiations between East and West. In Strauss's words:

A policy of strength in the age of the hydrogen bomb means in no case that one wants to use military pressure, with the risk of a third world war, in order to bring about some territorial changes, if necessary even by force. A policy of strength means rather that one's own freedom of decision cannot be influenced by pressure from hostile or unfriendly quarters. . . . Germany . . . must become so indispensable to her Western friends, and so respectable for her potential adversary, that both will value her presence in the negotiations.[58]

In actual fact, there is little reason to think that national nuclear weapons, as such, increase the positive influence of a country in international affairs. Britain and France lost their colonial empires, and the Soviet Union lost her influence over China and a significant part of the communist world, precisely in the decades during which each of these powers acquired national nuclear weapons. The United States also had far less control over world affairs in 1966, when its nuclear arsenal was large, than it had in 1946, when it

was small. The expectation that national nuclear weapons would give West Germany substantially greater positive influence in international politics may well be an illusion. As our data showed, it is an illusion which is not shared, at present, by a majority of the West German leaders or voters.

Another aspect of the present situation is brought out in an article by an observer of German foreign policy:

Nothing would be more mistaken than the belief that the Germans of today are out for "status symbols" in nuclear defense or elsewhere: the plan for a European multilateral nuclear force was not a German idea, and the complicated discussions about it have aroused remarkably little interest outside expert circles. Being NATO's most exposed frontline country the Germans naturally want to make sure they have adequate influence on Western nuclear planning; beyond that they would gladly renounce any claim to nuclear "equality" in return for one step of real progress toward national reunion.[59]

Since any increase of West Germany's influence in NATO, especially as a nuclear power, is likely to intensify Soviet fears, the same military strength that is expected, by some statesmen, to make West Germany an indispensable and influential party at all future top-level negotiations would also make her a high-priority target in any atomic war that might follow upon a failure of such negotiations. In practice, most of the likely uses of any increased bargaining power of a strongly rearmed Germany would involve heightened risks to that country, to her neighbors, to world peace, and to the cohesion of her alliance with the West.[60]

[58]Franz-Josef Strauss, "Sicherheit und Wiedervereinigung," *Aussenpolitik*, VI, No. 3 (March, 1957), 140–47.

[59]Richard Lowenthal, *New York Times*, p. 46.
[60]See Karl W. Deutsch, "The German Federal Republic," in *Modern Political Systems: Europe*, pp. 387–88.

Toward new decisions

The two views just cited—the hopes for prospective West German leadership in Europe, and for West German military power as a counter in diplomatic bargaining—indicate some of the limits of the space within which West German policy makers are confined. West Germany's foreign policy of the mid-1960's depends, for much of its prospective stability, on outside limits and on outside props. If economic prosperity in the Western world should give way to a serious depression; if American interest and investment should be withdrawn; if a sharply increased risk of war should put much greater short-term strains and burdens on West Germany; if the Soviet Union should make some substantially more favorable offer on matters of German reunification; if a further deterioration of the French position within the Western alliance should bring about a changed situation in Western Europe, and between France and West Germany in particular; or if some drastic change in some of the countries of the Eastern bloc should create new conditions among West Germany's neighbors—in any of these events, German foreign policy makers might find themselves face to face with the need for major new decisions.

Such decisions might easily entail a broad revision of West German foreign policy. What their outcome would be is hard to foresee. Here we encounter some of the limits of any political analysis based on the past and on the background conditions of the policymaking process. The past suggests that some German responses could be dramatic; but it does not tell us what they would be.

We can, however, look to some West German policies that are currently being chosen—sometimes as specific moves, sometimes as mere shifts of emphasis—which may indicate the possible ways in which larger decisions might be made if circumstances should demand them. Such a tell-tale indication is the current German attitude toward any effort to reduce East-West tensions or to limiting the arms race, particularly in nuclear weapons. Will West German leaders welcome such efforts as favoring later German reunification, or will they insist that reunification must come first? Related to this are changes in the emphasis on West Germany's need for greater military power, in order to make the U.S.S.R. and other countries more receptive to the West German point of view. Will such themes and hints diminish or increase as time goes on? What will happen when the West German army becomes stronger, and when the question of nuclear weapons for West Germany becomes acute?

What will be the next developments in German-Soviet relations? Some members of the West German foreign policy elite are urging "genuine and fruitful" diplomatic relations with the U.S.S.R. "It makes no sense," wrote an SPD leader, Carlo Schmid, "to act as if the Soviet Union did not exist as a genuine business partner. For that, our direct and indirect business dealings with them are too large."

In the same connection, the question of West German diplomatic relations to other Soviet-bloc countries has been raised. For more than fifteen years, the West German government has refused to recognize the German Democratic Republic, and, under the "Hallstein doctrine," has also declined to have normal diplomatic relations with its Eastern European neighbors which had recognized the East German regime. For the same reason, the

Federal Republic has avoided entering the United Nations—except for special U.N. organizations—in order not to offer the German Democratic Republic an opportunity to enter that world body. The Soviet Union would almost certainly use its veto power to insist on the admission of both German states, or none.

Although the official attitude toward any direct contact between the Bonn government and its East German counterpart remains unchanged, West Germany's policy toward its Eastern European neighbors is being revised. In 1963, a German-Polish agreement provided for the exchange of trade missions; since then, similar agreements have been signed with Hungary, Rumania, and Bulgaria, and new trade missions have been established. Using the semidiplomatic status of trade missions instead of full diplomatic relations, Bonn hoped to circumvent the Hallstein doctrine and yet challenge the German Democratic Republic as the sole representative of the German people in these countries. The success of this policy, however, remains to be seen; it will, to a large extent, depend on the attitude taken by the Eastern European governments toward Bonn's policy of "restricted diplomacy," and therefore, to some extent, on the economic incentives which the Federal Republic may decide to offer alongside it.

Other indications of possible decisions to be made by the Federal government are found in West German policies toward Western European integration. In particular, the decisions will involve two crucial choices: whether to press, or to postpone, German reunification and the claims to formerly German territories and properties in Eastern Europe; and whether to limit West German participation in the ongoing process of Western European

integration to the point where it might remain compatible with the strongest development of West German national capabilities. Will the Federal Republic, at any time in the near future, be ready to throw its resources and institutions more fully into the melting pot of the emerging West European Federation —if it means sacrificing, not just the trappings but the substance of, West German national sovereignty? As part of this decision, West Germany must choose whether it will continue the rather rigid policy it adopted, in 1961–'62, toward the entry of Great Britain into the EEC, or whether it will be more accommodating toward Britain and take a more positive stand on the question of Britain's membership in the Community, and with respect to strategies of integration in general.

Another series of decisions will have to involve arms control and disarmament. The West German elite—and, from all indications, also the West German public—has, in the mid-1960's favored the 1963 American-British-Russian treaty limiting nuclear bomb testing. They favor further agreements of this nature, as well as international agreements to limit the proliferation of nuclear weapons "to countries now possessing them," that is, to the United States, Britain, the Soviet Union, France, and China. They were skeptical of arms control limited to Central Europe, but favored it on a worldwide scale. Generally, they believed that Germany had more to gain than to lose from a relaxation of international tensions. Whether any Bonn government would act on these preferences, and whether they would find support in Washington, no one could say in 1966.[61]

Whatever the results may be, the decisions of German foreign policy in

[61]For sources see Karl W. Deutsch, *Arms Control in the European Political Environ-*

the late 1960's may well be more important than any which the government and people of the German Federal Republic have had to make in the preceding decade.

What kind of Germany?

Perhaps the most important of all current decisions that may indicate possible German behavior in the event of a drastic international change or major crisis are those which bear on the official and unofficial attitudes toward the remnants of Nazism and old-line militarism inside West Germany. Any major crisis in foreign policy is likely to strain the limited consensus of the different ideological and interest groups that have been held together by the conditions of the postwar era. Under such strains, any major decision about West German foreign policy may well become involved in a decision as to what kind of country West Germany is to become and what groups and ideas are to lead her. Some decisions of this kind—on the attitudes to the Nazi past, to the war criminals, to authoritarianism—have been made, but others have been shelved. If the rest of the world remains stable for another decade, West Germany's moderate foreign policy and constitutional domestic evolution may well remain secure. The current decisions about West Germany's foreign policies, however, and, even more, those about her internal democracy and her domestic prestige and power structure, may give us some inkling of

the inner conflicts that might erupt if times should again become critical or dangerous.

On the surface, the German Federal Republic looks like a stable political community, whose leaders are pursuing a steadfast policy of national recovery within a Western alliance, and who are backed in this enterprise by a solid consensus of public opinion. More closely considered, however, the Republic, more than two decades after World War II, still resembles a political and psychological convalescent. The political unity of her population is precarious, and could easily break under strain. Any policy designed to make West Germany bear the major burdens of maintaining Western power in Europe in a period of major stress might well prove hazardous in the extreme.

Under these conditions, time, wisely used, might well work for the West. Each additional year of peace, prosperity, and confidence might aid in the consolidation of West German democracy and help West Germany to become a full member of the Western community of nations, by inner conviction and tradition, rather than only by strategic association and expediency. The great humanitarian and democratic traditions are alive in West Germany today, and a constitutional system of government has had a few years to take root. Very much may depend on giving these traditions a chance to grow, but this requires an international environment that is sufficiently peaceful to permit them to become more firmly and deeply established in the social fabric and the living memories of the German people.

ment: Summary Report (New Haven: Yale University, Political Science Research Library), January, 1966; and American Political Science Review, June 1966.

SELECTED BIBLIOGRAPHY

Adenauer, Konrad, *Memoirs: 1945–53.* Chicago: Henry Regnery Co., 1966.

Allemann, Fritz Rene, *Zwischen Stabilitaet und Krise: Etappen der deutschen Politik, 1955–1963.* Munich: R. Piper, 1963.

Almond, Gabriel A., ed., *The Struggle for Democracy in Germany.* Chapel Hill: University of North Carolina Press, 1949.

———, and Sidney Verba, *The Civic Culture.* Princeton, N.J.: Princeton University Press, 1963.

Altmann, Ruediger, *Das Deutsche Risiko: Aussenpolitische Perspektiven.* Stuttgart: Seewald, 1962.

Arntz, Helmut, *Facts About Germany.* Press and Information Office, Federal German Government, 1963.

Balabkins, Nicholas, *Germany Under Direct Controls.* New Brunswick, N.J.: Rutgers University Press, 1964.

Bathurst, M. E., and J. L. Simpson, *Germany and the North Atlantic Community: A Legal Survey.* London: Stevens & Sons, Ltd., 1956.

Boelling, Klaus, *Republic in Suspense.* New York: Frederick A. Praeger, Inc., 1965.

Bracher, Karl Dietrich, *Deutschland zwischen Demokratie und Dikatur.* Bern-Munich-Vienna: Scherz, 1964.

Braunthal, Gerard, *The Federation of German Industry in Politics.* Ithaca, N.Y.: Cornell University Press, 1965.

Buchanan, William, and Hadley Cantril, *How Nations See Each Other: A Study in Public Opinion.* Urbana, University of Illinois Press, 1953.

Chalmers, Douglas A., *The Social Democratic Party of Germany.* New Haven: Yale University Press, 1964.

Commission on International Affairs, American Jewish Congress, *The German Dilemma.* 1959.

Dahrendorf, Ralf, *Gesellschaft und Freiheit in Deutschland.* Munich: R. Piper, 1961.

Davison, W. Phillips, *The Berlin Blockade: A Study in Cold War Politics.* Princeton, N.J.: Princeton University Press, 1958.

Deutsch, Karl W., *Arms Control and the Atlantic Alliance.* New York: John Wiley & Sons, Inc., 1966.

———, *Nationalism and Social Communication.* Cambridge, Mass.: The M.I.T. Press; New York: John Wiley & Sons, Inc., 1953.

———, "The German Federal Republic," in *Modern Political Systems: Europe,* (2nd ed.) ed. Roy C. Macridis and Robert E. Ward. Englewood Cliffs, N.J.: Prentice-Hall, Inc., 1967.

Deutsch, Karl W., and Lewis J. Edinger, *Germany Rejoins the Powers: A Study of Mass Opinion, Interest Groups, and Elites in Contemporary German Foreign Policy.* Stanford, Calif.: Stanford University Press, 1959.

Deutsch, Karl W., et al., *France, Germany and the Western Alliance.* New York: Charles Scribner's Sons, Inc., 1966.

Deutsch, Karl W., et al., *Political Community and the North Atlantic Area.* Princeton, N.J.: Princeton University Press, 1957.

Edinger, Lewis J., "Atomic Blackmail and German Democracy," *South Atlantic Quarterly,* LVII (1958), 311–24.

———, "Continuity and Change: Some Data on the Social Background of German Decision Makers," *Western Political Quarterly,* XIV, no. 1 (March, 1961), 17–36.

———, "Electoral Politics and Voting Behavior in Western Germany," *World Politics,* XIII, no. 3 (April, 1961), 471–84.

———, *German Exile Politics.* Berkeley: University of California Press, 1956.

———, *Kurt Schumacher: A Study in Personality and Political Behavior.* Stanford, Calif.: Stanford University Press, 1965.

———, *Politics in Germany.* Boston: Little, Brown and Company, 1967.

———, "Post-Totalitarian Leadership," *American Political Science Review,* LIV (1960), 58–82.

———, *West German Armament.* Maxwell Air Force Base, Ala.: Research Studies Institute, Air University, October, 1955.

————, and D. Chalmers, "Overture or Swan Song?" *Antioch Review*, XX, no. 2 (Summer, 1960) 163–75.

Ellwein, Thomas, *Das Regierungssystem der Bundesrepublik Deutschland*. Cologne: Westdeutscher Verlag, 1963.

Enzensberger, Hans Magnus, et al., "Katechismus zur deutschen Frage," *Kursbuch*, 1, no. 4, (1966).

Erler, Fritz, *Democracy in Germany*. Cambridge, Mass.: Harvard University Press, 1965.

Eschenburg, Theodor, *Staat und Gesellschaft in Deutschland*. Stuttgart: Schwab, 1962.

Faul, Erwin, ed., *Wahlen und Waehler in Westdeutschland*. Villingen: Ring, 1960.

Grewe, Wilhelm, *Deutsche Aussenpolitik der Nachkriegszeit*. Stuttgart: Deutsche Verlagsanstalt, 1960.

Grosser, Alfred, *Die Bonner Demokratie*. Dusseldorf: Karl Rauch, 1960.

————, *The Federal Republic of Germany*. New York: Frederick A. Praeger, Inc., 1964.

Grossman, Kurt R., *Germany's Moral Debt: The German-Israel Agreement*. Washington, D. C.: Public Affairs Press, 1954.

Haas, Ernst B., *The Uniting of Europe*. Stanford, Calif.: Stanford University Press, 1958.

Hallstein, Walter, *United Europe: Challenge and Opportunity*. Cambridge, Mass.: Harvard University Press, 1962.

Hartmann, Frederick H., *Germany Between East and West: The Reunification Problem*. Englewood Cliffs, N.J.: Prentice-Hall, Inc., 1965.

Hartmann, H., *Authority and Organization in German Management*. Princeton, N.J.: Princeton University Press, 1959.

Heidenheimer, Arnold J., *The Governments of Germany*, (2nd ed.). New York: Crowell-Collier & Macmillan, Inc., 1966.

Hiscock, Richard, *Democracy in Western Germany*. London: Oxford University Press, 1957.

Janowitz, M., "Social Stratification and Mobility in West Germany," *American Journal of Sociology*, LXIV, no. 1, 6–24.

Kaiser, Karl, "Ansatzpunkte einer deutschen Wiedervereinigungspolitik", *Frankfurter Hefte*, XXI, no. 1 (January, 1966), 40–56.

————, "Die Deutsche Frage: Rekapituliert," *Frankfurter Hefte*, XX, no. 11 (November, 1965), 752–62.

————, "Die Deutsche Frage: Wiedervereinigung und europaeisches Gleichgewicht," *Frankfurter Hefte*, XX, no. 12 (December, 1965), 861–69.

Kirchheimer, Otto, "Germany: The Vanishing Opposition," in *Political Opposition in Western Democracies*, ed. Robert A. Dahl. New Haven: Yale University Press, 1966.

Kitzinger, U. W., *German Electoral Politics*. Oxford: Clarendon Press, 1960.

Krippendorff, Ekkehart, "Zweimal deutsche Aussenpolitik," *Der Monat*, XVIII, no. 208 (1966), 33–39.

Meissner, Boris, "Zehn Jahre deutsch-sowjetische Beziehungen," *Aussenpolitik*, XVI, no. 9 (September, 1965), 597–609.

Merkl, Peter H., *Germany: Yesterday and and Tomorrow*. New York: Oxford University Press, 1965.

————, *The Origin of the West German Republic*. New York: Oxford University Press, 1963.

Merritt, Richard L., "West Berlin: Center or Periphery?" in *Comparing Nations*, ed. Richard L. Merritt and Stein Rokkan. New Haven: Yale University Press, 1966.

Parsons, Talcott, "Democracy and Social Structure in Pre-Nazi Germany," in *Essays in Sociological Theory* (rev. ed.). New York: Free Press of Glencoe, Inc., 1954, pp. 104–23.

————, "The Problem of Controlled Institutional Change," in *ibid.*, pp. 238–74.

Plischke, Elmer, *Contemporary Government of Germany*. Boston: Houghton Mifflin Company, 1961.

Pollock, James Kerr, and Homer Thomas, *Germany in Power and Eclipse*. Princeton, N.J.: D. Van Nostrand Co., Inc., 1952.

Richardson, James L., *Germany and the Atlantic Alliance*. Cambridge, Mass.: Harvard University Press, 1966.

Robson, C. B., ed., Berlin: Pivot of German Destiny. Chapel Hill: University of North Carolina Press, 1960.

Scheuch, Erwin K., and Rudolf Wildenmann, eds., "Zur Soziologie der Wahl," in Koelner Zeitschrift fuer Soziologie und Sozialpsychologie, Sonderheft 9, 1965.

Schmidt, Helmut, Defense or Retaliation: A German Contribution to the Consideration of NATO's Strategic Problem. Edinburgh: Oliver & Boyd Ltd., 1962.

Schroeder, Gerhard, "Germany Looks at Eastern Europe," Foreign Affairs, XLIV, no. 1, (October, 1965), 15–25.

Senghaas, Dieter, "Pathologie der deutschen Aussenpolitik," in Politik ohne Vernunft, ed. Carl Nedelmann and Gert Schaefer. Hamburg: 1965.

Shell, Kurt L. Bedrohung und Bewaehrung: Fuehrung und Bevoelkerung in der Berlin-Krise. Cologne: Westdeutscher Verlag, 1965.

Siegler, Heinrich Freiherr von, Dokumentation zur Deutschland: Frage. 3 vols. Bonn: Verlag fuer Zeitarchive, 1961.

———, ¡Dokumentation der Europaeischen Integration. 2 vols. Bonn: Siegler, 1961–1964.

Smith, Jean Eduard, The Defense of Berlin. Baltimore: The Johns Hopkins Press, 1965.

Speier, Hans, German Rearmament and Atomic War: The Views of German Military and Political Leaders. New York: Harper & Row, Publishers, Inc., 1957.

———, and W. P. Davison, eds., West German Leadership and Foreign Policy. New York: Harper & Row, Publishers, Inc., 1957.

Stahl, Walter, ed., Education for Democracy in West Germany. New York: Frederick A. Praeger, Inc., 1961.

———, The Politics of Postwar Germany. New York: Frederick A. Praeger, Inc., 1963.

Strauss, Franz-Josef, The Grand Design: A European Solution to German Reunification. New York: Frederick A. Praeger, Inc., 1966.

Wallenberg, Hans, Report on Democratic Institutions in Germany. New York: American Council on Germany, 1956.

Wallich, Henry C., Mainsprings of the German Revival. New Haven: Yale University Press, 1955.

Wildenmann, Rudolf, Macht und Konzens als Problem der Innen- und Aussenpolitik. Bonn-Frankfurt: Athenaeum, 1963.

Zapf, Wolfgang, ed., Beitraege zur Analyse der deutschen Oberschicht. Munich: R. Piper, 1965.

———, Wandlungen der deutschen Elite. Munich: R. Piper, 1965.

———, The Politics of Postwar Germany. New York: Frederick A. Praeger, Inc., 1963.

SOVIET FOREIGN 5 POLICY

VERNON V. ASPATURIAN

CONTINUITY AND CHANGE IN RUSSIAN FOREIGN POLICY

One of the most baffling aspects of Soviet foreign policy is its remarkable capacity for evoking the most variegated and contradictory responses to its diplomacy. "In its distant objectives," writes Edward Crankshaw, "the foreign policy of the Soviet Union is less obscure and more coherent than that of any other country," yet its immediate intentions and the motivations behind its day-to-day diplomacy often appear incoherent, capricious, and almost always enigmatic.[1]

The foreign policy of any country, the Soviet Union included, is not, however, simply the sum total of its avowed intentions, no matter how sincerely and devotedly they are adhered to, but must depend upon the capacity, in the present or in the future, to carry out its intentions. "In order to transform the world," Stalin told H. G. Wells in 1934, "it is necessary to have political power . . . as a lever of change."[2] Marxist ideology, reinforced by the early experiences of the Soviet regime, thus has persuaded the Kremlin that the capacity to transform intentions into reality is indistinguishable from power, a power which is objectively determined by the economic and social foundations of society, but which, in turn, can dictate the evolution of society towards particular ethical and political goals.

[1] *New York Times Book Review*, July 3, 1949, p. 4.

[2] J. V. Stalin and H. G. Wells, *Marxism vs. Liberalism* (New York: 1934), p. 14.

156

In order to draw a proper appraisal of Soviet diplomacy at any given time, the voluntaristic aspects of Soviet foreign policy must always be measured against its power to overcome the deterministic impediments of international reality. Thus, although the Soviet Union can plan the calculated growth of the economic and military foundations of its power, it cannot "plan" foreign policy. This fact was eloquently stated by Maxim Litvinov to the Central Executive Committee in 1929:

Unlike other Commissariats, the Commissariat for Foreign Affairs cannot, unfortunately, put forward a five-year plan of work, a plan for the development of foreign policy. . . . In . . . drawing up the plan of economic development, we start from our own aspirations and wishes, from a calculation of our own potentialities, and from the firm principles of our entire policy, but in examining the development of foreign policy we have to deal with a number of factors that are scarcely subject to calculation, with a number of elements outside our control and the scope of our action. International affairs are composed not only of our own aspirations and actions, but of those of a large number of countries . . . pursuing other aims than ours, and using other means to achieve those aims than we allow.[3]

The balance between the voluntaristic and deterministic components of Soviet foreign policy is neither fixed nor stable, but is in a state of continual and deliberate flux. In the initial stages of the Bolshevik Republic, its foreign policy was virtually at the mercy of external forces over which it could exercise little control, and Soviet diplomacy assumed the characteristic contours of a weak power struggling for survival under onerous conditions.

As its economic and military position improved, it gradually assumed the characteristics of a great power and, given its geographical and cultural context, it took on the distinctive features of its Tsarist predecessors and the impulse to subjugate its immediate neighbors.

The geographic and historical inheritance

"Marxism," writes a contemporary Soviet specialist on diplomacy, "teaches that economic factors determine the foreign policy and diplomacy of a state only in the long run, and that politics and diplomacy are, in a certain sense, conditioned by the concrete historical period and by many other elements (not excluding even, for instance, the geographical situation of a given country)."[4] Although Soviet writers may still tend to agree with the observation of the hapless Karl Radek, that "it is silly to say that geography plays the part of fate, that it determines the foreign policy of a state,"[5] geography is nonetheless the most permanent conditioning factor in a country's foreign policy; for location, topography, and natural resources are significant—and often decisive—determinants of a country's economic and military power. Geography's effects, however, are relative, rarely absolute, always dependent upon the more variable factors in a country's character, such as its cultural traditions, political institutions, the size and diversity of its population, the exploitation of its natural resources, and the skill of its statesmen. A country's geography, with rare exceptions,

[3]*Protokoly Zasedani Tsentralnovo Ispolnitelnovo Komiteta Sovetov*, Bulletin 14, (Moscow: 1930), p. 1.

[4]F. I. Kozhevnikov, "Engels on 19th Century Russian Diplomacy," *Sovetskoye Gosudarstvo i Pravo*, (No. 12), December, 1950, pp. 18–34.
[5]Karl Radek, "The Bases of Soviet Foreign Policy," in H. F. Armstrong, ed., *The Foreign Affairs Reader* (New York: Harper & Row, Publishers, Inc., (1947), p. 173.

cannot be remade; it can only be utilized more effectively. Thus, although Radek's contention that "the questions raised by geography are dealt with by each social formation in its own way . . . determined by its peculiar economic and political aims," remains incontestable, it was the blessing of Providence that this vast empire secreted all the basic ingredients for the erection of a powerful industrial and military state, given the necessary will and determination of its leadership. Had Russia been a wasteland with limited raw materials, she would have been doomed to be permanently a preindustrial society. The character of her foreign policy—her very existence —would have been vastly different, and her vaunted ideology would have long been relegated to the ash cans of history.

The Soviet Union, like Tsarist Russia before it, is the largest single continuous intercontinental empire in the world. Embracing fully half of two continents, the Soviet Union has the world's longest and most exposed frontier, which is at once both its greatest potential hazard and one of its prime assets in international politics. As a part of both Europe and Asia, and embracing more than 150 ethnic and linguistic groups ranging from the most sophisticated nations to the most primitive, the U.S.S.R. achieves a unique microcosmic character denied any other country, including the United States with its ethnically variegated but linguistically assimilated population. Russia's serpentine frontier is both a consequence of the indefensibility of the central Russian plain and, at the same time, an important conditioning factor in the further evolution and execution of its foreign policy. For a weak Russia, such a frontier affords maximum exposure to attack, but for a powerful Russian state, this extended frontier, bordering on nearly a dozen states, offers an enviable and limitless choice for the exertion of diplomatic pressure. Since 1939, the Soviet Union has annexed four of its former neighbors, seized territory from seven more, and has made territorial demands upon two others; most of this territory was previously lost by a weakened Russia. Of all her bordering states, only Afghanistan has not been imposed on to cede territory to the Soviet Union.

In the past, Russia's geographical position has exposed her to continuous depredations and subjugation from all directions—an inevitable consequence of political disunity in a geographically indefensible community. But if geography simplified the conquest of a divided Russia, it also facilitated the expansion of a united and powerful Russian state, which pushed out in all directions until it was arrested by superior force.

In the absence of more obvious geographical obstacles to her enemies, Russia's physical security became irrevocably attached to land space, while her psychological security became inseparable from political centralization. This conviction was confirmed by Stalin, himself, on the occasion of Moscow's 800th anniversary in 1947.

Moscow's service consists first and foremost in the fact that it became the foundation for the unification of a disunited Russia into a single state with a single government, a single leadership. No country in the world that has not been able to free itself of feudal disunity and wrangling among princes can hope to preserve its independence or score substantial economic and cultural progress. Only a country united in a single centralized state can count on being able to make substantial cultural-economic progress and assert its independence.[6]

[6]*Pravda*, September 11, 1947.

It is a persisting fact of Russian history that this dual quest for physical and psychological security has produced, in Russian foreign policy, a unique pattern. A divided Russia invites attack, but a united Russia stimulates expansion in all directions. The Revolutions in 1917, and the terrible purges of the Thirties which Stalin undertook to enforce unity at home exposed Russia's internal schisms to the world and stimulated foreign intervention. In each crisis, after surviving the initial assault from without, she embarked on a campaign designed to carry her beyond her self-declared national frontiers. The campaign failed in 1921, but she succeeded, after World War II, in bringing all of Eastern Europe under her hegemony.

The Bolsheviks fell heir not only to Russia's geography and natural resources, but also to the bulk of her population, her language, and the Russian historical and cultural legacy. Marxism gave Russia new goals and aspirations, but once the decision was taken to survive as a national state, even on a temporary and instrumental basis, the Soviet Union could not evade assuming the contours of a Russian state, and falling heir to the assets and liabilities of its predecessors. Although Lenin thought that he had irrevocably severed the umbilical cord with Russia's past, it was not entirely within his power to unburden the new Soviet Republic of the disadvantages of Tsarist diplomacy. Foreign attitudes remained remarkably constant; fears and suspicions, sympathies and attachments, were reinforced more than erased. Designs on Soviet territory still came from the same quarter, exposure to attack remained in the same places, and the economic and commercial lifelines of the Tsars became no less indispensable to the new regime. In short, even if the Soviet Union refused to remain Russia, Japan remained Japan, Poland remained Poland, and the Straits remained the Straits.

Moreover, the Russian language, permanently encrusted in its Cyrillic shell, became the official speech of Soviet diplomacy, and, as the vehicle of the Marxist dogma, it was pompously proclaimed the "language of the future." Russian cultural and scientific achievement became the basis for Soviet claims to cultural supremacy, of which Soviet science and culture were pronounced a continuation; the symbolism of Holy Russia was revived. Moscow eagerly laid claim to all the advantages of historic Russia, and the outside world just as assiduously refused to permit her to evade the liabilities and vulnerabilities of the Russian past. Thus, partly by choice and partly by necessity, the foreign policy of the Soviet Union could not but assume some of the contours of its predecessors.

The impact of a voluntaristic doctrine like Marxism on the geographical facts of Russia and her messianic traditions not only reinforced the psychological obsession for security, but provided an ideological rationale for assuming the implacable hostility of the outside world and sanctified Russian expansion with the ethical mission of liberating the downtrodden masses of the world from their oppressors. The hostile West of the Slavophils became the hostility of capitalism and imperialism; instead of the parochial messianism of the pan-Slav enthusiasts, Marxism provided Russia with a mission of universal transcendence—transforming the outside world into her own image, in fulfillment of her historic destiny and as the only permanent guarantee of absolute security. Up until the Twentieth Party Congress, in 1956, the Leninist-Stalinist thesis that "the destruction of capitalist encirclement and the destruction of the danger of capitalist intervention are possible only as a result of the victory of the proletarian revolution, at least in several large countries,"[7] continued to be in force. Although "capitalist encirclement" was declared ended by Stalin's successors, the recent events in Poland and Hungary may have convinced the Kremlin that this proclamation was premature.

To assume, however, that Soviet foreign policy is merely Russian imperialism in new garb would be a catastrophic mistake on both sides. Soviet foreign policy was bound to assume "Russian" characteristics during one phase of its metamorphosis, but now that the maximum, but still limited, aims of Tsarist imperialism have been virtually consummated, the aggressive (no longer necessarily expansionist) aspects of its foreign policy will assume a purely Marxist character, while only the defensive aspects (i.e., the preservation of its present power position) of its diplomacy will retain distinctively "Russian" features. That these two aspects of current Soviet foreign policy are in flagrant contradiction is self-evident, even to the Kremlin and other communist leaders. Chinese accusations of "Great Power chauvinism," the de-Stalinization campaign, and the uprisings in Poland and Hungary are all manifestations of this fundamental schism in Soviet foreign policy. Whereas in the past, when the Soviet Union was weak, indiscriminate emphasis on the revolutionary aspects of its foreign policy tended to undermine its basic instinct to survive, now, its defensive reflexes tend to subvert not only its continuing leadership of world communism, but the eventual success of the movement itself.

[7]*Kommunist*, (No. 2), January 1953, p. 15.

World revolution and national interest in Soviet diplomacy

Deciphering Soviet motives is an elusive and hazardous undertaking, yet it must be done systematically and with calculation, otherwise *ad hoc* and unconscious assumptions acquire priority by default. Miscalculation of motives can often be catastrophic since foreign policy expectations are built upon assumptions concerning the motives and capabilities of other powers, and diplomatic success or failure often depend on the degree of accuracy with which these assumptions approach actuality. Much of the agony of postwar Western diplomacy can be traced directly to illusory expectations resulting from false calculations of Soviet motives by Western leaders. Diplomacy, however, is not an intellectual exercise, and motives are not always susceptible to rational and logical analysis. Assessment of motives, in any event, is rarely certain and in most cases calls not only for acute analytical intelligence, but espionage, and, above all, for the intuitive wisdom of long experience in statecraft.

Information concerning Soviet motives is derived from three principal sources: (1) word; (2) conduct; and (3) personal contact with the Soviet leadership. In general, whenever there exists a discrepancy between publicly stated intention and conduct, the latter is a more reliable indicator of motives on a short-run basis. Actually there are three possible relations between speech and practice in Soviet diplomacy: (1) *identity;* (2) *approximation,* usually implying a temporary accommodation or modification of a preconceived intention; unless the latter itself receives explicit reformation; and (3) *divergence.* Cleavages between word and conduct may, in turn, result from faulty execution, misinformation, miscalculation, or deliberate confusion.

Analyzing Soviet diplomacy purely from documents, speeches, and ideological statements, gives undue weight to "rational" factors, since the irrational and accidental aspects of diplomacy can hardly be culled from documentary sources, and, although such a study may give a fairly lucid picture of the long-range outlines of Soviet policy, it is of limited validity as an investigation of Soviet diplomacy. On the other hand, calculating Soviet motives purely on the basis of day-to-day conduct and responses to particular situations can easily produce a distorted conception of Soviet foreign policy and lead to the erroneous conclusion that it is only slightly distinguishable from traditional Great Power diplomacy.

Diplomacy is neither impersonal nor automatic in its execution—although its working executors may often be both—but it is a human enterprise. Soviet motives cannot be separated from the character and personality traits of the principal decision makers in the Kremlin. Any evaluation of the foreign policy of the Soviet Union, whose principal decision makers are a well-defined oligarchy, without a prudent and careful examination and consideration of the various estimates and observations of the "human equations" in Soviet diplomacy is bound to be defective. The personal factor, particularly in the last fifteen years of Stalin's life, and during Khrushchev's incumbency, was of crucial significance in any evaluation of Soviet foreign policy. Personal observations of the Soviet leadership, however, are essentially subjective; they originate with observers who are free from neither ignorance, prejudice, nor gullibility, and the observations are apt to vary accordingly. Any attempt to distill the essence of Soviet diplomacy solely from personality considerations is in fact doomed to hopeless confusion and sterility. A sound analysis of Soviet motives must take into consideration ideology, conduct, and personalities, not as separate and independent entities, but as basic variables whose relative and relational significance is in a constant state of flux.

One question that inevitably arises is whether Soviet policy is actually motivated by ideological ends, such as world revolution, or by some other more mundane consideration, such as "power" or "national interest." Soviet ideology itself defines "national interest," "power," and "world revolution" in such a way as to make them virtually as indistinguishable and inseparable as the three sides of an equilateral triangle. The transcendental goal of Soviet foreign policy, world revolution, was defined by Lenin even before the existence of the Soviet state, when he declared in 1915 that "the victorious proletariat of [one] country . . . would stand up against . . . the capitalist world . . . raising revolts in those countries against the capitalists, and in the event of necessity coming out even with armed force against the exploiting classes and their states."[8] " 'The fundamental question of revolution is the question of power,' " wrote Stalin, quoting Lenin, and he went on to say that, as the effectiveness of the Soviet Union as an instrument of world revolution is measured in terms of power, "the whole point is to retain power to consolidate it, to make it invincible."[9] As a contrived and temporary nation-state, the Soviet Union assumed par-

[8]V. I. Lenin, *Selected Words* (New York: International Publishers Company, Inc., n.d.), V, 141.
[9]J. V. Stalin, *Problems of Leninism* (Moscow: Universal Distributors, 1947), p. 39.

ticular interests, but "the U.S.S.R. has no interests at variance with the interests of the world revolution, and the international proletariat naturally has no interests that are at variance with the Soviet Union."[10] Stalin's final fusion was to identify the consolidation and extension of his own power with the interests of the world revolution.

The abstraction of a Soviet national interest outside the context of Soviet ideology, no matter how superficially attractive it may appear to be as a useful analytical tool, ruptures the image of Soviet reality and results in the calculation of Soviet foreign policy on the basis of false assumptions. Soviet foreign policy is based on the image of reality provided by the Marxist-Leninist ideological prism, and whether this image be faulty or not is totally irrelevant in the calculation of Soviet motives, although such a foreign policy will eventually reap its toll in diplomatic failure. The Soviet conception of "interest" cannot be separated from class categories, and its determination is essentially horizontal rather than vertical. Although the legal expression of class interests is temporarily articulated through the nation-state, and assumes the character of a "national interest," nonetheless in the Soviet view there exist within each state not one but several parallel "national interests," corresponding to its socio-economic development. The "national interest" reflected by the state in its diplomacy, however, can only represent the interests of the "ruling class," and no other, regardless of its pretensions.

Soviet ideology recognizes the coexistence of three qualitatively distinct national interests in the modern world, owing to the uneven development of

10W. K. Knorin, *Fascism, Social-Democracy and the Communists* (Moscow: 1933).

society: (1) the national interest of the feudal aristocracy, surviving only in extremely backward societies; (2) the national interest of the bourgeoisie, which allegedly is the dominant expression of most non-communist states; and (3) the national interest of the proletariat, receiving diplomatic expression only in communist states, which is presumed by the dialectic to be coterminous with that of society as a whole.

Marxism tenaciously holds to the view that the community of interests that binds identical classes of different nations is more fundamental and decisive than that which binds different classes within the same nation-state. Although division and disunity are inherently characteristic of the bourgeois classes of different states, whose conflicts of interest are periodically expressed in war, the interests of all proletarians (together with their peasant and colonial allies) are considered to be in total harmony, their basic identity being temporarily obscured by artificially stimulated national distinctions.

Given the premise of the total identity of interests on a class basis, the Soviet Union, as the only avowed proletarian state in existence and the self-proclaimed embryo of a universal proletarian state, pronounced its interests to be identical with those of the world proletariat:

The Communist Party of the Soviet Union has always proceeded from the fact that "national" and international problems of the proletariat of the U.S.S.R. amalgamate into one general problem of liberating the proletarians of all countries from capitalism, and the interests . . . in our country wholly and fully amalgamate with the interests of the revolutionary movement of all countries into one general interest of the victory of socialist revolution in all countries.[11]

Although this view is vigorously contested, is far from universally recognized, and does not correspond to actual facts, it is not thereby invalidated as a basis for diplomatic action or analysis.

The presence of one of two factors, both capable of objective verification, is sufficient to impart to the national interests of a particular state an authentic international quality. These factors are: (1) the creation of appropriate forms of political organization designed to articulate the national interests of one state as those of the world at large; and (2) mass recognition in other countries that the national interests of a foreign state are identical with a higher transcendental interest. Not one, but both of these desiderata characterize Soviet foreign policy. It was a cardinal aim to replace the nation-state system with a world communist state, by shifting allegiance and loyalty from the nation-state to class. This not only invited the nationals of other countries to recognize a higher, class, loyalty to the Soviet Union, but meant active engagement in fostering the appropriate political institutions, such as the Comintern, foreign communist parties, front organizations, and the like, to implement this fusion.

The Soviet invitation to commit mass disloyalty has elicited wide response, and the formula identifying Soviet interests with the interests of the world proletariat has been accepted by millions of communists throughout the world as a basis for political action. This gives to Soviet national interests an undeniable transcendental quality

denied to the national interests of any other state except China. No matter how persistently a state may claim to be motivated by the interests of all mankind, if such a claim is accompanied neither by a serious effort at implementation nor evokes a response in other countries, it remains an empty and pious pretension. Transcendental ethical ends in foreign policy, irrespective of their substantive nature, have relevance only if they function as effective instruments or stimulants for the limitation, preservation, or further accumulation of power, or as instruments for its focalization. Otherwise, they are meaningless slogans and utopias, devoid of anything but peripheral significance in the calculation of a country's foreign policy.

Expansionism is thus inherent in the Leninist-Stalinist ideology, since the Soviet state was conceived as an ideological state without fixed geographical frontiers. Not only did this idea of the Soviet Union as the nucleus of a universal communist state receive expression in the basic documents of the Comintern,[12] but the Soviet Constitution of 1924 proclaimed the new Union to be open to all future Soviet republics and a "decisive step towards the union of workers of all countries into one World Socialist Soviet Republic."[13] And at Lenin's bier, Stalin vowed "to consolidate and extend the the Union of Republics."[14] Since it was the indispensable instrument and base of the world revolution, the ex-

[11]*Kommunist* (No. 2), January 1953, p. 15.

[12]*Cf.* W. C. Chamberlin, ed., *Blueprint for World Conquest* (Chicago: Human Events, Inc., 1946).

[13]Full text in M. W. Graham, *New Governments of Eastern Europe* (New York: Holt, Rinehart & Winston, Inc., 1927), p. 608.

[14]*History of the Communist Party of the Soviet Union* (New York: International Publishers Company, Inc., 1939), p. 269.

tension of Soviet power and territory, by any means, was equated with the exfoliation of the revolution.

Stalin's attempt to preserve the dominant and privileged status of the Soviet proletariat in the postwar communist fraternity of nations resulted in a specific form of Soviet imperialism that brought about Tito's defection and unleashed corrosive forces within the orbit as a whole. The subsequent failure of Khrushchev and Mao Tse-tung to reconcile their divergent national interests may have produced an irreparable schism in the movement as a whole. The failure of Stalin and his successors to calculate accurately the persistence and vitality of the community of interests based on national peculiarities is actually a reflection of the inadequacy of Marxist categories to deal with the conflicting interests of national communities, whether they be communist or bourgeois.

Paradoxically, as long as the Soviet Union was the only communist state, its universalistic pretensions were unchallenged by foreign communist parties. But with the eclipse of the Soviet monopoly of the interests of the world proletariat, occasioned by the emergence of a Communist China and national communism in Eastern Europe, the universalistic pretensions of the Leninist doctrine have been blunted, while, at the same time, stimulating a more limited "regional interest" aimed at synthetizing the various national interests of the communist orbit. The transmutation of several national interests into a single supranational interest remains an insuperable difficulty in the communist world, so long as the incompatibility of individual communist national interests, which the Marxist dogma fails to perceive accurately, prevails:

Marxism-Leninism has always strongly advocated that proletarian international-ism be combined with patriotism. . . . The Communist Parties of all countries must . . . become the spokesmen of the legitimate national interests and sentiments of their people [and] . . . effectively educate the masses in the spirit of internationalism and harmonize the national sentiments and interests of these countries.[15]

Less than seven years later, however, it had become quite clear that "the spirit of internationalism" could not prevail over the conflicting and incompatible national interests of the two great communist powers, each with its own national goals, aspirations, and image of the outside world. Since both the Soviet Union and China function within an identical ideological matrix, each has attempted to reshape and subordinate the interests of the communist movement to its own national interests, and each has provided an ideological rationalization for the transmutation of its national interests into the universal interests of all mankind. In 1963, Moscow denounced with eloquence the very vice which she had hitherto practiced with such consummate skill:

The statements of the Chinese leaders reveal a growing tendency to speak on behalf of the peoples of practically the whole world, including the Soviet people, the peoples of other socialist countries, and also the young national states of Asia, Africa, and Latin America. "Yet, who has given the Chinese leaders the right," the Soviet people inquire with indignation, "to decide for us, for the Soviet government, for the communist party, what is in keeping, and what is not in keeping with our interests? We have not given you the right and we do not intend to give it to you."[16]

[15]Statement by the Chinese Communist Party, "Once More on the Historical Experience of the Dictatorship of the Proletariat." Full text in *Pravda*, December 31, 1956.

[16]Soviet government Statement of August 21, 1963, *Pravda*, August 21, 1963.

SOVIET IDEOLOGY AND FOREIGN POLICY

The exact relationship between Soviet ideology and foreign policy has been subject to great controversy, ranging from the view that it is substantially irrelevant to the conviction that foreign policy is rigidly dictated by ideology. Actually, aside from providing the transcendental objectives of Soviet diplomacy, Soviet ideology performs five additional and distinct functions in foreign policy: (1) As a system of knowledge and as an analytical prism, it reflects an image of the existing social order and the distinctive analytical instruments (dialectical laws, and categories like the "class struggle," "historical stages," and so on) for its diagnosis and prognosis. (2) It provides an action strategy whereby to accelerate the transformation of the existing social order into the communist millennium. (3) It serves as a system of communication, unifying and coordinating the activities of its adherents. (4) It functions as a system of higher rationalization to justify, obscure, or conceal the chasms that may develop between theory and practice. (5) It stands as a symbol of continuity and legitimacy.

This compartmentalization of Soviet ideology is frankly arbitrary, and actually ruptures its basic unity, which is not necessarily to be found in its logic or reason, but in the intuitive faith and active experience of its partisans—factors which often elude rational analysis. Elements of Soviet ideology that appear logically incompatible, in fact, are, but these rational contradictions can be unified only in the crucibles of revolutionary action, not in the intellectual processes of the mind. The true meaning of the Marxist-Leninist insistence on the "unity of theory and practice" is that contradictions cannot be resolved by logic, but by action,

which is the final judge of "truth." Communist "truth" cannot be perceived without intuitive involvement, i.e., revolutionary action and experience, and to the outsider it remains as enigmatic as the mysteries of Zen.

The Soviet image of the world

The Soviet ideological prism reflects an image of the world that is virtually unrecognizable to a non-communist, yet it is on this image that Soviet foreign policy is based. It reflects a world of incessant conflict and change, in which institutions, loyalties, and philosophies arise and decay in accordance with the convulsive rhythm of the dialectic which implacably propels it on a predetermined arc to a foreordained future—world communism. This image is accepted as the real world by Soviet leaders. Their foreign policy rests upon the conviction that Marxism-Leninism is a scientific system that has uncovered and revealed the fundamental and implacable laws of social evolution and, hence, affords its adherents the unique advantage of prediction and partial control of events. This conviction has imparted to Soviet diplomacy an air of supreme confidence and dogmatic self-righteousness:

Soviet diplomacy . . . wields a weapon possessed by none of its rivals or opponents. Soviet diplomacy is fortified by a scientific theory of Marxism-Leninism. This doctrine lays down the unshakeable laws of social development. By revealing these norms, it gives the possibility not only of understanding the current tendencies of international life, but also of permitting the desirable collaboration with the march of events. Such are the special advantages held by Soviet diplomacy. They give it a special position in international life and explain its outstanding successes.[17]

[17] V. P. Potemkin, ed., *Istoriya Diplomatii* (Moscow: 1945), III 763–64.

The history of Soviet diplomacy, however, is by no means a uniform record of success, though "errors" in foreign policy are ascribed not to the doctrine, but to the improper apprehension and application of these infallible laws. Failure to apply these laws properly, according to the Soviet view, divorces foreign policy from international realities, and although it is true that "the record of Soviet diplomacy shows an inability to distinguish between the real and the imaginary, a series of false calculations about the capabilities and intentions of foreign countries, and a record of clumsy coordination between diplomacy and propaganda,"[18] still, it is fatuous to deny that Marxism-Leninism, on the whole, has furnished a system of analysis that gives a sufficiently accurate comprehension of power, its calculation and distribution in the world, and the opportunities and limitations such calculations afford for Soviet foreign policy. The dogmatic reliance on techniques and methods that have proven successful under other conditions, the frequent refusal to jettison concepts that either have outlived their usefulness or consistently produce dismal results in terms of foreign policy aims, and the concentration of all decision-making authority in one man or in a tight oligarchy—these practices at times tend to convert Marxism-Leninism from a unique asset for Soviet diplomacy into a strait jacket.

The dialectical image of history. Soviet ideology exposes the forces and tendencies operating in international pol-

[18]Max Beloff, *Foreign Policy and the Democratic Process* (Baltimore: The Johns Hopkins Press, 1955), p. 98. *Cf.,* also, V. V. Aspaturian, "Diplomacy in the Mirror of Soviet Scholarship," in *Contemporary History in the Soviet Mirror,* ed. J. Keep (New York: Frederick A. Praeger, Inc., 1964), pp. 243–74.

itics, but it is up to the leadership to calculate these forces properly, seek out the most decisive trends, and coordinate Soviet diplomacy with the inexorable march of history. The success of Soviet diplomacy, according to the Soviet view, is maximized as it is attuned to the rhythm of the historical dialectic, and its failures are multiplied as it falls out of harmony. Conversely, the occasional successes of bourgeois diplomacy are due to fortuitous and haphazard coordination with historical development, or to the equally accidental deviation of Soviet foreign policy from the implacable dictates of history. These accidental deviations are attributed to faulty application of historical laws by individual leaders.

Without attempting any extended discussion of Soviet dialectics, it can be said that, in the communist view, history progressively exfoliates as a series of qualitative stages, each with its own peculiar economic organization of society, which gives rise to corresponding social, political, and religious institutions. This inexorable movement, from lower to higher forms of economic and social organization is propelled by means of a dialectical duel between perpetually developing economic forces of society and the social and political institutions that attempt to preserve the economic order in the interests of a particular ruling class, whose servants they are. As long as the institution of private property survives, class distinctions between property holders and the propertyless, whose interests are irreconcilable, are perpetuated, and will eventuate in conflict, war, and revolution, only to be replaced by a new economic system that perpetuates class divisions and conflicts in new form. The class struggle, which is the principal motivating force of historical revolution, comes to an end only with the overthrow of the capitalist system by the proletariat, after which class distinctions, conflict, and war are finally eliminated. Once communism achieves victory on a world scale, the state itself and its coercive institutions are supposed to "wither away."[19]

The communists recognize five qualitative historical stages; primitive communism, slave-system, feudalism, capitalism, and socialism-communism, all of which, except for the first and last, are characterized by the institution of private property, two main contending classes (owners of the means of production and workers), and a state that represents the interests of the ruling class. Although the movement of history is from lower to higher stages, this movement is neither uniform nor without complications, and it does not pursue a uniform and rigid chronological evolution. This has been particularly true of the twentieth century. At the present time, communists acknowledge the coexistence of all historical stages; and this recognition has had a profound influence on Soviet foreign policy.

Soviet ideology is not self-executing; that is, it does not interpret itself automatically and does not reflect images of reality that can be unambiguously perceived, but rather it is based upon an authoritative interpretation of changing events by the Soviet leaders, who must choose from among a variety of possible interpretations, only one of which can be tested at a time for truth in the crucible of action. As long as Stalin was alive, interpretation of doctrine was a monopoly reserved for him alone and it was his interpretation.

[19]For a more elaborate statement of the author's views on the nature of Soviet ideology, see Vernon V. Aspaturian, "The Contemporary Doctrine of the Soviet State and Its Philosophical Foundations," *American Political Science Review*, XLVIII (December, 1954).

The two-camp image. Stalin's image of the world after the Russian Revolution was one of forced "coexistence" between a single socialist state and a hostile capitalist world surrounding it —a coexistence imposed on both antagonists by objective historical conditions. Neither side being sufficiently powerful to end the existence of the other, they were fated to exist together temporarily on the basis of an unstable and constantly shifting balance of power:

The fundamental and new, the decisive feature, which has affected all the events in the sphere of foreign relations during this period, is the fact that a certain temporary equilibrium of forces has been established between our country . . . and the countries of the capitalist world; an equilibrium which has determined the present period of "peaceful co-existence."[20]

The establishment, in a capitalistic world, of a socialist bridgehead which was inevitably destined to envelop the entire globe was, for Stalin, the supreme and ineluctable contradiction in the international scene. Although the capitalist world was infinitely stronger and could overwhelm the Soviet Republic if it could embark on a common enterprise, it was viewed as torn by internal divisions and conflicts that prevented the organization of an anti-Soviet crusade. Beside the overriding contradiction between the socialist camp and the capitalist camp, the bourgeois world was plagued with four additional inescapable contradictions: (1) the contradiction between the proletariat and the bourgeoisie in each country; (2) the contradiction between the *status quo* and the revisionist powers (Stalin referred to them as

[20]J. V. Stalin, *Political Report of the Central Committee to the Fourteenth Congress of the Communist Party of the Soviet Union (B)* (Moscow: 1950), p. 8.

"victor" and "vanquished" capitalist states); (3) the contradiction between the victorious powers over the spoils of war; (4) the contradiction between the imperialist states and their colonial subjects.

The contradiction between the socialist and capitalist camps was considered by Stalin the most fundamental and decisive, but it was not to be aggravated so long as the Soviet Union was in a weakened condition. War between the two camps was viewed as inevitable; however, it could be temporarily avoided and delayed by astute maneuvering within the conflicts raging in the capitalist world.

Stalin's postwar policy was predicated on an inevitable conflict with the West, organized by the United States. The organization of the Cominform and the forced unity of the communist orbit, the expulsion of Tito from the communist fraternity, the extraction of public statements of loyalty from communist leaders in all countries, the urgency with which Stalin sought to eliminate all possible power vacuums between the two blocs along the periphery of the communist world, all were preparatory measures based on the false assumption that the American ruling class was betraying anxiety at the growth of Soviet power and was preparing the final Armageddon. At the founding convention of the Cominform the late Andrei Zhdanov revealed the authoritative Soviet interpretation of the emerging bipolarization of power:

The fundamental changes caused by the war on the international scene and in the position of individual countries have entirely changed the political landscape of the world. A new alignment of political forces has arisen. The more the war recedes into the past, the more distinct become two major trends in postwar international policy, corresponding to the division of the political forces operating on the international arena into two major camps; the imperialist and antidemocratic camp, on the one hand, and the anti-imperialist and democratic camp, on the other. The principal driving force of the imperialist camp is the U.S.A. . . . The cardinal purpose of the imperialist camp is to strengthen imperialism, to hatch a new imperialist war, to combat Socialism.[21]

During the Korean war and just prior to the Nineteenth Party Congress in 1952, a "great debate" had apparently taken place in the Politburo concerning the validity of the expectation of imminent war between the two camps. Two essentially divergent views were discussed by Stalin in his *Economic Problems of Socialism*: (1) that wars between capitalist countries had ceased to be inevitable and hence war between the two camps was imminent, the view that was then current; and (2) that wars between capitalist states remained inevitable, but that war between the two camps was unlikely. Although the first view was the basis of Soviet postwar policy, Stalin ascribed it to "mistaken comrades," and elevated the second to doctrinal significance:

Some comrades hold that the U.S.A. has brought the other capitalist countries sufficiently under its sway to be able to prevent them going to war among themselves. It is said that the contradictions between capitalism and socialism are stronger than the contradictions among the capitalist countries. Theoretically, of course that is true. It is not only true now, today; it was true before the Second World War. . . . Yet the Second World War began not as a war with the U.S.S.R., but as a war between capitalist countries. Why? . . . because war with the U.S.S.R., as a socialist land, is more dangerous to capitalism than war be-

[21]Full text reprinted in *Strategy and Tactics of World Communism* (Washington, D.C.: Government Printing Office, 1948), pp. 216–17.

tween capitalist countries; for whereas war between capitalist countries puts in question only the supremacy of certain capitalist countries over others, war with the U.S.S.R. must certainly put in question the existence of capitalism itself. . . . It is said that Lenin's thesis that imperialism inevitably generates war must now be regarded as obsolete. . . . That is not true. . . . To eliminate the inevitability of war, it is necessary to abolish imperialism.[22]

Stalin's only modification of his two-camp image was thus to concede that war between the two blocs was no longer imminent, but would be preceded by a series of wars among the capitalist powers themselves—between the United States and its satellite allies, France and Britain, on the one hand, and its temporary vassals, Germany and Japan, on the other. The resentment of the ruling classes of these vassal countries over American domination would provoke national revolutions and a renewed war over the ever-shrinking capitalist market, occasioned by the emergence of a parallel communist market, which would remain outside the arena of capitalist exploitation. The Soviet Union would remain outside the conflict, which would automatically seal the doom of world capitalism. However, Stalin's policies actually accentuated the very conflict—that between the two camps —he wished to temporarily deemphasize, while submerging those—among the capitalist states—which he wished to exacerbate. Soviet policy, by predicting war, was threatening to make inevitable a nuclear holocaust which would destroy both worlds.

The post-Stalin image. At the Twentieth Party Congress, Stalin's image of the world was considerably modified,

[22]J. V. Stalin, *Economic Problems of Socialism* (New York: International Publishers Company, Inc., 1952), pp. 27–30.

in an attempt to bring it into closer focus with the realities of international politics. These modifications were made to eliminate the threatening schisms in the communist camp, to break up the unity of the non-Soviet world and dismantle anti-Soviet instruments like NATO, to head off the impending nuclear war that Stalin's doctrines and policies were unwittingly encouraging, and to enhance the flexibility of Soviet diplomacy in exploiting the contradictions of the capitalist world.

In place of Stalin's fatalistic image of a polarized world, the Twentieth Party Congress drew a more optimistic, and, in many respects, a mellower picture:

1. "Capitalist encirclement" was officially declared terminated, as major speakers like Molotov echoed the Titoist doctrine that "the period when the Soviet Union was . . . encircled by hostile capitalism now belongs to the past." The permanent insecurity of the Soviet Union, pending the worldwide victory of communism, as visualized by Stalin, was replaced with the image of a permanently secured Soviet Union, surrounded by friendly communist states in Europe and Asia, embracing nearly one-third of the world, with imperialism in an irrevocable state of advanced decay.

2. In place of Stalin's fixed vision of coexistence between two irreconcilable camps poised in temporary balance, which was declared obsolete and inapplicable to the postwar world, his successors recognized a third, "anti-imperialist" but nonsocialist, group of powers, carved out of decaying colonial empires, which had separated from the capitalist camp but had not yet joined the communist. Stalin's inflexible two-camp image needlessly alienated these new states and tended to force them into the capitalist orbit. This belt of neutralist states—a concept which Stalin refused to recognize —insulated the entire communist orbit from the capitalist world and, together

with the socialist states, was viewed as constituting "an extensive 'zone of peace,' including both socialist and nonsocialist peace-loving states of Europe and Asia inhabited by nearly 1,500,000,000 people, or the majority of the population of our planet."

3. Stalin's doctrine of the "fatal inevitability" of wars was pronounced antiquated, since its emphasis on coercive and violent instruments of diplomacy tended to render the Soviet peace campaign hypocritical, accelerated the formation of anti-Soviet coalitions, and, in an era of nuclear weapons, appeared to doom both worlds to a war of mutual annihilation.

4. Stalin's five main contradictions were retained as valid and persistent, but the radical shift in the equilibrium of class forces in the world dictated a change of emphasis and the reordering of priorities. Stalin stressed the conflicts among the major capitalist countries as the main object of Soviet diplomacy, relegating other contradictions to minor roles, but his successors saw the main contradiction of the current historical stage to be that between the anticolonial and the imperialist forces. In short, the world has moved out of the stage of the "capitalist encirclement" of the Soviet Union and, during the current phase of coexistence, is moving into the stage of the "socialist encirclement" of the United States, as a prelude to the final victory of communism.[23]

The new image of the world drawn by Khrushchev at the Twentieth Party Congress was by no means the consequence of a unanimous decision. It was opposed by at least four, and possibly five, full members of the eleven-man Presidium. Aside from his vigorous opposition to Khrushchev's adventurist innovations in industry and agriculture, Foreign Minister Molotov

[23]Full text as broadcast by Moscow Radio, February 18, 1956. See also the *New York Times*, February 19, 1956 (Mikoyan Report).

and the so-called Stalinist faction bitterly resisted the demolition of the Stalin myth and the entire de-Stalinization program; and they systematically sabotaged the foreign policy decisions of the Twentieth Party Congress, which they publicly accepted.

Molotov's doctrinal differences had practical consequences in the actual formulation and execution of foreign policy. His constant carping criticism of existing policies, together with the precarious nature of Khrushchev's majority in the Presidium, introduced an uncharacteristic hesitancy into Soviet diplomacy. The vacillations, abrupt reversals, hesitations, discrepancies between policy and administration, and other eccentricities of Soviet diplomacy after Stalin's death were due not only to the incapacitating incompatibilities in the Presidium but also to Molotov's use of the foreign ministry and Soviet missions abroad as instruments to subvert the Government's policy in favor of his own.

Molotov objected to the decisions to seek a reconciliation with Marshal Tito and to meet President Eisenhower at Geneva. When Khrushchev and Bulganin returned from Geneva, Molotov was waiting with sarcastic and biting comments on their personal diplomacy. As a result of his persistent criticism and obstructionism, he was disciplined by the Central Committee in July, 1955, and his "erroneous stand on the Yugoslav issue was unanimously condemned." This was followed shortly by his forced and pained confession of doctrinal error, which superficially appeared to have no connection with foreign policy but appeared designed to tarnish his ideological orthodoxy and was an unmistakable sign that he was on his way out. His unrelenting sabotage through the foreign ministry, in particular his determination to poison relations with Tito, finally led to his ouster as foreign minister in favor of Shepilov on the eve of Tito's visit to Moscow in June, 1956. Apparently Shepilov also fell out of sympathy with the foreign policy he was supposed to execute and for opportunistic reasons (Khrushchev scathingly characterized him as "the careerist Shepilov who . . . showed himself to be a most shameless double-dealer") cast his lot with the Stalinist faction. The Molotov group suddenly contrived a majority in the December, 1956, Plenum of the Central Committee, but when Khrushchev regained control at the February, 1957, Plenum, Shepilov was summarily dismissed as foreign minister in favor of Andrei Gromyko, who was a professional diplomat and thus could be counted upon not to pursue a personal foreign policy.

In the bill of particulars against Molotov, it was charged that:

1. For a long time, Comrade Molotov in his capacity as Foreign Minister, far from taking through the Ministry of Foreign Affairs measures to improve relations between the U.S.S.R. and Yugoslavia, repeatedly came out against the measures that the Presidium . . . was carrying out to improve relations with Yugoslavia.

2. Comrade Molotov raised obstacles to the conclusion of the state Treaty with Austria and the improvement of relations with that country, which lies in the center of Europe. The conclusion of the Austrian Treaty was largely instrumental in lessening international tension in general.

3. He was also against normalization of relations with Japan, while that normalization has played an important part in relaxing international tension in the Far East.

4. Comrade Molotov repeatedly opposed the Soviet Government's indispensable new steps in defence of peace and security of nations. In particular he denied the advisability of establishing personal contacts between the Soviet leaders and the statesmen of other countries, which is essential for the achievement of mutual understanding and better international relations.[24]

"Molotov," Khrushchev bluntly stated in a later speech, "found more convenient a policy of tightening all screws, which contradicts the wise Leninist policy of peaceful co-existence."[25] Thus, it can be assumed that Molotov advocated a continuation of the basic foreign policies of the Stalinist era, as modified during the Malenkov regime, based on a perpetuation of the two-camp image. It was Molotov's contention that Soviet policy could reap its greatest dividends by maintaining international tensions at a high pitch and running the risks of nuclear war, on the assumption that an uncompromising, cold-blooded policy would force Western statesmen, through lack of nerve and under pressure of public opinion to continually retreat in the face of Soviet provocation, for fear of triggering a war of mutual extinction. It appears that he considered as un-Marxist the idea that the ex-colonial countries could be regarded as having deserted the capitalist camp and as constituting an "extensive zone of peace" together with the Soviet bloc, but rather he considered their behavior in international politics to be motivated purely by considerations of opportunism and expediency. The main arena of rivalry for Molotov remained in Western Europe and the Atlantic area—the bastions of capitalism—

[24]The last point is probably a reference not only to the Geneva Conference but also to the various junkets of Bulganin and Khrushchev throughout Asia and Europe, none of which included Foreign Minister Molotov.

[25]The *New York Times,* July 7, 1957.

and not in Asia or Africa, and he continued to view the new countries of Asia and Africa with hostility and suspicion as appendages to the capitalist camp.

Molotov's policy of "tightening all screws" was opposed by the Soviet army, and also by Peking, which had its own reasons, although it was later revealed that the Chinese and Molotov seemed to agree on a wide range of issues. Speaking in Peking, Anastas Mikoyan, reputedly the principal Kremlin architect of the new diplomatic strategy, invoked Lenin in support of the current policy. Quoting Lenin's famous formula that "in the last analysis, the outcome of the struggle will be determined by the fact that Russia, India, China, etc. constitute the overwhelming majority of the world's population," he roundly condemned the Stalinist two-camp image to which Molotov still subscribed.

Soviet diplomatic strategy in the underdeveloped countries of Asia, Africa and Latin-America appears to contradict the basic revolutionary strategy of communism. Although Moscow's support of the so-called "bourgeois-nationalist" (roughly, "neutralist" under existing conditions) independence or revolutionary movements in the underdeveloped regions (colonies and "semi-colonies") against Western colonialism, economic dependence upon the West and internal feudalism, is fully compatible with Leninist-Stalinist doctrine on revolution in the underdeveloped world, the Soviet pattern of political and economic assistance to regimes like those in India, Egypt, Iraq, Ghana and, to a lesser extent, Cuba, does not fully conform to communist doctrine. Red China has stepped into this breach and has challenged Moscow's refusal to encourage and support indigenous communist parties in their efforts to overthrow native "bourgeois-nationalist" governments and establish authentic communist-controlled regimes. Instead, according to Peking, Moscow supports governments which persecute and imprison local communists.

The Soviet position on this point is extraordinarily non-doctrinaire and pragmatic, for whereas China stresses the view that the Communist Party is the only reliable instrument of revolution, Khrushchev and his successors appear to be toying with the idea that under favorable circumstances, particularly when the balance of power has shifted decisively in favor of the communist world, native bourgeois-nationalist leaders may be won over to communism and the revolution could be consummated from above rather than below. The transformation of the Castro regime in Cuba, from an anti-imperialist, nationalist regime into a communist regime, was apparently viewed by Khrushchev as a prototype of this process. As a practical diplomatic position, Moscow feels that any move to encourage communist insurrection in these areas would simply stampede them all into the capitalist and anti-communist camp, a development which Peking considers—along with Molotov—as inevitable in any event. Peking's present strategy seems to stem from the conviction that the bourgeois nationalists will betray the Soviet Union (as Chiang Kai-shek did in 1928) and that, by supporting the local communist parties now, China will have earned their gratitude and support.

THE FORMULATION OF SOVIET FOREIGN POLICY

Introduction

Any attempt to describe the formulation of Soviet foreign policy in the crucibles of its decision-making organs is bound to be a hazardous and frustrating enterprise. The absence of periodic or systematic publication of documents, the inaccessibility of archives and officials, the virtual nonexistence of memoirs or diaries of retiring statesmen, the puzzling duplication of state and party institutions, the perplexing fluctuations in their relationships, the ambiguity of Soviet ideology and the wide discrepancy between theory and practice, the bewildering profusion of constitutional and institutional changes, the arbitrary tendency to ignore or short-circuit elaborately detailed institutional channels, and, finally, the capricious and convulsive turnover of personalities, are the more familiar impediments that must be contended with.

The decision-making process itself is a dynamic interaction between institutions and personalities, whose character varies with the effectiveness of institutions to impose limits on the acts of individuals. In constitutional states, characterized by relatively permanent institutions, the restraints on officials are carefully defined, imposing ineluctable limits not only on the range of policy formulation but upon the choice of means as well. In a totalitarian system like the Soviet Union, where impermanently rooted institutions have been subordinated to relatively permanent personalities, the institutional aspects of the decision-making process are little more than ceremonial. Decision making is essentially personal, and bound to vary with the evolving ideological convictions, character, and judgment of those in control, the nature of the rivalries between them, and, finally, their reaction to the political and social pressures that bear upon them.

The Soviet political superstructure prior to 1953, was a complicated mosaic of shifting and interlocking institutions resting on an entrenched foundation of one-man dictatorship, in which all powers were delegated from above. The institutions of both Party and State, as well as their relationship to one another, were essentially creatures of the late Joseph Stalin and were designed, not to limit his own power, but to limit that of his subordinates and rivals, and to facilitate the solidification of his own authority. As the instruments of his creation and manipulation, they could not, and did not, function as restraints on his latitude of decision. Both institutions and subordinates were liquidated with remarkable dispatch when the occasion demanded.

The system of duplicating and overlapping political organs between the Party and State allegedly reflects a division of functions between the formulation and execution of policy, with policy formulation a monopoly reserved exclusively for the Party, while the function of the government was to be restricted to formalizing and legalizing the decisions of the Party into official acts of state. This dichotomy was never either rigid or absolute, but constantly varied in accordance with the degree of interlocking of personnel at the summits of the Party and State hierarchies.

The Party Congress

In theory the most exalted, but in practice the most degraded of the central Party institutions in the formulation of policy is the Party Congress. Traditionally the most important fundamental pronouncements on foreign policy have been made before the Party Congress, which is empowered to set the basic line of the Party and State, but in actual fact merely hears and rubber-stamps the decisions made elsewhere. All higher organs of the Party, including the Presidium and

Secretariat, are responsible and accountable to the Party Congress, which theoretically can remove and replace their membership.

The actual role of the Congress in foreign policy has varied throughout its existence. Under Lenin, and, in fact, as late as the Sixteenth Party Congress (in 1930), serious debate on foreign policy and international revolutionary strategy frequently ensued, although never with the same intensity or wide range of diversity as on domestic policy. Because of its massive size (nearly 2,000 delegates), the Congress became increasingly unwieldy as an organ of debate and discussion, and it gradually was converted into a forum which heard various sides and finally into a subdued sounding board for Stalin's deadly rhetoric. Discussion and debate first slipped behind the doors of the Central Committee and eventually vanished into the Politburo. All decisions were made in the Politburo, then reported to the Central Committee and, with increasing infrequency, to the Party Congress. The principal function of the Party Congress was reduced to the hearing of reports by the prominent figures of the Party.

The two most important reports to Party Congresses relating to foreign policy are the Main Political Report of the Central Committee, delivered in the past by Stalin (except at the Nineteenth Congress), and a report on the activities of the World Communist Movement. At the Nineteenth Congress, Malenkov delivered the Main Report. However, Stalin had ordered published his *Economic Problems of Socialism* on the eve of the Congress, and this set the tone and dominated the entire proceedings. At the Twentieth Congress, Khrushchev delivered the Main Report, incorporating radical doctrinal innovations affecting foreign policy, while Molotov confined himself to praising reluctantly the new policy and resentfully subjecting his own past conduct of foreign policy to self-criticism. The activities of foreign communist parties were reported by their own representatives.

A close examination of the Main Political Reports betrays an almost rigid uniformity in organization. The entire first section is devoted to international affairs; an authoritative interpretation of the world situation; an appraisal of the Soviet position; trends, developments, and opportunities to watch for; warnings, threats, boasts, and invitations to bourgeois powers; congratulations and words of praise for friendly countries; and, finally, a summary of the immediate and long-range objectives of Soviet foreign policy. This report, before the emergence of polycentric tendencies in the world communist movement and the onset of the Sino-Soviet dispute, set the line to guide communists everywhere in their activities, and, thus, the Congress became not a forum for debate, but a unique medium of communication.

Debate and discussion vanished after 1930, and meetings of the Congress became so infrequent that they threatened to vanish altogether. In his secret speech to the Twentieth Congress, Khrushchev gave this vivid description of the deterioration of the Party Congress:

During Lenin's life, party congresses were convened regularly; always when a radical turn in the development of the party and country took place, Lenin considered it absolutely necessary that the party discuss at length all basic matters pertaining to . . . foreign policy. . . . Whereas during the first years after Lenin's death, party congresses . . . took place more or less regularly, later . . . these principles were brutally violated. . . . Was it a normal situation when over 13 years [1939–1952] elapsed between the Eighteenth and Nineteenth Congresses? . . . Of 1,966 delegates [to the Seventeenth Congress in 1934] with either voting or advisory rights, 1,108 persons were arrested on charges of revolutionary crimes.[26]

The Central Committee

As the body that "guides the entire work of the Party in the interval between Congresses . . . and . . . directs the work of the Central and Soviet public organizations [i.e., the government],"[27] the Central Committee became the principal arena of debate and discussion of foreign policy during the period preceding 1934. According to the Party rules at that time, the Politburo was obliged to report to this body at least three times a year, so that its decisions might be examined, criticized, and judged. The Central Committee elected the members of the Politburo, the Orgburo, and the Secretariat, and theoretically was empowered to appoint, remove, or replace its members. The Central Committee, itself elected by the Party Congress, was empowered to replace its own members by a two-thirds vote, but Stalin removed and appointed members of the Central Committee virtually at will.

On some occasions, the Foreign Commissar (who invariably is at least a full member of the Central Committee), as well as high Soviet functionaries of the Comintern, reported to the Central Committee on foreign policy and international communist activities. More often, the Secretary-General (Stalin) would deliver a report on the nature and scope of the Politburo's

work and explain the precise application of the "line" under changing international conditions. A fairly large body, composed of full and alternate members (about equally divided), the Central Committee was empowered to alter the policies of the Politburo and support the views of the minority. Only full members exercised the right to vote, but candidates had the right to participate in debate. Some of these reports, but not all, were made public, particularly if important modifications of the policies announced at the previous Party Congress were made. The records of the Committee's proceedings during the Stalin era remain generally unpublished and inaccessible for examination.

The Central Committee too, in time, was reduced to little more than a sounding board; its meetings became increasingly infrequent, and there is reason to believe that, after 1934, its decisions were unanimous. In Khrushchev's secret speech, he said:

> Even after the end of the war . . . Central Committee plenums were hardly ever called. It should be sufficient to mention that during the years of the Patriotic War [World War II] not a single Central Committee plenum took place. . . . Stalin did not even want to meet and talk with Central Committee members. . . . Of the 139 members and candidates of the Party's Central Committee who were elected at the Seventeenth Party Congress [1934], 98 persons, i.e., 70 per cent, were arrested and shot.

The Party Politburo[28]

There is no question but that the most important organ of decision making in the Soviet Union has been, and continues to be, the Politburo of the

[26]This extract and all subsequent references to Khrushchev's secret report to the Twentieth Congress are taken from the full text, *New York Times*, June 5, 1956. The speech has been widely reprinted elsewhere.

[27]*The Land of Socialism Today and Tomorrow* (Moscow: International Publishers Company, Inc., 1939), p. 473.

[28]The Party's highest organ was called the Politburo, from 1917 to 1952, and the Presidium, from 1952 to 1966. In 1966, the name Politburo was restored.

Party. In accordance with the principle of "democratic centralism," the ultimate power of the Party is entrusted to this organ. Its internal organization and recruiting procedures, the composition and convictions of its factions, and its voting practices remain essentially a mystery. No proceedings of its deliberations have been made public in decades, and, in the absence of any recent defections from this body, information concerning its procedures and activities can be derived only from the following sources: (1) fragmentary records of very early meetings; (2) public exposure of its deliberations by Leon Trotsky and other rivals of Stalin during the period before 1930; (3) accounts by high-ranking diplomats or government and Party officials, whose activities brought them into close range of the Politburo, and who have defected from the Soviet Union; (4) personal accounts and memoirs of foreign statesmen who negotiated with members of the Politburo or with Stalin; (5) accounts of renegade officials of the Comintern and foreign communist parties; (6) secrets spilled as a result of the Stalin-Tito feud; (7) Khrushchev's secret speech at the Twentieth Party Congress and its aftermath; (8) calculated leaks by the Polish Party and government since the rise of Gomulka; (9) examination of the decisions already taken; (10) rare public disputes between leading press organs of the Party and government; (11) shifts in Party and government officials; and (12) rare Central Committee Resolutions like that of June 29, 1957.

Under Stalin, all decisions of the Politburo on questions of foreign policy were, in one form or another, his. All rival and dissident views were quashed and their adherents liquidated. The membership of the body was hand-picked by him. In his relations with the Politburo, Stalin could either announce his decisions and expect unanimous approval; submit them for examination and ask for discussion, with or without a vote; simply act without consulting his colleagues; or consult with various members on certain questions, to the exclusion of others. According to a former Soviet diplomat, who was an eye-witness to some Politburo meetings in 1933:

A thin appearance of collective work is still kept up at Politburo meetings. Stalin does not "command." He merely "suggests" or "proposes." The fiction of voting is retained. But the vote never fails to uphold his "suggestions." The decision is signed by all ten members of the Politburo, with Stalin's signature among the rest. . . . The other members of the Politburo mumble their approval of Stalin's "proposal." . . . Stalin not only is generally called "the Boss" by the whole bureaucracy, but *is* the one and only boss.[29]

This general description of Stalin's style of work has been confirmed many times by diplomats and statesmen of many countries who observed that Stalin often made important decisions without consulting anyone, while Molotov and others would request time to consult with their "government." The role of the other members of the Politburo could best be described as consultative, although within the area of their own administrative responsibility they exercised the power of decision. Testimony concerning Stalin's

[29]Alexander Barmine, *One Who Survived* (New York: G. P. Putnam's Sons, 1946), p. 213. Barmine writes that ". . . thousands of relatively unimportant, as well as all-important, problems, must pass through Stalin's hand for final decision. . . . Weeks are spent in waiting; Commissars wait in Stalin's office."

intolerance of dissent is uniformly consistent. "Whoever opposed . . . his viewpoint," complained Khrushchev, "was doomed to be removed."

The relationship between the Foreign Ministry and the Presidium has always been unique. Since relations with other states are viewed in terms of a struggle for power among various "ruling classes," and thus directly involve the security and the very existence of the Soviet state, the Party center has always retained a tight supervision over the Foreign Ministry. This supervision assumes different forms, depending upon the Party rank of the individuals who hold the posts of Foreign Minister and of Premier. The Premier has always been a Party figure of the highest rank, while the Foreign Minister may or may not be a member of the Party Presidium.

During the period when Maxim Litvinov was Foreign Commissar, his work was supervised by Molotov, the Premier of the government and his formal superior. Matters of routine interest, not involving questions of policy or fundamental maneuver, were decided by Litvinov himself in consultation with his collegium. More substantial questions were taken to Molotov, who, depending upon the nature of the question, would make a decision, or take it to Politburo.[30]

The Politburo itself was broken down into various Commissions dealing with different aspects of policy. Questions of foreign policy were first considered by the Politburo Commission on Foreign Affairs, which included the Politburo specialists on the Comintern, Foreign Trade, and Defense. In matters involving exceptional or immediate importance, Molotov

[30]*Cf.* Merle Fainsod, *How Russia Is Ruled* (Cambridge, Mass.: Harvard University Press, 1953), p. 282.

would deal directly with Stalin and get a decision.

The procedures of the Politburo were neither systematic nor rigid. Often Stalin would personally consult with the Foreign Commissar and his chief advisers; and Litvinov, on a few occasions, would be asked to make a report to the Politburo. The principal function of the Commission on Foreign Affairs was to act as a coordinating agency of all the departments concerned with foreign relations, to assemble and evaluate intelligence information flowing from different channels, to devise strategy and policy, examine analyses, projects, and reports drawn up by specialists in the Foreign Commissariat, study reports of diplomats abroad, and then make a comprehensive report either to Stalin or to the Politburo as a whole.

Once the decisions were made, they would be transmitted in writing or verbally by Molotov to Litvinov for execution. These bureaucratic channels were often ignored and Stalin would act directly with Molotov, his principal agent, and they would personally give instructions to Litvinov. Deviation or improvisation from instructions by the Foreign Commissar or his subordinates in the Commissariat was neither permitted nor tolerated. According to Khrushchev, the system of Politburo Commissions was not primarily for organizational efficiency, but was a sinister device whereby Stalin weakened the authority of the collective body:

The importance of the . . . Political Bureau was reduced and its work disorganized by the creation within the Political Bureau of various commissions —the so-called "quintets," "sextets," "septets" and "novenaries."

When Molotov replaced Litvinov in

May, 1939, this cumbersome procedure was simplified. The Nazi-Soviet Pact was worked out principally by Stalin and Molotov, with Zhdanov and Mikoyan the only other members of the Politburo apparently apprised of the crucial decisions contemplated. The Politburo Commission on Foreign Affairs gradually increased in size until, by 1945, it was large enough to be converted by Stalin from a "sextet" into a "septet." As it grew in size, so its importance diminished. During the war, Stalin appeared to consult only Molotov on questions of foreign policy and frequently made decisions on the spot at the Big Three conferences.

Khrushchev's description of how decisions were made by Stalin and the Politburo is probably exaggerated and self-serving, but accurate in its general outline:

After the war, Stalin became even more capricious, irritable, and brutal; in particular his suspicion grew. His persecution mania reached unbelievable dimensions. Everything was decided by him alone without any consideration for anyone or anything. . . . Sessions of the Political Bureau occurred only occasionally . . . many decisions were taken by one person or in a roundabout way, without collective discussion. . . . The importance of the Political Bureau was reduced and its work disorganized by the creation within the Political Bureau of various commissions. . . . The result of this was that some members of the Political Bureau were in this way kept away from participation in the decisions of the most important state matters.

Decision making in the post-Stalin period: the agonies of collective leadership and factional conflict

The death of Stalin stimulated the expression of various opinions, and unleashed a struggle for power among his successors. Six months before his death, at the Nineteenth Party Congress, Stalin radically reorganized the Party summit, abolishing the Orgburo and replacing the eleven-man Politburo with a Presidium of twenty-five members and eleven candidate members as the key decision-making organ of the Soviet system. Since many of the new members of the Presidium were burdened with permanent administrative responsibilities far from Moscow, and since it was much too large to function as a decision-making body, there was secretly organized, in violation of the new Party charter, a smaller Bureau of the Presidium, whose membership has never been revealed. Whether expansion of the Presidium was designed by Stalin to widen the area of decision making and prevent a struggle for power after his death— thus preparing the conditions for orderly transition from personal to institutional dictatorship—or whether it was a sinister device for liquidating his old associates in favor of a generation ignorant of his crimes, remains an intriguing enigma. According to Khrushchev:

Stalin evidently had plans to finish off the old members of the Political Bureau. . . . His proposal after the Nineteenth Congress, concerning the selection of 25 persons to the Central Committee's Presidium, was aimed at the removal of the old Political Bureau members and the bringing in of less experienced persons so that they would extol him. . . . We can assume that this was a design for the future annihilation of the old Political Bureau members, and in this way, a cover for all the shameful acts of Stalin.

Immediately after Stalin's death, the old members of Stalin's entourage reduced the Presidium to its former size. The removal of Beria and the dismantling of his secret police apparatus introduced an uneasy equilibrium among the various factions in the Presidium, none of which was powerful enough to overwhelm the others.

In the post-Stalin Presidium, decisions often were taken only after stormy controversies and agile maneuvering among the various factions. As a consequence, necessity was converted into ideology, and conflicting opinions, within carefully circumscribed limits, were given official sanction. The authoritative theoretical journal *Kommunist,* however, warned that "views that are objectively directed toward dethroning the leadership elected by the Party masses," would not be tolerated.[31] This danger is adumbrated in the Party Statutes, Article 28 of which reads:

A broad discussion, in particular on an all-Union scale concerning the Party policy, should be so organized that it would not result in the attempts of an insignificant minority to impose its will on the majority of the Party or in attempts to organize fractional groupings which would break down Party unity, or in attempts to create a schism that would undermine the strength and the firmness of the socialist regime.[32]

The Party Statutes, however, were revised in 1961, at the Twenty-second Party Congress, in order to reflect more realistically the more fluid situation which had developed since Stalin's death and, while factionalism was still proscribed, greater emphasis was placed on ensuring the expression of divergent views within the Party. Thus, Article 27 of the 1961 Party Statutes stipulates that:

Wide discussion, especially discussion on a countrywide scale, of questions of Party policy must be held so as to ensure for Party members the free expression of their views and preclude attempts

to form fractional groupings destroying Party unity, attempts to split the Party.

The proliferation of factional politics. Diversity and clash of opinion was allowed, initially, to filter down only to the level of the Central Committee. Eventually however, differences of opinion which reflected various factional views erupted—at first gingerly, and then more boldly, in Party Congresses, lower-level Party bodies, the Supreme Soviet, various professional conferences, newspapers and periodicals, and in professional organizations. The disagreements within the Presidium which were unleashed after Stalin's death threatened to crack the Party pyramid down to its very base. It was even possible to envisage the development of a multiparty system, and authoritative voices were openly advocating the nomination of more than one candidate for elective offices.

Decisions in the Politburo are reached by simple majority, with only full members entitled to vote, although alternate members participate in the debate and discussion. Meetings of the Politburo are held at least once a week and, according to both Khrushchev and Mikoyan, most decisions are unanimous. Mikoyan has further elaborated by stating that if a consensus were unobtainable, the Presidium would adjourn, sleep on the matter, and return for further discussion until unanimity was achieved. Since five full members out of eleven were expelled, on June 29, 1957, for persistent opposition and obstruction to the Party line, the unanimity of the Presidium's deliberations appear to have been exaggerated.

In view of Khrushchev's bitter attack on the organization of Politburo Commissions under Stalin, the Politburo's internal compartmentalization may not be as rigidly demarcated as before; foreign policy decisions, in-

[31]*Kommunist,* No. 10 (August, 1956), pp. 3–13.
[32]*Pravda,* October 14, 1952.

stead of being merely the concern of the Commission on Foreign Affairs, are discussed and made by the body as a whole. "Never in the past," said Molotov at the Twentieth Party Congress, "has our Party Central Committee and its Presidium been engaged as actively with questions of foreign policy as during the present period."

The sharp and close factional divisions in the Politburo have revived the prominence and activity of the moribund Central Committee. Factional differences have been displayed before Plenums of the Central Committee (which are held at least twice a year) where the actions of the Politburo have been appealed. In this relatively large body of 195 full members and 165 alternates, discussion of the various views current in the Politburo is still more ritualized than free, with each faction in the Politburo supported by its own retainers in the Central Committee. Voting is conditioned not only by divisions in the Politburo, but also by considerations of political survival and opportunism, with members being extremely sensitive to the course that the struggle assumes in the higher body. "At Plenums of the Central Committee," according to the revealing statement of one low-ranking member, "Comrade Khrushchev and other members of the Presidium . . . corrected errors in a fatherly way . . . regardless of post occupied or of record."[33]

It was in the Central Committee that Malenkov reputedly indicted Beria and where, in turn, he and Molotov were disciplined and attacked by the Khrushchev faction. Shifts in the balance of factions in the Politburo are almost always immediately registered in the Central Committee, whose proceedings inevitably sway with those of the higher body. The Central Committee, whose decisions are invariably reported as unanimous, is empowered to alter its own membership and that of its higher bodies by a two-thirds vote; and in the June, 1957, Plenum it expelled three full members and one alternate from the Presidium and the Central Committee, demoted one to alternate status, and cut off still another at full membership in the Central Committee. Correspondingly, the Presidium was expanded to fifteen full members and nine alternates.

The Central Committee assumed increasing importance during the Khrushchev era, and it is likely that, after the "anti-Party group" episode, of June, 1957, he considered this body as a counterweight to the opposition which might congeal against him in the Presidium. Khrushchev was almost fastidious in his zeal to enshrine Central Committee as the ultimate institutional repository of legitimacy in the Soviet system. The body was enlarged and convened regularly by Khrushchev, and all changes in personnel and major pronouncements of policy were either confirmed by or announced at Central Committee Plenums. Thus, the Central Committee was convened to expel Marshal Zhukov, former Premier Bulganin, Kirichenko, and Belyayev, as well as others, and met more often than the two annual meetings specified in the Party statutes. New appointments to the Presidium and the Secretariat were also announced after Central Committee meetings.

Immediately after the expulsion of the "anti-party group," in mid-1957, and the removal of Marshal Zhukov, the Khrushchev faction appeared to be in full control of both the Presidium and the Central Committee and Khrushchev appeared to be in full command of the ruling faction. Proceedings of the Central Committee

[33]Moscow Radio broadcast, February 21, 1956. Speech of Z. I. Muratov, first secretary of the Tatar Oblast Committee.

were also published more or less regularly under Khrushchev although selective censorship and suppression persisted. Khrushchev's behavior at Central Committee proceedings was often crude, rude and earthy; commanding, but not domineering. He would deliver a report on the main item on the agenda, which was then discussed in speeches delivered by the other members. These were freely interrupted by the First Secretary, who might affirm, criticise, chastise, admonish, correct, and even warn the speakers, and they would respond with varying degrees of deference, familiarity, meekness, fear, or audacity. At the December, 1958, Plenum, for example, seventy-five speakers discussed Khrushchev's report, and Bulganin, Pervukhin, and Saburov used the occasion to denounce themselves for complicity in the "anti-Party group" conspiracy to oust Khrushchev from power.

Factional conflict in the Politburo. Differences in the Politburo arise as a result of both personal ambitions for power and fundamental conflict over doctrine and policy. Both factors are so intricately interwoven that attempts to draw fine distinctions between personal and policy conflicts are apt to be an idle exercise. Although Soviet ideology neither recognizes the legitimacy of factional groupings in the Party nor tolerates the doctrinal schisms that are their ideological expression, the Party, throughout its history, has been constantly threatened with the eruption of both. After Stalin's death, the rival cliques he permitted—and may even have encouraged—to form among his subordinates developed into factions, each with its own aspirations and opinions. Since no single faction was sufficiently powerful to annihilate the others, necessity was converted into virtue and the balance

of terror in the Presidium was ideologically sanctified as "collective leadership."

Even before the revelations of the resolution that hurled Molotov and his associates from their places of eminence, it was unmistakable that serious factional quarrels kept the Presidium in a continual state of turmoil. At least three factions appear to have existed in the Presidium before June, 1957, although the members of each faction were not permanently committed to issues; and personality and tactical shifts, though not frivolous, were also not unusual. The Presidium was divided on four major issues that had important foreign policy repercussions: the Stalinist issue; the relations between the Soviet Union and other communist states and parties; economic policy and reorganization; and relations with the ex-colonial states.

The so-called Stalinist faction had at its core the veteran Politburo members, Molotov and Kaganovich, and was frequently supported by Malenkov. The nucleus of the anti-Stalinist faction was made up of Khrushchev, Mikoyan, Voroshilov, Bulganin, Kirichenko, and the alternate members of the Presidium. This faction was in decisive control of the Party apparatus and the Central Committee, and it found crucial support in the army, in Peking, Warsaw, and Belgrade. Pervukhin and Saburov made up the so-called "managerial-technical" faction, which appeared to have close connections with Malenkov in the past but generally cast its vote with the Khrushchev group on questions of Stalinism. The group deserted Malenkov for Khrushchev when Malenkov appeared to be the apostle for increased emphasis on the production of consumer goods and Khrushchev continued to rely on heavy industry. These factions were bound together by bonds of common ideological and policy considerations, but personal ambitions and opportunism played a considerable role, allowing wide room for maneuver and re-alignment of positions as the main chance presented itself.

The events in Poland and Hungary, together with the uncompromising attitude of Marshal Tito, encouraged the Stalinists to believe that the Khrushchev group had fumbled, while Khrushchev's sudden interest in decentralizing the economic structure of the state stampeded Pervukhin and Saburov foolishly to join the Stalinist faction in an anti-Khrushchev coalition that made a desperate effort to thwart the proposed dismantling of their economic empires. At the December, 1956, Plenum of the Central Committee, this combination was sufficiently powerful to arrest the de-Stalinization program temporarily and to guarantee the preservation of the centralized economic structure by installing Pervukhin as the virtual dictator of the economic system. Relations with Tito were once again inflamed, and Satellite policies appeared to harden. During this period, Malenkov—as representative of the new majority—accompained Khrushchev to the communist gathering held in Budapest, from which both Warsaw and Belgrade were deliberately excluded.

The inconclusive factional strife in the Kremlin, and the ideological ferment in Eastern Europe, provided an opportunity for Peking to intervene, and Chou En-lai embarked upon an emergency trip to Moscow and Eastern Europe to shore up the Khrushchev faction. Because of the unnatural and unstable amalgamation organized against him, Khrushchev's ouster was deferred; but once the crisis had subsided, and it was clear that the armed forces and China preferred Khrushchev's policies in preference to those of his opposition, a realignment of forces

in the Presidium enabled Khrushchev once again to reconstitute a majority at the February, 1957, Plenum, and Pervukhin was toppled from his brief perch on the economic throne. The economic levers of power were wrenched from his hands, while Shepilov was ousted from the Foreign Ministry in favor of Gromyko.

With the Presidium so sharply and evenly divided, "collective leadership" threatened to abandon Soviet foreign policy to the mercies of an inconclusive see-saw struggle plunging the Kremlin into a condition of perpetual indecision. While key Khrushchev supporters were out of town, Stalinist forces, by engineering a rump meeting of the Presidium—ostensibly to discuss minor matters—regrouped and resolved to unseat Khrushchev through a parliamentary ruse. When the meeting took place on June 17–18, 1957, the First Secretary found himself momentarily outmaneuvered and apparently irrevocably outvoted. Saburov and Pervukhin once again voted with the Stalinist faction, as did Khrushchev's erstwhile protégé, Shepilov. But the key figure in the new realignment was Bulganin, who miscalculated the power of the anti-Khrushchev forces and underrated the First Secretary's political agility (leading Khrushchev to confide later that some of his colleagues knew more about arithmetic than politics), and in an opportunistic maneuver voted to oust Khrushchev from power in the meeting over which he presided. Refusing to resign, Khrushchev conducted a filibuster while his supporters quickly assembled a special meeting of the Central Committee and its auditing commission (a total of 319 members), which sat from June 22–29, 1957.

After a bitter ventilation of all the contentious issues of doctrines and policy, during which 60 members reportedly took part in the debate and 115 filed statements, the Molotov-managerial coalition was overwhelmed by a unanimous vote tarnished only by a single obstinate abstention by Molotov—the first such publicly admitted dissonance in a Central Committee vote in almost thirty years. The Stalinist wing of the coalition was charged in the resolution which expelled them with engaging in illegal factional activity and cabalistic intrigue:

Entering into collusion on an anti-Party basis, they set out to change the policy of the Party, to drag the Party back to the erroneous methods of leadership condemned by the Twentieth Party Congress [i.e., Stalinism]. They resorted to methods of intrigue and formed a collusion against the Central Committee.

The others were not specifically condemned, but Saburov lost his seat on the Presidium and Pervukhin was demoted to alternate status. In their humiliating appearances before the Twenty-first Party Congress, held in February, 1959, both confessed their complicity in the plot against Khrushchev, although they maintained that they later switched to Khrushchev on the vote to actually oust him as First Secretary. Saburov was eventually exiled to the obscurity of a factory manager in Syzran, while Pervukhin wound up with the less than exalted post of ambassador to East Germany. Apparently for purposes of concealing the fact that a majority of the Presidium actually voted against him, Bulganin lingered on as Premier until March, 1958, and as a member of the Presidium until the following September, although it was clear that his position had been compromised. He was formally charged with being part of the anti-Khrushchev conspiracy on November 14, 1958, and at the December, 1958, Plenum, Bulganin made a grovelling confession in which he denounced himself as the "nominal leader" of the plot because of his position as chairman of the Council of Ministers. He made an abject plea for forgiveness, unleashed a vicious attack on Molotov and Kaganovich, and was consigned to the demeaning post of chairman of the Stavropol Economic Council.

The victorious group soon betrayed signs of splitting on a wide range of domestic and foreign policies. The leadership tended to polarize around two main factions, a "moderate" group, led by Khrushchev, and a "conservative" group, whose leaders appeared to be M. A. Suslov and F. R. Kozlov, later apparently supported by traditional elements of the professional military and representatives of heavy industry. Generally speaking, the moderate faction sought a relaxation of international tensions and a *détente* with the United States, even at the expense of alienating China; the conservative faction saw little value in a *détente* with the United States, especially at the expense of alienating the Soviet Union's most important ally. Domestically, Khrushchev and the "moderates" were willing to tolerate greater relaxation of controls at home and advocated a change in the economic equilibrium in the direction of producing more consumer goods at the expense of heavy industry. The "conservatives" were opposed to further relaxation at home and may have even demanded some retrenchment, and they were virtually dogmatic in their insistence that priority continue to be given to heavy industry over light industry and agriculture. Under these conditions, formalized debate in the Central Committee gave way to a genuine if largely esoteric, articulation of divergent factional viewpoints, which was also evident from the content of the speeches delivered at the Twenty-first and Twenty-second Party Congresses, in January, 1959, and October, 1961, respectively.

As long as Khrushchev's policy of seeking a relaxation of international tension and a *détente* with the United States seemed to be bearing fruit, he was able to isolate and silence his critics in the leadership, particularly after his meeting with President Eisenhower at Camp David, in mid-1959. Relations with China simultaneously deteriorated catastrophically when Khrushchev unilaterally nullified a secret, 1957, Sino-Soviet agreement on nuclear technology, just prior to his meeting with President Eisenhower. Since an improvement in relations with the United States inevitably meant a further deterioration of relations with China, this became an important and crucial issue which agitated the Soviet leadership. The factional opposition to Khrushchev was strengthened in January, 1960, when the Soviet leader alienated the traditional military by calling for a reduction of the ground forces by one-third and shifting the main reliance for Soviet security to its nuclear deterrent capability. This new strategic policy was based upon the expectation of an imminent settlement of all outstanding issues between Washington and Moscow on the basis of the "Camp David Spirit."

After the U-2 incident, Khrushchev's grip on the Central Committee and its Presidium was weakened and became under increasing attack at home, while criticism in Peking mounted simultaneously. Khrushchev's foreign policy was based upon a fundamental restructuring of the image and character of the American "ruling class", which, according to the "moderates" had split into a "sober" group, on the one hand, and an intractable group, made up of "belligerent," "aggressive," "irration-

al," and even "mad" elements, on the other. The sober group, whose leader, according to Khrushchev, was President Eisenhower, was dominant, and it appeared ready to negotiate a settlement with the Soviet Union, on a realistic basis, which to Khrushchev meant a *détente* based on supposed Soviet strategic superiority. Neither the "conservative" faction, nor the traditional military, nor the Chinese leaders subscribed to this image. The Soviet Union's leader was, in effect, relying upon the self-restraint of the sober forces in the American ruling class, and his opposition viewed his call for troop reductions and cutbacks in heavy industry with considerable alarm. From the Chinese viewpoint, Khrushchev's search for a *détente* with Eisenhower indicated an erosion in Moscow's commitment to revolutionary goals and a tacit alliance with Peking's principal national enemy.

Although Khrushchev's logic was undermined by the U-2 incident, he managed to remain in power. He pleaded that a new American administration would resume the earlier pacific course of Soviet-American relations, viewed the U-2 crisis as an unfortunate incident, and insisted that the sober American group was still dominant and would be so demonstrated by the forthcoming elections.

Kennedy was unknown to the Russians, but Nixon was a well-known and heartily disliked personality, and so Moscow placed its reliance on a Kennedy victory and a reversal of post-U-2 policy. But the Soviet leader was to be disappointed once again, as the new President embarked on a course of strengthening U.S. military capabilities, supported an attempt to overthrow the Castro regime in Cuba, and refused to be bullied into negotiating a settlement on Soviet terms. The Soviet failure to win a Berlin victory and the steadily growing power of the United States, increased the pressures upon Khrushchev both at home and from Peking and at the Twenty-second Party Congress, he adopted a harsher line towards the United States.

From the time of the Twenty-second Party Congress until Khrushchev's ouster, in October, 1964, the Soviet leadership was plagued by constant factional squabbles and these often found expression in the Central Committee Plenums. Khrushchev stayed in power only because the factional balance was extremely delicate, with some leaders supporting him on some issues and opposing him on others. Thus, Soviet factional politics was not only institutionally and functionally oriented but issue oriented as well, and it was the existence of issue-oriented factionalism which provided Khrushchev with the margins necessary to stay in power.

Khrushchev once again narrowly missed being ousted as a consequence of the Cuban missile crisis of October, 1962, when his opposition at home and his critics in Peking seemed perilously close to having a common point of view. His problems were aggravated, also, by President Kennedy's initial rejection of a Soviet proposal for a limited test-ban treaty based on three annual inspections. The Soviet Premier gained a temporary extension of power, however, when the leader of the "conservative" faction, F. R. Kozlov, suffered an incapacitating stroke in April, 1963. Although Khrushchev mused in public about his possible retirement, the incapacitation of Kozlov gave him a new lease on political power and he quickly took advantage of President Kennedy's offer, in a speech at American University, to reach an agreement on a limited test-ban treaty, which was signed the following month.

Khrushchev thus appeared to have vindicated himself for the "sober" forces were indeed in control in Washington and while the *détente* was based not upon the assumption of Soviet strategic superiority, but upon the implied assumption of U. S. strategic superiority, it enabled Khrushchev to turn his attention to pressing economic problems at home and to the dispute with Peking. The Chinese called the limited test-ban treaty an act of Soviet betrayal, and there was strong evidence that the treaty was not enthusiastically accepted by the "conservative" faction or the traditional military.

Khrushchev's inept handling of the dispute with China, his generally crude and unsophisticated behavior as a politician, and his constant boasting in public apparently finally alienated some of his supporters, who saw in his person an impediment to a reconciliation with China and an obstacle to a rational approach to domestic problems. In October, 1964, he was ousted, in a coup engineered largely by his own trusted subordinates, Brezhnev, Kosygin, and Mikoyan. He was indirectly accused of concocting "harebrained schemes," "boasting," and general ineptness. Khrushchev's ouster allegedly took place at a Central Committee Plenum, but the proceedings were not made public. The manner and abruptness of his dismissal caused considerable commotion and disturbance in other communist countries and parties, whose leaders demanded and received an explanation in a series of bilateral conferences.

The Chinese, the conservatives, the traditionalistic military, and the moderates all seemed to have a common interest in removing Khrushchev, if for widely differing and even contradictory reasons, and there seems to be little question that the factional situation at home and the criticisms from

Peking combined to bring about the Soviet Premier's political ouster.

The Central Committee is thus emerging as the most important political organ of power and authority in the Soviet system, although it has not yet eclipsed the Politburo, which, however, must be increasingly responsive to its deliberations. The growing power of the Central Committee reflects the increasingly pluralistic character of the Soviet social order. This body is composed of representatives from the most powerful and influential elite groups in Soviet society. It includes the entire membership of the Politburo and the Secretariat, the most important ministers of the government, the first secretaries of republican party organizations and important regional party organizations, the most important officials of the Union Republics, the marshals, generals, and admirals of the armed forces and the police, the important ambassadors, the trade union officials, the cultural and scientific celebrities and leaders, the leading Party ideologists, and the top Komsomol officials. Increasingly, these representatives perceive attitudes reflecting their institutional or functional roles and status in Soviet society and this provides the social basis for the political factions which now characterize the Soviet system.

The transition from Stalinist, one-man rule to quasi-pluralistic political behavior is now all but complete. The Khrushchev decade emerges as a sort of transition period between these two types of political behavior. Under Stalin, conflicts were rendered into decisions after a blood purge in which potential opponents were physically destroyed; under Khrushchev, conflicts were resolved into decisions by the clear-cut victory of one faction and the expulsion of the others from important positions of power. The

blood purge was replaced with public condemnation and disgrace, demotion, or retirement but, since the execution of Beria in 1954, no fallen leader has been executed or even brought to trial. With the element of terror removed from the political process, however, the risks of opposition and dissent were considerably reduced. Victorious factions divided into new factions, and so the factional conflict resumed on a new level, and around new issues. By late 1959, no single group could establish dominance, and control gradually came to be exercised by a kind of consensus, based on compromise, bargaining, and accommodation. This has introduced an element of instability and uncertainty with respect to any given government or administration, but it has simultaneously stabilized and regularized the Soviet political process and has removed much of the uncertainty which hitherto prevailed.

No formal charges of factionalism have been made against any group or individual in the Soviet Union's hierarchy since 1959. Such a charge can only be levelled if a particular faction is soundly defeated and expelled from the leadership, and this was characteristic of the rule by a single faction which flourished between 1953 and 1959. Factionalism is still prohibited by the Party rules, but its existence was tacitly admitted by Kozlov at the Twenty-second Party Congress:

Under present circumstances, need the statutes contain any formal guarantee against factionalism and clique activity? Yes . . . such guarantees as needed. To be sure there is no social base left in Soviet society that could feed opportunistic currents in the Party. But the sources of ideological waverings on the part of particular individuals or groups have not yet been entirely eliminated. Some persons may fall under the influence of bourgeois propaganda from the outside. Others having failed to comprehend the dialectics of society's development and having turned . . . into dying embers, will have nothing to do with anything new and go on clinging to old dogmas that have been toppled by life.[34]

Interest groups and factional politics. It is at once obvious that factions could neither arise nor flourish unless they received constant sustenance from powerful social forces in Soviet society. Just as Party factions do not organize into separate political organizations competing with the Party for political power, so interest groups in Soviet society do not constitute separate organizations, but rather seek to make their influence felt as formless clusters of vested interests. Within the context of Marxist ideology, an interest group can only be a social class with economic interests that conflict with the interests of other classes. After the Revolution only the interests of the working class, as distorted by the Marxist prism, were given legitimate recognition—although the concrete political articulation of these interests was usurped by the Communist Party —and all other interests and parties were condemned to oblivion. In 1936 Stalin declared the eradication of class conflict in Soviet society, but he continued to recognize the existence of separate social classes, whose interests had merged into a single identity. The Communist Party was transformed from a party representing only the interests of the working class into one representing the transcendental interests of all Soviet social classes. Consequently, Soviet ideology neither recognizes the legitimacy of competing interest groups nor tolerates their autonomous existence. In Soviet jargon, an interest group that develops in-

[34]*Pravda*, October 29, 1961.

terests that deviate from the Party line is a hostile class; the faction that represents it in the Party is an attempt to form a party within a party; and its articulated views on policy and doctrine constitute an ideological deviation.

Separate interest groups, however, continue to flourish in Soviet society, but not in conformity with the doctrinaire and contrived premises of nineteenth-century Marxism, nor within the synthetic social divisions given official sanction. The collective-farm peasantry and the working class constitute the numerically preponderant classes in Soviet society, but the major interest groups with sufficient power and influence to apply political pressure do not follow the artificial constructions of Soviet ideology; in accordance with the unique dynamic of Soviet society the privileged elites find their social differentiation within a single recognized group, the intelligentsia, which is not recognized as a social class, but is euphemistically called a *stratum*.

Although the Soviet intelligentsia (roughly identical with what Milovan Djilas labels the "New Class") is a variegated congeries of differentiated elites, they all have in common a desire to perpetuate the Soviet system from which they have sprung and from which they benefit as privileged groups. But each group is immediately concerned with its own vested stake in Soviet society and seeks to force doctrine and policy to assume the contours of its own special interests. Since these groups do not enjoy official recognition, they all seek to exert their influence through the Communist Party, not outside it, and political rivalry assumes the form of competing for control of the Party's decision-making organs and its symbols of legitimacy. Because Soviet ideology rigidly and inaccurately insists on the existence of a single monolithic interest, representing that of society in its collective entity, conflicts between major groups are resolved not by political accommodation, but by mutual elimination and by the attempt of one interest group to establish its supremacy and to impose its views as those of society as a whole. Thus the Communist Party, under the pressures of diverse groups seeking political articulation and accommodation, has become a conglomeration of interests whose basic incompatibilities are only partially obscured by a veneer of monolithic unity.

Not all interest groups in the Soviet Union are sufficiently powerful to exact representation for their views by factions in the Party hierarchy. There are six principal groups within Soviet society that have accumulated sufficient leverage, either through the acquisition of indispensable skills and talents or through the control of instruments of persuasion, terror, or destruction, to exert pressure upon the Party. These are: (1) the Party apparatus, consisting of those who have made a career in the Party bureaucracy; (2) the Government bureaucracy; (3) the economic managers and technicians; (4) the cultural, professional, and scientific intelligentsia; (5) the police; (6) the armed forces.

These major groups are by no means organized as cohesively united bodies, speaking with a single authoritative voice, but rather themselves are made up of rival personal and policy cliques, gripped by internal jealousies, and often in constant collision and friction with one another in combination or alliance with similarly oriented cliques in other social groups.

The Party apparatus itself was thus divided into rival cliques, the two main contending groups being those led by

Khrushchev and Malenkov. Since the denouncement of Malenkov, his supporters in the Party apparatus were replaced with followers of Khrushchev. Although the function of the Party bureaucracy is essentially administrative rather than policy-making, it has a tendency to feel that it "owns" the Party, and thus seeks first to subordinate the Party to its control and then to force the other major groups to submit to the domination of the Party. After Stalin's death, the serious and imminent threat posed to the Party by Beria and his secret police caused Khrushchev and Malenkov to temporarily bury their rivalry in the apparatus of the Party in order to crush the secret police, which had developed into an independent center of power and threatened to subjugate the Party to its will. The secret police was dismembered with the aid of the army.

TABLE 5.1

Major Groups Represented in the Central Committee

	1952	1956	1961	1966
Party apparatus	103	117	158	159
State and economic officials	79	98	112	134
Military officers	26	18	31	35
Cultural and scientific representatives	....*	....*	18	*
Police	9	3	2	**
Others	19	19	9	
Totals	236	255	330	

*Included in *others.*
**Included in military.

There appears to be no systematic attempt to select members of the Central Committee and its Politburo from among the major forces in Soviet society; the composition of these bodies appears to depend upon the balance of forces at any given time (see Tables 5.1 and 5.2). Ample evidence exists, however, that their composition reflects deliberate recognition of these major interest groups. Traditionally, the Party apparatus accounts for slightly less than half the total membership of the Central Committee, with the government bureaucracy (including the economic administrators) following close behind. The representation of the other groups is substantially less, although, because virtually all members of the Party's two highest bodies who are not career Party bureaucrats are employed by the state, it is often difficult to distinguish the main line of work pursued by a particular member of the Central Committee. This is especially true of individuals who move from one group to another. Consequently, all distinctions are provisional and, in some cases, arbitrary. The composition of the Politburo is more accurately differentiated, although even there, because of the interlocking of the top organs of state and Party, some ambiguity prevails.

Since the membership of the Central Committee is normally determined by the Party Congress, which meets every four years, its composition is not normally affected by day-to-day changes in the factional equilibrium. The Politburo, whose membership can be altered by the Central Committee, is peculiarly sensitive to the fluctuations in the balance of power and is a fairly accurate barometer of changing political fortunes.

Formerly, it could be said that the composition of the Central Committee was determined from the top, by the Politburo, but the relationship between the two bodies is becoming increasingly reciprocal. Changes in the composition of the Politburo now reflect, to some degree, changes in the factional balance in the Central Committee as groups and individuals maneuver for position and advantage— bargaining, negotiating, and accommodating. The Central Committee's authority becomes crucial, and perhaps even decisive, when the factional balance is delicate. Then, rival groups seek to gain wider support and alter their policies to meet the demands of wider constituencies. Thus, while the Politburo is the more accurate gauge of day-to-day politics, the composition of the Central Committee is apt to reflect more durable, long-range trends. Table 5.2 shows only institutional representation on the Politburo, and it should be noted that interest groups tend, increasingly, to cut across institutional entities.

The Party apparatus continues to be the dominant institutional actor in both the Central Committee and its Presidium, but its absolute and relative strength in both bodies, after reaching a post-Stalin high point in 1957, seems now to be diminishing as other groups demand greater representation. As factional cleavages develop within the apparatus, opportunities are created for other groups as they become targets of appeal for support by rival apparatus factions and in turn make demands upon the apparatus. The year 1957, after the expulsion of the "anti-party group" represented the zenith of single faction rule which was sustained substantially unimpaired until Khrushchev's assumption of the premiership in the following year. Factionalism, however, infected the victorious Khrushchev group itself and the overall representation of the ap-

TABLE 5.2

Major Institutions Represented on the Presidium or Politburo

	1952	1953	1956	1957	1961	1963	1966
Party apparatus	13(5)	2(2)	4(3)	10(6)	7(3)	8(4)	6(6)
State officials							
Economic sector	5(3)	4	4	1(2)	2	2	1
Other	4(2)	3(1)	3(1)	3	2(2)	2(2)	4(1)
Military	0	0	0(1)	1	0	0	0
Police	2	1(1)	0	0	0	0	0
Other	1(1)	0	0(1)	0(1)	0	0	0(1)
Totals	25(11)	10(4)	11(6)	15(9)	11(5)	12(6)	11(8)

paratus in the Presidium started to decline and by the time of the Twenty-second Party Congress in October, 1961, two main factions had once again materialized, a "moderate" faction led by Khrushchev and a "conservative" faction, supported by the traditional military, led by F. R. Kozlov, an erstwhile Khrushchev satrap. No less than four full members and four candidate members of the Presidium associated with the "moderate" position were dropped, and the overall size of the Presidium was substantially reduced. In the Secretariat, the "moderate" faction's dominance was eliminated by the appointment of new members associated with the "conservative" group and the size of this body was raised from five to nine. Thus the "moderate" faction suffered losses in the Presidium by a trimming of its membership while in the Secretariat, its presence was diminished through the addition of new members associated with the other faction. Khrushchev managed to hang on as both Premier and First Secretary, first in order to present a united front to both the United States and China and second, because he adjusted and accommodated his publicly stated views and policies to accord more with the demands of the "conservative" faction,

without at the same time abandoning his leadership of the "moderate" faction. From the Twenty-second Party Congress until his ouster in October, 1964, he presided over a regime which was characterized not by single faction rule but by factional consensus and accommodation.

During the Khrushchev era, the government bureaucracy suffered a drastic decrease in its representation on the Presidium, both in the economic and non-economic realms. Since 1958, there has been no active representation of either the professional military or heavy industry, while light industry was amply represented by Kosygin and Mikoyan, both of whom were in high favor with Khrushchev. The appointment of D. F. Ustinov as a candidate member of the Politburo and as a member of the Secretariat at the Twenty-third Party Congress (1966) marked the first direct representation of heavy industry in the Party's highest body in nearly a decade. A specialist in defense industry, Ustinov represents in his person the symbolic relationship between heavy industry and the traditional military in the Soviet social system. The police were also excluded, although the admission of Shelepin to the Presidium, after he stepped down from his position as chairman of the

Committee on State Security, may have given the police some marginal representation. The cultural intelligentsia was represented by professional ideologists like Suslov, who were closely identified with the Party apparatus.

The fall of Khrushchev, in 1964, did not produce any immediate major dislocations or dismissals in the Soviet hierarchy, except for the demotion of a few individuals who were personally close or related to the Soviet leader. The most conspicuous was his son-in-law, Alexei Adzhubei, who was unceremoniously booted out of the Central Committee and relieved of his job as chief editor of *Izvestia*. Shelepin and Shelest, neither of whom were candidate members, were admitted as full members of the Presidium, and Demichev was appointed a candidate member. Shelepin and Demichev were also members of the Secretariat, and their appointment broadened the overlapping membership in the two bodies. It is possible that their elevation was, in part, a reward for their support in ousting their erstwhile patron. There were other dismissals and appointments at lower levels, but they were accomplished with little fanfare. It was quite clear that Khrushchev's ouster had created a series of minor power vacuums which had to be filled, and this resulted in some maneuvering. Three Khrushchev supporters, Ilyichev, Polyakov, and Titov, were dropped from the Secretariat, reducing its size to eight.

In March, 1965, after a Central Committee Plenum, further changes were made. Mazurov was elevated from candidate membership to full membership in the Presidium, and D. F. Ustinov was added as a candidate member. Ustinov's star had appeared to rise, after the Cuban missile crisis, when Khrushchev seemed to be in deep trouble, but it dimmed after Koz-

lov's stroke and Khrushchev made a temporary political recovery.

Further changes were made in the Party summit in December, 1965, when Ustinov, Kapitonov, and Kulakov were appointed to the Secretariat to replace the three members who had been dropped after Khrushchev's political demise, raising its number once again to eleven. Six members of the Secretariat were also full or candidate members of the Presidium, which suggested a resurgence of the Party apparatus's representation at the Party summit. Podgorny, at this time, also replaced Mikoyan as Chairman of the Presidium of the Supreme Soviet, and subsequently relinquished his membership in the Secretariat.

The definitive post-Khrushchev composition of the Party summit was made at the Twenty-third Party Congress in April, 1966, when Mikoyan and Shvernik were retired from the Politburo and, Pelshe, a Latvian Party secretary, was appointed a full member over the heads of all the candidate members. Two new candidate members were appointed—Kunayev, a Kazakh Party leader, and Masherov, a Byelorussian Party secretary who had become a full member of the Central Committee only in November, 1964, immediately after Khrushchev's ouster, which suggests that he played a key role in the post-Khrushchev factional maneuvering. The composition of the Secretariat remained unchanged, except that Kirilenko, also a full member of the Politburo, replaced Podgorny in the Secretariat, since the latter's new post as Chairman of the Presidium of the Supreme Soviet is traditionally disassociated from the Secretariat.

The restructuring of the Party summit at the Twenty-third Party Congress strongly suggested that Brezhnev, the General Secretary of the Party, had strengthened his position and that he enjoyed a factional majority or consensus, but by no means had assumed the power of a Khrushchev or a Stalin, irrespective of the symbolic manipulation of nomenclature at the Congress. Of the eleven full members of the Politburo, four were members of the Secretariat, while of the eight candidate members, two were members of the Secretariat. This meant that six members of the eleven-man secretariat also sat on the Politburo. The clear dominance of the Party apparatus in the Politburo was further indicated by the presence of six Party secretaries of republics (Ukrainian, Latvian, Georgian, Uzbek, Byelorussian and Kazakh) as full or candidate members, thus broadening its ethnic base to include representation from six of the fourteen major non-Russian nationalities, including two Central Asian Moslem nationalities, the Uzbek and Kazakh, and giving the apparatus a total of six full members and six candidate members of the Politburo, or twelve votes out of nineteen, a clear majority. In addition to this, career Party bureaucrats like Podgorny and Mazurov moved into key state offices. The interlocking of institutions and personnel between the Party and the state after the Twenty-third Party Congress is shown in Table 5.3.

It is normal practice to divorce membership in the Secretariat from membership in the Council of Ministers, since the Secretariat is supposed to exercise an independent audit of the government's work and check on the execution and implementation of Party directives and resolutions. The only consistent deviation from this practice occurs when the same personality functions as General Secretary (First Secretary) of the Party and Chairman of the Council of Ministers, as was the case during the later years of the Stalin and Khrushchev eras. Similarly, the Chairmanship of the Presidium of the

Supreme Soviet is considered to be incompatible with membership in the Secretariat. Both Brezhnev and Podgorny relinquished their membership in the Secretariat upon their appointment as Chairman of the Presidium of the Supreme Soviet. It is traditional, however, for the General Secretary to be an ordinary member of the Presidium of the Supreme Soviet if he holds no other state post, and it is usual for the Presidium to include several other members of the Party Secretariat, thus ensuring Party audit and control over its activities. It is also customary for membership in the Presidium of the Supreme Soviet to be incompatible with membership in the Council of Ministers, since the latter is juridically responsible to the former. Since the death of Stalin, it has been normal practice to include high state and Party officials of the R.S.F.S.R. and the Ukraine in the Politburo.

Internal politics and Soviet foreign policy: interest groups and factional polarization on foreign policy issues[35]

The informal recognition of groups with distinctive special interests of their own and the admission of their representatives to the decision-making bodies of the Party cannot but influence the country's foreign policy, although how this influence is exerted, and in what direction, is difficult to determine. The removal of the managerial bureaucrats from both the Presidium and high government posts was motivated, at least in part, by the fear that their control of the key economic levers of society could be used to frustrate the decisions of the Party.

[35]This section is adapted from the author's "Internal Politics and Foreign Policy in the Soviet System," in *Approaches to Comparative and International Politics*, ed. B. Farrell, (Evanston, Ill.: Northwestern University Press, 1966).

TABLE 5.3

Interlocking of Government and Party Institutions and Personnel in the Soviet Union: 1966

First Secretaries of Republics	Presidium of the Supreme Soviet	Secretariat	Politburo	Presidium of the Council of Ministers	Premiers of Republics	Other
		Brezhnev (General Secretary)	Brezhnev			
			Kosygin	Kosygin (Chairman)		
		Suslov	Suslov			
	Podgorny (Chairman)		Podgorny			
		Kirilenko	Kirilenko			
			Polyansky	Polyansky (First Deputy)		
			Voronov		Voronov (R.S.F.S.R.)	
		Shelepin	Shelepin			
Shelest (Ukraine)			Shelest			
Pelshe (Latvia)			Pelshe			
			Mazurov	Mazurov (First Deputy)		
			Grishin			Grishin (Trade Union Chairman)
Mzhvanadze (Georgia)			Mzhvanadze			
Rashidov (Uzbek)			Rashidov			
			Shcherbitsky		Shcherbitsky (Ukraine)	
	Demichev	Demichev	Demichev			
		Ustinov	Ustinov			
Masherov (Byelorussia)			Masherov			
Kunayev (Kazakh)	Kunayev	Andropopov	Kunayev			
		Ponomarev				
		Kulakov				
		Kapitonov				
		Rudakov				

Marshal Zhukov's leadership of the army posed an even grimmer threat to the supremacy of the Party apparatus, had he been permitted to remain in the Presidium and the Defense Ministry where he could seriously question the basic decisions of the Party concerning military and foreign policy and frustrate their implementation. His removal, in October, 1957, from both strategic positions, was essentially preventive, designed to remove a popular and commanding personality who might at some future date challenge even more crucial decisions of the Party and thus produce an internal crisis of incalculable magnitude.

By 1958, the Party apparatus, under Khrushchev's direction, had dismembered the police, domesticated the managerial bureaucrats and decentralized their empire, exiled the leaders of factional groupings in the Party to Siberia, and subordinated the military to its will. As Table 5.2 indicates, neither major instrument of coercion in the Soviet system now has a representative in the Party Presidium, which is now overwhelmingly dominated by career Party *apparatchiki*.

As the Soviet system matures and becomes inextricably identified with the interests of its various privileged elites, the decision makers must give greater consideration in the calculation of foreign policy to factors affecting the internal stability of the regime; and they will show greater sensitivity to the effects of decisions on the vested interests of the various elites in Soviet society. The rise of powerful social and economic elites in the Soviet Union, and their insistent pressure for participation in the exercise of political power, could only introduce stresses, strains, conflicts, and hence new restraints into Soviet diplomacy.

Within the context of an ideology that imposes a single interest representing society as a whole, each interest group will tend to distort ideology and policy in an endeavor to give it the contours of its own interests; the next step is to elevate these to transcendental significance. Under these conditions, Soviet ideology may be constantly threatened with a series of fundamental convulsions if one interest group displaces another in the struggle for the control of the Party machinery. Hence, a rational system of accommodating conflicting interests appears to be evolving. As the vested stake of each major group becomes rooted in the Soviet system, the contours of Soviet diplomacy and national interest will inexorably tend to be shaped more by the rapidly moving equilibrium or accommodation of interests that develop internally than by abstract ideological imperatives, which may conflict with the concrete interests of specific major elites in Soviet society.

Although ideologically the basic purpose of external security and state survival is to develop into a power center for the purpose of implementing ideological goals in foreign policy (world communism), increasingly the purpose becomes in fact to protect and preserve the existing social order in the interests of the social groups who dominate and benefit from it. To the extent that the implementation of foreign policy goals, whether ideologically motivated or otherwise, are compatible with the preservation and enhancement of the social order and serve to reward rather than deprive its beneficiaries, no incompatibility between internal and external goals is experienced. If, however, the pursuit of ideological goals in foreign policy undermines or threatens the security of the state and the social groups who dominate it (or even arrests the progress of their material prosperity), the primacy of internal interests are ideologically rationalized and the energies and efforts devoted to external ideological goals are correspondingly diminished.

It must be realized that the relationship between internal interests and external ideological goals is a dynamic one and fluctuates in accordance with opportunities and capabilities, but in the long run the tendency is that ideological goals which threaten internal interests erode and are deprived of their motivating character. The persistence of ideological goals in Soviet foreign policy reflects socio-functional interests which have been traditionally associated with the Party apparatus and professional ideologues. The fact that the concrete policies which have resulted from the pursuit of ideological goals in foreign policy have created special vested interests for other sociopolitical or socio-institutional groups, like the Secret Police, the Armed Forces, and the heavy industrial managers, should not obscure the fact that the definition, identification, and implementation of ideological goals, whether in foreign or domestic policy, has been the special function of the Party apparatus and its attendant ideologues. An area of common interest among some members of the Party apparatus and the Armed Forces and heavy industrial managers in pursuing policies which are tension-producing has thus come into being. Tension-producing policies, however, in an era of increasing technological complexity, not only tend to automatically enhance the power of professionalized and technologically oriented groups in the Soviet Union, to the relative detriment of the status and power of the Party apparatus, but also tend to alienate from the apparatus other more numerous social groups in society whose interests are more in consonance with tension-lessening policies, such as the consumer goods producers and light industrial managers, the intellectuals, artists, professionals, agricultural managers, and finally, the great mass of Soviet citizenry, comprising the lower intelligentsia, workers, peasants, and others, whose priorities are always low during periods of high international tensions. Since these latter social forces are more numerous than those whose interests are served by tension-producing policies, the Party apparatus was in danger of alienating itself further from the great masses of the Soviet citizenry and becoming increasingly dependent upon the traditional military and heavy industry.

The Soviet Union like the United States is thus involved in a great debate over foreign policy and national security matters centering around the issue of whether heightening international tensions or relaxation of international tensions best serves the "national interests."

While only Molotov and the "anti-Party group" have been specifically identified by the Soviet leadership with a policy of favoring international tensions, the nature of the factional conflicts in the Soviet Union over budgets, military strategy, the likelihood of war and violence, the nature of imperialism, images of American "ruling class" behavior, and the proper balance between the production of consumer goods and services and heavy industry in the Soviet economy, clearly indicate that tension-producing policies tend to favor certain groups within Soviet society while tension-lessening policies tend to favor others. While the residual fervor of a purely ideological commitment to specific goals and policies remains operative in the thought and behavior of Soviet leaders, there has also been an inexorable tendency for individual leaders and functional interest groups to perceive the interests of society as a whole through their own prism and to distort and adjust the national interest to accord with their own. Ideological distortion takes shape in similar fashion in order to impart the necessary symbolic legitimacy to policies and interests which the Soviet system demands as part of its political ritual.

The foreign policy and defense posture of the Soviet state establishes a certain configuration of priorities in the allocation of money and scarce resources. Various individuals and groups develop a vested interest in a particular foreign policy or defense posture because of the role and status it confers upon them. Correspondingly, other individuals and groups in Soviet society perceive themselves as deprived in status and rewards because of existing allocation of expenditures and resources, and hence they might initiate proposals which might alter existing foreign policy and defense postures or support proposals submitted by other groups or individuals.

A particular interest group or social formation may often have a role or function imposed upon it by events, circumstances, policies, and the mechanism of a given social system in response to certain situations not of its own making, or, in some instances, which provided the basis for its very creation and existence. While particular interest groups may not have sought such a role, nor taken the initiative in acquiring it, or even did not exist before the function was demanded, once this role is thrust upon them, they adjust to it and develop a vested interest in the role and function imposed upon them, since it constitutes the source of their existence and status. As individual members adjust to their role, develop it, and invest their energies and careers in it, they almost

automatically resist the deprivation or diminution of this role or function in their self-interest.

The same is true of groups which have assigned to them limited or arrested roles or functions in society, except that they develop a vested interest in expanding their role, dignifying it with greater status and prestige, and demanding greater rewards. Consequently, it is extremely difficult to distill out of Soviet factional positions those aspects of thought and behavior which express conflicting perceptions of self-interest on the part of various individuals, factions, and groups as opposed to authentic "objective" considerations of a broader interest, whether national or ideological, since they are so inextricably intertwined and interdependent.

All that we can assert at this point is that certain individuals, factions, and socio-institutional functional groups seem to thrive and flourish and others to be relatively deprived and arrested in their development under conditions of exacerbated international tensions, while the situation is reversed when a relaxation of international tensions takes place. What might be assumed, therefore, because of these complicated psychological dialogues between perceptions of self-interest and perception of objective reality, is that groups that are favored by a particular policy or situation have a greater inclination to perceive objective reality in terms of their self-interest. Thus, groups that are objectively favored by heightened international tensions might have a greater propensity to perceive external threats and a corresponding disinclination to recognize that the nature of a threat has been altered, reduced, or eliminated, thus requiring new policies which might adversely affect them. On the other hand, groups that are objectively favored by relaxation of international tensions or a peacetime economy might be more prone to perceive a premature alteration, diminution or elimination of an external threat and a corresponding tendency to be skeptical about external threats which arise if they would result in a radical rise in defense expenditures and a reallocation of resources and social rewards.

The social and institutional groups in Soviet society which appear to benefit from an aggressive foreign policy and the maintenance of international tensions are (1) the traditional sectors of the Armed Forces; (2) the heavy industrial managers; (3) professional Party *apparatchiki* and ideologues. By no means do all individuals or sub-elites and cliques within these groups see eye-to-eye on foreign policy issues. Some individuals and sub-elites, for opportunistic or careerist reasons or functional adaptability, are able to adjust to a relaxation of tensions by preserving or even improving their role and status. The significant point is that the main impetus for an aggressive policy and the chief opposition to a relaxation of tensions find their social and functional foundations within these three socio-functional or socio-institutional groups, whose common perception of interests results in an informal "military-industrial-apparatus complex." Their attitudes stem almost entirely from the function and role they play in Soviet society and the rewards in terms of prestige, status and power which are derived from these functions in time of high international tensions as opposed to a *détente*.

The professional military, on the whole, has a natural interest in a large and modern military establishment and a high priority on budget and resources; the heavy industrial managerial groups have a vested stake in pre-serving the primacy of their sector of the economy; and the Party apparatus traditionally has had a vested interest in ideological conformity and the social controls which they rationalized, thus ensuring the primacy of the apparatus over all other social forces in the Soviet system. All of these functional roles are served best under conditions of international tension. Consequently, this group wittingly or unwittingly has developed a vested interest in either maintaining international tensions or creating the illusion of insecurity and external danger, which would produce the same effect.

To the degree that individuals or sub-elites within these groups are able to socially re-tool their functions and adapt them to peacetime or purely internal functions, then do they correspondingly lose interest in an aggressive or tension-preserving policy.

For purposes of analytical convenience, those social groups which would seem to benefit from a relaxation of international tensions can be classified into four general categories: (1) The state bureaucracy, in the central governmental institutions as well as in the Republics and localities; (2) Light industrial interests, consumer goods and services interests, and agricultural interests; (3) The cultural, professional and scientific groups, whose role and influence seem to flourish and thrive under conditions of relaxation both at home and abroad; and (4) The Soviet "consumer," the rank and file white collar employees, the working class, and the peasantry, who will ultimately benefit most from a policy which concentrates on raising the standard of living. The technical-scientific branches of the professional military, including the nuclear-missile specialists, also appear to benefit during periods of relaxed international tensions because during periods of *détente* they become the main reliance for national security while the traditional forces are subject to severe budget reductions.

While the contradiction between Soviet security interests and ideological goals in foreign policy has long been recognized by observers of the Soviet scene, a new variable in Soviet policy is the contradiction between enhancing economic prosperity at home and fulfilling international ideological obligations. In Soviet jargon, this emerges as a contradiction between the requirements of "building Communism" and the costs and risks of remaining faithful to the principle of "proletarian internationalism."

This new factor has not gone unnoticed by the Chinese who accuse Khrushchev of abandoning Soviet ideological and material obligations to international Communism and the national-liberation movement in favor of avoiding the risks of nuclear war and building an affluent society to satisfy the appetites of the new Soviet "ruling stratum," in the guise of pursuing peaceful coexistence and "building Communism." Thus, in a long editorial entitled; "On Khrushchev's Phoney Communism and Its Historical Lessons For the World," the authoritative Chinese organ, *Jen Min Jih Pao*, charged on July 14, 1964:

The revisionist Khrushchev clique has usurped the leadership of the Soviet party and state and . . . a privileged bourgeois stratum has emerged in Soviet society. . . . The privileged stratum in contemporary Soviet society is composed of degenerate elements from among the leading cadres of party and government organizations, enterprises, and farms as well as bourgeois intellectuals. . . . Under the signboard of "peaceful coexistence," Khrushchev has been colluding with U.S. imperialism, wrecking the socialist camp and the international communist movement, opposing the revolutionary struggles of the oppressed peoples and nations, practicing great-power chauvinism and national egoism, and betraying proletarian internationalism. All this is being done for the protection of the vested interest of a handful of people, which he places above the fundamental interests of the peoples of the Soviet Union, the socialist camp and the whole world.[36]

The same charge has also been leveled at Khrushchev's successors, who, Peking maintains, are simply practicing "Khrushchevism without Khrushchev."

THE ADMINISTRATION AND EXECUTION OF SOVIET FOREIGN POLICY

Party policy and state administration: conflict and harmony

Responsibility for the actual *execution* of foreign policy as distinct from its *formulation* rests with the Council of Ministers and its Presidium, which is nominally accountable to the Supreme Soviet and its Presidium but in fact is subordinate to the Party Politburo, with which it normally shares key personnel. The relationship between the Party's highest body and the Council of Ministers and its Presidium in the decision-making process, which is often ambiguous and is currently in a state of transition, depends more upon the degree of interlocking membership between the two organs than upon constitutional forms. Under Stalin, particularly after he became Premier in 1941, interlocking membership was virtually complete and was designed to ensure maximum harmony between Party policy and state administration. Distinctions between formulation and execution of policy were ambiguous to the point of complete irrelevance under these condi-

[36] *Jen Min Jih Pao*, July 14, 1964.

tions. Before Stalin held any formal executive position in the government, the institutions of the Party were the chief decision-making bodies of the regime, but with Stalin's assumption of the premiership, Stalin, the Secretary-General of the Party, made policy, and in his capacity as premier he was also in charge of its execution and administration. As head of both Party and government he did not need to employ all the institutions of decision making; and those of the Party virtually withered away. Since all diplomatic relations with the outside world are carried on through State institutions, the organs of the State had to retain sufficient vitality to legalize Stalin's decisions into formal acts of government.

The apparent rise of the State to a position superior to that of the Party was undoubtedly a major factor in Malenkov's decision to succeed Stalin as Premier rather than as First Secretary of the Party. Legally, as Premier, he had under his control the two principal instruments of violence, the Police and the Armed Forces; and thus he chose the State in preference to the Party Secretariat as his instrument with which to subdue his rivals in the Presidium. The Police and the Army, however, turned out to be virtually separate entities with their own informal lines of organization and loyalty which radically departed from constitutional and legal patterns. By relinquishing control of the Party Secretariat to Khrushchev in favor of the premiership, Malenkov abdicated the symbols of legitimacy in favor of the shell of power, since within the context of the Party rules and institutional controls bequeathed by Stalin, the Premier and the Government were mere creatures of the Party's will. As long as the Secretariat and the premiership are united in a single personality, relation-

ships of control and subordination are irrelevant, but once they are separated, custom and precedent, as well as ideology, favor the Secretariat in any rivalry for supremacy.

With the eruption of factional rivalry in the Presidium and the separation of the Party Secretariat from the Government, interlocking membership between the Council of Ministers and the Party's highest body, instead of ensuring harmony between policy and administration, in fact guaranteed conflict and friction, as the Party Presidium came under the control of one faction while key administrative organs of State were in the hands of members of rival factions.

The first overt instance of conflict between Party policy and state administration was Beria's attempt to thwart the decisions of the Party through his control of the Ministry and Internal Affairs. Since then, both major and minor discrepancies between policy administration have taken place. Thus, while Khrushchev could muster narrow majorities in the Presidium, members of the opposition were in strategic administrative positions where they could subvert the implementation of Party decisions. One of the major accusations against Foreign Minister Molotov, and also against Shepilov, was that he was using the Foreign Ministry and Soviet missions abroad to subvert and sabotage, rather than to carry out, the policies formulated by the Party. Similarly, Khrushchev's plan for breaking up the concentration of economic power in Moscow was probably opposed by the managerial bureaucrats like Kaganovich, Pervukhin, and Saburov, who controlled key economic levers in the nation's industrial system and could effectively frustrate the dismantling of their own source of power and influence. Thus, before the reorganization of the Presidium in June 1957, five of the nine members of the Presidium of the Council of Ministers were members of the opposition minority in the Party Presidium. It was untenable that the minority faction in the Party Presidium should enjoy a majority in the Presidium of the Council of Ministers, whose function it was to implement the very policies rejected, in the Party Presidium by a majority of its members.

The power of the Council of Ministers as a policy-making and executive institution was severely curtailed during the brief period of Bulganin's continued incumbency after the 1957 reorganization. Before June 29, 1957, the nine-man Presidium of the Council of Ministers included seven full members of the Party Presidium, but after the reorganization only Bulganin and Mikoyan remained members of both bodies. The displacement of Bulganin by Khrushchev in March 1958 marked a revival in overlapping membership in the two organs, whereby career Party workers moved into top government positions. By 1961, four of the seven-man Presidium of the Council of Ministers were also members of the Party Presidium. The situation became highly fluid as Khrushchev's grip on the leadership started to erode after the Twenty-second Party Congress and in particular after the Cuban missile crisis, when only four full members of the Party's Presidium of 12 full members were also members of the Government Presidium of 12 members.

The constitutional basis of Soviet foreign relations

Under the Soviet Constitution of 1936, as amended, foreign policy is administered and executed at four different institutional levels: (1) the Presidium of the Supreme Soviet; (2) the Supreme Soviet; (3) the Council

of Ministers; and (4) the Union Republics, of which there are now fifteen. Although the Soviet constitutional set-up is based on the principle of complete fusion of executive, legislative, and administrative power, each institutional level is invested with certain foreign policy functions, which may be permissive, exclusive, or concurrent. These legal relationships, however, do not function in any way as limitations on Soviet diplomacy.

The Presidium of the Supreme Soviet. The Presidium of the Supreme Soviet is vested under the Constitution with a wide range of ceremonial, executive, and legislative functions. Juridically a creature of the Supreme Soviet, for which it acts as legal agent, it is, in fact, its institutional superior and surrogate, since it is empowered with virtually the entire spectrum of authority granted to the Supreme Soviet during the long and frequent intervals between sessions of the Soviet legislature. Technically, all of its actions are subject to later confirmation by the Supreme Soviet, but, in practice, this is an empty ritual.

In the area of foreign affairs, the Presidium, in the person of its chairman, functions as the ceremonial chief of state, much like the American president and the British monarch:

In accordance with the universally recognized doctrine of international law, the supreme representation of the modern state is vested in the chief of state, whether he be an actual person (monarch, president of the republic) or a collective body (Presidium of the Supreme Soviet of the U.S.S.R., Federal Council of Switzerland). . . . As a general rule, the competence of the chief of state includes the declaration of war and conclusion of peace, nomination and reception of diplomatic agents, granting powers for the conclusion of international treaties and agreements of special significance, and the ratification and denunciation of these treaties and accords.[37]

In its ceremonial capacity, the Presidium confers all diplomatic ranks and titles of a plenipotentiary character, formally appoints and recalls diplomatic representatives of the U.S.S.R., and receives the letters of credence and recall from foreign envoys. Although foreign representatives almost always present their credentials to the Chairman of the Presidium, they are, in fact, accredited to the Presidium as a collective entity.

The Presidium's substantive powers are considerable. Article 49 of the Constitution authorizes it to interpret all Soviet laws, convene and dissolve the Supreme Soviet, annul decisions and orders of the Council of Ministers, appoint and remove the higher commands of the armed forces, and issue decrees in its own right, virtually without limits. Furthermore, the Presidium, during intervals between sessions of the Supreme Soviet, "proclaims a state of war in the event of armed attack . . . or whenever necessary to fulfill international treaty obligations concerning mutual defense against aggression," can order general or partial mobilization, and can proclaim martial law in separate localities or throughout the country. The exercise of many of these powers is not subject to later confirmation by the Supreme Soviet, although the Presidium remains technically accountable for all its activities to the Soviet legislature, which theoretically can replace its personnel.

Certain important powers vested in the Presidium are provisional and delegated. Thus, the Presidium, during periods when the Supreme Soviet is not in session, can appoint and dismiss ministers upon the recommendation of the chairman of the Council of Ministers, but this is subject to later confirmation. Similarly, if the Presidium promulgates decrees of a fundamental nature, outside its formal constitutional competence, they also are subject to confirmation, although this may be several years later.

Although the Constitution appears to give the Presidium a monopoly on the ratification and denunciation of treaties, a law of the Supreme Soviet, "On the Procedure for Ratification and Denunciation of International Treaties," passed on August 19, 1938, defines as treaties requiring its ratification: (1) treaties of peace; (2) mutual defense treaties; (3) treaties of nonaggression; and (4) treaties requiring mutual ratification for their implementation.[38] By implication, and in accordance with past practice, all treaties not specifically enumerated as requiring ratification by the Presidium are left to the discretion of the Council of Ministers. On the other hand, on rare occasions the Supreme Soviet has been asked to ratify or give preliminary approval to particularly important treaties, although there exists no constitutional imperative.

The Supreme Soviet. As the "highest organ of state authority in the U.S.S.R.," the power of the Supreme Soviet under the Constitution is coterminous with that of the Union.

Composed of two coordinate chambers—the Council of the Union and the Council of Nationalities—of approximately equal size, the constitutional competence of the Soviet legislature in foreign affairs surpasses that of any other organ. In practice, it has abdicated most of its powers to the Presidium and has been left only with

[37] *Istoriya Diplomatii,* III, 765.

[38] *Second Session of the Supreme Soviet of the U.S.S.R.* (New York: International Publishers Company, Inc., 1938), p. 678 verbatim report.

the empty shell of ceremony, which may sometimes border on consultation. Both chambers are equally potent or impotent, singly or together, and neither has specific functions or powers denied the other.

The formal authority of the Supreme Soviet in foreign policy falls into seven categories: (1) the enactment of basic legislation and constitutional amendments; (2) the confirmation of the decisions and decrees of the Presidium and the Council of Ministers; (3) ratification of selected treaties; (4) declaration of war and peace; (5) confirmation and authorization of territorial changes and of the creation, admission, promotion, demotion, and abolition of new republics; (6) hearing and approving of foreign policy reports delivered by the Premier or the Foreign Minister; and (7) the preliminary examination of treaties prior to ratification by the Presidium. Since Stalin's death, all these activities have been accorded greater publicity.

The sessions of the Supreme Soviet are short. Between 1946 and 1954, the Supreme Soviet sat for a total of only forty-five days, the longest session lasting seven days (June, 1950) and the shortest, sixty-seven minutes (March, 1953); its performance before and during World War II was even less auspicious. By far the most significant function of the Supreme Soviet is to hear reports on the foreign policy of the government. It is customary, but by no means the invariable rule, that the Foreign Minister review the government's foreign policy before this body, usually before joint sessions. It listens attentively and enacts the desired legislation. There is "discussion," but a close examination of the official records discloses not a single note of criticism, to say nothing of a negative vote, in all the deliberations of the Supreme Soviet.

In the words of *Kommunist,* "until recently its [the Supreme Soviet's] sessions concerned for the most part consideration of budget questions and approval of the decrees of the Presidium,"[39] but after the replacement of Malenkov by Bulganin, in 1955, it was given a more conspicuous role in foreign affairs. At that time, the Supreme Soviet issued an appeal to other parliaments for a program of parliamentary exchanges in the form of visiting delegations addressing each other's legislatures; more than a dozen such exchanges have taken place. In July, 1955, the Supreme Soviet adhered to the Inter-Parliamentary Union (ITU) and sent a delegation to its forty-fourth annual conference in Helsinki.

Although the two Foreign Affairs Commissions of the two chambers of the Supreme Soviet are supposed to make "a preliminary examination of all matters connected with foreign affairs to be considered by the Supreme Soviet (and its Presidium)," this function had all but withered away and the existence of these bodies was virtually rendered superfluous. They were suddenly brought back to life when the Soviet-Iranian Agreement of 1954, the denunciation of the Anglo-Soviet and Anglo-French Treaties of Alliance, the Warsaw Pact, and the agreement to establish diplomatic relations with West Germany were all submitted to joint sessions of the two Commissions (the Supreme Soviet was not in session) for consideration. After hearing reports by Molotov and his deputies, they recommended approval to the Soviet Presidium. At about the same time, the two chairmen of the chambers, together with allegedly prominent members of the two Commissions, appeared at diplomatic receptions, received foreign dignitaries, and

[39] *Kommunist,* No. 10 (August, 1956), pp. 3–15.

pompously pontificated on foreign policy in patent, but bogus, imitation of their counterparts in the American Congress.

It was the Supreme Soviet which proclaimed an end to the state of war with Germany, on January 25, 1955. On August 4, 1955, it was called into special session to hear Bulganin's report on the Summit Conference at Geneva, a procedure not used since Molotov had addressed a special session on the Nazi-Soviet Pact of 1939. On this same occasion, the Supreme Soviet, after "debating" the policy of the government and "interpellating" the Foreign Minister, issued an appeal to the parliaments and governments of the world to "put an end to the arms race." The regular session of the Supreme Soviet coincided with the return of Bulganin and Khrushchev from their tour of Southeast Asia, and both addressed the Supreme Soviet on the results of their trip.

Although the activities of the Supreme Soviet have been stepped up, there is little reason to believe that there has been a corresponding enhancement of its influence and power. It hears more reports on foreign policy, but it has also retained its absolute unanimity. The invocation of the formal prerogatives of the Supreme Soviet, however, is no idle exercise, since it creates certain advantages for Soviet diplomacy: (1) It serves to infuse the citizenry with the notion that their representatives participate in the formulation of foreign policy decisions. (2) As a propagandistic maneuver it strives to create the illusion of evolving constitutionalism in the Soviet system. (3) As a purely diplomatic device, it permits the Kremlin to invoke constitutional procedures as a stumbling or delaying mechanism in negotiations and affords a basis for demanding reciprocal action in the rati-

fication of treaties and other diplomatic instruments.

The possibility, no matter how slight, that ceremony may some day be replaced with substance cannot be ignored, but this expectation must yield to the realization that the flurry of activity we have noted can be arrested as abruptly as it began. Yet it must be stated that periodic suggestions are made in the Soviet press that the Supreme Soviet be given more legislative authority.

The Council of Ministers.[40] As the "highest executive and administrative organ" of the government, the Council of Ministers "exercises general supervision" over the execution and administration of the country's foreign policy, and also directs the state's foreign trade monopoly. Constitutionally, since 1944 the central government no longer exercises a monopoly over foreign affairs, but merely represents the Federal Union as a whole and establishes the "general procedure in mutual relations between the Union Republics and foreign states," and thus shares the conduct of diplomacy with its fifteen constituent republics. In practice, however, foreign policy in the Soviet Union is the most tightly centralized activity of the Soviet government.

The Council of Ministers has the following powers: (1) grant or withdraw recognition of new states or governments; (2) sever and restore diplomatic relations; (3) order acts of reprisal against other states; (4) appoint negotiators and supervise the negotiation of international treaties and agreements; (5) declare the adherence of the Soviet Union to international conventions not requiring formal ratification; (6) conclude agreements not requiring ratification

[40] Formerly the Council of People's Commissars, or *Sovnarkom.*

with other heads of governments (similar to American executive and administrative agreements); (7) ratify all treaties and agreements not requiring ratification of the Presidium; (8) give preliminary examination of all treaties submitted to the Presidium for its ratification; (9) oversee "the current work of the diplomatic organs, effectually direct that work and take the necessary measures in that field"; and (10) appoint and accredit all diplomats below plenipotentiary rank and foreign trade representatives.[41]

Actually, there appears to be a great area of overlapping activity between the Presidium and the Council of Ministers in the conduct of diplomacy, and were it not that the one-party system makes all basic decisions, rivalries and jealousies would almost certainly develop between these two organs, rendering coordination of diplomatic activity virtually impossible.

a) The Chairman and his Cabinet. The most influential member of the Council of Ministers is its Chairman, referred to in the West as the Premier, who is always an important figure of the highest rank in the Party hierarchy. This office, including its predecessors under previous constitutions, has been filled by only eight men since the establishment of the Soviet state: Lenin (1917–1924); Rykov (1924–1930); Molotov (1930–1941); Stalin (1941–1953); Malenkov (1953–1955); Bulganin (1955–1958); Khrushchev (1958–1964); and Kosygin (1964–   ). After Lenin's death, when Stalin refused to hold formal office, this post was reduced to a mere shadow of the Secretary-General of the Party, but after Stalin assumed formal responsibility

for the policies of the government in 1941, the post retrieved its former prestige and power. The rivalries that were unleashed after Stalin's death, in 1953, temporarily revived the division of power between the Premier and First Secretary of the Party, and the two positions were again separated, then reunited and later reseparated. Khrushchev's assumption of the office after Bulganin's resignation reflected the internal and external symbolic significance which it acquired during Stalin's long tenure as well as the fact that it was too risky to permit it to be separately occupied.

The sundering of the two positions, in October, 1964, reflected once again a division of power in the Soviet leadership. The post of Premier serves to legitimize and legalize the power of the First Secretary, just as the latter imparts to the premiership the necessary ideological sanctity. The position has suffered another setback with Khrushchev's ouster and the restoration of the title of General Secretary, but the premiership will continue to exert an attraction to any General Secretary.

The Chairman, or Premier, has primary responsibility for the conduct of foreign policy and, presumably, the authority to appoint and remove the ministers concerned with its day-to-day execution. Immediately below the Chairman are his first deputy chairmen and deputy chairmen, who normally are in charge of a specific ministry, or may be without portfolio. The Chairman, his first deputies, and his deputies constitute the Presidium (Cabinet) of the Council of Ministers.

The size and composition of the Presidium have undergone serious transformations in recent years and has varied in size up to more than a dozen members. Under Stalin, the Presidium became so large that a Bu-

[41]*Cf.* A. Y. Vyshinsky, *The Law of the Soviet State* (New York: The Macmillan Company, 1948), p. 376; *Istoriya Diplomatii,* III, 767–68, 806–7; Towster, *op. cit.,* p. 279.

reau—or inner cabinet—of the Presidium was secretly organized, whose composition and membership have never been made public. After his death, the Bureau of the Presidium was technically abolished, but in fact, the Presidium was reduced to the smaller size of the Bureau.

The Council of Ministers and its Presidium are actually subordinate to the Party Politburo and, in theory, to the Supreme Soviet and its Presidium. If the Premier of the government loses a vote of confidence in the Politburo, the decision is reviewed by the Central Committee; if it is upheld there, he submits his resignation to the Presidium of the Supreme Soviet. The Central Committee, through its First Secretary, nominates the next Premier to the appropriate state organs and a new government is thus formed.

Since the formation of the Bulganin government, the Premier and other key members of the Presidium of the Council of Ministers have played an increasingly personal and active role in the country's diplomacy. This pattern was further accelerated after Khrushchev became Premier. Not only the Premier, but important ministers and the Chairman of the Presidium of the Supreme Soviet, have made state visits to many countries as a part of the Kremlin's new diplomatic offensive. Kosygin and Brezhnev introduced a division of labor in international affairs, each assuming individual personal roles in Soviet diplomacy. While he was Foreign Minister, Molotov played an active personal role in the country's diplomacy, but he apparently objected to the interference of the other members of the government in Soviet diplomatic activity. In particular, he objected to the travels of Bulganin and Khrushchev and their meetings with the heads of various governments.

b) *The Foreign Minister.* In forty years of Soviet diplomacy, there have been only seven Foreign Ministers: Leon Trotsky (November, 1917– April, 1918); Georgi Chicherin (1918 –1929); Maxim Litvinov (1929– 1939); Vyacheslav Molotov (1939– 1949, and 1953–1956); Andrei Vyshinsky (1949–1953); Dimitri Shepilov (during 1956); Andrei Gromyko (1957–   ). The typical tenure of a Soviet Foreign Minister is ten years, and nearly forty-five years of Soviet diplomacy have been directed by only four individuals, thus giving Soviet diplomacy an enviable continuity except for a few years after Stalin's death, when the changes reflected the bitter conflicts that have raged over foreign policy in the past few years.

The Foreign Minister's influence depends almost entirely upon his Party rank. When the Minister is of relatively low rank in the Party, he is little more than a caretaker of the department. If he is of top Party rank, as Trotsky and Molotov were, he participates in the decisions he is asked to execute and, in at least two cases (Molotov and Shepilov), he has actually flouted the will of the decision makers. Chicherin and Litvinov, like Gromyko, were relatively low-ranking members in the Party hierarchy, but this by no means indicates that they were less effective as diplomats. There is ample evidence to suggest that the Party leaders would prefer a low-ranking Party member as Foreign Minister rather than one of first rank, except under critical circumstances, since it enhances the flexibility of Soviet diplomacy while hampering that of other countries, who are forced to accommodate their diplomacy to the bureaucratic channels of the Soviet Foreign Office. Normally, the Foreign Minister is at least a full member of the Central Committee, although both Chicherin and Litvinov achieved that status some time after they had become Foreign Commissars. Gromyko was elevated to full membership only at the Twentieth Party Congress. Trotsky and Molotov were the only Foreign Ministers who were full members of the Party's highest body; Vyshinsky and Shepilov were alternate members of the Presidium during their incumbency.

The Ministry of Foreign Affairs[42]

Evolution of the Ministry. The government department directly charged with the day-to-day administration of Soviet diplomacy does not materially differ in its structure and organization from its counterparts in the other Great Powers, although its evolution is unique. Since its establishment, it has undergone a triple metamorphosis.

In the beginning, its primary purpose was to trigger a world revolution and thus create the conditions for its own extinction. It was thought that if the world revolution failed, a Soviet diplomacy would be impossible, and, if it succeeded, unnecessary. It was Leon Trotsky's boast, "I will issue a few revolutionary proclamations to the people of the world, and then close up shop."[43] On November 26, 1917, a decree from Trotsky's Foreign Affairs Commissariat virtually disestablished the diplomatic apparatus of the Russian state: all members of the Russian foreign service abroad were summarily dismissed unless they expressed loyalty to the Bolshevik regime. In their places, Bolshevik émigrés abroad were appointed as "unofficial" agents of the new government (Litvinov was such an appointee to Great Britain). Trotsky even neglected to establish a permanent home office; he appeared at his office only once—to dismiss all employees reluctant to pledge loyalty to the new regime and to set up a committee to publish the secret treaties in the archives of the Russian Foreign Office.

The Treaty of Brest-Litovsk imposed upon the new regime diplomatic relations with Germany and its allies, so the Council of People's Commissars was forced to re-create a provisional diplomatic service. With obvious petulance, in a decree of June 4, 1918, they attempted to rewrite unilaterally the principle of diplomatic ranks adopted by the Congress of Vienna in 1815, by abolishing all Soviet diplomatic titles in favor of a single designation, "plenipotentiary representative" (*Polpred*). In a naive attempt to impose Soviet egalitarian principles upon foreign envoys, the decree peremptorily announced that "all diplomatic agents of foreign states . . . shall be considered equal plenipotentiary representatives regardless of their rank."[44]

Pending the eventual liquidation of the Foreign Affairs Commissariat, the functions of Soviet diplomacy during this initial period fell into three principal categories: (1) the publication of "secret treaties" in order to expose the duplicity and hypocrisy of the Allies and compromise them in the eyes of their own people; (2) the conduct of necessary negotiations and diplomatic relations, on a temporary basis, with capitalist states in a position to impose them; and (3) the utilization of Soviet

---

[42]Formerly the People's Commissariat for Foreign Affairs, or *Narkomindel.*

[43]Cited in E. H. Carr, *The Bolshevik Revolution, 1917–1923,* (London: Macmillan, 1953), III, 16.

[44]Full text in T. A. Taracouzio, *The Soviet Union and International Law* (New York: The Macmillan Company, 1935), p. 383.

embassies and legations abroad as centers of revolutionary propaganda, conspiracy, and activity, in clear violation of treaty obligations. In this connection, the Soviet government announced that "The Council of People's Commissars considers it necessary to offer assistance by all possible means . . . to the left internationalist wing of the labor movement of all countries [and] . . . for this purpose . . . decides to allocate two million rubles for the needs of the revolutionary international movement and to put this sum at the disposal of the foreign representatives of the Commissariat for Foreign Affairs."[45]

The failure of the revolution to spread beyond Russia, the success of the seceding border states in maintaining their independence, and the failure of foreign intervention to subdue the Bolshevik regime, forced the expansion of diplomatic contact with the bourgeois world. By 1921 the Soviet foreign office was prepared to pass out of its initial phase into its second, as a quasi-permanent agency for "normalizing" relations with the capitalist powers on the basis of "mutual interests" during the prolonged period of "co-existence" which Lenin now recognized as the inevitable interval between the first and final stages of the world revolution. From an instrument of world revolution the foreign office was converted into an instrument for furthering the interests of the Soviet state.

Since the revolutionary and conspiratorial activities of Soviet diplomats complicated the establishment of desirable trade and political connections with the bourgeois world, the new Commissar of Foreign Affairs,

Georgi Chicherin (who succeeded Trotsky in April 1918), was instrumental in shifting the function of revolutionary agitation from the Foreign Office to the Party. A new diplomatic service was organized from scratch by Chicherin, and shortly after he assumed office, the Foreign Commissariat was organized into more than a dozen departments. The first Statute on the Commissariat for Foreign Affairs was issued by the Council of Ministers on July 6, 1921; it defined the sphere of competence of each of the departments. After the formation of the Union and the centralization of diplomacy in Moscow, the Commissariat on November 12, 1923, received its definite statute which still constitutes the juridical basis for the organization and structure of the Foreign Ministry. However, it was not until 1924 that Soviet diplomacy was juridically relieved of its revolutionary mission and it entered into its current phase. According to a decree issued November 21, 1924 and still effective:

It goes without saying that diplomatic missions abroad are appointed by each of the parties establishing diplomatic relations for purposes which exclude propaganda in the country to which they are accredited. The Soviet diplomatic missions follow and are to follow this principle with absolute strictness.[46]

Although technically the Soviet Foreign Office is supervised by the Council of Ministers, it has always enjoyed a unique, direct relationship with the Party Presidium. Unlike the other departments of government in the new Bolshevik regime, the Foreign Commissariat was unencumbered with holdovers from the old bureaucracy, Chi-

[45]Jane Degras, ed., *Soviet Documents on Foreign Policy* (London: Royal Institute of International Affairs, 1951), I, 22.

[46]Full text in Taracouzio, *op cit.*, 389–390.

cherin being the only prominent figure who had previous diplomatic experience. Consequently, from the very beginning, it was cherished by Lenin:

The diplomatic apparatus . . . is quite exceptional in the governmental apparatus. We excluded everyone from the old Tsarist apparatus who formerly had even the slightest influence. Here, the whole apparatus, insofar as it possesses the slightest influence, has been made up of Communists. For this reason this apparatus has acquired for itself . . . the reputation of a Communist apparatus which has been tested and cleansed of the old Tsarist bourgeois and petty bourgeois apparatus to a degree incomparably higher than that attained in the apparatus with which we have to be satisfied in the other people's commissariats.[47]

This quality, in the words of a Soviet diplomat, "helped make it a peculiarly well-fitted apparatus for the expression of new policies."[48]

The Statute governing the Foreign Affairs Commissariat, decreed on November 12, 1923, which has been frequently amended, but never superseded, defined its principal duties as:

(a) The defence of the political and economic interests of the U.S.S.R. . . . (b) The conclusion of treaties and agreements with foreign countries in accordance with the decisions of the government. (c) Supervision over the proper execution of treaties and agreements concluded with foreign states, and enabling the corresponding organs of the U.S.S.R. and the Union Republics to exercise rights conferred by these treaties. (d) Supervision over the execution by the competent organs of treaties, agreements,

and accords concluded with foreign states.[49]

The Foreign Minister and his Collegium. The administration of the Foreign Commissariat was initially entrusted to a collegium in accordance with the Bolshevik principle of collective responsibility. The Foreign Commissar was forced to share authority and responsibility with a board of three or four other senior officials of the Commissariat.

With the promulgation of the first Constitution in March 1918, the germ of one-man management was implanted, when the Commissar was invested with the personal power of decision relating to matters within the competence of his department, but if this decision conflicted with the views of the collegium, the latter, without the power of stopping execution of the decision, could appeal its differences to the Council or to the Presidium. As a consequence, collective responsibility became a convenient evasion of concrete responsibility and the collegium frequently abused its powers by issuing orders in its own name, thus lowering the prestige and personal responsibility of the Foreign Commissar.

By 1934, defects of collective responsibility became so serious that Stalin condemned the collective principle as obsolete and subversive of efficient administration; the collegium was abolished and the Foreign Minister installed in complete charge of his department and, in turn, he assumed full personal responsibility for its work.

Four years later, in March 1938, the collegium was restored in modified

[47]*The New York Times,* July 1, 1956. Extract is from suppressed Lenin documents distributed at the 20th Party Congress and later made public.

[48]Alexi F. Neymann in S. N. Harper, ed., *The Soviet Union and World Problems* (Chicago: Chicago University Press, 1935), p. 279.

[49]The full text of this statute, with amendments through 1927, is reprinted in *Yezhegodnik Narodnovo Komissariata Po Inostrannym Delam Na 1928 God* (Moscow, 1928), pp. 182–193. All subsequent references and extracts refer to this text. Cf. also *Istoriya Diplomatii,* III, 770–71.

form, but was clearly divested of its former tyrannical power over the Commissar. The Council, which was too large and unwieldy as a decision-making or even advisory body, was retained as a convenient institution for the diffusion of policy and administrative decision, and the collegium retained its character as the executive committee of the Commissariat. The Commissar retained his plenary authority and responsibility, but the formal prerogatives of the collegium remained considerable.[50]

The institutional relationship established in 1938 between the Foreign Minister and his collegium has survived, substantially unaltered, till now. Its size and composition appear to vary, depending upon the discretion of the Foreign Minister, except in unusual circumstances, although appointments to the collegium continue to be made by the Council of Ministers. The collegium is presided over by the Minister or one of his First Deputies. It includes not only the First Deputy and Deputy Ministers, but also about four to six senior officials in the department, one of whom frequently is the Chief of the Press and Information Division. The number of First Deputies has varied from one to three; their rank roughly corresponds to that of the undersecretary in the American State Department. Immediately below the First Deputies are the Deputies, whose rank corresponds to that of Assistant Secretaries in the American hierarchy; there may be up to six Deputies (in 1966 there was one First Deputy and six Deputies). The other members of the collegium are normally department heads. Thus the size of the collegium may vary up to more than a dozen members.

The institutional prerogatives of the collegium fall just short of the power of actual decision, but without weakening in any way the full responsibility of the Minister. It cannot overrule the Minister's decisions, nor issue orders in its own name, but it is mandatory for the Minister to report any disagreement with his collegium to the Council for disposition. The collegium retains the right, individually or collectively, to appeal to the Council and the Central Committee of the party.[51]

The organization and structure of the Foreign Ministry. The basic organization and structure of the Soviet Foreign Ministry remain governed by the Statute of 1923, which established a flexible system of administration, permitting a wide latitude for internal reorganization at the discretion of the Minister. The Ministry is organized into "divisions according to the main geographical divisions of the world and the main functions of the department and . . . this apparatus both in its offices in Moscow and its missions in foreign countries does not present any striking differences in structure compared with similar departments in other countries."[52]

At the apex of the Ministry stands the Minister with his collegium, which is provided with a central secretariat —headed by a secretary-general— performing routine secretarial and staff administrative work for the Minister, his deputies, and members of the collegium. The functional divisions, which have become increasingly differentiated with the expansion of Soviet diplomatic activity, have been conventional: Protocol, Political Archives, Courier and Liaison, Passport and Visa, Treaty and Legal, Economic, Consular Affairs, Administration, Personnel, Finance, Supplies, and Press Information. Several related functional divisions are grouped together and supervised by Deputy Ministers, and perhaps also by

[50]*Cf. Vyshinsky*, pp. 387–89.

[51]*Ibid.*

[52]Neymann, *op. cit.*, pp. 226–27.

collegium members. As Soviet power and influence in international affairs has increased, the functional divisions have undergone substantial expansion in recent years. There are now seven functional divisions: Protocol, Press, Treaty and Legal, Consular Administration, Archives Administration, Personnel Administration and Administration for Servicing the Diplomatic Corps. In addition, the Foreign Ministry has attached to it two training institutions, The Institute of International Relations and The Higher Diplomatic School. The old Economic Division has since proliferated into a separate Ministry called The State Committee for Foreign Economic Relations, which is in charge of the extensive Soviet foreign aid program. Two other Ministries closely related to the Foreign Ministry are the old Ministry of Foreign Trade and The State Committee for Cultural Relations with Foreign Countries.

The political changes of the past twenty years, the massive expansion of Soviet diplomatic relations, and the creation of many new states in Asia and Africa, have profoundly affected the internal organization of the Foreign Office. In the past few years, the number of geographical divisions has been increased, while the number of functional divisions has remained fairly constant. As compiled from press accounts, there are now eight "Western" divisions and eight "Eastern" divisions, plus two separate departments for international organizations, and for international economic organizations. The geographical divisions, which closely resemble those of 1925, are as follows:

Western Divisions

1. United States of America Division
2. Latin-American Countries Division

3. First European Division (France, Benelux, Italy)
4. Second European Division (United Kingdom and white Commonwealth countries)
5. Third European Division (the two Germanies, Austria, Switzerland)
6. Fourth European Division (Poland and Czechoslovakia)
7. Fifth European Division (Balkan countries)
8. Sixth European Division (Scandinavian countries and Finland)

Eastern Divisions

1. First African Division (North African states with the exception of Egypt and Sudan.
2. Second African Division (Black African states)
3. Third African Division (Black African states)
4. Near-Eastern Countries Division
5. Middle-Eastern Countries Division
6. South-Asian Countries Division
7. Southeast-Asian Countries Division
8. Far-Eastern Countries Division (China, Mongolia, North Korea, and Japan)

Normally, a deputy minister exercises general administrative supervision over the work of several contiguous geographical divisions, and usually he is a former ambassador with diplomatic experience in the geographical area in question.

The appearance of kindred communist states in Eastern Europe and in the Far East has not modified the geographical divisions of the Ministry. Relations with communist countries through the Foreign Ministry, however, have been reduced to the bare minimum required by international law and protocol, since substantive and policy questions are handled through corresponding Party organizations. Soviet envoys to important communist countries are considered primarily as functionaries and emissaries from the Party, and secondarily as government agents. This has been confirmed and emphasized since Stalin's death, with the adoption of the practice of dispatching high Party functionaries as ambassadors to important communist states.

In view of the deterioration of relations with China, however, Party relations between the two countries have virtually ceased, and contact has been limited almost exclusively to formal state relations. Already in 1959, Moscow had replaced a highly placed Party official (Yudin) functioning as the Soviet ambassador, with a lower-level Party functionary. And in April, 1965, this lower ranking Party official (Chervonenko) was replaced by a career diplomat, S. G. Lapin, who is not even a candidate member of the Central Committee. There is little question but that the Party standing of Soviet ambassadors to communist countries is indicative of the state of Party relations existing between them.

The Soviet diplomatic service. The decree of 1918, reducing all diplomatic ranks to the single and equal rank of plenipotentiary representative, remained technically in force until 1941, although it was neither possible nor desirable to honor it in practice. The principle of diplomatic equality was based on the discarded theory that "the representatives of . . . the U.S.S.R. do not personify a quasi-mythical Leviathan state, but only . . . the plenipotentiary of the ruling class," and that diplomats from bourgeois countries were likewise emissaries of their ruling classes.[53] This view was condemned as doctrinaire and subversive of Soviet prestige and diplomacy

since, in practice, it amounted to unilateral renunciation of all the privileges and prerogatives of seniority and rank under traditional norms of diplomatic intercourse.

Soviet diplomacy gradually accommodated itself to existing international practice through the extralegal exchange of supplementary protocols granting informal recognition of rank so that Soviet diplomats might avoid forfeiting recognized privileges accorded to those of rank and seniority. On May 9, 1941, the Presidium issued a decree establishing three diplomatic categories: (1) ambassador extraordinary and plenipotentiary; (2) minister extraordinary and plenipotentiary; and (3) *chargé d'affaires*. This decree gave legal sanction to *de facto* distinctions. Two years later, on May 28, 1943, the Presidium decreed the establishment of eleven grades in the diplomatic service and thus brought Soviet diplomatic ranking into complete focus with general diplomatic practice: (1) ambassador extraordinary, and plenipotentiary; (2) minister extraordinary and plenipotentiary of the first class; (3) minister extraordinary and plenipotentiary of the second class; (4) counselor, first class; (5) counselor, second class; (6) first secretary, first class; (7) first secretary, second class; (8) second secretary, first class; (9) second secretary, second class; (10) third secretary; and (11) attaché.[54]

As a rule, career Soviet diplomats do not rank very high in the Party hierarchy. The foreign minister is at least a full member of the Central Committee and frequently a member or alternate member of the Presidium. First deputies are normally full members of the Central Committee, while

---

[53]E. Korovin, *Mezhdunarodnoye Pravo Perekhodnovo Vremeni* (Moscow, 1924), p. 63.

[54]*Cf. Istoriya Diplomatii,* III, 778–80. Date of the decree is mistakenly given as June 14, 1943, in this work.

career diplomats rarely achieve higher status than candidate membership in the Central Committee.

Since Stalin's death, the Soviet diplomatic service has been subjected to a unique infusion of new personnel. Alongside members of the career service, who serve as diplomatic technicians, there now exist numerous high-ranking Ministry officials and diplomats who are primarily State administrators and Party functionaries who appear to correspond to the political appointee in the American diplomatic hierarchy. The transfer of high Party officials and State administrators into the diplomatic service has gone through four distinct phases since Stalin's death, corresponding to the principal milestones in the struggle for power after 1953. Each time a major change in the power equilibrium took place in the Presidium, Party officials were shifted to diplomatic work. Consequently, the most obvious trend is that the Foreign Ministry is once again being used as a convenient post of exile from the centers of political power for Party bureaucrats wounded in the power struggles. A second trend is the assignment of career Party bureaucrats—not all of them in disgrace—to Communist capitals, which has resulted in the formation of a distinct parallel diplomatic pattern which serves to combine both Party and State relations in the Communist orbit. A third trend is that a Ministry long under the control of Molotov and exposed to the temptations of the outside world is being placed under quasi-surveillance and provided with Party ballast.

Since 1953, not counting Molotov and the late A. Y. Vyshinsky, no less than six full members and five alternate members of the Party Presidium elected in 1952 have been shifted to the diplomatic service, most of whom are still there. Many of these new Party diplomats enjoy higher Party rank than their technical superior, Foreign Minister Gromyko, and they constitute a distinct cluster of Party luminaries who outshine any combination of career diplomats. The year 1958 represented the high-water mark of Party infusion into the Foreign Ministry, when Gromoko's two First Deputy Ministers and at least six of his ambassadors appeared to outrank him in the Party galaxy, although in most cases their stars were in decline. Five of these new diplomats were admitted to the Party Central Committee in 1939, the same year in which Gromyko entered the diplomatic service as a junior official.

Since 1958 some of the Party officials have worked themselves back into the Party apparatus, others have died, and some have been appointed to quasi-diplomatic ministerial positions. None have fully recovered their former Party eminence, while additional Party and Government officials have been shifted to diplomatic careers.

The channels of Soviet diplomacy. It is general practice for Soviet envoys to report to the Ministry through routine bureaucratic channels, that is, through the appropriate geographical divisions in the Ministry, but ambassadors in important posts frequently report directly to the Foreign Minister. Reports of an exceptionally important character are also sent directly to the Foreign Minister or his First Deputies, rather than through normal channels. The close supervision of the diplomatic service by the Party center cannot be overemphasized; and diplomatic channels remain deliberately flexible.

Not all Soviet representatives abroad report to the Foreign Ministry. Envoys to Communist states, particularly those holding high Party rank, probably report to the Central Committee or the Presidium, except for reports of essentially protocol or legalistic significance, which are funnelled through normal channels. The jurisdiction of the Foreign Ministry over envoys to Communist countries appears marginal at best.

Although the Ambassador, as the chief legal representative of the Soviet Union in foreign countries, is charged with general supervision over the activities of Soviet representatives and missions abroad to ensure that they are in accord with the general policy of the government, this responsibility is often of little more than formal or legal significance. According to defectors like Igor Gouzenko and Vladimir Petrov, Soviet missions abroad are organized into five separate divisions, each with separate and independent channels of communication: (1) the Ambassador and his staff, reporting directly to the Ministry of Foreign Affairs; (2) the Commercial Counsellor, reporting to the Ministry of Foreign Trade; (3) the Secret Police representative, disguised as a minor diplomat, reporting directly to the foreign section of the Security Ministry (now Committee); (4) the Attachés, reporting directly to the Director of Military Intelligence in Moscow; (5) the Party representative, also disguised as a minor diplomatic functionary, communicating directly with the foreign section of the Central Committee of the Party.

All of these representatives, with the exception of the Ambassador and the embassy staff proper, may be actively engaged in the overt or clandestine collection of intelligence information. In order to comply with the letter of their agreements with foreign countries, the Ambassador is scrupulously insulated from all knowledge of illegal espionage activities organized by the other sections, and although the Foreign Ministry Statute gives him the power to determine whether their activities are in accordance with government policy, in practice the Ambassador rarely sees the reports dispatched by the other sections through their respective channels.

In addition to espionage and intelligence activities, the Secret Police and Party sections maintain general surveillance over the other members of the mission and over each other. If the accounts of high-ranking defectors from the diplomatic and police service are accurate, Soviet missions abroad are often centers of intrigue, personal vendettas, and institutional rivalries and jealousies.

Information coming through various channels is screened, coordinated, and evaluated by a special agency of the Central Committee, which then submits its reports to the Presidium to be used as a factor in the formulation of foreign policy and in the making of decisions.

As instruments, rather than makers of policy, professional Soviet diplomats play a minor role in the formulation of foreign policy. Their work is essentially technical and legalistic; their reports are concerned primarily, if not exclusively, with observations and suggestions for more effective implementation of existing policy. Their area of initiative is carefully circumscribed, and often they are ignorant about the exact intentions of their superiors in the Kremlin. Their reports constitute but a minute fraction of the information on which the Presidium acts, and final disposition of all information from routine diplomatic channels and intelligence sources is made by the Presidium as it sees fit. As Merle Fainsod points out, accurate evaluation of information in the Soviet Union is often subjected to special hazards:

But the mountains of material have to be reduced to manageable proportions before they are brought to the attention of the leadership. What the rulers read reflects the selection and emphasis of an editorial staff which may be guided by its own preconditioning as well as its sensitivity to the anticipated reactions of its readers. The tendency to embrace data that confirm established predilections while rejecting the unpalatable facts that offend one's preconceptions is a weakness . . . [to] which . . . totalitarian societies appear to be particularly susceptible. . . . Every dictatorship has a tendency to breed sycophancy and discourage independence in its bureaucratic hierarchy. When the pronouncements of the dictator are sacred and unchallengeable, the words which subordinates must throw back at him tend to flatter his whims rather than challenge his analyses. . . . The ideological screen through which facts are received, filtered, and appraised constitutes an additional possibility of misrepresentation. . . . Not even the most pragmatically oriented member of the ruling group can wholly liberate himself from the frame of responses that represent the residue of a lifetime in Communist thought patterns.[55]

Khrushchev's explanation of why Stalin ignored repeated warnings, from Churchill and from his own efficient espionage networks, that the Nazis were planning to attack the Soviet Union appears to confirm Fainsod's perceptive appraisal when he revealed that "information of this sort concerning the threat of German armed invasion of Soviet territory was coming in also from our own military and diplomatic sources . . . [but] because the leadership was conditioned against such information, such data were dispatched with fear and assessed with reservation."

[55] Merle Fainsod, *How Russia Is Ruled* (Cambridge, Mass.: Harvard University Press, 1953), p. 283.

SELECTED BIBLIOGRAPHY

Armstrong, H. F., ed., *The Foreign Affairs Reader*. New York: Harper & Row, Publishers, Inc., 1947. See articles by Bukharin, Radek, and "X" (George Kennan).

Aspaturian, Vernon V., *The Union Republics in Soviet Diplomacy*. Paris: Librairie Droz, 1960.

Barghoorn, F. C., *Soviet Russian Nationalism*. New York: Oxford University Press, 1956.

———, *The Soviet Cultural Offensive*. Princeton, N.J.: Princeton University Press, 1960.

———, *The Soviet Image of the United States*. New York: Harcourt, Brace & World, Inc., 1950.

Beloff, Max, *Soviet Policy in the Far East: 1944–1951*. London: Royal Institute of International Affairs, 1953.

———, *The Foreign Policy of Soviet Russia: 1929–1941*. New York: Royal Institute of International Affairs, 1947.

Carr, E. H., *German-Soviet Relations between the Two World Wars*. Baltimore: Johns Hopkins Press, 1951.

———, *The Bolshevik Revolution: 1917–1923*, Vol. III. London: Macmillan & Co., Ltd. 1953.

Dallin, Alexander, ed., *Soviet Conduct in World Affairs*. New York: Columbia University Press, 1960.

Dallin, D. J., *Soviet Espionage*. New Haven, Conn.: Yale University Press, 1955.

———, *Soviet Foreign Policy After Stalin*. New York: J. B. Lippincott Co., 1961.

Degras, Jane, ed., *Soviet Documents on Foreign Policy*. New York: Oxford University Press, 1951–1953. 3 Vols.

Dennet, R., and J. Johnson, eds., *Negotiating with the Russians*. Boston: World Peace Foundation, 1951.

Deutscher, I., *Stalin*. New York: Oxford University Press, 1949.

Dinerstein, Herbert, *War and the Soviet Union* (2nd ed.). New York: Frederick A. Praeger, Inc., 1963.

Fainsod, M., *How Russia Is Ruled* (2nd ed.). Cambridge, Mass.: Harvard University Press, 1963.

Falsifiers of History. Moscow: Soviet Information Bureau, 1948. Official explanation of the diplomacy of the Nazi-Soviet Pact and its aftermath.

Fischer, L., *The Soviet in World Affairs*. Princeton, N.J.: Princeton University Press, 1951. 2 Vols.

Hilger, G., and A. G. Meyer, *The Incompatible Allies*. New York: The Macmillan Company, 1953.

Keep, John, ed., *Contemporary History in the Soviet Mirror*. New York: Frederick A. Praeger, Inc., 1965.

Kennan, George, *Soviet Foreign Policy Under Lenin and Stalin*. Boston: Little, Brown and Company, 1961.

Kulski, W. W., *Peaceful Co-existence*. Chicago: Henry Regnery Co., 1959.

Laqueur, Walter, *Russia and Germany*. Boston: Little, Brown and Company, 1965.

Leites, Nathan, *A Study of Bolshevism*. New York: Free Press of Glencoe, Inc., 1953.

Lenczowski, George, *Russia and the West in Iran: 1918–1948*. Ithaca, N.Y.: Cornell University Press, 1949.

Mackintosh, J. M., *Strategy and Tactics of Soviet Foreign Policy*. New York: Oxford University Press, 1962.

Marx, K., and F. Engels, *The Russian Menace to Europe*. New York: Free Press of Glencoe, Ill., 1952.

Moore, Barrington, *Soviet Politics: The Dilemma of Power*. Cambridge, Mass.: Harvard University Press, 1950.

Mosely, Philip E., *The Kremlin and World Politics*. New York: Vintage Books, Inc., Alfred A. Knopf, Inc., 1960.

Nazi-Soviet Relations: 1937–1941. Washington, D.C.: Government Printing Office, 1948. Selected documents from the German archives.

North, Robert C., *Moscow and Chinese Communists*. Stanford, Calif.: Stanford University Press, 1953.

Reshetar, J. S., Jr., *Problems of Analyzing and Predicting Soviet Behavior*. New York: Doubleday & Company, Inc., 1955.

Roberts, H. L., *Russia and America*. New York: Harper & Row, Publishers, Inc., 1956.

Rossi, A., *The Russo-German Alliance: 1939–1941*. Boston: Beacon Press, 1951.

Rubinstein, Alvin Z., *The Foreign Policy of the Soviet Union*. New York: Random House, Inc. 1960.

Sokolovskii, V. M., ed., *Soviet Military Strategy*, tr. H. S. Dinerstein, L. Goure, and T. Wolfe. Englewood Cliffs, N.J.: Prentice-Hall, Inc., 1963.

Stalin, J. V., *Economic Problems of Socialism*. New York: International Publishers Company, Inc., 1952.

———, *Problems of Leninism*. Moscow: Universal Distributors, 1947.

———, *The Great Patriotic War of the Soviet Union*. New York: International Publishers Company, Inc., 1945.

Taracouzio, T. A., *The Soviet Union and International Law*. New York: The Macmillan Company, 1936.

———, *War and Peace in Soviet Diplomacy*. New York: The Macmillan Company, 1940.

Towster, Julian, *Political Power in the U.S.S.R.* New York: Oxford University Press, 1948.

Triska, Jan, and Robert Slusser, *The Theory, Law and Policy of Soviet Treaties*. Stanford, Calif.: Stanford University Press, 1962.

Ulam, A. B., *Titoism and the Cominform*. Cambridge, Mass.: Harvard University Press, 1952.

Wolfe, B. D., *Khrushchev and Stalin's Ghost*. New York: Frederick A. Praeger, Inc., 1957. Khrushchev's secret report in full text, with commentary.

Wolfe, Thomas, *Soviet Strategy at the Crossroads*. Cambridge, Mass.: Harvard University Press, 1964.

The Soviet Union and International Communism

6

VERNON V. ASPATURIAN

THE SOVIET UNION AND WORLD COMMUNISM UNDER LENIN AND STALIN

As rulers of the first country in which a Marxist revolutionary party had been elevated to power, the Bolsheviks early had to define their relationship with kindred Marxist parties engaged in revolutionary activity in other countries.

Although the international communist movement has been institutionalized only in two organizations, the Comintern and the Cominform, Moscow's relations with foreign communist parties before 1956 falls into three distinct, but closely interrelated, periods: (1) the Leninist period (1919–1928); (2) the Stalinist period (1928–1953), and (3) the residual-Stalinist period (1953–56). These distinctions are purely arbitrary, based neither on the programmatic nor the institutional metamorphosis of the world commu-

nist movement, but exclusively on the degree to which foreign communist parties participated in the formulation of decisions concerning revolutionary strategy or Soviet foreign policy.

The Leninist phase: partners in world revolution

The Comintern, founded by Lenin in 1919, was invested with two basic and interdependent functions: (1) to coordinate the strategy and direction of the world revolutionary movement; and (2) to defend the Soviet state against counterrevolution and foreign intervention. These two purposes, in turn, rested upon two fundamental assumptions concerning the world revolutionary movement: (1) the Russian Revolution was merely the first phase of a general revolution, and had neither a justification nor a purpose independent of it; (2) the revolution in Western Europe, particularly in Germany, was imminent.

The entire history of the relationship between Moscow and foreign communist parties has been determined by the two essentially contradictory purposes—world revolution, and the defense of the Soviet Union. The proper defense of the Soviet Union, in turn, has rested on the shifting assumptions concerning the fortune and direction of the revolutionary movement outside Russia.

When Lenin convened the first Congress of the Comintern, in 1919, neither the concept of a world communist movement nor of foreign communist parties existed. Under Bolshevik sponsorship, radical or left-wing factions of the social-democratic parties splintered off to form separate communist parties which affiliated with the new Third International. At the Second Congress, in 1920, statutes were drawn up defining: "The Communist International [as] . . . a universal Communist party of which the parties operating in each country [including Russia] form individual sections," whose aim was "the establishment of . . . the international Soviet Republic."[1] Although the Russian Party was the only Communist Party in power— except for the Hungarian during a brief period—and although a Russian, Grigori Zinoviev, was installed as president, the Party was not invested with a privileged and dominant status in the organization, but, like all the others, was subordinate to the decisions of the World Congress and its executive committee. However, since the Soviet Union was the only soviet state in the world, and since the headquarters of the Comintern could be established only in Moscow, it was inevitable that, as the prospects of the revolution faded, the position of the

Party would, correspondingly be enhanced.

Disagreements between Bolshevik leaders and foreign communist parties, particularly the German, were frequent. Revolutionary doctrine and strategy, and the role of Soviet diplomacy, were discussed in the World Congress and in the meetings of its executive committee. The participation of foreign communist parties was by no means a mere formality, and the Soviet state, which was conceived primarily as an instrument of the world revolution, frequently had to adjust its foreign policy to the views of these other parties, over which it did not exercise full control. The failure of revolution to take hold in Hungary and Germany, plus the ability of the Bolshevik regime to survive, forced a corresponding modification of the assumptions upon which the Comintern rested.

The struggle for power unleashed by Lenin's death, in 1924, also found its reflection in the Comintern and within communist parties abroad. A reexamination of the previous estimates of the revolution in Germany, and the victory of Stalin's policy of "socialism in one country," in opposition to Trotsky's idea of "permanent revolution," forced leaders in the Comintern and in foreign communist parties to choose sides. As Stalin squeezed out his rivals at home, his supporters in the Comintern and in foreign communist parties carried out corresponding purges in their organizations. By 1930, Stalin had established his mastery over the Party apparatus at home, and this was immediately followed by a corresponding subjugation of the Comintern.

The Stalinist phase: the primacy of soviet interests

The Soviet state soon assumed an identity and existence of its own, separate, yet related, to that of the

[1] W. H. Chamberlin, ed., *Blueprint for World Conquest* (Chicago: Human Events, Inc., 1946), p. 36.

Comintern. The entire history of Soviet relationships, first with foreign communist parties, then with other communist states, and then with rivals for leadership (i.e., China), has been determined by the Soviet Union's two essentially contradictory purposes—to serve the interests of foreign constituencies (world revolution, other communist states, China), and to reflect its internal interests (survival as a state, national interests, Soviet elites). This contradiction was resolved by adjusting the interests and behavior of the Comintern and foreign communist parties to those of the Soviet Union. From 1928 to 1953 foreign communist parties, even after they assumed power in their own countries, played little part in the formulation of Soviet foreign policy and were, on the contrary, completely subservient to it as pliable and expendable instruments.

The world communist movement during the Stalinist period rested upon assumptions radically divergent from those upon which the Comintern was originally founded. These were: (1) the Soviet Union is the center and bulwark (not simply the advanced guard) of the world revolution; (2) revolution independent of Moscow's support is impossible; and (3) the preservation of the Soviet as the indispensable base of the world revolution is the most important objective of all communists, who must owe undeviating loyalty to Russia as the "proletarian fatherland." These new assumptions were incorporated into the 1928 *Program of the Comintern,* and the extension of world revolution became identified with the expansion of Soviet power:

The U.S.S.R. inevitably becomes the base of the world revolutionary movement. . . . In the U.S.S.R., the world proletariat for the first time acquires a country that is really its own. . . . In

the event of the imperialist declaring war upon and attacking the U.S.S.R., the international proletariat must retaliate by organizing bold and determined mass action and struggle for the overthrow of the imperialist governments.[2]

The basic philosophy justifying this submission to Moscow's control was euphemistically defined by Stalin himself as "proletarian internationalism":

A *revolutionary* is he who without evasions, unconditionally openly and honestly . . . is ready to uphold and defend the U.S.S.R. . . . An *internationalist* is he who unconditionally, without hesitation and without provisos, is ready to defend the U.S.S.R. because the U.S.S.R. is the base of the world revolutionary movement, and to defend and advance this movement is impossible without defending the U.S.S.R.[3]

Communist parties abroad were subordinated as expendable instruments manipulated in the interests of the Soviet state. Orders transmitted through the Comintern were followed with unquestioning obedience, even if they invited self-destruction (China, Germany) or conflicted with the fundamental interests of their own people (France). As Moscow changed its policies, foreign communists followed suit, even if the new policies were diametrically opposed to the current line. The Kremlin functioned as a GHQ of the world communist movement, sacrificing a division or corps here and there in the interest of the movement as a whole.

The dissolution of the Comintern in 1943 did not materially alter the relationship between Moscow and foreign parties, except, as noted by Andrei Zhdanov at the founding of the Cominform in 1947, that "some comrades understood the dissolution of the

[2]*Ibid.,* pp. 220–223.
[3]J. V. Stalin, *Sochineniya* (Moscow, 1949), Vol. X, p. 61.

Comintern to imply the elimination of all ties, of all contact, between the fraternal Communist Parties [which] . . . is wrong, harmful and . . . unnatural."[4]

After World War II, when communist parties were installed in power in the countries of Eastern Europe and the Soviet Union was deprived of its unique position as the only communist state in the world, the theory of "proletarian internationalism" was transformed from a system justifying Moscow's control of parties into a system justifying her control of entire countries and subordinating their interests to those of Russia. Some satellite communist leaders considered the Soviet theory of "proletarian internationalism" applicable only to parties in capitalist countries, otherwise it became a philosophical justification for Soviet colonialism.

As satellite leaders betrayed signs of uneasiness and independence in their new role as government leaders with the interests of their own countries and peoples to consider, Stalin organized the Cominform, ostensibly as an organ of mutual consultation based on the equality and independence of its members, but in reality to solidify his control over the satellites and to root out all tendencies towards independence. Unlike the Comintern, the new organization was carefully restricted to only the seven communist states of Eastern Europe (Albania was denied membership) and to the two largest parties in the West, the Italian and the French. The refusal of Tito and other satellite leaders to place the interests of Russia above those of their own communist countries and to act as Moscow's subservient agents of plunder and exploitation of their own people led to the expulsion of Yugo-

slavia from the Cominform and the wholesale slaughter of satellite leaders who showed signs of independence. "Loyalty to the Soviet Union," ran the Moscow line, "is the touchstone and criterion of proletarian internationalism."[5] This was echoed by satellite communists and by communist leaders in capitalist countries, who agreed with Dimitrov that "proletarian internationalism . . . means complete coordination of the activities of Communist Parties and of the leading role of the Bolshevik [i.e., Soviet] Party."[6]

In rebuttal, Yugoslav leaders complained:

The leaders of the U.S.S.R. consider that Yugoslavia as a state should be subordinated . . . and its entire development in a general way should be made dependent upon the U.S.S.R. At the same time, they have forced other socialist states to act in a similar manner. . . . The political relations . . . are also based upon . . . the need to maintain in the various socialist countries the kind of regimes that will always be prepared to agree . . . to accept such unequal status and exploitation of their country. Thus—subservient and vassal governments and vassal states are actually being formed.[7]

Stalin's insistence that the communist parties in Eastern Europe and in the Far East continue their subservience to Russia's interests introduced serious strains in the communist orbit, of which Tito's defection was merely the most obvious manifestation. Moscow continued to interfere crudely in the internal development of the satellite states, while disclaiming interference;

[4]Strategy and Tactics of World Communism, p. 229.

[5]For a Lasting Peace, For a People's Democracy, June 30, 1950.
[6]G. Dimitrov, Report to the 5th Congress of the Bulgarian Communist Party (Sofia, 1948), p. 55.
[7]Milovan Djilas, Lenin on Relations between Socialist States (New York, 1949), pp. 16, 31.

it plundered their economies and called it disinterested aid; and it rigidly dictated their progress toward socialism, while paying lip-service to national peculiarities. On all these matters, satellite leaders were not consulted before decisions were taken in the Kremlin, but were simply commanded to carry them out as efficiently as possible.

Whereas the small communist states of Eastern Europe were at the mercy of Soviet power, the attempt to dictate to Peking provoked considerable resistance. Satellite leaders elsewhere were slaughtered by the score, but no Stalinist purges took place in the Chinese Party. One measure of Stalin's patent contempt for Chinese interests or national sensitivities was his refusal to relinquish the Soviet stranglehold on Manchuria, dissolve joint stock companies, or surrender the special extraterritorial interests in Port Arthur and Darien, although this refusal was clearly resented by the Chinese. According to Walter Ulbricht, Stalin's brazen attempts to treat China like an ordinary satellite almost forced Mao to desert the Soviet camp.

The residual Stalinist phase: the primacy of Soviet interests defied

When Stalin died, in March, 1953, the dominance of the Soviet Union in the communist system appeared fixed and permanent, and the primacy of its interests established and assured. His death, however, unleashed rivalries among his successors, and this created opportunities for other communist states to stir and come back to life. Since Stalinist sycophants were installed in all the satellite countries, and their constituency was in Moscow rather than at home, they had no vested interest in loosening the Soviet grip. With their patron dead, however, they faced an uncertain future. As

they anxiously sought to identify their new patron in Moscow, "collective leadership" was proclaimed. Malenkov was invested only with the formal trappings of state authority, and he clearly was forced to share power with Beria and Molotov. Factional groupings assumed shape in the satellite capitals, corresponding to those in the Kremlin, and Beria's arrest, in June, sent a ripple of fear through Eastern Europe. Soon, collective leadership became the new orthodoxy, as Party and state posts in Eastern Europe were separated and redistributed.

Stalin's successors were thus almost immediately confronted with the vexing problem of trying to perpetuate his system of vassalage, or of modifying it. This reexamination unleashed a "great debate" within the Kremlin, one which divided the leadership into one faction which insisted that the old system be retained with minor adjustments and another which advocated a liberalization that bordered on revolutionizing the entire relationship between Moscow and her allies. While Malenkov was Premier, no radical departures from Stalin's policies toward Eastern Europe could be detected, but it now appears that the faction headed by Khrushchev and Bulganin was pressing for a complete rupture with the past. Its program included: (1) elimination of the developing schism with Peking; (2) rapprochement with Marshal Tito; (3) halting the economic exploitation of the satellites; and (4) permitting the gradual evolution of partial political autonomy. These proposals presupposed not only a break with the past, but also an actual repudiation of Stalin's policies, and consequently they were strongly resisted by Molotov and others, as dangerous to the unity of the communist movement.

As the internal controversy became

more acute, uncertain, and incapable of resolution on the basis of the internal political balance, the factions in the Kremlin reached out into their empire for incremental support. Communist leaders were once again about to become power constituencies, starting with the most powerful and the most independent, China and Yugoslavia. China had been humiliated by Stalin, who had tried to make her subservient and this was clearly resented by the Chinese, not only as unconsonant with its national pride and dignity, but as contrary to proper relations between communist states.

Obviously, Chinese resentment promised possible political support to some in the Kremlin. We can date the beginnings of the Soviet Union's loss of primacy in the communist world from Khrushchev's opportunistic use of China and Yugoslavia against his rivals. Presumably, both Mao and Tito would reciprocate by supporting Khrushchev. And for the next three years, both China and Yugoslavia played significant roles in shoring up Khrushchev's position at home and vis-à-vis the Eastern European communist countries.

The defeat of the Malenkov-Molotov policy was clearly apparent by July, 1954. Neither Premier Malenkov nor Foreign Minister Molotov accompanied the Khrushchev-Bulganin mission to Peking, in the autumn of 1954, where it was their purpose to assuage Peking's resentments and inaugurate a new era in the relations between the two countries. The Soviet grip on Manchuria was relinquished, the joint stock companies liquidated, and full Chinese sovereignty restored over Darien and Port Arthur.

The Chinese apparently submitted an additional list of grievances and demands. Mao apparently interpreted the Soviet action as a sign of fear and weakness, and demanded further adjustments: the return of Mongolia; a rectification of Sino-Soviet frontiers in China's favor; and perhaps a demand that the Soviet Union cancel Chinese debts incurred as a result of the Korean War, which, after all, was fought in the interests of the socialist camp as a whole. All these were presumably rejected. The Mongolian issue and the general territorial question became a matter of public record only in August 1964, when Mao Tse-tung raised them in an interview with a visiting delegation of Japanese socialists:

In keeping with the Yalta Agreement the Soviet Union, under the pretext of insuring Mongolia's independence, actually placed this country under its domination. . . . In 1954 when Khrushchev and Bulganin were in China we took up this question but they refused to talk to us. . . . Some people have declared that the Sinkiang area and the territories north of the Amur must be included in the Soviet Union.[8]

The Soviet version of the 1954 events placed them in a broader context, as revealed in a rebuttal by *Pravda*:

Maps showing various parts of the Soviet Union . . . as Chinese territory continued to be published in the CPR. Chinese representatives recently began mentioning with increasing frequency hundreds of thousands of square kilometers of Soviet territory which allegedly belong "by right" to China. . . . In his talk, Mao Tse-tung bemoaned the fate of Mongolia which, as he said, was put by the Soviet Union "under its rule. . . ." The existence of an independent Mongolian state, which maintains friendly relations with the U.S.S.R. . . . does not suit the Chinese leaders. They would like to deprive Mongolia of its independence and make it a Chinese province. The CPR leaders offered "to reach agreement" on this with N. S. Khrushchev and other Soviet comrades during their visit

[8]*Pravda*, September 2, 1964.

to Peking in 1954. N. S. Khrushchev naturally refused to discuss this question.[9]

Thus, by 1954, China felt assertive enough to demand territorial restitution in the name of Chinese national interests. Mao was also apparently informed of the impending resignation of Malenkov, an unprecedented gesture on the part of Soviet leaders, in that it was an implicit request for clearance from a foreign communist leader.

The decision to seek a reconciliation with Tito proceeded more cautiously, but it, too, was a Khrushchev-Bulganin gesture in search of new external constituencies. And since the effort to return Yugoslavia to the communist fraternity was bound to have repercussions in Eastern Europe, Khrushchev saw a need to ameliorate conditions in other communist states as well. Comecon (Council of Mutual Economic Aid) was converted from a vehicle of exploitation into an institutionalized conference, and regular meetings were devoted to mutual economic problems. In November, 1954, a conference in Moscow laid the foundations for the Warsaw Pact, which was signed on May 14, 1955, binding all the European communist states in a military alliance. While the Pact did little more than legalize the presence of Soviet troops on the territories of the Eastern European states, it was significant psychologically. Unilateralism was replaced with formal multilateralism, and Stalin's devisive, bilateral arrangements were disowned.

The rapproachement with the Yugoslavs was preceded by a bitter controversy in the Kremlin, and Molotov, who was strenuously opposed to the whole idea, was overruled. At Tito's insistence, the following measures were taken: (1) Stalin's satellite policies

were openly condemned and repudiated; (2) Stalin's victims in Eastern Europe, like Rajk in Hungary and Kostov in Bulgaria, were posthumously rehabilitated, their trials pronounced a fraud, and Tito absolved of all implications of subversion and deviation; (3) "national deviationists" or "Titoists" still alive, like Gomulka in Poland and Kadar in Hungary, were released from prison and restored to high rank in the Party; (4) "Stalinists" in Eastern Europe were dethroned and replaced with personalities more acceptable to Tito; (5) the Cominform was liquidated; (6) Molotov was ousted as Foreign Minister because he was *persona non grata* to Tito; and (7) Moscow accepted the Yugoslav theory "that the roads and conditions of socialist development are different in different countries . . . that any tendency of imposing one's views in determining the roads and forms of socialist development is alien."[10] Never before had a foreign communist leader —and a former outcast, at that—demanded and received such an influential role in the policies of the Kremlin.

THE SOVIET UNION AND INTERNATIONAL COMMUNISM: THE EROSION OF SOVIET PRIMACY

The Twentieth Party Congress represented a new level in the evolution of Soviet relations with the rest of the communist world. Locally responsive communists, like Gomulka and Nagy, were catapulted into power in Poland and Hungary by powerful internal pressures which were set into motion by the revelations of the Twentieth Party Congress. The demolition of Stalinism at home could only have resulted in the progressive disintegration of Stalinist structures in Eastern Europe. The repercussions in China,

[9] *Ibid.*

[10] The *New York Times*, June 21, 1956.

Yugoslavia, and Albania were smallest, since they were governed largely by indigenous Stalinist regimes, particularly China and Albania.

The Polish and Hungarian "Octobers" were the immediate and most serious consequences of de-Stalinization, and the demands these two events placed upon the communist system, as then organized, threatened to reduce it to ruins. Nationalism of the Soviet variety could no longer be obscured and nationalism of the smaller states could no longer be denied. The year 1956, thus, inaugurated the gradual dissolution of proletarian internationalism into its constituent proletarian or communist nationalisms. This process unfolded gradually and pragmatically in response to situations and events.

Before Stalin's death, the flow of demands in the communist system had been in one direction only, from the center to the periphery. After Stalin's death, and especially after 1956, the flow was substantially and progressively altered. First Peking, in 1954, then Yugoslavia, in 1955, then Poland, in 1956, made demands upon the Soviet Union which were met and which have since been repeated by other communist states. By 1958, the Soviet Union was bombarded with demands, trivial and serious, from all directions. Moscow's demands on other communist states became more limited and less coercive. During the years 1957–1961, demands flowing in from the periphery gradually exceeded those flowing outward from the center.

The Council of Mutual Economic Aid (Comecon), for example, which was originally operated to the economic advantage of the Soviet Union, was reorganized to control and arrest Soviet exploitation. No sooner had this happened, than it was converted into a vehicle for channeling economic aid from the Soviet Union to the other commu-nist states, as demands came in for restitution, reparations, economic assistance, and commercial autonomy. The joint stock companies were dissolved, and deliveries of raw materials and finished goods were made in accordance with world market prices. Eastern European states asserted the right to receive economic assistance from, and engage in profitable commercial transactions with, capitalist countries.

Economic demands upon the Soviet Union spilled over into the political and ideological realms, as individual states demanded and received greater autonomy. Institutions modeled after those in the Soviet Union were, in many cases, dissolved or modified, while Soviet-type ideological controls over the arts, sciences, professions, education, and media of information were renounced in accordance with the local demands of each state. No overt attempt was made to organize joint or concerted action on Moscow until 1961, however, when China and Albania forged an anti-Soviet factional alliance.

The role of the Soviet Union underwent modification with each successive stage in the continuing evolution of the system and movement. Four distinct phases are discernible in the Soviet Union's relationship to the communist universe of states and parties during the period from 1956 to 1967.

The first phase was a short one, covering the period from the Twentieth Party Congress to the World Conference of Communist Parties in November, 1957. During this period, the Soviet Union was clearly a crippled leader, mauled and bruised as a consequence of its de-Stalinization program. Split and divided at home, with its prestige tarnished and its power tattered and ragged, using both Belgrade and Peking as crutches, it hobbled its way from one capital to another seeking to preserve its authority.

The World Conference of November, 1957, marks the end of the first phase and the beginning of the second, which lasted until the Twenty-second Party Congress of the Communist Party of the Soviet Union (CPSU), in October, 1961. Unable to assert its former primacy, the Soviet Union was soon challenged by China, which attempted to introduce Chinese interests as a prime factor in proletarian internationalism, by making successive demands on the Soviet Union, on the system, and then on the movement itself. Khrushchev's excommunication of China's echo, Albania, at the Twenty-second Party Congress, signaled a successful Soviet quashing of the Chinese bid for primacy and an attempt to reassert positive Soviet leadership in Eastern Europe and over Western communist parties.

The third phase, which covers the period from the Twenty-second Party Congress to the limited Test Ban Treaty of July, 1963, was marked by the progressive transformation of a polycentric communist universe into a movement grouped around two opposite poles, Moscow and Peking. This meant that not only was Marxism-Leninism incapable of guaranteeing an ideological consensus, but that the international communist movement was no longer even capable of containing the conflict.

The fourth phase, beginning with the limited Test Ban Treaty and still continuing, was marked by open mutual denunciation and abuse, the possible transformation of a polarized communist universe into two hostile camps, and the dissolution of the communist world as a military bloc. Peking accused Moscow of conspiring with the United States against her, while Moscow charged Peking with seeking to maneuver the Soviet Union into a thermonuclear war of mutual annihilation with the United States so that it might pick up the pieces and dominate the ruins. The ouster of Khrushchev, in October, 1964, postponed the climax of this phase, but China's refusal to send a delegation to the Twenty-third Congress of the CPSU in April, 1966, may have inaugurated a new phase in the evolution of the world communist movement, the phase of two hostile communist camps and movements, and the evolution of a Soviet-American *détente*.

Crippled leader: the primacy of soviet interests subdued

Theoretically, of course, proletarian internationalism demands that national interests be subordinated to an international interest. In the case of the Soviet Union, the subordination of its interests to proletarian internationalism could only mean to reverse roles and allow the national interests of other communist states to prevail over its own. This, Moscow was not prepared to do. From 1956 to 1958, therefore, an attempt was made to find a way to coordinate several national interests. The effort proved futile, however, as it became apparent that the Chinese were demanding a disproportionately large role for their national interests in the calculation of proletarian internationalism. Soviet recognition of the primacy of proletarian internationalism, under these conditions, would have been tantamount to the subordination of its national interests to those of the Chinese.

The cracking of the monolith in Eastern Europe approached its climax in October, 1956, with an independent-minded Gomulka in Warsaw and a secessionist-minded Nagy in Budapest. Moscow fluctuated between adventurism and paralysis. The Poznan uprising and its aftermath elicited a Soviet threat to intervene militarily but, according to Chinese accounts, Chinese pressures exerted a moderating influence and Poland was saved from Soviet military occupation. The Hungarian national uprising, which threatened to sweep communism out entirely, was met with hesitation and vacillation in Moscow; according to the Chinese version, it was only the wisdom and firmness of Mao Tse-tung which induced Khrushchev to save Hungary for the socialist camp.

Events in Eastern Europe soon outpaced both Soviet thought and action. The "palace revolution" in Warsaw introduced an autonomous and significant center of heretical pressure within the bloc. Gomulka successfully defied Soviet threats, purged Stalinists from key positions, and demanded and received a veto on the movement of Soviet troops in Poland. The Polish revolution was praised in Peking and Belgrade, but generally condemned by the Stalinist-oriented leaders in other satellite capitals.

Soviet intervention in Hungary also evoked divergent reactions in various capitals. Peking pressured for military intervention, the other satellites applauded it, Warsaw deplored it, and Belgrade condemned it. This brought Tito into direct conflict with Peking. Tito openly condemned the Soviet explanation of the revolution and deplored the use of troops. In his famous Pula speech, Tito revealed the existence of "Stalinist" and "anti-Stalinist" factions in the Soviet hierarchy and in the communist movement as a whole, and Yugoslavia was once again removed to the periphery of respectable communism. The situation over Hungary was so serious that Moscow asked Peking for support. A statement was issued condoning the Hungarian repression and repudiating the Yugoslav criticisms. Belgrade temporaily lost influence, but Peking and Belgrade were to emerge as the two poles of the communist axis.

On October 30, 1956, the Soviet leaders, in consultation with Peking, issued a statement entitled "The Foundations of the Development and Further Consolidation of Friendship and Cooperation between the Soviet Union and other Socialist States," in which Moscow conceded grave errors in its relationships with other communist states, promised amends (and eventually reparations), and called for the transformation of the communist system into a commonwealth of socialist nations:

In the process of constructing a new system and effecting profound revolutionary changes in social relationships, there have arisen many difficulties, unsolved problems and outright errors. The latter have included infringements of the mutual relationships between socialist countries and mistakes which have weakened the principle of the equality of rights in the mutual association of the socialist countries.[11]

Moscow also pledged that "the Soviet Government is ready to discuss, together with the governments of other socialist states, measures . . . to remove the possibilities of violating the principle of national sovereignty and . . . equality."

The dissolution of the Cominform —the only multilateral party organization in the entire movement—made it a matter of urgency to devise new processes and institutions of mutual consultation as quickly as possible. Since the Cominform was viewed as a discredited symbol of Soviet primacy and Stalinist domination, Moscow's stated preference for a new, permanent, multilateral organization was rejected

[11]*Pravda*, October 31, 1956.

by Peking, Warsaw, and Belgrade as too suggestive of the Cominform and Comintern. It was also opposed by the Italian Party. In all cases, the opponents of a revival of institutionalized multilateral forms betrayed a fear that this might relegitimize Soviet primacy, in view of Moscow's command of the loyalty of a majority of both communist states and parties. Moscow, accordingly, resigned itself to a position of flexibility, but called for immediate action:

The establishment of businesslike contact between Communist, Socialist, and Workers' Parties in order to eliminate the split in the international labor movement has become one of the most urgent problems of our times.[12]

With Tito discredited, Peking boldly moved in and unilaterally assumed the role of an honest broker between Moscow and its rebellious Eastern European client states. On December 29, 1956, the Chinese issued a long statement, in which they condemned the extremes of both Stalinism and Titoism, and, at the same time, attempted to suggest a new orthodoxy for the entire system. The legitimacy of national interests in determining common action was explicitly recognized:

Marxism-Leninism has always strongly advocated that proletarian internationalism be combined with patriotism. . . . The Communist Parties of all countries must . . . become the spokesmen of the legitimate national interests and sentiments of their people [and] . . .effectively educate the masses in the spirit of internationalism and harmonize the national sentiments and interests of these countries.[13]

Chou En-lai was dispatched by

[12]Mikoyan's speech to the Eighth Congress of the Chinese Communist Party, *Pravda*, September 18, 1956.
[13]*Pravda*, December 31, 1956.

Peking on a fence-mending tour designed to find a new common ground between Moscow and its recalcitrant satellites in Eastern Europe. The Chinese action was welcomed by Gomulka, who saw, in Peking's intervention, a useful counterpoise to Soviet pressure. Tito, however, viewed it with resentment and anxiety, since Peking was seeking to strike a compromise between Polish and Soviet positions, rather than between Yugoslav and Soviet. Chou En-lai carefully steered a course which simultaneously renounced "great power chauvinism" and preserved the "leading role" of the Soviet Union. Peking's intervention apparently also helped to improve Khrushchev's position in the Soviet hierarchy. As a consequence, the balance of factions in the Kremlin was altered, and the February, 1957, Plenum of the Central Committee reversed some of the key decisions of the December, 1956, Plenum, which seemed directed at Khrushchev.

The forging of a new international interest or communist consensus was, during most of 1957, restricted mainly to bilateral discussions between communist parties and leaders and consultations at various Party Congresses, but this soon proved inadequate and ineffective. Warsaw continued its refusal to accept even the formalities of Soviet primacy, while Peking became an increasingly assertive spokesman for the camp as a whole. During the "anti-Party group" crisis, in June, 1957, Khrushchev again apparently sought and received support from Mao, which further contributed to the image of China as virtually a codirector of the socialist camp. In return for Chinese support, Khrushchev apparently agreed to contribute to China's nuclear development, and an agreement on nuclear technology was signed in October, 1957.

Not only did the communist countries fail to agree upon new forms of supranational organizations of consultation, but they failed to find any operational consensus at all. In 1957, the Soviet Union was unable to convince the other communist countries of the necessity for a new multilateral communist organization similar to the Cominform in structural outlines. And by 1964, Moscow was unable even to persuade the communist states to convene a general conference of communist parties. None have been convened since November, 1960. An alternative pattern of multilateral consultation, reportedly suggested by Moscow, was the exchange of permanent Party representatives. Both suggestions were frowned upon by Peking, Warsaw, and the Italian Communist Party, and Belgrade was not consulted.

The principal resistance to a new Cominform came from Yugoslavia, although both Poland and China also opposed a revival of the organization in any form, which they still feared might once again be employed by Moscow as an instrument of centralization and domination. The Yugoslav-Polish view was that consultation be primarily a bipartisan affair:

Both parties recognized that the bilateral interparty relations in the present conditions constitute the most appropriate form of consultation between Communist and Workers' Parties. This does not exclude, however, a broader cooperation of Communist and Workers' Parties and progressive movements in connection with individual questions of common interest.[14]

Pending the formation of definitive institutions and methods of consultation, bilateralism and *ad hoc* multilateralism have been the general rule. This has followed three patterns: (1)

[14]The *New York Times*, January 1, 1957.

mutual exchanges of Party delegations to Party conferences and congresses; (2) bilateral discussions throughout the communist world, followed by the issuance of joint communiqués, which have deviated interestingly from the crude uniformity of the past; (3) multiparty conferences, in the form of periodic gatherings of delegates from all communist parties, and selective conferences restricted to parties which exercise power in their respective states. The first of these post-Cominform conferences was a rump meeting held in Budapest in January, 1957, which was attended only by delegates from Moscow, Budapest, Sofia, Prague and Bucharest.

November, 1957, saw the first attempt to establish a multilateral process for arriving at a communist consensus. Since two distinct consensuses were involved, one among communist states and another among all parties, two separate conferences were organized. The first, held from November 14 to 16, included only representatives from the communist states; the second, which met from November 16 to 19, included representatives from sixty-four communist parties. This was in line with the evolving formula that the communist camp as a whole should offer direction to the movement. It is now known that serious controversies between Moscow and Peking developed at the November Conference. The expulsion of the "anti-Party group" and the successful disposition of Zhukov had improved Khrushchev's position to the point where Peking's support was no longer required or desired. A number of Mao's proposals were successfully resisted, but the Chinese leader was successful in altering a Soviet draft declaration which proved unacceptable to Yugoslavia. On the issue of Soviet primacy, Peking was even more emphatic than Moscow in having the declaration incorporate the formulation, "the socialist camp headed by the Soviet Union."

The Yugoslav representatives refused to accept the declaration issued by the ruling communist parties, which embodied a common core of ideological principles and policy positions which had been hammered out after long and arduous negotiation. The purpose of the declaration was to restore the unity among the various ruling parties, but it became impossible to reconcile the extreme positions of China and Yugoslavia, in spite of the wide latitude which the November Declaration afforded for individual variation within a common program.

The concessions made by Moscow, however, did earn the public support of Peking for the ideological innovations introduced at the Twentieth Party Congress, as well as the denunciation of at least some aspects of Stalinism, but the Chinese could not accept positions which would be acceptable to Belgrade. Now that China supported the Russian position, Warsaw had no alternative but to alter its heretical position and support the declaration. The main points at issue, which the Yugoslavs could not accept, were the questions of the leading role of the Soviet Union in the communist world, the dogmatic insistence that all international tensions were generated by Western imperialism, that peace was possible only after the liquidation of capitalism but that peaceful coexistence would govern relations with the capitalist world pending its final liquidation and, finally, that revisionism (i.e., Titoism) constituted the chief threat to the unity of the communist orbit. Dogmatism (i.e., Stalinism) was condemned as a lesser deviationist evil and threat to communist unity.

The net result was the elimination of Yugoslavia as a factor in making decisions for the communist orbit, and the elevation of Peking to a position of rivalry with Moscow for power and influence in the communist world. The November, 1957, meeting signalled China's political and ideological independence from Moscow and underlined the voluntary character of her recognition of Soviet Russian primacy, with the implication that she could withdraw this recognition at will. The auspicious inauguration of the People's Communes in China in 1958, and the bitter attacks levelled against them by Soviet leaders betrayed a bold attempt on the part of China to claim primacy for the Chinese state as the most advanced society in the world.

The 1957 declaration also called for a new authoritative international journal of the communist movement, presumably to replace the defunct paper issued by the Cominform, and a third multiparty conference, held in Prague in March, 1958, without benefit of the Yugoslavs, could only agree to issue a theoretical and informational monthly, the *World Marxist Review*. This journal has, however, been repudiated by Peking and its followers in the international communist movement.

Outwardly, the 1957 conference seemed to reflect harmony and concord, and its declaration outlined new procedures for determining the content and direction of proletarian internationalism:

Following their exchange of views, the participants in the discussion have come to the conclusion that in the present circumstances it would be expedient, in addition to the meetings of leading officials and in addition to an exchange of information on a bilateral basis, to arrange more far-reaching conferences of the communist and workers' parties in order to discuss topical international problems, to exchange experiences, to get to know one another's views and attitudes and to coordinate the common struggle for common aims, for peace, democracy, and socialism.[15]

Challenged leader: the Chinese bid for primacy

The full implications of the resurgence of nationalism were not immediately apparent in 1956–'57. The enthronement of the nation-state as the definitive form of the communist state meant that the idea of a world communist state had been jettisoned in favor of a communist inter-state system for the indefinite future. Party conflicts would inevitably be transformed into state conflicts, and state conflicts would inexorably reflect national conflicts, as the nation-state once again pre-empted the highest loyalty of its citizens. Highest loyalty to the proletariat, yes, but to the *national* proletariat and its nation-state.

The Chinese were caught in a peculiar dilemma. They insisted that the movement required a center or leader, But more than any other communist state, they demanded autonomy. What Peking wanted, of course, was to assume direction herself, but since there was little immediate prospect of displacing Moscow directly, the Chinese sought to use Moscow as an unsuspecting instrument in their drive for power and influence.

The Chinese insisted that Moscow be recognized as the leader of the camp and movement because a leader was required, although the Soviet leaders had demonstrated their unworthiness since the Twentieth Party Congress. Peking refrained from criticizing the Soviet leadership openly and expected, in return for preserving the unity of the movement, that Moscow would cater to Chinese superior

[15]*Pravda*, November 22, 1957.

wisdom and advice. The Soviet Union would thus lead a world communist movement whose policies would reflect Chinese interests. Perhaps at the appropriate time, China would then displace Moscow as the *de jure* leader of the movement.

This strategy is only thinly concealed by subsequent Chinese explanations of why they followed an unworthy leader for so long a period of time. Thus, in February, 1964, in response to a Soviet charge that Peking wished to "seize the leadership," the Chinese rhetorically asked:

> From whom? . . . Who now holds the leadership? In the international communist movement, is there such a thing as leadership which lords it over all the fraternal parties? And is this leadership in your hands?

And then, somewhat inconsistently, Peking refers to the events of 1957:

> At the 1957 Moscow meeting of fraternal parties, our delegation emphasized that the socialist camp should have the Soviet Union at its head. The reason was that, although they had committed some mistakes, the leaders of the C.P.S.U. did finally accept the Moscow declaration. . . . Our proposal that the Socialist camp should have the Soviet Union at its head was written into the declaration.[16]

An earlier statement by the Chinese, issued in September, 1963, reveals that Peking's motivation, in pressing for the recognition of Soviet leadership, was a compound of cynicism, fear, and timing, while their behavior was arrogant, self-righteous, and patronizing:

> Ever since the 20th congress of the C.P.S.U. we have watched with concern as the C.P.S.U. leadership has taken the

[16]*Jen Min Jih Pao*, February 4, 1964. Citation is from the version published in the *New York Times*, February 7, 1964.

road of revisionism. Confronted with this grave situation our party has scores of times and for a long period considered: What should we do?. . . Should we keep silent about the errors of the C.P.S.U. leadership? We believed that the errors of the C.P.S.U. leadership were not just accidental errors . . . but rather a whole series of errors of principle which endanger the interests of the entire socialist camp and the international Communist movement. . . . We foresaw that if we criticized the errors of the leaders of the C.P.S.U. they would certainly strike at us vindictively and thus inevitably cause serious damage to China's socialist construction. . . . We took into consideration the fact that the C.P.S.U. . . . is the party of the first Socialist state, and that it enjoyed high prestige in the international Communist movement and among the people of the whole world. Therefore, over a considerable period of time we were particularly careful and patient in criticizing the leaders of the C.P.S.U., trying our best to confine such criticism to interparty talks between the leaders of the Chinese and Soviet parties. . . . But all the comradely criticism and advice given to the leaders of the C.P.S.U. by responsible comrades of the C.C.P. Central Committee in scores of inter-party talks did not succeed in enabling them to return to the correct path.[17]

Peking's description of Mao Tse-tung's behavior at the 1957 Moscow conference could scarcely conceal the manner in which he apparently lectured Khrushchev and other Soviet leaders:

The delegation of the C.C.P., which was headed by Comrade Mao Tse-tung, did a great deal of work during the meeting. On the one hand, it had full consultations with the leaders of the C.P.S.U., and where necessary and appropriate waged struggle against them, in order to help them correct their errors; on the other hand, it held repeated exchanges in views with the leaders of other fraternal parties in order that a common document acceptable to all might be worked out. . . . In their original draft of the declaration, the leadership of the C.P.S.U. insisted on the inclusion of the erroneous views of the 20th Congress on peaceful transition. . . . The Chinese Communist party resolutely opposed the wrong views contained in the draft declaration submitted by the leadership of the C.P.S.U. We expressed our views on the two successive drafts put forward by the Central Committee of the C.P.S.U. and made a considerable number of major changes of principles which we presented as our own revised draft. Repeated discussions were then held between the delegations of the Chinese and Soviet parties on the basis of our revised draft before the "joint draft declaration by the C.P.S.U. and the C.C.P." was submitted to the delegations of the other fraternal parties for their opinions.[18]

Under Khrushchev's direction, Soviet policies were gradually oriented toward the avoidance of thermonuclear war and a relaxation of international tensions, based on a limited accommodation with the United States. By achieving an agreement with the United States when Soviet prestige was high, the diplomatic consequences might be correspondingly advantageous. This strategy, however, conflicted with Chinese aspirations. Mao made dramatically clear, at the 1957 Moscow meeting, that he calculated the Soviet Union to be militarily superior to the United States and that instead of settling for an accommodation, his superior wisdom dictated that the Soviet Union should use its military superiority to oust American power from marginal areas, particularly in the Far East.

These divergent national interests were bound to collide, although Peking apparently thought that its leverage was still sufficient to force Mos-

[17]*Peking Review*, No. 37 (September 13, 1963), pp. 6–23.

[18]*Ibid*.

cow's acceptance of its demands. The Chinese decided to press the issue and confront Khrushchev with an agonizing choice between supporting a major ally or seeking an accommodation with the major enemy and thus risking a rupture with Peking. The Chinese leaders apparently thought that Khrushchev would hardly dare to alienate Peking in return for an uncertain and fragile accommodation with the United States. Mao probably calculated—on the basis of past experience—that Khrushchev would not dare oppose him for fear that his rivals might use his opposition as a pretext to successfully discredit his leadership.

From Peking's standpoint, China possessed all the necessary credentials for primacy in the communist world except nuclear power and stage of development. In 1958, China had the world's largest population, which was three times that of the Soviet Union and about twice the size of the combined populations of all party states. It was blessed with the longest and most continuous civilization and culture in the world; it was truly universal in an historical sense as the direct successor of the Celestial Empire, whose civilization and culture had extended to the Middle East and Eastern Europe by Genghis Khan and his successors, who destroyed 40 states, large and small, in order to erect a more beautiful civilization. Furthermore, China had the largest communist party in the world, nearly one-half the total of all communist party members on the globe. Its party and state were graced with the most politically adept, verbally eloquent, and ideologically elegant leader in the communist world, Mao Tse-tung, the true inheritor of the tradition of Marx, Lenin, and Stalin. Although the Soviet Union remained a powerful military and industrial state, this was only a temporary

phase, since its prestige and that of its leaders, was soiled by inept and fumbling behavior. The Soviet Union was an unworthy leader whose primacy had crumbled as a consequence of its own political opportunism and ideological sophistry. This was the perception which the Soviet leaders thought Mao held, and it probably was not too inaccurate. Thus, a Soviet leader was to complain in 1964:

It is known that beginning in ancient times the ideologists of China created a concept of their country as the "Middle Kingdom," the oldest civilization, the custodian of world order and spiritual harmony, as a "universal land" with power over everything under the sun. The imperial ideology concerning China's special role in the history of mankind to some degree affects the consciousness of China's present-day leaders.[19]

Sometime in late 1957 or early 1958, the Chinese leaders decided to overcome the two deficiencies in their credentials for an assertion of primacy: (1) the lack of nuclear weapons; and (2) a retarded stage of economic development. Apparently, Mao perceived an opportunity, in the summer of 1958, to force the issue of nuclear weapons with the Soviet Union and, at the same time, to disrupt Khrushchev's attempts to bring about a new summit meeting in order to establish some sort of accommodation with the United States.

Peking's fears and suspicions were apparently reinforced by Moscow's mild response to the landing of American Marines in Lebanon and Khrushchev's assent to Eisenhower's suggestion that a summit conference be held within the framework of the United Nations Security Council, to discuss the Middle Eastern crisis. Such a con-

[19]L. Ilyichev, "Revolutionary Science and the Present Day," *Kommunist*, No. 11, (July, 1964), pp. 12–35.

ference would not only exclude Peking, but possibly include India and even Chiang Kai-shek, since Nationalist China continued to occupy China's seat on the Security Council.

Peking's reaction was sufficiently violent to impel Khrushchev not only to withdraw his acceptance, but also to make a hurried and unannounced trip to Peking to offer explanations. On August 4, Khrushchev withdrew his suggestion for a summit meeting altogether.

The Chinese had apparently prevailed again. It appears, however, that they may have used the opportunity to make an additional demand, that Moscow supply China with sample atom bombs, but Moscow refused. The Chinese may also have demanded that Khrushchev be prepared to issue a public statement of nuclear support for a forthcoming Chinese initiative in the Taiwan Strait to test American determination and perhaps, also, to force Moscow to choose between communist unity and an agreement with the United States.

The unsatisfactory nature of the Soviet response during the Taiwan Straits crisis of 1958 was confirmed in 1963, when the entire episode was raked over in acrimonious public debate after the Test Ban Treaty was signed. In reply to a Soviet claim that China was spared nuclear destruction during the Taiwan Straits crisis because of the Soviet Union's readiness to retaliate with nuclear weapons if China were attacked, the Chinese delivered their own version of the episode:

It is especially ridiculous that the Soviet statement also gives all the credit to Soviet nuclear weapons for the Chinese people's victory in smashing the armed provocations of U.S. imperialism in the Taiwan Straits in 1958. What are the facts? In August and September, 1958, the situation in the Taiwan Straits was

indeed very tense. . . . The Soviet leaders expressed their support for China on 7 and 19 September respectively. Although at that time the situation in the Taiwan Straits was tense, there was no possibility that a nuclear war would break out and no need for the Soviet Union to support China with its nuclear weapons. It was only when they were clear that this was the situation that the Soviet leaders expressed their support for China.[20]

The issues of a Soviet nuclear capability for China and unspecified Soviet military demands upon China were revived in connection with the events of 1958.

Speaking for the Soviet Union, Suslov reported to the Central Committee in February, 1964:

It is known that the CPR leaders have stubbornly sought to get the Soviet Union to hand over atomic bombs to them. They took extreme offense that our country did not offer them samples of atomic weapons.[21]

It seems clear that the Soviet Union began to resist Chinese demands after Khrushchev's return from Peking in 1958, when he decided, instead, to pursue his policy of seeking an agreement with the United States. This was confirmed by the Chinese in September, 1963:

The leaders of the C.P.S.U., eager to curry favor with U.S. imperialism, engaged in unbridled activities against China. . . . They thought they had solved their internal problems and had "stabilized" their own position and could therefore step up their policy of "being friendly to enemies and tough with friends."[22]

The Chinese later complained bitterly

[20]*Peking Review*, No. 37 (September 13, 1963), pp. 6–23.
[21]*Pravda*, April 3, 1964.
[22]*Peking Review*, No. 37 (September 13, 1963), pp. 6–23.

that the Soviet refusal to supply them with nuclear assistance and bombs was a betrayal of "proletarian internationalism." Moscow retorted that, since the Chinese could always rely for their security upon Soviet nuclear power, Peking's desire for a separate nuclear capability had little to do with proletarian internationalism and probably was motivated by a desire to engage in adventures which would be subversive and detrimental to Soviet interests:

If the leaders of China are actually following the principles of proletarian internationalism, why are they striving so hard to obtain their own atom bomb? People who stop at nothing in their desire to provide themselves with new types of destructive weapons must have some motive. What is behind this desire? From our point of view, the very idea of the need to provide themselves with nuclear weapons could occur to the leaders of a country whose security is guaranteed by the entire might of the socialist camp only if they have developed some kind of special aims or interests that the socialist camp cannot support with its military force. But such aims and interests can manifest themselves only among those who reject proletarian internationalism, who depart from socialist positions on questions of foreign policy. . . . After all, it is impossible to combine with the peaceloving foreign policy course of the countries of the socialist system plans for nuclear weapons of one's own order, for example, to increase one's influence in the countries of Asia, Africa and Latin America or to create for oneself a "position of strength" in disputed international questions or, finally, to exacerbate international tension.[23]

Further insight into China's motivations during this period, was provided when Chen Yi, the Chinese Foreign Minister, conceded, in 1963:

Atomic bombs, missiles and supersonic aircraft are reflections of the technical level of a nation's industry. China will have to resolve this issue within the next several years; otherwise, it will degenerate into a second-class or third-class nation.[24]

The Chinese demands, in 1958, for a nuclear arsenal of some sort were paralleled by a series of bold moves designed to secure an ideological foundation for a future Chinese claim to primacy. According to a subsequent account, Moscow interpreted Chinese behavior at that time as follows:

In the spring of 1958 the Chinese leadership began to change its line sharply. Instead of the approximately 15 years that had been envisioned for setting up the base for socialism in China, in 1958 a period of only three years was proclaimed to be adequate even for the transition to communism. The so-called "great leap" was announced—a political-economic adventure unprecedented in both design and scale. This was a policy . . . built on the desire to solve grandiose tasks faster and to "teach" others the newly invented methods of building socialism and communism. It was then that the slogan was proclaimed of the "people's communes," which formed the basis of the attempt to leap over natural stages of socialist construction in the . . . effort to get "ahead of progress" here.[25]

Khrushchev, a resourceful politician, quickly perceived the challenge, and while he did not overtly condemn the communes or criticize the Chinese Great Leap at the time, he ignored it publicly and ridiculed it privately. The Soviet press was conspicuously silent about the entire affair, but the Yugoslavs openly denounced the communes and other Eastern European leaders

[23]*Pravda*, September 21, 1963.

[24]As reported by *Kyodo* (Tokyo), October 28, 1963.

[25]L. Ilyichev, "Revolutionary Science," pp. 12–35.

privately expressed disgust and apprehension over Mao's abrupt leftward turn. In April, 1964, Khrushchev revealed what he had obviously discerned, six years earlier, to be the motivation behind China's behavior:

But in that same year, 1958, the Chinese leaders unexpectedly proclaimed the so-called course of the "great leap" and the "people's communes." The idea behind this course consisted in skipping over the stages of socialist development into the phase of communist construction. At the time, Chinese propaganda asserted that China would show everyone an example of entry into communism ahead of schedule.[26]

Who was ahead of whom was no idle question, since both Moscow and Peking were aware that spearheading the dialectic of history was a necessary ideological prerequisite for a serious and legitimate claim to primacy, although it could not by itself be sufficient. Nuclear power was also necessary. Consequently, Khrushchev took immediate and effective steps to deny both nuclear weapons and economic success to the Chinese. Moscow curtailed its economic and technical assistance to China on the pretext that the Great Leap forward was disrupting and distorting Chinese economic development, and aid, hence, constituted a waste of Soviet resources. Although Peking later confessed that the Great Leap had failed, the episode remained a sobering experience for the Soviet Union's leaders.

The Chinese then sought new ways to press their demands upon Moscow and enhance their power and influence in the communist movement. They shifted to the strategy of denying the ideological significance of the Soviet Union's material and social achievements, and maintained that both the Soviet Union and China were in a transitional stage of development and more or less equidistant from communism. This shift in design was fully appreciated in Moscow.

The mania of hegemonism drove them onto the path of adventurist leaps in the economy. . . . The first successes in economic development and in the cooperation of the peasants turned the heads of the Chinese leaders, gave them the idea that the transitional period was already past and that through communes China would be able to reach communism fast—before the socialist countries of Europe, the Soviet Union included. . . . Then the Chinese leadership, to conceal its miscalculations, launched a noisy propaganda campaign designed to present matters as though not only in China but in the U.S.S.R. and all socialist countries the tasks of the transitional period have not been carried out, that the U.S.S.R. is a country somewhat richer than China, but, in the sense of social gains, as far from communism as China is.[27]

Since Soviet interests required a rapprochement with the United States, and Chinese interests dictated an aggravation of Soviet-American relations, the interests of the two countries were to drift further and further apart. On this point, compromise was impossible. Each was convinced that its vital interest—the avoidance of thermonuclear war, from the Soviet point of view, and the expulsion of the Americans from the Far East, from the Chinese—dictated the proper course to pursue. If Moscow, China's chief ally, were to become reconciled to the United States, her major enemy, then of what value was the Sino-Soviet alliance to the Chinese? On the other hand, if solidarity with China required that the Soviet Union risk nuclear

[26]*Pravda*, April 16, 1964.

[27]*Pravda*, April 21, 1964.

annihilation in a confrontation with the United States, her alliance with China was tantamount to a suicide pact. These divergent interests made it imperative that each chart its own policy towards the United States in accordance with its individual goals.

Khrushchev, in a series of ripostes to the Chinese bid for primacy, continued to apply various forms of political, military, and economic pressure. The Chinese were later to complain about this period rather bitterly:

In 1958 the leadership of the C.P.S.U. put forward unreasonable demands designed to bring China under Soviet military control. These unreasonable demands were rightly and firmly rejected by the Chinese Government. Not long afterward, in June, 1959, the Soviet Government unilaterally tore up the agreement on new technology for national defense concluded between China and the Soviet Union in October, 1957, and refused to provide China with a sample of an atomic bomb and technical data concerning its manufacture.[28]

Two months after the nuclear agreement with China was nullified by Moscow, on August 3, 1959, it was announced in Moscow that Khrushchev would meet with Eisenhower in the United States. Almost simultaneously, Marshal Peng Teh-huai was dismissed by Peking. The Chinese military leader, who had been Peking's observer to the Warsaw Pact Organization, apparently shared Khrushchev's misgivings about Mao and, furthermore, was professionally concerned over the imminent suspension and withdrawal of Soviet military support. The Chinese have hinted that Khrushchev tried to bring about the ouster of Mao by intriguing with his rivals.

On more than one occasion, Khrush-

chev has gone so far as to tell leading comrades of the Central Committee of the C.P.C. that certain anti-party elements in the Chinese communist party were his "good friends." He has praised Chinese anti-party elements for attacking the Chinese party's general line for socialist construction, the big leap forward and the people's communes, describing their action as a "manly act."[29]

On August 7, while the Chinese Central Committee Plenum which dismissed Marshal Peng was still in session, the Sino-Indian border conflict flared up, leading to an invasion of Indian territory by the Chinese which continued into September. The Sino-Indian dispute, which Moscow interpreted as a device to frustrate the Eisenhower-Khrushchev meeting, unleashed acrimonious discussion between the two communist giants, culminating in a Soviet statement deploring the conflict and virtually disassociating Moscow from Chinese actions. Three years later, Peking complained:

On the eve of the Camp David talks in September, 1959—on September 9, 1959, to be exact . . . a socialist country, turning a deaf ear to China's repeated explanations of the true situation and to China's advice, hastily issued a statement on a Sino-Indian border incident through its official news agency. Here is the first instance in history in which a socialist country, instead of condemning the armed provocations of the reactionaries of a capitalist country, condemned another fraternal socialist country when it was confronted with such armed provocation.[30]

All these anti-Chinese moves by Moscow, according to Peking, were

[29]*Jen Min Jih Pao*, February 4, 1964.
[30]*Whence The Differences? A Reply to Comrade Thorez and Other Comrades* (Peking: 1963), pp. 11–12.

[28]*Peking Review*, No. 37 (September 13, 1963).

sacrificial offerings at the altar of a détente with the United States:

The tearing up of the agreement on new technology for national defense by the leadership of the C.P.S.U. and its issuance of the statement on the Sino-Indian border clash on the eve of Khrushchev's visit to the United States were presentation gifts to Eisenhower so as to curry favor with the U.S. imperialists and create the so-called "spirit of Camp David."[31]

Peking charged that Khrushchev further sacrificed Chinese interests by informing Eisenhower that the Soviet Union would not give nuclear weapons to China and that Moscow would accept a "two Chinas" solution to the Taiwan problem. After the Camp David talks, which Khrushchev considered a signal success, the Soviet leader's stature and prestige visibly increased. In his next confrontation with Mao in Peking, almost immediately afterward, his self-assertion did not go unnoticed:

Back from the Camp David talks, he went so far as to try to sell China the U.S. plot of "two Chinas" and, at the state banquet celebrating the 10th anniversary of the founding of the C.P.R. he read China a lecture against "testing by force the stability of the capitalist system."[32]

Serious conflicts of national purpose and interests were only obliquely revealed in the Sino-Soviet dialogue but, as the conflict continued and intensified, they gradually broke through the ideological shells in which they were encrusted. Although ideology and national interests are so intimately intertwined in communist politics that they cannot be distilled out completely, yet they were separating out as visible quantities in the equation of conflict.

[31]*Peking Review*, No. 23 (September 13, 1963).
[32]*Ibid.*

Soviet interests veered more and more in the direction of an acceptance of the *status quo*, whereas Chinese interests demanded that the United States be expelled from the Far East.

What the Chinese failed to do, Gary Francis Powers and the flight of an American U-2 over Soviet territory succeeded in doing, on May Day, 1960. The Chinese felt themselves justified and congratulated themselves on their superior wisdom. Three years later, they were still exulting: "The 'spirit of Camp David' completely vanished. Thus, events entirely confirmed our views." Khrushchev, however, berated both Eisenhower and Mao, the former for cupidity or stupidity, and the latter for belligerent dogmatism. Relations with China deteriorated even faster than those with the United States, however. In June, Moscow suggested that the forthcoming Rumanian Party Congress be turned into an *ad hoc* meeting of ruling parties to discuss the implications of the abortive summit meeting with the West, and Peking accepted only grudgingly, because it was opposed to Moscow's purpose in calling the meeting. Moscow's interest in seeking a *détente* with the United States seemed to coincide with the interests of the Eastern European states, and the Chinese were unenthusiastic about placing themselves in the minority, so they had the meeting broadened into a general conference of communist parties. Peking's relations with the Kremlin were not visibly improved by the shooting down of the U-2, but it appears that Khrushchev's rivals at home were strengthened and Soviet attitudes towards the United States hardened.

The Chinese initiated their new strategy of reaching outward from the fraternity of communist countries into the larger movement for support by engaging in factional activity against

Soviet positions at a WFTU meeting held in Peking on June 5-9, 1960. This was the first instance of one communist state, other than the Soviet Union, organizing opposition against another. This factional activity was to accelerate and become the main organizational weapon against Moscow's seemingly permanent majority in the fraternity.

Anticipating China's factional strategy, Khrushchev laid an ambush for the Chinese at Bucharest:

At Bucharest, to our amazement, the leaders of the C.P.S.U. . . . unleashed a surprise assault on the Chinese Communist Party. . . . In the meeting, Khrushchev took the lead in organizing a great converging onslaught against the Chinese Communist Party as "madmen," "wanting to unleash war" . . . "being pure nationalist" on Sino-Indian boundary question and employing "Trotskyite ways" against the C.P.S.U.[33]

Khrushchev's crude, but probably warranted, retaliation against the Chinese failed to halt them. Instead, the Chinese escalated the level of their demands, expecting that Moscow would back down eventually. Moscow had no alternative but to retaliate again. In the words of the Chinese:

Apparently the leaders of the C.P.S.U. imagined that once they waved their baton, gathered a group of hatchetmen to make a converging assault, and applied immense political and economic pressures, they could force the Chinese Communist Party to abandon its Marxist-Leninist and proletarian internationalist stand and submit to their revisionist and great power chauvinist behests. But the tempered and long-tested Chinese Communist Party and the Chinese people could neither be vanquished nor subdued. Those who tried to subjugate us by engineering a converging assault and applying pressures miscalculated.[34]

[33]*Ibid.*
[34]*Ibid.*

Nationalism continued to spill over from the communist system into the larger movement. Non-ruling parties were drawn more and more into the struggle, as the twelve communist ruling parties failed to find an area of common agreement for the movement as a whole. A separate conference of parties has not been convened since 1957, and is not likely to occur in the future, although the European group has met, as the Warsaw Pact Organization and as Comecon.

The second conference of all the communist parties was convened in November, 1960. Both the Chinese and Soviet leaders lobbied vigorously before, during, and after the conference. The Chinese found themselves in the minority. They made virtually no headway among the European and Western parties, and their behavior completely bewildered and confused the others, most of whom did not want to be placed in the uncomfortable position of being forced to choose, although they were not averse to exploiting the dispute to their own ends. Stung by Chinese charges of great power chauvinism, the Soviet leaders emphasized that theirs was the majority position and correctly claimed that, of the eighty-one parties represented at the conference:

The overwhelming majority of the fraternal parties rejected the incorrect views and concepts of the C.C.P. [Chinese Communist Party] leadership. The Chinese delegation at this meeting stubbornly upheld its own particular views and signed the Statement only when the danger arose of its complete isolation. Today it has become absolutely obvious that the C.C.P. leaders were only maneuvering when they affixed their signatures to the 1960 Statement.[35]

The Chinese ruefully conceded a

[35]*Pravda*, July 14, 1963.

Soviet majority at the conference, which reaffirmed the primacy of the Soviet Union as the senior partner in an association of equal members:

The communist and workers' parties unanimously declare that the Communist Party of the Soviet Union has been, and remains, the universally recognized vanguard of the world communist movement, being the most experienced and steeled contingent of the international communist movement.[36]

The Soviet Party was thus unambiguously enthroned as an ambiguous leader. Khrushchev, in a widely publicized speech on January 6, 1961, virtually renounced the dubious distinction of being the leader of a movement which was fractured beyond repair. It was also, simultaneously, a signal that Moscow could no longer be held responsible for, or be associated with, Peking's actions:

The C.P.S.U. in reality does not exercise leadership over other parties. All communist parties are equal and independent. . . . The role of the Soviet Union does not lie in the fact that it leads other socialist countries but in the fact that it was the first to blaze the trail to socialism, has the greatest positive experience in the struggle for the building of socialism, and was the first to enter the period of comprehensive construction of communism. . . . It is stressed in the Statement that the universally acknowledged vanguard of the world communist movement has been and still remains the C.P.S.U. . . . At the moment, when there exists a large group of socialist countries, each of which is faced with its own tasks, when there are eighty-seven communist and workers' parties functioning, each of which, moreover, is faced with its own tasks, it is not possible for leadership over socialist countries and communist

parties to be exercised from any center at all.[37]

Rump leader: polarization of the international communist movement

The course of the controversy between the Soviet Union and China since the conference in November, 1960, and the nature of the demands each has placed upon the other has resulted in the release of more information, greater employment of abuse and invective, less sophistication and discretion in argumentation, and greater visibility of underlying motives and intentions—all, more or less, variations on themes which are now familiar.

The deterioration of the ideological quality of the conflict revealed the naked national interests which were in conflict. This did not signify that ideology was rendered insignificant, but it did mean that it was becoming progressively national and internationalized. Furthermore, issues of national interest are more likely to mobilize popular support than are abstract ideological imperatives. The emergence of Communist China as well as of national communist states in Eastern Europe required the dozen communist states involved to reconcile their divergent interests into a common ideology which could command universal respect. The result appears to be little more than a demand that the non-ruling communist parties subordinate their interests to those of the twelve communist states. The debilitating struggle between Moscow and Peking has further revealed the degeneration of a once universalistic ideology into a vehicle of national power.

The polarization of the communist system and movement has largely followed lines of geography, stage of

[36]Cited from full text in the *New York Times*, December 7, 1960.

[37]*Kommunist*, No. 1 (January, 1961) p. 34.

economic development, and even race, rather than ideology, although each pole continues to justify its position ideologically. More and more, the Soviet Union is being forced to surrender its pretensions to universalism as it emerges as essentially the leader of a coalition of European communist nations and a group of Western communist parties.

By the time of the Twenty-second Party Congress in October, 1961, the crystallization of national conflicts was already yielding to a new polarization. Soviet primacy had been dethroned, and the Chinese bid for leadership rebuffed. Each communist state was chartering its own road to socialism, and Soviet classifications of each country's stage of development seemed to be essentially a barometer of its relationship to Moscow. The Soviet position in the communist world was largely defined by its military power and economic strength, rather than by its ideological wisdom. Moscow adjusted to the new distribution of power in the system with grudging grace, although residual aspects of its former aspiration to centralized control continued to assert themselves. More out of habit than conviction, Soviet leaders continued to pose as the source of ideological innovation. Khrushchev announced a grandiose plan for the construction of communism, promulgated new statutes for the Party, which introduced the principle of rotation, and proclaimed a new Party Program, after discussion of a draft which had been widely circulated. Innovations like "all-people's state" and "all-people's party" were evidences more of the ideological exhaustion of the Soviet regime than its creativity. Although these enunciations were offered as guides to other states and parties, it was evident that each communist country and party would examine the new ideological wares and carefully select and reject in accordance with its own needs.

After halfhearted attempts to oust the Albanian leader, Enver Hoxha, had failed, Khrushchev publicly excommunicated the Albanian Party. As the most outspoken defender of the Chinese position, Tirana was a thorn in Khrushchev's side and had to be removed from the communist bloc. Albania also served as a useful surrogate target for Peking, since China's darts were hitting closer and closer to Moscow, although they were ostensibly aimed at Belgrade. The Chinese reacted by defending Albania, and by ordering Chou En-lai to leave the Congress in a huff. Khrushchev and other Soviet leaders appeared indifferent.

Albania was China's first recruit in her anti-Soviet campaign within the system. She was soon joined by North Korea (which has since assumed a neutral position), and then by an ambivalent, but practical, North Vietnam. The Chinese were also ultimately able to entice the numerically powerful Indonesian Party (which has since been all but destroyed) to their side, but they succeeded in generating factionalism and splinter groups in other countries more often than they won over their parties. Some communist states and parties, in Europe and elsewhere, offered and tried to mediate, since most of the parties had a vested interest in preventing an open and formal break, though few were really interested in healing the split. As long as the two most powerful communist states were locked in controversy, it allowed the widest latitude of autonomy for the others. The advantages for the non-ruling parties, however, were not as clear.

As early as December, 1961, the Italian communist leader, Luigi Longo, openly admitted the pattern of polarization which was assuming shape in the communist world:

The quarrel between the Soviet and the Chinese Communist Parties refers to a much more important question than that of peaceful coexistence, possibilities of avoiding atomic war or the dispute over the cult of Stalin's personality. The real issue is a difference between their views on the true way to socialism and communism. The Chinese believe that the development of communism in the various countries of the socialist bloc should be indivisible. The countries that are more advanced economically should therefore take more interest in the troubles and sufferings of the more backward socialist countries and place all their material resources at their disposal. Those who hold this view cannot accept the competition between the Soviet Union and the United States and the capitalist countries. Nor can they accept peaceful coexistence or Soviet aid to underdeveloped countries. This help should be given to the economically backward countries in the socialist camp. The Chinese comrades do not hide their misgivings but we Italian communists believe that the Soviet policy of competition with the United States is more useful for the development of world communism than a concern for the equal economic development of all the countries in the socialist camp. The effect of Soviet policy is to accelerate the development of conflicts within the capitalist camp and to draw the colonial peoples in the socialist camp.[38]

The Cuban missile crisis, resulting at least in part from a Soviet attempt to demonstrate its ability to protect all socialist countries, accelerated the fragmentation and polarization and brought into question the credibility of what Moscow was seeking to demonstrate. Accusing Khrushchev of engaging in both "adventurism" and

[38]*L'Unita*, December 23, 1961.

"capitulationism," and of risking thermonuclear war without prior consultation of other communist states (by dispatching missiles and then withdrawing them over Cuban objections), the Chinese sought to cast doubt on Moscow's willingness to defend other communist states against American imperialism. The Chinese gesture backfired, as the European parties rallied to the support of the Soviet Union, although Castro was obviously humiliated and peeved by the quick Soviet retreat. Moscow sought to salve his wounds by dispatching Mikoyan on a fence-mending mission and by promising additional economic assistance. Peking's charge of a Caribbean "Munich" struck most of the other parties as unnecessarily inflexible and a verification of China's belligerence.

The episode served to isolate China even more. Moscow organized its counterstroke against the Chinese, as Peking was subjected to an unprecedented crossfire of invective and abuse at a series of European Party Congresses, held from November, 1962, to January, 1963 (Bulgarian, Hungarian, Italian, Czechoslovak, and East German). Moscow concentrated its fire on Albania, while the European parties converged upon the Chinese directly. Some parties, including the Cuban, attempted to preserve a posture of neutrality, but as the conflict escalated, polarization accelerated. Peking struck back in a series of unusually long, documented, and systematically organized attacks on Western parties, still adhering to the phrase "certain comrades" when referring to the Soviet leaders, but naming Italian and French leaders in their indictments. The conflict flared into the open in March, 1963, when Khrushchev's position seemed precarious at home. But the Test Ban Treaty was soon signed, and the first phase of the long sought-after *détente* with the United States was a reality.

Compromised leader: the Soviet-American detente and world communism

The Soviet Union's relations with both the United States and Yugoslavia improved rapidly, and Moscow's image of American intentions underwent a radical change. From the Chinese point of view, something resembling a *reversement des alliances* had taken place, and they saw the Soviet Union and the United States as conspiring to deny China nuclear weapons and plotting to jointly dominate the world.

The leaders of the C.P.S.U. have completely reversed enemies and comrades. . . . The leaders of the C.P.S.U. are bent on seeking Soviet-United States cooperation for the domination of the world. They regard United States imperialism, the most ferocious enemy of the people in the world as their most reliable friend and they treat the fraternal parties and countries adhering to Marxism-Leninism as their enemy. They collude with United States imperialism, the reactionaries of various countries, the renegade Tito clique and the right-wing Social Democrats in a partnership against the socialist fraternal countries. When they snatch at a straw from Eisenhower or Kennedy or others like them, or think that things are going smoothly for them, the leaders of the C.P.S.U. are beside themselves with joy, hit out wildly at the fraternal parties and countries adhering to Marxism-Leninism, and endeavor to sacrifice fraternal parties and countries on the altar of their political dealings with United States imperialism.[39]

The Chinese, having failed in their bid for primacy, and Moscow, having failed equally to bring the Chinese to heel, are now both looking for an appropriate occasion to fasten re-

[39]The *New York Times*, February 7, 1964.

sponsibility for an organizational split upon the other. Recognizing that few Eastern European or Western communist parties can identify their interests with those of the Chinese, Peking has virtually abandoned Eastern Europe states and Western parties as possible instruments with which to organize a new revolutionary movement which would embrace both communists and noncommunist revolutionaries. Since Moscow has succeeded in virtually isolating Peking from the European communist states, the Chinese have retaliated by trying to freeze the Soviet Union out of Asia, Africa, and Latin America. Resorting to bonds of race and under-development, Peking appears to be seeking to mobilize the nonwhite under-developed world against the white developed world, whether communist or noncommunist. Chinese representatives vigorously propagate the view that racial bonds are stronger than class bonds in Soviet calculations, and that Moscow will inevitably associate itself with whites against nonwhites. According to a Soviet indictment, the Chinese reason that, since nonwhites outnumber whites, the most effective road to Chinese hegemony is to organize them under Chinese direction, in preparation for the day when they will displace the white race as the dominant element on the globe. This, according to Moscow, is the real meaning of the Chinese slogan, The East Wind prevails over the West Wind:

The Chinese leaders represent matters as though the interests of the peoples of Asia, Africa, and Latin America were especially close and understandable to them, as though they were concerned most of all for the further development of the national liberation struggle in order to turn them into a tool for the realization of the hegemonic plans. . . . The Chinese . . . suggested to the representatives of the African and Asian countries that inasmuch as the Russians, Czechs, and Poles are white, "you can't rely on them," that they will allegedly "always be in collusion with the Americans—with whites," that the peoples of Asia and Africa have their special interests. . . . The Chinese leaders are trying to fan these feelings, in the hopes of setting the peoples of the former colonies against the socialist countries, against the working people of the developed capitalist countries. . . . China, they reason, is the largest country of the East and embodies its interests; here are born the "winds of history" that are to prevail over the "winds of the West." Thus this slogan is nothing but an ideological and political expression of the hegemonic aspirations of the Chinese leadership.[40]

The Chinese strategy now seems as follows: (1) to undermine the traditional Soviet claims to a special position in the communist world, by charging its leaders with "modern revisionism" and "the restoration of capitalism"; (2) to undermine the credibility of Soviet promises to defend and look after the military security of its smaller allies; (3) to isolate the Soviet Union from the under-developed countries and from the revolutionary movement in Latin America, Africa, and Asia. They are, in effect, energetically preparing the groundwork for a separate and rival revolutionary movement, in these continents.

One of the consequences of the Sino-Soviet split is that it leaves the Soviet Union as a badly wounded leader of a rump, essentially Western communist movement. And within this orbit, it is now defied even by its formerly most servile minions, the leaders of the Rumanian Communist Party, who, in an unexpected and unusual gesture of defiance, refused to accept the agricultural role assigned

[40]*Pravda*, April 3, 1964.

to Rumania under the new Comecon plan for the international socialist division of labor. Rumania has not only offered itself as a mediator in the Sino-Soviet dispute, but also deals with both Peking and Moscow, while it seeks expanded and more profitable commercial relations with the West. This is likely to be the pattern pursued by other communist states remaining in the Soviet sphere, as they exercise their right to adopt and pursue policies tailored to their national interests, just as does the Soviet Union.

The sudden and unexpected ouster of Khrushchev from his posts of authority in October, 1964, diminished Soviet prestige further. The humiliating manner of Khrushchev's removal conveyed the impression that Chinese pressure and demands on the Soviet Union had somehow prevailed again. And the sense of outrage expressed by Eastern European leaders and by Western parties, most of whom had associated their interests with Khrushchev's policies, indicated that they were using the removal of their champion as an occasion to assert their increasing independence and autonomy. Some parties, like the Polish, Hungarian, Yugoslav, Italian, and French, were critical of Khrushchev mainly because he did not pursue the ultimate logic of de-Stalinization with sufficient vigor. Disturbed in particular by the nature of Khrushchev's ouster, they demanded and received an explanation. Togliatti's testament, issued in September, 1964, explicitly called for a greater public disclosure of factional and policy differences among Soviet leaders:

It is not correct to refer to the socialist countries (including the Soviet Union) as if everything were always going well in them. . . . Some situations appear hard to understand. In many cases one has the impression there are differences of opinion among the leading groups, but one does not understand if this is really so and what the differences are. Perhaps it could be useful in some cases for the socialist countries also to conduct open debates on current problems, the leaders also taking part. Certainly, this would contribute to a growth in the authority and prestige of the socialist regime itself.[41]

This represented a further development in the reverse flow of demands from the periphery to the center in the communist world. Up to now, only Moscow exercised the right to interfere and intervene in the factional squabbles in other communist states, while changes in Moscow were immune from outside scrutiny and intervention. The chorus of demands and criticisms which descended on Khrushchev's detractors and successors resulted, first, in arresting any further design to downgrade and degrade Khrushchev and, second, in accepting the demands for a detailed explanation of the sudden change in Soviet leadership. Further, the concern expressed by Eastern European and Western party leaders is a reflection of their determination to complete the transition from pawns to actors in the world communist system and movement. Either they participate in decisions pertaining to communism as a whole, and their interests are taken into account in arriving at these decisions, or they will assert their right to chart their own course.

Although the escalation of the Vietnamese war in 1965, and the systematic bombing of North Vietnam by the United States, has caused a deterioration in Soviet-American relations and has arrested the *détente*, it has poisoned Sino-Soviet relations even more. In March, 1966, just prior to the opening of the Twenty-third Communist Party

Congress, which the Chinese refused to attend, Moscow and Peking once again exchanged denunciations. These summarized their complaints against one another, revealed new information about their past relations, and disclosed additional sources of continuing conflict and rivalry. In a secret letter circulated to communist parties, Moscow levelled a series of charges against the Chinese leaders which seemed almost deliberately designed to provoke the Chinese into absenting themselves from the Congress. In this letter, the Soviet leaders made the following charges: (1) China has interfered with Soviet attempts to send material and military assistance to North Vietnam; (2) Chinese leaders have rebuffed all Soviet overtures for a meeting in order to settle their differences; (3) the Chinese have organized anti-Soviet demonstrations and have tried to incite the Soviet population against its leadership; (4) "the C.P.R. [Chinese People's Republic] leadership propagates ever more obstinately the thesis of potential military clashes between China and the Soviet Union"; (5) the Chinese have been "provoking border conflicts . . . [which] have increased again in recent months . . . [and] allegations are being spread to the effect that the Soviet Union unlawfully holds Chinese territory in the Far East"; (6) and, finally:

There is every reason to assert that it is one of the goals of the policy of the Chinese leadership in the Vietnam question to cause a military conflict between the U.S.S.R. and the United States. They want a clash of the U.S.S.R. with the United States so that they may, as they say themselves, "sit on the mountain and watch the fight of the tigers."[42]

In conclusion, the Soviet letter reiterat-

[41]Quoted in the *New York Times*, September 5, 1964.

[42]Quoted in the *New York Times*, March 24, 1966.

THE SOVIET UNION AND INTERNATIONAL COMMUNISM

ed the charge that Peking was manipulating the international communist movement and the national liberation movement for its own hegemonic purposes.

The Chinese leaders retorted, in a public statement, that the circulation of "an anti-Chinese letter to other parties, instigating them to join you in opposing China," was eloquent proof of insincerity in inviting the Chinese to attend the Twenty-third Congress of the CPSU. Peking accused Moscow of spreading false rumors that China was obstructing Soviet assistance to Vietnam, and "encroaching on Soviet territory." The Soviet leaders were charged with stating that China was no longer to be viewed as a socialist country and of viewing the Chinese Communist Party as an "enemy." The Chinese statement made a brief but spirited defense of Stalin, and accused Khrushchev's successors of intensifying his "revisionism" and "splittism," but the main burden of its attack was that Moscow, far from wanting to aid North Vietnam, was encouraging the North Vietnamese to negotiate with the United States in order to clear the way for the Soviet Union and the United States to accelerate their joint conspiracy against China:

Despite the tricks you have been playing to deceive people, you are pursuing United States-Soviet collaboration for the domination of the world with your whole heart. . . . You have all along been acting in coordination with the United States in its plot for peace talks, vainly attempting to sell out the struggle of the Vietnamese people against United States aggression and . . . to drag the Vietnam question into the orbit of Soviet-United States collaboration. You have worked hand in glove with the United States in a whole series of dirty deals inside and outside the United Nations. In close coordination with the counter-revolutionary "global strategy" of United

States imperialism, you are now trying to build a ring of encirclement around socialist China. . . . You have even aligned yourselves with United States imperialism . . . and established a holy alliance against China, against the movement and against the Marxist-Leninists.[43]

Thus, beginning in late 1958 and continuing into the Sixties, was the gradual emergence of Peking and Moscow as the two poles of ideology and power in the communist camp. A new Soviet policy was to seek to solidify Soviet control and influence over the Eastern European communist states, as a separate and distinct process from maintaining the unity of the communist world as a whole. This has led to the existence of a European communist bloc, led by the Soviet Union. Only Albania, whose special fear is Yugoslavia—the main focus of attack by Peking—remains outside the Soviet bloc, playing a strange game of pitting Peking against Moscow. China has not yet organized a comparable regional communist bloc, but indications are that Peking would like to organize such a regional grouping, made up of the four Asian communist states— China, North Korea, Mongolia, and North Vietnam, but her geographical position vis-à-vis the smaller Asian countries, is not as decisive as the Soviet position with respect to Eastern Europe since three of the four Asian communist countries border on the U.S.S.R. itself. Mongolia, which fears Chinese power, has solidly associated itself with Moscow, while North Korea has issued a plague on both houses, and North Vietnam straddles the fence, using the Soviet Union as a counterpoise against Chinese domination, and relying upon Chinese threats to deter the U.S. from carrying the war to the north.

[43]*Ibid.*

The Soviet Union and China appear to be significantly divided on questions of ideology and policy sufficient to prevent the development of a common outlook and the forging of a common policy toward the noncommunist world. These divisions reflect a basic conflict of national interests between a maturing social and industrial order—the Soviet Union and the European satellites—which has a greater stake in avoiding nuclear war, and a pre-industrial revolutionary society which feels that its political and economic goals can be achieved only by destroying the vestiges of the old social and economic order.

Irrespective of the detailed nature, causes, and motivations of Sino-Soviet controversies—and these range from traditional, historical and territorial questions to fundamental differences between the basically European character and culture of Moscow and the orientalism of China and transcend ideological matters—the significant point is that the world communist movement has been divested of its single directing center and threatens to fragment into several centers. Regardless of what institutional forms of cooperation are adopted, the Kremlin has abdicated its monopoly on making decisions for the entire communist world and to some extent must coordinate its foreign policy with that of its allies, rather than the other way around.

SELECTED BIBLIOGRAPHY

Aspaturian, Vernon V., *The Soviet Union in the International Communist System*. Stanford, Calif.: Hoover Institution Studies, 1966.

Borkenau, F., *The Communist International*. London: Faber & Faber, Ltd., 1938.

———, *European Communism*. New York: Harper & Row, Publishers, Inc., 1953.

Brzeninski, Zbigniew K., *The Soviet Bloc*. Cambridge, Mass.: Harvard University Press, 1960.

Chamberlin, W. H., ed., *Blueprint for World Conquest*. Chicago: Human Events, Inc., 1946.

Dallin, Alexander, *et al.*, eds., *Diversity in International Communism*. New York: Columbia University Press, 1963.

Floyd, David, *Mao Against Khrushchev*. New York: Frederick A. Praeger, Inc., 1963.

Goodman, Elliot R., *The Soviet Design for a World State*. New York: Columbia University Press, 1960.

Griffith, William E., *Albania and the Sino-Soviet Rift*. Cambridge, Mass.: The M.I.T. Press, 19⟨3.

———, *The Sino-Soviet Rift*. Cambridge, Mass.: The M.I.T. Press, 1964.

Grzybowski, Kazmierz, *The Socialist Commonwealth of Nations*. New Haven, Conn.: Yale University Press, 1964.

Laqueur, Walter, and Leopold Labedz, eds., *Polycentrism*. New York: Frederick A. Praeger, Inc., 1962.

Lowenthal, Richard, *World Communism*. New York: Oxford University Press, 1964.

McKenzie, Kermit, *Comintern and World Revolution*. New York: Columbia University Press, 1962.

Russian Institute of Columbia University, *The Anti-Stalin Campaign and International Communism*. New York: Columbia University Press, 1956. A selection of documents.

Schwartz, Harry, *Tsars, Mandarins and Commissars*. New York: J. B. Lippincott Co., 1964.

The Soviet-Yugoslav Dispute. London: Royal Institute of International Affairs, 1948.

Triska, Jan, *The World Communist System*. Stanford, Calif.: Stanford Studies of the Communist System, 1964.

Zagoria, Donald, *The Sino-Soviet Conflict: 1956–1961*. Princeton, N. J.: Princeton University Press, 1962.

Zinner, P. E., ed., *National Communism and Popular Revolt in Eastern Europe*. New York: Columbia University Press, 1947. A selection of documents.

Throughout its history, the United States has pursued a consistent foreign policy. Beneath the clamor of contending philosophies, the controversies of factions, the contradictions and reversals of individual moves on the international scene, the foreign policy of the United States presents a simple and coherent pattern. This pattern results from the character of the interests which the United States has traditionally pursued on the international scene.

In the Western Hemisphere, the United States has always endeavored to preserve its unique position as the predominant, unrivalled power. The United States has recognized from the very beginning that its predominance could not be effectively threatened from within the hemisphere without support from outside it. This peculiar situation has made it imperative for the United States to isolate the Western Hemisphere from the political and military policies of non-American nations. The interference of these nations in the affairs of the Western Hemisphere, especially through the acquisition of territory, was the only way in which the predominance of the United States could have been challenged from within the hemisphere itself. The Monroe Doctrine, and the policies implementing it, express the permanent national interest of the United States in the Western Hemisphere.

Since the interests of the United States in the Western Hemisphere can be effectively threatened only from outside—historically, from Europe—the United States has always striven to prevent the development of conditions in Europe which would be conducive to interference in the affairs of the Western Hemisphere, or contemplation of a direct attack upon the United States. These conditions would be most likely to arise if a European nation having unchallenged predominance in Europe could look across the sea for conquest without fear of being threatened at the center of its power.

It is for this reason that the United States has consistently pursued policies

7

HANS J. MORGENTHAU

THE AMERICAN TRADITION IN FOREIGN POLICY

aiming at the maintenance of the balance of power in Europe. The War of 1812 is the sole major exception to this tradition. It has opposed whatever European nation was likely to gain ascendancy over its European competitors and jeopardize the hemispheric predominance and, eventually, the very existence of the United States as an independent nation. Conversely, it has supported whatever European nation appeared capable of restoring the balance of power by offering successful resistance to the would-be conqueror. While it is hard to imagine a greater contrast in political philosophy than that between Alexander Hamilton and Woodrow Wilson, they agree in their concern for the maintenance of the balance of power in Europe. It is with this in mind that the United States has intervened in both World Wars on the side of the initially weaker coalition, and has pursued European policies largely paralleling those of Great Britain; for from Henry VIII to Sir Edward Grey, on the eve of the First World War, Great Britain's single objective in Europe was the maintenance of the balance of power.

Asia has vitally concerned the United States only since the turn of the century, and the meaning of Asia for American interests has never been obvious or clearly defined. In consequence, American policies in Asia have never as unequivocally expressed the permanent national interest as have the hemispheric and European policies. Yet beneath the confusions and incongruities which have sometimes marred American policy in Asia, one can detect a consistency that reflects, however vaguely, the permanent interest of the United States in Asia. And this interest is again the maintenance of the balance of power.

The principle of the "open door" in China expresses this interest. At the beginning, its meaning was purely commercial. But when other nations, especially Japan, threatened to close the door to China, not only commercially but also militarily and politically, the United States sought to keep the door to China open in order to safeguard the latter's territorial integrity and political independence for political rather than commercial reasons. However unsure the United States may have been in the particular moves of its Asian policy, it has always assumed that the domination of China by another nation would create so great an accumulation of power as to threaten the security of the United States.

This extraordinary position of safety, which could be threatened only sporadically from afar, gave rise to a peculiarly American attitude toward foreign policy and war. All other politically active nations have been forced, by their continuous exposure to danger from abroad, to recognize the truth of Karl von Clausewitz's dictum that war is the continuation of policy by other means. The peaceful and warlike means by which a nation pursues its interests vis-à-vis other nations form a continuous process in which, though one means may replace the other, the end remains the same. Foreign policy itself is a continuum beginning with the birth of the nation and ending only with its death.

Yet under the impact of the extraordinary position in which the United States found itself vis-à-vis other nations from the beginning of its history to the end of the Second World War, Americans came to embrace a different philosophy. According to this philosophy, it was "normal" for a nation to have no foreign policy at all. If a crisis should require a temporary departure from that normalcy in the form of an active foreign policy or of intervention in a foreign war, it was taken for granted that after the crisis was settled the nation ought to return to the normalcy of detachment. On this assumption, that the nation had a choice between involvement in or detachment from world affairs, and that the latter was to be preferred, both the isolationists and internationalists of the interwar period agreed. They disagreed only in their assessment of the urgency of intervention in a particular crisis situation. Furthermore, the internationalists believed that, in order to forestall the next crisis and meet it with the greatest chance for success, the United States should participate in the development and support of international organizations seeking to maintain international order and peace.

Foreign policy was thus regarded as something like a policeman's night stick, to be used only when necessary to bring a disturber of the peace to reason; war, in turn, was assigned the function of the policeman's gun, to be used only *in extremis* to rid the world of a criminal. But here the analogy ends: the policeman always carries his gun with him, but the United States threw its gun away twice, after it had done the job in two World Wars.

The United States could see that war did have a necessary connection with the criminal aggression that preceded and provoked it, but it did not realize the organic relation that exists between war and what follows it. The purpose of war appeared to be the elimination of a disturbance by eliminating the disturber; once that was done, the world would presumably settle back into normalcy and order. War, as prepared for and waged by the United States, was a mere technical operation to be performed according to the rules of the military art—a feat of military engineering like building a dam or flattening a mountain. The organic relationship between foreign and military policy was lost and, in consequence, foreign policy was without strength, and military policy lacked purpose.

THE REVOLUTION IN AMERICAN FOREIGN POLICY

The aftermath of World War II witnessed a drastic change, not in the traditional interests, but in the traditional policies and attitudes of the United States. This change was imposed by the conditions of unprecedented novelty under which the United States had to pursue its traditional interest in the preservation of the balance of power in Europe and Asia. What is the nature of the unusual threat with which the Soviet Union confronts the balance of power in Europe, and with which China confronts the balance of power in Asia? When the United States was called on, in the two World Wars, to redress the European balance of power, the German threat was being contained, however precariously, by a counterweight located in Europe itself. The Japanese threat, in turn, was contained on the Asian mainland by the power of China. The United States only needed to add its strength to these counterweights until victory was achieved, and then it expected to return to the normalcy of isolation. This is what it did after the First World War, and what it was prepared to do after the Second. After some months of hesitation and confusion, the United States realized that the nations of Western Europe had become too weak to contain the Russian threat to the European balance of power and that the United States, in order to prevent the Russian conquest of all of Europe, had to commit itself in virtual permanence to the defense of Western

Europe. When, in 1948, China fell to communism and nothing stood in the way of its expansion except Chiang Kai-shek's forces, the United States took upon itself similar permanent obligations in Asia.

By 1947, the new pattern of American foreign policy was set. It manifested itself in four political innovations: the Truman doctrine, containment, the Marshall Plan, and the American alliance system. Foreign aid and liberation were added to them in the Fifties. These policies have in common the permanent assumption, by the United States, of responsibilities beyond the limits of the Western Hemisphere.

The Truman doctrine is contained in President Truman's message to Congress of March 12, 1947. The President recommended the appropriation of $400 million for assistance to Greece and Turkey and the authorization to send civilian and military personnel as well as commodities, supplies, and equipment to these two countries. The immediate occasion for these requests was the inability of Great Britain to continue the historic function, which she had performed for almost a century and a half, of protecting the eastern shores of the Mediterranean from Russian penetration. Since the end of the Napoleonic Wars, one of the basic assumptions of British foreign policy had been that Russian control of Greece and of the Dardanelles constituted a threat to the European balance of power. Great Britain was no longer able to shoulder the over-all responsibility for the maintenance of the balance of power in Europe, and she had just notified the United States that she no longer possessed the military and economic resources to defend Greece against communist attack.

The interest of the United States in the maintenance of the European balance of power had been historically identical with that of Great Britain and, by the beginning of 1947, the United States had already become— by the logic of the distribution of power, if not by design—the successor to Great Britain as the main counterweight against a threat to the independence of the nations of Europe. It was then almost inevitable that the United States take over the particular British burden for the protection of the independence of Greece and the territorial integrity of Turkey, an action justified both by traditional interest in the European balance of power and by the particular conditions prevailing in the eastern Mediterranean at the beginning of 1947.

Yet the Truman doctrine went beyond the immediate occasion by committing the United States to the defense of democratic nations everywhere in the world against "direct or indirect aggression" and against "subjugation by armed minorities or by outside pressure." At this point, the Truman doctrine merges into the policy of containment.

The policy of containment was never officially formulated. It grew as an almost instinctive reaction to the threat of Russian imperialism. It called a halt to the territorial expansion of Russian power beyond the line of military demarcation drawn at the end of the Second World War between the Soviet orbit and the Western world. It said, in effect, to the Soviet Union: "Thus far and no farther, else you will be at war with the United States." Or as the London *Economist* of December 2, 1950, put it: "The object of the endeavor in which the nations of the free world are now united is to contain Russian imperialism without having to fight another world war."

The United States recognized that

the policy of containment could not succeed while the nations of Western Europe remained economically prostrate and politically unstable. Thus, Secretary of State George Marshall declared, in an address at Harvard on June 5, 1947, that the United States would welcome the initiative and cooperation of the European countries in the elaboration of an economic program of self-help combined with American assistance. The Western European nations quickly responded to this "Marshall Plan," forming as their vehicle of cooperation a Committee of European Economic Cooperation which laid the foundation for the establishment, the following year, of the Organization for European Economic Cooperation (OEEC). In April, 1948, Congress approved the bill creating the Economic Cooperation Administration (ECA) as the instrument for channeling billions of dollars to the nations of Europe over a four-year program.

The American tradition limited to the Western Hemisphere the continuous presence of the United States on the stage of foreign policy. The great reversal of 1947 extended the permanent military commitments of the United States immediately beyond the Rhine and, potentially, to any region, anywhere, threatened by communist aggression or subversion. It further committed the economic resources of the United States immediately to the support of the nations of Western Europe, of Greece and Turkey, and potentially of any nation anywhere which needed it to preserve its freedom. It had become the policy of the United States, in the words of the Truman Doctrine, "to support free peoples who are resisting attempted subjugation by armed minorities or by outside pressures." Since peoples throughout the world, in Europe, Africa, Asia, and Latin America, are resisting such subjugation, the commitments of the United States, by virtue of the Truman Doctrine, have become worldwide, unlimited geographically, and limited only by the lack of need for support or a nation's unwillingness to accept it.

Of the traditional foreign policy of the United States, this revolution in America's relations to the outside world made short shrift. Nothing is left of it but a memory and, in some, a vain desire to return to an age when the United States was committed to defend only its own territory and the Western Hemisphere, not the nations of Western Europe, Berlin, Greece, Turkey, Australia, New Zealand, Pakistan, Thailand, South Vietnam, South Korea, Japan, and Taiwan, and when the United States endeavored to transform the world by its own example rather than by intervening, assisting, and advising.

America, once its policy of containment had met successfully the Russian military threat to Western Europe, had to achieve three difficult tasks. First of all, it had to create, out of the makeshift arrangements aimed at meeting the Russian military threat, a viable international order which would translate common interests into a common purpose, fuse the power of individual nations, and assign to them responsibilities commensurate with their interests and power. Second, it had to create a relationship with the uncommitted new nations of Africa and Asia which would be conducive to the development of domestic and international stability. Third, it had to establish a relationship conducive both to peace and freedom, with those nations who were unwilling objects of communist domination, such as the nations of Eastern Europe.

How did the United States endeavor to meet these tasks? It developed three policies to serve them: alliances; foreign aid; and liberation.

The policy of alliances

Since the end of the Second World War, the United States had concluded four collective alliances: The Inter-American Treaty of Mutual Assistance of 1947, also called the Rio Pact; the North Atlantic Treaty of 1949, under which the North Atlantic Treaty Organization (NATO) was established; the Security Treaty with Australia and New Zealand, called ANZUS, of 1951; and the Southeast Asia Treaty Organization of 1954, called SEATO. To these collective agreements must be added individual alliances the United States has concluded with Japan, the Philippines, South Korea, South Vietnam, and the Republic of China. The Baghdad Pact of 1955, concluded among Turkey, Iraq, Great Britain, Pakistan, and Iran, and succeeded, after the defection of Iraq in 1958, by the Cento Pact, has been actively supported, but was not formally joined, by the United States.

The Rio Pact, of which the United States and all Latin-American nations are members, serves the common defense of the Western Hemisphere by transforming the Monroe Doctrine from a unilateral American declaration into a collective arrangement. NATO, to which the United States and all nations of Western Europe—with the exception of Austria, Ireland, Sweden, Switzerland and Spain—as well as Greece and Turkey, belong, serves the defense of Western Europe. The ANZUS Treaty serves the defense of the Pacific. SEATO, of which the United States, Great Britain, France, Australia, New Zealand, the Philippines, Thailand, and Pakistan are members, serves the defense of South and Southeast Asia.

The relationships within an alliance are determined by two fundamental factors—the interests and the power of its members. In this respect, the alliance between the United States and the nations of Western Europe must be distinguished from the other American alliances. The interests which tie the United States to its European allies are more profound, more comprehensive, and more stable than the interests upon which alliances have traditionally been based. Far from concerning nothing more than a limited territorial advantage against a temporary enemy, these interests enclose the national identity of all the members within a common civilization, threatened by an alien and oppressive social system. Thus, this alliance was not formed through a process of bargaining among suspicious temporary associates, but rather sprang naturally and almost inevitably from a concern with a common heritage which had a chance to survive only through common support. The members of the alliance had to choose between the alliance and the loss of their national identity and cultural heritage; that is to say, they had no choice at all.

The cement that has maintained that alliance has been the paramount power of the United States. While, in past alliances, power had been unequally distributed, with one ally predominant, rarely had there been such a concentration of power, with all other allies in a subordinate position. The United States was not only paramount in the military and economic fields, but also in the intangible sphere of the values of Western civilization, and had become, in every respect, the predominant power of the alliance.

If the institutions and operations of the alliance had been as comprehensive and intense as its underlying interests, and if the influence of the United States had been commensurate with its power, the alliance might have amounted to a confederation of states merging their most vital activities in the fields of foreign policy, defense, finance, and economics. However, during the Fifties, the United States did not play its required role in the Western alliance. Three inherited patterns of thought and action prevented this: the traditional limitation of the direct exercise of American power to the Western Hemisphere; the principle of equality; and the military approach to foreign policy.

On the two previous occasions when American power went beyond the limits of the Western Hemisphere, America retreated to its traditional confines after it had failed to establish itself firmly beyond them. The liquidation of the conquests of the Spanish-American War, in view of its accidental and peripheral connection with the American tradition of foreign policy, could begin as soon as the conquests had been made. The failure of Wilson's attempt to make the world safe for democracy rendered pointless the presence of American power in Europe. The nature of the Russian threat after the Second World War left the United States no rational choice but to establish its power in virtual permanence at the circumference of the Russian empire. But should that power be established in terms of American supremacy, which would reduce America's allies to the status of satellites, or was it to be the equality of all members of the alliance, which would, ideally, result in the harmonious co-operation of like-minded nations? This dilemma had to be solved in a way that would not deny either of these essentials of American policy.

American power had to operate in the territory of friendly nations whose consent provided the only title for the American presence, the purpose of which was the defense of the freedom and territorial integrity of the allies. If the United States had reduced its allies to the status of satellites, the very purpose of the European alliance would have been defeated. On the other hand, the establishment of the alliance on the basis of complete equality was feasible only on the assumption that the identity of interests among the allies was so complete that they could pursue common ends, with common measures, through free and equal cooperation. If this cooperation fell short of the ideal expectation, the purpose of the alliance, as a cooperative effort on behalf of the common interests, would be defeated.

Of these alternatives, the United States chose the latter. It refused to bring its superior power to bear on the alliance on behalf of common interests which would compete with divergent ones. When the United States left the Western Hemisphere, it carried only its military and economic power, not its creative imagination and its constructive will. Significantly, this imagination and will played its greatest role in that sphere closest to the American tradition in foreign affairs, the military sphere.

The United States emerged from the Second World War as the most powerful nation on earth by chance and not by design, and it assumed the leadership of the coalition of free nations by virtue of necessity and not of choice. In consequence, its will and mind were not equal to its power, responsibility, and opportunity. Since America's responsibility was not the result of conscious choice, it approached the tasks incumbent upon the paramount power of the Western alliance with unbecoming humility and unwarranted self-restraint. The political predominance required by its power was incompatible with its anti-imperialist tradition, which is the manifestation abroad of the principle of equality. Confronted with the choice between assuming the position of leadership and treating its allies as equals, the United States chose the latter. Accustomed to expanding its rule into political empty spaces but not to imposing it on existing political entities, it endeavored to establish a consensus within the Western alliance by the same methods of rational persuasion and economic inducements with which the American commonwealth had been created, maintained, and developed.

Yet the application of the equalitarian principle of democratic consensus to alliances resulted in disintegration and anarchy. The integrating effects of the domestic equalitarian consensus depend upon a pre-established hierarchical relationship in the form of a sovereign central government; any equality among allies drastically differing in power and responsibility must be subordinated to a hierarchical relationship between the paramount power and the rest. This relationship was lacking between the United States and its allies. As a result of this lack, the alliance was either incapable of pursuing new, positive policies in common, or else the most determined ally was able to impose its will on the United States.

NATO is the outstanding example of the former consequence. The principle of equality among its fifteen members, applied to the political operations and over-all military planning of the alliance, put a virtually insurmountable obstacle in the way of new policies to be pursued in response to new opportunities or threats. The principle of equality would have been compatible with new departures in policy only on the unattainable conditions that all members of the alliance had an equal interest in such depar-

tures, were equally aware of these interests, and agreed completely on the means to be used in support of them. Short of an open threat of military conquest or revolution, such as confronted the members of NATO in the late 1940's, these conditions cannot be expected to be present at the same time. In the absence of one of them, the best an alliance can achieve is to translate the lowest common denominator of agreed interests into common action. While the objective conditions under which the fifteen allies live require a degree of unity in purpose and action far transcending that of a traditional alliance, and while NATO was designed to be the instrument of that kind of unity, NATO has become more and more undistinguishable from a traditional, loosely knit alliance.

The other consequence of the equalitarian approach to alliances has been most marked in the bilateral relations between the United States and its allies. Governments which govern only because the United States maintains them or which have no alternative to the American association have been able to play a winning game in which the United States holds all the trumps. The United States has not been disposed to play these trumps for two reasons. Its commitment to the principle of equality made it impossible to bring its superior power to bear upon a weak ally on behalf of its interests. These interests were conceived in terms of what might be called the "collector's approach" to alliances. The United States, in the Fifties, was primarily interested in the conclusion of alliances per se, regardless of the specific and concrete interests these alliances were supposed to serve. An alliance thus conceived is a standing invitation for a weak ally to make the alliance serve its specific and concrete interests. Thus the United States has paid for the willingness of weak and even unviable nations to become its allies by underwriting the interests of these nations, regardless of whether these interests coincide with, or even run counter to, its own.

This relationship, unhealthy even by the standards of traditional foreign policy, is a far cry from the new order through which the United States was called on to realize the common purpose of the nations of Western civilization in the atomic age. The United States was not able to free itself from the pattern of thought and action established both by its tradition and its successful reaction to the threat of Russian power in the aftermath of the Second World War—it continued to conceive of its relations to the outside world primarily in military terms. It saw itself surrounded by allies, by uncommitted nations which thus far had refused to become allies, and by satellites which Russian power had thus far prevented from becoming allies. From this picture of the world, three militarily oriented objectives ensued. The allies had to be kept in the American orbit, the uncommitted nations had to be drawn into it, and the satellites had to be liberated in order to enable them to join it. SEATO and the abortive Eisenhower Doctrine of March, 1957, were open-ended—and largely unsuccessful—invitations to the uncommitted nations of Asia and the Middle East, respectively, to become allies of the United States, or at least to accept military assistance from it.

These policies were largely unsuccessful because the picture of the world from which they derived was at odds both with the facts of experience and the interests of the United States. What the United States had to cope with, outside Europe, was not the threat of Russian military power but the promise of a new political and economic order. A policy of military alliances was irrelevant to the problems raised by that promise. It was also counter-productive, for by strengthening the forces of the *status quo* and the military establishments in the allied nations, it tended to identify the United States with those forces and with preparations for war. This, in turn, gave communism the opportunity to identify itself with the forces of progress and peace.

The policy of foreign aid

The policy of foreign aid, considered the main instrument for strengthening the uncommitted nations in their uncommitted position, has similarly suffered from this predominantly military orientation. But it has also suffered from two other handicaps.

The American theory and practice of foreign aid, during the Fifties, was derived largely from certain unexamined assumptions which are part of the American folklore of politics. The popular mind has established a number of simple and highly doubtful correlations between foreign aid, on the one hand, and a rising standard of living, social and political stability, democratic institutions and practices, and a peaceful foreign policy on the other. The simplicity of these correlations is so reassuring that the assumption of a simple and direct relationship between foreign aid and economic, social, and political progress is rarely questioned.

Thus, fundamental questions like the following were hardly ever asked explicitly: What are the social, political, and moral effects of foreign aid likely to be under different circumstances? Does successful foreign aid require a particular intellectual, political, and moral climate, or will the injection of capital and technological capability from the outside create this climate? To what extent, and under what conditions, is it possible for one nation to transform, through outside intervention, the economic and technological life of another nation? More specifically, in terms of the political objective of keeping the uncommitted nations uncommitted, how is one to create that positive relationship in the mind of the recipient between the aid and its beneficial results, on the one hand, and the political philosophy, system, and objectives of the giver, on the other? As long as the recipient disapproves of the politics of the giver, the political effects of the aid are lost. These effects are similarly lost as long as the recipient remains unconvinced that the aid received is but a natural manifestation of the politics of the giver. Foreign aid, then, remains politically ineffective as long as the recipient says either, "Aid is good, but the politics of the giver are bad," or "Aid is good, but the politics of the giver have nothing to do with it."

Answers to questions such as these require policies of extraordinary subtlety and intricacy. The simple correlation between foreign aid and what the United States desires in the uncommitted nations could not provide the answers. That correlation is a projection of the domestic experience of America onto the international scene. Capital formation and investment and technological innovation created the wealth and prosperity of America, and so it was assumed that the export of American capital and technology into the underdeveloped nations would bring forth similar results there. The similarity between this and the Wilsonian expectation is striking. Wilson wanted to bring the peace and order of America to the rest of the world by exporting its democratic institutions. His contemporary heirs wanted to bring the wealth and prosperity of America to the rest of the world through the export of American capital and technology. Yet, the failure of the Wilsonian experiment was quick and drastically revealed; the failure of foreign aid, simplistically conceived, has been less obvious, albeit no less drastic.

However, even if the United States had developed a well-planned philosophy of foreign aid, its application would have come up against the same equalitarian principle which has frustrated the alliance policy of the United States. While the application of this principle to the alliance policy was not warranted by the objective situation, foreign aid has confronted the United States with a real dilemma. If you apply the equalitarian principle, expressed in the slogan "No strings attached," to foreign aid, you put yourself at the mercy of unenlightened or corrupt governments which might misuse foreign aid through incompetence or by design. If, on the other hand, you assume responsibility for the way your aid is used, you feed the nationalistic suspicion of "imperialist" motives. By choosing the former method, the United States gave the recipient governments at least a potential leverage against itself, similar to that its allies enjoy. This leverage is increased by the competitive participation of the Soviet Union in foreign aid, which allows the recipient governments to play one superpower against the other. Yet, while the Soviet Union used foreign aid as an integral part of its political policy, seeking the expansion of its influence either directly or through communist movements, the United States was at a disadvantage in trying to serve consistently either its own purpose or the purposes of the underdeveloped nations.

The policy of liberation

The weakness of the foreign policies of the United States, as conducted in the Fifties, came to a head in the total failure of its policies toward the satellites of the Soviet Union. The character of that failure suggests, as we shall see, the nature of the remedy. The inspiration from which the policies towards the satellites are derived is within the American tradition of seeking the expansion of the area of freedom. These policies continue the anti-imperialistic tradition of America, yet with one significant difference. The anti-imperialistic tradition has operated on two levels, the general one of revulsion against the normal practices of European power politics, and the specific one of revulsion against a particular case of oppression of one nation by another. The political consequences of the first type were the abstention and isolationism of the Farewell Address. The second type had almost no political consequence at all, but led to emotional commitment to what appeared to be the cause of freedom and humanitarian assistance to its suffering supporters. Thus, the American anti-imperialism of the nineteenth century favored the national movements of Europe against monarchical enemies and opposed certain colonial ventures of European nations, and the American anti-imperialism of the early twentieth century took its stand against Imperial and Nazi Germany and against Tsarist and Soviet Russia, and both received the fighters in the lost causes of freedom as citizens.

The new anti-imperialism, aimed at the conquests of the Soviet Union, obviously partook of these characteristics, but possessed a quality its predecessors lacked. It became an integral and crucial part of the foreign policy of the United States. The traditional anti-imperialism of America was without a political objective, either by virtue of its very nature or else because the radius of an active American foreign policy was limited to the Western Hemisphere. The new anti-imperialism could no longer afford to condemn the suppression of liberty from afar and limit its tribute to freedom to charitable deeds. Committed to the containment of communism, to the preservation of national freedom wherever it was threatened by Soviet Russia imperialism, the United States could reconcile itself to the loss of national freedom only if it altogether ceased being anti-imperialistic. If it wanted to remain faithful to its anti-imperialist tradition, it would have had to embark upon positive political and military policies on behalf of both the preservation and the expansion of national freedom. Yet at this point, when it came to adapting the traditional attitude of America to the opportunities and limitations of the contemporary world, American foreign policy failed.

The traditional American goal of expanding the area of freedom encountered a new opportunity and a new limitation in the foreign policy of the United States. It did not come to terms with either. Of this failure, the policy of liberation and the explicit inaction on the occasion of the Hungarian revolution of 1956 have been the outward manifestations. The policy of liberation manifested unconcern with the limitations; inaction on the occasion of the Hungarian revolution demonstrated unawareness of the opportunities.

The policy of liberation must be seen as a logical extension of the policy of containment and as the positive implementation of the American refusal to recognize the Soviet Union's European conquests. Stalin and his successors attempted to liquidate the Cold War by concluding an agreement with the United States which divided Europe into two spheres of influence, with the European conquests of the Soviet Union recognized as definite and legitimate. The United States has consistently refused to consider even the possibility of such an agreement. The United States could let it go at that, satisfied with containing Russian power within the limits reached in 1945, and that is essentially what it did up to the beginning of 1953. The impulse to go beyond this negative policy of containment and nonrecognition, and to give that policy a positive implementation, stems from the traditional American purpose of expanding the area of freedom. But once America yielded to that impulse, it was up against the problem of what kind of positive policy should be pursued.

In accordance with its general conception of foreign policy, the United States conceived of liberation essentially in military terms, as the evacuation of Eastern Europe by the Red Army. Such evacuation could be brought about only through military pressure which carried the risk of war. As the London *Economist* put it on August 30, 1952, when the policy of liberation was first proclaimed: "Unhappily 'liberation' applied to Eastern Europe —and Asia—means either the risk of war or it means nothing. . . . 'Liberation' entails no risk of war only when it means nothing." Since liberation was to be achieved without resort to war, according to repeated official statements, it was, as conceived by American policy, incapable of achievement.

Thus, what pretended to be a new dynamic policy turned out to be no policy at all, nothing more than a verbal commitment incapable of implementation by action. However, that commitment was taken as a threat by the Soviet Union and as a promise by the satellites. Instead of contributing anything to the liberation of the satellites, it served as a pretext for the Soviet Union to maintain its military rule of Eastern Europe, and as an incentive for the satellites to entertain illusions about what the United States might do, only to be disillusioned with American policy and reconciled to their fate when no action was forthcoming. The policy of liberation not only did not liberate, it actually strengthened the forces opposed and detrimental to liberty.

The Hungarian revolution of 1956 provided the ultimate test of the self-defeating unreality of the policy of liberation. For here the United States was faced, not with the impossible task of liberating without resort to war, but with the opportunity to support a liberation already achieved. By remaining inactive under these most favorable circumstances, it demonstrated that there was no such thing as a policy of liberation, but only verbal pronouncements designed to give the appearance that there was one. The United States declared from the outset, through its most authoritative spokesman, the President, that it would abstain from active interference. While it is a moot question as to how much the United States could have done, it is obvious, in view of the since-revealed dissension within the Soviet government over the use of force, that it could have done more than nothing.

THE REVOLUTION IN THE INTERNATIONAL ENVIRONMENT

These weaknesses, inherent in the foreign policy of the United States as it developed during the Fifties, were aggravated by fundamental changes in the international environment to which American foreign policy did not adapt itself. At the end of the period, the international scene was different in four fundamental respects from what it had been at its beginning.

First of all, the balance of military power had changed radically. In the aftermath of the Second World War, the United States was unquestionably the most powerful nation on earth. Under the umbrella of its monopoly of atomic weapons, the United States formed the European alliance, implementing the policy of containment. The monopoly provided a virtually absolute protection for the nations which felt themselves threatened by communist aggression. This protection has disappeared. It has been replaced by a stalemate, or by what Sir Winston Churchill has called a "balance of terror." The United States is able to destroy the Soviet Union and the Soviet Union is able to destroy the United States in an all-out war.

In view of this stark and simple situation, an alliance with the United States is no longer regarded as an unmixed blessing. It still provides a certain protection, but it also implies a certain liability. Can the United States be relied upon to come to the aid of an ally at the risk of its own destruction? And wouldn't such aid, even if provided, seal the doom of the ally, since it would probably be in the nature of nuclear war to be countered in kind by the enemy? The allies of the United States are raising questions such as these, and they answer them by seeking safety in greater independence from the United States. Either they try to develop foreign and military policies of their own, and especially try to get nuclear weapons, or else they tend to move away from the United States into a neutral or at least a more detached position.

The second great transformation in the political world during the Fifties is the restoration of the economic and, to a certain extent, the political health of most of the nations of Western Europe. At the beginning of the Fifties, the alliance with the United States was, for nations such as Italy, France, and Great Britain, a matter not of choice but of life and death. Without the economic, political, and military support of the United States, those nations might not have survived as independent national entities and would have been in great danger of being subverted by communism or swallowed up by the Soviet Union. Today, this dependence on the United States has to a great extent disappeared, especially in the economic area. It has become rather ineffective in the political area, and its military ambivalence has become obvious.

Furthermore, and most importantly, the foreign policy of the Soviet Union has fundamentally changed. In the years immediately following the Second World War, the greatest asset of United States foreign policy was the foreign policy of Stalin. Whenever there was a slackening in the Western effort or a weakening of the alliance system, Stalin would make a drastic move which demonstrated how necessary the American connection was for survival.

Khrushchev's foreign policy, during the Fifties, was of an entirely different nature. His was not a policy of direct military aggression or of direct military threats. Even the threat against the Western presence in Berlin, uttered for the first time in November, 1958, and repeated many times since, was quite different from the threats Stalin would have uttered or would have followed up by action, as in the case of the Berlin blockade in 1948. Khrushchev's policies aimed not so much at the conquest of territories by diplomatic pressure or military threats as at the subversion of the whole non-communist world through the impact of Soviet power and technological and economic accomplishments. This is a much more insidious, a much subtler way of undermining the position of the United States and of the Western world.

To these three fundamental changes must be added a fourth: the rise of the former colonial nations in Africa and Asia. These enormous masses of land and populations no longer belong to any of the power blocs. They are no longer under the control of any of the great powers. But they will, in all likelihood, have to seek the support of stronger nations and fashion their political, economic, and social lives in the image of one of the great political and social systems competing for their allegiance. Hence, they have become the great prize in the struggle between East and West. Whoever can attract the loyalties of these uncommitted nations and impress them with the excellence and superiority of his form of government, of his social and economic system, will in all probability win the struggle for the world. And Khrushchev proclaimed that the Soviet Union, through the attractiveness and achievements of communism, would conquer the minds of the uncommitted peoples and thereby inherit the earth.

These four fundamental changes in the international environment imposed on the United States the task of rethinking and refashioning American foreign policy in five major areas: the relations with the allies; the relations with the uncommitted nations; the relation between domestic politics and foreign policy; the relations with the communist bloc; and, finally, the supranational control of nuclear power.

The several alliances of which the United States is a member owe their existence, as we have seen, to two different factors: the need our European allies, as well as our former enemies, found, after the Second World War, to have American economic, military, and political support; and the objective of the United States to contain, by military means, the Soviet Union throughout the world and Communist China in the Middle East and Asia. During the Fifties, the foundations for the first type of alliance changed radically; the foundations for the second type were weak from the very outset.

The economic recovery of the nations of Western Europe and the former enemies made them less dependent on American support than they once had been. As a consequence, they have, at times, been able to pursue their own narrower interests regardless of the common interests of the alliance. The United States must find a new foundation for these alliances. France is the principal case in point. These alliances were primarily conceived in military terms. They must now be given an economic, political, and cultural content as well.

The transformation of the Cold War into what is now called "competitive coexistence" has revealed the essential unsoundness of the policy of military containment as extended to Asia and the Middle East. The conflict between East and West has taken on the aspects of a struggle for the minds of men, especially in the uncommitted nations of Asia, Africa, and Latin America: a struggle to be fought with the weapons of prestige, subversion, political pressure, foreign aid, and foreign trade. Military alliances—in any contest for men's minds—are likely to be, at best, of minor importance and, at worst, a political handicap.

If the United States is to wage this struggle for the minds of men with any chance of success, it must devise a new grand strategy. Two fundamental reforms are called for: the integration of all the factors involved in the struggle—military, political, economic—for the single purpose of maintaining and expanding the influence of the noncommunist world; and the adaptation of these various factors to the local conditions prevailing in any country. The United States must develop, and act on, a coherent philosophy of foreign aid and foreign trade.

The uncommitted nations also confront the United States with a problem in political organization. Many of the new nations owe their existence to mere accidents of colonial history, and are therefore not likely to become viable political, economic, and military units within the boundaries they now occupy. They present a standing invitation for a new imperialism to establish a new order where the old colonial order has disappeared, or they are threatened with an anarchy which might well involve the rest of the world. This enormously complex problem will test the political creativity and determination of the United States.

It is obvious that the domestic policies pursued by the United States, especially in the field of race relations, are bound to have a direct influence upon its ability to wage the struggle for the minds of men. The United States needs to be fully aware of this influence in its conduct of domestic policies. Where it cannot entirely control these policies, it must at least give moral support to the positions which conform most closely to the best traditions of America. Throughout the better part of American history, the foreign policy of the United States drew strength and its attractiveness to other nations from the character of its domestic politics. The American experiment in government and social

organization was intended, from the very outset, not only for America but for the world. It was meant as a model for other nations to emulate. The United States must restore that meaning.

The outcome of these new policies will depend upon the kind of relations the United States is able to establish with the communist world. If these relations should deteriorate further, the very success of the new policies might turn out to be self-defeating, bringing closer the probability of a third world war fought with nuclear weapons. Thus, the United States must accomplish the supreme task of statesmanship—it must successfully wage the competitive struggle with the communist world, without at the same time increasing the risk of war.

The first condition for minimizing that risk is the stabilization of the contested territorial frontiers. The second condition is the maintenance of the Western deterrent to nuclear war. The risk of war will diminish only in the measure that the points of conflict which might ignite a war can be reduced, at the same time that deterrence to the starting of a war is maintained. The third condition is the abatement of the nuclear armaments race through arms control, that is, the stabilization of nuclear arms and delivery systems sufficient to maintain the balance.

Finally, even if the United States should be successful in the pursuit of all these policies, the United States and the world will still be confronted with the mortal danger of the spread of atomic weapons to an indefinite number of nations. This danger the United States can cope with only in cooperation with the other great nations of the world. The prospect of such a spread is bound to become a reality unless the present trend is reversed; if the trend continues, it is likely to cause unprecedented anarchy which will finally go beyond the control of the big powers. To bring nuclear weapons under supra-national control is the overriding task of the age. History is likely to judge the United States by its approach to this task and its success in accomplishing it.

THE CONDUCT AND FORMATION OF AMERICAN FOREIGN POLICY

The character of a foreign policy conducted in a democracy is not determined by the requirements of sound foreign policy alone. It is also characterized by the willingness of the domestic political forces, whose approval is either required by the Constitution or necessary for political reasons, to support the foreign policies favored by the executive branch of the government. To secure that support becomes a prerequisite for the conduct of foreign policy. While it is certainly an exaggeration to say, as an eminent observer of American foreign policy has done, that 90 per cent of American foreign policy consists of domestic politics, it is no less certain that an American administration which fails to secure domestic political support for its foreign policies will find itself incapable of pursuing those policies effectively.

To secure support is bound to be a difficult task, for there exists an inevitable incompatibility between the requirements of good foreign policy and the preferences of a democratically controlled public opinion. As de Tocqueville wrote, with special reference to the United States,

Foreign politics demand scarcely any of those qualities which are peculiar to a democracy; they require, on the contrary, the perfect use of almost all those in which it is deficient . . . a democracy can only with great difficulties regulate the details of an important undertaking, persevere in a fixed design, and work out its execution in spite of serious obstacles. It cannot combine its measures with secrecy or await their consequences with patience.

The history of foreign policy conducted under democratic conditions illustrates the truth of these observations. The conditions under which popular support can be obtained for a foreign policy are not necessarily identical with the conditions under which a foreign policy can be successfully pursued. Whenever these two sets of conditions diverge, those responsible for the conduct of foreign policy are confronted with a tragic choice. Either they must sacrifice what they consider good policy on the altar of public opinion, or they must, by devious means, gain popular support for policies whose true nature is concealed from the public.

Nations with a long experience in the conduct of foreign policy and a vivid awareness of its vital importance, such as Great Britain, have developed constitutional devices and political practices which tend to minimize the dangers to the vital interests of the nation inherent in the democratic conduct of foreign policy. Parliamentary democracy, especially under the conditions of the two-party system, provides in the Cabinet a mechanism which ensures the support, by the majority of the elected representatives of the people, of the foreign policies pursued. The collective parliamentary responsibility of the Cabinet compels the government to speak in foreign affairs with one voice, so that there can be no doubt, either at home or abroad, about the government's foreign policy at a particular moment.

It is the peculiar quality of the conduct of foreign policy in the United

States that it maximizes the weaknesses inherent in the formulation and execution of foreign policy under democratic conditions, and that it aggravates these inherent weaknesses by unique constitutional devices and political practices.

The method of conducting foreign policy is determined by four general characteristics of the American Constitution: (*a*) its lack of definition in assigning functions to the different agencies of the Government; (*b*) the separation of powers, which allows the executive and legislative branches of the government to hold office and, within certain limits, to pursue policies, without regard to the other; (*c*) the system of checks and balances, which, within certain limits, makes it possible for one branch of the government to prevent another branch from pursuing its policies; and (*d*) the requirement that, under certain conditions, measures can be taken by neither branch alone, but only through the concerted action of both.

The Constitution nowhere makes clear with whom the ultimate responsibility for the conduct of foreign policy rests. It assigns to the President alone certain specific functions, such as the reception of foreign diplomatic representatives; it assigns others, such as the regulation of foreign commerce and the declaration of war, to Congress alone; it provides for still others, such as the conclusion of treaties, which the President can discharge only in cooperation with the Senate. Apart from these specific grants, the Constitution limits itself to an over-all distribution of powers between the President and Congress by vesting in the former the executive power and making him Commander-in-Chief of the armed forces, and by vesting all legislative powers and the power of appropriations in Congress.

To locate, with the guidance of these "great generalities" and specific instances, the ultimate authority for the conduct of foreign policy is a task for constitutional theory and political practice. Jefferson's dictum that "The transaction of business with foreign nations is executive altogether" has claimed that ultimate authority for the President. On the other side of the argument, there is a chorus of voices which claim for the Senate, if not for both Houses of Congress, at least an equal share in the conduct of foreign policy. Constitutional theologies have covered these two positions with clusters of legalistic cobwebs, and have left the issue where the Constitution has left it—undecided. For, in view of the affirmative powers granted by the Constitution to the President and Congress, the issue cannot be decided through constitutional interpretation. By giving some powers to the President, some to the Senate, some to Congress, and by remaining silent on the ultimate responsibility for the conduct of foreign policy, the Constitution, in the words of Professor Corwin, an eminent expounder of its law, "is an invitation to struggle for the privilege of directing American foreign policy." Just as the question of the location of sovereignty in the United States, an issue similarly held in abeyance by the Constitution, had to be answered by a civil war, so the issue of the ultimate responsibility for the conduct of American foreign policy is being decided individually each time it arises, in a series of running battles between the Senate or the two Houses of Congress, on one side, and the executive branch, on the other. Each side uses the weapons provided by the Constitution as well as the extra-constitutional ones which have grown in its shadow.

The political relations between the President and Congress are determined by the fact that the President can hardly ever be certain of the support of a majority of both Houses of Congress for his policies. This is obviously so when the President and the majority of Congress belong to different parties, but even if the President is a member of the majority party, a minority of his own party will regularly vote against the policies with which he is identified. This defection is somewhat offset by a minority of the opposition party generally voting in favor of the President's policies. Yet the traditional jealousy with which any Congress guards its prerogatives against any President tends to give the edge to the hostile minority of the President's party. The President operates under the perpetual threat that his policies will be disavowed by a bipartisan majority of Congress.

To make such a threat come true, Congress has at its command legislation, appropriations, and resolutions. To the same end, the Senate alone has power over treaties and over the appointment of diplomatic representatives and the high officials of the executive branch. This power of the Senate over appointments, by virtue of Article II, Section 2, of the Constitution, is a potential threat in the field of foreign policy rather than an active weapon. The Senate has sometimes refused to confirm individuals nominated by the President to ambassadorial positions or high positions in the Department of State, but it has not used that power for the purpose of making it impossible for the President to pursue a certain foreign policy.

The weapon of legislation can be used in two different ways. Whenever a foreign policy needs to be implemented by legislation, Congress can modify, emasculate, or negate the foreign policy pursued by the executive branch. Congress can also take the initiative and, as in the case of the neutrality legislation of the Thirties and the successive Immigration Acts, limit the President's freedom of action through restrictive statutory provisions.

The weapon of appropriations can be wielded in two different ways. Congress can either withhold, in part or in whole, appropriations necessary to the execution of a certain foreign policy, and thus cripple that policy or make its execution altogether impossible. The customary congressional changes in appropriations for the Department of State, for foreign aid, and for information policies illustrate the potentialities of this weapon. The financial requirements of present American foreign policy make it the most potent of all the weapons at the disposal of Congress. Or Congress can attach a rider to an appropriation bill, providing expenditures for purposes not contemplated by the executive branch. In that case, the President must either reject the appropriation *in toto* and forego the policy for which the appropriation was to be used, or he must accept the appropriation *in toto* and, against his better judgment, execute a policy imposed upon him by Congress. Thus Congress, in 1948, earmarked, in the bill providing aid to Western Europe, an appropriation for aid to China, a rider which the President had to accept since he did not want to jeopardize the European aid program.

Through resolutions, either joint or by one of the Houses, Congress expresses its preference for certain policies. While such expression of preference has no legally binding effect upon the executive branch, it indicates what kind of foreign policies Congress is likely to approve when called upon to act by way of legislation or appropriation. The Vandenberg Resolution of 11th June, 1948, for instance, calling for the conclusion of regional compacts for the purpose of mutual defense, influenced the form in which the North Atlantic Treaty was submitted to the Senate.

Public opinion has come to regard the constitutional provision which requires approval of two-thirds of the Senate for treaties negotiated by the President as the main weapon by which one-third of the Senate members, plus one, can veto the foreign policies of the executive branch which have taken the form of international treaties. In view of the relations between majority and minority party mentioned above, and given a politically controversial issue calling for a partisan stand, the chances of a treaty being approved by two-thirds of the Senate are slim. "A treaty entering the Senate," wrote Secretary of State Hay summing up his bitter experience, "is like a bull going into the arena. No one can say just how and when the final blow will fall. But one thing is certain —it will never leave the arena alive." The death blows which the Senate dealt, in the interwar years, to presidential policies of international cooperation are remembered, for whatever different reasons, by President and Senate. Their memory has exerted a powerful influence toward avoiding conflict situations and securing, in advance, bipartisan support for the foreign policies to be pursued by the executive branch.

The general power of Congress in the field of foreign affairs has been met by the President with the general weapon put at his disposal by his position as Chief Executive and Commander-in-Chief. The President has a natural eminence in the conduct of foreign affairs from which constitutional arrangements and political practices can detract, but which they cannot obliterate. His powers in this field are, in the words of the Supreme Court, "delicate, plenary, and exclusive." Short of the expenditure of money, the binding conclusion of treaties, and the declaration of war, the President can almost do as he pleases in formulating and executing foreign policies. He can, without reference to any other agency of government, make a public declaration of policy, such as the Monroe or Truman Doctrines. He can recognize or refuse to recognize a foreign government, as successive Presidents did with respect to the government of the Soviet Union. He can give advice, make promises, and enter into informal commitments as he sees fit. He can send the armed forces of the United States anywhere in the world and can commit them to hostile acts short of war. In sum, he can narrow the freedom of choice which constitutionally lies with Congress to such an extent as to eliminate it for all practical purposes. If, for instance, the President had wanted to use armed force during the Berlin crisis of 1948, or in response to the military operations of China in the Straits of Taiwan during the late Fifties, he could have done so on his own responsibility, and thus he could have committed Congress to a declaration of war regardless of the latter's preferences. The course of American policy toward Germany and Japan during the initial phase of the Second World War was determined primarily by presidential action, and it was left to Congress to ratify or, at worst, to retard and weaken the consummation of that course.

The ascendancy of the President over Congress in the determination of American foreign policy is dramatically revealed by the extent to which the President has been able to circumvent Senate participation by substituting executive agreements, not requiring legislative approval, for formal treaties. The executive agreement has recently become the normal medium for international compacts. Most of the great political understandings of the war years, from the destroyer deal to Potsdam, were concluded by the President alone, in the form of executive agreements. In 1939, 10 treaties were concluded by the United States as opposed to 26 executive agreements. The corresponding figures for the following years are eloquent: 1940, 12 and 20, respectively; 1941, 15 and 39; 1942, 6 and 52; 1943, 4 and 71; 1944, 1 and 74; 1945, 6 and 54. They are even more eloquent for the decade starting in 1950: 1950, 12 and 59; 1951, 13 and 200; 1952, 20 and 356; 1953, 12 and 128; 1954, 9 and 251; 1955, 23 and 291; 1956, 10 and 241; 1957, 19 and 227; 1958, 6 and 178; 1959, 13 and 227.

The relations between President and Congress, however, must be conceived not only in terms of actual or potential conflict, but also in terms of cooperation. For while the power of the President is pre-eminent in starting the course of American foreign policy, Congress's potential for obstruction remains, and the dependence of the Executive upon congressional consent has increased with the expanding financial requirements of American foreign policy. Since the end of the Second World War, successive Presidents and Secretaries of State have developed a system of cooperation with Congress in the formulation and execution of foreign policy. Its main purpose is the avoidance of the situation, which was the undoing of Wilson, in which the minority party opposes presidential policies primarily because they are the President's and his party's policies. It has become the established practice of the executive branch to brief, and consult with, the foreign policy experts of the two parties, especially those of the Senate, in advance

of major steps to be taken, to secure their consent, and to take their advice into account. This practive has worked with different results in different fields of American foreign policy. At times, the executive branch has not dared to take a step for fear of Congressional disapproval and, on other occasions, Congress has not dared to oppose certain policies proposed or initiated by the executive branch for fear it be accused of partisan obstruction. The over-all result, however, has been the formation of a coalition, composed of the majority of the two parties, in support of the President's foreign policy.

Bipartisanship, as originally conceived at the end of the Second World War, carried the negative implication that a foreign policy ought not to be opposed by one party solely because the President and the Secretary of State, who belonged to the other party, were carrying it out. In positive terms, bipartisanship implied that the opposition party should support sound foreign policies and oppose unsound ones, regardless of the party affiliation of those carrying them out. Conceived in these terms, bipartisanship recognized the elementary fact that the consequences of foreign policy are not limited, as are those of many domestic ones, to a particular segment of the population identified with one or the other party, but affect the whole nation for generations to come. Bipartisanship drew from this fact the sound and indispensable conclusion that party strife for its own sake must stop at the point where the whole nation meets other nations in defense of its interests and its very existence.

Thus far, we have referred to the President and the executive branch in their relations with Congress and foreign powers as though the President and the executive branch were one single entity pursuing one single policy. Nothing could be farther from the truth. It is true that the President, as chief executive and Commander-in-Chief, has the constitutional power to impose his own conception of most foreign affairs upon the executive and military departments. In reality, however, even so strong and astute a President as Franklin D. Roosevelt was unable to assume full control even of the State Department, the constitutional executor of his foreign policies.

The reason for this anomaly must be sought in two factors. One is the absence of a Cabinet which could integrate the policies of the different executive departments in the field of foreign policy, the American Cabinet being an informal advisory body. The other factor is the frequent inability of the President to definitely resolve major dissensions between executive departments or to meet head-on resistance to his policies on the part of an executive department, without risking inopportune conflicts with Congress. Congress is always ready to take advantage of open dissensions within that branch. President Roosevelt, rather than taking on a reluctant State Department, entrusted the execution of his more delicate and controversial foreign policies to special representatives, operating directly from the White House, or created special agencies for the performance of special functions. Sometimes Roosevelt pursued foreign policies of his own without even the knowledge of the State Department. The classic example is Roosevelt's approval, in June, 1944, of the division of the Balkans into British and Russian spheres of influence, while for almost three weeks afterwards the State Department continued to pursue a policy of opposition to the Anglo-Russian agreement. Sometimes, as with regard to certain phases of Middle Eastern policy, the State Department emerges victorious from the struggle with the President.

The problem of unity of action arises not only between the President and the executive departments, but also, and especially when strong leadership from the White House is lacking, among the executive departments themselves, and even within them. Washington is the scene of continuous inter-office feuds, sometimes growing from real differences of policy, more often the result of a mere struggle for power. The Hoover Commission on Organization of the Executive Branch of the Government counted about forty-five executive agencies, aside from the State Department, which are concerned with some phase of foreign policy. While most of them deal only with minor matters, some have exerted an important influence upon the conduct of American foreign policy. Among them, the military establishment is outstanding. The main vehicle for its influence is the National Security Council, composed of the President, the Vice-President, the Secretaries of State and Defense, and the director of the Office of Civil and Defense Mobilization, as statutory members. Its purpose is "to advise the President" in those fields of policy "relating to the national security." In a period of Cold War, the whole field of foreign policy becomes the proper object of the Council's advice. The National Security Council has become the key agency through which the views of the executive departments are filtered. Through the daily reports of its executive secretary it exerts a potent influence upon the President's mind.

The task of coordinating American foreign policy under the President's direction does not end with the settlement of disputes between executive departments. It extends to the executive departments themselves and their representation abroad. Certain ambassadors, such as Dodd in Berlin and Kennedy in London, in the Thirties, and Hayes in Madrid, during the Second World War, were able for months to pursue foreign policies at variance with the policies of the State Department, if not the President. Generals Clay in Germany and MacArthur in Japan, during the period immediately following the Second World War, in large measure formulated and executed their own policies which the executive departments concerned could do little else but ratify.

The success of the American way of conducting foreign affairs is due to that elusive factor which gives direction and unity to the American political system on all levels—public opinion. The Constitution makes public opinion the arbiter of American policy by calling upon the American voter to pass judgment on the President and his party every four years, and on all members of the House of Representatives and one-third of the membership of the Senate every other year. The American people live perpetually in a state of pre-election or election campaigns. Presidential and Congressional policies are always fashioned in anticipation of what the voter seems likely to approve. The President, as the most exalted mouthpiece of the national will and the initiator of foreign policies, will test the state of public opinion by submitting new policies in the tentative form of public addresses and messages to Congress. These new policies will then be pursued or shelved, according to the reaction of the public. Democratic control of American foreign policy will depend largely on the correctness of the President's estimate of the willingness of public opinion to support his policies, and on his ability to marshal public opinion to that support. It is here that another, perhaps fundamental, weakness of the conduct of American foreign policy becomes apparent.

The state of American public opinion is ascertained by a special branch of the State Department and by the intuitive estimates of individuals through the media of press, radio, public opinion polls, Congress, and private communications. Yet these paint a distorted picture of the actual state of the American mind. While they may point with approximate accuracy to its lack of information, they give only a hint of its susceptibility to strong and wise leadership, derived from its native intelligence and moral reserves. The President and State Department seem to be taking at face value the picture conveyed, by the mouthpieces of public opinion, of the moral and intellectual qualities of the American people. In particular, fear of what Congress might do to their policies has become a veritable obsession with many members of the executive department, a fear derived from a misjudgment of the powers of Congress as an organ of public opinion.

That this fear is not justified by the actual control of Congress over the conduct of foreign affairs has already been pointed out. That the temper of Congress, and especially of the Senate, is not necessarily representative of public opinion is evident from a consideration of the four factors which limit the representative function of Congress: the disproportionate influence of rural over urban representatives by virtue of the apportionment of Congressional districts favoring the former; the disproportionate influence of the less populous states by virtue of the representation of all states, regardless of population, by two Senators; the disproportionate influence, on members of Congress, of the spokesmen of special interest groups; and finally, the limited representative character of members of Congress from a number of Southern states by virtue of the limitation of the franchise to a small fraction of the population.

The mistaken identification of press, radio, polls, and Congress with public opinion has had a distorting as well as a paralyzing influence on American foreign policy. It is here that the way American foreign policy is conducted has a direct bearing on the kind of foreign policy pursued by the United States. By equating what Congress will approve with what the American people might be willing to support, President and State Department underrate the intellectual and moral resources of the American people. In consequence, the foreign policies they present to public opinion for approval often stop short of what they deem necessary in the national interest.

This fear of public opinion, especially in the form of Congressional opinion, together with the ever-present risk of conflict between the Executive and Congress and within the executive branch itself, constitutes a very serious handicap for any fresh departure in foreign policy. If one wants to win the next election, if one wants to advance in the bureaucratic hierarchy, if one wants to retain and increase the powers of one's office, it is well to avoid conflict and to swim with the prevailing current. Yet any fresh departure in foreign policy means conflict—conflict with a half-informed and at times hysterical public opinion, conflict with a suspicious and reluctant Congress, conflict between and within

executive departments. Thus the foreign policy of the Cold War, with its emphasis on military preparations and its minimization of the traditional methods of diplomacy, is in a sense the foreign policy which the procedures of the American government are best fitted to conduct, although it is not the best fitted to preserve peace. The overriding concern for the preservation of peace makes imperative a change in the methods and, more important, in the spirit in which American foreign policy is conducted.

The factors which determine the conduct of American foreign policy cooperate as a brake upon executive initiative in foreign affairs. The evils which de Tocqueville finds in the democratic conduct of foreign affairs are compounded by the peculiarities of the American constitutional and political system. Not only does Congress act as a brake upon the executive branch, as it should, but so does public opinion, which ought to provide the fuel to carry American foreign policy forward. In that task of reestablishing public opinion as an independent positive force, the responsibility of the President is paramount.

The President must reassert his historic role as both the initiator of policy and the awakener of public opinion. Only a strong, wise, and shrewd President can marshal, to the support of wise policies, the strength and wisdom latent in that slumbering giant, American public opinion. Yet while it is true that great men have rarely been elected President of the United States, it is upon that greatness, which is the greatness of its people personified, that the United States has had to rely in the conduct of its foreign affairs. It is upon that greatness that Western civilization must rely for its survival.

SELECTED BIBLIOGRAPHY

Almond, Gabriel, The American People and Foreign Policy. New York: Harcourt, Brace & World, Inc., 1950.

Bemis, Samuel Flagg, American Foreign Policy and Diplomacy. New York: Holt, Rinehart & Winston, Inc., 1959.

Bloomfield, Lincoln P., The United Nations and U.S. Foreign Policy. Boston: Little, Brown & Company, 1960.

Gordon, Morton, and Kenneth N. Vines, Theory and Practice of American Foreign Policy. New York: Thomas Y. Crowell Company, 1955.

Halle, Louis, Dream and Reality: Aspects of American Foreign Policy. New York: Harper & Row, Publishers, Inc., 1959.

Jacobson, Harold K., America's Foreign Policy. New York: Random House, Inc., 1960.

Kennan, George F., American Diplomacy: 1900—1950. Chicago: University of Chicago Press, 1951.

———, Realities of American Foreign Policy. Princeton, N.J.: Princeton University Press, 1954.

Kissinger, Henry A., The Necessity for Choice. New York: Harper & Row, Publishers, Inc., 1960.

Lefever, Ernest, Ethics and United States Foreign Policy. New York: Meridian Books, 1957.

Morgenthau, Hans J., In Defense of the National Interest. New York: Alfred A. Knopf, Inc., 1951.

———, The Purpose of American Politics. New York: Alfred A. Knopf, Inc., 1960.

Osgood, Robert, Ideals and Self-Interest in America's Foreign Relations. Chicago: University of Chicago Press, 1953.

Perkins, Dexter, The American Approach to Foreign Policy. Cambridge, Mass.: Harvard University Press, 1952.

———, The Evolution of American Foreign Policy. New York: Oxford University Press, 1948.

Spanier, John W., American Foreign Policy Since World War II. New York: Frederick A. Praeger, Inc., 1960.

Stillman, Edmund, and William Pfaff, The New Politics: America and the End of the Post-War World. New York: Coward-McCann, Inc., 1961.

Wolfers, Arnold, ed., Alliance Policy in the Cold War. Baltimore: Johns Hopkins Press, 1959.

8

The Foreign Policy of MODERN JAPAN

ROBERT A. SCALAPINO

THE BACKGROUND OF JAPANESE FOREIGN POLICY

In geopolitical terms, there are some obvious reasons for making a rough comparison between Japan and Great Britain. Both are island societies lying within the Temperate Zone and close to a great continental mass. From earliest times, cultural interaction with the continent has been vital in shaping the character of each society; each has definitely been a part of the larger cultural orbit centering upon the continent. The sea, however, has been both a lane and a barrier, It has prevented recent invasions, enabling the development of a relatively homogeneous people who, despite many foreign adaptations, have retained a strong quality of uniqueness. Thus the encircling sea has been important to culture as well as to livelihood and defense. It has also been central to the historic dilemma over isolation versus continental involvement. This has been the basic foreign policy issue of both societies throughout their existence. And in recent eras, the interaction between internal and external pressures has been such as to present essentially the same answer to this question in both Japan and Great Britain. The growth of foreign pressures and the needs flowing from modernization—the scarcity of certain domestic resources combined with the rise of unused power—these and other factors led to regional and then global commitment. There is the temptation to add that, for both societies, there now exists the need to adjust to a permanent decline in world power. This analysis, of course, stresses the similarities, not the differences. The latter will become apparent as we turn now to the Japanese scene.

The Tokugawa era

The diplomacy of modern Japan opened in the mid-nineteenth century on a decidedly reluctant and confused note. Prior to Perry's arrival in 1853, the Japanese government had pursued a rigorous policy of isolation from the outside world for over two hundred years. It abandoned that policy only under strong pressure and with many misgivings. Isolation had first been imposed as a method of maintaining internal stability. When the Tokugawa family first came to power in Japan in 1606, the West had already been represented in the country for fifty years. Missionaries and traders had come in a steady stream, first from Portugal and Spain, then from the Netherlands and England. In the first years of the Tokugawa era, however, abuses were regularly reported to the government. Christian converts among the provincial nobility sought Western arms or alliances to fortify their position against the central regime. Western trade also became a means of augmenting local power, especially in the Kyushu area. Between 1616 and 1641, therefore, the Tokugawa government applied a series of anti-Christian and anti-trade edicts, leading up to a policy of almost total exclusion of the West. As is well known, only the Dutch were allowed to trade, very restrictedly, at Nagasaki. This, together with some limited relations with China and Korea, constituted Japanese foreign relations until the middle of the nineteenth century.

To draw up a balance sheet for the policy of isolation is not easy. It can be argued that, had Western intercourse been allowed to continue, Japan might well have been plunged into chaos and warfare, subsequently suffering the colonial fate of Southeast Asia. On the other hand, isolation clearly exacted its price. This is true not merely in terms of institutions and material developments, but also in the realm of emotions and attitudes. Isolation always breeds some of the symptoms of the garrison state—exclusivism, ethnocentrism, and mounting fear of the unknown, outside world. Most of these factors have been present in the Japanese scene, helping to shape the foreign policies and attitudes of that nation.

But in its time, isolation seemed to present only one major problem to Japan: How to maintain it? The expansion of the West in Asia was building up an intense pressure on Japan by the beginning of the nineteenth century. From the north, the Russians were moving forward on a broad front; Saghalien, the Kuriles, and even Hokkaido seemed threatened. Overtures for trade and coaling stations were rejected, but, at the same time, English intrusions began to take place in the southwest. These events were climaxed by news of the Opium War and repeated warnings from the Dutch. A debate began to shape up in Japan over fundamental policies.

This debate enabled Japanese nationalism to come forward, borne aloft by intellectuals from the agrarian-military class, and rooted in the primitive mythology of Shintoism. It was a movement with many facets: in part, dedicated to a restitution of imperial prerogatives and their defense against usurpation by Tokugawa; in part, an attack on the long-standing intellectual subservience to China and a simultaneous insistence on the unique character of Japan; and finally, a fierce assault on Western encroachment born out of an admixture of condescension and fear. All these factors were implied in the chief slogan of the era, *sonno-joi*, ("Revere the Emperor; oust the barbarians").

In the precise form just described, this movement did not enjoy complete success, but within it was carried the destiny of modern Japan. Its evolution followed, in some measure, the broad stages characteristic of the whole panorama of Asian-Western relations during this period, whether stated in political or intellectual terms: an initial stage, dominated by the total rejection of Westernism as barbarian, inferior, and completely incompatible with the Asian way of life; a second stage, in which Western science and technology —distilled into the unforgettable spectacle of Western power—were accorded a begrudging but nonetheless deeply felt respect, from which followed, after much soul-searching and confusion, a conscious majority decision to attain these sources of power while holding firmly to traditional values; and thence, inevitably, there developed that stage in which such a rigid and unrealistic dichotomy as that between technology and values had to be abandoned in favor of a more broadly based and integral synthesis, the exact ingredients and balance of which have depended on the background and convictions of each individual or group. It is within this general trend—its various exceptions, time lags and all-important local distinctions not to be ignored—that the major elements of foreign policy in modern Asia have taken shape. Japan has been no exception.

Even before the arrival of Perry, a small group of Japanese intellectuals had begun to question the policy of rigid isolation. Out of "Dutch learning" had come exciting ideas; and there grew, in some minds, the desirability of leading the commercial revolution rather than fighting it, and of using foreign trade to develop power. How else could the intriguing slogan, "A rich country; a powerful soldiery," be made a reality? How else could Japan defend herself against Western imperialism? But this group was a small minority in the early period. Even the Tokugawa government supported the opening of the country only as a temporary expedient until force could be garnered to throw out the West. In accepting Perry's demands, it decided to accede rather than risk war, but it gave as little ground as possible. With the initial step taken, however, it was impossible to retreat. Our first envoy, Townsend Harris, secured major liberalization of the Perry treaty in 1858, and similar rights were soon granted to other Western powers. From this date, Japan was truly opened up to Western commerce, and shortly the Tokugawa regime was even to seek assistance in developing arsenals and shipyards. "Support the government" and "Open the country" seemed to be slogans indissolubly linked.

Yet basically, Tokugawa policy remained more a product of pressure than of purpose, and this fact worked against the effectiveness of the policy. Beset by many problems, the regime grew steadily weaker; its capacity to act vigorously in any direction diminished. It satisfied neither the West, which complained of its inability to control unruly elements, nor the provincial samurai, who regarded the central government as arch-appeasers. As so often happens in history, the regime in power found, by tortuous means, the only feasible policy for national survival—in this case, the policy of opening the country—but in the course of reaching that policy it was itself fatally weakened, so that the actual execution and fulfillment of the policy had to pass to other hands.

Meiji foreign policy

In 1867, the Tokugawa regime was finally overthrown and the young Emperor Meiji was "restored" to the position of ruler, a position which the nationalists claimed the Tokugawa family had stolen. But real power in Meiji Japan gravitated into the hands of a small group of court officials and young leaders of the former military class. Their first major objective in foreign policy became that of removing the blemish of the unequal treaties, thereby attaining "complete independence" and equity with the Western powers. This task proved more difficult than they had expected; to accomplish it took nearly three decades. The Western powers, and particularly Great Britain, saw no reason to revise the treaties until Japanese standards came close to Western norms. The Japanese discovered that treaty revision was closely connected with basic reform in such fields as law and commerce. Thus the Iwakura mission, which left for the West so hopefully, in 1871, to persuade the powers to abandon the fixed tariffs and extraterritoriality, came home realizing that many internal developments had first to be undertaken.

Through the years, "modernization" progressed by means of German, French, British, and American models. Japanese economic and military power showed remarkable gains. Law and order prevailed despite occasional domestic crises. Finally, in 1894, after repeated failures, the first great objective of Japanese foreign policy was

obtained: agreements on basic treaty revisions were concluded with the West, all of which went into effect by 1899. As the nineteenth century ended, Japan had become the first nation of Asia to attain nearly complete parity with the West in legal terms. She had done so, in part, by satisfying the West that she was prepared to abide by the general rules of Western conduct, in part by the obvious facts of her internal progress and stability, and in part by her persistence and by certain clear signs that inequity toward Japan had reached a point of diminishing returns.

In the long struggle for treaty revision, latent elements of anti-foreignism occasionally came to the surface in various forms. Officials deemed obsequious to foreign powers, too pro-Western in their personal habits, or disrespectful of Japanese tradition ran grave risks. The history of these years is filled with records of assassination plots, some successful, against more moderate leaders. This was one price to be paid for cultivating a nationalist movement so assiduously, while scarcely daring to admit its excesses. But quite apart from its extremists, Japanese society as a whole tended to react in pendulum-like fashion to the West. In many respects, this was most natural. Periods of intensive borrowing and adaptation at both individual and group levels would be followed by noticeable retreats, with the primary targets being those excesses and absurdities most easily discernible, but with secondary attacks ranging over as broad a front as conditions would permit. On the one hand, Japan wanted to catch up with the West, be accepted as a "progressive" and "civilized" nation, and match the West in the areas of its own talents; in addition, a very genuine fondness for things Western was entertained by many Japanese great and small. But on the other hand, in this period of intensive nationalist indoctrination, and when the old anti-foreign traditions were not yet completely dead, the periodic cry of "excessive Europeanization!" or "un-Japanese practices!" could have telling effect. Moreover, if selected aspects of Westernism appealed to almost everyone, there was no widespread desire to abandon the main stream of Japanese culture or customs. These factors are not completely absent from contemporary Japan.

During the early Meiji era, there were strong overtones of defensiveness in Japanese policy and psychology. But the climate was also ripe for the rise of expansionism. Northeast Asia was largely a vacuum of power, tended haphazardly by the sick man of Asia, China, on the one hand, and the somewhat stronger, but essentially unstable and overcommitted Czarist forces, on the other. The Japanese mission seemed even clearer when it could be posed against the prospects of continuous Korean turmoil and the increasing threat of Western imperialism in this entire area. The theme of "Asia for the Asians" was first applied here, and sometimes by sincere men who had a vision of liberating other Asians from backwardness and Western domination, sharing with them the fruits of the new era in Japan. Private societies like the *Genyosha* (Black Current Society) and the *Kokuryukai* (Amur River Society) emerged, to exercise a great influence on Japanese foreign policy as influential pressure groups on behalf of a forceful continental policy with some such objectives in mind.

The ideology of expansionism was complex, and it knew no single form of expression. Groups like the Kokuryukai represented the past: they held firm to Japanese Confucianism, exalted

the primitive mythology that surrounded the Emperor-centered state, and were ultranationalists of a peculiarly medieval type. Yet, from another point of view, these same men were radicals associated with the new era. Wherever Asian nationalism took root, they were willing to give it nourishment, even when its ideological bases were greatly different from their own. To movements as widely disparate as those of Aguinaldo and Sun Yat-sen their assistance was given freely, and in this they often went beyond what the Japanese government was willing or prepared to do. Moreover, there was an element of radicalism in their approach to internal affairs as well, though its source might be largely traditional. Decrying the corruption, materialism, and excessive wealth of the new order, they demanded stringent internal reforms, some of which could be considered socialist in character. Thus were connected the themes of internal reform and external expansion as twins that were to have recurrent echoes throughout modern Japanese history.

The expansionists made their first major advance in the extraordinary decade between 1895 and 1905. Prior to that time, Japan had already added the Ryukyu islands and the Bonins to her domain, and made more secure her northern outpost, Hokkaido, by extensive colonization, but these were not spectacular ventures. By 1894, however, Japanese leadership was ready to challenge China, the weakest of her rivals, for influence on the Korean peninsula. For Japan, the war was unexpectedly short and easy, the first of a series of wars that "paid." The Western-style training and the nationalist indoctrination of her conscript military forces stood the initial test with flying colors. For China, defeat at the hands of a foe long regarded with some contempt, and treated at best as a pupil, was a profound shock. Demands for fundamental reform were now renewed, especially by younger intellectuals, and China was pushed toward accelerated change and revolution despite Manchu resistance.

In Japan, the implications of victory were fourfold. The beginnings of the Japanese Empire were laid, and the first tentative steps as a modern continental power were taken; China ceded Formosa, the Pescadores, and for a time, the Liaotung Peninsula, until the intervention of Russia, France, and Germany forced its return. And China was eliminated as a serious competitor in the Korean contest. Second, the war served as a further stimulus to industrial growth and general economic development. In an atmosphere of patriotic fervor, industrial investment and expansion were undertaken, with an emphasis upon heavy industry. The war boom brought prosperity; and afterwards, Japan received both indemnities and new China markets. Third, Japan enjoyed a sharp rise in prestige; most of the West looked on approvingly as their most apt pupil demonstrated her progress and valor, and it was in the aftermath of this victory that Japan began to be received in Western circles with some semblance of equality. Finally, these factors naturally accrued to the credit of the nationalist movement and to the prestige of the military class. The professional soldier, his samurai traditions now supplemented by Western science and by a new sense of mission not present in the Tokugawa era, promised to play a vital role in determining the future of his society.

In the aftermath of the Sino-Japanese War, a crucial decision had to be made. Japan was dedicated to increasing her ties with other Asian societies and providing leadership for them when possible. But to obtain these objectives and to have any basic security for herself, she needed a major alliance with a non-Asian power. This was still the world of the nineteenth century, when Europe collectively exercised a global influence, and when the unfolding of European power politics had a direct and immediate effect upon the non-European world. With the United States, Japan needed only to achieve some general agreement that would serve to neutralize potential conflict; indeed, she could expect no more, since American commitments toward the Pacific were still very limited, even after the annexation of the Philippines. The major powers in Asia were Great Britain and Russia, and the choice had to be made between these two.

Initially, top political circles in Japan were divided. Men like Ito and Inoue hoped for an agreement with Russia that would establish long-term peace in northeast Asia on the basis of satisfying mutual interests. Had such an agreement been reached, Japanese expansion might have been directed south at a much earlier point. An alliance with Great Britain, on the other hand, was recognized as a step toward stabilization in the south and fluidity in the northeast. Not merely in this respect, however, but in every respect, Japanese foreign policy was affected for nearly two decades by the Anglo-Japanese Alliance of 1902. This pact was widely heralded as insuring the peace of Asia. Within certain limits, perhaps it did contribute to that end. England, now finished with isolation, needed global alliances to protect her global interests. In the Western hemisphere, she cultivated the United States; in Asia, she directed her attentions to Japan. Once established, the alliance not only supported the *status quo* in South and Southeast

Asia; it also provided, within the limitations of British policy, some protection for China. In exchange, Japanese "special interests" in Northeast Asia were given recognition by the leading power of the world. Under such conditions, Japan could scarcely afford not to advance those interests.

Thus the first fruit of the Anglo-Japanese Alliance was not peace, but war. The question of Japanese or Russian hegemony over Northeast Asia, having its antecedents back as far as the seventeenth century, was now given over to military decision. As is well known, Japanese victory against a weary and distracted foe was swift. From the Portsmouth Treaty, Japan emerged in control of much of Northeast Asia, and became the first Asian world power. The fruits of defeat and victory were similar to those of the Sino-Japanese War: for the defeated —soul-searching, unrest, and revolution; for the victor—a new gain of territory and fame. Clear title was obtained to the Kuriles, and southern Saghalien was added to the Empire; control over Korea could no longer be challenged, although outright annexation did not come until 1910; the Manchurian-Mongolian area also fell within the shadow of expanding Japanese power, a situation placing new pressure upon China. Again, Japanese industry had enjoyed great expansion as a part of the war effort, with some support from British and American loans. And once more Japanese nationalism had risen to the test. Only a handful of intellectual pacifists and radicals denounced the war; the great majority of the people had been deeply loyal to the cause of a greater Japan.

Some of the costs of victory could also be tabulated. One lay on the surface. Nationalist propaganda had been carried so far during the war that many patriots assumed that the peace would be dictated in Moscow, not realizing that a long war of attrition might be dangerous for a smaller country. Consequently, ugly riots broke out over the Portsmouth settlement, and the government had difficulty in restoring order. There were also deeper costs to be tallied. At home, militarism had grown stronger; the nonconformist had little protection, either in law or by the customs of his society. Abroad, Japan was moving into a new orbit of power and influence but as a result, she was now the object of new suspicions and fears, some of them coming from such traditional supporters as the United States and Great Britain. Already it seemed likely that the critical test might be China.

In partial recompense, immediately ahead lay an era of unprecedented influence for Japan throughout Asia. It was an influence, moreover, derived from much more than mere military prowess. There is no doubt that most of the Asian world experienced a thrill at the Japanese victory over Russia, because it gave hope that the West could be beaten at its own game. But in the broader sense, Japan had become the symbol of the new Asia, a society that had successfully made the transition toward modernization by a process of synthesizing new ideas with its indigenous culture. Western science and progress had come alive within the Japanese context, and from this experience the rest of Asia had much to learn. The success of Japanese nationalism was also a tremendous stimulus, even though its precise ideological forms might not be acceptable elsewhere. Thus, as this era unfolded, Japan embarked upon an extensive career as model, tutor, and leader to eager Asians everywhere. Thousands of students flocked to Tokyo and other Japanese centers of learning and industry. The majority came from China, but every section of Asia was represented in some degree. Likewise, Asian nationalist movements found in Japan a haven and source of support. Their leaders in exile wrote polemics, collected funds, and sometimes obtained official encouragement. Tokyo became a revolutionary center for the Far East. Japan was riding the crest-tide of the developing "Asia for the Asians" movement.

Already, however, the central problem of Japanese foreign policy was becoming that of distinguishing the thin line between acceptable leadership in Asia and unwelcome domination. This problem could be put in various forms. Would Japanese national interests, in the long run, be made compatible with the Asian march toward independence? Would Japanese technological, economic, and political assistance to Asia rest on mutual benefit and truly cooperative bases, or were the methods and intentions such as to be readily labelled the underpinnings of Japanese imperialism? Did the Japanese have, or would they acquire, a fitting psychology for world leadership, or would their actions and attitudes be marked by ethnocentrism, insecurity, and brutality, thereby producing the hatred of those whom they wished to persuade? From these, the universal questions of twentieth-centry relations between advanced and lagging societies, Japanese foreign policy was by no means immune. The events of the first World War accentuated the issues.

The rise of Japan as a world power

The First World War was the third conflict within a generation to pay handsome and immediate dividends to the cause of Japanese prestige. It is not difficult to understand why later glorification of war by Japanese mili-

tarists produced such weak rebuttals from the society as a whole. Against the true desires of her ally, Japan entered the war "to fulfill her obligations under the Anglo-Japanese Alliance." She proceeded to capture, without difficulty, the German holdings on the Chinese Shantung Peninsula and in certain other parts of the Pacific. With this mission accomplished, she directed her energies to supplying the Asian markets cut off from their normal European contacts, and to providing her Western allies with the materials of war. These tasks required enormous industrial expansion. Indeed, it was at the close of this period that industrial productivity overtook agrarian productivity in yen value, and Japan could thereby claim to have moved into the ranks of industrial societies.

These trends, and complemental factors elsewhere, stimulated the drive for a more intensive policy toward China. The Manchu dynasty had fallen in the Revolution of 1911, but that revolution had failed in its major objectives. The Chinese scene was now marked by deep political cleavages, with rival factions striving desperately for both internal and external support. With Europe fully engaged in a bloody "civil war" and the United States prepared to go no further than a policy of moral suasion, Japan was soon heavily involved in Chinese politics. In 1915, the Japanese government demanded an extensive list of concessions from the Yuan Shih-k'ai regime, known as the "Twenty-one Demands." These were bitterly resisted by China, with some success. Japanese influence moved steadily forward by means of loans, advisers, and technical assistance, yet Japan soon acquired a new image in China: that of the chief enemy to Chinese nationalism. This era was climaxed by the historic May

Fourth Movement, now widely heralded by the Chinese Communists as their point of origin, a fervent demonstration against Versailles and against Japanese imperialism, spearheaded by Peking students and spreading throughout China in May, 1919.

At the close of the First World War, however, there could be no question that Japan had become a world power. She was the one major nation besides the United States to emerge from that war in a stronger position. Her pre-eminence in East Asia could not be doubted, despite the uncertain new force of Bolshevism. What were the ingredients of this power as the third decade of the twentieth century began?

One source of Japan's new power clearly was her evolving economic capacities. Perhaps the full secret of the Japanese industrial revolution still escapes us. However, in its essence, it seems to have involved the capacity of Japanese society to utilize selected elements of Western technique and experience, adapting these to its own culture and timing, without duplicating either the historical context of Western development or the precise set of Western drives, impulses, and incentives. Toward this process were contributed both the conscious purposes of state and the remarkable talents of a people who could display creativeness through integration and discipline. By 1920, Japan was already becoming the workshop of Asia. Her large factories, equipped in many cases with the most modern machinery, contributed such basic products as textiles in great volume; at the same time, an infinite variety of cheap manufactured items flowed out of the thousands of small and medium-sized plants that formed the base of the pyramidal Japanese industrial structure. Sharing with management the credit for such

productivity was the new Japanese labor force, abundant in numbers, cheap in cost, malleable, within limits, to its new task, moving out of the paddy fields into the factories, and acquiring sufficient know-how to give Japan an industrial character of which their fathers could not have dreamed.

But if manpower was a strength, it was also a problem—and one that now began to have an overt influence upon policy. Shortly after the First World War the Japanese population reached sixty million, more than double the figure at the beginning of the Meiji era. In many respects, the facilities existing within Japan to accommodate this great mass already seemed seriously strained, yet no levelling off was in sight. Increasing talk of *lebensraum* was inevitable. And if the population explosion had produced an abundance of cheap labor, by the same token it had placed certain limits on their consumption of goods, by throwing increased emphasis on foreign trade.

Other factors underlined Japanese dependence on foreign lands. The four main islands of Japan were not richly blessed with those natural resources vital to the industrial development of this period. Coal was present in sufficient quantities, except for high-grade coking coal, but the supply of iron ore was very limited, that of petroleum was negligible, and most essential metals were either absent or available only in modest quantity. Moreover, because of her limited land space and her location, Japan had to import many of the agricultural resources needed for industry; raw cotton and rubber were two prominent examples. The Japanese Empire of this period was helpful; from Formosa, Saghalien, and particularly from Korea, came important raw materials and foodstuffs. However, the more important supplies lay outside these areas, and the Manchuria-Mongolian region could be depicted in impressive economic terms.

To revert to our discussion of the sources of Japanese power, the military and political ingredients certainly cannot be overlooked. The Japanese navy had become the third largest in the world. Her army, in size, equipment, and training, dwarfed other forces readily available in this part of the world. There was no foreign force that seemed prepared to challenge a Japanese force that was fully committed in its own territories or in any part of East Asia. The size and equipment of the Japanese military was a testament to the lavish yearly budgetary contributions of the people; the morale of that force was a tribute to intensive indoctrination, sustained by the realities of great political power and prestige within the society.

Politics, in its broader reaches, was also a wellspring of power. For a society without totalitarian restraints (albeit one strongly paternal and authoritarian in character), Japan presented a picture of remarkable stability up to this point. Besides a handful of intellectual radicals, there were few who would dare (or think) to question *Kokutai*—"the national polity" or, more vaguely, "the Japanese way of life." Thus decisions of state, especially in the realm of foreign policy, could be taken on the assumption that they would be accepted with a maximum of conformity. The oracles of national interest could speak without fear of discordant responses, at least so long as they spoke within a consistently nationalist framework. What leadership group has not found some advantage in this?

Yet, as the postwar era began, there were indications that Japanese politics might be drastically affected by the democratic tide. The influence of Western liberalism, crowned by the global idealism of Woodrow Wilson, was strongly felt in Japanese intellectual and urban circles. Party government had assumed new importance, the office of Premier was held for the first time by a commoner, and the movement for universal suffrage was receiving widespread support. Japan's liberal era was opening, bringing with it some serious efforts to establish parliamentary and civilian supremacy in Japanese politics. Temporarily, at least, the long-entrenched bureaucrats and even the military had to move to the defensive. For the latter, the Siberian Expedition was the first clearly unrewarding venture abroad. And however strong the attempt to shift the blame to political timidity and lack of resolution at home, the army could not prevent some questions from arising in the public mind.

Hence, moderation in foreign policy was possible during this period. At the Washington Conference, Japan accepted the famous 5-5-3 naval ratio with the United States and Great Britain, despite the bitter protests of her naval authorities. She agreed to the return of the Shantung concessions. Withdrawal from Siberia was slowly and cautiously undertaken. One Cabinet even had the audacity to cut the military budget sharply, and there were some discussions (although no action) on a permanent reduction in the institutional power of the military in Japanese government. During this era, no figure symbolized moderation in foreign policy more than Kijuro Shidehara, Foreign Minister under the Minseito Cabinets. Shidehera was a conservative, a nationalist, and a loyal servant of the Emperor. He believed that Japan had special interests in Northeast Asia and a special responsibility toward China. But he wanted to avoid a "get-tough" policy which would only provoke boycotts, anti-Japanese hostility, and possibly war. Rather, he hoped Japanese influence could be exerted through trade, financial agreements, and political negotiation.

Militarism and defeat

The liberal era was short-lived. With its collapse went much of the hope for moderation, either at home or abroad. This is not the place to spell out the story of democratic failure in prewar Japan, but its more immediate causes are familiar: economic crisis and depression; political confusion and corruption; and the consequent rise of opponents from left and right. The repercussions were felt almost immediately in Japanese foreign policy. In 1928, under the Tanaka Cabinet, there was a sharp turn toward a more militant nationalism in both the economic and political fields. State support to home industry was combined with a more "positive" program of support for Japanese interests abroad, especially in China. Overtures from Chiang Kai-shek—who had just broken with the communists—were rejected, partly because of fear that his successful northern expedition would jeopardize the future Japanese position in Manchuria and northern China. Ironically, while the Tanaka China policy was provoking sharp Chinese reaction because of its strengths, it was under simultaneous attack by Japanese military extremists because of its weaknesses. Some of these elements, working through the Kwantung Army in Manchuria, engineered the murder of Chang Tso-lin in June, 1928, hoping to force a decisive Japanese move in this area. The Japanese government was posed with the first of a series of direct military challenges to civilian control, challenges which went unmet.

Japanese foreign policy, in the fif-teen years between 1930 and 1945, represented the natural culmination of these new trends. To be sure, not all the old themes were reversed, particularly those that could be read with different inflections. Stress continued to be placed upon Sino-Japanese cooperation, and on the need for a stable, friendly China, purged of communist and anti-Japanese elements. But action continually interfered with words. As the Japanese militarists gained control of the strategic heights of policy, especially in the field, any cooperation had to be strained through the tightening net of aggression, fanatical patriotism, and individual, sometimes mass, acts of brutality. Through these field actions, and as a result of a contrived incident, war came to Manchuria in September, 1931. The weaker Chinese forces were quickly defeated, but Manchukuo remained, to the great body of the Chinese, an acceptable symbol of Japanese aggression.

With the Manchurian region at last under complete Japanese control, the militarists could not avoid spreading outward toward Mongolia and northern China. Thus the Second China Incident erupted, in 1937, and led eventually to total war and defeat. Throughout this entire era, Japan could always find some Chinese allies, whether as a result of the acrid internal rivalries for power in China, sheer opportunism, or some genuine hopes that this route might lead to a new and better Asia, freed from Western control. Indeed, the allies garnered from all of these sources were not inconsiderable either in number or in influence. In Wang Ch'ing-wei, Japan finally found an able if embittered leader. But, as against these facts, Japanese policy achieved what had always been feared most: a union of the dominant wing of the Kuomintang with the communists and many independents, into a nationalist popular front that was bitterly anti-Japanese. Though it had as one of its supreme goals the salvation of Asia from communism, Japanese policy, in the end, contributed more than any other single factor to communist success.

To concentrate solely on China, however, would be to examine only the weakest link of a general Asian policy which, for all its militant, aggressive qualities, had elements of real power and appeal. Building from the old "Asia for the Asians" theme, Japanese policy moved, in the 1930's, toward the concept of a Greater East Asia Co-Prosperity Sphere. The economic background for this policy lay in the rapid strides made by Japanese trade throughout Asia. By means of general deflation, changes in currency valuation, industrial rationalization, and extensive state support, Japanese trade came to enjoy highly favorable competitive conditions in East Asia by the mid-Thirties. Western Europe complained vigorously about the practice of "social dumping" onto the colonial markets. Japan retorted with charges of economic discrimination and attempted monopoly. The fact remained, however, that Japanese penetration of the Asian market, during this period, was substantial. The basis was thus provided for later proposals of greater economic integration of an Asian region led by Japan and divorced from Western control.

The center of the Japanese appeal to greater Asia, however, remained in the sphere of political nationalism. As Japan drifted toward the fascist bloc, Western imperialism in Asia could be attacked with less inhibition than in the past. These attacks were particularly effective in areas where nationalism was still treated as subversive by Western governors, and where Japanese policies could not yet be tested.

Once again, an attempt was made to develop an expanded program of cultural relations and technical assistance. Students flocked to Japan from all parts of Asia; cultural missions were exchanged on an increasing scale; Japanese technicians went forth; and, as the Pacific War approached, the Japanese government provided underground assistance to various Asian nationalist movements in the form of funds, political advice, and even the training and equipping of military forces.

Most of the presently independent governments of South and Southeast Asia owe an enormous debt to Japanese propaganda, military successes, and political concessions—even when the latter were self-serving, empty, or last-minute gestures. There can be no doubt that Japan, both in victory and in defeat, contributed mightily to the end of the old era and the emergence of a more independent, dynamic Asia. Yet her record was tarnished, and today she must combat a legacy of suspicion and even hatred in many of these countries. In part, this can be attributed to such factors as the misconduct of her troops but, more importantly, it is the product of the great cultural barriers that separated her from the regions she occupied and of her inability—through lack of experience, insecurity, and because of her own traditions—to develop the type of flexibility and broad tolerance necessary in leadership. In considerable degree, Japanese hopes for cooperation and friendship were strangled by the nationalism that pushed them forward.

As a corollary to her new Asian policy, Japan naturally developed a new policy with respect to the West. Nearly a decade earlier, at the time of the Washington Conference of 1921, Japan had reluctantly given up the Anglo-Japanese alliance, her shield and support for twenty years. In its place were substituted the more general agreements among the major powers. This concept of collective agreement (not, it should be emphasized, collective security) was especially attuned to the American position. The United States wanted an end to exclusive alliances, but it was prepared to undertake only the most limited of commitments, and it still wished to rely essentially upon moral suasion for policy enforcement. The great symbol of this hope and this era was the famous Kellogg-Briand Peace Pact, outlawing war.

Thus the decline of Japanese liberalism at home was complemented by the absence of effective external checks or controls. The old system of alliances, and the type of checks they imposed upon unilateral action, had been declared obsolete in the Pacific, but no effective international order had replaced them. Consequently, in the name of her national interests, Japan could successfully defy the Nine Power Agreement and the League of Nations, with no single nation or group making an effective stand against her. Inevitably, as she challenged the *status-quo* powers, Japan gravitated toward Germany and Italy, the dissidents of Europe. The Anti-Comintern Pact sealed an alliance of mutual interest, though not one of great intimacy.

But the real decision that confronted Japan as the Pacific War approached had a familiar ring: Was she to seek a stabilization of her northern or her southern flanks? Who was to be engaged, the Soviet Union or the Western allies? The decision was not an easy one. In the late 1930's, Japan had participated in large-scale clashes with Russian forces in the Mongolian region, and her historic rivalry was augmented by her hatred of communism. In the final analysis, however, she de-

cided to count on a German victory on the steppes of Russia, and she turned to the south, whose resources had to be unlocked and whose Western masters had to be overthrown if the Japanese vision of the future were to be attained. Possibilities for agreement with the West to avoid this fateful step were explored, as all the moderates desired, but hopes were broken on the rock of China. Too much had been invested in blood and treasure to concede to Chiang Kai-shek, and so, infinitely more was to be invested—and all in vain.

THE FORMULATION OF FOREIGN POLICY IN PREWAR JAPAN

In the Tokyo trials of major war criminals that followed the Japanese surrender, the Allied prosecutors repeatedly sought the answer to one central question: Who bears the responsibility for leading Japan toward aggression and war? If they did not obtain a completely satisfactory answer, no blame should be assigned. Few questions involve greater difficulties. The problem has taken on universal dimensions as the modern state has grown in complexity and as foreign policy has developed into the composite, uncertain product of a myriad of technicians, men rigidly compartmentalized, skilled and jealous of these skills, but almost always frustrated by the limits of their power; an indeterminate number of free-roaming generalists, yet not so free, being bound by the limits of the single mind, the niceties of group decision, and the pressures—subtle or direct—of subalterns; and, finally, the larger, vaguer public, varying in size but never comprising the whole of its society nor the sum of its parts—alternately indifferent and excited, overwhelmed by the complexities and focusing on some vital issue, ignored and watched with anxiety, molded and breaking out of molds.

Japan was a modern state. In the narrow sense, Japan appeared as a society of great personal absolutism. In both the family and the nation, the head was invested with absolute powers. Inferiors owed complete and unswerving obedience. There seemed no measure of egalitarianism or individualism to alleviate the rigidities of a hierarchical system which, through primogeniture and an Emperor-centered mythology, found its apex in a single source. But in fact, the essence of power in Japanese society has not been that of personal absolutism. The vital center of decision making has uniformly lain in its collective or group character, and in its extensive reliance on consensus as the primary technique. It is critical to understand that, despite all superficial signs to the contrary, the basic nature of Japanese society can only be approached by a thorough appreciation of the intricate refinements of group interaction, the great importance of induced voluntarism, and the generally eclectic quality of final agreements.

In all likelihood, it is only because these things were true that the outward signs of rigid hierarchy and absolutism were so well maintained into the modern era. Elaborate methods had already been developed to integrate theory and appearance with the needs of a dynamic society. Just as the system of adopted sons had long preserved the necessary flexibility in the Japanese family, so the institutions of senior councillor, adviser, and go-between had each, in its own way, facilitated the making of group decisions. That process, giving extraordinary attention to form and status, was often wearisome and prolonged, but every care had to be taken to make concessions and consensus possible, with a minimum of violence to the position and prestige of those involved. Necessarily, equals were wary of confronting each other in person until the formula for consensus seemed assured; and inferiors developed, to a fine art, all forms of subtle pressures and persuasive devices, so that successful superiors paid silent homage to these in the course of final action.

Not all these conditions sound strange to Western ears, although the aggregate process might seem foreign or extreme. In any case, how were such basic factors in Japanese social relations translated into politics and the making of foreign policy? In theory, the Meiji Constitution of 1889 paid its highest tribute to imperial absolutism but, for successful practice, it demanded a unity or consensus of its disparate working parts. The weakest of these, the two-house Diet, its lower house elected, had at least the power to withhold its consent from basic policies. The administrative bureaucracy, culminating in such executives as the Prime Minister, and the members of the Cabinet and the Privy Council, had a vast range of powers and had legal responsibility only to the Emperor, but it could not be effective alone. The military also drew their power from the Emperor and had direct access to him; in practice, moreover, this branch acquired a potent weapon in that the Ministers of War and Navy had to come from its ranks, which served to limit sharply the independent power of the Japanese Cabinet. The military, however, could operate effectively only in conjunction with the other major branches.

There was never any serious thought of having these forces coordinated by the Emperor personally, despite the awsome nature of his stipulated powers. Instead, that task was handled, for some thirty years, by a small oligarchy of Restoration leaders who acted in the name of the Emperor as his "chief advisers." Ultimately, this group came to be known as the Genro or "senior councillors," an institution without a vestige of legal recognition or responsibility, but central to the process of Japanese politics. Every basic policy decision was placed before the Genro, and their approval was a prerequisite to action. Even the daily affairs of state frequently engaged their attention. With protégés in every branch of government, and with their own vast accumulation of experience, these men were at once the source of integration, the court of final appeal, and the summit of power. To be sure, agreement among them was not always easy; there were deep personal and political cleavages in this, as in other Japanese groups. Timed withdrawals and temporary concessions, however, enabled a consensus to operate with a minimum of crises. Until the close of the First World War, with rare exceptions, the fountainhead of Japanese foreign policy was this group.

With the postwar era, however, basic changes in government began to emerge, paralleling those in society. The members of the Genro became old, and their ranks were not refilled. No group came forth to undertake the integrative role. Instead, Japanese politics was marked by an increasing struggle for supremacy and control among the parties, the bureaucracy, and the military. It is interesting to note that, at the outset of this era, an attempt was made to establish a liaison council under the aegis of the Prime Minister for the development of a unified foreign policy. It was intended to include major party, official, and military representation, but it was never accepted by the major opposition party, and it ultimately faded away.

Without a supreme coordinator such as the Genro, Japanese constitutionalism, in both its written and unwritten aspects, revealed serious flaws. In the hectic party era, foreign policy decisions taken in Cabinet or government party circles were not only subject to legitimate attacks in the Diet, but also to extensive sabotage by the ranks of the subordinate bureaucracy, and to angry challenges by the military groups. The parties never attained more than a quasi-supremacy and, as they faded, the military moved from verbal challenge to open defiance. Japanese society, in the period after 1928, was a classic example of a government divided against itself. Important segments of the military operated, both in the field and at home, in such a manner as to scorn the government. They received substantial support from within the bureaucracy, and from certain party figures as well. Every branch of government was riddled with dissension. Within the Ministry of Foreign Affairs, various cliques maneuvered for position—the militarist clique, the Anglo-American clique, and numerous others. For a time, consensus was impossible, and conditions close to anarchy prevailed.

Gradually, however, greater stability was achieved. Making full use of traditional procedures, top court officials surrounding the Emperor involved themselves in unending conferences with representatives of all major groups; innumerable go-betweens explored the possible bases of compromise; certain voluntary withdrawals, strategic retreats, and silent acquiescences were effected. Slowly a new basis for interaction developed, one which gave due recognition to military superiority but still was broad enough to include essential elements of the civil bureaucracy, court officials, and important pressure groups. Once again the basic decisions were reached by consensus, but with somewhat greater cognizance of the realities of power. In this period, a new group of senior councillors, the Jushin, was organized. Although lacking the influence of the Genro, it was fashioned after its model, indicating the continuing search for an integrative center. That search was destined never to be completely successful. Another experiment was conducted in a liaison council, the purpose being to pool military and civilian policy with particular reference to the foreign scene. Ultimately, the Imperial Conference, with the Emperor himself presiding over a small group of top military and administrative officials, became the final decision-making body. Indeed, it was this group that determined the Japanese surrender, the Emperor personally settling this great issue. Perhaps this was the only basis left for the organic unity envisaged by the Meiji Constitution.

The foregoing trends are not completely meaningful without some brief reference to other important social groups. First, however, it should be noted that the type of consensus being developed during the militarist era was abetted by an increasing control over all media of communication. One of the most literate societies in the world, Japan had national newspapers and magazines with massive circulation. After the early Thirties, prominent dissent from ultranationalism became increasingly dangerous and, after the Second China Incident, all the public organs were echoing the official line.

Meanwhile, a process of accommo-dation had been taking place between conservative militarists and the industrial and commercial world of Japan. In the initial stages of the military revolt against liberalism and a weak-kneed foreign policy, the strong notes of a radical, anti-capitalist theme were heard; the historic cry of "internal reform, external expansion" once again sounded forth. However, after the February 26th Incident, of 1936, when army units in Tokyo under radical command rebelled, this type of revolutionary activity was suppressed. Although some liberal business elements were regarded with suspicion, and certain onerous controls were sharply protested by entrepreneurs, still the necessary compromises were made, and all of Japanese industry rose to the war effort.

Japanese labor reacted in the same way. Its radical and liberal elements had long since been silenced, and the great masses worked with patriotic fervor. It was from the rural areas, however, that the bedrock of Japanese conservatism derived. The alliance between peasant and soldier now held more meaning than at any time since the Restoration. As is so frequently the case, rural provincialism bred its own type of ultranationalism. The Japanese common man played a role in the formulation of foreign policy in his own way: he posed no obstacles to expansionism, his complete loyalty was assured, and no sacrifice would be too great if it contributed to the nationalist cause.

JAPAN SINCE 1945: OCCUPATION AND ITS AFTERMATH

When Japan surrendered, in August, 1945, both her leaders and her people were forced to reconcile themselves to being a vanquished nation. By the terms of the Yalta and Potsdam agreements, the Japanese Empire was to be dissipated and Japan reduced in size to the approximate boundaries of the Restoration era. The homeland was to be occupied for an indefinite period by foreign forces. For the first time in recorded history, Japanese sovereignty was to be superseded by foreign rule. Some of the broad objectives of this rule had already been stipulated: action was to be taken to insure that Japan never again would become a world menace, or a world power. Total disarmament was to be carried out, and those responsible for past aggression were to be punished; even the fate of the Emperor was unclear, although Japanese leaders sought desperately to gain assurances on this point during the surrender negotiations. Along with these essentially negative tasks, the occupation was also to encourage Japanese democratic forces and movements, so that Japan could eventually take her place in a peaceful world. Thus was inaugurated, in September, 1945, a radically new era for Japan, one that might well be labelled "the era of the American Revolution."

If the contemporary processes and substance of Japanese foreign policy are to be discussed meaningfully, certain pertinent aspects of this period must be set forth. In the first place, the American Occupation and its aftermath can easily be divided into three broad phases: (*a*) the early revolutionary era, when the emphasis was upon punishment and reform; (*b*) the era of reconstruction, when the stress was shifted to stabilization and economic recovery; and (*c*) the era of proffered alliance, which is continuing at present. Each of these eras, in its own way, has contributed to the current nature and problems of Japanese society.

The revolutionary era

The American Revolution in Japan was that of 1932, not that of 1776, although some of the spirit of the latter, as it applied to basic democratic values, was certainly present. The New Deal had new opportunities along the bombed-out Ginza and in the rice fields. But first, the old order had to be eradicated. Japanese miiltary forces were totally disbanded in a remarkably short time; before the end of 1947, some six million Japanese troops and civilians had been returned from overseas, demobilized, and poured into the homeland. The military forces within Japan proper had also been completely dissolved. The Ministries of War and Navy were abolished. And, in an effort to seal these actions with the stamp of permanency, the now-famous Article Nine was written into the new Japanese Constitution:

Aspiring sincerely to an international peace based on justice and order, the Japanese people forever renounce war as a sovereign right of the nation and the threat or use of force as means of settling international disputes.

In order to accomplish the aim of the preceding paragraph, land, sea, and air forces, as well as other war potential, will never be maintained. The right of belligerency of the state will not be recognized.

The American vision for Japan during this period became widely associated with the phrase "the Switzerland of the Far East," although, in this, pacifism was added to neutralization. It was a vision that had a powerful appeal to many Japanese who lived amidst rubble, without adequate food or warmth, and with vivid memories of lost ones, fire raids, and the final holocaust of the atom bomb. There could be no question as to whether this war had paid. Moreover, the extraordinary vulnerability of the great Japanese cities had been fully demonstrated during the war's last, terrible months. For most thoughtful Japanese, the early postwar era was a period of deep reflection. Its dominant theme was trenchant criticism of past leaders and institutions. Once more, there was a Japanese surge toward new ideas and ways; MacArthur, no less than Perry, symbolized the end of an old order, and a war-weary people turned hopefully to *demokurashi*, without being precisely sure of its contents. These sentiments, widespread as they were, aided the revolution that was getting under way.

Among the various SCAP[1] actions, none had more long-range implications than those which affected the nature and position of Japanese pressure groups. As we have noted, for more than a decade the most powerful group in Japanese society had been the military. Suddenly it was entirely liquidated, and it has not yet reappeared as a significant force. Liquidation was not merely demobilization, but also the purge that barred all professional military officers from future political activity, and the war crimes trials, after which the top military men of the nation were executed or sentenced to prison. Although many of these actions were subsequently modified or rescinded, their total effect, combined with other circumstances, has thus far been

[1]SCAP is the commonly used abbreviation for the term, Supreme Commander of the Allied Powers. It is used to designate General MacArthur, personally, and the Occupation force, collectively.

sufficient to render postwar militarism in Japan impotent.

Through the purge and other measures, SCAP ate still further into prewar conservative ranks. For the old guard it seemed like the reign of terror, though without violence or brutality. Most professional politicians of the old conservative parties had to step aside because they had belonged to some ultranationalist group or had been endorsed by the Tojo government in the elections of 1942. Conservative leadership was hastily thrust into the hands of the one group that could be cleared: the so-called Anglo-American group, from within the Foreign Ministry. Kijuro Shidehara, Shigeru Yoshida, and Hisashi Ashida, all from this group, became the top conservative leaders of Japan for nearly a decade. Even the commercial and industrial world felt the shock of reform. Beset by purges, a program to break down the *zaibatsu* ("big combines"), and the general toll of wartime ravage and postwar inflation, most business elements sought merely to survive, as if seeking shelter during a gale.

Meanwhile, with American encouragement, the labor union movement attained a massive size; within a brief period it numbered some six million workers, whereas, in the prewar period, *bona fide* union membership had never exceeded one-half million. These postwar figures masked many divisions and weaknesses, but there could be no doubt that Japanese organized labor was a new force with which to reckon on the economic and political scene. And in the rural areas, the American Revolution was operating in the most forceful fashion. Under a far-reaching program of land reform, absentee landlordism was almost completely abolished, tenancy was reduced to less than 10 per cent of total agrarian families, and land holdings were equalized beyond the wildest imagination of prewar advocates of land reform. Basically, this program was dedicated to the creation of a huge independent yeomanry. The repercussions in the rural areas, especially among younger age groups, are only now becoming measurable.

Certain reforms cut across class lines and into the broadest categories of society. Legal attempts were made to abandon primogeniture and to emancipate women. Women were given full equality before the law, including equal rights of inheritance, divorce, and suffrage. Sweeping reforms in education were inaugurated, with the purpose of developing freer, more independent students, unshackled from the old chauvinism and submissiveness. Even that very special category of men, the subordinate government officials, were given lectures on democracy, in the hope that some of the old attitude of *kanson mimpi* ("officials honored, people despised") could be removed.

To recite these various efforts in such bald fashion may lead to the supposition that a total social revolution took place in Japan during the first years after 1945. Any such impression would be false. Conservatism, both in the form of certain dominant classes and in the form of certain traditions that operated in every class, was a sturdy force. Moreover, as might be surmised, not all SCAP experiments were successful and, by the end of 1947, in any case, the era emphasizing reform was drawing to a close. In its ripest forms, it had lasted only about two years. The conservatives definitely survived.

It would be equally misleading, however, to underestimate the changes that took place during this era, whether be-cause of SCAP reforms or as a result of the total complex of postwar circumstances. Some of these changes should be regarded as part of the continuum inherited from prewar days. Others were largely the product of foreign intervention or the new conditions prevailing as a result of military defeat. In any case, the changes which developed during this period had a direct influence on the processes and substance of Japanese foreign policy. Most important have been the altered composition of Japanese pressure groups and the accelerated movement toward a mass society.

The nature of Japanese conservatism has been strongly affected by the demise of the military, the levelling of agriculture, and the combined impact of defeat and technology. Japanese reformism has been equally affected by the rise of organized labor and the freedom accorded the intellectuals and students. It is still too early to be certain about the political path that will be taken by a rapidly changing Japanese society. One thing, however, seems apparent: the trend has been toward a closer balance of competing pressure groups within that society than there was in the prewar era. As a result of this and other factors, the Japanese common man has become the object of increasing political solicitation and concern. As we shall note, public opinion has become an important factor in the shaping of Japanese foreign policy.

Stabilization

Before we turn to the current status of foreign policy, some brief consideration should be given to the second and third phases of the Occupation and the gradual emergence, once again, of an independent Japan. The shift of emphasis in Occupation policy, from punishment and reform to economic stabilization and recovery, began as early as 1947. The change was motivated by many problems. Certain earlier American premises about the postwar world now seemed unjustified. The prospects for a China that would be friendly and democratic by American definition were dim; the honeymoon with the Soviet Union was clearly over and the Cold War was beginning; the threat of communism throughout Europe and Asia, as a result of postwar chaos and economic misery, was a matter of profound concern. In Japan itself, the close relation between economic recovery and the prospects for democratic success could no longer be slighted or ignored. In addition, the expenses of occupation and relief constituted a heavy burden for the American taxpayer; at its peak, the cost ran close to one-half billion dollars a year.

The new emphasis brought many changes. Increasingly, the supreme test to which any policy could be put was, Does it advance productivity and economic stabilization? An assessment was made of the primary obstacles—war damage, inflation, the lack of raw materials, and low industrial morale. SCAP began to interest itself in Japanese productive efficiency, and moved from merely keeping Japan alive to furnishing her with raw materials and acquainting her entrepreneurs with the most advanced machinery and techniques. The complex problem of inflation was finally faced. Under the Dodge Nine-Point Stabilization Program, stringent reforms were put into effect. These were unpopular in many quarters, but the inflationary tide was at last turned.

Meanwhile, other disruptions to production were dealt with. The deconcentration program was relaxed and gradually abandoned, after successful initial attempts to reduce certain large *zaibatsu* families and cartels. The United States also progressively receded from its early severity on the issue of reparations. By the end of this era, the American government had indicated its acceptance of the thesis that the Japanese ability to repay war damages was strictly limited, that large reparations would indirectly become a responsibility to the United States, and that the heavy industry on which the Japanese future was so dependent could not be used for these purposes. Finally, SCAP took a sterner attitude toward the labor movement, amending its earlier generous legislation on unionism to give the employer, and especially the government, a stronger position.

The net effect of these actions, accompanied by certain broader trends at home and abroad, was to stimulate rapid economic recovery. Japanese society could build on an industrial revolution already well advanced, and on a legacy of technical knowhow. Deflation and internal readjustments were followed by new opportunities for industrial expansion. The Korean War and the great prosperity of the free world were of major assistance. Beginning in 1950, therefore, Japan entered a period of amazing economic development. For the next fifteen years, the average annual rise in gross national product was approximately 10 per cent, one of the most spectacular rates of growth in the world.

This second phase of the Occupation, which triggered the economic surge, was not without internal political reverberations. In the revolutionary era, American actions had been an anathema to the conservatives; now, the conservatives became the new allies. The liberal left, which had cheered in the early days, was filled with dismay and resentment at many actions of which it did not approve but from which it had no recourse. Japanese democracy was still under the tutelage of American military rule, and criticism and opposition were strictly limited by that fact. Inevitably, however, the United States and its policies became the central issue in Japanese politics, paving the way for the sharp divergencies that came into the open later. For every political group, moreover, this second era was one of reflection and reconsideration of Western values. There was an unmistakable tendency, at all levels, to emphasize synthesis and adjustment rather than uncritical acceptance of foreign concepts. The pendulum had begun to swing back.

As can be seen, the beginnings of postwar Japanese foreign policy were established in this era, albeit under American direction. These beginnings followed a course that Japanese leadership itself might well have taken and even labelled "in the national interest," had it been an independent agent. Indeed, on issues like reparations and trade, the United States was widely accused of being excessively pro-Japanese. One policy which was emphasized was that of rehabilitating Japanese heavy industry and encouraging its orientation toward the needs and markets of the late-developing societies, particularly those of noncommunist Asia. Again, the concept of Japan as the workshop of Asia was advanced, but without certain former connotations. As a concomitant to this policy, the United States also tried to adjust Japanese political and economic relations with erstwhile enemies. Like a benevolent warden convinced of the successful rehabilitation of his charge, the United States pressed for Japanese reentry into the world community.

But with the second phase of the Occupation, there also began an intimate and largely new relationship between Japan and the United States, a relationship founded on a rising tempo of economic interaction. Japanese products began to flow into the United States in exchange for American raw materials, foodstuffs, and machinery. Technical assistance from the United States smoothed the way for investments and patent sharing. The economic interaction was thus very broadly based. It was supported, moreover, by an expanding cultural exchange of customs, ideas, and patterns of life.

The era of alliance

Within these trends lay the seeds of the third era, that of alliance proffered by the United States to Japan. By 1949, American authorities realized, on the one hand, that the Occupation was reaching a point of diminishing returns, and, on the other, that continuing economic and political ties between the two countries were a mutual necessity. The explorations which led to the San Francisco Peace Treaty of 1951 involved a series of decisions that added to the new Japanese foreign policy and provoked heated political debate.

The critical issue pertained to the question of Japanese defense. Two broad alternatives seemed to exist. One was Japanese pacifism, which involved seeking universal agreements guaranteeing the sanctity of Japanese territory and backing these with pledges of protection by the United Nations, and possibly by the United States, separately. The alternative was to acknowledge the Japanese need for, and right to, military defense, and to underwrite Japanese rearmament with American power. Obviously, the choice between these two broad courses would affect and shape most other aspects of Japanese foreign policy.

The Yoshida government did not hesitate to support the second alternative, that of political, military, and economic alliance with the United States, as the only course compatible with world conditions and Japanese needs. To adopt a policy of neutralism, the conservatives argued, would make Japan dependent on the mercurial policies of the communist world. It would provide neither security nor prosperity. They insisted that both the economic and the political interests of Japan were best served by alignment with the free world, particularly the United States.

These arguments prevailed. While making known its desire for an over-all peace treaty, the Japanese government agreed to sign a treaty with the noncommunist allies alone, if necessary. The Cold War had become hot in Korea while preliminary treaty negotiations were getting under way. Because of this, and the wide divergence between Soviet and American views on Japan, no serious attempt was made to obtain communist approval for the treaty draft, as the Japanese socialists had wished. In exchange for their willingness to sign a separate treaty, the conservatives were given a treaty considered generous by all, and soft by some. Reparations, and certain territorial issues (the Kurile and Ryukyu islands), were left open, providing Japan with some bargaining power. The treaty contained no stipulations concerning SCAP reforms. Japan was left free to make any changes desired in her internal institutions. This included the right to rearm.

Official independence for Japan finally came on April 28, 1952, the day on which the Treaty of San Francisco came into effect. Accompanying the main treaty was a bilateral mutual security treaty with the United States providing for the continuance of American bases in Japan until adequate defenses were prepared by the Japanese government. At least as early as 1949, the creation of a Japanese defense force was being urged in some American and Japanese circles, and Japanese rearmament was first started in the summer of 1950, shortly after the outbreak of the Korean War. The National Police Reserve was activated in August of that year with an authorized component of 75,000 men. With the coming of Japanese independence in May, 1952, this number was increased to 110,000, and a small Maritime Safety Force was established. In August, these were brought together under the National Safety Agency. Two years later, on July 1, 1954, the name was changed to the Defense Agency, and the armed forces were brought directly under the office of the Prime Minister, and authorized to add a small Air Self-Defense Force. The slow build-up of Japanese defense forces continued. By the end of 1955, there were about 200,000 men in the total defense force. Twelve years later, in 1967, the force numbered some 275,000 men in all branches, and while this represented a small force in comparison with Communist China's military establishment, it was ultramodern, and capable of being rapidly expanded. Indeed, some observers were prepared to accord Japan seventh or eighth status in world power. Despite these trends—or perhaps because of them—the military aspect of the American-Japanese alliance continued to be somewhat unstable for reasons we shall discuss later.

In economic terms, however, the alliance has flourished during the past 15 years. Between 1954 and 1963, Japanese-American trade tripled. Japan, obtaining nearly one-third of all her imports from the United States, became its second best customer, next to Canada. Japanese exports to the United States skyrocketed to nearly $2 billion yearly. United States sales to Japan were somewhat larger. By 1970, it was estimated, the United States would be selling $3 to $3.5 billion worth of goods to Japan, and buying goods valued at $2.8 billion. Trade between Japan and the United States has become the most powerful stimulus to continuing alliance.

If the alliance has been largely attuned to the business community and conservative circles, however, it has not been totally lacking in a larger cultural component. Heightened cultural exchange began during the Occupation, and seldom, if ever, have people from two such diverse societies had so great an opportunity to see each other at work and play. For various complex reasons, rapport between Americans and Japanese was rather easily established. Studies of attitudes give indications of the reasons for this: on the Japanese side, there was a general appreciation of American humanism, friendliness, and energy; on the American side, Japanese politeness, discipline, cultural achievements, and industriousness were respected. Favorable attitudes have facilitated an exchange between the two cultures, and exchanges between the elite of the two countries have probably been even more significant than mass interaction. In spite of language the Japanese and American elite can communicate with each other on an increasingly meaningful basis as their two societies move closer together. The development of communications concerning industrial techniques, social science methodology, and scientific theory is of profound importance.

Having thus survived the transition from Occupation to independence, the alliance between Japan and the United States continues. As we suggested earlier, however, this alliance is more applicable and more acceptable to some segments of Japanese society than to others. It is supported by the conservatives and opposed by the socialists. Relations between socialists and American authorities rapidly deteriorated after 1948, due in part to a major shift in Occupation policy. Differences concerning foreign policy became especially pronounced: the Socialist Party favored an over-all peace treaty with noncommunist, communist, and neutral states. To the argument that, given present circumstances, this was unrealistic, the socialists answered that no real attempt had been made because of American opposition. The socialists were also strongly antagonistic to Japanese rearmament; they bitterly denounced the new defense forces as illegal, and they charged an American-conservative coalition with undermining the Constitution of 1947. They were equally opposed to the Mutual Security Pact that accompanied the Treaty of San Francisco, and to the post-independence American bases in Japan that it sanctioned.

Against the conservative policy of alignment with the United States, the socialists advanced a policy of neutralism. In part, this policy was a product of their own historic traditions. Both the pacifist and the Marxist streams in Japanese socialism have been strong, and each of these streams has, in its own way, contributed to the modern socialist proclivity for neutralism. The socialist movement in Japan emerged partly as a Christian humanist protest against social injustice, militarism and war; and it existed long before the similar sentiments generated in the Japanese public after the disastrous Second World War. In the second stage of its development, moreover, the Japanese socialist movement was strongly influenced by Marxism. This separated many Japanese socialists from the ideology and practice of Western-style parliamentarism, and yet, because of the particular academic and "deviationist" qualities of Marxism in its Japanese socialist setting, it did not connect them with Moscow. In the initial postwar era, the Japanese socialists took as their ideal the foreign policy of Nehru. More recently, however, the Soviet policies of peaceful coexistence have won considerable support in Japanese socialist circles and Peking also has had a substantial influence upon one group within the Party. The Japanese socialists, as a result, have been brought closer to the international communist movement than at any point in their previous history.

The socialist case for neutralism has encompassed many arguments: the danger of involvement in war via an alliance with the United States; the extreme vulnerability of Japan; the importance of serving as a balance-wheel in a polarized world; identifying more closely with the aspirations of the Asian-African states; the threats to Japanese democracy implicit in a revitalized military force; and the need for Japan to free itself completely from American influence and control. The conservatives have answered with counter-arguments: the lack of realism in seeking to meet communism with a policy of pacifism and isolation; the moral and political rightness of associating with those who share a common ideology; the economic value in doing so; the difficulty of gaining great influence in the world without military potential and connections with a world power; and the possibility of having an independent foreign policy while still being aligned with the West, especially the United States.

Not only have the conservatives maintained their political supremacy and hence their foreign policy views; issues of foreign policy have been involved in the various splits that have occurred in socialist ranks. The first of these took place shortly after the San Francisco peace conference. The right-wing socialists, who plainly leaned toward the West in an ideological sense, were willing to accept the peace treaty even though it did not constitute an over-all agreement. The left-wing socialists, who sought to adhere closely to the neutralist position, remained sharply opposed to the treaty. Both groups rejected the Mutual Security Treaty. However, the arguments over the peace treaty both exacerbated and reflected a wide range of differences within socialist ranks. The party split into two wings and was not reunited until 1954.

Another division occurred in 1959 and continues to the present. The right-wing Nishio faction, joined by a few other moderates, left the Socialist Party in revolt against the strongly Marxist orientation of the dominant left wing. The new Democratic Socialist Party recognized the importance of a balance of armed strength between the two major blocs, accepted the need for some military protection until a new international order could be attained and supported the idea of friendly relations with neighboring states regardless of ideological or political differences (including both China and Taiwan). The Democratic Socialist Party, however, currently obtains only 5-8 per cent of the national vote, whereas the Socialist Party gets approximately 30 per cent. The left is still in decisive command of Japanese socialism, although there are some indications of a moderate movement within the left itself.

In conservative ranks also, the concept of alliance has its limits. It must be remembered that after more than a thousand years of relative isolation, Japan comes to any alliance with difficulty. Even her modern alliances with Great Britain and, later, with the Axis powers were essentially superficial despite their importance to Japan. They involved minimum policy coordination or bilateral ties. Actually, the alliance with the United States is the most far-reaching alliance in Japanese history. But the conservatives as well as other Japanese have been involved in the resurgence of nationalism that naturally followed the Occupation. They never approved of many of the American Occupation policies, and proceeded to overturn a number of these quickly. They did more than merely talk about "an independent foreign policy aligned with the West"; they proved to be tough bargainers on a number of issues affecting the alliance, including the revised security treaty of 1961. Some might say, in this connection, that they wanted equality of rights but not equality of responsibility. Notwithstanding these facts, however, the era of alliance continues.

THE FORMULATION OF FOREIGN POLICY IN POSTWAR JAPAN

To compare the decision-making and administrative processes in Japanese foreign policy before and after World War II is a very difficult undertaking. A vast amount of detailed research is still necessary before generalizations can be advanced with any certainty. In some respects—for example, in terms of the constitutional allocation of responsibility—greater clarity and simplicity have been realized in the postwar era. Against this fact, one must acknowledge the increasing complexity that is the product of a more even balance of pressure groups and the rising importance of public opinion.

The new Japanese Constitution of 1947 did much to clarify the ultimate responsibility for policy, domestic and foreign. Patterned almost wholly after Anglo-American institutions, it drastically altered the old system. Under its provisions, the Emperor's functions became ceremonial and symbolic. Sovereignty was assigned to the people, to be exercised by their elected representatives. A parliamentary system modelled after that of Great Britain was established, with certain modifications of a distinctly American flavor.

The Diet, instead of being peripheral to the political process, is now its center, and both houses are elective. The upper house, the House of Councillors, is constructed in a complicated fashion, with both nationwide and prefectural constituencies; the lower house, the House of Representatives, is based on medium-sized election districts (three to five members chosen from each district, depending upon its size, with each voter having one vote). Executive responsibility to the Diet is clearly stipulated. The Prime Minister must be approved by the Diet, and if the houses disagree, by the lower house. In case of a vote of no confidence, the government must either dissolve the lower house and call for new elections, or resign.

A new law pertaining to the Diet was enacted to accompany the Constitution of 1947. Among other things, it provided for a system of standing committees, in contrast to the prewar, British style, *ad hoc* committees. Thus, both houses of the Diet now have Foreign Affairs Committees. After agreement among the parties on the allocation of committee seats, members are selected by each party, on the basis of training, experience, and political connections. The standing committees exist to hold hearings on government legislation or any policy matters within their general jurisdiction. Special, *ad hoc* committees, however, are still used extensively in the Japanese Diet, sometimes on issues involving foreign policy. The Japanese committee system, as it currently operates, does not give either to the Diet as a whole or to individual Diet members the degree of power possessed in the United States Congress. Of course, party or, more precisely, factional discipline interacts with the institutional framework of the Diet to make this true. In any case, initiative and power in foreign policy lie mainly with the executive branch of government.

Thus older political practices combine with the new legal framework to place a premium on the cooperation of bureaucracy and party leadership in the formulation of Japanese foreign policy. Under a Western-style parliamentary system, major party leaders constitute the apex of authority. The Emperor no longer serves as an independent and legally omnipotent channel of power. The military branch of government is no longer a separate and competitive source of influence. And even the civil bureaucracy is now clearly subordinated in law to a political administration that must be consonant with a majority of the popularly elected members of the House of Representatives.

In concrete terms, how do the bureaucracy and the parties cooperate in foreign policy formulation? Generally speaking, the party (that is to say, the dominant party, the Liberal Democratic Party) provides the broad policy framework and the Foreign Office drafts specific policy within this framework. The draft is then subject to scrutiny and approval by the party, after which the Foreign Office proceeds to execute policy in its final forms. To understand how this actually works out, however, one must have a general appreciation of the present Japanese party system and bureaucracy.

Perhaps four general trends within the party system are significant for foreign policy. First, the conservatives have continued to hold a commanding position in Japanese politics. They have consistently polled close to two-thirds of the total vote, and at all times—divided or united—they have held a large majority of the seats in both houses of the Diet. Perhaps the major reasons for regular conservative victories have been their prewar ties and strength at local levels, especially in rural areas; their prominent, well-known candidates; the funds at their disposal; the relative prosperity in Japan since 1950; the divided and weak nature of the opposition; and last, but by no means least, the capacity of the conservatives to adjust to changing conditions. For these reasons, the Liberal Democratic Party is the government, now and for the foreseeable future.

The growing importance of the postwar socialists, however, cannot be ignored. Although they are currently weak and divided, as we have said, they have moved a considerable distance from their pre-1945 position of total impotence. Socialists occupy roughly one-third of the Diet seats, and their percentage of the vote has generally increased since 1949. In the election of November, 1963, the two socialist parties got a combined total of 36.4 per cent of the vote, and the communists obtained an additional 4 per cent. The conservatives, therefore, have to be aware of competition in a sense that was unnecessary before World War II. The Japanese left cannot be disregarded.

These facts lead to a second generalization about Japanese politics, namely, that the party system can be variously defined as "two-party," "one and one-half party," or "federation type." Despite the socialist split of 1959, there are only two significant parties in Japan at present: the massive Liberal Democratic Party, which received 55 per cent of the vote in 1963, and the Socialist Party, which obtained over 29 per cent. The splinter Democratic Socialist Party, the moderate group, got only 7 per cent of the 1963 vote and the communists 4 per cent. In one sense, therefore, Japan has a two-party system.

In functional terms, however, Japan can be said to have a one and one-half party system: one dominant party that knows only how to govern, and a half party (or parties) that know only how to oppose. The socialists' position creates some serious problems. It is not easy to acquire responsibility, whether in foreign or domestic policy matters, if one has never had power and, hence, never had the responsibility that goes with formulating and defending policy.

There is still another way in which the Japanese party system can be defined and explained: as a system of rival federations within which operate the real parties, namely, the small factions that are based upon intimate personal ties and mutual interests. Each of the major parties is composed of such factions. Thus the Liberal Democratic Party currently has Sato, Ikeda, Miki, Ono, and Fujiyama factions, among others. The shifting alliances among these factions determine leadership of the "federation," or party. Factional loyalty generally takes precedence over loyalty to the federation; hence, in many respects, the real party is the faction.

Considering the circumstances noted above, it is not surprising that bipartisanship on foreign policy issues does not exist in Japan. Indeed, such issues are even used, on occasion, as weapons in the struggle for power among rival factions *within* a major party. Within the Liberal Democratic Party, recently, such issues as policy toward China and even the revised Security Treaty with the United States were made intraparty issues against Kishi and his supporters. Needless to say, socialist opposition is much more continuous and absolute. When we talk about Japanese foreign policy or government attitudes, it must be borne in mind that there is a vigorous and adamant opposition.

Finally, the party system as a whole is still on trial with the Japanese people. It is not yet thoroughly ingrained, either in institutional practice or in public behavior. Popular commitments to parties and to the party concept may be growing, but they are still weak. There is some danger that, with increasing mass participation in politics, the parties and the Diet will be circumvented. There is a tendency on the part of the left to protest via the streets, and on the part of the ultraright to protest via the knife.

The Japanese bureaucracy merits special attention. Its policy-making role is a vital one, especially with respect to foreign affairs. Once again, a few broad trends need to be noted. First, the general prestige and power of the Japanese bureaucracy continues to be great. To be sure, there are powerful, new challenges. Industry, commerce, and the professions, are also becoming prestigious. In relative terms, therefore, the prestige of the Japanese official has been declining. This is indicated by the popular homage he receives, by his emoluments, and by his own attitude toward his status. But these are changes relative to the Japanese past; in comparison with other democratic societies, the Japanese official enjoys great prestige and power.

Despite the efforts of the Occupation to encourage local autonomy, the forces of centralization triumphed, and the national government is as powerful as ever. Despite the new constitutional position of the Diet, the central bureaucracy wields enormous power, partly because of its legacy and partly as a natural result of its technical expertise. Under these conditions, it is not surprising that many young Japanese aspire to careers as officials. Indeed, competition for the available civil service positions is as intense as for top positions in industry or the leading professions.

In some respects the bureaucracy has changed less than most other facets of postwar Japan. It remains strongly hierarchical, and its modes of operation have been slow to change. Yet in composition and in background, the Japanese bureaucracy is undergoing significant evolution. Young men from the upper and upper-middle classes still have sizeable advantages—the educational opportunities and the proper social connections—but others have been pushing their way into the civil service in increasing numbers. Tokyo University, moreover, does not have the monopoly of training it possessed before 1945; a larger proportion of successful candidates come from other institutions. Above all, Japanese civil servants are now receiving a much broader college education, on the one hand, and much more advanced technical training, where it is desired, on the other hand. The premium on specialized skills has grown steadily. Some observers believe that the Japanese civil service not only attracts top talent in such fields as economics, but gives it more opportunity than does the academic world.

Another vital fact cannot be ignored. As in the prewar period, an increasing bureaucratic infiltration of the conservative party has been taking place. The percentage of conservative Diet members who have been officials in the national civil service has steadily risen since 1946. Approximately one-fourth of the Liberal Democratic Diet members are in this category, and the percentage of party leaders and Cabinet members who are former officials is much higher. This fact explains the close interaction between party leadership and government bureaucracy in contemporary Japan.

The Japanese Foreign Office is small, and simply organized. It has less than 2,000 men of civil service rank. Its major subdivisions are bureaus of two types, those covering geographic areas and those representing specialized functions. The latter include economic affairs, treaties, information and culture, and international cooperation. Within the Ministry, there is also a Secretariat which serves as a central coordinating and administrative unit. It includes a policy planning staff charged with over-all evaluation and planning of basic policy positions. Official liaison with the Diet is maintained through a parliamentary vice-minister, normally appointed from the Diet membership.

Today, a fairly high degree of coordination, efficiency, and continuity exists in the formulation of Japanese foreign policy. In the prewar period, as we have seen, the struggle to control foreign policy was a complex one waged by diverse forces. The ultimate cost to Japan was enormous. In the immediate post-surrender period, the Japanese Foreign Office could play only a minor role. Both foreign and domestic policy were laid down by Occupation authorities. The Japanese function was, essentially, to discern what the policy was and then to exercise—with uncertain results—the right of suggestion. In any case, diplomacy had to be directed primarily toward the United States. As the Occupation drew to a close, Japanese initiative was gradually reasserted. Initially, diplomacy, which was in the hands of Prime Minister Yoshida, himself a former Foreign Office man, was highly personalized. His opponents charged him with "one-man diplomacy." Party participation in foreign policy was very limited, and the Foreign Office still struggled to overcome its earlier weak and ineffectual position.

As Japan regained her independence, however, the conduct of foreign policy was gradually placed on a broader base. This base is the network of collaboration between the Liberal Democratic Party and the Foreign Office. By the time of the Kishi era (Kishi became Prime Minister in February, 1957), bureau chiefs in the Foreign Office had begun to have close contacts with party leaders. Many of these contacts were with the pertinent committees of the Liberal Democratic Party: the Research Committee on Foreign Relations, the Policy Research Committee, and the General Affairs Board. These committees, particularly the General Affairs Board, determine the foreign policy of the party.

Relations between the Foreign Office and the Liberal Democratic Party have not always been smooth or uncomplicated. The factional character of Japanese parties can be a major problem, especially if a faction is encouraged by external pressure groups. Thus, at the time of negotiations between Japan and the Soviet Union for a treaty of peace, some leaders within the Liberal Democratic Party, supported by certain fishery and commercial groups, built up pressure for a rapid settlement. This was resisted by top Foreign Office officials but, for a time, Japan suffered once again from dual diplomacy. The Foreign Office has also faced jurisdictional and policy quarrels with other ministries, on occasion. Japan, however, does not have the massive problem of reconciling and integrating a Pentagon-CIA-State Department triumvirate in the foreign policy field. On the whole, coordination of the formulation and execution of foreign policy has been more satisfactory in recent years than at any other time in the history of Japan.

There is another side to the coin. Japanese pressure groups, public opinion, and opposition parties have added many new complexities to the scene. As we noted earlier, pressure groups of all types exist. Their number, diversity and influence on Japanese foreign policy has increased greatly. It is not appropriate here to attempt any detailed discussion; only a few salient points can be presented. As in the prewar era, the commercial and industrial groups have the greatest single influence on the Liberal Democratic Party, especially in the field of foreign policy. These speak through the Japan Employers Association and many similar organizations. It would be a mistake, however, to assume that the Japanese business and industrial world speaks with a single voice. On such an issue as trade with China, for example, it is far from unanimous. Still, the broad outlines of Japanese foreign policy at present are deeply influenced by the interests and views of leading industrial and commercial pressure groups. They remain the chief financial support for the Liberal Democratic Party, they include the most intimate confidants of conservative politicians and, hence, they are the most powerful unofficial influence on public policy, domestic and foreign.

On certain issues, pressures emanating from rural Japan can also be important. Almost every Japanese farm-er belongs to an Agricultural Cooperative Association, and these Associations are vital to the fortunes of individual politicians and to the Liberal Democratic Party as a whole. Rural Japan constitutes approximately 25 per cent of the electorate, a portion that votes overwhelmingly conservative. The greatest agrarian pressures are exercised on domestic issues, but standing agrarian interests and attitudes do not need to be articulated constantly to establish certain guidelines and limits in foreign policy.

The more serious of the factors that complicate the formulation of Japanese foreign policy, however, are not the traditional Japanese pressure groups, but certain new ones, and the force of public opinion as it is revealed in countless polls. Among the opposition pressure groups, the most important is organized labor. Sohyo, the General Council of Trade Unions of Japan, has been especially vocal on foreign policy. It has hewed closely to, and helped to shape the socialist position on neutralism, relations with the communist world, American imperialism, and many other issues. In addition, it has supported these positions with demonstrations, work stoppages, and quantities of political literature.

Sohyo, with more than three million members, is probably the most formidable of the opposition pressure groups (though it should not be implied that it can commit all its members on any issue). There are, however, a number of others. Most of them represent intellectual, student, and labor elements in Japanese society. This opposition, as we indicated earlier, cannot be ignored. It maintains a substantial forum by means of newspapers, magazines, and radio. Its message reaches the Japanese public, especially the urban public, regularly. So,

since 1950, foreign policy has become a vital part of the political battlefield in Japan, probably the most vital part. The conservatives have been forced to recognize a far more significant opposition than any experienced in the prewar era, and they have had to devise new methods of meeting that opposition. Suppression or indifference are no longer feasible. Thus the conservatives are also resorting to the media of mass communication and seeking public support more actively than in the past.

It is a most difficult task to assess the influence of Japanese public opinion on foreign policy. In recent years, polling has become very popular in Japan. It is carried out by a variety of organizations, the most widely regarded polls being those which resemble the leading American polls. The major Japanese newspapers, in particular, poll the public at regular intervals on a wide variety of subjects, including many issues of foreign policy. Opinions on rearmament, a security treaty with the United States, and relations with China have been asked for frequently. And, in a number of cases, the polls have indicated that either a large minority or an actual majority of those polled differed with government policy.

There is little doubt that public opinion, now being presented in these concrete, measured forms, has had a rising impact on decision making in Japan. Increasingly, it is a factor which Japanese leaders take seriously. Sometimes, to be sure, public opinion is used to justify a decision based mainly on other grounds. But more frequently, when the polls indicate substantial public opposition to a given policy, conservative leaders respond with modifications, a shift in timing, or a more intensive public relations campaign. The reluctance of recent conservative administrations to rearm rapidly or fully, the long and fairly firm Japanese bargaining in connection with the revised security treaty, and the cautious, ambivalent position toward China are all indications of the new power of the Japanese common man.

However, the Japanese conservatives are well aware of the fact that elections in Japan are not won primarily on the basis of issues, particularly issues of foreign policy. In recent elections, the Liberal Democrats have stressed domestic issues—notably prosperity and progress—and they count heavily on their superior organization, their greater funds, and their local leadership. Thus they can afford to take chances, even when they know or suspect that there is strong public opposition to specific foreign policies. This is the more true because they believe (with reason) that a mere numerical count of opposition is misleading. Opposition of the intensity likely to be translated into political action is largely confined to urban centers, especially Tokyo. Thus, when it is confronted with evidence of hostile public opinion, the government tactic is to camouflage or alter a policy slightly, so as to disarm some of the opposition, but rarely if ever to make changes. With respect to the socialists also, a *caveat* must be entered regarding the influence of public opinion. The record would indicate that the Japanese socialists have often ignored public opinion when it conflicted with their ideological purity.

In sum, the process of formulating, executing, and defending Japanese foreign policy today is in the hands of a conservative elite. The formal and informal institutional processes have been greatly refined in the postwar era, and now operate at a fairly high level of efficiency. Collaboration between the Foreign Office and the Liberal Democratic Party is close and continuous. Despite some problems, the old rivalries have largely been eliminated. With the military clearly subordinated, and with cooperation between party and government at a peak, Japanese foreign policy has achieved an unprecedented degree of coordination and continuity. The new Japanese Foreign Office men, moreover, are more broadly recruited and trained than they were before World War II, and they possess a higher level of technical proficiency.

The conservative elite that directs Japanese foreign policy is sustained and influenced mainly by the industrial, commercial, and agrarian segments of Japanese society. Contradictory pressures, however, sometimes flow from these elements. In any case, no simple economic analysis does justice to the realities of the situation. Among other things, Japan is becoming a mass society in which the conservative elite is forced to pay increasing attention to public opinion. In part, this is reflective of the fact that the public has a choice: the socialist opposition, while weak, is infinitely more important than it was before 1945, and it offers the Japanese people a dramatically different foreign policy. But the influence of public opinion in Japan today can easily be exaggerated. With respect to foreign policy, it would be most accurate to say that public opinion serves to effect certain modifications, both of substance and of timing, and causes the conservatives to give more attention to the public image of their policies.

CONTEMPORARY ISSUES IN JAPANESE FOREIGN POLICY

At present, three dominant considerations underlie the debates and decisions pertaining to foreign policy in

Japan. First, there are the interrelated issues of nationalism and security, issues involving Japanese relations with the United States, the communist bloc, and the world. Second, there is the high priority that must be accorded economic considerations in foreign policy—the extreme importance attached to such matters as trade, technical assistance opportunities, and equality of economic treatment by others. Finally, there exists within Japanese society an ardent search for some basic purpose or function, especially one that will relate Japan in a suitable manner to the Asian world, catering to her special interests there, while allowing her a major place on the world stage. We must study these general considerations further in the context of specific issues, for they are likely to be the enduring as well as the underlying forces motivating Japanese society. Indeed, if the background that we have projected is examined closely, these forces will be seen to have persisted, in different forms, throughout the history of modern Japan.

Nationalism, security and foreign policy

Given the years of defeat, occupation, and subordination to foreign authority, the recent resurgence of Japanese nationalism is completely understandable. Indeed, it is surprising that nationalism has not been a more important component of Japanese foreign policy. Currently, however, Japanese nationalism is not as narrow as it was before World War II. It runs the entire political gamut. Old-line conservative and ultra-rightist doctrines are once more in evidence, although they are largely lacking in public appeal. Some attempt to preserve or revive the Emperor cult has been made, and assassination is again a sporadic factor in the political scene.

Elements of the right, moreover, occasionally join the left in an anti-American, Pan-Asian chorus, evoking memories of earlier attempts to exclude the West from Asia and establish a Greater East-Asian Co-Prosperity Sphere.

Meanwhile, the left also finds nationalism a potent political weapon. American bases in Japan, the Okinawan occupation, and all issues revolving around the so-called subordination to America are approached nationalistically. In foreign policy, particularly, socialist and communist attacks on the conservatives are generally spearheaded by nationalist slogans. On domestic issues, the situation is sometimes reversed. When the Liberal Democrats attack the new Constitution, they do so partially in nationalist terms, referring to it as a document unsuitable for Japan in certain of its American-imposed provisions. It is the socialists who defend many of the foreign innovations as representing the true will of the Japanese people. And there are other respects in which the nationalist mantle seems to be worn by the conservatives, particularly on matters of education and culture.

In some respects, Japanese nationalism today is reminiscent of the Meiji era. Its dominant notes are defensive in character: Japan is an island of weakness surrounded by a sea of power. But this time the power is Asian as well as Western. The continent is no longer a vacuum; China, possessed of a huge standing army and rapidly acquiring nuclear weapons, is becoming a major power. Indeed, the containment of China is likely to be the major Asian problem for the decades that lie ahead. Fortunately for Japan, the Sino-Soviet alliance currently lies in shreds; but, by itself, the Soviet Union is another major

Asian power, and one having certain basic differences in national interest from Japan.

Under these conditions, it seems highly unlikely that Japanese nationalism will revert quickly or easily to its former themes of expansionism and a militant messianic mission. The burning issues are more likely to concern the best way in which to preserve the territorial integrity and the true independence of Japan. And these have been the issues of the day. On the one hand, questions of extraterritoriality, foreign bases, equality of treatment in commercial agreements—in short, questions of true independence from the United States—have come to the fore. But there is another way in which the basic issue can be posed: Under present conditions, how can Japan achieve security, lasting prosperity, and meaningful independence, except in close alliance with the United States?

Thus the great debate in Japan is over neutralism versus alliance. It is clear that neutralism has substantial support, and not merely from the organized left. World War II left terrible scars that will not soon be eradicated. Over two hundred thousand Japanese still suffer from radioactive diseases as a result of the atom bombs dropped on Hiroshima and Nagasaki. There are additional thousands who bear combat injuries or the marks of the great fire raids on major Japanese cities. The living symbols of the last war contribute strongly to a Japanese distaste for rearmament or heavy involvement in international power politics. And there is the widespread fear that alliance with the United States and, particularly, the presence of American bases on Japanese territory, will greatly increase the risk of Japanese involvement in war, especially in view of the troubled Asian scene.

The Japanese also ask whether the United States will or can actually provide security for Japan. Indeed, this may well be the crucial question of the next decade. Hence, American fortunes elsewhere in Asia will have a major, possibly decisive effect on trends in Japan. Many Japanese argue that, since China and the Soviet Union are major military powers, Japan should reconcile herself to the status of a minor power and seek security in some kind of international guarantee, rather than seeking to play a larger political and military role with American support. The Japanese population, which is now approaching one hundred million, must import 80 per cent of its industrial raw materials and about 20 per cent of its foodstuffs. Its cities are massive, densely packed, and highly vulnerable. They lie minutes away from communist bases. The American lines of supply and communication are long, and in the event of war, uncertain.

Perhaps all these points add up to a feeling, in some Japanese circles, that military and political developments, especially in Asia, make warfare a suicidal undertaking for modern Japan.

Some of these feelings lay behind the serious political crisis that developed, in the spring of 1960, over the revised security treaty with the United States. This crisis produced the most substantial mass movement in Japanese political history. Millions of Japanese signed petitions asking that the Diet be dissolved and new elections held. Hundreds of thousands demonstrated in Tokyo and other major cities. The acute stage of the crisis lasted for nearly one month, from mid-May to early June.

Naturally, the organized left played an important part in this crisis. But to dismiss the episode as communist or even socialist-controlled is to misunderstand seriously the climate of Japanese politics and public opinion. No one knows this better than the Japanese conservatives. The May-June Incident was the product of many complex factors: the increasing unpopularity of the Kishi government; the almost unanimous opposition of the metropolitan press to government actions, which helped to mobilize public sentiment; factionalism inside the Liberal Democratic Party, which helped to weaken Kishi's internal base of support; and the tactics used in forcing the treaty through the House of Representatives which gave opponents a new slogan, "for the protection of democracy," an appeal enlisting support even from some conservatives.

Certainly, the socialists cannot be exempted from responsibility for the crisis. In addition to their policy positions, the socialists hold certain special views on tactics. In socialist circles, a considerable ambivalence toward the concept of parliamentarism still exists. A number of socialists believe in parliamentarism plus, and are willing to go beyond parliamentary procedures, if necessary, to attain their ends. They do not accept completely the right of the majority to govern, and they do not eschew violence if it offers a chance of success.

Actually, the May-June Incident revealed some of the continuing weaknesses of Japanese parties and parliamentarism. No party really gained as a result of the crisis. With the revised treaty safely enacted, Kishi resigned, but after playing a major role in selecting his successor, Hayato Ikeda. Ikeda took office with conciliatory offers to consult with the opposition and operate in democratic fashion, to pay attention to public opinion, and to build a prosperous, peaceful Japan. Armed

with these pledges, the Liberal Democrats easily won in the elections of November, 1960, garnering 58 per cent of the vote, and 296 of the 467 seats in the House of Representatives. Majority control was also maintained in the thirtieth general election of November, 1963, when the Liberal Democrats won 55 per cent of the vote, and 283 seats. The disunited left received 39 and 40 per cent of the votes in the 1960 and 1963 elections.

Despite their sizeable electoral victories, the Japanese conservatives are well aware of the deep division in Japanese public opinion over security issues, and of the political hazards involved. Omitting the Democratic Socialists, who take a moderate view, the socialists and communists who have repeatedly registered their violent opposition to rearmament and to the military alliance now poll about one-third of the vote. Public opinion polls, moreover, indicate that about one-third of the electorate share socialist views on these issues, and that another sizeable element is uncertain or disinterested. Consequently, the conservatives have been cautious in approaching such questions. In recent budgets, appropriations for the Japan Self-Defense Force have totalled about 10 per cent, a very low figure in comparison with most of the other major nations of the world.

There is every indication that Japan will retain a military tie with the United States but will not become a major military ally in the near future. The Japanese military will probably be restricted to limited, non-nuclear (but modern) armaments, for defense only, at least for the next five years. In all likelihood, public opposition will preclude the addition of atomic weapons to the arsenal of the defense force, or the storage of such weapons on Japanese soil by the Americans. The numerical growth of the defense force will be very gradual and limited. As we noted earlier, its present total size is only about 275,000 men. There will be no attempt in the near future to commit these forces abroad, even for use by an international body like the United Nations. It is also unlikely that Article 9 of the Constitution will be repealed or altered, since the conservatives do not have the votes to accomplish this.

Nevertheless, there are some indications that a broad reconsideration of Japanese foreign policy, including its military component, has begun. Slowly, a recognition is developing that China presents both a military and a political threat to the other Asian states including Japan, a threat that can be met only by some balancing force, in which the leading noncommunist Asian states must play a significant role. Already, Japan has begun cautiously to play a more active political role in Asia, aligning herself with such states as India in the international scene. The extent to which she will also upgrade her military commitments as her political commitments in the world, and especially in Asia, grow, is yet uncertain. There can be no doubt, however, that a heightened discussion of this matter is under way, even in intellectual circles.

Meanwhile, in a major address to the Diet, on January 25, 1965, Prime Minister Sato outlined the twin themes that currently dominate Japanese foreign policy. Speaking of his recent visit to the United States, Sato asserted:

I emphasized that, for the maintenance of world peace, stability in Asia is essential and explained our country's policy to contribute to the promotion of the welfare of the Asian peoples by helping stabilize their livelihood and elevating their standard of living in the spirit of devoting ourselves to the cause of peace. . . .

I also reaffirmed Japan's policy to maintain firmly the Japan-United States Mutual Cooperation and Security Treaty arrangements in the belief that it is essential for the stability and peace of Asia that there be no uncertainty about our country's security.

The prospects for the continuance of the Japan-American alliance are good. However, to make that alliance more acceptable and to advance Japanese national interests, the conservatives will continue to approach issues of military security with an admixture of caution and tough bargaining. Under Japanese pressure, various adjustments have been made with respect to American military installations and their uses. With regard to Okinawa, a Japan–United States Consultative Committee has been established, and recently that Committee has expanded its authority to include not only questions of economic assistance but "various other problems concerning the promotion of the well-being of the Okinawans." The Japanese government continues to press for the return of administrative authority over Okinawa to Japan, and clearly, the establishment of this Committee represents an intermediate step in that direction.

The Sato government, like the conservative governments before it, is firmly committed to close cooperation with the United States, but it wants a heightened emphasis on Japanese interests, a partnership between equals, a continuous movement away from the heavy dependency of the Occupation era. This is both logical and politically expedient. Most recently, Sato expressed his views in the following words:

I perceived in the attitude of the American authorities a firm determination to cooperate with Japan for the attainment of world peace and at the same time to address themselves to the task of settling the problems pending between Japan and the United States while fully respecting each other's standpoints and national interests. I believe that I was able to achieve success because I discussed pressing problems instead of merely abstract questions frankly and in a concerted manner. I am convinced that through the recent talks, Japanese-American relations have entered a new stage of development. . . .

It is my intention to conduct an independent diplomacy and fully pursue our country's national interest and security, keeping as the supreme goal the establishment and maintenance of world peace based on freedom and justice. Needless to say, the national interest I seek is one closely tied to the cause of world peace and based on international cooperation. I would like to assert without hesitation our country's rightful interest in international community while discharging the responsibilities commensurate with our elevated international position.

Japan also continues to seek friendly, or at least normal, relations with the communist bloc. Shortly after the Korean War ended, an attempt to normalize these relations began. Negotiations with the Soviet Union, which culminated in the Treaty of 1956, were the opening move, but, in keeping with the past, Russia made very few concessions. Until recently, therefore, Russo-Japanese relations have been minimal. Within Japan, antipathy to the U.S.S.R. has been relatively strong, a product of historic rivalries, the last-minute attack in 1945, Russian treatment of Japanese prisoners, and its "get-tough" policy toward Japan on most postwar issues.

Recently, however, the Soviet Union has made some gains, at least with the Japanese public. The policy of peaceful coexistence, begun by Khrushchev and continued by his successors, has had a generally favorable impact upon the Japanese, especially on the socialists, who are today more pro-Russian than at any time in their postwar history. There is also some evidence that the Soviet Union has decided to woo Japan in more meaningful fashion than in the past. Recently, Soviet Premier Kosygin wrote Sato expressing a desire for personal contact, and a number of other minor indications of a possible shift in Russian policy can be found. The Russians, it should be remembered, are no longer *persona grata* with the main stream of the Japanese Communist Party, hence their main effort has recently been to cultivate the broader, more meaningful noncommunist left. Up to date, however, no specific concessions to Japan have been made. The Russians have even refused to yield the two small islands of Habomai and Shikotan off Hokkaido, unless the security treaty with the United States is abandoned. And other problems remain. But if official Soviet-Japanese relations are thawing only slowly and with difficulty, one cannot rule out the possibility of a significant Soviet effort in this direction. The Japanese conservatives are almost certain to view such a drive with caution, while hopeful that the widening Sino-Soviet breach will make possible the redress of certain Japanese grievances. Beyond this, one can muse on the possibility of a Russo-Japanese alliance against China, in place of or in conjunction with an American-Japanese alliance. Some variant of current Indian policy might be attempted; namely, the movement toward an "equilibrium" policy vis-à-vis the United States and the Soviet Union, whereby the American alliance was retained, but a more positive relationship with Russia was established to counteract the threat from China.

At the moment, however, relations

with China are still regarded as much more important by most Japanese. Japan has had a lengthy historic relationship with China, and it is inconceivable to many Japanese that the ties can remain as limited as they now are. Within Japan, pressures for a realistic policy toward China have mounted. Various business interests continue to believe that the China trade can again become meaningful, even if it is different and smaller than before 1945, and there is evidence to support this, trade is increasing. Certain conservative leaders are at odds with the present policy, which they regard as the result of excessive deference to the United States. The socialists, of course, have sought to make a major political issue out of policy toward China. They have long demanded full and unqualified recognition of the Chinese People's Republic, and have denounced the conservatives for preventing this by a policy of military alliance with the United States. On two occasions now, the Socialist Party has made common cause with Peking in joint communiqués denouncing "American imperialism" as "the enemy of the peoples of the entire world."

Despite the substantial internal pressures, however, official policy toward China has remained cautious. The attempt has been to seek some readjustment of policy toward China that will accord with the realities of the situation without conceding on all points to the Chinese communists and thereby jeopardizing relations with the United States and Taiwan. Prime Minister Sato reiterated the official, conservative position when he stated, on January 25, 1965:

It needs no expatiation that the problem of China holds a very great importance in present-day international politics. Especially for our country, which has a close relationship with China both his-torically and geographically, this problem is one of great importance with a variety of implications. I believe, therefore, that our country should deal with this problem prudently and from its own independent viewpoint, without making unnecessary haste to reach a conclusion. At the present stage, our country intends to promote economic and cultural interchange with Communist China on the basic principle of separation of political matters and economic matters, while maintaining the friendly relations with the Republic of China with which Japan has regular diplomatic relations.

Clearly, the Japanese government would like to realize a "two Chinas" policy or, more properly, a "one China, one Taiwan" policy. It can be expected to work to this end, and to put increasing pressure on the United States. The Chinese communists are aware of this, and determined to prevent it if possible. This is why they have been pursuing a tough policy, rejecting full economic relations unless they are accorded formal recognition and Taiwan is accepted as an internal problem of China. Moreover, there can be no doubt that the Chinese communists see the American-Japanese military alliance as a potential threat to them, and would like to break it up. Whether they will attempt this by pursuing a tough policy or a soft policy in the future is yet unclear; in the past, they have alternated uncertainly between the two approaches.

Thus once again, Japan is faced with the problem of finding a workable China policy, and this time it must be based more upon the strength than the weakness of that nation. Her success cannot be predicted; the variables are too numerous and they go far beyond Japan. Even if improvements are scored, however, it is very doubtful, given the political realities, that Sino-Japanese relations will be marked by great intimacy in the near future. The chances are strong that China will remain communist and Japan anticommunist; that economic as well as political rivalries will build up in the Asian area; that both states will reflect their differences by seeking alliances outside Asia as well as within. Nevertheless, Japan will attempt to follow a flexible, realistic policy under conservative leadership, exploring every economic opportunity and moving toward a "one China, one Taiwan" policy, if at all possible.

In sum, all forces in Japan today pay homage to the idea of an independent foreign policy, and the removal of those inequities remaining from the Occupation era. Increasingly, the conservatives believe that independence can only be truly achieved and maintained if Japan has her own military force, and is, at the same time, connected with the military power of the United States. Therefore they support the alliance, emphasizing its economic and political advantages and balancing its military risks against those of neutralism. If the internal prosperity of Japan continues, and no general war occurs, the conservatives will probably remain in power for the indefinite future, and they are not likely to undertake drastic shifts in this policy. Two major and interrelated debates, however, are likely to get hotter in the years ahead, namely those over neutralism versus alliance and full-scale rearmament versus limited defensive armament. The year 1970, when the Mutual Security Treaty can be revised, is likely to bring these issues to a climax, if crises prior to that time do not do so.

The economic basis of Japanese foreign policy

The high priority given to economic considerations in formulating Japanese foreign policy stems from many factors. In 1965, the Japanese population was approaching 100 million. This vast number of people live in a country the size of California, and only approximately 16 per cent of the land is arable. It is calculated that the population will probably be stabilized within the next twenty years, but there will then be 110 to 120 million people. Meanwhile, many millions of new workers will come onto the labor market, requiring further industrialization. Japanese industry, moreover, is very dependent on foreign trade. As we have already noted, over 80 per cent of all industrial raw materials are imported.

In addition, there are some dynamic, new factors in the scene. We have noted that the recent rate of Japanese economic growth rate has been spectacular, averaging 10 per cent annually. The major gains, of course, have been in industrial production, but agricultural production has also been increasing. The result has been an unprecedented degree of prosperity for Japan, albeit with occasional recessions. The per capita income, still low compared with that of the United States and certain parts of Western Europe, is growing fast. The result is that Japan is one of the very few countries of the Afro-Asian region where the revolution of rising expectations is really in progress. Almost all segments of Japanese society have participated in the boom.

But once this pace is set, it becomes imperative, from a political standpoint, to retain and, if possible, advance it. The Japanese conservatives are well aware of the fact that their future depends heavily on their capacity to meet the new desires and expectations of their people. Thus, the new ten-year economic program has been named The Plan for Doubling the People's Income. Furthermore, many conservatives talk frankly about the need for a welfare state. Indeed, they are doing more than talking; they are putting increasing sums of money into housing, road construction, and social security. To sustain these expenditures, and to increase them, general economic expansion—and particularly the expansion of trade—is vital.

Economic relations with the United States are likely to remain the single most important factor in determining the fate of the Japanese economy. Approximately one-third of Japanese trade is presently with this country. In 1965, trade between the United States and Japan exceeded $4 billion. Inevitably, this rapidly expanding trade has created certain problems for both parties. The United States has periodically been disturbed about the obstacles to foreign investment in Japan that have hampered American concerns seeking to establish themselves there. Some American producers, notably of textiles, marine products, and flatware, have demanded protection against "low-wage" Japanese goods and against alleged malpractices. The Japanese have complained, too— about unscrupulous American buyers who take advantage of the highly competitive nature of Japanese small and medium-scale industry, pursuing cut-throat tactics and encouraging illegal or immoral practices; about the penchant of American industry to exaggerate Japanese competition; about the trade deficit with the United States; and about the "unequal treatment" accorded Japan in certain commercial agreements.

Currently, such problems as Japanese air routes over the United States and Japanese fishing rights in the North Pacific are creating difficulties. To solve problems like these, the Joint United States-Japan Committee on Trade and Economic Affairs was established at the outset of the Kennedy Administration, and it has continued to function via yearly meetings attended by top-level American and Japanese officials. A number of vexing questions have been handled or discussed frankly at these meetings, and both sides agree that the Committee has been a valuable mechanism. Increasingly, as in the political field, Japan is pressing for equal economic rights, and bargaining on some points has been spirited.

The remainder of Japanese trade is very diverse. Outside the United States, no single country accounts for more than a small fraction of Japanese exports. In part, this pattern reflects the serious decline in Japanese trade with the Northeast Asian area, including China, Manchuria, and the former Japanese Empire. In the prewar period, when Japan controlled Taiwan, Korea, and Manchuria, and used these areas both for investments and as markets, this trade was of major importance.

While Japan recognizes that the old trade patterns cannot be reestablished, its interest in this region continues high. As we noted earlier, there is considerable doubt, in some commercial circles, as to whether trade with China can become truly significant in the near future. Problems of Chinese foreign exchange, the availability of Chinese products desired in Japan, and the omnipresent political factors involved in such trade are all obstacles to rapidly increased Japanese-Chinese economic relations. Trade in recent years has fluctuated, depending on both economic and political conditions. It currently stands at only 2 per cent of total Japanese trade, and is conducted via private trade agreements between Chinese authorities and Japanese firms, many of them classified by the communists as "friendly." The Japanese government, beset with numerous pressures, will undoubtedly continue to explore methods of improving her economic relations with China.

The trade with Taiwan is significant, and Japan has no intention of allowing this to be scrapped. Moreover, the conclusion of a treaty between Japan and the Republic of Korea in 1965, after many years of negotiations and political crises, promises greatly expanded economic relations with South Korea. Thus, gradually, Japan is rebuilding her economic ties with Northeast Asia, China remaining the great question mark.

Meanwhile, the quest for new markets and economic opportunities continues, with particular emphasis on the markets of Asia, the Middle East, and Africa. The export goal for fiscal 1965 was set at $8,000 million. Japanese businessmen have canvassed possibilities on every continent. There is hope of breaking down the restrictive trade practices practiced by certain European countries against Japanese goods, and of thus expanding Japanese trade with a prosperous Europe, but Japan continues to place her greatest faith in the Afro-Asian world. She expects to export major goods and services to societies *en route* to modernization. She is continuing to shift her emphasis toward heavy industrial and chemical products, recognizing that new competition and increasing self-sufficiency in light industry are probable. At the same time, she is anxious to explore every cooperative way of advancing technical assistance and capital to these countries, hoping to participate in all such programs. Thus, Prime Minister Sato hailed the Asia Development Bank scheme and immediately announced that Japan would increase her commitments to this region. By 1965, incidentally, Japan had already completed the payment of 53 per cent of her total reparations, which were $1,019 million, and much of this money went to the nations of Southeast Asia.

In sum, the conservative leaders will continue to give very heavy weight to economic considerations in determining Japanese foreign policy, because this is required by the political and economic facts of life in contemporary Japan. They will count strongly on favorable and expanding economic relations with the United States. At the same time, they will be anxious to lessen their dependency on American trade, not by reducing it, but by expanding their trade with all other regions of the world. Their emphasis will be upon the markets of Africa and Asia, especially the latter. Gradually, moreover, they will assume some of the global responsibilities of a major, advanced society.

Basic Japanese goals

In many respects, Japan is still searching for a basic purpose, a role to play in the modern world. The fact that this purpose or role has not been easy to find in the shattering aftermath of total defeat helps to account for some of the unrest in Japanese society, especially among the youth. There has been a certain tendency, in the postwar period, to go from moods of black despair to quests for lofty, idealistic causes. Perhaps this accounts in part for the enthusiasm shown in Japan for the United Nations and for the eagerness with which Japanese participation was greeted.

The great support accorded the United Nations may also reflect the initial Japanese acceptance of the status of a minor state after 1945. But here, there is increasing ambivalence. The recent pronouncements of Japanese leaders refer repeatedly to Japan's "responsibilities" as "one of the major, advanced societies." At present, these responsibilities are being defined primarily in economic and political terms, but there may ultimately be a reconsideration of Japan's military program, as we observed earlier. The problem of how to contain China is certain to be a major issue in Japan, as elsewhere in Asia, in the years that lie ahead.

Meanwhile, Japan hopes to play an increasingly significant role in the United Nations and other international bodies, in part as a bridge between Asia and the West. She knows that she has numerous competitors for this role, and that she has some lost ground to regain. However, she has certain unique capacities—among them, the fact that she is still the only advanced industrial society in the Asian area. This uniqueness is not an unmixed blessing, as we have noted earlier. It produces conflicting sentiments. In part, Japan sees herself as *sui generis*, and displays, on occasion, a strong ethnocentrism, finding it difficult to understand, communicate with, or adjust to others, including her fellow Asians. But Japan also sees herself as a synthesis of Asian and Western culture, an embodiment of the *modern*, non-Western society, and when this image predominates, she can display a highly sophisticated universality and a capacity to understand, adjust, and lead.

For twenty years, the Anglo-Japanese Alliance underwrote Japanese policy in Asia. Then through the disintegration of that alliance and Japanese abuses, Japanese plans and hopes came to naught. Now an American alliance has given Japan a second opportunity for an Asian policy which, if it is to be successful, however, must be marked by moderation and a cooperative spirit. How long will this new alliance last? To this question, there can be no certain answer. For the past fifteen years, it has been a logical alliance in terms of the needs and goals of both nations as viewed by their respective leaders and the majority of their peoples. Needs, goals, and leaders sometimes change. It is likely, moreover, that the international climate that surrounds this alliance— particularly the climate in Asia—will become more stormy in the years ahead. Thus the premium will be upon flexibility, a capacity of both parties in the alliance to adjust to new conditions. From Japan, in particular, this may require some major commitments for which, as yet, her people are scarcely prepared.

No doubt political storms lie ahead, particularly over the military aspects of the alliance. If economic relations retain a vital meaning for both societies, however, and cultural ties continue to expand, the hazards may be surmounted. Naturally, the attitudes and the actions of the communists— particularly the Chinese—will have a major influence on American-Japanese relations. On balance, there is every reason to believe that this alliance will remain one of the most meaningful between the West and the Asian world, and an important anchor-point for the foreign policies of both the United States and Japan. At the same time, the next decade should see the reemergence of Japan as a world power, not only economically, but politically as well.

SELECTED BIBLIOGRAPHY

There is a wealth of primary and secondary source materials on Japanese foreign policy for the reader who can use the Japanese language. Memoirs of prominent statesmen are abundant; a number of documentary collections and good secondary works exist; and many of the Japanese Foreign Office Archives, having been microfilmed during the Occupation, are obtainable through the Library of Congress. To list even the most essential Japanese materials would be a lengthy task, and one not appropriate here. Fortunately, the reader of Japanese can refer to a number of sources for bibliographic assistance. We shall merely suggest some English-language materials, with emphasis upon more recent books.

Although English materials are still far too limited, the last ten years have seen an increasing number of worthy articles, monographs, and general studies, many of which deal in some fashion with Japanese foreign policy.

To start with the historical background of Japanese international relations, one might mention the older work of R. H. Akagi, Japan's Foreign Relations: 1542–1936 (Argus, 1936), but the historical writings of Sir George Sansom provide an excellent introduction to this as to other facets of traditional Japan: Japan—A Short Cultural History (New York: Appleton-Century-Crofts, 1943); A History of Japan to 1334 (Stanford, Calif.: Stanford University Press, 1958); A History of Japan, 1334–1615 (Stanford Calif.: Stanford University Press, 1960); and The Western World and Japan (New York: Alfred A. Knopf, Inc., 1950).

To these should be added C. R. Boxer's Christian Century in Japan (Berkeley: University of California Press, 1951), for a careful exposition of initial Western contacts.

In the modern period, a few general works include materials on foreign policy. One might select Hugh Borton's Japan's Modern Century (New York: The Ronald Press Company, 1955); and Chitoshi Yanaga's Japanese People and Politics (New York: John Wiley & Sons, Inc., 1956), as recent works of this type.

For those particularly interested in the early Meiji period, we are fortunate in having the work of W. G. Beasley. Great Britain and the Opening of Japan: 1834–1858 (Luzac, 1951) has been followed by Select Documents on Japanese Foreign Policy: 1853–1868 (Oxford, 1955). These serve as an admirable introduction to the problems of the early Meiji era, which began in 1867.

The memoirs and accounts of Western diplomats and other residents are also of interest: E. M. Satow, A Diplomat in Japan (Philadelphia: J. B. Lippincott Co., 1921); Sir Rutherford Alcock, The Capital of the Tycoon, 2 vols. (London, 1863); J. H. Gubbins, The Progress of Japan: 1853–1871 (Oxford, 1911).

There are also a few monographs of special interest, mainly pertaining to the later Meiji period. Two of these are Hilary Conroy, The Japanese Seizure of Korea (Philadelphia: University of Pennsylvania Press, 1960); and Marius B. Jansen, The Japanese and the Chinese Revolutionary Movement: 1895–1915.

The Taisho period (1912–1926) is rather sparsely covered as yet. Masamichi Royama has written one work in English, entitled The Foreign Policy of Japan: 1914–1939 (Tokyo, 1941; the older work by T. Takeuchi, War and Diplomacy in the Japanese Empire (Garden City, N.Y.: Doubleday & Company, Inc., 1935), may still have some utility.

The books by A. M. Young, especially his Japan in Recent Times: 1912–1926 (New York: William Morrow & Co., Inc., 1928), are of interest as contemporary accounts; and the Young newspaper, the Kobe (later Japan) Chronicle, is a most important source for many events of the entire period between the mid-Meiji and prewar Showa eras.

For most readers, the Showa period is likely to be of greatest interest. For the militarist era of the 1930's, the most important materials are contained in two memoirs: the so-called *Harada-Saionji Memoirs* and the *Kido Diary;* neither of these has been published in English, but both are available at certain leading libraries in the United States in mimeographed form, in whole or in part.

Perhaps no single English source is as valuable as the voluminous *War Crimes Trial Documents,* running into thousands of pages, which were translated for the famous Tokyo trials. These also can be obtained; a complete set exists, for instance, at the Berkeley library.

Among existing Western memoirs, special mention should be made of J. C. Grew, *Ten Years in Japan* (Simon & Schuster, 1944), and Sir R. Craigie, *Behind the Japanese Mask* (London: Hutchinson & Co. (Publishers), Ltd. 1946).

From the Japanese side, see Mamoru Shigemitsu, *Japan and Her Destiny* (New York: E. P. Dutton & Co., Inc., 1958).

We have a general account of this wartime period in F. C. Jones, *Japan's New Order in East Asia: Its Rise and Fall, 1937–1945* (Oxford, 1954).

A growing number of monographs dealing with this general period are available. Yale Maxon explores the problems involved in formulating Japanese foreign policy in his *Control of Japanese Foreign Policy: A Study of Civil-Military Rivalry, 1930–1945,* (Berkeley: University of California, 1957).

For other worthy studies, see Harry J. Benda, *The Crescent and the Rising Sun* (Institute of Pacific Relations, 1958), Robert Butow, *Japan's Decision to Surrender* (Stanford, Calif.: Stanford University Press, 1955); Willard H. Elsbree, *Japan's Role in Southeast Asian Nationalist Movements, 1940–1945* (Cambridge, Mass.: Harvard University Press, 1953); Ernst Preusseisen, *Germany and Japan: A Study in Totalitarian Diplomacy, 1933–1941* (The Hague, 1958); and Paul Schroeder, *The Axis Alliance and Japanese-American Relations, 1941* (Ithaca, N.Y.: Cornell University Press, 1958).

Japanese accounts of the war can be obtained from T. Kase, *Journey to the Missouri*

(New Haven, Conn.: Yale University Press, 1950); M. Kato, *The Lost War* (New York.: Alfred A. Knopf, Inc., 1946); and Saburo Hayashi, in collaboration with Alvin D. Coox, *Kogun: The Japanese Army in the Pacific War* (Marine Corps Association, 1959).

Various aspects of the postwar period are covered in certain general books: Ardath Burks, *Government in Japan* (New York: Frederick A. Praeger, Inc., 1961); Allan B. Cole, *Japanese Society and Politics* (Boston, 1956), Esler Dening, *Japan* (New York: Frederick A. Praeger, Inc., 1961); Nobutaka Ike, "Japan" in *Major Governments of Asia.* ed. George Kahin (Ithaca, N.Y.: Cornell University Press, 1958), Kazuo Kawai, *Japan's American Interlude* (Chicago: University of Chicago Press, 1960), Ivan Morris, *Nationalism and the Right Wing in Japan* (Oxford, 1960); and Harold Quigley and John Turner, *The New Japan: Government and Politics* (Minneapolis: The University of Minnesota Press, 1956).

See also *Parties and Politics in Contemporary Japan* by Robert A. Scalapino and Junnosuke Masumi (Berkeley: University of California Press, 1962).

In his book, *The Japanese People and Foreign Policy,* Douglas Mendel, Jr., presents an important collection of public opinion polls pertaining to foreign policy issues (Berkeley: University of California Press, 1962).

Naturally, the American reader will tend to have a special interest in American-Japanese relations. A substantial number of books has been written on this subject. Among the older works, those of Payson J. Treat are well known: *Japan and the United States* (rev. ed.; Stanford, Calif.: Stanford University Press, 1928); and *Diplomatic Relations between the United States and Japan,* 3 vols. (Stanford, Calif.: Stanford University Press, 1932, 1938).

There is also Foster Rhea Dulles, *Forty Years of American-Japanese Relations* (New York: Appleton-Century-Crofts, 1937).

A broad cultural account is to be found in T. Dennett, *Americans in Eastern Asia* (Macmillan, 1922).

More recently, such an approach has been effectively used by Robert Schwantes in his

Japanese and Americans: A Century of Cultural Relations (Harper & Row, Publishers, Inc., 1955).

For current political relations, the reader can refer to E. O. Reischauer, *The United States and Japan*, rev. ed. (Cambridge, Mass.: Harvard University Press, 1957); R. A. Scalapino, "The United States and Japan," a section in the American Assembly publication. *The United States and the Far East*, rev. ed. (Englewood Cliffs, N.J.: Prentice-Hall, Inc., 1962); and *United States Foreign Policy: Asia*, a study prepared for the Committee on Foreign Relations, United States Senate (Washington, D.C.: Government Printing Office, 1959); and *The United States and Japan* ed. Herbert Passin (Prentice-Hall, Inc., The American Assembly, 1966).

Official publications from the State Department, such as the series on *Foreign Relations of the United States and Japan*, contain useful major documents.

In addition there are a number of more specialized accounts, limited in scope or time. Only three will be mentioned here: H. L. Stimson, *The Far Eastern Crisis* (New York: Harper & Row, Publishers, Inc., 1936); Herbert Feis, *The Road to Pearl Harbor* (Princeton, N.J.: Princeton University Press, 1950); and Ray W. Curry, *Woodrow Wilson*

and Far Eastern Policy (Twayne, 1957).

No serious study of Japanese foreign policy should be undertaken, of course, without reference to the periodical literature. Among the English-language journals, those carrying articles of significance at rather regular intervals include *Contemporary Japan, The Japan Quarterly*, (formerly *The Far Eastern Quarterly*), *Foreign Affairs, Pacific Affairs*, and *Asian Survey* (formerly *Far Eastern Survey*).

Some reference should also be made to the increasing number of English-language materials being published by the Japanese government, including valuable items pertaining to foreign policy problems and policies from the Ministries of Finance, Trade and Commerce, and the Foreign Office. In reference to contemporary issues it will be helpful to consult the translations of the vernacular press and translations of selected articles from Japanese vernacular magazines which are put out by the American Embassy, if one can obtain access to these.

Such newspapers as the *Japan Times* (formerly *Nippon Times*), the *Osaka Mainichi* English edition, and the *Asahi Evening News* should also be examined. Naturally, many of the above materials will contain further leads and much fuller bibliographies.

China, like Japan, is a relative newcomer to orthodox conduct of foreign relations. For centuries, relations between the imperial court at Peking and the outside world remained tributary in nature. No concept of sovereignty or equality interfered with domination by the Middle Kingdom over dependencies such as Tibet and Mongolia, or vassal states such as Korea and Annam. Beyond these peripheral areas the presence of "foreign barbarians" only occasionally interrupted the splendid isolation of the emperor.

Not until the nineteenth century did Western pressure forcefully break down this isolation. During the first decades, demands for trade, backed with arms, won limited concessions from Peking, but negotiations were restricted to provincial officials immediately concerned with coastal areas. Even when British and French troops shot their way to Peking, forcing establishment of the Tsungli Yamen as an office to deal with foreign governments, Chinese officialdom remained hostile to conventional Western practices of international law and comity.

The collapse of the Manchu Empire and the birth, in 1912, of the Republic of China offer a convenient point of demarcation in the foreign relations of modern China. Still, the resemblance with Western states is more apparent than real. To be sure, the Waichiao Pu, with its consular establishments abroad and its acceptance of international protocol at home functioned as did most ministries of foreign affairs. The difference lay in China's political fragmentation, which left nominal authority with a central government but permitted local warlords to conduct *de facto* if not *de jure* foreign relations.

Civil war rent China apart during the decade 1918–1928, as a northern government at Peking, dominated by shifting military factions, vied for power with a southern government at Canton, headed by Sun Yat-sen and his Kuomintang cohorts. Officially, Peking enjoyed recognition as the legal voice of China until its final defeat by the nationalist army in 1928. Its actual power, however,

9

foreign policy of communist china

allen s. whiting

extended through only a small section of the country. During the turbulent Twenties, most of South China, Tibet, Sinkiang, Mongolia, and Manchuria lay beyond control of the capital.

Thus, an examination of foreign policy during this period would have to consider not only Waichiao Pu activities, but also relations between Soviet Russian advisers and the Canton government. These important clandestine relations continued even after recognition was established between Moscow and Peking in 1924. Similarly, Russian troops assisted a revolutionary regime in Outer Mongolia to eliminate Chinese control in 1921. Despite the recognition, in 1924, of Peking's sovereignty over the area, the Soviet Russian Commissar for Foreign Affairs continued to describe its "autonomy" as permitting "independence in its foreign policy."[1] In like fashion, Moscow ignored Chinese protests and concluded an agreement with Marshal Chang Tso-lin for operation of the Chinese Eastern Railway, which ran through his bailiwick of Manchuria, although a similar agreement had been concluded with Peking only four months before.

In fact, in the history of modern China before 1949, there are few years wherein a central government exercised sufficient authority throughout the legal limits of its declared competence to preclude local conduct of foreign affairs. Japan overran Manchuria in 1931, and set up the independent state of Manchukuo. Soviet Russian authorities concluded extensive agreements with local governors in the border province of Sinkiang, covering loans, trading privileges, and mineral exploitation rights, all without reference to the central government. Even the

miniscule Chinese Communist Party took on itself the power to declare war against Japan in 1932, acting as a Chinese Soviet Republic.

We see then, that an analysis of Chinese foreign policy requires a continual adjustment of scope depending on the time span considered, for it would be fictive to ignore these side currents, some of which proved critical in determining the fate of large sectors of China. The Communist victory over the forces of Chiang Kai-shek in 1949, however, provides a partial solution to the problem, albeit not a wholly successful one. Communist control over the mainland of China and its general acceptance by Asia, if not by the world, as the *de jure* as well as the *de facto* government, compels us to study the regime of Mao Tse-tung. Yet another claimant to China conducts foreign policy in its name—the regime of Chiang Kai-shek, which withdrew to Taiwan in 1949 and continued to function there as the Republic of China. In view of the relatively small domain under his control, and the impossibility of this group reconquering the mainland, we shall focus solely on the People's Republic of China (PRC).

PROBLEMS OF ANALYSIS

The obstacles to an analysis of Soviet China's foreign policy are formidable. Our general perspective is limited by the language barrier, which restricts the number of Western scholars able to read original documents, and extensive translation of nineteenth-century materials on foreign policy has occurred only during the past decade. Furthermore, the turbulence of recent Chinese politics and the authoritarian tendencies of most modern Chinese regimes have seriously limited the materials available. Again, it has been only in the past decade that volumes of doc-

[1]Commissar for Foreign Affairs, Chicherin, to the Congress of Soviets, *Pravda*, No. 54 (2,985), March 6, 1925, p. 5.

uments on the important T'ai P'ing rebellion of a century ago were published
by the Peking regime.

The present government of China is
as secretive about its foreign policy
process as is its mentor, the Soviet
Union. A determined appearance of
"monolithic unity" within the authoritarian elite masks whatever differences
may exist. Complete control over all
media of communication limits the information made available to the West.
Public discussion comes only after
policy has been decided within the
highest levels of the Chinese Communist Party. Government spokesmen
rationalize policy, but need not defend
it in the absence of an organized opposition.

Compounding these physical obstacles to analysis is the interpretive
debate among noncommunists as to
the nature of policy making in Peking.
Is it principally Chinese, and therefore comprehensible only within a continuous flow of policies which date
back to Nationalist or even Manchu
days? Or is it principally communist,
necessitating close study of Marxist-
Leninist-Stalinist precedents for clues
and insights?

Our analysis admits elements of
both arguments, without supporting
either side exclusively. The present
rulers of China are Chinese. They have
lived there, with few exceptions, during most of their past. The environment within which they operate is
essentially the same as that which prevailed in China in the last century. At
the same time, they view that environment through communist lenses. The
elite possesses a highly articulated
ideology which it consciously proclaims
as the basis of behavior: the Marxist-
Leninist creed of communism.

Therefore, we must examine the
Chinese component of policy in terms
of the external environment within

which it operates. Part of this may be
termed "objective"—the physical factors, such as territory, accessibility,
and material development. Part of this
environment is subjective, in that it is
influenced by the way in which historical trends are experienced and perceived by decision makers. Insofar as
the subjective factor has remained
relatively constant in governments
which preceded the communists, we
may term it a Chinese component of
policy.

Then we shall analyze the communist component of policy. Its ideological content is defined by the canons
of Marx, Lenin, Stalin, and Mao. Its
institutional structure springs from
ideological convictions about the role
of the Party, the nature of government,
and the function of authoritarian rule
—or "democratic centralism," as it is
termed. By combining these varied
factors, we can discern more clearly
not only the goals of Soviet China's
foreign policy, but the means available
to the elite and likely to be adopted by
them in support of that policy.

EXTERNAL ENVIRONMENT: THE CHINESE COMPONENT

Physical factors

Although the days of the Chinese
Empire are long past, contemporary
Chinese leaders continue to pay obei-
sance to the memory of vanished glory
in their delineation of China's territorial
sovereignty. Chiang Kai-shek, borrowing Adolf Hitler's concept of *lebensraum*, ("living-space"), laid claim to
past holdings on the basis of population pressure as well as of historical
possession:

In regard to the living space essential
for the nation's existence, the territory
of the Chinese state is determined by the
requirements for national survival and

by the limits of Chinese cultural bonds. Thus, in the territory of China a hundred years ago [*circa* 1840], comprising more than ten million square kilometers, there was not a single district that was not essential to the survival of the Chinese nation, and none that was not permeated by our culture. The breaking up of his territory meant the undermining of the nation's security as well as the decline of the nation's culture. Thus, the people as a whole must regard this as a national humiliation, and not until all lost territories have been recovered can we relax our efforts to wipe out this humiliation and save ourselves from destruction.[2]

Although Chiang does not specify his "lost territories," a Chinese textbook published shortly after his statement contains a table listing them (see Table 9.1).

TABLE 9.1
China's "Lost Territories"

Date	Area, in square kilometers	Location	New ownership
1689	240,000	North side Khingan Mountains	Russia
1727	100,000	Lower Selenga Valley	Russia
1842	83	Hong Kong	United Kingdom
1858	480,000	North of Heilungkiang	Russia
1858	8	Kowloon	United Kingdom
1860	344,000	East of Ussuri River	Russia
1864	900,000	North of Lake Balkhash	Russia
1879	2,386	Liuchiu Islands	Japan
1882–1883	21,000	Lower Ili Valley	Russia
1883	20,000	Irtysh Valley east of Lake Zaysan	Russia
1884	9,000	Upper Koksol Valley	Russia
1885–1889	738,000	Annam and all Indochina	France
1886	574,000	Burma	United Kingdom
1890	7,550	Sikkim	United Kingdom
1894	122,400	West of the upper Salween	United Kingdom
1894	91,300	West of the upper Yangtze	United Kingdom
1894	100,000	Upper Burma, Savage Mountains	United Kingdom
1895	220,334	Korea	Japan
1895	35,845	Taiwan	Japan
1895	127	Pescadores	Japan
1897	760	The edge of Burma	United Kingdom
1897	2,300	The edge of Burma	United Kingdom
Total	4,009,093		

SOURCE: Hou Ming-chiu, Chen Erh-shiu, and Lu Chen, *General Geography of China* (in Chinese), 1946, as cited in G. B. Cressey, *Land of the 500 Million* (New York: McGraw-Hill Book Company, Inc., 1955), p. 39

Nor do communist leaders remain indifferent to China's past holdings, although they temper their immediate claims according to time and place. Thus Mao Tse-tung staked out his future realm in an interview more than thirty years ago:

It is the immediate task of China to regain all our lost territories. . . . We do not, however, include Korea, formerly a Chinese colony, but when we have re-established the independence of the lost territories of China, and if the Koreans wish to break away from the chains of Japanese imperialism, we will extend them our enthusiastic help in their struggle for independence. The same

[2]Chiang Kai-shek, *China's Destiny* (New York: Roy Publishers, 1947), p. 34.

thing applies for Formosa. . . . The Outer Mongolian republic will automatically become a part of the Chinese federation, at their own will. The Mohammedan and Tibetan peoples, likewise, will form autonomous republics attached to the Chinese federation.[3]

True to his word, at least in part, Mao, despite Indian protests, drove his Red Armies to the Tibetan heights one year after the establishment of the People's Republic of China in 1949. His implicit definition of Korea as within China's sphere of interest received implementation when Chinese armies hurled back United Nations troops from the Yalu River to the thirty-eighth parallel during 1950–'51. Sinkiang, presumably referred to above as "the Mohammedan people" because of its predominantly Moslem population, became an autonomous region in 1955 after considerable pacification by the Red Army. Only Taiwan, held by Chiang Kai-shek, and Outer Mongolia, recognized as independent by the Treaty of Friendship and Alliance concluded between the nationalist government and Moscow in 1945 and adhered to in this particular by Peking, remained beyond Mao's control in 1958.

Similarly, both nationalist and communist maps place China's borders far down in the South China Sea, off the shores of Borneo. Mao would subscribe to the statements of the official nationalist handbook:

Both the southernmost and westernmost borders remain to be defined. The Pamirs in the west constitute a contested area among China, the U.S.S.R., and Afghanistan. The sovereignty of the Tuansha Islands (the Coral Islands) in the south is sought by China, the Republic of the Philippines, and Indo-China.[4]

The movement of Chinese communist forces into the disputed area bordering India, during 1959–'60, aroused protests in New Delhi. Subsequent Indian efforts to recoup the usurped territory through the peaceful deployment of border guards brought a violent reaction from Peking in the form of a one-month massive offensive along the entire Sino-Indian border in 1962, marking Peking's most flagrant act of aggression since the Korean War. Thus did Peking show its unwillingness to renounce "lost territory," even when it possessed little economic or strategic value and when its attainment involved far-reaching unfavorable repercussions.

This persistent pattern of behavior stems from the traditional Chinese definition of a government possessing the Mandate of Heaven as one capable of defending the frontiers against barbarian incursions while maintaining the peace against domestic insurrection. So remote an area as Outer Mongolia became the subject of political controversy in 1912, when young nationalists agitated against Peking's concessions to Mongolian demands for autonomy under Russian protection. These nationwide protests proved a useful political weapon against the regime of Yuan Shih-k'ai. Similarly, in 1950, nationalist propagandists sought to embarrass communist Peking by charging it with "selling out" Chinese soil to the Soviet Union by accepting Outer Mongolian independence.

The leaders may not believe in this expansive definition of China's territory, but its acceptance may be dic-

[3]E. Snow, *Red Star over China* (New York: Modern Library, Inc., 1944), p. 96. Interviews with Mao Tse-tung in 1936.

[4]*China Handbook, 1955–56* (Taipei, Taiwan, 1955), p. 15.

tated by political expediency. Whatever the cause, the effect is to saddle the government with serious international problems. Vague territorial claims, based on concepts of suzerainty and tributary relations or on disputed treaties, give no objective basis for determining international boundaries. Thus, it is moot whether the Chinese invasion of Tibet in 1950 can legally be called "aggression."

Where such boundaries are fixed with rough approximation, precise definition is impeded by the absence of natural lines of demarcation. Except for the coast and the relatively short Yalu and Amur rivers in the northeast, none of China's frontiers can be readily identified by natural phenomena. They twist tortuously through jungle, mountain, and desert, according to the temporary dictates of local needs and the relative power available to interested parties. The absence of natural demarcation is paralleled by an absence of natural barriers against migration or invasion, complicating the responsibilities facing the central government responsible for its citizens' welfare and defense.

Few lines of communication traverse the great distances from China's traditional capitals to its remote border provinces, and these remote provinces are relatively close to rival centers of power. Not until the Chinese communists came to power was a railroad constructed linking Outer Mongolia with North China. At this same time, the first rough road joined Tibet with South China.

Despite Sino-Soviet friction along the extensive Sinkiang frontier, Peking has laid railroad track linking the vast province with Central China only as far as the provincial capital of Urumchi, some 300 miles short of the border. Even Manchuria's transport ties with China proper, although infinitely better than those to other areas, were weak, considering the strategic importance of this region.

Besides these obstacles, those responsible for China's security have been confronted with British pressure on Tibet, from India; Russian pressure on Sinkiang from adjacent Kazakhstan, on Mongolia from Siberia, and on Manchuria, from the Far-Eastern territories; and Japanese pressure, first on Korea, and from there on Manchuria, as well as upon the Ryukyu Islands and Taiwan. China's traditional attraction for invaders was food and wealth, luring from the interior certain nomadic groups against whom the Great Wall was originally designed. Modern invaders came after markets (Great Britain), raw materials (Japan), or imperial prestige (Germany).

Throughout the past 300 years, the seriousness of these conditions has been magnified by the inferiority of China's economic development as compared with that of predatory powers arrayed against her. Russia's piecemeal nibbling at Chinese territory was facilitated by the remoteness of Sinkiang and Outer Mongolia from the base of China's strength. Bringing the contest nearer this base, however, revealed that the strength was more apparent than real. Despite the striking disparity of populations, the Japanese took Korea, Manchuria and, finally, much of China proper from the "land of the 400 million." Only industrialization could remedy the material weakness which left China vulnerable to all comers.

Thus, during the nineteenth and twentieth centuries, China grappled with problems of defense against outer pressures to a degree unique among the countries under survey in the present work. These pressures were varied, but they were alike in their threat to Chinese civilization. Military attack literally tore off chunks of territory. Economic concessions carved out sheltered spheres of influence, disrupting domestic economic development through artificial emphasis on coastal points under foreign control. Finally, ideological pressures were exerted by foreign missionaries, who, protected with force when necessary, challenged the Confucian order with destructive vigor.

Virtually no point along the 12,600 miles of China's perimeter has been safe from one or another of these pressures during the last 300 years. So vulnerable were they at the turn of the century that many wondered whether China was not to be the "sick man" of Asia, to be carved up by other countries as was the Ottoman Empire. These physical factors pose an objective challenge for the makers of Chinese foreign policy, be they Manchu, nationalist, or communist. Taken in conjunction with the subjective factor of historical experience, they provide an important clue to the behavior of Mao Tse-tung and his followers.

Historical factors

China's defensive attitudes intermittently explode into xenophobia. Their subjective evaluation of events during the past century convinces Chinese nationalist and communist alike that many, if not all of China's ills stem from contact with the "foreign devil," now castigated as "Western imperialism." Two hundred years ago, Li Shih-yao, viceroy of Kwangtung and Kwangsi, memorialized the throne on regulations for the control of foreigners, warning:

It is my most humble opinion that when uncultured barbarians, who live far beyond the borders of China, come to our country to trade, they should establish no contact with the population, except for business purposes.[5]

Events since Li Shih-yao's day show little break in continuity, so far as interpretation of foreign relations is concerned. Chiang Kai-shek blamed the chaotic years of interregnum following the collapse of the Manchu Dynasty on "secret activities of the Imperialists . . . the chief cause of civil wars among the warlords."[6] Indeed, he attributed the Empire's disintegration to the so-called unequal treaties which "completely destroyed our nationhood, and our sense of honor and shame was lost. . . . The traditional structure of the family, the village, and the community was disrupted. The virtue of mutual help was replaced by competition and jealousy. Public planning was neglected and no one took an interest in public affairs."[7]

This simplistic explanation errs in attributing cause and effect where coincidence is the phenomenon. Western pressures hastened the collapse of the Empire and its Confucian traditions, but they came after the process of disintegration had begun. The ability of Japanese society to respond to the combined impact of feudal decline and Western influence by adapting the old content to new forms demonstrates the distortion of history in Chiang's analysis.

However, it is not the facts of history that condition political behavior but the way in which men view those facts. Hence the similarity of the following communist analysis to those preceding it is highly suggestive of xenophobia as a component of Chinese policy:

[5]Hu Sheng, *Imperialism and Chinese Politics* (Peking, 1955), p. 9.
[6]Chiang Kai-shek, *China's Destiny*, p. 78.
[7]*Ibid.*, pp. 79 and 88.

They [the imperialists] will not only send their running-dogs to bore inside China to carry out disruptive work and to cause trouble. They will not only use the Chiang Kai-shek bandit remnants to blockade our coastal ports, but they will send their totally hopeless adventurist elements and troops to raid and to cause trouble along our borders. They seek by every means and at all times to restore their position in China. They use every means to plot the destruction of China's independence, freedom, and territorial integrity and to restore their private interests in China. We must exercise the highest vigilance. . . . They cannot possibly be true friends of the Chinese people. They are the deadly enemies of the Chinese people's liberation movement.[8]

Thus, the Chinese communist devil-theory of imperialism coincides with the popular mythology that evil is inherent in foreign contacts, and produces suspicion and hostility at various levels. The popular mythology derives from perceived experience, the rape and pillage by Western troops during the nineteenth century. Western insistence on extraterritorial privileges so that their nationals could be tried by foreign law for crimes committed on Chinese territory rubbed salt in the wound. Insult was added to injury. While the Chinese viewed white behavior as barbaric, the whites viewed Chinese punishment as brutal. The inevitable cultural gap, widened by racial prejudice, reinforced the hostility on both sides.

Injustice was also encountered at higher levels of diplomatic relations. Chinese experience in the international arena gave good reason for bitter resentment at being cast in the role of "a melon to be carved up by the

[8]K'o Pai-nien, "Hsin min chu chu yi te wai chiao tse" ("The Foreign Policy of the New People's Democracy"), *Hsüeh Hsi* ("Study") I, No. 2 (October, 1949), 13–15.

powers." Throughout the nineteenth century, gunboat diplomacy forced China to abdicate her customary rights of sovereignty without reciprocal privileges. Extraterritorial law, economic concessions, and the stationing of foreign troops in Chinese cities were sanctified by treaty but won by force. Punitive expeditions, in 1860 and 1900, delivered the supreme insult of foreign military occupation of the venerated capital of Peking.

The twentieth century brought little relief. Japan fought Russia on Chinese soil for control of the rich provinces of Manchuria. China's own allies in World War I swept aside her protests at Versailles, and awarded to Japan concessions in China held by defeated Germany. During World War II, the Yalta Conference of 1945 rewarded Soviet Russia with important military, economic, and political privileges in China, all without consultation with Chiang Kai-shek. Although President Roosevelt reminded Premier Stalin that those inducements for Russian entry into the war against Japan would have to be affirmed by Chiang, Allied pressure left China no alternative but capitulation.

In sum, China was the object of international relations but seldom the subject. Acted on by others, she was unable to act in her own right. Long the primary power in Asia, she has been cut deeply, during the past century, by an induced feeling of inferiority. Her fear of Japan followed a defeat caused by material inferiority. Her resentment against the West followed a capitulation caused by military inferiority and a humiliation caused by sensed cultural and ideological inferiority. Small wonder that, today, Peking's militant insistence upon being heard in regional and world councils strikes a responsive chord among wide sectors of the populace. At long last, a determined elite is working to restore China's place in the sun.

To be sure, irredentist claims to lost territories, denunciation of unequal treaties, and the playing off of power against power—"use barbarians against barbarians"—are all traditional techniques of foreign policy. The difference in their use by the Chinese lies in the psychological convictions behind these techniques. Among Western states, the exploitation of grievances is an accepted strategem among assumed equals who are struggling for limited gains and for the coveted position of *primus inter pares*. Between China and the rest of the world, however, the bitter remembrance of things past heightens the defensive and offensive aspects of foreign policy.

The communists' emphasis on imperialist aggression fits well into the objective and subjective factors, conditioning Chinese views of world politics. The resulting xenophobia, manifested in exaggerated attitudes of belligerence, has ultimately worked even to Russia's disadvantage. Whereas originally it was exploited by Soviet Russian leaders against the West, eventually it exploded again over such real and sensed grievances as Soviet Russian looting in Manchuria after World War II, the resentment against dependence on Russian economic assistance, and the suspected Soviet Russian subversion in Sinkiang. In the decade 1949–1959, official affirmations of the "monolithic unity of Sino-Soviet friendship" sought to repress the hostility with which many Chinese viewed the Sino-Soviet alliance. When Mao challenged Khrushchev for primacy in the communist world, however, such protestations of friendship disappeared in a wave of anti-Russian invective which found ready acceptance among large sectors of the populace, always ready to believe the worst of any foreigner in his dealings with China.

THE PROCESS OF POLICY: THE COMMUNIST COMPONENT

Ideological content: Marxism-Leninism

Besides those aspects of continuity in policy which we ascribe to the Chinese component, there are differences in degree or substance which stem from the dedication of the present Chinese leaders to communism. As Mao Tse-tung declared in 1945, "From the very beginning, our Party has based itself on the theories of Marxism, because Marxism is the crystallization of the world proletariat's most impeccable revolutionary scientific thought."[9]

General protestations of fidelity to Christianity, international law, and justice appear throughout statements of Western political figures. Rarely do these protestations enable us to determine the ends and means of these leaders, especially in foreign policy. Marxism-Leninism, however, carries with it a construct of goals and ways of seeking those goals that imparts form to ideology and institutions to a degree unknown in the noncommunist world.

Foremost in this ideology is its determination to advance communism throughout the world. Almost three decades ago, the fugitive Chinese Communist Party, beleaguered by nationalist armies in Kiangsi, proclaimed, "The Provisional Government of the Soviet Republic of China declares that it will, under no condition, remain content with the overthrow of im-

[9]Mao-Tze-Tung [sic], *The Fight for a New China*. A report of April 24, 1945, to the Seventh National Congress of the Chinese Communist Party as quoted in O. Edmund Clubb, "Chinese Communist Strategy in Foreign Relations," in "Report on China," *The Annals*, Vol. 277 (September, 1951), 156.

perialism in China, but, on the contrary, will aim as its ultimate objective in waging a war against world imperialism until the latter is all blown up."[10]

In terms of "progress" and "revolutionary scientific thought" this goal is justified as a desirable one, the "good society" found in utopian drives common to world philosophies. An additional element, however, distinguishes this compulsion toward ideological expansion from counterparts in Islam, Christianity, Wilsonian democracy, and Nazism. For the Marxist, destruction of the imperialist is not only desirable but necessary. The maximum goal of world conquest is the only guarantee for achieving the minimum goal of communist survival.

Basic to this argument is the assumption of conflict as omnipresent in human relations. The "contradictions of the dialectical process" exist in various forms; conflict need not be military in manifestation. Marx posited all historical development as a process of struggle, whether between classes within a nation or between nations themselves. The highest and final conflict is to come between classes on the international plane, in the world revolution springing from the basic contradiction between international communism and international capitalism.

This struggle is not one that is created by the communists. According to their credo, it is the imperialists who are to blame, engaging in a death struggle to stave off the inevitable victory of the communist ideal. As expressed by Peking's official voice, the *Jen Min Jih Pao* (*Peking People's Daily*), "Although we have consistently held and still hold that the socialist and capitalist countries should co-exist in peace and carry out peaceful com-

petition, the imperialists are bent on destroying us. We must therefore never forget the stern struggle with the enemy, i.e., the class struggle on a world scale."[11]

Thus, the minimum goal of survival requires policies employing offensive means, which simultaneously serve the maximum goal of world communist domination. One such means is that of applying the classic Chinese dictum of "using barbarian against barbarian" so as to take advantage of the conflict that assumedly exists among capitalists. Mao Tse-tung wrote, in 1940, "Our tactical principle remains one of exploiting the contradictions among them [the imperialists] in order to win over the majority, oppose the minority, and crush the enemies separately.[12]

However, "the enemy" will not rest content and permit the socialist camp to develop peacefully. His efforts to split that camp apart compel the communist countries to unite and, particularly, to support the Soviet Union. An important statement of this principle came after the Hungarian uprising of 1956, when Peking justified Moscow's armed suppression of the insurgents:

There are before us two types of contradictions which are different in nature. The first type consists of contradictions between our enemy and ourselves (contradictions between the camp of imperialism and that of socialism, contradictions between imperialism and the people and

[11]From "More on Historical Experience of Proletarian Dictatorship," an article prepared by the Editorial Department of the *Jen Min Jih Pao* on the basis of a discussion at an enlarged meeting of the Political Bureau of the Central Committee of the Communist Party of China. *Jen Min Jih Pao* (Peking), December 29, 1956.

[12]Mao Tse-tung, "On Policy" (December 25, 1940), as translated in *Selected Works of Mao Tse-tung* (Bombay, India, 1954), III, 218.

[10]*Central China Post* (Hankow), November 25, 1931, as quoted in O. E. Clubb, *ibid.*, p. 157.

oppressed nations of the world, contradictions between the bourgeoisie and the proletariat in the imperialist countries, etc.). *This is the fundamental type of contradiction, based on the clash of interests between antagonistic classes.* The second type consists of contradictions within the ranks of the people (contradictions between different sections of the people, between comrades within the Communist Party, or in socialist countries, contradictions between the government and the people, contradictions between socialist countries, contradictions between Communist Parties, etc.). *This type of contradiction is not basic*; it is not the result of a fundamental clash of interests between classes, but of conflicts between right and wrong opinions or of a partial contradiction of interests. *It is a type of contradiction whose solution must, first and foremost, be subordinated to the over-all interests of the struggle against the enemy.*[13] [Italics supplied.]

These assumptions of conflict are reinforced by the attitudes and actions of the noncommunist world. In part, this results from Chinese communist behavior and illustrates the phenomenon of the self-fulfilling prophecy. When Mao Tse-tung proclaimed the establishment of the People's Republic of China in October, 1949, Great Britain extended recognition. Twisting the lion's tail, Peking rejected the recognition with protests against the phraseology of the British note, as well as against British consular relations with the nationalist authorities on Taiwan. The maltreatment of British business concerns in China undermined the economic arguments advanced in England for wooing Peking. The subsequent British refusal to vote for Peking's admission to the United Nations, and British support for the United States' action in Korea aroused a

[13]*Jen Min Jih Pao,* December 29, 1956, *op cit.*

violent reaction in China against the "Anglo-American imperialist bloc." In one sense, that bloc came about, in spite of the contradictions within it, largely because of the Chinese predisposition to hostility.

To a lesser extent, America's relations with the new regime were also a product of its own actions. As early as 1948, American consular officials were put under house arrest in communist-held Mukden, jailed, tried, and eventually expelled from China. The seizure of Economic Cooperation Administration stocks in 1949, the inflaming of public opinion against American personnel, both official and unofficial, and the confiscation of American consular property held through treaty agreement, in January, 1950, all served to obstruct a rapprochement between Washington and Peking. Chinese intervention in the Korean War, and the attendant defeat of American troops at the Yalu in November, 1950, wiped out whatever possibility remained of normal relations between the two countries, at least for many years to come. Yet, prior to this war, the record shows a number of instances where normal adherence by Peking to international custom might have strengthened the hand of groups within the United States which were seeking to establish ties with the new regime.

It would be misleading to attribute all Chinese communist fears and resentments against the United States to this self-fulfilling prophecy. America's support of Chiang Kai-shek in the civil war, its obstruction of Chinese representation in the United Nations, and its promulgation of an economic embargo against Peking exacerbated relations between the two countries during the 1950's. The combination of expectation and realization reinforced the ideological content of Chinese communist policy, which posits conflict, overt or covert, with the noncommunist world.

The most famous formulation of this principle came in Mao Tse-tung's "lean to one side" declaration on July 1, 1949:

"You lean to one side." Precisely so . . . Chinese people either lean to the side of imperialism or to the side of socialism. To sit on the fence is impossible; a third road does not exist. . . . Internationally we belong to the anti-imperialist front headed by the U.S.S.R. and we can look for genuine friendly aid only from that front, and not from the imperialist front.[14]

The implementation of this principle came quickly, with the signing of the Treaty of Friendship, Alliance, and Mutual Aid of February 14, 1950, between the Chinese People's Republic and the Union of Soviet Socialist Republics. Mao and Stalin agreed that "in the event of one of the Contracting Parties being attacked by Japan or any state allied with her and thus being involved in a state of war, the other Contracting Party shall immediately render military and other assistance by all means at its disposal." A proliferation of subsequent agreements regulated Russian economic assistance to China (loans and technical assistance), as well as military aid, cultural exchange, and routine international arrangements about telecommunications and postal regulations.

The "lean to one side" policy, excluding assistance from, much less alliance with, noncommunist countries, was antithetical to traditional Chinese politics of playing off one country

[14]Mao Tse-tung, "On People's Democratic Dictatorship," July 1, 1949, as translated in *A Documentary History of Chinese Communism*, eds. C. Brandt, B. Schwartz, and J. K. Fairbank (Cambridge, Mass.: Harvard University Press, 1952), pp. 449 ff.

against another. It can only be explained in terms of the communist component of Chinese foreign policy.

Ideology: Maoism

So far we have been discussing aspects of Chinese communist policy that stem from the communist component as developed in Marxism-Leninism. Assumptions of conflict, antagonism against capitalism, and unity within the socialist camp were all compatible with the ideological concepts dominant in Soviet Russia, at least until the death of Stalin in 1953.

Within the Marxist-Leninist framework, however, divergent strategies have developed. The course of Chinese communism over the past decades suggests a number of points in domestic and foreign policy that conflict with the Russian view. Although divergencies on conduct of the Chinese revolution appear as far back as the 1930's, disagreements on foreign policy remained hidden until the mid-Fifties. Isolated from the outside world during most of the civil war, the Chinese elite faced no need and experienced no contradicting evidence to challenge Russian interpretations of foreign affairs. With victory came a pressing need for reliance on Russian economic and military aid, precluding disagreement with Stalin's policies. Seconding the Kremlin's expulsion of Tito from the Cominform was politically expedient for Peking.

China's involvement in the Korean War, combined with the United Nations' embargo, furthered Peking's dependence upon Moscow. As the official *Handbook of World Knowledge, 1954* stated, "It is erroneous to think that we have no need for international assistance and can still succeed. . . . Who can help us? Only the camp of peace, democracy, and socialism under the leadership of the Soviet Union can give us genuine friendly assistance."[15]

Beneath the surface, however, relations were strained. One bone of contention within China was the establishment of joint Sino-Soviet stock companies in 1950 to exploit oil and nonferrous metals in Sinkiang, as well as to operate a civil airline.[16] It is significant that these companies, established in 1950 for a period of thirty years, were dissolved by joint agreement in 1954, when Khrushchev and Bulganin visited Peking after the death of Stalin.

In addition, Chinese participation in the Korean War, albeit aided by Russion military deliveries, saddled Peking with debts. By 1957, China owed the Soviet Union more than $2.4 billion, and there was open criticism within China.[17] The belated revelation of past grievance merits quotation at length:

It was unreasonable for China to bear all the expenses of the Korean war. . . . During the First and Second World War, the United States lent funds to its allies. . . . Afterward some of the countries repudiated their debts while in some cases the United States waived its claim for repayment. The Soviet loan . . . is

[15]*Shih chieh chih shih shou p'eng, 1954* (Handbook of World Knowledge) (Peking, 1954), p. 7.

[16]For a sampling of adverse comment reported by the Chinese communist press, see A. S. Whiting, "Communist China and 'Big Brother,'" *Far Eastern Survey*, No. 10 (October, 1955).

[17]For China's indebtedness to the Soviet Union see Li Hsien-nien, "Final Accounts for 1956 and the 1957 State Budget," delivered to the fourth session of the First National People's Congress on June 29, 1957; NCNA, Peking, June 29, 1957. A calculation of the timing of the loans, as revealed by Li's report, and a comparison with previously announced loans and related references to military assistance from Russia, compels the conclusion that almost $2 billion was military, as distinguished from purely economic, aid.

repayable in full in ten years. The time is too short and moreover interest has to be paid. I propose that repayment be extended to 20 or 30 years so as to ease the tense economic situation in our country. . . . When the Soviet Union liberated our Northeast [Manchuria], it dismantled some machinery equipment in our factories. Was there compensation for it? Will there be repayment?[18]

The dramatic events of 1956, commencing with Khrushchev's denunciation of Stalin at the Twentieth Congress in February and climaxed in the Hungarian revolt of November, brought Sino-Soviet differences to the fore. Commenting on Stalin's "cult of personality," *Jen Min Jih Pao* saw his errors not merely as the result of personality but as a product of "contradictions" in the socialist system. Reviving Mao Tse-tung's 1937 theory on the "universality of contradition," the editorial stated: "It is naive to assume that contradictions can no longer exist in a socialist society. To deny the existence of contradictions is to deny dialectics."[19] Yet *Pravda* implicitly denied this assertion by deleting all por-

[18]Lung Yün, "My Ideological Review," *Jen Min Jih Pao*, July 14, 1957, as translated in *Current Background* (Hong Kong: United States Consulate General), No. 470 (July 26, 1957). Lung here recapitulated the criticisms he voiced before the Standing Committee of the National People's Congress, of which he is a member. As vice-chairman of the National Defense Council and travelling companion of Politburo member P'eng Chen on a tour of Soviet Russia and East Europe in late 1956, Lung's words merit attention. He recanted in this article but only "subjectively," leaving intact his factual assertions. There was no official refutation of these facts, although he was criticized for his motives.

[19]*Jen Min Jih Pao*, "On Historical Experience concerning the Dictatorship of the Proletariat," April 5, 1956, as translated in *Current Background*, No. 403. Mao's original statement of this theory is in his essay of August, 1937, *On Contradictions*, (published in English in Peking, 1952).

tions relating to it from its translation of the editorial. Although a fuller version was subsequently published in Russia, Khrushchev explicitly denied the applicability of the formula to the Soviet Union in a television interview one year later.[20]

Soviet Russia's sensitivity to this analysis from Peking is understandable in view of its implications for relations within the bloc. It postulated that "contradictions" among socialist countries, rather than Stalinism, was basic to the cause of tension. The explicit attention to Yugoslavia's difficulties in this editorial signalled growing Chinese concern with East European developments, vital to China's economic developments as well as to its strategic interests.

Despite Khrushchev's open hostility to Gomulka, reliable reports indicated that the Polish leader received encouragement for independence from Mao Tse-tung personally.[21] When Hungary erupted in revolt, Peking's press offered a fuller version of the events, and one different from that of Moscow. Recalling its ambassador to the Soviet Union for consultation, the Chinese formulated an analysis in the *Jen Min Jih Pao* editorial of December 29, 1956, which marked the fullest statement thus far of disagreement with Soviet policy, albeit tempered by a desire to compromise for the sake of unity within the bloc:

. . . Contradictions between socialist countries, between Communist Parties . . . are not basic, not the result of a fundamental clash of interests but . . . of a *partial* contradiction of interests. . . . Recent controversies in the international Communist movement, for the most part, have had to do with one's appraisal of the Soviet Union. . . . The Communist Party of the Soviet Union has been taking measures to correct Stalin's mistakes and eliminate their consequences. *These measures are beginning to bear fruit.* . . . Since Stalin's mistakes were not of short duration, their thorough correction cannot be achieved overnight but demands fairly protracted efforts and thoroughgoing ideological education. . . . Only by adopting an objective and analytical attitude can we correctly appraise Stalin and *all those comrades who made similar mistakes under his influence.* . . . We need therefore to adopt a comradely attitude towards these people and *should not treat them as enemies* . . . should not blankly denounce everything they did. . . . Their mistakes have a social and historical background.[22] [*Italics supplied.*]

The faint touch of condescension and paternalism is apparent. For Peking, the case was far from closed on Stalin or on Soviet policy. As another comment on Russo-Polish relations noted, "In future relations between socialist countries, if only the bigger nations pay more attention to avoiding the mistake of big-nation chauvinism (this is the main thing) and the smaller nations avoid the mistake of nationalism (this is also important), friendship and solidarity based upon equality will undoubtedly become con-

[20] R. Schlesinger, "Soviet Historians Before and After the XX Congress," in *Soviet Studies*, VII, No. 2 (October, 1956), 165–66 and fn. 31. *Pravda* published the full text as a pamphlet that went to press on June 10, 1956. Khrushchev's denial was deleted from Russian and Chinese versions of the interview.

[21] *The New York Times* issues of October 16, 1956, and January 11, 1957, tell of two instances of intervention by Mao on behalf of Gomulka, both apparently related by authoritative sources.

[22] *Jen Min Jih Pao*, "More on Historical Experience," December 29, 1956. Although Ambassador Liu Hsiao's return to Peking went unreported in the press, his presence at a Moscow reception in November, and his subsequent departure for Moscow, from Peking with Chou En-lai on January 7, 1957, lend support to this analysis.

solidated."[23] The source of such "big-nation chauvinism" was explained by *Jen Min Jih Pao*. "The time-worn habits of big countries in their relations with small countries continue to make their influence felt in certain ways, while a series of victories achieved by a Party of a country in its revolutionary cause is apt to give rise to a certain sense of superiority."[24]

In keeping with its insistence upon "equality" and "independence" in relations among socialist countries, *Jen Min Jih Pao*, in the December 29 editorial, dealt relatively lightly with Tito's criticism of the Soviet Union. Expressing "amazement," the editorial termed his views "wrong" insofar as they could "only lead to a split in the communist movement. . . . Clearly the Yugoslav comrades are going too far. Even if some part of their criticism of brother parties is reasonable, the basic stand and method they adopt infringe the principles of comradely discussion." Thus, Peking did not castigate Belgrade in the same severe terms as Moscow, but reproached "Comrade Tito" and gave him "our brotherly advice" against washing dirty linen in public. As Chou En-lai observed after his trip to Russia and Eastern Europe in January, 1957, "Even if no unanimity can be reached for the time being, it would also be normal to reserve the differences while upholding our solidarity."[25]

In 1958–1960, Sino-Soviet differences flared into open debate on a wide range of domestic and foreign policy issues. Thinly veiled by Peking's attacks against "modern revisionists" and Moscow's warnings against "dogmatism and leftist adventurism," the debate nonetheless spilled over into communist parties inside and outside the bloc, as well as into various communist-front international organizations. By November, 1960, relations between the two allies had deteriorated to the point where rival Chinese and Russian policy statements circulated among eighty-one communist delegations summoned to Moscow in a vain attempt to resolve the conflict.[26] Simultaneous reports of Russian technicians withdrawing from China and sudden petroleum shortages on the Chinese mainland, long dependent on shipments of oil by the bloc, suggested the degree of strain in the alliance.

The debate turned around a host of issues related to differing Chinese and Russian estimates of the degree to which war might be risked, considering that the Soviet Union's intercontinental ballistic missiles appeared to be superior to those of the United States. It is impossible to say with certainty whether this difference grew out of Chinese disappointment with Russian support for China's nuclear bomb program or out of disputes over Sino-Soviet strategy in the abortive bombardment, in 1958, of the Chinese nationalist offshore islands, Quemoy and Matsu.[27] By early 1960, however, it was vented as a scathing Chinese attack against Russian policy vis-à-vis the West, specifically against Khrushchev's demands for summit

[23]NCNA, Peking, November 21, 1956, "International Significance of the Soviet-Polish Talks."

[24]*Jen Min Jih Pao*, December 29, 1956.

[25]Chou En-lai to the third annual plenary session of the Second National Committee of the Chinese Communist Party on March 5, 1957. In *Current Background* (Hong Kong: United States Consulate General), No. 439.

[26]Donald S. Zagoria "Strains in the Sino-Soviet Alliance," *Problems of Communism*, IX, No. 3 (May–June, 1960). See also his "Sino-Soviet Friction in Underdeveloped Areas," *Problems of Communism*, X, No. 2 (March–April, 1961), 1–12.

[27]Alice Langley Hsieh, "Communist China and Nuclear Warfare," *The China Quarterly*, I, No. 2 (April–June, 1960).

conferences and disarmament negotiations.

More important differences arose in areas where China could act independently, as it could not in Soviet-Russian-American relations. Mao's emphasis on armed struggle challenged Khrushchev's championing of the parliamentary path to power for communist parties in newly independent countries. Chinese attacks against the national bourgeoisie in these countries contrasted with Russian vacillation on the domestic anticommunism of Nasser and Kassim. Perhaps the most ominous aspect, at least from a noncommunist vantage point, was Peking's demand for bloc support for national liberation struggles, whether in Laos or in Algiers, explicitly flouting Moscow's warnings against encouraging local wars which might explode into general thermonuclear catastrophe.

In sum, the ideological ingredients that posit similar goals for the elite of the two countries do not also necessarily posit identical means or identical timing. Peking's characterizing of "relations among socialist countries" as marked by a "partial contradiction of interests" signalled, albeit with understatement, the degree to which China's alliance with Soviet Russia was a voluntary partnership, subject to deeply divisive forces. Even should the split be healed in a post-Maoist phase of Peking leadership, Chinese foreign policy can at best remain related to, but not dictated by, that of the Soviet Union.

Institutional structure

Decision making in the People's Republic of China is the exclusive prerogative of the Chinese Communist Party (CCP). Within that Party it is confined principally to the Political Bureau (Politburo) or, more probably, its standing committee. Teng Hsiao-p'ing analyzed the relationship between party and state in his report to the Eighth National Congress of the CCP, in September, 1956, as follows:

The Party is the highest form of class organization. It is particularly important to point this out today when our Party has assumed the leading role in state affairs. . . . [This] means first, that Party members in state organs and particularly the leading Party members' groups formed by those in responsible positions in such departments should follow the unified leadership of the Party. Secondly, the Party must regularly discuss and decide on questions with regard to the guiding principles, politics, and important organizational matters in state affairs, and the leading Party members' groups in the state organs must see to it that these decisions are put into effect with the harmonious cooperation of non-Party personalities. Thirdly, the Party must . . . exercise constant supervision over the work of state organs.[28]

This frank analysis lends substance to an analysis of Party control of state organs based upon interlocking direction by high-ranking Party members. The State Council, corresponding to the Council of Ministers in the Soviet Union or the Western Cabinet, allocates controlling positions to Party members—the premiership, all ten vice-premierships, and in such key ministries as foreign affairs, defense, public security, finance, state planning agencies, machine industries, electric power, railways, and foreign trade. Noncommunists hold ministries concerned primarily with consumption, such as food, textiles, and aquatic products, or posts concerned with cultural affairs and health.

Similarly, the Standing Committee of the National People's Congress is

[28]Teng Hsiao-p'ing, "Report on Revision of Party Constitution," delivered to the CCP Eighth National Congress on September 16, 1956, as quoted by NCNA, Peking, September 18, 1956.

studded both with Politburo members (its chairman and secretary-general) and with Party members (six of its fifteen vice-chairmen). Although this group is vested, by the Constitution of 1954, with powers akin to those of legislative bodies in the West, its membership seems politically impotent in view of the extreme range of decree power held by the State Council. The inclusion of such dignitaries as Madame Sun Yat-sen (Soong Ch'ingling); China's outstanding literary polemicist, Kuo Mo-jo; and Tibet's Panchen Lama among its vice-chairmen suggests that this body is an honorific gathering to provide public sanction for decisions arrived at elsewhere.

The Party's constitution makes clear the absolute duty of all members to carry out policies and practices decreed by the Central Committee or, in its absence, by the Politburo:

Article 19. (6) The decisions of the Party must be carried out unconditionally. Individual Party members must yield to Party organizations, the minority to the majority, the lower organizations to the higher organizations, and all the organizations throughout the country must yield centrally to the National Congress and the Central Committee.[29]

That such decisions are seldom those of the Central Committee is evidenced by the infrequency of its sessions, the size of its membership, and the relatively short intervals during which lengthy reports are read and accepted. The Eighth Central Committee, elected in 1956, now has more than 190 regular and alternate members. Although it meets approximately twice yearly, as stipulated by the Party constitution,

its plenums seldom last more than five days. Moreover, in crisis-ridden 1960, no Central Committee plenum was reported, despite famines, reorganization of the communes, and the growing differences with Soviet Russia.

Decisions are not basically made by the Central Committee, then, but by an inner group. This elite is composed of seventeen regular and six alternate members of the Politburo. Of its workings we know virtually nothing, except that only twice in the past two decades has its composition been shaken by purge, and then only three men fell from power. Essentially, the core, represented by the active members of the Standing Committee of the Politburo —Mao, Liu Shao-Ch'i, Chou En-lai, and Teng Hsiao-p'ing (plus P'eng Chen, next in line for Standing Committee membership), is a united group whose internal differences have remained concealed through more than thirty years of civil war and governmental responsibilities.

The political institutions of the People's Republic of China resemble those of noncommunist countries in name only. To be sure, other "democratic parties" exist, as they do not in the Soviet Union, but they play no part in policy formation. These groupings, such as the China Democratic League and the Revolutionary Committee of Kuomintang, are small in membership and limited in function. Less than one-third of the government ministries and chairmen of commissions under the State Council are headed by representatives of these parties and so-called nonparty persons.[30] Of the 1,226 deputies in the National People's Congress, only 269 came from the democratic parties in 1956.

[29]"The Constitution of the Communist Party of China," adopted by the Eighth National Congress of the CCP on September 26, 1956, as translated in *Current Background* (Hong Kong: United States Consulate General), No. 417 (October 10, 1956).

[30]*Biographic Information* (Hong Kong: United States Consulate General), No. 1 (November 29, 1959).

Basically, these organizations communicate from the center to the periphery, according to the nature of their membership, which may consist chiefly of intellectuals, businessmen, or overseas Chinese. Control of these parties is facilitated by the enrollment of some members in the CCP. In addition, the CCP never neglects its role as political leader, even while stressing "long-term co-existence and mutual supervision" between the CCP and the democratic parties. As a spokesman for one of these groups warned, "We must not one-sidedly emphasize the political freedom and organizational independence of the democratic parties."[31] That their role is to implement, but not formulate, policy is clear from an official explanation of their responsibility "following the victory of socialism. . . . Important results might be obtained then in our task of ideological remoulding if education and transformation is conducted through the democratic parties."[32]

These groupings perform, on a limited scale, functions parallel to those carried out by mass organizations. The Communist Youth League, the Sino-Soviet Friendship Association, the All-China Federation of Trade Unions, and the All-China Democratic Women's Federation enmesh millions in a closely coordinated network of communications media directed from the Department of Propaganda of the CCP. Annual gatherings, such as the National Committee of the Chinese People's Political Consultative Conference, bring together representatives of

[31]Huang Ch'i-hsiang, "Two Problems in Work of Democratic Parties," *Kuang Ming Jih Pao*, Peking, January 3, 1957.

[32]Shih Ch'i and Sun Nan, "How to Understand the Policy of Long-Term Coexistence between the Communist Party and the Democratic Parties," *Cheng Chih Hsüeh Hsi* (Political Study), No. 9 (September 13, 1956).

"democratic parties and mass organizations" to receive reports from government leaders and to endorse the contemporary program of the CCP. Additional *ad hoc* meetings convene these groups for ritualized avowals of support for particular campaigns of domestic or international import.

Thus, both parties and interest-group organizations exist in the PRC, but their function is basically one-way communication from the top downward, as distinguished from their dual role of influencing and explaining policy in the West. In this sense, public opinion exists to be mobilized by the Party but not to direct the Party. It may fail to respond to Party propaganda, thereby compelling some revision of policy. It may articulate grievances by indirection, thereby stimulating examination of policy at the top. When it comes to placing external pressure on the government, however, public opinion in China is not an articulate force.

It is important, in formulating foreign policy, that parties, interest groups, and public opinion act to unify the populace. Mass campaigns are carried out for months at a time over all the media of communications, and with thousands of study groups. These means are useful in three different types of situations.

Mass campaigns may serve a contingency purpose, preparing the populace for possible action without committing the government to such action. In 1954-'55, all China signed petitions in blood, applauded speeches, and endorsed resolutions calling for the "immediate liberation of Taiwan." No invasion of Taiwan followed, nor were any decisive preparations for invasion evident. Similarly, in 1956, a shorter, less intensive campaign pledged "volunteers for Egypt" during the Anglo-French attack upon that country.

Again, no action followed. Such instances serve to confuse the outside world as to the intent of Chinese policy, in addition to whatever domestic stimuli they may provide for increasing production, renewing bonds of allegiance, or promulgating symbols of national unity.

Such campaigns may also serve the function of whipping up public support for an action already decided on. In 1950, an attack on Tibet was preceded by public rallies, exhortatory articles, and ringing declarations by prominent leaders. Undoubtedly, the most extensive use of this technique came in the celebrated "Resist-American-Aid-Korea" movement which accompanied Chinese intervention in the Korean War. During the three years of that action, a steady barrage of propaganda carried the movement to every corner of China.

Finally, these campaigns serve the purpose of "feedback," as polls of public opinion are supposed to do in the noncommunist world. Study group meetings are active discussions. They seek to bring out all questions of doubt and opposition, for the purpose of achieving final unity under the skilled leadership of prepared Party personnel, activists, and cadres. Following Soviet Russian intervention in the abortive Hungarian revolt of 1956, meetings at Chinese universities, factories, and farms discussed Peking's support for the Russian action and attempted to quell what was reported by the communist press as "shock and confusion."

The limits on public participation in policy are extreme and explicit, however. An authoritative Chinese analysis warned against "practicing democracy merely for the sake of democracy." Specifically, it advised the youth:

Before the liberation the forms used by the people in demanding democracy from the Kuomintang consisted mainly of strikes (of workers and students), demonstrations, and parades, bringing loss to the Kuomintang and applying pressure on the enemy so that they had to accept our demands. Today, in dealing with the Anglo-French imperialists who carry out aggression against Egypt, we still adopt the form of demonstration and parade. However, in dealing with divergences of views within the internal ranks of the people, the defects and mistakes of the people, we must resort principally to argument . . . and not the form of applying pressure. . . . The country today belongs to us, and we ourselves will bear the losses, political and economic, arising out of such forms as strikes of workers, strikes of students, and demonstrations and parades for the solution of questions.[33]

Another caveat cautioned against "exaggerating" defects, particularly in Chinese or Russian policy:

Some people find certain inappropriate measures carried out by individual socialist countries, and begin to doubt the superiority of the socialist system, and lose confidence. . . . Those who begin to waver as soon as they see mistakes in socialist countries are even more susceptible to pessimism and despair, and lose their political direction. And if counter revolutionaries should be watching at the time, who can say but such young people will be utilized by the counter revolutionaries? The experiences of some Hungarian youth these past few weeks should give us cause for vigilance.[34]

The interaction of institutions and ideology produces a foreign policy, formulated by a small, authoritarian, continuously functioning elite. The process of policy making, as such, remains veiled from observation, but the content of that policy may be deter-

[33]Chiang Ming, "Democracy Is the Means, Not the End," *Chung Kuo Ching Nien (China Youth)*, No. 23 (December 1, 1956).
[34]Fang Chun, "Do Not Deny Everything," *China Youth*, No. 23 (December 1, 1956).

mined with a high degree of probability because of the explicit and detailed nature of the Chinese communist ideology and the conscious dedication of this relatively stable elite to that ideology. Allowing for the modifications of time, then, we may now proceed to examine the most likely policies to be formulated by the People's Republic of China in the near future.

THE SUBSTANCE OF POLICY

Ends

The foreign policy of the People's Republic of China embraces a range of goals. Maintenance of internal security is a minimum goal not peculiar to Peking. Intermediate goals, however, projecting what might be called "friendly domination" of Asian political and economic developments, stem from Chinese as well as communist components of policy. They are not, for instance, so evident in Burma or Thailand. Finally, the maximum goal of Peking, direct control of Asia through communist regimes that are political and economic satellites of China, is a more ambitious aim than is evident in any other ruling group in the area.

These different goals may be furthered by similar means. Wooing the uncommitted or neutral groups of Southeast Asia, following the Korean armistice in 1953, served the minimum goal of security by offsetting United States negotiations for the Southeast Asia Treaty Organization. It also smoothed the way for the increase of Peking's prestige and influence, an intermediate goal in the move to dominate governments in the area.

Yet it is important to recognize that this priority of goals is dictated by the necessity of circumstance. In the first decade, the People's Republic of China grappled, through its foreign policy, with the problems of uniting tradi-

tionally Chinese territory on the Asian mainland while at the same time, reducing the external threats to the new state's existence. Chou En-lai's skillful diplomacy at Geneva and Bandung provided a peaceful counterpart to military intervention in Korea, but both were aimed basically at the minimum goal of security.

The intermediate goal is capable of realization only with the economic development hoped for in the Second and Third Five Year Plans, and with the achievement of a more flexible political atmosphere within China following the elimination of counterrevolution and the completion of collectivization. These domestic developments, accompanied by armistices in Korea and Indochina, are a prerequisite for extending Peking's leadership in Asian affairs. Not until this process is completed, perhaps several decades distant, can the maximum goal, a Chinese bloc of communist regimes in Asia, be realistically contemplated by Peking.

Thus, although both China and the Soviet Union may hold the identical maximum goal, that of extending communism throughout the world, they are not in the same stage of development toward attaining this goal. Moscow has long since disposed of its concern over internal security and has advanced well along the path of attaining the intermediate goal, that of influencing governments along its periphery in Europe and the Middle East. Its economic and military means are far ahead of those available to China. This differentiation of ends attainable within a given time period provides further justification for distinguishing between Moscow and Peking, not only in our present analysis but in respect to their future policies.

This difference in development may be the basis for specific conflicts of policy between the two communist capitals. The prolongation of the Korean War, in 1952–'53, may have served the Soviet Russian ends of increasing the strains on the North Atlantic Treaty Organization and weakening its available force in Europe. This would facilitate Soviet influence over its Eastern European satellites, and extend its influence, at least negatively, into Western Europe. China's need for security, however, called for throwing back the United Nations troops from the Yalu, but not necessarily beyond the thirty-eighth parallel. The continuation of the war drained the Chinese economy, shaky at the start, and increased the danger of retaliation upon China proper by United States airpower. Not until the death of Stalin, in March, 1953, did Peking's negotiators at Panmunjom agree to armistice terms essentially similar to those they had rejected months previously. Although not conclusive, the timing of this move lends credibility to our analysis.

This example suggests a spatial difference in goals, in addition to one derived from temporal differences of development. Europe is the Soviet Union's primary sphere of interest and concern, offensively and defensively. The Asian periphery, extending from Tokyo to Kabul, demands China's prior attention. Both countries share interests as well as concern with Japan, but basically they are oriented in opposite directions. This increases the possibility of conflict between Peking and Moscow, at least with respect to specific points of policy. It also suggests differences in the degree of conflict they will have with the United States.

Means

Any construct of probable means to be adopted must take into consideration the availability of the means, as well as the likelihood of their being adopted. The latter consideration assumes rational decision making, insofar as a decision is logically consistent with ideology. For reasons stated earlier, we cannot assume such rationality to be uniformly present in Chinese foreign policy. Compulsive belligerency, for instance, during the early years of the People's Republic of China was irrational, even from the point of view of Peking's perceived interests, and much more so in terms of an objective appraisal of her assets and liabilities. However, such behavior seems less evident with the elite's maturing responsibility and its growing experience with international affairs. Therefore, the likelihood of rash or essentially irrational action lessens with time, although it by no means disappears entirely.

The means least likely to be employed by Peking, in pursuit of goals in Asia, are those of open military force. In the northeast, only South Korea and Japan might be targets of Chinese aggression. South Korea is definitely under United States protection; Japan is less vulnerable, given the relative air and sea weakness of Chinese military forces. In South Asia, transportation is sparse and primitive. The only rail lines venture from China into North Vietnam. Air bases are scattered and isolated. Terrain along the frontier is predominantly thick jungle or rugged mountains. Although this favors border incursions, it argues against mass invasions of the distant capitals of Delhi, Rangoon, Bangkok, or Phnom Penh.

In addition, the base strength of China, presently located along the coast and the northeastern sectors, is moving gradually toward the north and northwest. This is more secure from United States bases of attack and closer to the Soviet Russian hinterland, which is safeguarded by alliance. It leaves China's south and southwestern areas extremely deficient in the manpower and economic strength necessary for supporting large-scale military action.

Finally, open use of force would risk the loss of influence and prestige that might be won through less costly means. It might drive uncommitted countries to the side of the United States. If Soviet Russian precedent serves as example, military force is used only when all other alternatives are exhausted. The Russian attack upon Finland, in 1939, provides this precedent, but the singularity of the occurrence argues against assuming a high probability that military means would be used.

More likely is Chinese military assistance to local insurrections or civil wars that advance Peking's interests. Strengthening North Vietnam, bolstering insurgent Pathet Lao forces, and aiding guerilla groups in Malaya served China well during 1950–1954. Increased emphasis on the so-called Bandung spirit, however, brought abandonment of this strategy, for several years. The resumption of a bellicose posture, in 1958–1960, endangered the positive influence won by Peking in circles sensitive to armed insurrection. Peking's doctrine of armed struggle and advocacy of wars of national liberation raised increasing doubt in the minds of its former friends, particularly in Africa, as newly independent regimes lost their revolutionary ardor and preferred the Soviet Union's emphasis on peaceful coexistence as a means for taking aid from all sides without being dominated by one.

The least expensive and the least dangerous means of advancing intermediate goals would appear to be economic and political. Dramatic announcements of economic assistance, as in the case of food and factories to Cuba in 1960, or token teams of technical experts accompanied by loans or grants, as in Nepal, also in 1960, reap rewards far out of proportion to their expense. Chinese experience is closer than that of Western countries to the experience of underdeveloped countries. The cultural gap is easier to bridge. Finally, accomplishments by Chinese communists appear more striking in contrast with recent conditions in their country than does continued industrial expansion by the United States.

The political channels available for exporting influence are several. Much of Asia is opposed to ρrivate capital and to foreign investment. The communist credo supports this prejudice. Key groups in India, Burma, Indonesia, and Japan support varying degrees of Marxist or socialist ideology and are responsive to Peking's planned economy. Official support for Buddhism and Islam lessens the antipathy of Burmese and Indonesians, while communist strictures against corruption, nepotism, and sloth provide a positive appeal throughout Asia.

Local agents for communicating Chinese messages may be found in various cultural groups organized to promote Sino-Nepali or Sino-Burmese friendship. They may be assisted by local communist parties of some strength, as they were in Indonesia. In these personal contacts at the popular level, Peking enjoys a political advantage generally denied to Western capitals.

Furthermore, personal contact plays a major role in Chinese diplomacy, which exploits shared attitudes of anticolonialism and bonds of so-called Afro-Asian unity. In addition to the shared sense of economic deprivation attributed to Western usurpation, this appeal masks an attempt at solidarity based on a negative color line, i.e., anti-white sentiments. The possibilities of this approach are suggested by the fact that, of fifty-one states having diplomatic relations with Peking in August, 1965, twenty-one are from the Afro-Asian world.

Exploiting these contacts to the fullest, Chinese leaders conclude pacts of non-aggression and friendship with weaker neighbors and exchange support for their grievances, whether in West Irian (Indonesia) or Kashmir (Pakistan), receiving support, in turn for Chinese claims to Taiwan and representation in the United Nations. In addition, growing technical assistance programs place a proliferation of efficient Chinese communist experts throughout Africa and Asia. Their exemplary behavior and their contributions to local needs mitigate the negative impact of Peking's brutal suppression of the Tibet revolt, or its bellicose posture on various international problems.

Finally, Chou En-lai, suave and sophisticated, has played a signal role, lingering for days in little Cambodia or sipping long cups of tea in Rangoon, assuring his audiences of China's need for peace, of its exclusive concern with domestic problems, and of its interest in assisting fellow Asians. This approach pays dividends in countries where individuals play an important role in policy, unimpeded by opposition parties or by rival leaders in the bureaucracy.

These various tactics serve the familiar united-front strategy intermittently employed by communists throughout the world since the days of Lenin. They may act from above, joining forces at the elite level, or they may act from below, infiltrating mass organizations to undermine present leadership. Either strategy is a temporary one designed to facilitate ultimate overthrow of the government.

In view of China's power compared with that confronting it, both from local sources and from the United States, this strategy maximizes Peking's assets while minimizing its liabilities. So long as societies in South and Southeast Asia continue to suffer from political and economic instability, and so long as the United States places its primary emphasis on military development within the area, we may expect increased economic and political action from the People's Republic of China.

This decade has witnessed a new growth, both geographic and strategic, in China's foreign policies. Chinese activity in Africa has increased dramatically as Peking strengthens, by diplomatic contacts and economic assistance, its access to newly independent regimes. Its challenge to Moscow has spread its influence among nascent communist parties and splinter groups in Latin America where it has no official presence. And as Peking's nuclear weapons increase, its prestige is certain to expand among the weaker, less developed countries, especially in Asia. Whether this is accompanied by more militant behavior depends on many unknown factors, including the composition of the regime after Mao Tse-tung passes from the scene, the alternative means of advancing its goals, and the counterforce available to noncommunist countries. As final determinants of Chinese policy, of course, the actions of Moscow and Washington are of prime importance. In this sense, no analysis can predict the future course of China by focusing solely on the decision makers in Peking. Only a continuous correlation of their views with the changing environment within which they must operate can enable us to outline the alternatives which lie before the People's Republic of China, the most powerful country of Asia.

SELECTED BIBLIOGRAPHY

Barnett, A. Doak, *Communist China and Asia—Challenge to American Policy.* New York: Harper & Row, Publishers, Inc., 1960. Published for the Council on Foreign Relations.

Boormann, H., *et al., Moscow-Peking Axis.* New York: Harper & Row, Publishers, Inc., 1957. Published for the Council on Foreign Relations.

Boyd, R. G., *Communist China's Foreign Policy.* New York: Frederick A. Praeger, Inc., 1962.

Levi, Werner, *Modern China's Foreign Policy.* Minneapolis: University of Minnesota Press, 1953.

North, Robert C., *Moscow and Chinese Communists.* Stanford, Calif.: Stanford University Press, 1953.

In addition, the reader should consult the bibliographies published each August in *The Far Eastern Quarterly,* renamed *The Journal of Asian Studies* in 1957.

10

India's Foreign Policy

Richard L. Park

India's policy of nonalignment, and the conciliatory diplomacy advocated by the late Prime Minister Jawaharlal Nehru, have combined to elevate the Republic of India to a major role in the conduct of world affairs, despite its relatively low rank on the ladder of great powers. This remarkable achievement of international eminence, reduced in stature only in part by recent conflicts with China (1962) and Pakistan (1965), involved skillful strategy and a shrewd reading of current events. History also helped to shape the circumstances.

The emergence of India as an independent state in 1947, and the coming to power of the Chinese communists two years later, represent the consequences of two major forces in the social and political revolutions that have been waged in Asia throughout the present century. The results of the competition between a liberal, democratic Republic of India and a communist People's Republic of China are recognized as being of critical importance to the ultimate success or failure in the spread of the communist movement throughout the world. More than half the people on earth are encompassed in the great arc of nations, from Japan and Korea in East Asia, and westward to Pakistan and the Middle East. What happens in India and in China, and between them, will affect the whole of Asia. For the noncommunist as well as for the communist worlds, what comes of the Indian experiment with democratic govern-

with some contempt, and treated at best as a pupil, was a profound shock. Demands for fundamental reform were now renewed, especially by younger intellectuals, and China was pushed toward accelerated change and revolution despite Manchu resistance.

In Japan, the implications of victory were fourfold. The beginnings of the Japanese Empire were laid, and the first tentative steps as a modern continental power were taken; China ceded Formosa, the Pescadores, and for a time, the Liaotung Peninsula, until the intervention of Russia, France, and Germany forced its return. And China was eliminated as a serious competitor in the Korean contest. Second, the war served as a further stimulus to industrial growth and general economic development. In an atmosphere of patriotic fervor, industrial investment and expansion were undertaken, with an emphasis upon heavy industry. The war boom brought prosperity; and afterwards, Japan received both indemnities and new China markets. Third, Japan enjoyed a sharp rise in prestige; most of the West looked on approvingly as their most apt pupil demonstrated her progress and valor, and it was in the aftermath of this victory that Japan began to be received in Western circles with some semblance of equality. Finally, these factors naturally accrued to the credit of the nationalist movement and to the prestige of the military class. The professional soldier, his samurai traditions now supplemented by Western science and by a new sense of mission not present in the Tokugawa era, promised to play a vital role in determining the future of his society.

In the aftermath of the Sino-Japanese War, a crucial decision had to be made. Japan was dedicated to increasing her ties with other Asian societies and providing leadership for them when possible. But to obtain these objectives and to have any basic security for herself, she needed a major alliance with a non-Asian power. This was still the world of the nineteenth century, when Europe collectively exercised a global influence, and when the unfolding of European power politics had a direct and immediate effect upon the non-European world. With the United States, Japan needed only to achieve some general agreement that would serve to neutralize potential conflict; indeed, she could expect no more, since American commitments toward the Pacific were still very limited, even after the annexation of the Philippines. The major powers in Asia were Great Britain and Russia, and the choice had to be made between these two.

Initially, top political circles in Japan were divided. Men like Ito and Inoue hoped for an agreement with Russia that would establish long-term peace in northeast Asia on the basis of satisfying mutual interests. Had such an agreement been reached, Japanese expansion might have been directed south at a much earlier point. An alliance with Great Britain, on the other hand, was recognized as a step toward stabilization in the south and fluidity in the northeast. Not merely in this respect, however, but in every respect, Japanese foreign policy was affected for nearly two decades by the Anglo-Japanese Alliance of 1902. This pact was widely heralded as insuring the peace of Asia. Within certain limits, perhaps it did contribute to that end. England, now finished with isolation, needed global alliances to protect her global interests. In the Western hemisphere, she cultivated the United States; in Asia, she directed her attentions to Japan. Once established, the alliance not only supported the *status quo* in South and Southeast

Asia; it also provided, within the limitations of British policy, some protection for China. In exchange, Japanese "special interests" in Northeast Asia were given recognition by the leading power of the world. Under such conditions, Japan could scarcely afford not to advance those interests.

Thus the first fruit of the Anglo-Japanese Alliance was not peace, but war. The question of Japanese or Russian hegemony over Northeast Asia, having its antecedents back as far as the seventeenth century, was now given over to military decision. As is well known, Japanese victory against a weary and distracted foe was swift. From the Portsmouth Treaty, Japan emerged in control of much of Northeast Asia, and became the first Asian world power. The fruits of defeat and victory were similar to those of the Sino-Japanese War: for the defeated —soul-searching, unrest, and revolution; for the victor—a new gain of territory and fame. Clear title was obtained to the Kuriles, and southern Saghalien was added to the Empire; control over Korea could no longer be challenged, although outright annexation did not come until 1910; the Manchurian-Mongolian area also fell within the shadow of expanding Japanese power, a situation placing new pressure upon China. Again, Japanese industry had enjoyed great expansion as a part of the war effort, with some support from British and American loans. And once more Japanese nationalism had risen to the test. Only a handful of intellectual pacifists and radicals denounced the war; the great majority of the people had been deeply loyal to the cause of a greater Japan.

Some of the costs of victory could also be tabulated. One lay on the surface. Nationalist propaganda had been carried so far during the war that many patriots assumed that the peace would be dictated in Moscow, not realizing that a long war of attrition might be dangerous for a smaller country. Consequently, ugly riots broke out over the Portsmouth settlement, and the government had difficulty in restoring order. There were also deeper costs to be tallied. At home, militarism had grown stronger; the nonconformist had little protection, either in law or by the customs of his society. Abroad, Japan was moving into a new orbit of power and influence but as a result, she was now the object of new suspicions and fears, some of them coming from such traditional supporters as the United States and Great Britain. Already it seemed likely that the critical test might be China.

In partial recompense, immediately ahead lay an era of unprecedented influence for Japan throughout Asia. It was an influence, moreover, derived from much more than mere military prowess. There is no doubt that most of the Asian world experienced a thrill at the Japanese victory over Russia, because it gave hope that the West could be beaten at its own game. But in the broader sense, Japan had become the symbol of the new Asia, a society that had successfully made the transition toward modernization by a process of synthesizing new ideas with its indigenous culture. Western science and progress had come alive within the Japanese context, and from this experience the rest of Asia had much to learn. The success of Japanese nationalism was also a tremendous stimulus, even though its precise ideological forms might not be acceptable elsewhere. Thus, as this era unfolded, Japan embarked upon an extensive career as model, tutor, and leader to eager Asians everywhere. Thousands of students flocked to Tokyo and other Japanese centers of learning and industry. The majority came from China, but every section of Asia was represented in some degree. Likewise, Asian nationalist movements found in Japan a haven and source of support. Their leaders in exile wrote polemics, collected funds, and sometimes obtained official encouragement. Tokyo became a revolutionary center for the Far East. Japan was riding the crest-tide of the developing "Asia for the Asians" movement.

Already, however, the central problem of Japanese foreign policy was becoming that of distinguishing the thin line between acceptable leadership in Asia and unwelcome domination. This problem could be put in various forms. Would Japanese national interests, in the long run, be made compatible with the Asian march toward independence? Would Japanese technological, economic, and political assistance to Asia rest on mutual benefit and truly cooperative bases, or were the methods and intentions such as to be readily labelled the underpinnings of Japanese imperialism? Did the Japanese have, or would they acquire, a fitting psychology for world leadership, or would their actions and attitudes be marked by ethnocentrism, insecurity, and brutality, thereby producing the hatred of those whom they wished to persuade? From these, the universal questions of twentieth-century relations between advanced and lagging societies, Japanese foreign policy was by no means immune. The events of the first World War accentuated the issues.

The rise of Japan as a world power

The First World War was the third conflict within a generation to pay handsome and immediate dividends to the cause of Japanese prestige. It is not difficult to understand why later glorification of war by Japanese militarists produced such weak rebuttals from the society as a whole. Against the true desires of her ally, Japan entered the war "to fulfill her obligations under the Anglo-Japanese Alliance." She proceeded to capture, without difficulty, the German holdings on the Chinese Shantung Peninsula and in certain other parts of the Pacific. With this mission accomplished, she directed her energies to supplying the Asian markets cut off from their normal European contacts, and to providing her Western allies with the materials of war. These tasks required enormous industrial expansion. Indeed, it was at the close of this period that industrial productivity overtook agrarian productivity in yen value, and Japan could thereby claim to have moved into the ranks of industrial societies.

These trends, and complemental factors elsewhere, stimulated the drive for a more intensive policy toward China. The Manchu dynasty had fallen in the Revolution of 1911, but that revolution had failed in its major objectives. The Chinese scene was now marked by deep political cleavages, with rival factions striving desperately for both internal and external support. With Europe fully engaged in a bloody "civil war" and the United States prepared to go no further than a policy of moral suasion, Japan was soon heavily involved in Chinese politics. In 1915, the Japanese government demanded an extensive list of concessions from the Yuan Shih-k'ai regime, known as the "Twenty-one Demands." These were bitterly resisted by China, with some success. Japanese influence moved steadily forward by means of loans, advisers, and technical assistance, yet Japan soon acquired a new image in China: that of the chief enemy to Chinese nationalism. This era was climaxed by the historic May

Fourth Movement, now widely heralded by the Chinese Communists as their point of origin, a fervent demonstration against Versailles and against Japanese imperialism, spearheaded by Peking students and spreading throughout China in May, 1919.

At the close of the First World War, however, there could be no question that Japan had become a world power. She was the one major nation besides the United States to emerge from that war in a stronger position. Her pre-eminence in East Asia could not be doubted, despite the uncertain new force of Bolshevism. What were the ingredients of this power as the third decade of the twentieth century began?

One source of Japan's new power clearly was her evolving economic capacities. Perhaps the full secret of the Japanese industrial revolution still escapes us. However, in its essence, it seems to have involved the capacity of Japanese society to utilize selected elements of Western technique and experience, adapting these to its own culture and timing, without duplicating either the historical context of Western development or the precise set of Western drives, impulses, and incentives. Toward this process were contributed both the conscious purposes of state and the remarkable talents of a people who could display creativeness through integration and discipline. By 1920, Japan was already becoming the workshop of Asia. Her large factories, equipped in many cases with the most modern machinery, contributed such basic products as textiles in great volume; at the same time, an infinite variety of cheap manufactured items flowed out of the thousands of small and medium-sized plants that formed the base of the pyramidal Japanese industrial structure. Sharing with management the credit for such

productivity was the new Japanese labor force, abundant in numbers, cheap in cost, malleable, within limits, to its new task, moving out of the paddy fields into the factories, and acquiring sufficient know-how to give Japan an industrial character of which their fathers could not have dreamed.

But if manpower was a strength, it was also a problem—and one that now began to have an overt influence upon policy. Shortly after the First World War the Japanese population reached sixty million, more than double the figure at the beginning of the Meiji era. In many respects, the facilities existing within Japan to accommodate this great mass already seemed seriously strained, yet no levelling off was in sight. Increasing talk of *lebensraum* was inevitable. And if the population explosion had produced an abundance of cheap labor, by the same token it had placed certain limits on their consumption of goods, by throwing increased emphasis on foreign trade.

Other factors underlined Japanese dependence on foreign lands. The four main islands of Japan were not richly blessed with those natural resources vital to the industrial development of this period. Coal was present in sufficient quantities, except for high-grade coking coal, but the supply of iron ore was very limited, that of petroleum was negligible, and most essential metals were either absent or available only in modest quantity. Moreover, because of her limited land space and her location, Japan had to import many of the agricultural resources needed for industry; raw cotton and rubber were two prominent examples. The Japanese Empire of this period was helpful; from Formosa, Saghalien, and particularly from Korea, came important raw materials and foodstuffs. However, the more important supplies lay outside these areas, and the Manchuria-Mongolian region could be depicted in impressive economic terms.

To revert to our discussion of the sources of Japanese power, the military and political ingredients certainly cannot be overlooked. The Japanese navy had become the third largest in the world. Her army, in size, equipment, and training, dwarfed other forces readily available in this part of the world. There was no foreign force that seemed prepared to challenge a Japanese force that was fully committed in its own territories or in any part of East Asia. The size and equipment of the Japanese military was a testament to the lavish yearly budgetary contributions of the people; the morale of that force was a tribute to intensive indoctrination, sustained by the realities of great political power and prestige within the society.

Politics, in its broader reaches, was also a wellspring of power. For a society without totalitarian restraints (albeit one strongly paternal and authoritarian in character), Japan presented a picture of remarkable stability up to this point. Besides a handful of intellectual radicals, there were few who would dare (or think) to question *Kokutai*—"the national polity" or, more vaguely, "the Japanese way of life." Thus decisions of state, especially in the realm of foreign policy, could be taken on the assumption that they would be accepted with a maximum of conformity. The oracles of national interest could speak without fear of discordant responses, at least so long as they spoke within a consistently nationalist framework. What leadership group has not found some advantage in this?

Yet, as the postwar era began, there were indications that Japanese politics might be drastically affected by the democratic tide. The influence of Western liberalism, crowned by the global idealism of Woodrow Wilson, was strongly felt in Japanese intellectual and urban circles. Party government had assumed new importance, the office of Premier was held for the first time by a commoner, and the movement for universal suffrage was receiving widespread support. Japan's liberal era was opening, bringing with it some serious efforts to establish parliamentary and civilian supremacy in Japanese politics. Temporarily, at least, the long-entrenched bureaucrats and even the military had to move to the defensive. For the latter, the Siberian Expedition was the first clearly unrewarding venture abroad. And however strong the attempt to shift the blame to political timidity and lack of resolution at home, the army could not prevent some questions from arising in the public mind.

Hence, moderation in foreign policy was possible during this period. At the Washington Conference, Japan accepted the famous 5-5-3 naval ratio with the United States and Great Britain, despite the bitter protests of her naval authorities. She agreed to the return of the Shantung concessions. Withdrawal from Siberia was slowly and cautiously undertaken. One Cabinet even had the audacity to cut the military budget sharply, and there were some discussions (although no action) on a permanent reduction in the institutional power of the military in Japanese government. During this era, no figure symbolized moderation in foreign policy more than Kijuro Shidehara, Foreign Minister under the Minseito Cabinets. Shidehera was a conservative, a nationalist, and a loyal servant of the Emperor. He believed that Japan had special interests in Northeast Asia and a special responsibility toward China. But he wanted to avoid a "get-tough" policy which would only provoke boycotts, anti-Japanese hostility, and possibly war. Rather, he hoped Japanese influence could be exerted through trade, financial agreements, and political negotiation.

Militarism and defeat

The liberal era was short-lived. With its collapse went much of the hope for moderation, either at home or abroad. This is not the place to spell out the story of democratic failure in prewar Japan, but its more immediate causes are familiar: economic crisis and depression; political confusion and corruption; and the consequent rise of opponents from left and right. The repercussions were felt almost immediately in Japanese foreign policy. In 1928, under the Tanaka Cabinet, there was a sharp turn toward a more militant nationalism in both the economic and political fields. State support to home industry was combined with a more "positive" program of support for Japanese interests abroad, especially in China. Overtures from Chiang Kai-shek—who had just broken with the communists—were rejected, partly because of fear that his successful northern expedition would jeopardize the future Japanese position in Manchuria and northern China. Ironically, while the Tanaka China policy was provoking sharp Chinese reaction because of its strengths, it was under simultaneous attack by Japanese military extremists because of its weaknesses. Some of these elements, working through the Kwantung Army in Manchuria, engineered the murder of Chang Tso-lin in June, 1928, hoping to force a decisive Japanese move in this area. The Japanese government was posed with the first of a series of direct military challenges to civilian control, challenges which went unmet.

Japanese foreign policy, in the fif-teen years between 1930 and 1945, represented the natural culmination of these new trends. To be sure, not all the old themes were reversed, particularly those that could be read with different inflections. Stress continued to be placed upon Sino-Japanese cooperation, and on the need for a stable, friendly China, purged of communist and anti-Japanese elements. But action continually interfered with words. As the Japanese militarists gained control of the strategic heights of policy, especially in the field, any cooperation had to be strained through the tightening net of aggression, fanatical patriotism, and individual, sometimes mass, acts of brutality. Through these field actions, and as a result of a contrived incident, war came to Manchuria in September, 1931. The weaker Chinese forces were quickly defeated, but Manchukuo remained, to the great body of the Chinese, an acceptable symbol of Japanese aggression.

With the Manchurian region at last under complete Japanese control, the militarists could not avoid spreading outward toward Mongolia and northern China. Thus the Second China Incident erupted, in 1937, and led eventually to total war and defeat. Throughout this entire era, Japan could always find some Chinese allies, whether as a result of the acrid internal rivalries for power in China, sheer opportunism, or some genuine hopes that this route might lead to a new and better Asia, freed from Western control. Indeed, the allies garnered from all of these sources were not inconsiderable either in number or in influence. In Wang Ch'ing-wei, Japan finally found an able if embittered leader. But, as against these facts, Japanese policy achieved what had always been feared most: a union of the dominant wing of the Kuomintang with the communists and many independents, into a nationalist popular front that was bitterly anti-Japanese. Though it had as one of its supreme goals the salvation of Asia from communism, Japanese policy, in the end, contributed more than any other single factor to communist success.

To concentrate solely on China, however, would be to examine only the weakest link of a general Asian policy which, for all its militant, aggressive qualities, had elements of real power and appeal. Building from the old "Asia for the Asians" theme, Japanese policy moved, in the 1930's, toward the concept of a Greater East Asia Co-Prosperity Sphere. The economic background for this policy lay in the rapid strides made by Japanese trade throughout Asia. By means of general deflation, changes in currency valuation, industrial rationalization, and extensive state support, Japanese trade came to enjoy highly favorable competitive conditions in East Asia by the mid-Thirties. Western Europe complained vigorously about the practice of "social dumping" onto the colonial markets. Japan retorted with charges of economic discrimination and attempted monopoly. The fact remained, however, that Japanese penetration of the Asian market, during this period, was substantial. The basis was thus provided for later proposals of greater economic integration of an Asian region led by Japan and divorced from Western control.

The center of the Japanese appeal to greater Asia, however, remained in the sphere of political nationalism. As Japan drifted toward the fascist bloc, Western imperialism in Asia could be attacked with less inhibition than in the past. These attacks were particularly effective in areas where nationalism was still treated as subversive by Western governors, and where Japanese policies could not yet be tested.

Once again, an attempt was made to develop an expanded program of cultural relations and technical assistance. Students flocked to Japan from all parts of Asia; cultural missions were exchanged on an increasing scale; Japanese technicians went forth; and, as the Pacific War approached, the Japanese government provided underground assistance to various Asian nationalist movements in the form of funds, political advice, and even the training and equipping of military forces.

Most of the presently independent governments of South and Southeast Asia owe an enormous debt to Japanese propaganda, military successes, and political concessions—even when the latter were self-serving, empty, or last-minute gestures. There can be no doubt that Japan, both in victory and in defeat, contributed mightily to the end of the old era and the emergence of a more independent, dynamic Asia. Yet her record was tarnished, and today she must combat a legacy of suspicion and even hatred in many of these countries. In part, this can be attributed to such factors as the misconduct of her troops but, more importantly, it is the product of the great cultural barriers that separated her from the regions she occupied and of her inability —through lack of experience, insecurity, and because of her own traditions —to develop the type of flexibility and broad tolerance necessary in leadership. In considerable degree, Japanese hopes for cooperation and friendship were strangled by the nationalism that pushed them forward.

As a corollary to her new Asian policy, Japan naturally developed a new policy with respect to the West. Nearly a decade earlier, at the time of the Washington Conference of 1921, Japan had reluctantly given up the Anglo-Japanese alliance, her shield and support for twenty years. In its place were substituted the more general agreements among the major powers. This concept of collective agreement (not, it should be emphasized, collective security) was especially attuned to the American position. The United States wanted an end to exclusive alliances, but it was prepared to undertake only the most limited of commitments, and it still wished to rely essentially upon moral suasion for policy enforcement. The great symbol of this hope and this era was the famous Kellogg-Briand Peace Pact, outlawing war.

Thus the decline of Japanese liberalism at home was complemented by the absence of effective external checks or controls. The old system of alliances, and the type of checks they imposed upon unilateral action, had been declared obsolete in the Pacific, but no effective international order had replaced them. Consequently, in the name of her national interests, Japan could successfully defy the Nine Power Agreement and the League of Nations, with no single nation or group making an effective stand against her. Inevitably, as she challenged the *status-quo* powers, Japan gravitated toward Germany and Italy, the dissidents of Europe. The Anti-Comintern Pact sealed an alliance of mutual interest, though not one of great intimacy.

But the real decision that confronted Japan as the Pacific War approached had a familiar ring: Was she to seek a stabilization of her northern or her southern flanks? Who was to be engaged, the Soviet Union or the Western allies? The decision was not an easy one. In the late 1930's, Japan had participated in large-scale clashes with Russian forces in the Mongolian region, and her historic rivalry was augmented by her hatred of communism. In the final analysis, however, she de-

cided to count on a German victory on the steppes of Russia, and she turned to the south, whose resources had to be unlocked and whose Western masters had to be overthrown if the Japanese vision of the future were to be attained. Possibilities for agreement with the West to avoid this fateful step were explored, as all the moderates desired, but hopes were broken on the rock of China. Too much had been invested in blood and treasure to concede to Chiang Kai-shek, and so, infinitely more was to be invested—and all in vain.

THE FORMULATION OF FOREIGN POLICY IN PREWAR JAPAN

In the Tokyo trials of major war criminals that followed the Japanese surrender, the Allied prosecutors repeatedly sought the answer to one central question: Who bears the responsibility for leading Japan toward aggression and war? If they did not obtain a completely satisfactory answer, no blame should be assigned. Few questions involve greater difficulties. The problem has taken on universal dimensions as the modern state has grown in complexity and as foreign policy has developed into the composite, uncertain product of a myriad of technicians, men rigidly compartmentalized, skilled and jealous of these skills, but almost always frustrated by the limits of their power; an indeterminate number of free-roaming generalists, yet not so free, being bound by the limits of the single mind, the niceties of group decision, and the pressures—subtle or direct—of subalterns; and, finally, the larger, vaguer public, varying in size but never comprising the whole of its society nor the sum of its parts—alternately indifferent and excited, overwhelmed by the complexities and focusing on some vital issue, ignored and watched with anxiety, molded and breaking out of molds.

Japan was a modern state. In the narrow sense, Japan appeared as a society of great personal absolutism. In both the family and the nation, the head was invested with absolute powers. Inferiors owed complete and unswerving obedience. There seemed no measure of egalitarianism or individualism to alleviate the rigidities of a hierarchical system which, through primogeniture and an Emperor-centered mythology, found its apex in a single source. But in fact, the essence of power in Japanese society has not been that of personal absolutism. The vital center of decision making has uniformly lain in its collective or group character, and in its extensive reliance on consensus as the primary technique. It is critical to understand that, despite all superficial signs to the contrary, the basic nature of Japanese society can only be approached by a thorough appreciation of the intricate refinements of group interaction, the great importance of induced voluntarism, and the generally eclectic quality of final agreements.

In all likelihood, it is only because these things were true that the outward signs of rigid hierarchy and absolutism were so well maintained into the modern era. Elaborate methods had already been developed to integrate theory and appearance with the needs of a dynamic society. Just as the system of adopted sons had long preserved the necessary flexibility in the Japanese family, so the institutions of senior councillor, adviser, and go-between had each, in its own way, facilitated the making of group decisions. That process, giving extraordinary attention to form and status, was often wearisome and prolonged, but every care had to be taken

to make concessions and consensus possible, with a minimum of violence to the position and prestige of those involved. Necessarily, equals were wary of confronting each other in person until the formula for consensus seemed assured; and inferiors developed, to a fine art, all forms of subtle pressures and persuasive devices, so that successful superiors paid silent homage to these in the course of final action.

Not all these conditions sound strange to Western ears, although the aggregate process might seem foreign or extreme. In any case, how were such basic factors in Japanese social relations translated into politics and the making of foreign policy? In theory, the Meiji Constitution of 1889 paid its highest tribute to imperial absolutism but, for successful practice, it demanded a unity or consensus of its disparate working parts. The weakest of these, the two-house Diet, its lower house elected, had at least the power to withhold its consent from basic policies. The administrative bureaucracy, culminating in such executives as the Prime Minister, and the members of the Cabinet and the Privy Council, had a vast range of powers and had legal responsibility only to the Emperor, but it could not be effective alone. The military also drew their power from the Emperor and had direct access to him; in practice, moreover, this branch acquired a potent weapon in that the Ministers of War and Navy had to come from its ranks, which served to limit sharply the independent power of the Japanese Cabinet. The military, however, could operate effectively only in conjunction with the other major branches.

There was never any serious thought of having these forces coordinated by the Emperor personally, despite the awsome nature of his stipulated powers. Instead, that task was handled, for some thirty years, by a small oligarchy of Restoration leaders who acted in the name of the Emperor as his "chief advisers." Ultimately, this group came to be known as the Genro or "senior councillors," an institution without a vestige of legal recognition or responsibility, but central to the process of Japanese politics. Every basic policy decision was placed before the Genro, and their approval was a prerequisite to action. Even the daily affairs of state frequently engaged their attention. With protégés in every branch of government, and with their own vast accumulation of experience, these men were at once the source of integration, the court of final appeal, and the summit of power. To be sure, agreement among them was not always easy; there were deep personal and political cleavages in this, as in other Japanese groups. Timed withdrawals and temporary concessions, however, enabled a consensus to operate with a minimum of crises. Until the close of the First World War, with rare exceptions, the fountainhead of Japanese foreign policy was this group.

With the postwar era, however, basic changes in government began to emerge, paralleling those in society. The members of the Genro became old, and their ranks were not refilled. No group came forth to undertake the integrative role. Instead, Japanese politics was marked by an increasing struggle for supremacy and control among the parties, the bureaucracy, and the military. It is interesting to note that, at the outset of this era, an attempt was made to establish a liaison council under the aegis of the Prime Minister for the development of a unified foreign policy. It was intended to include major party, official, and military representation, but it was never accepted by the major opposition party, and it ultimately faded away.

Without a supreme coordinator such as the Genro, Japanese constitutionalism, in both its written and unwritten aspects, revealed serious flaws. In the hectic party era, foreign policy decisions taken in Cabinet or government party circles were not only subject to legitimate attacks in the Diet, but also to extensive sabotage by the ranks of the subordinate bureaucracy, and to angry challenges by the military groups. The parties never attained more than a quasi-supremacy and, as they faded, the military moved from verbal challenge to open defiance. Japanese society, in the period after 1928, was a classic example of a government divided against itself. Important segments of the military operated, both in the field and at home, in such a manner as to scorn the government. They received substantial support from within the bureaucracy, and from certain party figures as well. Every branch of government was riddled with dissension. Within the Ministry of Foreign Affairs, various cliques maneuvered for position—the militarist clique, the Anglo-American clique, and numerous others. For a time, consensus was impossible, and conditions close to anarchy prevailed.

Gradually, however, greater stability was achieved. Making full use of traditional procedures, top court officials surrounding the Emperor involved themselves in unending conferences with representatives of all major groups; innumerable go-betweens explored the possible bases of compromise; certain voluntary withdrawals, strategic retreats, and silent acquiescences were effected. Slowly a new basis for interaction developed, one which gave due recognition to military superiority but still was broad enough to include essential elements of the civil bureaucracy, court officials, and important pressure groups. Once again the basic decisions were reached by consensus, but with somewhat greater cognizance of the realities of power. In this period, a new group of senior councillors, the Jushin, was organized. Although lacking the influence of the Genro, it was fashioned after its model, indicating the continuing search for an integrative center. That search was destined never to be completely successful. Another experiment was conducted in a liaison council, the purpose being to pool military and civilian policy with particular reference to the foreign scene. Ultimately, the Imperial Conference, with the Emperor himself presiding over a small group of top military and administrative officials, became the final decision-making body. Indeed, it was this group that determined the Japanese surrender, the Emperor personally settling this great issue. Perhaps this was the only basis left for the organic unity envisaged by the Meiji Constitution.

The foregoing trends are not completely meaningful without some brief reference to other important social groups. First, however, it should be noted that the type of consensus being developed during the militarist era was abetted by an increasing control over all media of communication. One of the most literate societies in the world, Japan had national newspapers and magazines with massive circulation. After the early Thirties, prominent dissent from ultranationalism became increasingly dangerous and, after the Second China Incident, all the public organs were echoing the official line.

Meanwhile, a process of accommo-dation had been taking place between conservative militarists and the industrial and commercial world of Japan. In the initial stages of the military revolt against liberalism and a weak-kneed foreign policy, the strong notes of a radical, anti-capitalist theme were heard; the historic cry of "internal reform, external expansion" once again sounded forth. However, after the February 26th Incident, of 1936, when army units in Tokyo under radical command rebelled, this type of revolutionary activity was suppressed. Although some liberal business elements were regarded with suspicion, and certain onerous controls were sharply protested by entrepreneurs, still the necessary compromises were made, and all of Japanese industry rose to the war effort.

Japanese labor reacted in the same way. Its radical and liberal elements had long since been silenced, and the great masses worked with patriotic fervor. It was from the rural areas, however, that the bedrock of Japanese conservatism derived. The alliance between peasant and soldier now held more meaning than at any time since the Restoration. As is so frequently the case, rural provincialism bred its own type of ultranationalism. The Japanese common man played a role in the formulation of foreign policy in his own way: he posed no obstacles to expansionism, his complete loyalty was assured, and no sacrifice would be too great if it contributed to the nationalist cause.

JAPAN SINCE 1945: OCCUPATION AND ITS AFTERMATH

When Japan surrendered, in August, 1945, both her leaders and her people were forced to reconcile themselves to being a vanquished nation. By the terms of the Yalta and Potsdam agreements, the Japanese Empire was to be dissipated and Japan reduced in size to the approximate boundaries of the Restoration era. The homeland was to be occupied for an indefinite period by foreign forces. For the first time in recorded history, Japanese sovereignty was to be superseded by foreign rule. Some of the broad objectives of this rule had already been stipulated: action was to be taken to insure that Japan never again would become a world menace, or a world power. Total disarmament was to be carried out, and those responsible for past aggression were to be punished; even the fate of the Emperor was unclear, although Japanese leaders sought desperately to gain assurances on this point during the surrender negotiations. Along with these essentially negative tasks, the occupation was also to encourage Japanese democratic forces and movements, so that Japan could eventually take her place in a peaceful world. Thus was inaugurated, in September, 1945, a radically new era for Japan, one that might well be labelled "the era of the American Revolution."

If the contemporary processes and substance of Japanese foreign policy are to be discussed meaningfully, certain pertinent aspects of this period must be set forth. In the first place, the American Occupation and its aftermath can easily be divided into three broad phases: (*a*) the early revolutionary era, when the emphasis was upon punishment and reform; (*b*) the era of reconstruction, when the stress was shifted to stabilization and economic recovery; and (*c*) the era of proffered alliance, which is continuing at present. Each of these eras, in its own way, has contributed to the cur-

rent nature and problems of Japanese society.

The revolutionary era

The American Revolution in Japan was that of 1932, not that of 1776, although some of the spirit of the latter, as it applied to basic democratic values, was certainly present. The New Deal had new opportunities along the bombed-out Ginza and in the rice fields. But first, the old order had to be eradicated. Japanese miiltary forces were totally disbanded in a remarkably short time; before the end of 1947, some six million Japanese troops and civilians had been returned from overseas, demobilized, and poured into the homeland. The military forces within Japan proper had also been completely dissolved. The Ministries of War and Navy were abolished. And, in an effort to seal these actions with the stamp of permanency, the now-famous Article Nine was written into the new Japanese Constitution:

Aspiring sincerely to an international peace based on justice and order, the Japanese people forever renounce war as a sovereign right of the nation and the threat or use of force as means of settling international disputes.

In order to accomplish the aim of the preceding paragraph, land, sea, and air forces, as well as other war potential, will never be maintained. The right of belligerency of the state will not be recognized.

The American vision for Japan during this period became widely associated with the phrase "the Switzerland of the Far East," although, in this, pacifism was added to neutralization. It was a vision that had a powerful appeal to many Japanese who lived amidst rubble, without adequate food or warmth, and with vivid memories of lost ones, fire raids, and the final holocaust of the atom bomb. There could be no question as to whether this war had paid. Moreover, the extraordinary vulnerability of the great Japanese cities had been fully demonstrated during the war's last, terrible months. For most thoughtful Japanese, the early postwar era was a period of deep reflection. Its dominant theme was trenchant criticism of past leaders and institutions. Once more, there was a Japanese surge toward new ideas and ways; MacArthur, no less than Perry, symbolized the end of an old order, and a war-weary people turned hopefully to *demokurashi*, without being precisely sure of its contents. These sentiments, widespread as they were, aided the revolution that was getting under way.

Among the various SCAP[1] actions, none had more long-range implications than those which affected the nature and position of Japanese pressure groups. As we have noted, for more than a decade the most powerful group in Japanese society had been the military. Suddenly it was entirely liquidated, and it has not yet reappeared as a significant force. Liquidation was not merely demobilization, but also the purge that barred all professional military officers from future political activity, and the war crimes trials, after which the top military men of the nation were executed or sentenced to prison. Although many of these actions were subsequently modified or rescinded, their total effect, combined with other circumstances, has thus far been

[1]SCAP is the commonly used abbreviation for the term, Supreme Commander of the Allied Powers. It is used to designate General MacArthur, personally, and the Occupation force, collectively.

sufficient to render postwar militarism in Japan impotent.

Through the purge and other measures, SCAP ate still further into prewar conservative ranks. For the old guard it seemed like the reign of terror, though without violence or brutality. Most professional politicians of the old conservative parties had to step aside because they had belonged to some ultranationalist group or had been endorsed by the Tojo government in the elections of 1942. Conservative leadership was hastily thrust into the hands of the one group that could be cleared: the so-called Anglo-American group, from within the Foreign Ministry. Kijuro Shidehara, Shigeru Yoshida, and Hisashi Ashida, all from this group, became the top conservative leaders of Japan for nearly a decade. Even the commercial and industrial world felt the shock of reform. Beset by purges, a program to break down the *zaibatsu* ("big combines"), and the general toll of wartime ravage and postwar inflation, most business elements sought merely to survive, as if seeking shelter during a gale.

Meanwhile, with American encouragement, the labor union movement attained a massive size; within a brief period it numbered some six million workers, whereas, in the prewar period, *bona fide* union membership had never exceeded one-half million. These postwar figures masked many divisions and weaknesses, but there could be no doubt that Japanese organized labor was a new force with which to reckon on the economic and political scene. And in the rural areas, the American Revolution was operating in the most forceful fashion. Under a far-reaching program of land reform, absentee landlordism was almost completely abolished, tenancy was reduced to less than 10 per cent of total agrarian families, and land holdings were equalized beyond the wildest imagination of prewar advocates of land reform. Basically, this program was dedicated to the creation of a huge independent yeomanry. The repercussions in the rural areas, especially among younger age groups, are only now becoming measurable.

Certain reforms cut across class lines and into the broadest categories of society. Legal attempts were made to abandon primogeniture and to emancipate women. Women were given full equality before the law, including equal rights of inheritance, divorce, and suffrage. Sweeping reforms in education were inaugurated, with the purpose of developing freer, more independent students, unshackled from the old chauvinism and submissiveness. Even that very special category of men, the subordinate government officials, were given lectures on democracy, in the hope that some of the old attitude of *kanson mimpi* ("officials honored, people despised") could be removed.

To recite these various efforts in such bald fashion may lead to the supposition that a total social revolution took place in Japan during the first years after 1945. Any such impression would be false. Conservatism, both in the form of certain dominant classes and in the form of certain traditions that operated in every class, was a sturdy force. Moreover, as might be surmised, not all SCAP experiments were successful and, by the end of 1947, in any case, the era emphasizing reform was drawing to a close. In its ripest forms, it had lasted only about two years. The conservatives definitely survived.

It would be equally misleading, however, to underestimate the changes that took place during this era, whether because of SCAP reforms or as a result of the total complex of postwar circumstances. Some of these changes should be regarded as part of the continuum inherited from prewar days. Others were largely the product of foreign intervention or the new conditions prevailing as a result of military defeat. In any case, the changes which developed during this period had a direct influence on the processes and substance of Japanese foreign policy. Most important have been the altered composition of Japanese pressure groups and the accelerated movement toward a mass society.

The nature of Japanese conservatism has been strongly affected by the demise of the military, the levelling of agriculture, and the combined impact of defeat and technology. Japanese reformism has been equally affected by the rise of organized labor and the freedom accorded the intellectuals and students. It is still too early to be certain about the political path that will be taken by a rapidly changing Japanese society. One thing, however, seems apparent: the trend has been toward a closer balance of competing pressure groups within that society than there was in the prewar era. As a result of this and other factors, the Japanese common man has become the object of increasing political solicitation and concern. As we shall note, public opinion has become an important factor in the shaping of Japanese foreign policy.

Stabilization

Before we turn to the current status of foreign policy, some brief consideration should be given to the second and third phases of the Occupation and the gradual emergence, once again, of an independent Japan. The shift of emphasis in Occupation policy, from punishment and reform to economic stabilization and recovery, began as early as 1947. The change was motivated by many problems. Certain earlier American premises about the postwar world now seemed unjustified. The prospects for a China that would be friendly and democratic by American definition were dim; the honeymoon with the Soviet Union was clearly over and the Cold War was beginning; the threat of communism throughout Europe and Asia, as a result of postwar chaos and economic misery, was a matter of profound concern. In Japan itself, the close relation between economic recovery and the prospects for democratic success could no longer be slighted or ignored. In addition, the expenses of occupation and relief constituted a heavy burden for the American taxpayer; at its peak, the cost ran close to one-half billion dollars a year.

The new emphasis brought many changes. Increasingly, the supreme test to which any policy could be put was, Does it advance productivity and economic stabilization? An assessment was made of the primary obstacles— war damage, inflation, the lack of raw materials, and low industrial morale. SCAP began to interest itself in Japanese productive efficiency, and moved from merely keeping Japan alive to furnishing her with raw materials and acquainting her entrepreneurs with the most advanced machinery and techniques. The complex problem of inflation was finally faced. Under the Dodge Nine-Point Stabilization Program, stringent reforms were put into effect. These were unpopular in many quarters, but the inflationary tide was at last turned.

Meanwhile, other disruptions to production were dealt with. The deconcentration program was relaxed and gradually abandoned, after successful initial attempts to reduce certain large *zaibatsu* families and cartels. The United States also progressively receded from its early severity on the issue of reparations. By the end of this era, the American government had indicated its acceptance of the thesis that the Japanese ability to repay war damages was strictly limited, that large reparations would indirectly become a responsibility to the United States, and that the heavy industry on which the Japanese future was so dependent could not be used for these purposes. Finally, SCAP took a sterner attitude toward the labor movement, amending its earlier generous legislation on unionism to give the employer, and especially the government, a stronger position.

The net effect of these actions, accompanied by certain broader trends at home and abroad, was to stimulate rapid economic recovery. Japanese society could build on an industrial revolution already well advanced, and on a legacy of technical knowhow. Deflation and internal readjustments were followed by new opportunities for industrial expansion. The Korean War and the great prosperity of the free world were of major assistance. Beginning in 1950, therefore, Japan entered a period of ámazing economic development. For the next fifteen years, the average annual rise in gross national product was approximately 10 per cent, one of the most spectacular rates of growth in the world.

This second phase of the Occupation, which triggered the economic surge, was not without internal political reverberations. In the revolutionary era, American actions had been an anathema to the conservatives; now, the conservatives became the new allies. The liberal left, which had cheered in the early days, was filled with dismay and resentment at many actions of which it did not approve but from which it had no recourse. Japanese democracy was still under the tutelage of American military rule, and criticism and opposition were strictly limited by that fact. Inevitably, however, the United States and its policies became the central issue in Japanese politics, paving the way for the sharp divergencies that came into the open later. For every political group, moreover, this second era was one of reflection and reconsideration of Western values. There was an unmistakable tendency, at all levels, to emphasize synthesis and adjustment rather than uncritical acceptance of foreign concepts. The pendulum had begun to swing back.

As can be seen, the beginnings of postwar Japanese foreign policy were established in this era, albeit under American direction. These beginnings followed a course that Japanese leadership itself might well have taken and even labelled "in the national interest," had it been an independent agent. Indeed, on issues like reparations and trade, the United States was widely accused of being excessively pro-Japanese. One policy which was emphasized was that of rehabilitating Japanese heavy industry and encouraging its orientation toward the needs and markets of the late-developing societies, particularly those of noncommunist Asia. Again, the concept of Japan as the workshop of Asia was advanced, but without certain former connotations. As a concomitant to this policy, the United States also tried to adjust Japanese political and economic relations with erstwhile enemies. Like a benevolent warden convinced of the successful rehabilitation of his charge, the United States pressed for Japanese reentry into the world community.

But with the second phase of the Occupation, there also began an intimate and largely new relationship between Japan and the United States, a relationship founded on a rising tempo of economic interaction. Japanese products began to flow into the United States in exchange for American raw materials, foodstuffs, and machinery. Technical assistance from the United States smoothed the way for investments and patent sharing. The economic interaction was thus very broadly based. It was supported, moreover, by an expanding cultural exchange of customs, ideas, and patterns of life.

The era of alliance

Within these trends lay the seeds of the third era, that of alliance proffered by the United States to Japan. By 1949, American authorities realized, on the one hand, that the Occupation was reaching a point of diminishing returns, and, on the other, that continuing economic and political ties between the two countries were a mutual necessity. The explorations which led to the San Francisco Peace Treaty of 1951 involved a series of decisions that added to the new Japanese foreign policy and provoked heated political debate.

The critical issue pertained to the question of Japanese defense. Two broad alternatives seemed to exist. One was Japanese pacifism, which involved seeking universal agreements guaranteeing the sanctity of Japanese territory and backing these with pledges of protection by the United Nations, and possibly by the United States, separately. The alternative was to acknowledge the Japanese need for, and right to, military defense, and to underwrite Japanese rearmament with American power. Obviously, the choice between these two broad courses would affect and shape most other aspects of Japanese foreign policy.

The Yoshida government did not hesitate to support the second alternative, that of political, military, and economic alliance with the United States, as the only course compatible with world conditions and Japanese needs. To adopt a policy of neutralism, the conservatives argued, would make Japan dependent on the mercurial policies of the communist world. It would provide neither security nor prosperity. They insisted that both the economic and the political interests of Japan were best served by alignment with the free world, particularly the United States.

These arguments prevailed. While making known its desire for an over-all peace treaty, the Japanese government agreed to sign a treaty with the noncommunist allies alone, if necessary. The Cold War had become hot in Korea while preliminary treaty negotiations were getting under way. Because of this, and the wide divergence between Soviet and American views on Japan, no serious attempt was made to obtain communist approval for the treaty draft, as the Japanese socialists had wished. In exchange for their willingness to sign a separate treaty, the conservatives were given a treaty considered generous by all, and soft by some. Reparations, and certain territorial issues (the Kurile and Ryukyu islands), were left open, providing Japan with some bargaining power. The treaty contained no stipulations concerning SCAP reforms. Japan was left free to make any changes desired in her internal institutions. This included the right to rearm.

Official independence for Japan finally came on April 28, 1952, the day on which the Treaty of San Francisco came into effect. Accompanying the main treaty was a bilateral mutual security treaty with the United States providing for the continuance of American bases in Japan until adequate defenses were prepared by the Japanese government. At least as early as 1949, the creation of a Japanese defense force was being urged in some American and Japanese circles, and Japanese rearmament was first started in the summer of 1950, shortly after the outbreak of the Korean War. The National Police Reserve was activated in August of that year with an authorized component of 75,000 men. With the coming of Japanese independence in May, 1952, this number was increased to 110,000, and a small Maritime Safety Force was established. In August, these were brought together under the National Safety Agency. Two years later, on July 1, 1954, the name was changed to the Defense Agency, and the armed forces were brought directly under the office of the Prime Minister, and authorized to add a small Air Self-Defense Force. The slow build-up of Japanese defense forces continued. By the end of 1955, there were about 200,000 men in the total defense force. Twelve years later, in 1967, the force numbered some 275,000 men in all branches, and while this represented a small force in comparison with Communist China's military establishment, it was ultra-modern, and capable of being rapidly expanded. Indeed, some observers were prepared to accord Japan seventh or eighth status in world power. Despite these trends—or perhaps because of them—the military aspect of the American-Japanese alliance continued to be somewhat unstable for reasons we shall discuss later.

In economic terms, however, the alliance has flourished during the past 15 years. Between 1954 and 1963, Japanese-American trade tripled. Japan, obtaining nearly one-third of all her imports from the United States, be- came its second best customer, next to Canada. Japanese exports to the United States skyrocketed to nearly $2 billion yearly. United States sales to Japan were somewhat larger. By 1970, it was estimated, the United States would be selling $3 to $3.5 billion worth of goods to Japan, and buying goods valued at $2.8 billion. Trade between Japan and the United States has become the most powerful stimulus to continuing alliance.

If the alliance has been largely at- tuned to the business community and conservative circles, however, it has not been totally lacking in a larger cultural component. Heightened cul- tural exchange began during the Oc- cupation, and seldom, if ever, have people from two such diverse societies had so great an opportunity to see each other at work and play. For various complex reasons, rapport be- tween Americans and Japanese was rather easily established. Studies of attitudes give indications of the reasons for this: on the Japanese side, there was a general appreciation of Ameri- can humanism, friendliness, and en- ergy; on the American side, Japanese politeness, discipline, cultural achieve- ments, and industriousness were re- spected. Favorable attitudes have facilitated an exchange between the two cultures, and exchanges between the elite of the two countries have prob- ably been even more significant than mass interaction. In spite of language the Japanese and American elite can communicate with each other on an increasingly meaningful basis as their two societies move closer together. The development of communications con- cerning industrial techniques, social science methodology, and scientific theory is of profound importance.

Having thus survived the transition from Occupation to independence, the alliance between Japan and the United States continues. As we suggested earlier, however, this alliance is more applicable and more acceptable to some segments of Japanese society than to others. It is supported by the conservatives and opposed by the so- cialists. Relations between socialists and American authorities rapidly de- teriorated after 1948, due in part to a major shift in Occupation policy. Dif- ferences concerning foreign policy be- came especially pronounced: the So- cialist Party favored an over-all peace treaty with noncommunist, communist, and neutral states. To the argument that, given present circumstances, this was unrealistic, the socialists answered that no real attempt had been made because of American opposition. The socialists were also strongly antagonis- tic to Japanese rearmament; they bitter- ly denounced the new defense forces as illegal, and they charged an Ameri- can-conservative coalition with under- mining the Constitution of 1947. They were equally opposed to the Mutual Security Pact that accompanied the Treaty of San Francisco, and to the post-independence American bases in Japan that it sanctioned.

Against the conservative policy of alignment with the United States, the socialists advanced a policy of neutral- ism. In part, this policy was a product of their own historic traditions. Both the pacifist and the Marxist streams in Japanese socialism have been strong, and each of these streams has, in its own way, contributed to the modern socialist proclivity for neutralism. The socialist movement in Japan emerged partly as a Christian humanist protest against social injustice, militarism and war; and it existed long before the similar sentiments generated in the Japanese public after the disastrous Second World War. In the second stage of its development, moreover, the Japanese socialist movement was strongly influenced by Marxism. This separated many Japanese socialists from the ideology and practice of Western-style parliamentarism, and yet, because of the particular academic and "deviationist" qualities of Marxism in its Japanese socialist setting, it did not connect them with Moscow. In the initial postwar era, the Japanese socialists took as their ideal the foreign policy of Nehru. More recently, however, the Soviet policies of peaceful coexistence have won considerable support in Japanese socialist circles and Peking also has had a substantial influence upon one group within the Party. The Japanese socialists, as a result, have been brought closer to the international communist movement than at any point in their previous history.

The socialist case for neutralism has encompassed many arguments: the danger of involvement in war via an alliance with the United States; the extreme vulnerability of Japan; the importance of serving as a balance-wheel in a polarized world; identifying more closely with the aspirations of the Asian-African states; the threats to Japanese democracy implicit in a revitalized military force; and the need for Japan to free itself completely from American influence and control. The conservatives have answered with counter-arguments: the lack of realism in seeking to meet communism with a policy of pacifism and isolation; the moral and political rightness of associating with those who share a common ideology; the economic value in doing so; the difficulty of gaining great influence in the world without military potential and connections with a world power; and the possibility of having an independent foreign policy while still being aligned with the West, especially the United States.

Not only have the conservatives maintained their political supremacy and hence their foreign policy views; issues of foreign policy have been involved in the various splits that have occurred in socialist ranks. The first of these took place shortly after the San Francisco peace conference. The right-wing socialists, who plainly leaned toward the West in an ideological sense, were willing to accept the peace treaty even though it did not constitute an over-all agreement. The left-wing socialists, who sought to adhere closely to the neutralist position, remained sharply opposed to the treaty. Both groups rejected the Mutual Security Treaty. However, the arguments over the peace treaty both exacerbated and reflected a wide range of differences within socialist ranks. The party split into two wings and was not reunited until 1954.

Another division occurred in 1959 and continues to the present. The right-wing Nishio faction, joined by a few other moderates, left the Socialist Party in revolt against the strongly Marxist orientation of the dominant left wing. The new Democratic Socialist Party recognized the importance of a balance of armed strength between the two major blocs, accepted the need for some military protection until a new international order could be attained and supported the idea of friendly relations with neighboring states regardless of ideological or political differences (including both China and Taiwan). The Democratic Socialist Party, however, currently obtains only 5-8 per cent of the national vote, whereas the Socialist Party gets approximately 30 per cent. The left is still in decisive command of Japanese socialism, although there are some indications of a moderate movement within the left itself.

In conservative ranks also, the concept of alliance has its limits. It must be remembered that after more than a thousand years of relative isolation, Japan comes to any alliance with difficulty. Even her modern alliances with Great Britain and, later, with the Axis powers were essentially superficial despite their importance to Japan. They involved minimum policy coordination or bilateral ties. Actually, the alliance with the United States is the most far-reaching alliance in Japanese history. But the conservatives as well as other Japanese have been involved in the resurgence of nationalism that naturally followed the Occupation. They never approved of many of the American Occupation policies, and proceeded to overturn a number of these quickly. They did more than merely talk about "an independent foreign policy aligned with the West"; they proved to be tough bargainers on a number of issues affecting the alliance, including the revised security treaty of 1961. Some might say, in this connection, that they wanted equality of rights but not equality of responsibility. Notwithstanding these facts, however, the era of alliance continues.

THE FORMULATION OF FOREIGN POLICY IN POSTWAR JAPAN

To compare the decision-making and administrative processes in Japanese foreign policy before and after World War II is a very difficult undertaking. A vast amount of detailed research is still necessary before generalizations can be advanced with any certainty. In some respects—for example, in terms of the constitutional allocation of responsibility—greater clarity and simplicity have been realized in the postwar era. Against this fact, one must acknowledge the increasing complexity that is the product of a more even balance of pressure groups and the rising importance of public opinion.

The new Japanese Constitution of 1947 did much to clarify the ultimate responsibility for policy, domestic and foreign. Patterned almost wholly after Anglo-American institutions, it drastically altered the old system. Under its provisions, the Emperor's functions became ceremonial and symbolic. Sovereignty was assigned to the people, to be exercised by their elected representatives. A parliamentary system modelled after that of Great Britain was established, with certain modifications of a distinctly American flavor.

The Diet, instead of being peripheral to the political process, is now its center, and both houses are elective. The upper house, the House of Councillors, is constructed in a complicated fashion, with both nationwide and prefectural constituencies; the lower house, the House of Representatives, is based on medium-sized election districts (three to five members chosen from each district, depending upon its size, with each voter having one vote). Executive responsibility to the Diet is clearly stipulated. The Prime Minister must be approved by the Diet, and if the houses disagree, by the lower house. In case of a vote of no confidence, the government must either dissolve the lower house and call for new elections, or resign.

A new law pertaining to the Diet was enacted to accompany the Constitution of 1947. Among other things, it provided for a system of standing committees, in contrast to the prewar, British style, *ad hoc* committees. Thus, both houses of the Diet now have Foreign Affairs Committees. After agreement among the parties on the allocation of committee seats, members are selected by each party, on the basis of training, experience, and political connections. The standing committees exist to hold hearings on government legislation or any policy matters within their general jurisdiction. Special, *ad hoc* committees, however, are still used extensively in the Japanese Diet, sometimes on issues involving foreign policy. The Japanese committee system, as it currently operates, does not give either to the Diet as a whole or to individual Diet members the degree of power possessed in the United States Congress. Of course, party or, more precisely, factional discipline interacts with the institutional framework of the Diet to make this true. In any case, initiative and power in foreign policy lie mainly with the executive branch of government.

Thus older political practices combine with the new legal framework to place a premium on the cooperation of bureaucracy and party leadership in the formulation of Japanese foreign policy. Under a Western-style parliamentary system, major party leaders constitute the apex of authority. The Emperor no longer serves as an independent and legally omnipotent channel of power. The military branch of government is no longer a separate and competitive source of influence. And even the civil bureaucracy is now clearly subordinated in law to a political administration that must be consonant with a majority of the popularly elected members of the House of Representatives.

In concrete terms, how do the bureaucracy and the parties cooperate in foreign policy formulation? Generally speaking, the party (that is to say, the dominant party, the Liberal Democratic Party) provides the broad policy framework and the Foreign Office drafts specific policy within this framework. The draft is then subject to scrutiny and approval by the party, after which the Foreign Office proceeds to execute policy in its final forms. To

understand how this actually works out, however, one must have a general appreciation of the present Japanese party system and bureaucracy.

Perhaps four general trends within the party system are significant for foreign policy. First, the conservatives have continued to hold a commanding position in Japanese politics. They have consistently polled close to two-thirds of the total vote, and at all times—divided or united—they have held a large majority of the seats in both houses of the Diet. Perhaps the major reasons for regular conservative victories have been their prewar ties and strength at local levels, especially in rural areas; their prominent, well-known candidates; the funds at their disposal; the relative prosperity in Japan since 1950; the divided and weak nature of the opposition; and last, but by no means least, the capacity of the conservatives to adjust to changing conditions. For these reasons, the Liberal Democratic Party is the government, now and for the foreseeable future.

The growing importance of the postwar socialists, however, cannot be ignored. Although they are currently weak and divided, as we have said, they have moved a considerable distance from their pre-1945 position of total impotence. Socialists occupy roughly one-third of the Diet seats, and their percentage of the vote has generally increased since 1949. In the election of November, 1963, the two socialist parties got a combined total of 36.4 per cent of the vote, and the communists obtained an additional 4 per cent. The conservatives, therefore, have to be aware of competition in a sense that was unnecessary before World War II. The Japanese left cannot be disregarded.

These facts lead to a second generalization about Japanese politics, namely, that the party system can be variously defined as "two-party," "one and one-half party," or "federation type." Despite the socialist split of 1959, there are only two significant parties in Japan at present: the massive Liberal Democratic Party, which received 55 per cent of the vote in 1963, and the Socialist Party, which obtained over 29 per cent. The splinter Democratic Socialist Party, the moderate group, got only 7 per cent of the 1963 vote and the communists 4 per cent. In one sense, therefore, Japan has a two-party system.

In functional terms, however, Japan can be said to have a one and one-half party system: one dominant party that knows only how to govern, and a half party (or parties) that know only how to oppose. The socialists' position creates some serious problems. It is not easy to acquire responsibility, whether in foreign or domestic policy matters, if one has never had power and, hence, never had the responsibility that goes with formulating and defending policy.

There is still another way in which the Japanese party system can be defined and explained: as a system of rival federations within which operate the real parties, namely, the small factions that are based upon intimate personal ties and mutual interests. Each of the major parties is composed of such factions. Thus the Liberal Democratic Party currently has Sato, Ikeda, Miki, Ono, and Fujiyama factions, among others. The shifting alliances among these factions determine leadership of the "federation," or party. Factional loyalty generally takes precedence over loyalty to the federation; hence, in many respects, the real party is the faction.

Considering the circumstances noted above, it is not surprising that bipartisanship on foreign policy issues does not exist in Japan. Indeed, such issues are even used, on occasion, as weapons in the struggle for power among rival factions *within* a major party. Within the Liberal Democratic Party, recently, such issues as policy toward China and even the revised Security Treaty with the United States were made intraparty issues against Kishi and his supporters. Needless to say, socialist opposition is much more continuous and absolute. When we talk about Japanese foreign policy or government attitudes, it must be borne in mind that there is a vigorous and adamant opposition.

Finally, the party system as a whole is still on trial with the Japanese people. It is not yet thoroughly ingrained, either in institutional practice or in public behavior. Popular commitments to parties and to the party concept may be growing, but they are still weak. There is some danger that, with increasing mass participation in politics, the parties and the Diet will be circumvented. There is a tendency on the part of the left to protest via the streets, and on the part of the ultra-right to protest via the knife.

The Japanese bureaucracy merits special attention. Its policy-making role is a vital one, especially with respect to foreign affairs. Once again, a few broad trends need to be noted. First, the general prestige and power of the Japanese bureaucracy continues to be great. To be sure, there are powerful, new challenges. Industry, commerce, and the professions, are also becoming prestigious. In relative terms, therefore, the prestige of the Japanese official has been declining. This is indicated by the popular homage he receives, by his emoluments, and by his own attitude toward his status. But these are changes relative to the Japanese past; in comparison with other democratic societies, the Japanese official enjoys great prestige and power.

Despite the efforts of the Occupation to encourage local autonomy, the forces of centralization triumphed, and the national government is as powerful as ever. Despite the new constitutional position of the Diet, the central bureaucracy wields enormous power, partly because of its legacy and partly as a natural result of its technical expertise. Under these conditions, it is not surprising that many young Japanese aspire to careers as officials. Indeed, competition for the available civil service positions is as intense as for top positions in industry or the leading professions.

In some respects the bureaucracy has changed less than most other facets of postwar Japan. It remains strongly hierarchical, and its modes of operation have been slow to change. Yet in composition and in background, the Japanese bureaucracy is undergoing significant evolution. Young men from the upper and upper-middle classes still have sizeable advantages—the educational opportunities and the proper social connections—but others have been pushing their way into the civil service in increasing numbers. Tokyo University, moreover, does not have the monopoly of training it possessed before 1945; a larger proportion of successful candidates come from other institutions. Above all, Japanese civil servants are now receiving a much broader college education, on the one hand, and much more advanced technical training, where it is desired, on the other hand. The premium on specialized skills has grown steadily. Some observers believe that the Japanese civil service not only attracts top talent in such fields as economics, but gives it more opportunity than does the academic world.

Another vital fact cannot be ignored. As in the prewar period, an increasing bureaucratic infiltration of the con- servative party has been taking place. The percentage of conservative Diet members who have been officials in the national civil service has steadily risen since 1946. Approximately one-fourth of the Liberal Democratic Diet members are in this category, and the percentage of party leaders and Cabinet members who are former officials is much higher. This fact explains the close interaction between party leadership and government bureaucracy in contemporary Japan.

The Japanese Foreign Office is small, and simply organized. It has less than 2,000 men of civil service rank. Its major subdivisions are bureaus of two types, those covering geographic areas and those representing specialized functions. The latter include economic affairs, treaties, information and culture, and international cooperation. Within the Ministry, there is also a Secretariat which serves as a central coordinating and administrative unit. It includes a policy planning staff charged with over-all evaluation and planning of basic policy positions. Official liaison with the Diet is maintained through a parliamentary vice-minister, normally appointed from the Diet membership.

Today, a fairly high degree of coordination, efficiency, and continuity exists in the formulation of Japanese foreign policy. In the prewar period, as we have seen, the struggle to control foreign policy was a complex one waged by diverse forces. The ultimate cost to Japan was enormous. In the immediate post-surrender period, the Japanese Foreign Office could play only a minor role. Both foreign and domestic policy were laid down by Occupation authorities. The Japanese function was, essentially, to discern what the policy was and then to exercise—with uncertain results—the right of suggestion. In any case, diplomacy had to be directed primarily toward the United States. As the Occupation drew to a close, Japanese initiative was gradually reasserted. Initially, diplomacy, which was in the hands of Prime Minister Yoshida, himself a former Foreign Office man, was highly personalized. His opponents charged him with "one-man diplomacy." Party participation in foreign policy was very limited, and the Foreign Office still struggled to overcome its earlier weak and ineffectual position.

As Japan regained her independence, however, the conduct of foreign policy was gradually placed on a broader base. This base is the network of collaboration between the Liberal Democratic Party and the Foreign Office. By the time of the Kishi era (Kishi became Prime Minister in February, 1957), bureau chiefs in the Foreign Office had begun to have close contacts with party leaders. Many of these contacts were with the pertinent committees of the Liberal Democratic Party: the Research Committee on Foreign Relations, the Policy Research Committee, and the General Affairs Board. These committees, particularly the General Affairs Board, determine the foreign policy of the party.

Relations between the Foreign Office and the Liberal Democratic Party have not always been smooth or uncomplicated. The factional character of Japanese parties can be a major problem, especially if a faction is encouraged by external pressure groups. Thus, at the time of negotiations between Japan and the Soviet Union for a treaty of peace, some leaders within the Liberal Democratic Party, supported by certain fishery and commercial groups, built up pressure for a rapid settlement. This was resisted by top Foreign Office officials but, for a time, Japan suffered once again from

dual diplomacy. The Foreign Office has also faced jurisdictional and policy quarrels with other ministries, on occasion. Japan, however, does not have the massive problem of reconciling and integrating a Pentagon-CIA-State Department triumvirate in the foreign policy field. On the whole, coordination of the formulation and execution of foreign policy has been more satisfactory in recent years than at any other time in the history of Japan.

There is another side to the coin. Japanese pressure groups, public opinion, and opposition parties have added many new complexities to the scene. As we noted earlier, pressure groups of all types exist. Their number, diversity and influence on Japanese foreign policy has increased greatly. It is not appropriate here to attempt any detailed discussion; only a few salient points can be presented. As in the prewar era, the commercial and industrial groups have the greatest single influence on the Liberal Democratic Party, especially in the field of foreign policy. These speak through the Japan Employers Association and many similar organizations. It would be a mistake, however, to assume that the Japanese business and industrial world speaks with a single voice. On such an issue as trade with China, for example, it is far from unanimous. Still, the broad outlines of Japanese foreign policy at present are deeply influenced by the interests and views of leading industrial and commercial pressure groups. They remain the chief financial support for the Liberal Democratic Party, they include the most intimate confidants of conservative politicians and, hence, they are the most powerful unofficial influence on public policy, domestic and foreign.

On certain issues, pressures emanating from rural Japan can also be important. Almost every Japanese farm-er belongs to an Agricultural Cooperative Association, and these Associations are vital to the fortunes of individual politicians and to the Liberal Democratic Party as a whole. Rural Japan constitutes approximately 25 per cent of the electorate, a portion that votes overwhelmingly conservative. The greatest agrarian pressures are exercised on domestic issues, but standing agrarian interests and attitudes do not need to be articulated constantly to establish certain guidelines and limits in foreign policy.

The more serious of the factors that complicate the formulation of Japanese foreign policy, however, are not the traditional Japanese pressure groups, but certain new ones, and the force of public opinion as it is revealed in countless polls. Among the opposition pressure groups, the most important is organized labor. Sohyo, the General Council of Trade Unions of Japan, has been especially vocal on foreign policy. It has hewed closely to, and helped to shape the socialist position on neutralism, relations with the communist world, American imperialism, and many other issues. In addition, it has supported these positions with demonstrations, work stoppages, and quantities of political literature.

Sohyo, with more than three million members, is probably the most formidable of the opposition pressure groups (though it should not be implied that it can commit all its members on any issue). There are, however, a number of others. Most of them represent intellectual, student, and labor elements in Japanese society. This opposition, as we indicated earlier, cannot be ignored. It maintains a substantial forum by means of newspapers, magazines, and radio. Its message reaches the Japanese public, especially the urban public, regularly. So,

since 1950, foreign policy has become a vital part of the political battlefield in Japan, probably the most vital part. The conservatives have been forced to recognize a far more significant opposition than any experienced in the prewar era, and they have had to devise new methods of meeting that opposition. Suppression or indifference are no longer feasible. Thus the conservatives are also resorting to the media of mass communication and seeking public support more actively than in the past.

It is a most difficult task to assess the influence of Japanese public opinion on foreign policy. In recent years, polling has become very popular in Japan. It is carried out by a variety of organizations, the most widely regarded polls being those which resemble the leading American polls. The major Japanese newspapers, in particular, poll the public at regular intervals on a wide variety of subjects, including many issues of foreign policy. Opinions on rearmament, a security treaty with the United States, and relations with China have been asked for frequently. And, in a number of cases, the polls have indicated that either a large minority or an actual majority of those polled differed with government policy.

There is little doubt that public opinion, now being presented in these concrete, measured forms, has had a rising impact on decision making in Japan. Increasingly, it is a factor which Japanese leaders take seriously. Sometimes, to be sure, public opinion is used to justify a decision based mainly on other grounds. But more frequently, when the polls indicate substantial public opposition to a given policy, conservative leaders respond with modifications, a shift in timing, or a more intensive public relations campaign. The reluctance of recent conservative administrations to rearm rapidly or fully, the long and fairly firm Japanese bargaining in connection with the revised security treaty, and the cautious, ambivalent position toward China are all indications of the new power of the Japanese common man.

However, the Japanese conservatives are well aware of the fact that elections in Japan are not won primarily on the basis of issues, particularly issues of foreign policy. In recent elections, the Liberal Democrats have stressed domestic issues—notably prosperity and progress—and they count heavily on their superior organization, their greater funds, and their local leadership. Thus they can afford to take chances, even when they know or suspect that there is strong public opposition to specific foreign policies. This is the more true because they believe (with reason) that a mere numerical count of opposition is misleading. Opposition of the intensity likely to be translated into political action is largely confined to urban centers, especially Tokyo. Thus, when it is confronted with evidence of hostile public opinion, the government tactic is to camouflage or alter a policy slightly, so as to disarm some of the opposition, but rarely if ever to make changes. With respect to the socialists also, a *caveat* must be entered regarding the influence of public opinion. The record would indicate that the Japanese socialists have often ignored public opinion when it conflicted with their ideological purity.

In sum, the process of formulating, executing, and defending Japanese foreign policy today is in the hands of a conservative elite. The formal and informal institutional processes have been greatly refined in the postwar era, and now operate at a fairly high level of efficiency. Collaboration between

the Foreign Office and the Liberal Democratic Party is close and continuous. Despite some problems, the old rivalries have largely been eliminated. With the military clearly subordinated, and with cooperation between party and government at a peak, Japanese foreign policy has achieved an unprecedented degree of coordination and continuity. The new Japanese Foreign Office men, moreover, are more broadly recruited and trained than they were before World War II, and they possess a higher level of technical proficiency.

The conservative elite that directs Japanese foreign policy is sustained and influenced mainly by the industrial, commercial, and agrarian segments of Japanese society. Contradictory pressures, however, sometimes flow from these elements. In any case, no simple economic analysis does justice to the realities of the situation. Among other things, Japan is becoming a mass society in which the conservative elite is forced to pay increasing attention to public opinion. In part, this is reflective of the fact that the public has a choice: the socialist opposition, while weak, is infinitely more important than it was before 1945, and it offers the Japanese people a dramatically different foreign policy. But the influence of public opinion in Japan today can easily be exaggerated. With respect to foreign policy, it would be most accurate to say that public opinion serves to effect certain modifications, both of substance and of timing, and causes the conservatives to give more attention to the public image of their policies.

CONTEMPORARY ISSUES IN JAPANESE FOREIGN POLICY

At present, three dominant considerations underlie the debates and decisions pertaining to foreign policy in

Japan. First, there are the interrelated issues of nationalism and security, issues involving Japanese relations with the United States, the communist bloc, and the world. Second, there is the high priority that must be accorded economic considerations in foreign policy—the extreme importance attached to such matters as trade, technical assistance opportunities, and equality of economic treatment by others. Finally, there exists within Japanese society an ardent search for some basic purpose or function, especially one that will relate Japan in a suitable manner to the Asian world, catering to her special interests there, while allowing her a major place on the world stage. We must study these general considerations further in the context of specific issues, for they are likely to be the enduring as well as the underlying forces motivating Japanese society. Indeed, if the background that we have projected is examined closely, these forces will be seen to have persisted, in different forms, throughout the history of modern Japan.

Nationalism, security and foreign policy

Given the years of defeat, occupation, and subordination to foreign authority, the recent resurgence of Japanese nationalism is completely understandable. Indeed, it is surprising that nationalism has not been a more important component of Japanese foreign policy. Currently, however, Japanese nationalism is not as narrow as it was before World War II. It runs the entire political gamut. Old-line conservative and ultra-rightist doctrines are once more in evidence, although they are largely lacking in public appeal. Some attempt to preserve or revive the Emperor cult has been made, and assassination is again a sporadic factor in the political scene.

Elements of the right, moreover, occasionally join the left in an anti-American, Pan-Asian chorus, evoking memories of earlier attempts to exclude the West from Asia and establish a Greater East-Asian Co-Prosperity Sphere.

Meanwhile, the left also finds nationalism a potent political weapon. American bases in Japan, the Okinawan occupation, and all issues revolving around the so-called subordination to America are approached nationalistically. In foreign policy, particularly, socialist and communist attacks on the conservatives are generally spearheaded by nationalist slogans. On domestic issues, the situation is sometimes reversed. When the Liberal Democrats attack the new Constitution, they do so partially in nationalist terms, referring to it as a document unsuitable for Japan in certain of its American-imposed provisions. It is the socialists who defend many of the foreign innovations as representing the true will of the Japanese people. And there are other respects in which the nationalist mantle seems to be worn by the conservatives, particularly on matters of education and culture.

In some respects, Japanese nationalism today is reminiscent of the Meiji era. Its dominant notes are defensive in character: Japan is an island of weakness surrounded by a sea of power. But this time the power is Asian as well as Western. The continent is no longer a vacuum; China, possessed of a huge standing army and rapidly acquiring nuclear weapons, is becoming a major power. Indeed, the containment of China is likely to be the major Asian problem for the decades that lie ahead. Fortunately for Japan, the Sino-Soviet alliance currently lies in shreds; but, by itself, the Soviet Union is another major

Asian power, and one having certain basic differences in national interest from Japan.

Under these conditions, it seems highly unlikely that Japanese nationalism will revert quickly or easily to its former themes of expansionism and a militant messianic mission. The burning issues are more likely to concern the best way in which to preserve the territorial integrity and the true independence of Japan. And these have been the issues of the day. On the one hand, questions of extraterritoriality, foreign bases, equality of treatment in commercial agreements—in short, questions of true independence from the United States—have come to the fore. But there is another way in which the basic issue can be posed: Under present conditions, how can Japan achieve security, lasting prosperity, and meaningful independence, except in close alliance with the United States?

Thus the great debate in Japan is over neutralism versus alliance. It is clear that neutralism has substantial support, and not merely from the organized left. World War II left terrible scars that will not soon be eradicated. Over two hundred thousand Japanese still suffer from radioactive diseases as a result of the atom bombs dropped on Hiroshima and Nagasaki. There are additional thousands who bear combat injuries or the marks of the great fire raids on major Japanese cities. The living symbols of the last war contribute strongly to a Japanese distaste for rearmament or heavy involvement in international power politics. And there is the widespread fear that alliance with the United States and, particularly, the presence of American bases on Japanese territory, will greatly increase the risk of Japanese involvement in war, especially in view of the troubled Asian scene.

The Japanese also ask whether the United States will or can actually provide security for Japan. Indeed, this may well be the crucial question of the next decade. Hence, American fortunes elsewhere in Asia will have a major, possibly decisive effect on trends in Japan. Many Japanese argue that, since China and the Soviet Union are major military powers, Japan should reconcile herself to the status of a minor power and seek security in some kind of international guarantee, rather than seeking to play a larger political and military role with American support. The Japanese population, which is now approaching one hundred million, must import 80 per cent of its industrial raw materials and about 20 per cent of its foodstuffs. Its cities are massive, densely packed, and highly vulnerable. They lie minutes away from communist bases. The American lines of supply and communication are long, and in the event of war, uncertain.

Perhaps all these points add up to a feeling, in some Japanese circles, that military and political developments, especially in Asia, make warfare a suicidal undertaking for modern Japan.

Some of these feelings lay behind the serious political crisis that developed, in the spring of 1960, over the revised security treaty with the United States. This crisis produced the most substantial mass movement in Japanese political history. Millions of Japanese signed petitions asking that the Diet be dissolved and new elections held. Hundreds of thousands demonstrated in Tokyo and other major cities. The acute stage of the crisis lasted for nearly one month, from mid-May to early June.

Naturally, the organized left played an important part in this crisis. But to dismiss the episode as communist or even socialist-controlled is to misunderstand seriously the climate of Japanese politics and public opinion. No one knows this better than the Japanese conservatives. The May-June Incident was the product of many complex factors: the increasing unpopularity of the Kishi government; the almost unanimous opposition of the metropolitan press to government actions, which helped to mobilize public sentiment; factionalism inside the Liberal Democratic Party, which helped to weaken Kishi's internal base of support; and the tactics used in forcing the treaty through the House of Representatives which gave opponents a new slogan, "for the protection of democracy," an appeal enlisting support even from some conservatives.

Certainly, the socialists cannot be exempted from responsibility for the crisis. In addition to their policy positions, the socialists hold certain special views on tactics. In socialist circles, a considerable ambivalence toward the concept of parliamentarism still exists. A number of socialists believe in parliamentarism plus, and are willing to go beyond parliamentary procedures, if necessary, to attain their ends. They do not accept completely the right of the majority to govern, and they do not eschew violence if it offers a chance of success.

Actually, the May-June Incident revealed some of the continuing weaknesses of Japanese parties and parliamentarism. No party really gained as a result of the crisis. With the revised treaty safely enacted, Kishi resigned, but after playing a major role in selecting his successor, Hayato Ikeda. Ikeda took office with conciliatory offers to consult with the opposition and operate in democratic fashion, to pay attention to public opinion, and to build a prosperous, peaceful Japan. Armed

with these pledges, the Liberal Democrats easily won in the elections of November, 1960, garnering 58 per cent of the vote, and 296 of the 467 seats in the House of Representatives. Majority control was also maintained in the thirtieth general election of November, 1963, when the Liberal Democrats won 55 per cent of the vote, and 283 seats. The disunited left received 39 and 40 per cent of the votes in the 1960 and 1963 elections.

Despite their sizeable electoral victories, the Japanese conservatives are well aware of the deep division in Japanese public opinion over security issues, and of the political hazards involved. Omitting the Democratic Socialists, who take a moderate view, the socialists and communists who have repeatedly registered their violent opposition to rearmament and to the military alliance now poll about one-third of the vote. Public opinion polls, moreover, indicate that about one-third of the electorate share socialist views on these issues, and that another sizeable element is uncertain or disinterested. Consequently, the conservatives have been cautious in approaching such questions. In recent budgets, appropriations for the Japan Self-Defense Force have totalled about 10 per cent, a very low figure in comparison with most of the other major nations of the world.

There is every indication that Japan will retain a military tie with the United States but will not become a major military ally in the near future. The Japanese military will probably be restricted to limited, non-nuclear (but modern) armaments, for defense only, at least for the next five years. In all likelihood, public opposition will preclude the addition of atomic weapons to the arsenal of the defense force, or the storage of such weapons on Japanese soil by the Americans. The numerical growth of the defense force will be very gradual and limited. As we noted earlier, its present total size is only about 275,000 men. There will be no attempt in the near future to commit these forces abroad, even for use by an international body like the United Nations. It is also unlikely that Article 9 of the Constitution will be repealed or altered, since the conservatives do not have the votes to accomplish this.

Nevertheless, there are some indications that a broad reconsideration of Japanese foreign policy, including its military component, has begun. Slowly, a recognition is developing that China presents both a military and a political threat to the other Asian states including Japan, a threat that can be met only by some balancing force, in which the leading noncommunist Asian states must play a significant role. Already, Japan has begun cautiously to play a more active political role in Asia, aligning herself with such states as India in the international scene. The extent to which she will also upgrade her military commitments as her political commitments in the world, and especially in Asia, grow, is yet uncertain. There can be no doubt, however, that a heightened discussion of this matter is under way, even in intellectual circles.

Meanwhile, in a major address to the Diet, on January 25, 1965, Prime Minister Sato outlined the twin themes that currently dominate Japanese foreign policy. Speaking of his recent visit to the United States, Sato asserted:

I emphasized that, for the maintenance of world peace, stability in Asia is essential and explained our country's policy to contribute to the promotion of the welfare of the Asian peoples by helping stabilize their livelihood and elevating their standard of living in the spirit of devoting ourselves to the cause of peace. . . .

I also reaffirmed Japan's policy to maintain firmly the Japan-United States Mutual Cooperation and Security Treaty arrangements in the belief that it is essential for the stability and peace of Asia that there be no uncertainty about our country's security.

The prospects for the continuance of the Japan-American alliance are good. However, to make that alliance more acceptable and to advance Japanese national interests, the conservatives will continue to approach issues of military security with an admixture of caution and tough bargaining. Under Japanese pressure, various adjustments have been made with respect to American military installations and their uses. With regard to Okinawa, a Japan–United States Consultative Committee has been established, and recently that Committee has expanded its authority to include not only questions of economic assistance but "various other problems concerning the promotion of the well-being of the Okinawans." The Japanese government continues to press for the return of administrative authority over Okinawa to Japan, and clearly, the establishment of this Committee represents an intermediate step in that direction.

The Sato government, like the conservative governments before it, is firmly committed to close cooperation with the United States, but it wants a heightened emphasis on Japanese interests, a partnership between equals, a continuous movement away from the heavy dependency of the Occupation era. This is both logical and politically expedient. Most recently, Sato expressed his views in the following words:

I perceived in the attitude of the American authorities a firm determination to cooperate with Japan for the attainment of world peace and at the same time to address themselves to the task of settling the problems pending between Japan and the United States while fully respecting each other's standpoints and national interests. I believe that I was able to achieve success because I discussed pressing problems instead of merely abstract questions frankly and in a concerted manner. I am convinced that through the recent talks, Japanese-American relations have entered a new stage of development. . . .

It is my intention to conduct an independent diplomacy and fully pursue our country's national interest and security, keeping as the supreme goal the establishment and maintenance of world peace based on freedom and justice. Needless to say, the national interest I seek is one closely tied to the cause of world peace and based on international cooperation. I would like to assert without hesitation our country's rightful interest in international community while discharging the responsibilities commensurate with our elevated international position.

Japan also continues to seek friendly, or at least normal, relations with the communist bloc. Shortly after the Korean War ended, an attempt to normalize these relations began. Negotiations with the Soviet Union, which culminated in the Treaty of 1956, were the opening move, but, in keeping with the past, Russia made very few concessions. Until recently, therefore, Russo-Japanese relations have been minimal. Within Japan, antipathy to the U.S.S.R. has been relatively strong, a product of historic rivalries, the last-minute attack in 1945, Russian treatment of Japanese prisoners, and its "get-tough" policy toward Japan on most postwar issues.

Recently, however, the Soviet Union has made some gains, at least with the Japanese public. The policy of peaceful coexistence, begun by Khrushchev and continued by his successors, has had a generally favorable impact upon the Japanese, especially on the socialists, who are today more pro-Russian than at any time in their postwar history. There is also some evidence that the Soviet Union has decided to woo Japan in more meaningful fashion than in the past. Recently, Soviet Premier Kosygin wrote Sato expressing a desire for personal contact, and a number of other minor indications of a possible shift in Russian policy can be found. The Russians, it should be remembered, are no longer *persona grata* with the main stream of the Japanese Communist Party, hence their main effort has recently been to cultivate the broader, more meaningful noncommunist left. Up to date, however, no specific concessions to Japan have been made. The Russians have even refused to yield the two small islands of Habomai and Shikotan off Hokkaido, unless the security treaty with the United States is abandoned. And other problems remain. But if official Soviet-Japanese relations are thawing only slowly and with difficulty, one cannot rule out the possibility of a significant Soviet effort in this direction. The Japanese conservatives are almost certain to view such a drive with caution, while hopeful that the widening Sino-Soviet breach will make possible the redress of certain Japanese grievances. Beyond this, one can muse on the possibility of a Russo-Japanese alliance against China, in place of or in conjunction with an American-Japanese alliance. Some variant of current Indian policy might be attempted; namely, the movement toward an "equilibrium" policy vis-à-vis the United States and the Soviet Union, whereby the American alliance was retained, but a more positive relationship with Russia was established to counteract the threat from China.

At the moment, however, relations

with China are still regarded as much more important by most Japanese. Japan has had a lengthy historic relationship with China, and it is inconceivable to many Japanese that the ties can remain as limited as they now are. Within Japan, pressures for a realistic policy toward China have mounted. Various business interests continue to believe that the China trade can again become meaningful, even if it is different and smaller than before 1945, and there is evidence to support this, trade is increasing. Certain conservative leaders are at odds with the present policy, which they regard as the result of excessive deference to the United States. The socialists, of course, have sought to make a major political issue out of policy toward China. They have long demanded full and unqualified recognition of the Chinese People's Republic, and have denounced the conservatives for preventing this by a policy of military alliance with the United States. On two occasions now, the Socialist Party has made common cause with Peking in joint communiqués denouncing "American imperialism" as "the enemy of the peoples of the entire world."

Despite the substantial internal pressures, however, official policy toward China has remained cautious. The attempt has been to seek some readjustment of policy toward China that will accord with the realities of the situation without conceding on all points to the Chinese communists and thereby jeopardizing relations with the United States and Taiwan. Prime Minister Sato reiterated the official, conservative position when he stated, on January 25, 1965:

It needs no expatiation that the problem of China holds a very great importance in present-day international politics. Especially for our country, which has a close relationship with China both his-

torically and geographically, this problem is one of great importance with a variety of implications. I believe, therefore, that our country should deal with this problem prudently and from its own independent viewpoint, without making unnecessary haste to reach a conclusion. At the present stage, our country intends to promote economic and cultural interchange with Communist China on the basic principle of separation of political matters and economic matters, while maintaining the friendly relations with the Republic of China with which Japan has regular diplomatic relations.

Clearly, the Japanese government would like to realize a "two Chinas" policy or, more properly, a "one China, one Taiwan" policy. It can be expected to work to this end, and to put increasing pressure on the United States. The Chinese communists are aware of this, and determined to prevent it if possible. This is why they have been pursuing a tough policy, rejecting full economic relations unless they are accorded formal recognition and Taiwan is accepted as an internal problem of China. Moreover, there can be no doubt that the Chinese communists see the American-Japanese military alliance as a potential threat to them, and would like to break it up. Whether they will attempt this by pursuing a tough policy or a soft policy in the future is yet unclear; in the past, they have alternated uncertainly between the two approaches.

Thus once again, Japan is faced with the problem of finding a workable China policy, and this time it must be based more upon the strength than the weakness of that nation. Her success cannot be predicted; the variables are too numerous and they go far beyond Japan. Even if improvements are scored, however, it is very doubtful, given the political realities, that Sino-Japanese relations will be marked by great intimacy in the near future. The chances are strong that China will

If Thomas Jefferson was the first great North-American exponent of this sector of the Western Hemisphere idea, Franklin D. Roosevelt was the last. In January, 1937, he declared:

Among the nations of the great Western Hemisphere the policy of the "good neighbor" has happily prevailed. In this achievement, every American nation takes an understanding part. There is neither war, nor rumor of war, nor desire for war. The inhabitants of this vast area, 250 million strong, spreading more than 8,000 miles from the Arctic to the Antarctic, believe in, and propose to follow, the policy of the "good neighbor." They wish with all their heart that the rest of the world might do likewise. The rest of the world—ah! there is the rub.[14]

Whether or not the Western Hemisphere idea was ever a true picture of the real world is not a question it is necessary to settle here. Two points, however, are worth making at this juncture. One is that the idea, during the past century or more, has shaped much thinking in the United States about policies toward Latin America. The second is that the three elements of the hemisphere concept are dynamic. They grow and move. They come and go. They are now gone.

The death of the geographic element of the Western Hemisphere idea has been a slow and lingering process. As long ago as the 1890's, Alfred Thayer Mahan announced the proposition that the seas unite rather than divide. And, at the end of World War I, Sir Halford J. Makinder, a British geographer who exerted a strong influence on twentieth-century geographic thought, argued that conventional eighteenth and nineteenth-century maps had declined in

utility, since "the geographical perspective of the twentieth century differs . . . from that of all previous centuries."[15] Writing in 1941, Eugene Staley, building on Mahan's point that land divides while water unites, noted that "no capital in Europe, including Moscow, is as far from Madison [Wisconsin] as is Buenos Aires, and only one European capital [Athens] is as far as Rio de Janeiro . . . This is direct-line distance, and by actually travelled routes Europe is relatively closer."[16] A year later, Nicholas Spykman asserted that the relations of Latin America "to Washington can never be as important as those of the great powers of Europe and Asia," and branded the Western Hemisphere idea as a disguised isolationism.[17] By the end of World War II, the concept of the geographic unity of the Americas had been largely abandoned.

Whether or not they were needed, additional lethal attacks against the geographic component of the Western Hemisphere idea continued to come in the years after World War II. Travel by air had become increasingly commonplace and rapid. Experimentation with artificial satellites and the exploration of outer space became, in the 1960's, a major preoccupation of the governments of the United States and the Soviet Union. The full implications of these technological developments are by no means clear, but it seems safe to say that increased use of air and space travel can be expected to render the old myths of land and water, of continents and oceans, even

---

[14]Quoted in United States Department of State, *Peace and War: United States Foreign Policy, 1931–1941* (Washington, D.C.: Government Printing Office, 1943), p. 528.

[15]Halford J. Makinder, *Democratic Ideals and Reality* (New York: Holt, Rinehart & Winston, Inc., 1942), p. 29.

[16]Eugene Staley, "The Myth of the Continents," *Foreign Affairs*, XIX (1941), 481–94.

[17]Nicholas J. Spykman, *America's Strategy in World Politics* (New York: Harcourt, Brace & World, Inc., 1942), pp. 352–53.

more irrelevant to questions of foreign policy.

The notion that political commonality joins Latin America to the United States also fell during World War II. The Western Hemisphere had long been advertised as the home of free republican institutions, essentially similar in Latin America and the United States. It is to be doubted whether this was ever true, even in the nineteenth century. Three Latin-American states —Brazil, Mexico, and Haiti—had attempted monarchical forms of government; and Chile, regarded early in the twentieth century as a leading Latin-American democracy, employed the parliamentary rather than the presidential system. As World War II focused North-American attention on dictatorships abroad, it became increasingly difficult to overlook the dictatorships that flourished in many Latin-American states. The celebrated Argentine question dramatized this problem during the war, and hastened the collapse of the second element of the Western Hemisphere idea.

In the heyday of the Western Hemisphere idea, the United States' Latin-American policies were frequently based on the geopolitical assumption that the American nations bore a special fraternal relationship to each other. The Monroe Doctrine, of course, long was the chief statement of that assumption.[18]

In the years since the philosophical abandonment of the Western Hemisphere idea, the Washington government has nevertheless clung, from time to time, to the notion of a special relationship to Latin America.

Many fields of activity illustrate the claim of the United States to a peculiar relationship with the other American republics. Only one of those fields— social, political, and economic change —is chosen for discussion here. In general, such change may be said to take two major forms in contemporary Latin America, revolution and economic development.

The United States and political change in Latin America

It may well be that Latin America has acquired a formidable reputation as a theater of frequent and chronic revolutions. Insofar as this is true, it should be noted that much of this reputation rests on a loose usage of the word "revolution." An amazing array of dissimilar and unrelated occurrences go by the name of "revolution" in the Americas. The Wars of

[18]The essence of the Monroe Doctrine may be said to be contained in the following excerpts from U.S. President James Monroe's celebrated foreign policy statement of December 2, 1823:

"The American continents, by the free and independent condition which they have assumed and maintain, are henceforth not to be considered as subjects for future colonization by any European powers . . .

"The Political system of the European powers is essentially different . . . from that of America. . . . We should consider any attempt on their part to extend their system to any portion of this hemisphere as dangerous to our peace and safety. . . .

"With the existing colonies or dependencies of any European power we have not interfered and shall not interfere. . . .

"In the wars of the European powers in matters relating to themselves we have never taken any part, nor does it comport with our policy to do so. . . ."

The works of Dexter Perkins are still regarded as standard and authoritative on the Monroe Doctrine. Chief among these books are *The Monroe Doctrine: 1823–1826* (Cambridge, Mass.: Harvard University Press, 1927); *The Monroe Doctrine: 1827–1867* (Baltimore: John Hopkins University Press, 1933); and *The Monroe Doctrine:1867–1907* (Baltimore: John Hopkins University Press, 1937).

Independence have been so dubbed, as well as minor changes in government, the promulgation of new written constitutions, political violence of almost any variety, and, true revolutions.[19]

Partly because of this variety of so-called revolutions, the policy of the United States toward these occurrences in Latin America has been varied and open to the charge of inconsistency. In general, and especially since World War II, Washington has attempted to refrain from interfering with revolutions thought to be superficial in character. But it has intervened in revolutionary situations believed to be of more far-reaching significance, especially where the government of the United States has been persuaded that communists have been involved in the revolutions in question—in Cuba, in Dominica, and in Guatemala.

The Guatemalan Revolution, which overthrew the fourteen-year-old dictatorship of General Jorge Ubico, generated a spirit of crusade. The mission of the Revolution, as understood by the crusaders, was the liquidation of oppression as symbolized by the Ubico regime. In the years after 1944, it was believed that, as this oppression had two aspects—one political and the other economic—the Revolution, unable to cope with both simultaneously, must therefore move in two successive phases.

The administration of President Juan José Arévale (1945–1951) was re-

[19]See Russell H. Fitzgibbon, "Revolutions: Western Hemisphere," *The South Atlantic Quarterly*, LV (July, 1956), 263–79; Harold E. Davis, ed., *Government and Politics in Latin America* (New York: The Ronald Press Company, 1958), pp. 119–46; and Gabriel A. Almond and James S. Coleman, eds., *The Politics of the Developing Areas* (Princeton, N.J.: Princeton University Press, 1960), pp. 496–501.

garded by the custodians of the Revolution as its first, or political, phase. During that period, attempts were made to dismantle the machinery of the old Ubico dictatorship. Under Arévalo's guidance, a new constitution was written and promulgated, political parties were legalized and permitted to function, and a relatively free press emerged. Thus the political phase. The economic phase fell to President Jacobo Arbenz Guzman, who was inaugurated early in 1951. His administration was concerned with such matters as agrarian reform and the containment of what he called the "foreign monopolies" operating in Guatemala. The latter were symbolized by the United Fruit Company, a United States corporation.

Communist influence and activity came to be matters for concern during Arbenz's administration. Guatemala now had a multiparty system, and Arbenz was formally supported by a coalition of four political parties. One of these was the Guatemalan Labor Party, which had formerly called itself the Communist Party, and whose members were still called "communists." This Party did not represent the majority of the Arbenz government's supporters, and it was frequently engaged in squabbles with other elements of his administration. President Arbenz was probably not himself a communist, although he was more friendly toward the communists than President Arévalo had been. One student of the Guatemalan situation found that, during the Arbenz period, the communists were:

. . . able to entrench themselves in the key organs of state power, in the official and semi-official press and radio, and in the leadership of the labor and peasant organizations, not as the result of a widespread popular revolutionary movement, but through a well-managed conspiracy unwittingly helped by the non-Communists and ineffectually opposed by the anti-Communists.[20]

The growth of communist influence led directly to a crisis, in July, 1954, in which the government of President Arbenz was overthrown. At that time, Colonel Carlos Castillo Armas, a Guatemalan who had been exiled to Nicaragua, led an uprising which found material support not only within Guatemala, but also in Nicaragua, in other states of Central America, and in the United States. In the course of some weeks of armed conflict, Castillo's Army of Liberation was triumphant and the Arbenz government was deposed. Castillo Armas, pledged to an anticommunist program, assumed the presidency of Guatemala late in 1954.

The role of the United States in the Guatemalan affair, though small in comparison with the Cuban and Dominican cases discussed below, was clear. The Washington government had not only helped to arm the Army of Liberation, but also lent it moral and diplomatic support. Moreover, when a conflict developed within the anti-Arbenz forces, John Puerifoy, the United States Ambassador to Guatemala, intervened as mediator to give the support of the North-American government to Castillo Armas. Indeed, for many years after 1954, some embittered Guatemalans continued to say that Puerifoy's last words were *"No me gusta este coronel. Tráigame*

otro."[21] Clearly opposed to the Guatemalan Revolution, the United States helped to bring it down in 1954.[22]

The relationship between revolution and economic development is not clear. Three hypotheses might be advanced with respect to this relationship. One is that political change, such as revolution, is a prerequisite for, or at least a stimulus to, economic development. This view is supported by many students of the Mexican scene, who have regarded Mexico's Revolution of 1910 as indispensible to the spectacular rapid industrialization and economic development after World War II.[23] A second hypothesis might be the reverse of the first—namely, that industrialization and economic development lead to political revolution. This view is held, sometimes with trepidation, in some sectors of Latin-American society. Finally, a third formulation is that political revolution and economic development are mutually exclusive alternatives, suggesting that many Latin-American societies stand at a species of crossroads and must make the choice between one of these paths or the other.[24]

[20]Theodore Geiger, *Commmunism versus Progress in Guatemala* (Washington, D.C.: National Planning Association, 1953), p. 30. See Also K. H. Silvert, *A Study in Government: Guatemala* (New Orleans: Middle American Research Institute, Tulane University, 1954), *passim.*

[21]"I do not like this colonel. Bring me another." After the fall of Arbenz, Puerifoy was transferred to Burma, where he died in an automobile accident.

[22]See Philip B. Taylor, Jr., "The Guatemalan Affair: A Critique of United States Foreign Policy," *American Political Science Review,* L (September, 1956), 787–806.

[23]See Howard F. Cline, "Mexico: A Matured Latin-American Revolution, 1910–1960, in "Latin America's Nationalistic Revolutions," ed. Robert N. Burr, *Annals of the American Academy of Political and Social Science,* March, 1961, pp. 84–94; and Robert E. Scott, *Mexican Government in Transition* (Urbana: University of Illinois Press, 1964), *passim.*

[24]See, for example, K. H. Silvert, *The Conflict Society: Reaction and Revolution in Latin America* (New Oreans: The Hauser Press, 1961), *passim.*

Whatever the relationship between political revolution and economic development, it seems clear that the United States has taken differing positions on these forms of change as they have occurred in Latin America in the years since World War II. The Washington government has made an unmistakable attempt to stimulate economic development in the Americas, yet it has opposed revolution. Thus, if the two are different facets of the same process of change, this fact may well be the basic dilemma of the Latin-American policy of the United States in the 1960's. To oppose revolution while trying to promote economic development may be inconsistent. Yet if the stimulation of economic and social development is basic to North-American policy in the 1960's, so is opposition to revolution. This has been amply demonstrated by the Cuban and Dominican cases.

Fidelismo. The Cuban affair may be said to revolve around Fidel Castro Ruz and *fidelismo,* his political movement. In 1947, Castro, then a twenty-one-year-old Cuban law student, took part in an invasion of the Dominican Republic in an unsuccessful attempt to overthrow the government of Generalissimo Rafael Leónidas Trujillo Molina. The following year, he took part in the *bogotazo,* the tumultuous rioting which began at Bogotá during the Ninth International Conference of American States. In 1952, Dr. Castro, during the course of his legal practice in Cuba, filed a brief with the Court of Constitutional Guarantees asking that body to declare unconstitutional the government of General Fulgencio Battista y Zaldivar, who had resumed power by *coup d'état* in March of that year. When the court rejected Castro's legal plea, he turned to revolutionary activity against the Batista regime. On July 26, 1953— *fidelismo* is known officially as the 26th of July movement—Castro led an unsuccessful attack on a military post at Santiago, in eastern Cuba. He was imprisoned, and then freed in an amnesty in 1955. He then left Cuba to spend almost two years in exile, principally in Mexico, preparing for his major contest with Batista. In December of 1956, Castro and a small band of guerilla invaders landed in eastern Cuba. During the following two years, while the island was gripped by civil war, Fidel Castro acquired legendary stature as the guerrilla leader of the rebels. Batista at length fell from power on January 1, 1959. *Fidelismo* then took up the reins of government.

No doubt, much of *fidelismo* is peculiar to Castro, and much is indigenous to Cuba. Yet a substantial sector of the movement is recognizably a part of the revolution of our time. For the purpose of analysis of *fidelismo* in that context, it is helpful to identify the four major components of the movement. These components—let us call them the keys to *fidelismo*—are the historic political instability of Cuba, the political contrast between metropolitan Havana and the remainder of the island, domestic social and economic changes in Cuba, and problems in the country's relations with the United States. All of these components, of course, merit systematic examination. However, as space is limited, the present discussion is restricted to the fourth key only.[25]

[25]I have dealt with the first three in another place. See George I. Blanksten, "Fidel Castro and Latin America," *The Revolution in World Politics,* ed. Morton A. Kaplan (New York: John Wiley & Sons, Inc., 1962), pp. 113–36.

Cuba's history has been markedly influenced by the colossus of the North. The United States, of course, played a major role in achieving the island's independence from Spain. But although the first Cuban president, Tomás Estrada Palma (1902–'09), expressed "the immense gratitude which the people feel towards the American nation,"[26] it is worth remembering that Jose Martí, the major national hero of the island's independence, saw the United States as beginning "to bring into the open its latent spirit of aggression."[27] Martí's view of the *Yanquis'* part in the struggle for insular independence is much more widely held among Cubans than Estrada's attitude.

Indeed, the fateful Platt Amendment was to become the major symbol of their image of the United States. Adopted by Congress, in 1901, as an amendment to an appropriation for the United States Army, the Platt instrument was later written into Cuba's first constitution and also, in 1904, into a treaty between the Washington and Havana governments. The Amendment, so-called, provided, among other things, for limitations of Cuba's authority to conduct its own foreign relations and to contract public debts. At the same time, the United States was guaranteed the right to intervene militarily in the island to maintain order there, and to hold naval bases in Cuba.[28] The first *Yanqui* military oc-

[26]Quoted in Graham H. Stuart, *Latin America and the United States* (5th ed., New York: Appleton-Century-Crofts, 1955), p. 212.

[27]Quoted in Donald Marquand Dozer, *Are We Good Neighbors?* (Gainesville: University of Florida Press, 1959), p. 2.

[28]The Platt Amendment has become so controversial in the relations between the United States and Cuba that the relevant clauses of that instrument deserve quotation in full:

"(a) That the Government of Cuba

shall never enter into any treaty or other compact with any foreign Power or Powers which will impair or tend to impair the independence of Cuba, nor in any manner authorize or permit any foreign Power or Powers to obtain by colonization or for military or naval purposes, or otherwise, lodgment in or control over any portion of said Island.

"(b) That said Government shall not assume or contract any public debt to pay the interest upon which, and to make reasonable sinking-fund provision for discharge of which, the ordinary revenues of the Island, after defraying the current expenses of the Government, shall be inadequate.

"(c) That the Government of Cuba consents that the United States may exercize the right to intervene for the preservation of Cuban independence, the maintenance of a government adequate for the protection of life, property, and individual liberty, and for discharging the obligations with respect to Cuba imposed by the Treaty of Paris on the United States, now to be assumed and undertaken by the Government of Cuba.

"(d) That all acts of the United States in Cuba during its military occupation thereof are ratified and validated, and all lawful right acquired thereunder shall be maintained and protected.

"(e)That the Government of Cuba will execute, and as far as necessary extend, the plans already devised or other plans to be mutually agreed upon, for the sanitation of the cities of the Island to the end that a recurrence of epidemic and infectious diseases may be prevented, thereby assuring protection to the people and commerce of Cuba, as well as to the commerce of the Southern ports of the United States and the people residing therein.

"(f) That the Isle of Pines shall be omitted from the proposed constitutional boundaries of Cuba, the title thereto left to future adjustments by treaty.

("g) That to enable the United States to maintain the independence of Cuba, and to protect the people thereof, as well as for its own defense, the Government of Cuba will sell or lease to the United States lands necessary for coaling or naval stations at certain specified points, to be agreed upon with the President of the United States.

"(h) That by way of further assurance the Government of Cuba will embody the foregoing provisions in a permanent treaty with the United States."

cupation was terminated in 1902. Under the Platt Amendment, however, North-American armed forces returned four years later to occupy the country until 1909. During the administration of President Alfredo Zayas (1921–'25), the Amendment was invoked repeatedly. At length, President Franklin D. Roosevelt abrogated the Platt Amendment, in 1934, as an early step in his administration's Good Neighbor Policy toward Latin America. Provision was made at that time for the retention of the United States naval base at Guantánamo Bay, originally acquired under the Amendment.

As the forms of United States influence in Cuba changed, however, the influence itself grew. *Yanqui* investments in the island, valued at $80 million as early as 1901, rose steadily in the following half-century. Most of these investments were connected with the sugar industry, with North-American firms owning or controlling 54 per cent of the island's sugar mills during the Batista period (1933–1944; 1952–1958). United States interests invested heavily in other sectors of Cuba's economy as well, particularly in tobacco, fruit, transportation, docks, electric light and power, telecommunications, banks, luxury hotels, and steamship and air lines. Late in the Batista regime, the island's imports achieved an annual average value of $640 million, and exports were valued at $766 million. Approximately two-thirds of each of these figures represented trade with the United States.

See *United States Statutes at Large*, XXXI, 897, or *House Document No. 2*, 57th Congress, 1st Session, p. 47. The reader may also wish to consult Raymond L. Buell, "Cuba and the Platt Amendment," *Foreign Policy Reports*, V, No. 3, (April 17, 1929); and Graham H. Stuart, *Latin America and the United States*, pp. 186–230, especially pp. 213–14.

Under Batista, Cuba—principally Havana—became an increasingly attractive vacation resort for *Yanqui* tourists. Many, originally oriented toward the pleasures of Miami Beach, suddenly discovered an even more beckoning playground less than an hour away by commercial airline. Crowding into the luxury hotels, night clubs, and gambling casinos of Havana, these fun-seeking vacationers fed a Cuban image of the *Yanqui* as a shallow and insensitive materialist with unlimited amounts of money to devote to amusing himself.

Such continuing North-American economic, cultural, and social influence in Cuba has given rise on the island to a phenomenon that has been called "Plattism."[29] This might be defined as the circumstance that, despite the abrogation of the Platt Amendment more than a generation before the rise of Fidel Castro, Cuba has "continued to experience a significant degree probably of economic and certainly of psychological subordination to the United States."[30] No doubt, Plattism is essentially psychological in nature. It is widely believed, in Cuba, that the Platt Amendment is still in force. While quantitative data on this are not available, it is probably true that the overwhelming majority of the Cubans who have heard of the document have *not* heard that it was abrogated. The heavy economic and other influences of the *Yanquis,* and the retention of the United States naval base at Guantánamo Bay are, for most Cubans, more than ample evidence that the Platt Amendment still lives.

And Plattism is a major element of

[29]See Russell H. Fitzgibbon, "The Revolution Next Door: Cuba," in "Latin America's Nationalistic Revolutions," ed. Robert N. Burr, p. 114.
[30]*Idem.*

fidelismo, governing many of its attitudes and policies toward the United States. In this context, it was necessary to eliminate *Yanqui* economic influence in the island; Plattism no doubt motivated much of the nationalization and expropriation of United States business interests in Cuba in 1960. The same psychological phenomenon strains to do battle at Guantánamo Bay. Such *fidelista* policies would certainly have brought renewed United States military intervention in Cuba if the Platt Amendment had still been in force. But that intervention would have been, to the Cubans, largely indistinguishable from the invasion of the island at the Bay of Pigs, which the *Yanqui* aided in April of 1961.

Much of the interplay between *fidelismo* and communism has derived its curious course and character from Plattism. The Cuban Communist Party had long been one of the four or five most important communist organizations in Latin America, lagging behind only those of Brazil, Chile, and perhaps Argentina and Mexico.[31] It has been estimated that, on the eve of the fall of Batista, the Cuban communists had from 20,000 to 30,000 members, roughly equivalent to a Communist Party of more than 670,000 members in the United States. Despite its influence among some of the rural sugar workers, Cuban communism was essentially an urban movement. Its strength was concentrated in, almost restricted to, Havana. Before the fall of Batista—that is, when *fidelismo* was essentially a rural movement warring against the urban capital—there was little evidence of communist association with the 26th of July movement. It was not until Castro took Havana, in 1959, that the island's communist

organization clearly threw its support to him. Many observers of the Cuban scene in the early days of the Castro revolution have thought it significant that "the Communists mounted the Castro bandwagon . . . late in its parade to success.[32] Fidel Castro reacted sympathetically to the communists. Plattism furnished the *fidelistas* and the communists with a common enemy, the United States.

Under *fidelista* leadership, Cuba's relations with the Soviet Union, China, and other communist states have been redefined. Diplomatic relations with these countries became cordial in the years immediately following Castro's rise to power, and trade and other economic agreements were entered into with communist governments in an endeavor, sometimes desperate, to fill the vacuum in the Cuban economy left by the departing *Yanquis*. Finally, in December of 1961, Fidel Castro declared, in a major address, that he was a "Marxist-Leninist." He asserted that he had been so oriented since his student days, but that he had withheld public statements to that effect for fear of alienating anticommunist Cubans from the Revolution. By the end of 1961, Castro asserted, he no longer feared the consequences of such alienation.

A second, and more spectacular, climax came in October, 1962. Planes, tanks, and other conventional armaments had been delivered to Cuba before then by the Russian and other communist governments, but, in 1962, Russian nuclear missile bases were established on the island. Their discovery by the United States precipitated a major international crisis, in consequence of which the Soviet Union withdrew its missiles from Cuba. The missile crisis of 1962 was a turning

---

[31]See Robert J. Alexander, *Communism in Latin America* (New Brunswick, N.J.: Rutgers University Press, 1957), *passim*.

[32]Russell H. Fitzgibbon, *"The Revolution Next Door,"* p. 117.

point. Thereafter, Soviet Russian interest in Cuba appeared to wane, and Havana's relations with China became somewhat strained. Refusing to compromise with the Castro regime, the United States continued to pursue a policy of rejection and containment of the influence of the Cuban revolution in the Americas.

The Dominican affair. The curious contradiction between the determination of the United States to promote development, on the one hand, and to oppose revolution, on the other, was dramatically illustrated by events in the Dominican Republic in 1965. One of the smallest of the Latin-American countries, this Caribbean island nation has historically been among the most politically and economically unstable states of the Western Hemisphere. Indeed, the country has been militarily occupied by the United States on a number of occasions. The most celebrated of the earlier interventions began in 1916, when President Woodrow Wilson (1913–'21) sent a detachment of United States Marines to occupy the island republic in consequence of a cluster of economic difficulties centering on the inability of the Dominican Republic to service its foreign debt. That intervention lasted for eight years, ending with the withdrawal of the Marines in 1924.

In subsequent years, the Dominican army came to dominate the nation's politics. Military dictatorship was accompanied by accelerated political instability; in 1930, the country suffered its one hundred and second revolution since the achievement of independence from Spain in the nineteenth century. The 1930 revolution brought General Rafael Leónidas Trujillo Molina to power. The Trujillo regime came to be notorious throughout the Americas, and it was remark-able on a number of counts. For one thing, it lasted until 1961, thus becoming the second longest dictatorship in the history of Latin America. (The longest was that of General Porfirio Díaz, who ruled Mexico from 1877 until 1911.) Further, Trujillo was noted for his brutal and terroristic methods, and dealt with his critics and political opponents with ruthless violence. Moreover, Trujillo and his family became extremely wealthy during the regime and spent huge amounts of money in spectacularly conspicuous, and often frivolous, ways.

The dictatorship came to a violent end in 1961, when Trujillo was killed by a group of assassins. Thereafter, attempts were made to establish civilian democratic constitutional government, and the country's first free election in over a half-century was held in 1962. Dr. Juan Bosch, a civilian, was elected president, and inaugurated on February 27, 1963. Bosch legalized political parties and sought changes in land tenure and the country's tax structure, measures which alarmed high-ranking officers of the Dominican army, who had been in power during the Trujillo era and who feared that Bosch's reforms would lead the country to communism. On September 25, 1963, the Bosch government was overthrown by a group of Dominican Army officers led by General Elías Wessín y Wessín. The United States government expressed doubt that Bosch had tended toward communism and withheld diplomatic recognition from the Wessín y Wessín regime. That group thereupon formed a civilian junta, headed by Dr. Donald J. Reid Cabral, which the United States recognized late in 1963.

The Cabral government was overthrown in a rebellion which was launched, on April 24, 1965, with the announced purpose of restoring the government of Bosch, who had been exiled in Puerto Rico. Colonel Francisco Caamaño Denó, leader of the revolt, proclaimed that its objective was "to return to the people what was taken from the people." Wessín y Wessín, repeating his charge that the Bosch government would be procommunist, led a military movement to prevent its restoration, and about 2,000 Dominicans were killed in the fighting between the supporters of Bosch and Wessín y Wessín. A detachment, initially of 405 United States Marines, called for by United States Ambassador W. Tapley Bennett, Jr., arrived in Santo Domingo on April 28. It was at first announced that the purpose of the intervention was to save the lives of about 2,500 United States citizens in the Dominican Republic, but the number of United States troops sent there was soon increased to about 20,000.

The charge of extensive communist involvement in, or influence on, the Bosch rebellion was not substantiated. The United States government identified three procommunist political parties in the Dominican Republic—the Moscow-oriented Dominican Popular Socialist Party, the pro-Chinese Dominican Popular Movement, and the pro-Castro 14th of June organization—and published a list of fifty-three Dominicans said to be communists or procommunists, but it offered no public statement of the degree to which it was thought that these organizations and persons exercised a controlling influence on the pro-Bosch rebellion. Caamaño Denó denied that such influence existed, and Bosch declared categorically that the "revolutionary forces . . . are not communists." Denied transportation to his country by the United States, Bosch asserted bitterly in his Puerto Rican exile that "this was a democratic revolution smashed by the leading democ-

racy of the world, the United States. That is why I think my time is over. I belong to a world that has ended politically."

Seeking to establish a provisional Dominican regime to balance against the pro-Bosch rebels, the United States persuaded Brigadier General Antonio Imbert Barreras, the sole surviving assassin of Trujillo, to form an anti-rebel junta. While the formal position of the United States was that it was neutral in the struggle between the Imbert group and the pro-Bosch forces led by Caamaño Denó, the United States nevertheless paid the salaries of the Imbert junta and United States military officers frequently participated in the command of Imbert's troops. Charges that the Imbert forces were torturing and executing political prisoners and then mutilating their bodies were made by the rebels; a committee of criminologists later sent to the Dominican Republic by the Organization of American States (OAS) found that forty-one suspected rebels had been tortured and killed by Imbert troops.

Meanwhile, there were flurries of activity in the United Nations and the OAS. The United Nations Security Council took up the Dominican crisis and heard attacks against the United States intervention from delegates of the Soviet Union, France, and Uruguay. United States Ambassador Adlai E. Stevenson argued that United Nations action would be unnecessary since the case was already before the OAS. Nevertheless, the Security Council unanimously asked Secretary General U Thant to send a representative to the Dominican Republic.

Meeting in Washington at the call of the OAS, the foreign ministers of the American Republics heard attacks against the United States action by the delegations from Uruguay, Venezuela, Mexico, and Chile, and then decided to send a five-man peace committee to the Dominican Republic to attempt to restore order there. The OAS foreign ministers also agreed to send an inter-American military force to the island. Guatemala, Brazil, Paraguay, Costa Rica, and Honduras contributed troops to this force, and the same number of United States soldiers were withdrawn from the intervention as were sent by these countries. After protracted negotiations with the Caamaño Denó and Imbert forces, the OAS proposed that a provisional Dominican Government be established under the leadership of Héctor García Godoy, who had been Foreign Minister in President Bosch's cabinet. The García regime was inaugurated on September 3, 1965, and Caamaño Denó and Imbert dissolved their respective forces. Wessín y Wessín reluctantly left the Dominican Republic. Ex-President Bosch at last returned to Santo Domingo to lead a strongly anti-United States political campaign. An election was held in June of 1966 at which time Joaquín Balaguer, identified with the Trujillo era, defeated Bosch in the race for the Presidency.

The repercussions of the Dominican affair were very great. Throughout Latin America, attitudes were generally critical of the intervention. In the United States, however, President Lyndon B. Johnson's actions in the Dominican Republic were praised by former President Dwight D. Eisenhower (1953–1961), former Vice-President Richard M. Nixon (1953–1961), and former Senator Barry M. Goldwater (1953–1965), who had been defeated by Johnson in the 1964 presidential campaign. On September 20, 1965, the House of Representatives adopted, by a vote of 312-52, a resolution endorsing unilateral intervention in the Western Hemisphere to prevent "intervention, domination, control, and colonization . . . by . . . international communism." However, critical voices were also raised. Prominent among these were those of Senators Robert F. Kennedy; Wayne Morse, chairman of the Senate Subcommittee on American Republic Affairs; and J. William Fulbright, chairman of the Senate Foreign Relations Committee. In a major Senate speech on October 22, 1965, Fulbright said:

> If the United States had really been intervening to save American lives, as it had a moral if not a strictly legal right to do, it could have done so promptly and then withdrawn and the incident would soon have been forgotten. But the United States did not intervene primarily to save American lives; it intervened to prevent what it conceived to be a Communist takeover. That meant, in the terms in which the United States defined the situation, that it was intervening against the rebels, who, however heavily they might or might not have been infiltrated by Communists, were also the advocates of the restoration of a freely elected constitutional government which had been forcibly overthrown. It also meant that the United States was intervening for the military and the oligarchy—to the detriment of the Dominican people and to the bitter disappointment of those throughout Latin America who had placed their hopes in the United States and the Alliance for Progress.[33]

Mexico: The preferred revolution. In 1910, Francisco Ignacio Madero, a curiously quixotic lawyer, launched a rebellion that in the following year brought down the government of General Porfirio Díaz, who had ruled Mexico since the 1870's. Madero's ac-

[33]*Congressional Record*, No. 198, Part 2, October 22, 1965, p. 3. See also Theodore Draper, "A Case of Political Obscenity," *The New Leader*, XLIX, No. 10 (May 9, 1966), pp. 3-7.

tion inaugurated a generation of turmoil and reconstruction. This Revolution—the celebrated "wind that swept Mexico"—has been as profound as that which struck France in the eighteenth century or Russia less than a decade after the fall of Díaz. Although its initial objectives were more limited, the Mexican Revolution later launched a frontal attack on fundamental problems—such as land tenure, the temporal position of the Roman Catholic Church, the situation of the lower classes, and foreign economic influence in the country—that have historically troubled not only Mexico but also much of the rest of Latin America.

Land tenure has, of course, long been a problem in Mexico. It has been estimated that, in 1910, on the eve of the Revolution, about 1 per cent of the population owned approximately 70 per cent of the arable land of Mexico. The Revolution was committed to, and has achieved, a substantial change in the pattern of land ownership. Determined that the large landed estates should be reduced, the Mexicans introduced two other land systems which are held to be mutually compatible. The first of these is designed to create a large group of individual owners of small parcels of land. The second is the *ejido* system, intended to deliver collectively owned lands to rural communities. Particularly in the early years of the Revolution, Mexico sought a solution to its historic land problem through these devices, notably the *ejido* system.

The Revolution has also altered the traditionally dominant role of the Roman Catholic Church in the temporal life of Mexico. Against an historic background of frequent unions of church and state, the church had become a major social, economic, and political, as well as religious, force in the predominantly Catholic country. In the wake of the Revolution, the church has been disestablished and its position weakened. It has been deprived of much of the land it had acquired; and church officials are forbidden to vote or to present themselves as candidates for public office. In short, much of the Revolution is distinctively anticlerical in nature.

Some redefinition of the place of the lower classes in national life has also been accomplished. The small upper class, variously known as "creoles" or "whites," had long dominated the political and economic life of the nation, excluding the two lower groups, the *mestizos* and the Indians, from effective participation. The new Mexican government has sought a new national role for these lower classes, partly through the *ejido* system, partly through education of the illiterates, and partly through fostering a renaissance of Indian culture. An attempt has been made, with some success, to destroy the older class system and to multiply the opportunities available to the lower classes.

The Revolution has also challenged the role of foreign capital in Mexico's economy. Especially during the regime of General Díaz (1876–1911), capital, particularly from the United States, was encouraged to enter Mexico on a large scale and to develop and exploit natural resources. Especially affected were oil, communications, transportation, and electrical energy. In an endeavor to reduce these outside economic influences, Mexico has placed restrictions and limitations on the ability of foreigners to acquire most types of property. Expropriation and related steps have deprived foreigners of many of their earlier holdings, particularly in oil, land, and transportation, and outsiders attempting to do business in Mexico frequently find themselves discriminated against by the pattern of the laws.

If we succumb to the temptation to compare the Mexican and Cuban Revolutions, we find certain obvious differences. For one thing, Mexico was in a vastly different stage of economic development, in 1910, than Cuba was a half century later. Industrialization had hardly begun in Mexico when the Díaz regime fell, and revolution came to what was in many ways a primitive economy. Fifty years and two World Wars later, revolution in Cuba gripped a more advanced economy which, despite its many problems, boasted the third highest standard of living in Latin America. In short, the Castro revolution does not appear to have either sprung from or contributed to modernization, which was already well under way in Cuba before the fall of the second Batista regime.

Time is significant in another way, also. Students of the process of revolution argue that all major revolutions, during the course of their development, pass through a more or less uniform set of steps or stages. The first of these, in most formulations, is a period of social unrest, frequently attributed to economic causes. From this initial stage emerges what is sometimes called the "desertion or the defection of the intellectuals," a phase in which the writers, artists, teachers, and preachers of the affected society set up a running attack against the existing order. In the third stage, it is held, the output of the intellectuals takes on a more positive quality, and the social myth or ideology of the revolution then emerges. Next, the established armed forces, for one reason or another, are unable to defend the tottering old regime. Moderates rise briefly to

power, during a violent physical change in government, after which the revolution enters upon a stage variously called "the accession of the extremists," "the reign of terror," "the era of revolutionary virtue," or "the period of dictatorship." Finally, the stage of Thermidor arrives, when the extremists are displaced by new moderates, under whose leadership compromises are made as the social myth of the revolution is reinterpreted.[34]

If some such formulation is accepted, we can say that Mexico's spectacularly rapid economic development and modernization are largely characteristic of the Thermidorean stage, which had set in at about the time of World War II. The Cuban Revolution is still too young to judge even its durability.

Technological considerations also account for some of the differences between the two. Since we are viewing

[34]There is, of course, a voluminous literature on revolution in general, and in Latin America in particular. The reader may be interested in the following particularly relevant works: Crane Brinton, *The Anatomy of Revolution* (New York: W. W. Norton & Company, Inc., 1938); Lyford P. Edwards, *The Natural History of Revolution* (Chicago: University of Chicago Press, 1927); Robert Hunter, *Revolution: Why, How, When?* (New York: Harper & Row, Publishers, Inc., 1940); Harold E. Davis, ed., *Government and Politics in Latin America* (New York: The Ronald Press Company, 1958), especially pp. 119–46; Kalman H. Silvert, *The Conflict Society: Reaction and Revolution in Latin America* (New Orleans: Hauser Press, 1961); Russell H. Fitzgibbon, "Revolutions: Western Hemisphere," *The South Atlantic Quarterly*, LV (July, 1956), 263–79; Alfred Meusel, "Revolution and Counterrevolution," *Encyclopedia of the Social Sciences* (New York: The Macmillan Company, 1937), IV, pp. 259–62; and Robert N. Burr, ed., "Latin America's Nationalistic Revolutions," *Annals of the American Academy of Political and Social Science*, CCCXXXIV (March, 1961).

economic development as the process
of technological innovation, resulting
in greater efficiency of production, we
can say that a more effective technology draws a higher level of production—that is, a greater gross national
product per capita—from a fixed input
into an economy. In the first decade
of the twentieth century, when revolution struck Mexico, that country's
major cities had not yet become the
great source of technological innovation and beginning industrialization
that they were a generation or two
later. In Fulgencio Batista's Cuba,
however, the industrializing "middle
sectors" were centered in the metropolitan area of Havana.

Placing the Mexican and Cuban
revolutions into the context of international relations uncovers additional
differences. There is, for one thing,
the overriding question of the relationship of the revolutions to the Soviet
Union and the communist movement.
The Mexican Revolution began a full
seven years before the Russian. Those
seven years were decisive; during that
hectic period between the rise of
Francisco Ignacio Madero and the fall
of Alexander Kerensky, the Mexican
Revolution acquired its own course,
character, and definition—its own
identity as a major social and political
movement. Although there are obvious
similarities between the Mexican and
Russian revolutions, especially in
ideology, the two movements did not
coincide in time and so went off in
different directions. Not so in the Cuban case. Born in—and, to some extent, of—the Cold War, the Castro
revolution has been, perhaps inevitably,
influenced by the Soviet Union.

An additional consideration related
to international politics is perhaps
more directly relevant to the process

of modernization. This has to do with
participation in foreign aid programs
designed to stimulate economic growth
through technical assistance. Mexico
has participated in these programs,
virtually without interruption, since
their inception on the eve of World
War II, and has presumably benefited.
Cuba has been excluded, from the early
days of the Castro revolution, from
programs of technical cooperation and
from participation in the Alliance for
Progress, and thus the Cuban regime
has presumably lost a boost to its economic development and modernization.
The trade embargoes imposed against
Cuba by the United States and other
American republics no doubt have a
similar effect. While the Soviet Union,
China, and a number of the states of
Eastern Europe have made gestures of
economic assistance to Cuba, these
have not been sufficient to fill the gaps
left by the American nations and other
states of the West.

The United States and economic change in Latin America

Economic development constitutes a
second major form of change in contemporary Latin America. By "economic development," we mean technological innovation which results in
greater productive efficiency. A more
effective technology draws a higher
level of production—that is, a greater
gross national product per capita—
from the same initial input into an
economy.[35] Thus defined, economic
development is widespread in contemporary Latin America, and is a par-

[35]See George I. Blanksten, "The Aspira-
tion for Economic Development," in "Latin
America's Nationalistic Revolutions," ed.
Robert N. Burr, *Annals of the Academy of
Political and Social Science*, March, 1961,
pp. 10–19.

ticularly rapid vehicle of change in such countries as Brazil and Mexico.[36]

North American policies designed to promote economic development in Latin America antedate World War II, having been begun in the 1930's. Over the years, the names given these foreign aid programs have varied. They were known originally as "technical assistance," but were called "Point Four" during the administration of President Harry S. Truman (1945–1953); "technical cooperation," during the presidency of General Dwight D. Eisenhower (1953–1961); and the "Alliance for Progress," after 1961.

In general, the programs have been designed to increase the efficiency of the productive arts in at least one of the participating countries. Thus conceived, technical cooperation is concerned primarily with the international transfer of technology. The Mutual Security Act of 1954 defines "technical cooperation programs" as "programs for the international interchange of technical knowledge and skills designed to contribute primarily to the balanced and integrated development of the economic resources and productive capacities of economically underdeveloped areas."[37] The bulk of the technical cooperation programs in which the United States has participated in Latin America have been in the fields of agriculture, education, health and sanitation, industrial productivity, and public administration.

Economic assistance in World War II. United States technical assistance to Latin America was born of war, and the early participants in the cooperative programs thought of them as war measures. In May, 1939—a period of taut, prewar international tension—the Congress of the United States enacted legislation authorizing the President to engage in technical cooperation in Latin America and the Philippines "whenever he finds that the public interest renders such a course advisable."[38] In August of the same year —less than a month before the war formally began—additional legislation expanded the statutory bases of technical cooperation "in order to render closer and more effective the relationship between the American Republics."[39]

Meetings related to the war were held by the foreign ministers of the American republics at Panama, in 1939, and at Havana, in 1940. The third meeting, at Rio de Janeiro, in January of 1942, was called immediately after Pearl Harbor and took place in an atmosphere of hectic mobilization. "Inch by inch," Brazilian President Getulio Vargas told the conference, "we Brazilians will defend our country against all and any invaders, and we shall not permit either our land or our seaboard to serve the purpose of a base for attack against any of our sister nations."[40] Among the instruments adopted at the Rio conference was Resolution XXX, establishing an inter-American framework for technical cooperation. The text of Resolu-

---

[36]See T. Lynn Smith, "Brazil: The Giant Awakes," in Burr, *op. cit.*, pp. 95–102; George I. Blanksten, "Brazil: Too Many Economic Pressures?" *Challenge*, XI (January, 1963), 35–38; and Howard F. Cline, "Mexico: A Matured Latin-American Revolution, 1910–1960," in Burr, *op. cit.*, pp. 84–94.

[37]Public Law 665, 83rd Congress, Title III, Section 302.

[38]Public Law No. 63, 76th Congress, May 3, 1939.

[39]Public Law No. 355, 76th Congress, August 9, 1939.

[40]Quoted in *New York Times*, January 15, 1942.

tion XXX cited two reasons for the step: the preservation of the vital and strategic products of the Western Hemisphere, and contribution to "reconstruction of the world order."[41]

Later in 1942, the Institute of Inter-American Affairs (IIAA) was established as a United States government corporation designed to carry forward technical cooperation in Latin America, and the first IIAA projects were soon established in Latin America. The concept during this early period, when technical cooperation was viewed as an additional instrument for the winning of the war against the Axis, clearly emerges from the writings of the United States personnel who helped to launch the cooperative projects in the field. Lieutenant Colonel Edward A. Westphal, the first United States chief of field party in Peru, wrote:

Primary purpose of the activities of the Office of Inter-American Affairs was the fostering of good will between the United States and the other American Republics by means of propaganda and the carrying out of various types of cooperative aid programs along health and sanitation lines. A considerable proportion of these cooperative activities were aimed at facilitating the extraction or the production of raw materials needed to further war effort.[42]

A similar picture of the situation in Brazil was drawn by a pioneer in technical cooperation with that country:

Few "North Americans" visualized remaining in the cooperative program after the war was won. A large number of employees did not interpret the development of SESP[43] as something more fundamental than a wartime activity. Many who left at the end of the war did not have faith that their own contributions would be more lasting than those of a purely military nature.[44]

Thus, public technical cooperation was conceived and actively participated in by the United States, during World War II, and the record indicates that the people who were associated with it thought of it as a contribution to the defensive strength of the Western Hemisphere.

Once the war came to a close in 1945, and before the Alliance for Progress was launched in 1961, technical cooperation became a tenuous and uncertain policy. During the postwar years, budgets for cooperative programs were continued, but on a reduced basis, because this seemed the easiest way of meeting expiration dates. No clear and positive formulation of technical cooperation appeared in the period immediately following the war. Diplomatic correspondence about the cooperative programs reached a low point at this time.

The Alliance for Progress. The launching of the Alliance for Progress in 1961 decided the question. Technical cooperation, a war measure until 1945, confused and indecisive during the Truman and Eisenhower administrations, became a legitimate foreign pol-

---

[41]Quoted in Serviço Especial de Saúde Pública, *Notas Diplomáticas e Contratos entré o Brasil e os Estados Unidos da América de 1942 a 1952 para Desenvolvimiento de um Programa Cooperativo Bilateral de Saúde* (Rio de Janeiro: Serviço Especial de Saúde Pública, 1953), p. 11.

[42]Lt. Col. Edward A. Westphal, "A Report on the Operations of the Servicio Cooperativo Inter-Americano do Salud Pública and on the Activities of the Division of Health and Sanitation of the Institute of Inter-American Affairs in Peru from July 1942 to December 1945" (Lima: Unpublished manuscript, 1946), p. 1.

[43]After the initial letters of Serviço Especial de Saúde Pública.

[44]Serviço Especial de Saúde Pública, *op. cit.*, pp. 58–59.

icy objective, war or no war, during the presidency of John F. Kennedy (1961–'63). Sharply increased funds were made available for the Alliance, conceived, in 1961, as a ten-year program for the economic development of Latin America. In Table 11.1, economic development is depicted in terms of per-capita income.

TABLE 11.1

Economic Development in Latin America (Rank Order of Countries Based on Gross National Product, per Capita, in U.S. Dollars)*

Rank	Country	Gross National Product Per Capita, in U.S. Dollars
1	Argentina	$ 688
2	Venezuela	457
3	Cuba	454
4	Uruguay	382
5	Panama	382
6	Chile	335
7	Brazil	278
8	Colombia	231
9	Costa Rica	203
10	Mexico	199
11	Dominican Republic	189
12	Guatemala	182
13	Nicaragua	168
14	El Salvador	167
15	Paraguay	166
16	Honduras	134
17	Peru	118
18	Bolivia	109
19	Ecuador	93
20	Haiti	62
	United States	2,200

SOURCES: Harold E. Davis, ed., *Government and Politics in Latin America* (New York: The Ronald Press Company, 1958), pp. 50–93; Gabriel A. Almond and James S. Coleman, eds., *The Politics of the Developing Areas* (Princeton, N. J.: Princeton University Press, 1960), pp. 455–531; and Robert E. Burr, ed., "Latin America's Nationalistic Revolution," *Annals of the American Academy of Political and Social Science*, March 1961, pp. 10–19, especially p. 11.

In the Alliance for Progress, there developed a new kind of combination of the long-standing foreign-aid programs of the United States. The Alliance has joined economic aid with technical assistance. These had been united once before but, at that time, technical assistance, that is developmental assistance, was made to serve the objective of the other aid programs. Economic aid included in the Alliance for Progress is made to serve the ends of technical assistance. There is now economic aid directed toward technological innovation, economic growth, and improvement in the standard of living in Latin America. In a sense, technical assistance has become the dog rather than the tail. As government policies, many of the components of the Alliance for Progress are, of course, fairly old. What is new is, first, that the aid programs were planned to foster economic development rather than short-run political objectives. Second, it has a wider multilateral basis: the United States has attempted to enlist the participation of all the American republics, except Cuba.

Since economic aid was now related to economic development and technological change, the participating governments were expected to establish a favorable climate for certain internal social and economic reforms. This was to ensure that economic assistance would be more effectively related to economic growth and development. Grants or loans could now be used, for example, for the purchase of technical or industrial equipment needed to carry out a growth project developed through technical assistance.

The Alliance for Progress faced frustrating obstacles. Only a few of the specific programs undertaken under the name of the Alliance have been related to one another. A housing project, for example, was undertaken without reference to an educational program in the same locality. Both are needed and, indeed, each is useful, but they would be more effective if they were related to each other.

The Alliance still is in danger of being something of an omnibus operation, sponsoring great numbers of small foreign aid projects without much thought to the relationship of these projects to economic development and to the Alliance as a whole. The Alliance would be more effective if there were some integration of the various programs. In most cases coordination could be accomplished without much difficulty and without any great damage to the vested interests that have become involved in the Alliance.

A second type of problem which the Alliance faces is the intransigence of some of the Latin-American elite. There are governments which are reluctant to make the social and economic reforms proposed by study teams. Critics may say this was to have been expected: governing groups always resist change. In Latin-America, however, two types of elite exist. There are, of course, the groups which resist change and which regard any reform as threats to their traditional controlling position. Thus, landowners' associations may resist agrarian reform, a church hierarchy may oppose steps toward a greater separation of church and state, or a group of army officers may resist attempts to free civilian government from military control.

On the other hand, some governing groups welcome change, and seek to promote and stimulate it. That is because some governing groups in Latin-American countries are under pressure to produce change. A revolutionary government is usually required to show that life is now better in some way, or at least different. To think of all the governing groups as opposed to change, especially in the more rapidly chang-

ing countries where a new elite desires a new order and finds itself opposing an older elite that is still wedded to the *status quo*, is inaccurate and unrealistic.

In some Latin-American countries, the *Alianza para Progreso* has become subject of jest: "*Alianzi si; progreso no.*" Statements such as these have resulted from the obstacles which have been placed in the way of reform. Some plans for development, for example, have included tax reform, or the introduction of the income tax into areas where it has been unknown. Some programs have involved proposals for land reform. And some Latin-American governments have sought to obtain economic aid without making reforms, saying in effect, "We do not have time to make the reforms, but we need the money in a hurry." The administration of the Alliance has attempted to resist such pressures, but they are serious, nonetheless.

It is not easy to evaluate the Alliance in such flat terms as "Is it a success?" or "Is it a failure?" One of the problems is failure to place its operation in perspective. It should be remembered that this is a ten-year program. It is not fair at this stage to write it off as a failure.[45]

INTERNATIONAL ORGANIZATION

The states of the Western Hemisphere have been involved in two types of international organizations, universal and regional. On the universal level, two organizations should be mentioned, the League of Nations and the United Nations.

Although the United States never became a member of the League of

[45]See George I. Blanksten, "The Alliance for Progress," in *Explosive Forces in Latin America*, ed. John J. TePaske and Sydney Nettleton Fisher (Columbus: Ohio State University Press, 1964), pp. 175–85.

Nations, formed at the end of World War I, ten of the Latin-American countries were charter members of the League. And, after the Dominican Republic joined that organization in 1924,[46] all of the Hispanic-American states except Mexico and Ecuador had become members of the organization. Participation in the United Nations, formed at the close of World War II, has been complete; the United States and all of the countries of Latin America have been members of that organization.

So far as the American republics are concerned, regional international organization has been more significant than universal organization. The Pan-American Union, formed in 1910, served until 1948 as the basic organization for collaboration among the twenty states of Latin America and the United States. In 1948, the inter-American system was revamped so that it would function as the regional agent of the United Nations in the Western Hemisphere. The present Organization of American States (OAS) grew out of that reorganization. Although the OAS functions well as an agency of social, cultural, and economic collaboration among its members, it has been criticized as being politically weak and an instrument for the subservience of the Latin-American states to the foreign policy of the United States.[47]

The next decade may well see a significant change in the cultural and political composition of the OAS. At present, its membership is limited to the United States and the twenty states of Latin America, Canada having declined to join because of her participation in the British Commonwealth of Nations and the North Atlantic Treaty Organization. In recent years, some of the British West Indies have become independent, the most recent of the new states among them being Jamaica, Trinidad and Tobago, and the Republic of Guyana, formerly British Guiana. When and if these new states become members of the OAS, it seems reasonable to expect that Canada will do likewise. At this writing, it would be foolhardy to attempt to predict the ramifications of such a major change in the OAS, but the indications that it is coming seem clear enough.

Meanwhile, the Western Hemisphere is a restive theater of change. The United States, accepting economic development but thus far rejecting political change, is a confused and inconsistent policeman of the Americas. It is not a happy lot, but the prescription for its improvement is by no means clear or simple.

[46]"The Dominican Republic, whose national life had suffered a hiatus owing to the intervention of the United States . . . became a member in September, 1924, as soon as American military intervention was relaxed." J. Fred Rippy, *Historical Evolution of Hispanic America* (New York: Appleton-Century-Crofts, 1940), p. 521.

[47]See United States Senate Committee on Foreign Relations, *United States—Latin-American Relations: The Organization of American States* (Washington, D.C.: Government Printing Office, 1959), *passim.*

SELECTED BIBLIOGRAPHY

Adams, Richard N., et al., Social Change in Latin America Today: Its Implications for United States Policy. New York: Harper & Row, Publishers, Inc., 1960.

Alexander, Robert J., Communism in Latin America. New Brunswick, N. J.: Rutgers University Press, 1957.

Castaneda, Jorge, Mexico and the United Nations. New York: Carnegie Endowment for International Peace, 1958.

Dozer, Donald M., Are We Good Neighbors? Gainesville: University of Florida Press, 1959.

Geiger, Theodore, Communism versus Progress in Guatemala. Washington: National Planning Association, 1953.

Guerrant, Edward O., Roosevelt's Good Neighbor Policy. Albuquerque: University of New Mexico Press, 1950.

Huberman, Leo, and Paul Sweezy, Cuba: Anatomy of a Revolution. New York: Monthly Review Press, 1960.

Johnson, John J., Political Change in Latin America: Emergence of the Middle Sectors. Stanford, Calif.: Stanford University Press, 1958.

Lieuwen, Edwin, Arms and Politics in Latin America. New York: Frederick A. Praeger, Inc., 1960.

Maier, Joseph, and Richard W. Weatherhead, eds., Politics of Change in Latin America. New York: Frederick A. Praeger, Inc., 1964.

Martz, John D. ed., The Dynamics of Change in Latin-American Politics. Englewood Cliffs, N. J.: Prentice-Hall, Inc., 1965.

National Planning Association, Technical Cooperation in Latin America: Recommendations for the Future. Washington: National Planning Association, 1956.

Silvert, Kalman H., The Conflict Society: Reaction and Revolution in Latin America. New Orleans: The Hauser Press, 1961.

TePaske, John J., and Sydney N. Fisher, eds., Explosive Forces in Latin America. Columbus: Ohio State University Press, 1964.

United States Senate Committee on Foreign Relations, United States—Latin-American Relations: The Organization of American States. Washington, D.C., Government Printing Office, 1959.

Index

Absolutism, in Japan, 283
Acheson, Dean, 137
Adenauer, Konrad:
  Chancellorship, 121–123
  and Christian Democratic Union, 126
  and Common Market, 140–141
  and de Gaulle, 89
  popularity, 105, 120
  and reunification of Germany, 143–144
  and Soviet Russia, 145–146
  and West German sovereignty, 133–139
Adzhubei, Alexei, 191
Afro-Asian bloc, in UN, 354
Agricultural Cooperative Association, Japan, 299
Agriculture, French, 64
Akbar, 340
Albania, 223, 224, 239, 244
Algeria, 73, 88
Alliance for Progress, 386–388
Alliances, U.S., 259
Allied High Commission, 133
Almond, Gabriel, 47
Americanismo, 360–362
Analytical approach, foreign policy, 1–4, 27
Anglo-Japanese Alliance (1902), 275–276, 277, 281–282, 310
Anti-Americanism, in Latin America, 362, 363
Anti-Comintern Pact, 282
Anti-communist posture, U.S., 24
Anti-foreignism, Japan, 273–274 (*see also* xenophobia)
Anti-Semitism, in West Germany, 117
Anti-Stalinist faction, Soviet politics, 181
Antofagasta, 369
ANZUS, 251
Appropriations, Congressional, and U.S. foreign policy, 262–263
Arab nationalism, and British policy, 59–60
Arbenz Guzman, Jacobo 373–374
Arévalo, Juan José, 373
Argentina, 359, 367–368
Aron, Raymond, 93
Ashida, Hisashi, 287

Asia, U.S. policy, 247, 248
Asian nationalism, and Japan, 274, 276–277, 281
Assimilation, French empire, 72
Atom bomb, France, 75, 81, 90–93
Australia, 50, 51

Bagdad Pact, 351
Balaguer, Joaquín, 381
Balance of payments, Britain, 52–53
Balance of power, U.S. and U.S.S.R., 258
Balance of power policy, France, 67–68, 82–84
Banda Oriental, 367
Barmine, Alexander, 176
Basic Law of 1948, West Germany, 116, 120–121, 124, 125
Batista, Fulgencio, 365, 375, 377
Beria, 178, 180, 188, 199, 220
Berlin crisis, 57–58
Berlin Wall, 109, 143
Bevin, Ernest, 35
Bidault, Georges, 78
Bipartisanship, and U.S. foreign policy, 265
Bismarck, Otto von, 102–103
Bohlen, Charles E., 6
Bolívar, Simón, 360, 368
Bolivia, disputes with Peru and Chile, 368–369
Bonn government, 135
Bosch, Juan, 379–380, 381
Brazil, 359, 363, 367–368
Brazzaville conference (1944), 72
Brest-Litovsk, Treaty, 206
Brezhnev, Leonid, 191–192
British foreign policy:
  background, 30–34
  Cabinet, 34–36, 38
  in China, 324
  Common Market, 93–94, 140–142
  Commonwealth relations, 47–50
  cultural and ideological ties, 50–52
  economic policy, 52–56
  Foreign Secretary, 35–36
  Foreign service, 36–37

391

DATE DUE

DEC 1 7 1999			